Contents

4 Map of principal sights

8 Map of touring programmes

12 Places to stay

14 Leisure – Austrian-style

17 Austria

19 Introduction

20 Description of the country

26 Historical table and notes

32 The Austrian provinces

33 Economic activity

36 Art

43 Music

46 Some Austrian folklore

49 Food and drink

51 Sights

341 Practical information

353 Calendar of events

357 Admission times and charges

377 Index

See list of Federal Provinces p 32

Principal sights

De   in Deutsch
En   in English
Es   en Español
Fr   en Français
It   in Italiano
Ne   in het Nederlands
Po   em Português

WÜRZBURG   NÜRNBERG

STUTTGART

Ulm

AUGSBURG

DONAU

DEUTSCHLAND

Lech

FRIEDRICHSHAFEN

Füssen

BODENSEE

Plansee   ZUGSPITZE   Seefelder Sattelstraßen

Pfänder   Lermoos   Seefeld i. Tirol
Bregenz   Mösern

ZÜRICH   Fernpaßstraße

Rappenlochschlucht   Oberes Lechtal   Seefelder Joch

Bregenzerwald   Holzleitner Sattel

Neßlegg   Stams

Rankweil   Zuger Hochlicht   LECH   Imst

Feldkirch   Zürs   Ötztal   Stubaital

Bludenz   Flexenpaß   VALLUGA   Landeck   PITZTAL

Arlbergpaß   St. Anton   Trisannabrücke

Brandnertal   Inntal   KAUNERTAL   Sölden

LIECHTENSTEIN   Montafon   Arlberg   Jochdohle

ZÜRICH   Lünersee   Gaschurn   Ischgl   Mittelberg   Ventertal   Obergurgl

RHEIN   Vermunt-Stausee   Finstermünzpaß   Nauders   Vent   Hohe Mut

Silvretta-Stausee   HOHES RAD   Weißseeferner   S. Leonardo

SCHWEIZ   Schweiz
SUISSE   Suisse
SVIZZERA   Svizzera
          De/En/Fr

LUGANO   Inn   Adige

4

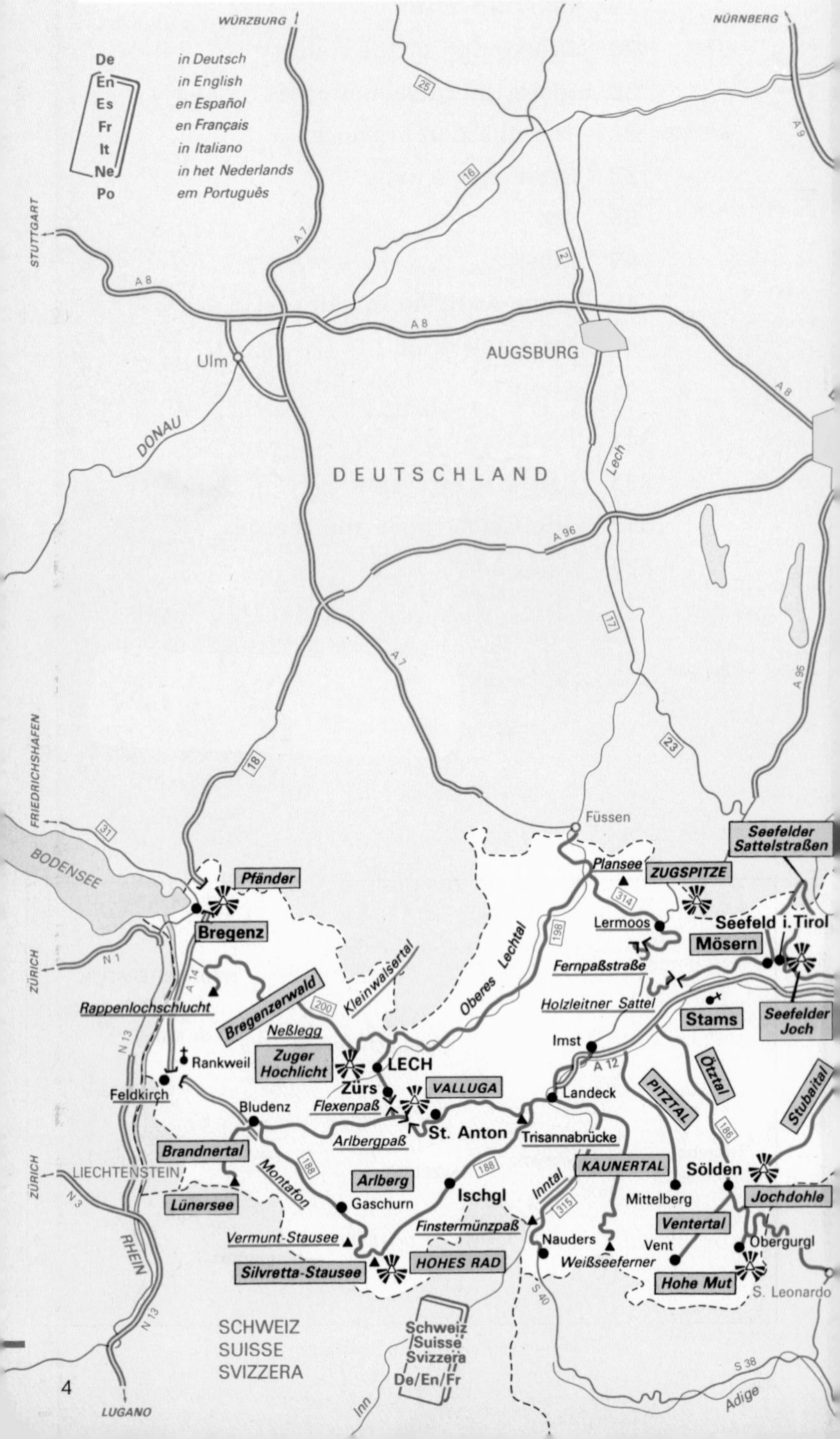

Touring programmes

Altenburg ★★

★ Krems

Göttweig

Herzogenburg ★

Melk ★★

DONAU

Klosterneuburg

★ Wienerwald

WIEN ★★★

Schloßhof

BRATISLAVA

Petronell

Rohrau

Leitha

★ Neusiedler See

‡‡ Baden

★ Mariazell

Semmering ★

★ Aflenzer Seebergstraße

Vorau

Bruck an der Mur ★

★ Pöllau

Pöllauberg ★

★ Herberstein

Österreichisches ★★★
Freilichtmuseum

★ Rein

★★ Eggenberg

Piber

GRAZ ★★

Stainz

★ Packsattelstraße

Riegersburg ★

Bad Gleichenberg ‡

MAGYARORSZÁG

Bad Radkersburg

★ Steirische Weinstraße

Mura

SLOVENSKÁ
REPUBLIKA

SLOVENIJA

HRVATSKA

ZAGREB

Aust. 2

0   50 km

Places to stay

The seasons – Austria, two thirds covered by mountains, is justly favoured for its ski slopes in **winter**. The sweep of resorts, enjoyed equally by those just learning to ski as by the highly skilled, begins on the frontier around the Arlberg Pass, itself famous in sporting history. The resources of the Tyrol, the most popular area, benefited considerably from the Olympic Games held in Innsbruck in 1964 and 1976. The Salzburg region is also well developed for skiing, with major resorts such as the Sportwelt Amadé. Styria offers a variety of opportunities for skiers in the resorts of the Dachstein-Tauern and Schladming areas.

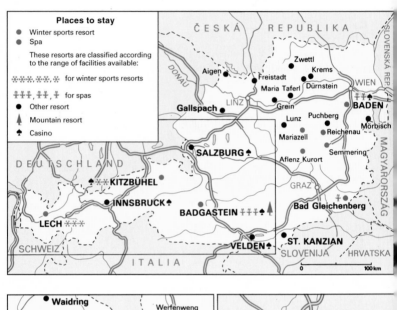

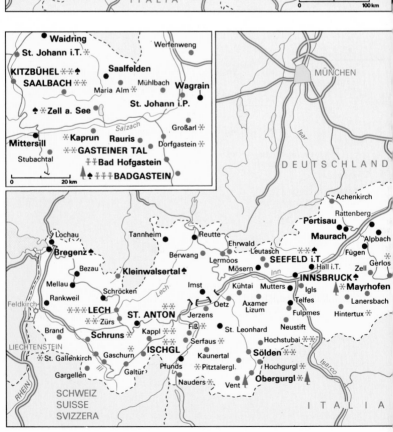

In the **spring** the longer days make it possible to ski at a high altitude, and add hiking to the holiday's activities. The season is also enlivened by carnival processions. **Summer** is the time for enjoying Austria's mountain scenery to the full and making the most of the varied cultural events on offer. Welcoming Carinthia, with its warm-water lakes, attracts swimmers, water-skiing enthusiasts and anglers. Colder, but more romantic, are the picturesque lakes of the Salzkammergut. Mountaineers will choose the glaciers of the Ötztal or the Hohe Tauern, or the slopes of the Karwendel, the Kaisergebirge, the Dachstein or the Gesäuse.

Autumn, with the sun shining and a nip in the air, sheds a particularly beautiful light on the old stone buildings in the towns. This is a good season to discover the wealth of Austria's museums. The wooded valleys of Styria and Carinthia are a pleasure to explore on foot. Night falls swiftly, however. A journey through the vineyards of the Burgenland or Lower Austria, or along the Danube beneath the Wachau, is unforgettable at this time of year, which is marked in Vienna by the reopening of the theatrical and musical seasons (1 September and October respectively).

Mountain weather – The mountain climate varies considerably according to difference in altitude, physical relief or exposure to sunshine.

At the end of morning, the warm expanded air of the valleys creeps up the natural corridors to the heights, causing the formation of clouds round the summits. These clouds are a sign of settled fine weather. About 5pm this valley breeze ceases to blow, and coolness suddenly sets in; it is now the turn of the **mountain breeze**, cold and generally stronger, to sweep the valley in the opposite direction.

The **Föhn** wind is most strongly felt north of the Alps, in the Alpine Valleys of the Rhine, the Inn (especially in the Ötztal) and the Salzach. It is caused by the passage of a deep depression along the north slope of the Alps. Having shed its moisture on the Italian slope of the range, where storms and rain are frequent, the air drawn in by the depression spills over the crest-line and, warmed by compression as it loses altitude (1 ºC per 100m or 5 ºF per 100ft), is transformed into a dry and burning wind, while the atmosphere becomes wonderfully clear. In the mountains everyone is on the alert. Torrents are in spate, avalanches rumble and the risk of fire is great. Citizens live in such a state of nervous exhaustion that examinations are sometimes suspended in the schools in Innsbruck. The *Föhn* can even be submitted as a defence in criminal trials.

However, the *Föhn* has some beneficial effects. It melts the snow, so flocks can be taken up to the Alpine pastures early in the spring. In certain valleys, which are suitably oriented, maize and fruit trees can be cultivated at unexpectedly high altitudes.

Leisure – Austrian-style

For information on winter sports and other resorts, refer to the Practical information section at the end of the guide.

MOUNTAINEERING

In spite of political frontiers, the Bavarian and Austrian Alps and the Dolomites form a single playground in Central Europe, with about 1 100 mountain huts and refuges. In Austria, hundreds of mountain-guides and ski-guides are at the disposal of tourists. In winter, one Austrian in three goes skiing.

The Heroic Period – The conquest of the Großglockner (alt 3 797m – 12 458ft) in 1800 was a victory not only over the difficulties presented by the mountain itself but also over the superstitions that surrounded it. It was however only in the second half of the 19C that climbing became widely popular among the students of the Universities of Munich, Vienna, Innsbruck and Graz. What the students lacked in money, they made up for in courage and spirit of adventure, much to the horror of experienced French and Swiss mountaineers, as they frequently went climbing in the eastern Alps without guides.

Nowadays all the rock-walls of the Austrian Alps are listed in specialized guides, while the citizens of Vienna are able to practise their technique on the Raxalpe (elementary) and on the Gesäuse (advanced), both a day trip away from the city.

Contempt for Danger – After the First World War, young German and Austrian climbers undertook desperate enterprises, sometimes alone, with a contempt for danger bordering on insanity. This daring brought about much of the tragic atmosphere associated with the rock-walls of the Dolomites and even more with the north wall of the Matterhorn, the Great Jurasses and the Eiger, regarded as the last great problems of the Alps and only conquered in 1931, 1935 and 1938 respectively. But technique was being perfected and mountaineering became a recognised sport. In 1925, Wilo Welzenbach of Munich drew up a scale of difficulty in six degrees of which the sixth corresponded with the limit of human endurance. Several Austro-German expeditions have taken part in the conquest of the peaks in the Himalayas and the Karakoram. They attacked Nanga Parbat (8 125m – 26 657ft), the highest peak in Kashmir, which, with walls 5 000m – 16 400ft high, has the greatest relative difference of level in the world. In 1895 the British Alpine climber Albert F Mummery sought to climb the mountain but died in the attempt. Many other climbers tried but none succeeded (owing to terrible weather conditions or avalanches); it was a Tyrolese, Hermann Buhl, who completed the climb alone in 1953. Mount Kangchenjunga, at 8 586m – 28 169ft the third highest peak in the world, was also conquered by a joint Austro-German team. The Charles Evans British Expedition scaled the peak in 1955, but turned back from the summit itself at the request of the Sikkim authorities, who consider the mountain sacred.

In 1975, Reinhold Messner, of Italy, and Peter Habeler, of the Tyrol, stunned the mountaineering world by climbing the Gasherbrum (Hidden Peak, alt 8 068m – 24 470ft) in only four days, without making intermediate camps on the way in what had been the traditional method for Himalayan expeditions. This pair astounded the world a second time in 1978, when they climbed Mount Everest for the first time without using oxygen apparatus. Prior to this, Habeler had conquered the infamous north face of the Eiger in Switzerland in a record nine hours.

P. Habeler/ÖSTERREICH WERBUNG

Peter Habeler's first mountaineerings boots

SKIING

MatthiasZdarsky, an Austrian, published one of the first skiing manuals in 1897, based on his adaptation of Scandinavian techniques to the slopes of the Eastern Alps.

The Arlberg Period (1920-1930) – Although not the pioneer of Austrian skiing, **Hannes Schneider** (1890-1955), from the Arlberg, was the first to devise a coherent doctrine of Alpine skiing. He banned the Scandinavian Telemark swing (a turn made by lifting the weight from the outside and leaning over the inside ski) and drew on the technique of the snow plough to develop the *Stemmbogen* and the *Stemmschwung*, which enabled pupils to control their speed and thus gain confidence.

Schneider was well in touch with modern methods of communication. In 1926 he made a film, *The Wonders of Skiing*, which was a huge success. In 1927 Schneider met Arnold Lunn of England, founder of the Kandahar Ski Club who had revolutionized competitive skiing by codifying the downhill race and the slalom. The two men agreed to introduce a combination of the downhill run and the slalom at St. Anton. The Arlberg-Kandahar began in 1928. Around 1930 many contacts were made between the Tyrolese masters and instructors and the champions of other Alpine countries. Toni Seelos, an expert at the slalom whose elegant style was to influence the until then somewhat rough Arlberg technique, was in charge at Seefeld, which became an advanced training centre and attracted skiers who were highly proficient including the young Frenchman Émile Allais. Allais, by critical observation and experiment, helped to create a new style: skidding, *Stemmschwung* with parallel skis – known as pure drops – diving with the body forward, etc. Since 1956 Austrian skiing has maintained its excellent reputation. The *Wedeln (scull)*, which was devised by the instructor, Kruckenhauser, and the "Jet Wedeln" are systems used by skiers throughout the world. Among the Austrian skiers with international reputations for downhill skiing and ski-jumping are Toni Sailer, Karl Schranz, Franz Klammer and Anne-Marie Moser-Pröll.

Austria, a winter sports paradise – In addition to Innsbruck (Winter Olympics Capital in 1964 and 1976), Austria also offers a selection of smaller winter sports resorts with good facilities, such as St. Anton, Seefeld and Kitzbühel, to which must be added spa resorts, notably Badgastein with its numerous ski-lifts, and mountain villages such as Saalbach. In total there are more than 800 villages fitting snugly into the landscape. Between them they offer visitors 22 000km – 13 670 miles of downhill slopes, 12 000km – 7 460 miles of cross-country trails and 400 ski-schools. The mountains are so densely settled that there has been hardly any necessity to build special ski resorts which might spoil the local atmosphere for the many foreigners who come to Austria not only for the excitement of skiing but also for the traditional friendliness of the local population.

Summer skiing – A number of cable-cars take visitors beyond the 3 000m – 10 000ft level. This makes it possible to ski all year round on the slopes of (among others) the Kitzsteinhorn, the Hunerkogel, the upper valleys of the Stubai (Hochstubai) and the Tux, Mayrhofen, and thanks to the Ötztal Glaciers Route, the Ötztal.

Cross-country skiing – This can be enjoyed practically anywhere in Austria. The gentle slopes of the Eastern Alps provide good conditions for long-distance enthusiasts, while small villages as well as the bigger resorts like Seefeld or Kitzbühel have their network of trails *(Loipen)*. Some resorts like Ramsau am Dachstein have come into their own by specializing in this ever more popular type of skiing.

15

HIKING

Austria is also a hiker's paradise. Tourist resorts offer numerous maintained footpaths, many of which are accessible even in winter, so that visitors can explore the countryside along a dense network of waymarked paths all year round.

Mountain hiking is of course a very popular activity in Austria, offering not only physical exercise in fresh mountain air, but also incredible views. To meet the growing interest in this particular holiday pastime, a number of hikes and rambles to some of the more spectacular viewpoints are described in the main body of this guide.

Austrian National Parks

Nationalpark Hohe Tauern – This vast protected Alpine region stretches over the provinces of Salzburg, east Tyrol and Carinthia.

Nationalpark Neusiedler See-Seewinkel (Burgenland) – This is the only national park on the Central European steppe nearly half of it lies (in Hungary).

Nationalpark Nockberge (Carinthia) – This park between the Lieser valley and the Turracher Höhe range was founded as part of a project to conserve its eco-system.

LOCAL CRAFTS

Those looking for good quality souvenirs should visit the **Heimatwerk**, an official outlet for the work of local artisans.

Burgenland – *Eisenstadt Heimatwerk*. China (Stoob), basket-weaving (Piringsdorf and Weiden am See), jade jewellery and serpentine marble (Bernstein).

Carinthia – *Klagenfurt, Spittal and Villach Heimatwerk*. Costumes, ceramics, carved wooden boxes; wrought iron (Friesach).

Salzburg – *Salzburg and Neukirchen am Großvenediger Heimatwerk*. Pewter, china, regional costumes.

Styria – *Graz and Kapfenberg Heimatwerk*. Printed linens, jewellery (Bad Aussee), carved wooden masks (Mitterndorf), painted pottery (Gams), *Loden* cloth (Ramsau and Mandling).

Tyrol – *Innsbruck Heimatwerk*. Wooden Christmas cribs, tablecloths and embroidered fabrics, wrought iron; majolica (Schwaz), cut and engraved glassware (Kufstein and Kramsach).

Upper Austria – *Linz Heimatwerk*. Painted glassware and painted wooden boxes; handwoven linen (Haslach); leather-work, candles (Braunau); wrought iron, steel-engravings (Steyr); china (Gmunden); head-dresses and silver jewellery (Bad Ischl).

Vienna – Petit point, Augarten porcelain, embroidered blouses. Viennese enamel.

Vorarlberg – *Bregenz Heimatwerk*. Wooden articles, painted glassware, hand weaving; embroidery (Schwarzenberg and Lustenau); candles (Schruns).

SPAS

Austria has a wide selection of spa resorts equipped for the most varied treatment. In the skiing season many of these country resorts (Badgastein) keep their warm swimming pools open.

Sulphur-springs – These are used mainly to remedy ailments of the joints, muscles, the nervous system and skin troubles at resorts such as Baden whose thermal beach draws many Viennese and, in the Salzkammergut, at Bad Ischl, Bad Goisern, etc.

Salt-springs – Waters impregnated with sodium chloride (salt) from natural springs or "mother-waters", the residues of the refining of industrial salt, are exploited alongside the salt-mines themselves. They are used in douches and baths and are good for gynaecological and infantile diseases, and for inhaling, when they clear the bronchial tubes. To this group may be added the bicarbonate bearing waters, like those of Bad Gleichenberg in Styria, which are also recommended for drinking to treat the stomach, intestines and kidneys.

Iodized-springs – These are invaluable for curing metabolic and circulatory disorders, and for vision and glandular troubles. They are particularly well represented by Bad Hall in Upper Austria. In addition to the true mineral springs, some hot springs such as those at Badgastein also have radioactive properties.

Special Treatment – Mud baths and applications of mud are features of many resorts. Patients suffering from inflammation of the joints or the after-effects of wounds have a good chance of a permanent cure.

The **Kneipp Cure** was perfected by Sebastian Kneipp, the parish priest of the Bavarian village of Wörishofen from 1855 to 1897. The system uses every kind of hydrotherapy in specialized establishments, combined with a healthy and balanced diet.

Austria

Through inheritance Austria acquired a vast empire which included, under the authority of a single sovereign in Vienna, countries as different as southern Italy and Galicia, Hungary and the Netherlands, but the boundaries of the modern republic, more modest in size, were laid down in 1919. Nevertheless, she reflects the character of her former empire, and the place she occupies in the Europe of today is due as much to her historic past as to her geographical position.

Enchanting Landscapes – From the Vorarlberg, which resembles eastern Switzerland, to the Burgenland which is similar to the Balkans, and from the Drava valley to the foothills of the Bohemian massif and the Carpathians, the Austrian landscape is one of continued variety. Here are the Tyrolean Alps, their snowy summits given over to skiers and lovers of mountaineering; the Salzkammergut, dotted with lakes and villages; the Danube valley, marked in the Wachau by ruined castles and by vineyards; the Vienna Woods, which one can hardly think of without humming a waltz; the moving beauty of Salzburg, the town of Mozart and the prince-archbishops; the charm of Graz, the capital of fertile Styria; the prestige of Vienna, impregnated with world history and rich in priceless art treasures, and the wistful horizons of the Burgenland stretching away into the Hungarian plain *(puszta)*.

Art Treasures – Cities like Innsbruck, Graz, Salzburg and, above all, Vienna are of tremendous interest to tourists; they have fine buildings and incredibly rich museum collections. Smaller towns like Feldkirch, Hall in Tirol, Rattenberg, Steyr, Freistadt, St. Wolfgang and Bruck an der Mur proudly display their links with the past.

Innumerable castles, surviving from the Middle Ages, dot the landscape and are powerfully placed on spurs guarding important routes. Many of them have been turned into hotels or restaurants which can be enjoyed by tourists.

The parish churches and above all the abbeys, for the most part remodelled in the Baroque style, contain decoration and furnishings – picture galleries, statues and altarpieces – evidence of one of the most brillant periods of religious art. At least one of these churches should be visited during the course of a service, when the singing, the tones of the organ, the rising incense, and the presence of the congregation heighten the already theatrical atmosphere of the Baroque.

The course of Austrian history has very often been marked by some musical festivity. Thus it was Beethoven's Fidelio which was performed at the reopening of the Vienna Opera on 5 November 1955, a moment of high emotion coinciding with the lifting of Allied occupation and the restoration of the country's sovereignty. The national anthem of Republican Austria is sung to a tune popularly attributed to Mozart, but which was in fact composed by Johann Holzer, one of his contemporaries. The lyrics were written by Paula von Preradovic in 1947.

A Warm Welcome – To the charm and interest of scenes and buildings is added the attraction of a kind and smiling welcome, showing the pleasant habit of the Austrians, which they call *Gemütlichkeit*, of making people feel at home.

Tourists are rarely treated as foreigners in Austria. They can mix freely with local people, even taking part in lively folk festivals, especially in the Tyrol. In a wine-producing village in the Viennese suburbs they may spend an evening in a wineshop *(Heuriger)*, sipping this year's wine to the sound of violins and accordions. Its variety makes Austria an attractive country for holidays, having something to offer all tastes. The culturally-inclined go to the art and museum towns, while the sophisticates prefer the fashionable resorts on the Carinthian lakes. Nature-lovers have a wide choice of small, hospitable mountain villages which offer, in summer, opportunities for numerous excursions, and in winter excellent skiing, both downhill and cross-country. For real skiing fanatics, facilities make year-round skiing possible on some of the glaciers.

The Modern Face of Austria – The idea of Austria as a nation of operetta-lovers is of course but a simplistic caricature. As far as the arts are concerned, the country has more than its fair share of innovative architects, sculptors, poets, painters and other graphic artists...

In the domain of industry and technology, Austria plays an equally leading role, particularly in its relations with the re-emerging countries of Eastern and Central Europe. The country's changing landscapes can be appreciated by driving along the great mountain roads such as those of the Silvretta, the Großglockner, or the Felbertauern, the Brenner motorway, or the new highway which follows the Danube through the Wachau; by crossing the great Europa Bridge which spans the Sill valley, the Kaprun Dam, high in the mountains, or the Altenwörth Dam on the Danube; by passing through industrial towns in full development such as Linz and Graz, whose modern suburbs are constantly expanding.

Austria has used its neutral status (based on the Constitutional Law on neutrality enacted by its Parliament on 26 October 1955) to act as an international meeting-place for exchanges of all kinds. Until recently, it was something of an outpost of the West, bounded to north, east and southeast by the "Iron Curtain". The changes taking place in the former Communist countries have enhanced its chosen role as an intermediary between the halves of a once-divided Europe.

Helligenblut

Introduction

GEORG MIKES

Description of the country

At the heart of the Alps, Austria covers an area of 84 000km² - 32 430 sq miles, stretching for 580km - 360 miles from Switzerland to Hungary. For a distance of 2 600km - 1 616 miles, it shares a border with Germany, the Czech and Slovak Republics, Hungary, Slovenia, Italy, Switzerland and Liechtenstein.
The river Danube, which acts as a catchment for virtually all the rivers of Austria, flows west-east for 360km - 224 miles across the Danube plain, a vast uplands abutting the foothills of the Bohemian mountains to the north and encompassing the mountainous Wachau region. This is the historical heart of Austria. Two thirds of the country is covered by the Alpine chain, beginning with the eastern end of the Alps in the south. To the east, Austria runs into the Puszta, or Hungarian plain.

Diverse influences - Austria has received many different influences from the north, south and east, as great natural areas have rarely corresponded to the political frontiers. To the north, Austria and Bavaria share the limestone chain of the Alps and there have always been close contacts between the two countries. To the east, where the Alps slope away to the great Hungarian plain, Austria has an eastern window open to the cultural and climatic influences coming from the Balkans. Vienna arose at the crossroads of Germanic and Balkan influences. To the south, Austria once had links to the Adriatic, lost since 1919. Nevertheless, the spread of the old Austro-Hungarian Empire, far beyond present-day frontiers, favoured the earlier penetration of many Mediterranean influences.

AN ALPINE COUNTRY

The Austrian Alps are divided from north to south into three chains: the Northern Limestone Alps, the High or Central Alps, and the Southern Limestone Alps, separated from each other by the great furrows which form the valleys of the Inn, the Salzach and the Enns in the north; and the Drava and the Mur in the south.

The Northern Limestone Alps - These overflow to a large extent into Bavaria and spread out west to east into the massifs of Rätikon, Lechtal, Karwendel, Kaisergebirge, Steinernes Meer, Tennengebirge, Dachstein, the Alps of Ennstal, Eisenerz, Hochschwab and Schneeberg, where the dark green forests stand out against the grey limestone cliffs. The highest point is the 3 038m - 9 967ft Parseierspitze. The Limestone Alps do not form an unbroken barrier that is difficult to cross. Transverse valleys along which the waters of the Lech, Ache (the Alz in Bavaria), Saalach and Enns flow towards the Danube plateau, divide the Northern Limestone Alps into distinct massifs which tourists with cars can easily cross or go round, and whose cliffs have been explored by mountaineers.
The Alps east of the Ache have a characteristic outline: the Dachstein, the Hochschwab and the Raxalpe rise sharply to summits of more than 2 000m - 6 562ft. The porous nature of their limestone rocks makes these plateaux

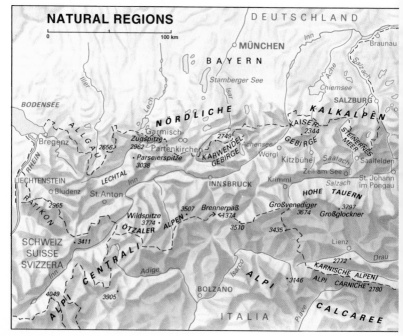

into stony deserts, scored here and there with narrow furrows, between which rise small sharp crests formed by water courses through the limestone. Here, the flow of the water is almost entirely subterranean and results in the formation of numerous caves, the most well-known being those of the Dachstein. The climb by cable-car to the Krippenstein *(see DACHSTEIN)* or the Raxalpe will reveal all the characteristic features of this formation.

The Northern Limestone Alps are bounded to the south by a deep cleft, separating them from the High Alps. This cleft is divided into valleys, each with its own river, the Inn (between Landeck and Wörgl), the Salzach (between Krimml and St. Johann im Pongaa), and the Enns (between Radstadt and Hieflan). The presence of this major break in the landscape has been of great benefit to east-west communications, making it possible to drive along the chain for its entire length.

The High or Central Alps – The High Alps, mostly of crystalline rock, appear as a succession of ridges topped by glaciers, comprising (west to east): the Ötztal Alps (Wildspitze, 3 774m – 12 382ft), the Hohe Tauern (Großvenediger, 3 674m – 12 054ft – and Großglockner, 3 797m – 12 458ft) with their dazzling glaciers and the Niedere Tauern. The line of the crests hardly drops below 3 000m – 10 000ft for a distance of more than 250km – 150 miles; mountain passes are rare, making the barrier no easy matter to cross. The Brenner Pass (1 374m – 4 508ft), the medieval route to Venice, links the valleys of the Inn and the Adige. The Großglockner road and the Felbertauern tunnel enable tourists to cross the imposing massif of the Hohe Tauern. To the south of the High Alps, the furrows of the Drava, Mur and Mürz rivers play a role that is comparable to the great valleys of the north and form the natural link between Vienna and Venice or Milan.

Nationalpark Hohe Tauern – Some of the eastern slopes of the Großglockner and part of the Schobergruppe massif have been designated a national park, with the aim of conserving the varied landscapes, rich flora and wildlife of the area. The extensive network of signposted footpaths gives access to areas of virtually virgin landscape as well as to those parts of the park where a traditional mountain economy and culture still flourish.

The Southern Limestone Alps – The Carnic Alps and the Karawanken are Austrian on their northern slopes only, following Austria's cession, in 1919, of the southern part of the Tyrol to Italy and the Julian Alps to then Yugoslavia.

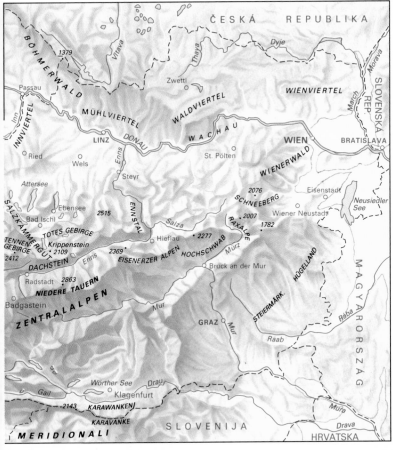

Alpine relief

The following summary gives an idea of how the formation of the Alps was influenced by the action of water or ice.

FLUVIAL RELIEF	GLACIAL RELIEF

Upper valley: erosion

Stream headwaters
① Funnel-shaped basin, deeply ravined.
② Overflow channel.

Former glacial hollow (natural amphitheatre, cirque or corrie)
① Smoothed surface.
② Steep back walls.

Middle valley: transport of material

River valley
① V-shaped valley.
② Steeply-incised valley.

Former glaciated valley
① U-shaped valley – wide valley floor (filled with material) and steep sides.
② Bench ("Alp").

Lower valley: deposition of material

Alluvial fan
The material is deposited in the form of an alluvial fan at the point where the slope is no longer steep enough for the stream to transport it.

Moraines
① Terminal moraine.
② Lateral moraine.
③ Medial moraine.

The work of the glaciers

About 10 000 years ago, the Alpine glaciers advanced northwards, extending over the Bavarian plateau almost as far as the site of modern Munich. These solid rivers of ice were immensely thick; the glacier which occupied the valley of the Inn reached a maximum depth of 1 700m – nearly 6 000ft.

The action of the glaciers led to a complete remodelling of the relief of the Alpine valleys *(see sketch opposite)*. They scooped out natural amphitheatres known as cirques, like the one closing off the Brandnertal, scoured valleys into a U-shaped section (like the steep-sided Saalach valley north of Saalfelden), and created hanging valleys (one of the best examples being the one above the Achensee), often marked by high waterfalls where they join the main valley.

Glaciers tended not to follow the existing continuous slope of a valley but to carve out a series of well-defined steps, natural sites for modern hydro-electric installations. Carrying along a mass of rocky debris, which when deposited is known as a moraine, the glaciers added an extra, complex layer to the landscape of the pre-alpine plateau. The terminal moraines, semi-circular in shape, created natural dams behind which water accumulated to form the lakes of the Bavarian plateau and of the northern Salzkammergut (Attersee).

FAUNA

Austria has a rich and varied animal world. The most interesting fauna are to be found around the shores of the Neusiedler See, a paradise for waterfowl and waders, of which the area can boast over 250 species: kingfishers, river terns, spoonbills, herons, bitterns, snipes and hoopoes. Storks are also regular visitors here. On the lakes of the Salzkammergut and Upper Austria, swans add a fairytale element to the scene.

The Danube is home to 60 of the 80 species of fish to be found in Austria, such as eels, perch and catfish.

Various kinds of deer, wild boar, badgers and foxes make their home in Austria's forests, while the fields and woodlands are a playground for rabbits and hares. But the real stars among Austrian fauna, as far as tourists are concerned, are undoubtedly the inhabitants of the mountains.

Alpine fauna – Visitors never fail to succumb to the charms of Austria's cutest Alpine resident, the grey-brown **marmot**, which can be up to 60cm – 24in long and which lives on slopes exposed to the sun. Unfortunately, being of a somewhat shy disposition, it only rarely grants lucky ramblers a public audience. The blue hare is equally cautious, and has the added advantage of a coat which changes colour with the seasons, helping it to blend in better with its surroundings.

Herds of nimble **chamois** are to be seen principally in the Limestone Alps. **Alpine ibex**, equally agile and also very strong, live from the tree line up to an altitude of 3 500m – 11 483ft. **Red deer** are common throughout Austria. The snow-mouse makes its home above the forest line, while the Alpine salamander prefers the shores of mountain lakes.

Typical Alpine birdlife includes the snow-partridge, the Alpine jackdaw, the griffon vulture and the capercaillie, which is more rare a sight, tending to keep to lower-lying areas, as does the blackcock. On the whole, and especially during the mating season, these birds are more likely to be heard than seen. King of them all, however, is surely the **golden eagle**, a truly majestic bird with a wingspan of 2m – 7ft, which sadly rather tends to make itself scarce.

FLORA

In mountain areas the pattern of vegetation is not only influenced by soil type and climate but also strongly linked to altitude and aspect. Tree species in particular tend to succeed one another in clearly defined vertical stages, though this staging is much modified by human influences as well as by the orientation of the particular slope. Northern, ie south-facing, sunny slopes offer the best conditions for settlement and agriculture and have therefore been the most subject to deforestation. Southern, ie north-facing, slopes by contrast have tended to keep their trees, which flourish in the prevailing wetter and more shady conditions. This pattern is seen at its best in valleys running east-west.

Bird-watching

Burgenland – Neusiedler See, Seewinkel/Lange Lacke; **Carinthia** – Landskron ruins (eagles), Grossedlinger Teich near Wolfsberg, Völkermarkt reservoir; **Lower Austria** – Danube, March and Thaya river plains, Thaya valley (near Hardegg); **Salzburg** – Pinzgau between the Gasteiner and Habach valleys, south shore of the Zeller See; **Upper Austria** – Danube river plain near the Linz basin, Schmiding bird reserve.

Stemless Trumpet Gentian
gentiana acaulis
May to August

Edelweiss
leontopodium alpinium
July to September

Alpine Sea Holly
eryngium alpinum
July and August

Martagon Lily
lilium martagon
June to August

Orange Lily
lilium bulbiferum
June and July

Alpenrose
rhododendron ferrugineum
July and August

In most parts of the Alps, farming is practised up to about the 1 500m – 5 000ft contour; beyond this there is a belt of conifer forest. At around 2 200m – 7 000ft, the trees give way to alpine pastures with their rich mixture of grasses, herbs and myrtles, while beyond the 3 000m – 10 000ft level bare rock prevails, relieved in places by mosses and lichens.

Trees of the Alps – The Alpine forests consist mainly of conifers, four of which are characterised below. There are many different species of pine, all of which have their needles grouped in bunches of 2 to 5, while their cones have hard, coarse scales.

Spruce (Fichte) – This is the typical tree of north-facing slopes. It has a pointed outline and drooping branches, while its reddish bark (hence its German name of *Rottane* = red fir) becomes deeply fissured with age. It has sharp needles and its downward-hanging cones fall in one piece from the tree.

Larch (Lärche) – The only European conifer to lose its needles in winter, the larch is the characteristic tree of south-facing slopes. Its delicate light-green foliage casts a relatively light shade, favouring the growth of a rich grass and herb layer, an attractive feature of larch woods. The small cones are carried upright on the twigs.

Austrian pine (Schwarzkiefer, Schwarzföhre) – A tree of medium height, the Austrian pine has a dense crown, dark green foliage and a pale and darkly fissured bark. Its needles grow in pairs. Undemanding in terms of soil and climate, it is the dominant tree of the limestone heights bordering the Vienna basin. It is frequently used in reclamation work in difficult conditions (eg on thin limestone soils).

Arolla pine (Zirbel) – This pine is easily recognised by its upward-curving branches which give it the look of a candelabra. It grows right up to the tree line, often tortured into fantastic shapes by the wind. Its bluish-green needles grow in clusters of five. The dense wood of this pine is much appreciated by woodcarvers and makers of rustic furniture.

Austrian Pine

Alpine flora – The name "Alpine" is normally used to describe those plants which grow above the tree line. Because of the short growing season (June to August), they flower early, while the disproportionate development and colouring of the flower is a result of exposure to intense ultra-violet light. Resistance to drought is often important (woolly leaf surfaces, thick leaves for water storage).

Remote origins – Most Alpine plants originated elsewhere. Some came from the lower mountains and plains but adapted to the harsher conditions at high altitude (dandelion, centaury); others are from the Mediterranean (pinks and narcissus), the Arctic (buttercup, white poppy), or even Asia (edelweiss, primula). The few truly indigenous species (valerian, columbine) managed to survive the Quaternary glaciations.

The influence of site – Mountain plants do not grow at random; some need alkaline, others an acid soil; some flourish on scree, in a cleft in the rock or in a boggy patch, depending on their particular environmental requirements. Each type of site has a corresponding plant – or plant association – able to thrive in the given conditions.

Historical table and notes

976-1246	Rule of the house of Babenberg.
1260	Ottokar (King of Bohemia, 1253) invested with the Duchies of Austria and Styria by Richard, King of the Germans, Earl of Cornwall and brother of Henry II of England.

The Habsburgs

1273-1291	**Rudolf I**, founder of the Habsburg dynasty, elected by the German princes to succeed the Babenbergs, defeated Ottokar and divided Austria and Styria between his sons.
1335	Carinthia and Carniola annexed to the Habsburg territory.
1358-1365	Reign of **Rudolf IV**.
1363	The Tyrol annexed to Austria.
1440-1493	Friedrich III, Duke of Styria, inaugurated a policy of political succession and intermarriage which raised the Habsburgs to the highest rank in the west. His son Maximilian was the first to benefit from this.
1477	Marriage of Maximilian, son of Friedrich III, to Mary of Burgundy, only daughter of Charles the Bold and sole heiress of the powerful Duchy of Burgundy. Her dowry included territories which France tried to regain in subsequent centuries.
1483-1498	Austria became a most formidable rival for Charles VIII of France.

Expansion of influence

1493-1519	By his marriage, **Maximilian I**, Emperor of the Holy Roman Empire, had gained possession of most of the Burgundian States (Low Countries, Franche-Comté). He married his eldest son, Philip the Handsome, to the Infanta of Spain. Their son, Charles V, inherited the whole of their possessions.
1519-1556	Reign of **Emperor Charles V**. Rivalry between Charles V and François I of France (1517-1547). Charles V became Head of the Holy Roman Empire. Struggle between the Empire and France for supremacy in Europe.
1529	Vienna besieged by the Turks.
1556	Abdication of Charles V and partition of the Empire. Charles's brother, Ferdinand I, became Emperor and head of the Austrian branch of the House of Habsburg. He founded the Austrian Monarchy and also reigned over Bohemia and Hungary. Charles's son, Philip II, was given Spain and Portugal, Sicily, Naples and northern Italy, the Low Countries and Burgundy.
1618-1648	Thirty Years War caused by the mutual antagonism of Protestants and Catholics and European fears of the political ambitions of Austria.
1635	France entered the war against Austria; previously Richelieu had been supporting Austria's enemies in secret.
1648	Austria signed the Treaty of Westphalia which ended the Thirty Years War and marked the failure of Habsburg efforts to reorganise and strengthen Germany.
1164	Louis XIV of France (1643-1715) sent 6 000 young nobles under the command of Jean de Coligny to assist in the defence of Austria against the Turks (victory of St Gotthard).
1685	Revocation of the Edict of Nantes: the League of Augsburg – Austria, Spain, Sweden and various German princes – made war against France.
1697	Peace of Ryswick following the French victory.

Consolidation of the Empire

1657-1705	Reign of Leopold I.
1683	Vienna again besieged by the Turks.
1687	The Hungarian monarchy fell to the Habsburgs.
18C	Throughout this century, Austrian policy was overshadowed by three great problems: the Succession to the Empire; the territorial threat from the Turks, the Piedmontese and the French; the unified administration of very different countries.
1701-1714	War of the Spanish Succession. A new coalition against France formed by Austria, the United Provinces and England.

1704	The Battle of Blenheim in which Vienna was saved from the French by English and Dutch armies under the command of the Duke of Marlborough.
1713	To ensure his daughter's succession to the Imperial Crown in the absence of male heirs, Karl VI sacrificed territorial rights to the great European countries and promulgated the Pragmatic Sanction. When the king died Maria Theresa had to defy its signatories in order to keep her empire.
1733-1738	War of the Polish Succession: Louis XV of France (1715-1774) supported his father-in-law, Stanislas Leszczinski of Poland; the Emperor Charles VI supported Augustus III; France acquired Lorraine.
1736	Maria Theresa of Austria married Duc François de Lorraine who attracted artists from his native country to Vienna.
1740-1748	War of the Austrian Succession: France and Prussia contested the validity of Maria Theresa's claim to the Imperial Throne. The Austrian cause was supported by the United Kingdom and Holland against Prussia, France and Spain.
1743	French defeat at Dettingen by an army of Austrians, Hanoverians and British commanded by George II, the last time an English king fought in person on the battlefield.
1745	Anglo-Austrian defeat at Fontenoy.
1756-1763	Seven Years War: re-alignment of the alliances: Austria, France, Russia, Saxony and Sweden fought against Britain and Prussia to recover Silesia.
1740-1765	Reign of **Maria Theresa.** With the help of able ministers, she became popular for her financial and administrative reforms.
1763	Marie-Antoinette, daughter of Maria Theresa, married Louis XVI, future king of France.
1765-1790	Reign of **Joseph II,** who in the authoritarian manner of enlightened despotism, continued the work of reorganization begun by his mother.
1781	Abolition of serfdom.
1786	Secularization: Dissolution of 738 houses of contemplative orders in favour of the parishes.
1792-1835	Reign of **Franz II.**
1792-1815	**Napoleonic Wars.**
1792	Declaration of War by the French government (Assemblée législative) against the "king of Bohemia and Hungary". French victory at Valmy.
1796-1797	Following Napoleon's campaigns in Italy, the French Army reached Leoben where peace preliminaries were signed; they became the terms of the Treaty of Campoformio.
1803, 1805, 1809	Austria defeated three times by the French under Napoleon.
1805	Austria received the territory of the Archbishops of Salzburg as compensation for the losses of territory suffered by her under the Treaty of Pressburg.
1808	Franz II renounced the title of Head of the Holy Roman Empire and adopted that of Emperor of Austria under the name of **Franz I.**
1809	Austrian policy directed by Chancellor **Metternich** who worked for revenge against France. Rebellion of the Tyrol led by Andreas Hofer against the Franco-Bavarian alliance.
1810	Marriage of Marie-Louise, daughter of the Emperor Franz I, to Napoleon.
1811-1832	Napoleon II, the Duke of Reichstadt, son of Napoleon and Marie-Louise, resident at Schönbrunn with Franz I.
1813-14	Austria joined the sixth coalition which broke through the French lines at Leipzig, forced Napoleon back on to the defensive in France and then to abdication.

Trouble and Downfall of the Monarchy

1814-1815	**Congress of Vienna** to redraw the map of Europe. Austria recovered Lombardy and Venetia lost in her wars with France and took a leading position in the Germanic Confederation of which Metternich was the mastermind.
1848-49	Revolution in Vienna. Fall of Metternich, Hungarian rebellion suppressed with the help of Russia.
1853-56	**Crimean War.** Austrian intervention forced Russian withdrawal from Balkan invasion and the sinking of the Turkish fleet at Sinope. Britain and France declared war on Russia in 1854.

1852-70	Napoleon III intervened on the side of Piedmont; Austrian defeat at Magenta and Solferino, resulting in the loss of Lombardy.
1861-65	Civil War.
1848-1916	Reign of **Franz Joseph**.
1866	War between Austria and Prussia. Austria was defeated at Sadowa, gave up her intervention in German politics and cast her eyes upon the Balkans.
1867	Creation of the dual Austro-Hungarian monarchy, with common foreign, defence and economic policies.
1878	Austrian occupation of Bosnia and Herzegovina.
1914-18	Outbreak of the First World War, provoked by the assassination of the Crown Prince Franz Ferdinand at Sarajevo

Emperor Franz Joseph

in Bosnia and Austria's subsequent attack on Serbia.

1916-1918	Reign of **Karl I** and collapse of the Dual Monarchy.

The Republic

1919	Treaty of St Germain-en-Laye. Cession of South Tyrol to Italy. A plebiscite determined that southern Carinthia should remain in Austria and not be ceded to Yugoslavia. Karl Renner became the first State Chancellor.
1930	**Great Depression.**
1933	Chancellor Dollfuß inaugurated an authoritarian regime, hostile both to the Social-Democrats and to the Nazis.
1934	Social Democratic Party banned. Nazi putsch. Assassination of Chancellor Dollfuß. His successor Schuschnigg sought to avoid war with Germany.
1936	Recognition by Germany of the territorial sovereignty of Austria.
1938	Nazi invasion of Austria which became Ostmark, the Eastern March of the Greater German Reich; the annexation (Anschluß) was approved by a referendum.
1939-45	Second World War. Austria, annexed by Germany, entered the war against the Allies.
1940	The ashes of the Duke of Reichstadt, l'Aiglon, transferred from the Capuchin Crypt in Vienna to Les Invalides in Paris.
1943	At the Moscow Conference the Allies undertook to restore Austria's independence after the war within the frontiers of 1 January 1938.
1945	The Russians occupied Vienna on 11 April. On 27 April a government was formed under the premiership of Karl Renner. The democratic constitution of 1920 was put into practice. Austria and Vienna divided into four occupied zones: British, French, American and Russian.
15 May 1955	Belvedere Treaty. Withdrawal of occupying troops. Proclamation of Austrian neutrality.
26 October 1955	Austria declares its neutrality.
1955-56	Coalition of social democrats (SPÖ) and conservatives ("people's party", or ÖVP).
1956	Accepted onto the Council of Europe.
1971-83	Social democratic government under Chancellor Kreisky, for the first time with an absolute majority in Parliament.
1986	Election as President of Kurt Waldheim, Secretary-General of the UNO (1972-81).
1989	Austria applies for membership of the European Community.
	Death of Zita of Bourbon-Parma, last Empress of Austria and Queen of Hungary, in exile since 1919.
Spring 1992	Election as President of Thomas Klestil (ÖVP).
1 January 1995	Austria becomes a member of the European Union.

GREAT DAYS AND ADVERSITIES

The Eastern March – The Romans arrived in the Danube Valley at an early date. All along the river there arose a defensive system of forts and castles, of which Carnuntum (Petronell), capital of the province of Pannonia, was the hub. The mixing of peoples which occured in Europe following the Celtic occupation had its greatest effect in Austria.

After defeating the Avar tribes, who lived in the area that is now Hungary, Charlemagne reinforced the defensive system of his empire by forming, on the banks of the Danube, the Eastern March – Ostmark or Ostarrîchi – whose name became Österreich in German and finally Austria in English.

This Eastern March was granted to the Babenberg family by Emperor Otto I, son of Heinrich I Duke of Saxony and successor to the Germanic branch of the Carolingian dynasty.

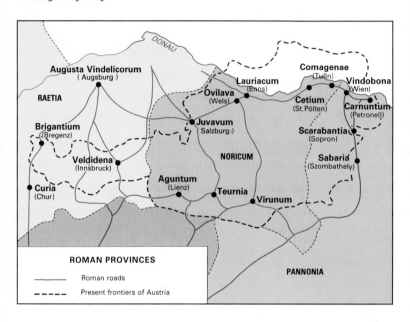

The House of Babenberg (976-1246) – This family brought unity to a country wrestling with opposing influences and cleverly preserved it through the quarrels of the Papacy and the Empire which set popes against emperors. They chose as residences Pöchlarn, Melk, Tulln, the Leopoldsberg and finally Vienna. They were devout and favoured the foundation of abbeys such as Kremsmünster, St. Florian, Melk, Göttweig and Klosterneuburg.

Under Heinrich II Jasomirgott, Austria was elevated to the rank of a hereditary Duchy. The last of the Babenbergs, Frederick the Warrior, was killed while fighting the Magyars.

Bohemian Intervention (1246-78) – The vacancy left by Frederick aroused the envy of the kings of Bohemia and Hungary. Ottokar of Bohemia got the better of his rival and imposed his rule on the former possessions of the Babenbergs, but ended by finding an opponent in Rudolf of Habsburg, who had been chosen by the Prince-Electors to succeed the Babenbergs.

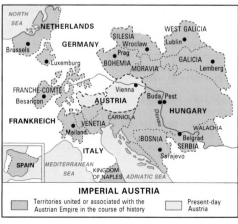

Rudolf the Founder – Rudolf, who was crowned in 1273, immediately attacked Ottokar, occupied Vienna and won the victory of Marchfeld in 1278. The opening phase had begun of what was to be the remarkable destiny of the House of Habsburg.

A.E.I.O.U.

Austria Est Imperare Orbi Universo – Austria shall rule the world. The meteoric career of the Habsburg dynasty *(see genealogical tree opposite)* in less than three centuries was such that it could adopt this proud motto. To the political wisdom of those Habsburg representatives wearing the imperial crown was added great diplomatic skill.

A clever marriage policy brought Austria, in the 16C, more territory than the most fortunate of wars: Maximilian I, a prince who was a friend of the arts *(see INNSBRUCK)*, acquired the Franche-Comté and the Low Countries by his marriage to Mary of Burgundy, daughter of Charles the Bold; his son, Philip the Handsome, married Joan the Mad, Queen of Castille, the child of this union being **Charles V**. As Holy Roman Emperor, King of Spain, possessor of Naples, Sicily and Sardinia and immense territories in the two Americas, Emperor Charles V, the successor of the Habsburgs through his father, was the most powerful sovereign in Europe. This vast Empire remained united but a short time beneath a single crown. On the abdication of Charles V, the territories were divided between Charles's son, Philip II, and his brother, Ferdinand I, who reigned over the Habsburg's German possessions and Bohemia and Hungary.

"Long Live Our Maria Theresa!" – This was the cry of the Hungarian noblemen, preparing in 1740 to defend the rights of their young sovereign, aged 23. Maria Theresa, the daughter of Karl VI, found a difficult situation when she came to the throne, despite her father's efforts to secure succession for her, in the absence of a male heir.

The Elector of Bavaria, elected Emperor under the name of Karl VII, showed himself, at first, to be a dangerous rival. War broke out between Austria on the one hand, Bavaria, Prussia and France on the other. Maria Theresa faced it with tireless energy, and her forty-years' reign brought positive gains. She shared her ruling powers with her husband, Duc François de Lorraine, later Emperor Franz I Stephan, and after his death, with her son, **Joseph II**. Remarkably supported by first-class ministers and generals, she carried out useful financial and administrative reforms.

The Struggle with France (1792-1815) – For the twenty-three years during which Revolutionary, then Imperial, France was at war with the rest of Europe, Austria was, together with England, her most determined opponent.

It was France which on 20 April 1792 declared war on Franz II, Emperor of Austria and Germany. The war went badly for the Austrians; they were beaten at Jemappes in 1792, at Marengo and Hohenlinden in 1800 and threatened, after Napoleon's daring campaign, in Italy in 1797.

The accession of Napoleon to the Imperial French throne in 1804 dealt a heavy blow to the Habsburg monarchy. Napoleon I opened his reign with the victories of Ulm and Austerlitz (1805) and forced Franz II to sue for peace and renounce the crown of the Holy Roman Empire. In 1809 the defeat of the French on the battlefields of Essling and Aspern and the successes of the Tyrolese partisans under the leadership of **Andreas Hofer** brought new hope to the Austrians; but the victory of Napoleon at Wagram was followed by the **Treaty of Vienna**. In 1810 the victor married Marie-Louise, daughter of the vanquished Emperor. Metternich however refused to accept humiliation and after the Russian campaign of 1812 threw all the forces of Austria against Napoleon. In 1814 the Austrian troops under Schwarzenberg entered Paris.

The **Congress of Vienna** consolidated not only the triumph of Metternich, who was virtually directing the politics of all Europe, but renewed the power of the Habsburgs.

The Century of Franz Joseph – Franz Joseph's reign of sixty-eight years (1848-1916), one of the longest in history, ended in failure, since the Habsburg monarchy collapsed two years after his death. Nevertheless, he was a significant figure, loved and respected by his people, and made profound social, economic and political changes in his reign.

Few monarchs have had to face so many political difficulties: the revolution of 1848, on his accession to the throne, marked by a terrible revolt of the Hungarians, which was checked by aggressive Russian intervention; the compromise *(Ausgleich)* of 1867 which created a dual Austro-Hungarian government; disastrous wars in Italy against Napoleon III in 1859 and against Prussia in 1866; not to mention also family misfortunes: death of the Emperor's brother, the Emperor Maximilian of Mexico, shot in 1867; death of his only son, the Crown Prince Rudolf, at Mayerling in 1889; assassination of his wife, the Empress Elisabeth (the beautiful Sissi) at Geneva in 1898; assassination of his nephew, the Archduke Franz Ferdinand at Sarajevo in 1914.

Yet his reign resulted in economic prosperity and a relatively easy-going way of life, reflected in the middle class of the period, and by an artistic and cultural revival and development of town-planning of which, in Vienna, the layout of the Ring was typical.

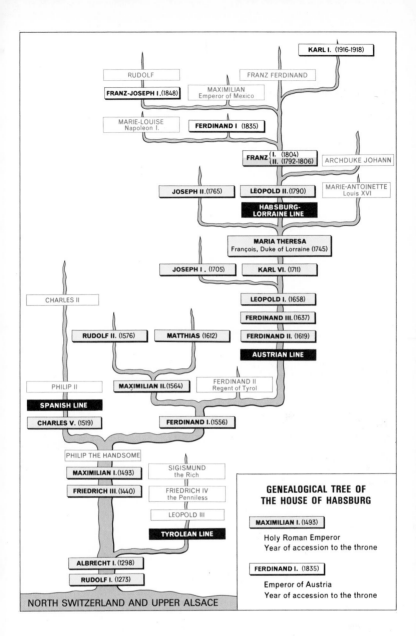

GENEALOGICAL TREE OF THE HOUSE OF HABSBURG

KARL I. (1916-1918)

RUDOLF

FRANZ FERDINAND

FRANZ-JOSEPH I.(1848)

MAXIMILIAN
Emperor of Mexico

MARIE-LOUISE
Napoleon I.

FERDINAND I (1835)

FRANZ { I. (1804)
{ II. (1792-1806)

ARCHDUKE JOHANN

JOSEPH II.(1765)

LEOPOLD II.(1790)

MARIE-ANTOINETTE
Louis XVI

HABSBURG-
LORRAINE LINE

MARIA THERESA
François, Duke of Lorraine (1745)

JOSEPH I . (1705)

KARL VI. (1711)

CHARLES II

LEOPOLD I. (1658)

FERDINAND III.(1637)

RUDOLF II. (1576)

MATTHIAS (1612)

FERDINAND II. (1619)

AUSTRIAN LINE

PHILIP II

MAXIMILIAN II.(1564)

FERDINAND II
Regent of Tyrol

SPANISH LINE

CHARLES V. (1519)

FERDINAND I.(1556)

PHILIP THE HANDSOME

MAXIMILIAN I.(1493)

SIGISMUND
the Rich

FRIEDRICH III.(1440)

FRIEDRICH IV
the Penniless

LEOPOLD III

**GENEALOGICAL TREE OF
THE HOUSE OF HABSBURG**

MAXIMILIAN I. (1493)

Holy Roman Emperor
Year of accession to the throne

TYROLEAN LINE

FERDINAND I. (1835)

Emperor of Austria
Year of accession to the throne

ALBRECHT I. (1298)

RUDOLF I. (1273)

NORTH SWITZERLAND AND UPPER ALSACE

THE AUSTRIAN DEMOCRACY

Austria is a Federal State formed by nine provinces *(Länder - see overleaf)*. Each province seeks to maintain its independent character but strictly within the framework of the Austrian state as a whole.

The "Bundesland" – The population of the province *(Land)* elects the members of the **Provincial Diet** every 5 or 6 years. The number varies between 36 and 56 in proportion to the size of the population of the province. Only the Diet of Vienna has 100 members.
The diet elects the members of the **Provincial Government** *(Landtag)* on the basis of proportional representation. This government is the administrative organ of the *Land*; it has to have the confidence of the diet, and takes its decisions on a majority vote.

Federal organization – The **Federal Assembly** *(Bundestag)* consists of the members of the National Council and of the Federal Council, who share the legislative power.
The **National Council** *(Nationalrat)* has 183 members elected for 4 years by universal suffrage, by men and women over nineteen years of age. It is convoked or dissolved by the Federal President.
The **Federal Council** *(Bundesrat)* is formed by 63 representatives elected by the provincial diets. Its role is to safeguard the rights of the provinces in the

administrative and legislative fields *vis-à-vis* the Federation. On the federal level, it has the right to propose laws and its approval is necessary for international agreements and treaties.

The **Federal President** *(Bundespräsident)* or President of the Republic, elected by the people for 6 years, holds executive power together with the Federal Government. He represents the Republic abroad, appoints the Chancellor and senior civil servants, and promulgates the laws.

The **Federal Government** *(Bundesregierung)* is made up of a Chancellor, a Vice-Chancellor, Ministers and Secretaries of State, appointed by the Federal President on the advice of the Chancellor.

THE AUSTRIAN PROVINCES

See the map on p 3, which shows the boundaries and the capital of each Federal Province.

Since 1920, when it adopted a federal constitution similar to that of Switzerland, the Austrian Republic has been a Federal State consisting of nine autonomous provinces.

BURGENLAND - 3 965km² - 1 531sq miles - pop 270 880
Until 1918 this region was part of the kingdom of Hungary. It owes its name to three castles *(Burgen)* which lie beyond the present boundary of this frontier province. Its population includes small Hungarian and Croat minorities.

BURGENLAND

CARINTHIA (Kärnten) - 9 533km² - 3 681sq miles - pop 547 798
This southern province has the only considerable national minority in Austria (4% of the inhabitants speak Slovene). In 1920 a plebiscite was held in the southern districts being claimed by Yugoslavia, which decided in favour of Austria.

SALZBURG

LOWER AUSTRIA (Niederösterreich) - 19 172km² - 7 402sq miles - pop 1 473 813
Emperor Heinrich II bestowed part of this marchland province as a hereditary estate on Margrave Heinrich I of Babenberg, whose successors, Dukes of Austria from 1156, expanded it as far east as the river Leitha. This province is thus considered the historical cradle of the Austrian nation. It is also now Austria's most prosperous agricultural region.

UPPER AUSTRIA (Oberösterreich) - 11 978km² - 4 624sq miles - pop 1 333 480
This region between the Salzkammergut and Bohemia is highly developed agriculturally and industrially.

KÄRNTEN

SALZBURG - 7 154 km² - 2 763sq miles - pop 482 365
The former domains of the prince-archbishops of Salzburg were united with Austria only in 1805. Their economy was based on salt. The Salzburg Festival, together with the province's spas and ski resorts, give it a high tourist profile.

STEIERMARK

STYRIA (Steiermark) - 16 387km² - 6 327sq miles - pop 1 184 720
The "green province" of Austria (half its surface is covered by forest) is one of the oldest industrial regions in Europe, with important timber and steel industries.

TYROL (Tirol) - 12 648km² - 4 883sq miles - pop 631 410
Once a duchy extending as far south as Merano in Italy, the Tyrol escaped from the clutches of the Habsburgs in 1335, only to fall into them in 1363. It was expanded to include Kufstein, Kitzbühel and Rattenberg in 1505, and handed over to Napoleon's ally Bavaria in 1806. It was returned to the Austrians in 1815, but lost the Alto Adige (Trentino and Brixen) to Italy in 1919. Now one of the world's most famous holiday destinations, the Tyrol is also an important industrial region and a pivotal junction for European traffic.

TIROL

NIEDERÖSTERREICH

VIENNA (Wien) - 414 km² - 165sq miles - pop 1 539 848
The services and ministries of the Federal Government and of the *Land* (District) of Vienna have their headquarters in the capital, as do a number of international organisations.

VORARLBERG - 2 601km² - 1 004sq miles - pop 331 472
Smallest of the federal provinces, this "Ländle" (little country) is by no means the least lively; apart from tourism, it has a thriving textile industry and is a major producer of hydro-electric power.

OBERÖSTERREICH

WIEN

VORARLBERG

Economic activity

In 1991, Austria's total population numbered 7 795 786. About a third of the inhabitants live in the five cities, Vienna, Graz, Linz, Salzburg and Innsbruck, which have a population of more than 100 000. Austria has a population density of 93 people per km^2 – one of the lowest in Europe (population density of the UK: 227 people per km^2).

Immediately after the break-up of the Austro-Hungarian Empire in 1919, Austria, small and mountainous, appeared on the map as a rump, cut off from its traditional commercial markets and the suppliers of its raw materials. The situation was made even more complicated by the fact that Austrian industry had been developed in the 19C to meet the needs of its own huge empire and had not been geared to compete in international markets.

The vicissitudes undergone by the country following the Anschluß – subordination to the demands of the Third Reich, war damage and Four-Power occupation – took time to overcome, but Austria now enjoys the benefits of a flourishing economy. Austria has been a member of the European Union since January 1995.

TOURISM

Tourism is extremely important to the Austrian economy both in terms of job creation and as a source of revenue which makes an invaluable contribution to the country's balance of payments. In 1993, it brought in takings of 161 billion Austrian schillings. However, Austria's attitude towards tourists is by no means all take and no give; it has completely adapted to meet visitors' needs and now offers an excellent tourist infrastructure. Most people travel to Austria in search of unspoiled natural surroundings and a healthy environment, but at least three quarters of these visitors appreciate comfort and a welcoming atmosphere, with the opportunity to relax and recuperate from everyday stresses and strains. A third of Austria's visitors are interested in pursuing healthy activities or some kind of sport. A further interesting fact is that 45 % of holiday makers in Austria value the varied programme of cultural activities the country has to offer.

Austria has 18 700 hotels, guesthouses and pensions, and about 39 500 guest rooms in private houses (with a capacity for accommodating up to 1 230 000 people). In 1994, the number of foreign visitors to Austria was 17 890 000, the majority of whom were German. Foreigners account for three quarters of all overnight stays. By far the most popular of the Austrian provinces is the Tyrol, which is some way ahead of Salzburg and Carinthia.

AGRICULTURE, FORESTRY AND THE TIMBER INDUSTRY

Although vast areas of mountainous land in Austria are not suitable for cultivation, with the result that there is a steady fall in farming jobs available, **agriculture** is nonetheless an important contributor to the Austrian economy, providing for almost 100% of national food requirements. With a payroll of 187 500, around 5.4% of Austria's workforce is employed in agriculture and forestry. In 1993, there were still 267 000 going concerns in agriculture and forestry, 53% of which were smaller than 10ha – 25 acres, and just under 3% of which were larger than 100ha – 247 acres. **Livestock** headcounts remain stable, at about 2 300 000 cattle (including 1 million dairy cows) and 3 800 000 pigs in 1993. The quantities of cereals (barley and maize) produced continue to grow as a result of the large increases in yields on farms in the Lower Austrian hills and the Danube valley. The area covered by vineyards and orchards is expanding slowly.

Forests are one of Austria's richest natural resources. They are made up mainly of coniferous trees and cover about 47% of the country's total surface area – a statistic surpassed elsewhere in Europe only by Sweden and Finland. In 1993, over 12 million m^3 – 9 700 acre-feet of timber were felled. Austria is the world's fifth largest exporter of cut timber, with 77% of her sales made within the EU alone.

POWER RESOURCES

Water power was developed at an early date and is now one of the country's most important resources.

If dams were constructed on all the sites theoretically suitable, production could rise to 54 billion kWh (output in the United Kingdom in 1983 = 276 billion kWh), which would make Austria, for its size, one of the larger producers of electrical energy in Europe. In fact only about 50% of the national resources have been developed to date, but already there are spectacular achievements to be seen, such as that at Kaprun, that in the Upper Valley of the Ill at Malta, at Zemm and as well there are the dams and power stations along the Danube.

Nearly half of the railways are electrified but approximately 90% of the traffic is hauled by electric locomotives. Electrical consumption per person per year is among the highest in Europe and the country has begun to export electricity.

Oil, another of the natural resources which has been developed since 1938, still plays a role in the Austrian economy though production is declining. The wells are mostly located around Matzen, Aderklaa and Zistersdorf in Lower Austria; the oil is refined at Schwechat on the edge of the Vienna conurbation but supplies only a fraction of the country's needs.

The construction in 1970 of a pipeline leading off to Vienna from the great transalpine Trieste-Ingolstadt oil pipeline (TAL) has allowed the refinery at Schwechat, whose capacity is nearly 10 million tons, to work to full production and also supply one quarter of the total Austrian industrial, automobile and domestic oil requirements.

Production of **natural gas** is at a modest level about 860 million m³ – 30 370 million ft³. Most of the country's demand (5.2 billion m³ – 184 billion ft³) is met by supplies from abroad. Part of the requirement is supplied via the CIS to Italy pipeline (Trans-Austria Gas Pipeline – TAG) and by the CIS to West Germany pipeline (West Austria Gas Pipeline – WAG).

MINING AND HEAVY INDUSTRY

Austria is a country with a long tradition in mining and heavy industry; in the Tyrol especially deposits of gold, silver and copper were mined intensively up to the 17C. Salt mining and the mining of non-ferrous minerals are still carried on, in particular in the production of **magnesite**. Austria is among the most important producers in the world of this mineral, which is used in the fire-proof linings for blast-furnaces and smelting ovens and also in construction work. So far as building resources are concerned, Austria is self-sufficient in cement.

Current development of **heavy industry** in Austria is governed, above all, by production in the metallurgical basin in Styria where the well known Iron Mountain, the Erzberg, is situated. The biggest opencast mine in Europe, it supplies the blast furnaces of Donawitz which produce steel sections and those of Linz producing sheet metal. Domestic iron ore production reached 1.43 million tons in 1993, and a further 3.6 million tons were imported.

The relative lack of iron ore and, above all, of scrap-iron for the smelting ovens has stimulated research, especially at the School of Mining Engineering at Leoben. Austrian engineers have perfected the "Linz-Donawitz", or steel-blasting, technique (L.-D.-Verfahren), now used under licence by more than 200 steel firms abroad, enabling them to process up to 300 tons of raw iron ore into steel in 20 minutes, and that of metallurgical powders (Plansee works near Reutte).

TEXTILE AND CHEMICAL INDUSTRIES

Austria has succeeded in modernising its textile industry but a modern chemical industry has had to be built up from scratch.

Textile industries – These go back to a famous craft tradition, for the materials woven in Vorarlberg were much sought after in the fairs of central Europe in the time of the Thirty Years War. Even today Viennese embroidery and lace from Vorarlberg are amongst the most important, in terms of volume, of Austria's textile exports.

At the time of the industrial revolution in the 19C, production of yarn and cloth was concentrated in the Vorarlberg (the cotton-belt) which followed a parallel course to the neighbouring Swiss cantons of Appenzell and St Gallen, and also in the region of Vienna, where the proximity of a great city directed production particularly towards the manufacture of fabrics for clothes and furnishings.

The textile industry now represents 4% of total industrial production.

The chemical industry – The nitrogen works at Linz produce 1.5 million tons and more than cover the domestic requirements for chemical fertilizers, exporting the surplus, as does the Lenzing factory producing approximately 105 000 tons of staple fibre a year, putting it amongst the most important in the world. Rubber is produced at the factories at Traiskirchen (tyres) and Wimpassing (synthetic rubber).

The chemical industry generates 12% of total industrial production.

SALT

Salt-mining is now only of minor importance. Nonetheless, since prehistoric times the precious mineral has played such a part in the civilization of the eastern Alps that tourists can hardly overlook the various enterprises still being worked in the Salzburg area. Moreover, the salt waters of Bad Aussee, Bad Ischl and Hall in Tirol in the Tyrol still play an important part in the treatment of a variety of illnesses. Place-names often include the syllable *Salz* or *Hall* – synonymous terms, meaning salt, salt-works. Tours through the mine galleries still attract tourists. The miners stick faithfully to their traditional vocabulary – the greeting *"Glück auf!"* (Hope you come up again!) is still heard – and they still have their dress uniform and tell the old legends about the underground world with its gnomes and goblins.

Melting Mountains – Except in the natural springs *(Solequellen)* of Bad Reichenhall, the mineral deposits in the Austrian Alps consist of a mixture, called *Haselgebirge*, of salt, clay and gypsum. The miners begin by making a pit in the bed, which they flood and keep supplied regularly with fresh water. This water dissolves the rock on the spot and, so being saturated with salt (27%), sinks to the bottom of the basin, from which it can be pumped, while impurities are left behind. Mod-

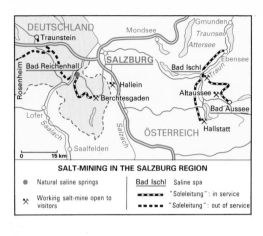

SALT-MINING IN THE SALZBURG REGION

● Natural saline springs	<u>Bad Ischl</u> Saline spa
✕ Working salt-mine open to visitors	▪▪▪▪▪ "Soleleitung" : in service
	▪ ▪ ▪ "Soleleitung" : out of service

ern methods of extraction involve the drilling of boreholes and the dissolving of the deposit by the injection of hot water. The brine *(Sole)* is brought to the surface and pumped into the vats of the salt factories *(Sud-hütten)*, for the production of domestic or industrial salt.

The First Pipelines – By the 17C much of the woodland around the salt-mines had disappeared, burnt up as fuel in the furnaces. This, coupled with the remoteness of many of the mines, led to attempts by the authorities to site the centres of salt production closer to the market for the product. This involved the construction of impressive lengths of pipeline made of timber, lead or cast iron, to bring the brine down from the mountains to the lowlands. The longest of these **Soleleitungen** ran 79km – 49 miles from Bad Reichehall to Rosenheim in Bavaria and was in use from 1810 to 1958.
Pumping stations *(Brunnhaus)* kept up a constant flow of brine, over hill and dale. To prevent too sudden a drop the aqueducts included long mountainside sections as in the water-conduits *(bisses)* of the Swiss Valais. The footpaths *(Soleleitungsweg)* which followed them made splendid *corniche* routes; such is the mine-road from Hallstatt to Bad Ischl, clinging to the mountainside above the Lake of Hallstatt. When the salt had been refined it was sent on by water – on the Inn below Hall in Tirol and the Lower Traun – or in carts. Many salt-roads *(Salzstraßen)* in Austria, one of the best known being the Ellbögen road, recall memories of this traffic, so fruitful for the country's economy and the public treasury.

FAMOUS AUSTRIANS OF THE 19C AND 20C

See also the sections on architecture and music.

Franz **GRILLPARZER** (1791-1872): poet and dramatist (historical plays).
Adalbert **STIFTER** (1805-68): novelist and short story writer *(Indian Summer)*.
Gregor Johann **MENDEL** (1822-84): biologist specialising in heredity.
Marie von **EBNER-ESCHENBACH** (1830-1916): author, editor of short stories.
Bertha von **SUTTNER** (1843-1914): novelist *(Lay Down Your Arms!)* and prominent pacifist, winner of the Nobel Peace Prize in 1905.
Sigmund **FREUD** (1856-1939): founder of psychoanalysis.
Hugo von **HOFMANNSTHAL** (1874-1929): poet and dramatist *(Everyman)*, wrote the libretti of a number of Richard Strauss' operas including *Rosenkavalier*.
Rainer Maria **RILKE** (1875-1926): one of the great poets of the 20C.
Lise **MEITNER** (1878-1968): physicist.
Robert von **MUSIL** (1880-1942): novelist and short story writer *(The Man without Qualities)*.
Stefan **ZWEIG** (1881-1942): novelist influenced by psychology *(Amok)* and biographer *(Marie Antoinette)*.
Erich von **STROHEIM** (1885-1957): film-maker and actor *(La Grande Illusion; Sunset Boulevard)*.
Georg Wilhelm **PABST** (1885-1967): film-maker *(The Trial, 1947)*.
Karl von **FRISCH** (1886-1982): behaviourist, Nobel Prize for Medecine in 1973.
Fritz **LANG** (1890-1976): film producer *(Metropolis, 1926; "M", 1931)*.
Josef von **STERNBERG** (1894-1969): film producer, discovered Marlene Dietrich *(The Blue Angel, 1930)*.
Konrad **LORENZ** (1903-89): behaviourist, Nobel Prize for Medecine in 1973.
Herbert von **KARAJAN** (1908-89): conductor, founder of the Salzburg Festival (1967).
Ingeborg **BACHMANN** (1926-73): poet (novel *Malina*)
Alfred **HRDLICKA** (b 1928): sculptor and draughtsman.
Thomas **BERNHARD** (1931-89): controversial novelist and dramatist.
Peter **HANDKE** (b 1942): producer, novelist and film script-writer with Wim Wenders.

Art

Over the course of the centuries Austria has been a meeting place for very varied cultures and its artistic achievement has often reflected these external influences which provided some of its best sources of inspiration. At certain periods however a style developed which was appropriate to the nation's aspirations, particularly in the 18C, under the enlightened rule of the Habsburgs, when Austrian Baroque blossomed so vigorously that previous achievements were relegated to second place. The Roman occupation has left traces at Carnuntum (Petronell), in the Danube valley, upstream of Vienna, which was then called Vindobona, in Enns (Lauriacum) where St Florian was martyred and especially in Carinthia, at Teurnia (near Spittal), Aguntum (near Lienz) and Magdalensberg overlooking St. Veit an der Glan.

THE MIDDLE AGES

The Romanesque style

From the 12C onwards church building flourished in Austria as in all Christian Europe. The main centres of the Romanesque style were the episcopal seats of Salzburg, Passau and Brixen. The style was also promoted by the foundation of many Benedictine, Cistercian and Augustinian convents and monasteries, such as those at Melk, Göttweig, Klosterneuburg, Zwettl, Seckau and Heiligenkreuz, or the transformation of those already in existence. The best preserved buildings from this period are the cathedrals of Gurk and Seckau, but the cloisters at Millstatt and the great door of the Stephansdom in Vienna are particularly impressive examples of Austrian Romanesque art. Mural paintings developed most extensively in the Archbishopric of Salzburg (interior decoration of the cathedral of Gurk). Salzburg was already an art centre, while Vienna as yet had no bishop. The frescoes at Lambach Abbey, dating from 1090 and completely restored in 1967, are of great interest.

Gurk Cathedral

The Gothic style

In the 14C and 15C the Gothic style invaded Austria. The Cistercians drew inspiration from the French pointed arch and the Franciscans kept to their traditional Italian architecture.

Most Gothic churches are of the **hall-church** *(Hallenkirche)* type with nave and aisles of equal height, as in Vienna in the Augustinerkirche, the Minoritenkirche, and the church of Maria am Gestade. The Stephansdom too is of this type (particularly the chancel); this, the most characteristic building of the Gothic period in Austria, was begun in 1304 by architects who were in touch with their contemporaries in Regensburg and Strasbourg.

Until the 16C there was a preference for sectional vaulting where decorative ribs form a pattern of groined or star vaulting in which richness of design contrasts boldly with the bare walls. This **Late Gothic** *(Spätgotik)* developed into a style of long straight lines – the exact opposite of the ornamental opulence of the Flamboyant Gothic to be seen in France at this period.

Paired naves were the fashion in the Alps: two naves at Feldkirch, four at Schwaz.

The great Gothic altarpieces, which were a synthesis of all the plastic arts – architecture, sculpture, painting – have, for the most part, suffered mutilation. Two are of exceptional quality: Kefer-

Kefermarkt Altarpiece

markt, which was restored at the instigation of the writer Adalbert Stifter, and especially St. Wolfgang, painted and carved in 1481 by a Tyrolese, Michael Pacher, the greatest Late Gothic artist.

A few 15C secular buildings have fortunately been preserved, such as the Bummerlhaus at Steyr and the Kornmesserhaus at Bruck an der Mur. Oriel windows *(Erker)* were added at this period to the façades of mansions and other buildings, such as the delightful Goldenes Dachl at Innsbruck.

THE RENAISSANCE

The architectural heritage of a Renaissance inspired by Italian models was not to be preponderant in Austria, except at Salzburg, which the prince-archbishops dreamed of making a new Rome. In spite of a great outpouring of ideas, reflected in Emperor Maximilian I's character (1493-1519), the Gothic tradition dominated in the 16C. Even Maximilian's tomb at Innsbruck, which is regarded as a typical product of the German Renaissance, is still influenced by the famous tombs of the Dukes of Burgundy in Dijon, surrounded by figures of mourners.

Notwithstanding, buildings can be found all over the country in which a Classical style elegance bears eloquent witness to the influence of the Italian Renaissance in Austria, for example the arcaded courtyards of Schloß Schallaburg near Melk, Schloß Porcia in Spittal an der Drau and the Landhaus in Graz.

THE BAROQUE WORLD (17C-18C)

The revolution in the arts which took place in Italy at the end of the 16C derives its name from the Portuguese word "barroco" meaning an irregularly shaped stone. It affected all aspects of art, architecture, painting, sculpture and music.

In Austria, the Baroque gave the country its most brilliant artistic period since the Gothic. In essence a religious art, it accorded perfectly with the mood of mystical joyfulness which followed the Council of Trent. It enjoyed the favour of the Habsburgs, ardent supporters of the Counter-Reformation, and benefited from the euphoria which followed the defeat of the Turks before Vienna in 1683, when the whole country was seized by a passion for building. Another factor in the triumph of the Baroque style was the Austrian love of show, of dramatic effects, of elegance and colour and joie de vivre.

For a long time, Baroque was thought of as a degenerate form of Classical art, but the relationship between the two was aptly expressed by the art historian, Eugenio d'Ors, who stated: "Both styles have their own integrity; Classicism is inspired by reason and economy, Baroque by music and abundance. Both are forms of feeling that recur eternally."

Admont Abbey Library

The churches, monasteries and palaces of the Baroque can only be understood fully in relation to the new liturgical and festive music which emerged ever more strongly in the years after 1600, in which a dominant melodic line supplanted the older vocal polyphony. Virtuosi, instrumentalists as well as singers, occupied a prominent place in choirs and chapels. The pomp and circumstance of the new liturgies were backed by the rich and powerful sounds of ever more sophisticated church organs.

Principal Baroque churches

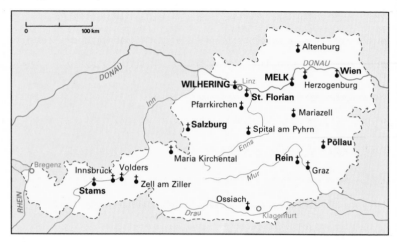

Architecture

Austrian Baroque needs to be understood as an essentially local phenomenon, the expression of an authentically Austrian sensibility, and not as an import. With its irregular outlines, abundance of forms and richness of ornament, the Baroque is above all a style of movement. Its dynamism results from colour (the use of both bright and delicate colours, the contrast of black, white and gilt), line (curves and undulations), the exuberant treatment of features like pediments, cornices, balustrades, statues and a delight in unexpected effects of angle and perspective.

The great Baroque abbeys – St. Florian, Melk, Altenburg, Kremsmunster, Göttweig... these great abbeys show Austrian Baroque at the peak of its achievement, surpassing in their magnificence any civic edifices of the period. Often prominently sited, these "monuments of militant Catholicism" (Nikolaus Pevsner) draw together bold terraces, elegant entrance pavilions, inner and outer courtyards and main wings of imposing dimensions into harmonious compositions of unparallelled splendour. The scale and lavishness of ornamentation of these vast structures give rise to a certain duality of feeling; places of worship, they are also temples dedicated to art, to which the Baroque assigned a key role in celebrating the splendours of God's creation.

Churches – All over Austria stand graceful onion-domed churches, their elegant exteriors giving little hint of the delights within. It is only beyond the church door that the Baroque gives full and joyous voice to that love of exuberant decoration which is capable of transcending the most modest of structures.
Not a few such churches are in fact Gothic (Rattenberg, Mariazell) or even Romanesque (Rein, Stams) buildings, remodelled in the Baroque style in the course of the 17C and 18C by local masons working alongside famous sculptors, painters and decorators. The rigours of the Reformation and its separation of soul and body were overcome by these artists who knew how to stir the soul by appealing to the senses.

Civic buildings – Their façades alive with colour and movement, palace and town house alike were treated as stage sets for the urban theatre by local masters as well as by Italian architects like dell'Allio or the Carlones. In the 17C, sumptuous residences arose on the edge of towns like Graz (Eggenburg) and Salzburg (Hellbrunn) as well as Vienna (the Belvedere - early 18C).

Great architects – Contributing to the triumph of Baroque in Austria were a number of figures of local origin. Though they succeeded in creating a truly national style, they were by no means immune to external influences; Italy in particular excited their admiration, and those of them who had not received their architectural training there made at least one Italian tour.
After a stay in Italy and a study of French architecture, **Johann Bernhard Fischer von Erlach** (1656-1723) created a monumental, national style based on his own interpretation of foreign (particularly Italian) influences. The Dreifaltigkeitskirche at Salzburg is one of the prototypes of this style. Many of the most

beautiful buildings in Vienna bear the mark of his genius: the Nationalbibliothek (then the Imperial Library), the Palais Schwarzenberg and winter palace belonging to Prince Eugene, etc. Most of these buildings were completed after his death by his son, Joseph Emmanuel (1693-1742), who also built the wing of the Imperial Chancellery and the indoor riding school (Winterreitschule) in the Hofburg.

Johann Lukas von Hildebrandt (1668-1745) settled in Vienna in 1696 and worked with Fischer von Erlach. In Vienna he designed the two palaces at the Belvedere, the Peterskirche with its oval cupola, the Piaristenkirche and the Palais Kinsky, and in Salzburg Schloß Mirabell; his considerable body of work had a significant influence on the artists of his generation.

The Tyrolean architect **Jakob Prandtauer** (1660-1726) had a masterly touch in relating massive structures to their landscape setting. Thus, while his interiors are conventional or even somewhat heavy, his staircase at St. Florian and the two pavilions and great bastion at Melk are achievements of a very high order. The villa at Hohenbrunn is another example of this great architect's talent. The monastery at Melk was to be completed by Prandtauer's son-in-law, **Joseph Munggenast**, who later went on to work at Dürnstein, Altenburg and Geras. Prandtauer did not restrict his talents to religious architecture alone, however – he was responsible for a number of beautiful civic buildings as well, such as Schloß Hohenbrunn.

Painting and sculpture

Baroque building is unimaginable without its natural complements of painting and sculpture, which, together with artists' brilliantly realistic stuccowork creations, breathe joyful life into the spaces created by the architect. Church walls disappear beneath elaborate altarpieces, myriads of saints and angels people the ceilings and an army of statues puts to flight their Gothic predecessors, now deemed "barbarous".

Palaces and abbeys are endowed with huge stairways, while cheerfully coloured and stuccoed façades bring a theatrical air to both village street and town square. Great painters and sculptors lent their talent to the decoration of palaces and churches. Among them were **Michael Rottmayr**, Fischer von Erlach's preferred collaborator and the precursor of a specifically Austrian pictorial style, Balthasar Permoser whose famous marble of the Apotheosis of Prince Eugene graces the museum of Baroque art in Vienna, **Daniel Gran** who executed the painting of the Nationalbibliothek in Vienna, **Paul Troger**, master of all tones of blue, responsible for the ceiling paintings at Geras, Altenburg and Klagenfurt, **Martin Johann Schmidt** ("Kremser Schmidt") whose altarpieces are to be found all over Lower Austria, **Bartolomeo Altomonte** who decorated the splendid library at Admont, and his nephew Martino Altomonte whose airy frescoes grace the ceilings at Wilhering. It is however with **Franz Anton Maulbertsch** that Austrian painting of this period attains its peak. **Georg Raphaël Donner**, sometimes referred to flatteringly as the "Austrian Michaelangelo", is best known for the fine fountain in the Neuer Markt in Vienna.

The Rococo Style

Inspired by the French *Rocaille*, this style reached its highest form of development in Bavaria. It carries the decorative refinements of the Baroque to their limit; painting in *trompe-l'œil*, marble, stucco, bronze and wood are used in profusion by artists who were frequently masters of several arts. The stuccoists brought together garlands, medallions, vegetation and shell-work. The painted figure passes indistinguishably into sculpture; a head may be in *trompe l'œil*, the body in relief, without the transition between the two being apparent. The burning passion of the Baroque gives way to a delight in sophisticated effects, monumentality to delicacy and playfulness. Baldaquins, sham draperies, superimposed galleries, niches overladen with gilding and painted in pastel shades add to the prevailing impression of being in a theatre rather than a church. The interior of the church at **Wilhering** near Linz is the most accomplished example of a Rococo religious building. In the east of the country Rococo is found again at **Schönbrunn**, with its profusion of ornament in the somewhat precious manner sometimes called "Maria-Theresa Baroque".

THE 19th CENTURY

Neo-Classicism

After the excesses of Rococo came the triumph of neo-Classicism, inspired by Greece and Rome, a cold style characterized by the columns and pediments of Classical antiquity. This tendency, which had little in common with the Austrian and even less with the Viennese character, was patronized by certain German rulers, including Ludwig I of Bavaria who transformed Munich. Vienna saw the construction of a number of buildings of great sobriety like the Technische Hochschule, the Schottenstift and the Münze (Mint). The equestrian statue of Joseph II in the Hofburg by Franz Anton Zauner is a fine example of neo-Classical sculpture.

Biedermeier (early 19C)

Biedermeier is the name given to the style which dominated the "Vormärz" (Pre-March), the period between the Congress of Vienna in 1814 and the insurrections of March 1848, the "Year of Revolutions". It is an essentially middle-class style, reflecting the prosperity and settled way of life of this increasingly important section of society.

Furniture – The cosy interiors inhabited by the rising Vienna bourgeoisie were furnished with simple yet elegant pieces, frequently fashioned in pleasingly light-coloured woods, their design reflecting new ideas of function and comfort. The discretion and modesty of the style eventually fell out of fashion, only then (around 1900) earning it the unflattering title of "Biedermeier" (a combination of "bieder", meaning solid, and "Meyer", the commonest German surname, a name originally applied to a character invented by a pair of German authors. The Ehemaliges Hofmobiliendepot (national furniture collection) in Vienna has an important collection of Biedermeier furniture.

Biedermeier chair

Painting – Austrian painting, and Viennese painting in particular, developed in a remarkable way during this period. Georg Ferdinand Waldmüller showed himself to be a master of light and colour in his rendering of landscape, while Friedrich Gauermann captured the atmosphere of the age with great accuracy and left many fine drawings of outstanding quality. The art of watercolour evolved too; **Rudolf von Alt** was the greatest master in the medium, becoming honorary president of the Viennese Secession at an advanced age.

Historicism (late 19C)

Between 1840-80, under Emperor Franz Joseph's influence, Vienna's encircling fortifications were pulled down and work begun on replacing them with the great processional way known as the Ringstraße, or "Ring". The buildings along the new boulevard were designed according to the dictates of **Historicism**, an eclectic movement inspired by a great variety of past styles: Florentine Renaissance (Museum für angewandte Kunst), Grecian (Parlament), Flemish Gothic (Rathaus), and French Gothic (Votivkirche). Having triumphed in the capital, Historicism went on to leave its mark on the other cities of the Empire. Its fall from grace came at the end of the century with the founding of the Secession.

Painting and sculpture

Sculpture flourished at this time, not least because of the abundance of public commissions. These included the martial statues of Prince Eugene and Archduke Karl (by Fernkorn) in Vienna's Heldenplatz and the moving Hofer monument (by Natter) on the Bergisel in Innsbruck.

The late 19C was a turning point for Austrian painting. The great tradition of Realism continued in the work of landscapers like **Emil Jakob Schindler**, whose *Mill at Goisern* in the Oberes Belvedere recalls the work of Corot. However, the highly original talent of **Anton Romako** marks a break with the opulence and joie de vivre which had suffused painting for centuries past; though still influenced by the formal language of Romanticism, the morbid nature of his subject-matter heralds the torments his successors strove to express.

JUGENDSTIL (early 20C)

In the final years of the 19C, a radical artistic movement known as Jugendstil affected all the German-speaking countries; with its epicentre in Munich, it took its name from the illustrated magazine "Jugend" (Youth), published between 1896-1940. In Vienna, the movement was headed by two exceptionally talented figures, the painter **Gustav Klimt** and the architect **Otto Wagner**. Its influence was felt in the provinces too, albeit in a more subdued form, and there are good examples of Jugendstil buildings in places like Wels or Graz.

Jugendstil drawing and painting are characterised by a love of flat surfaces, curvilinear forms and floral decoration. The movement was parallelled in other countries; Art Nouveau in France, Modern Style in Britain (whose Charles Rennie Mackintosh was much admired by his Viennese contemporaries), and in Italy, where it was known as "Stile Liberty".

The Secession

On 25 May 1897 a small group of friends led by Klimt founded the **Association of Austrian Artists**, the **Vienna Secession**. The following year the architect Olbrich built an exhibition hall in the Karlsplatz. Completed in only six months, this building remains one of the purest expressions of Jugendstil aspirations, even though contemporaries nicknamed it the "Golden Cabbage" because of its dome of gilded laurel leaves. Its façade proclaims the slogan "Der Zeit ihre Kunst – der Kunst ihre Freiheit" (To each century its art, to art its liberty). Olbrich's Secession building was home to numerous exhibitions of contemporary, progressive art, many of them international in scope. It became a focus of opposition to the values represented by academic art and the pastiche architecture lining the Ring. For the artists of the Secession art was above all a matter for personal expression, requiring sincerity and a quest for truth as well as a rejection of social and aesthetic conventions.

Gustav Klimt (1862-1918) – Klimt was in many ways the typical Secession artist. Early in his career he put his academic training behind him and abandoned all attempts at naturalism in favour of rich and subtle decorative effects carried out on a two-dimensional surface. His sinuous line, his use of colour (especially greens and gold), his stylised foliage, his cult of the sensual and the delicacy of his female portraits led to a revolution in Viennese artistic circles. Symbolism was an additional influence in the work of this major figure, the forerunner of what was later known as **"Viennese Expressionism"** represented by painters like Egon Schiele and Oskar Kokoschka.

Otto Wagner (1841-1918) – Wagner was the dominant architectural figure of the whole of the Jugendstil period. Born in Biedermeier times and educated in the most classical tradition, he rose to become Professor at the Academy of Fine Arts and Imperial Architectural Advisor for Vienna. For more than 20 years his career was one of conventional success; he designed a number of buildings in neo-Renaissance style along the Ring for example. But then, at the age of 50, Wagner broke decisively with his past, joining the Secession in 1899. His uncompromisingly contemporary views on architecture had already been published in his "Modern Architecture" of 1895, a work still referred to today. Wagner favoured the use of glass and steel, a rational approach to spatial design and the omission of superfluous ornament. His finest works include the Karlsplatz underground railway station (1894), the Postsparkasse (1904-06) and the Steinhof church (1907). Wagner exercised a decisive influence on a whole generation of students and, through them, on the evolution of modern European architecture in general.

Wiener Werkstätten (Vienna Workshops)

Founded in 1903 by the Banker Waerndorfer, the architect Josef Hoffmann and **Kolo Moser**, one of the most gifted members of the Secession movement, the Wiener Werkstätten were intended to make good art accessible to all and to put both artist and craftsman on a firm professional footing. A wide range of products was made, from household utensils and wallpaper to fashion garments and jewellery. Beauty of form and the use of high quality materials were considered to be more important than functional suitablity. Though expensive, the products were a great commercial success, with a strong appeal to a wealthy and leisured clientele. Financial problems led to the workshops' closure in 1932. Together with Klimt's paintings, the output of the Wiener Werkstätten marks the high point of Austrian Jugendstil.

Josef Hoffmann (1870-1956) – This highly versatile figure was a pupil of Otto Wagner. He graduated in 1895, winning the Prix de Rome in the same year. As well as designing buildings, he was also responsible for their interior design, furniture and fittings. His collaboration with the Wiener Werkstätten included the magnificent **Palais Sto-clet** in the suburbs of Brussels, his greatest achievement. Built regardless of cost between 1905-11, this palatial residence had the character of a total work of art. Both Klimt and Moser contributed to its decoration.
As well as his designs for private clients, Hoffmann also worked extensively for the city council of Vienna, particularly in the field of mass housing in the years 1923-25. His influence on a number of modern architects was considerable.

Museum für angtwandte Kunst, Wien – G. Zugmann

Tea service by Josef Hoffmann
(Österreichisches Museum für angewandte Kunst, Vienna)

Adolf Loos (1870-1933)

Educated by the Benedictine monks of Melk, this innovatory architect called himself a stonemason, though he was considered by Le Corbusier to be the forerunner of architectural Modernism. An admirer of the sober Classicism of Palladio, Loos made a violent attack in 1898 in the pages of the Secessionist journal "Ver Sacrum" on the Historicist architecture of Vienna's Ring. He was soon to break with the architects of the Secession, accusing them of "gratuitous ornamentalism". He himself propagated a purely functional architecture. His buildings in Vienna included villas, blocks of flats and cafés, and in addition he designed sculpture and furniture. His work reached maturity in the Golman and Salatsch store (1909) and in his Michaeler Platz building (1908) which attracted bitter criticism because of its total lack of ornament. Loos has gone down in history as one of the high priests of 20C functionalism.

ART AND ARCHITECTURAL TERMS USED IN THE GUIDE

Apse: semi-circular vaulted space terminating the east end of a church
Archivolt: moulding around an arch
Baldaquin: altar canopy supported on columns
Barbican: outwork of a fortified place
Barrel vault: simple, half-cylindrical vault
Bas-relief: sculpture in which the figures project only slightly from the background
Blind arcading: series of arches attached to a wall
Bond: pattern of brick or stonework
Capital: moulded or carved top of a column supporting the entablature
Cartouche: ornamental panel with inscription or coat of arms (Baroque)
Champlevé (enamel): enamelling with relief design in metal
Chapter-house: building attached to religious house used for meetings of monks or clergy
Chiaroscuro: treatment of areas of light and dark in a work of art
Ciborium: lidded vessel used to hold Communion wafers
Corbel: stone bracket
Cupola: small dome
Curtain wall: stretch of castle wall between two towers
Entablature: projecting upper part of building supporting the roof
Flamboyant: final phase of French Gothic style (15C) with flame-like forms
Fleuron: small floral ornament
Fresco: watercolour wall-painting on plaster
Grisaille: monochrome painting in shades of grey
Hall-church: Germanic church in which aisles are of the same height as the nave
Lantern: windowed turret on top of a dome
Lintel: horizontal beam over a door or window
Narthex: rectangular vestibule between the porch and nave of a church
Oriel: bay window corbelled out from an upper floor level
Ossuary: place where the bones of the dead are stored
Pendentive: triangular section of vaulting rising from the angle of two walls to support a dome
Peristyle: colonnade around a building
Pilaster: shallow rectangular column projecting from a wall
Predella: altar platform divided into panels
Putto (pl. putti): painted or sculpted cherub
Quadripartite vaulting: vault divided into four quarters or cells
Reredos: screen to the rear of an altar
Reticulated: patterned like a net
Rib: projecting band separating the cells of a vault
Saddleback roof: roof with a ridge between two gables, suggesting a saddle shape
Scotia: concave moulding
Sgraffito: decoration made by scratching through a layer of plaster or glaze to reveal the colour of the surface beneath
Shingle: wooden tile
Stucco or stuccowork: decorative plasterwork
Torus: convex moulding
Transept: wing or arm of a church at right angles to the nave
Triptych: set of three panels or pictures, often folding and used as an altarpiece
Trompe-l'œil: use of techniques such as perspective, or the combination of sculptures and painted figures, to deceive the viewer into seeing three dimensions where there are only two
Tympanum: space between the lintel and arch of a doorway
Volute: spiral scroll on an Ionic capital

Music *See also "Vienna, capital of music" under WIEN*

Middle Ages

9C	Musical culture flourished in the monasteries where Gregorian chant was sung. The earliest examples of written music in Austria are the Lamentations from the abbey at St. Florian and the Codex Millenarius Minor from Kremsmünster.
12C and 13C	The Germanic troubadours known as the **Minnesänger** celebrated the joys and sorrows of courtly love at the court of the Babenbergs in Vienna as well as at St. Veit an der Glan in Carinthia, drawing their inspiration from the Volkslied (folksong), the authentic expression of popular feeling.
14C and 15C	The burgher-class **Meistersinger** (Mastersingers), organised into guilds, continued the aristocratic *Minnesang* tradition, setting strict rules and testing achievement by means of competitions.

Renaissance

This was the age of polyphony, pioneered in Austria by the Tyrolean Oskar von Wolkenstein, who worked at the Court at Salzburg, then developed throughout the Empire in the work of a number of musicians belonging to the Franco-Flemish school.

The 17C century

1619	The accession to the Imperial throne of Archduke Ferdinand of Styria marked the beginning of the supremacy of Italian music in Austria, notably in opera and oratorio. A long line of Italian masters directed the music of the Court Chapel, the last of their number being none other than Mozart's great rival, Salieri *(see overleaf)*.

Gluck and the reforming of the opera

Vienna was the setting for the reform of opera, thanks to the German composer, Gluck.

1714-1787	**Christoph Willibald Gluck** considered opera as an indivisible work of art, both musical and dramatic; he sought, above all, natural effects, truth, simplicity and a faithful expression of feeling. Gluck's operas are characterised by their strong melodic line accompanied by highly original orchestration, in which the inclusion of parts for chorus and ballet increased the opera's dramatic impact.
1754	Gluck is named *Kapellmeister* of the Opera at the Imperial Court of Maria Theresa.
1774	Two of his operas are performed for the first time in Paris: *Iphigenia in Aulis* and *Orpheus*. The enthusiasm of the Gluckists clashed with the Piccinnists (traditionalists).

The Viennese Classics

This was the age of Haydn, Mozart, Beethoven and Schubert, all Viennese by birth or adoption. Their primarily instrumental work dominated the musical world for almost a century and made Vienna its uncontested capital.

Lesser known composers of the Viennese Classical School include **Matthias Georg Monn** (1717-50), an organist and composer who wrote concerti in the Classical rather than the Baroque style and who is thought to be the first composer to write a symphony in four movements, instead of three as was then common practice. **Leopold Hoffmann** (1738-93) wrote more than thirty concerti for the cembalo. **Carl Ditters von Dittersdorf** (1739-99) was an acclaimed violinist and composer, who won particular renown as a pioneer of the **Singspiel**, or 18C comic German opera. He was a friend of Gluck and later of Haydn, and played in string quartets with Mozart.

1732-1809	**Joseph Haydn** – Conductor and composer attached to the service of Prince Esterházy at Eisenstadt for thirty years, Haydn was the creator of the string quartet and laid down the laws of the classical symphony, showing a remarkable care for balance and grace. His ground-breaking compositions made him one of the most influential musicians in the history of music, and won him international renown and – unusually, for a great composer – financial security.

1750-1825	**Antonio Salieri** was a prolific composer, particularly of operas but also of oratorios, religious and chamber music. He enjoyed the support of Gluck early on in his career, and went on to become a life-long friend of Haydn, and of Beethoven, whom he had also taught for a period. Other famous students of his include Liszt and Schubert. The Viennese public of the 18C frequently preferred Salieri's compositions to those of his famous contemporary. Mozart.
1756-91	**Wolfgang Amadeus Mozart** – Arguably the greatest composer the world has ever known, although tragically his gifts were not fully recognised during his lifetime, Mozart brought every form of musical expression to perfection, owing to his exceptional fluency in composition and constantly renewed inspiration. His dramatic genius, trained in the school of the German *Singspiel* then in Italian *opera buffa*, led to the great operas of his maturity: *The Marriage of Figaro*, *Don Giovanni*, *Così fan Tutte* and *The Magic Flute (for details of Mozart's life and work see SALZBURG)*.

1770-1827 **Ludwig van Beethoven** – Heir to Haydn (under whom he studied briefly) and Mozart, Beethoven had a Romantic conception of music. He was much affected by the ideas of the French Revolution and felt himself to be the bearer of a message for the whole of mankind. This brilliant musician had to cope with the onset of deafness from 1800 onwards; by about 1812, he was chronically deaf, and he finally lost his hearing altogether a few years later. He never married, and unlike many of his fellow composers he did not travel. Besides his devastating disability, he had to endure a long and bitter struggle for custody of his

ROGER VIOLET

Ludwig van Beethoven

nephew Karl, of whom he was very fond. The latter's failed attempt to commit suicide in 1826 put a great strain on Beethoven's health, which was by then rather fragile.

1805	First performance of *Fidelio* at the theatre "An der Wien".
1824	The Ninth or Choral Symphony concluding with the *Ode to Joy* with words by Schiller.

Romanticism

1797-1828	**Franz Schubert** – Blessed with a great sensibility, Schubert was an outstanding improviser, who rediscovered in the *Lieder* the old popular themes of the Middle Ages. His *Lieder*, even more than his symphonies, masses, impromptus and compositions of chamber music, made him secure as the leading lyrical composer of the 19C.

The waltz and operetta

1820	In Vienna, a musical genre, the **waltz**, which had its origins in popular triple-time dance, was triumphant. Adopted first in the inns and then in the theatres on the outskirts of the city, the waltz scored such success that it appeared at the Imperial Court. Two men, **Joseph Lanner** (1801-1843) and **Johann Strauss** (1804-1849), helped to give this music form such an enviable place that the waltz known everywhere as the "Viennese Waltz" enjoyed worldwide popularity. The Strauss sons, Joseph and Johann, carried the waltz to a high degree of technical perfection, taking it further and further from its origins to make it a symphonic form. With the performance at the Carltheater in 1858 of Offenbach's *Die Zerlobung bei der Laterne*, Vienna's enthusiasm for **operetta** knew no bounds. Encouraged by Offenbach, **Johann Strauss the Younger** (1825-99) enjoyed equal success with his "*Fledermaus*" and "*Gipsy Baron*". For many years the operetta, that child of the waltz, carried all before it with compositions by Suppé, Stolz, Benatzky (*White Horse Inn - see ST. WOLFGANG*) and Lehár (*The Merry Widow, The Land of Smiles*).

Symphonic renewal

1824-1896	**Anton Bruckner** was one of the most fertile composers of church music, having spent many years as organist of St. Florian and at Linz Cathedral before his appointment as professor at the Vienna Conservatory. His great symphonies, still reflecting the influence of Beethoven, reached a high level of dramatic intensity.
1833-1897	Of German origin but settled in Vienna, **Johannes Brahms** composed a large body of work of a lyrical nature, inestimable in its impact (1868, *Ein deutsches Requiem – A German Requiem*).
1842	Founding of the Vienna Philharmonic Orchestra playing under the guidance of illustrious conductors (Richard Strauss, Furtwängler) chosen by the players themselves.
1860-1903	**Hugo Wolf,** a tormented spirit who became insane, composed fine *Lieder* in his lucid periods, based for the most part on the works of Goethe, Mörike and Eichendorff.
1860-1911	**Gustav Mahler** a disciple of Bruckner, was the last of the great Romantic composers. An inspired conductor, he composed many *Lieder* as well as his nine symphonies. He helped to set in motion the revolutionary changes in music at the turn of the century.

ROGER VIOLET

Johannes Brahms

The 20th century

From 1903 onwards the "New School of Vienna" led by Schœnberg is a major influence in the evolution of modern music as seen in the work of composers such as Ernst Krenek and Pierre Boulez.

1864-1949	The German composer/conductor **Richard Strauss** carried on the Classical/Romantic Austrian tradition, composing symphonic poems and operas. He was one of the founders of the Salzburg Festival.
1874-1951	**Arnold Schœnberg**, whose early works clearly reflect the influence of Wagner, Brahms and Mahler, revolutionized music by rejecting the tonal system which had prevailed for 300 years. Together with his followers **Anton von Webern** (1883-1945) and **Alban Berg** (1885-1935) he introduced a new method of atonal composition, based on the concept of series. This is known as dodecaphony, or in its more advanced form, as serial composition. His change of style did not meet instant approval with the public, however – the première of his first chamber symphony provoked a riot! Having pursued his study of atonality in Berlin, Schœnberg was exiled from Germany under the Nazis, and settled in the United States, where he finally adopted US citizenship.
1894-1981	The conductor **Karl Böhm** helped to stage two operas composed by his friend Richard Strauss. His fame rests on his seminal interpretations of the works of the great German composers.
1908-1989	The conductor **Herbert von Karajan** brought classical music to a wide audience by his mastery of audio-visual techniques. For many years he presided over the destinies of the Salzburg Festival as well as directing both the Vienna Philharmonic and Berlin Philharmonic.
1947	Salzburg première of the opera *Danton's Death* by **Gottfried von Einem** (b 1918).
1958	*"Die Reihe"* ensemble founded by **Friedrich Cerha** (b 1926).
1979	World première at the Paris Opera of *Lulu* by Alban Berg based on the work of the playwright Frank Wedekind; the third act was completed by Cerha.

Some Austrian folklore

Religious belief

Austria is a country steeped in tradition, where old customs are kept very much alive, particularly in rural communities. A religious faith which is deeply rooted in Austria's people has left its mark on town and countryside alike.

Roofed crosses *(Wiesenkreuze)*, set up at the roadside or in the middle of a field, are thus very much a feature of Austria's rural landscape, being particularly prevalent in the Tyrol. A common sight in Carinthia is a post *(Bildstock)* with a little roof protecting a facetted pole decorated with paintings of Biblical scenes. Crucifixes are also frequently on display inside Austrian homes, in the *Herrgottswinkel* (God's corner) – in the Tyrol these are to be found in virtually every house, including guest-houses and inns.

Religious figures are also a favourite subject for the paintings to be found on many an Austrian façade *(Lüftlmalerei)* : St Florian features particularly prominently in these, in his role as protector against fire. Another popular figure is St George, the dragon slayer. From time to time, visitors will come across a church containing an enormous painting of St Christopher, such as that in Imst. These arose in response to the popular belief that looking at the image of this saint would protect the viewer from a violent death for another day. The figure of St John of Nepomuk is often to be found adorning bridges and fountains, of which he is the patron saint (having been martyred by being thrown off a bridge in Prague).

Roadside cross

A custom for all seasons

See also the Calendar of events at the back of the guide.

The year begins on 6 January, with the feast of the Epiphany, when Christmas celebrations are brought to a close by commemorating the journey of the Three Kings guided by the Star of Bethlehem (children's carol-singing and processions, *Sternsingen* and *Dreikönigsritten*; *Perchtenläufen* carnival parade in Badgastein). In some places, such as Bad Aussee, Ebensee, Gmunden or Bad Ischl, local people parade in giant head-dresses decorated with bells *(Glöcklerläufen)*. Carnival time, or **Fasching** (Fasnacht in western Austria), is ushered in as early as January in Vienna with the start of the ball season. Elsewhere, Fasching is celebrated with traditional carnival parades, to which a colourful note is added by the masks handed down from generation to generation. Some of the most famous of these parades include : the Imster Schemen (Imst), the Telfser Schleicherlaufen (Telfs), the Thaurer Mullerlaufen (Thaur) and the Schellenschlagen (Lans), in the Tyrol ; the Bad Aussee carnival with its original and colourful *Trommelweiber* and *Flinserln*; and the *Fetzenfasching* in Ebensee.

Bildstock

St. Wolfgang

Palm Sunday is marked by the blessing of the "palm branches" – generally willow catkins or box. This religious festival is closely followed by the pagan one of May Day celebrations (1 May), complete with maypole *(Maibaum)* and dancing. The feast of Corpus Christi sees more processions, which vary according to the particular traditions of the region: carrying flower-bedecked poles *(Prangstangen)* in Bischofshofen; laying down a carpet of flowers *(Blumenteppich)* in Deutschlandsberg; processions on horseback, as in Brixental in Tirol, or on water, as in Traunkirchen. Most villages celebrate the festival of *Kirtag,* or the consecration of the local church, in August or September. Also in August, Styria is the scene of *Samsonumzüge*, parades involving a giant figure of Samson. On 15 August, bouquets of flowers known as *Kräuterbuschen* or *Frauenbuschen* are blessed in honour of the Assumption of the Blessed Virgin Mary. September is Harvest Festival *(Erntedankfest)* season, and October is when livestock is brought down from the mountain pastures to its winter quarters. The feast of St Hubert is celebrated on 3 November (church services, parades on horseback etc), and that of St Leonard (patron saint of livestock) on 6 November. The feast of St Martin, with torchlit processions, brightens up the darker months. The periods of Advent and Christmas make December full of events, from the feast of St Nicholas (6 December), with the *Nikolospiel* parade in Bad Mitterndorf, through to the crib scenes on show in Bad Ischl, Traismauer and even in people's private homes in the Tyrol, and finally Christmas Eve (24 December), marked by the *Turmblasen* (wind instruments).

Traditional costumes

Although traditional local costumes are no longer worn every day, they occasionally make an appearance on religious festivals and local fête days, much to the admiration of onlookers.

The velvet corsages of the women of Bad Ischl, the embroidered silk blouses of those from the Wachau, the colourful beribboned bodices of the Montafon, the finely pleated costumes of the Bregenzerwald and the lace aprons of the Burgenland are all evidence of a rich tradition of local folklore. Men wear leather or *Loden* wool breeches (tight at the knee) or shorts (which are less restrictive for the brisk movements of Tyrolean dancing), wide braces with a decorated chest panel and short, collarless jackets. The shape of the hat indicates the region its wearer comes from.

Traditional costumes from the Kitzbühel

The traditional *dirndl* (pleated skirt, pastel coloured apron, full white blouse with short puffed sleeves and a buttoned or laced bodice) and the *Steirer Anzug* ("Alpine dinner jacket", consisting of grey or brown *Loden* breeches embroidered in green, white socks and a long flared coat with green embroidery and gilt buttons) are not that common a sight these days. However, they are the original inspiration behind the so-called "traditional Austrian look", so popular with tourists, in which modern styles are combined with traditional decorative features and natural materials such as linen, cotton, felt and heavy woollen *Loden*.

Scenes of Austria

Farmscapes– The distinctive fences woven from laths which were once the most common style delimiting fields in the Salzburg, Tennengau and Pinzgau regions are becoming more rare. But it is still not unusual to see farmers piling hay at harvest time onto special drying racks made of metal wire or wooden stakes, to keep it off the damp ground while it is drying.

In the Carinthian Alps cereals are grown on the sunny slopes up to a height of 1 500m – 4 500ft, but the harvest often has to be gathered early on account of frost. The sheaves are spread out on wooden driers with horizontal struts, sometimes covered, so the grain is able to ripen.

Fences in Abtenau

Drying rack for grain

Drying hay in Carinthia

Rural architecture – From Tyrolean mountain chalets to the huge farmsteads of Lower Austria and the Burgenland, Austria displays a great variety of country dwellings.

House in Bezau in the Bregenzerwald

Tyrolean chalet

In this part of the Vorarlberg, with its Alemannic civilization, the farmer's house hardly differs from the Appenzell type found on the Swiss bank of the Rhine. A characteristic feature is the shingle-covered façade, in which each row of windows peeps from under a protective ledge.

The Lower Inn Valley was colonized by the Bavarians and the farmhouses resemble those in the Chiemgau Alps. The handsome wooden houses have long balconies on the upper floors and low-pitched roofs, surmounted by a miniature belfry and often weighted with blocks of stone.

Farm in the Danube Plain
(south of the Danube)

Heuriger in Lower Austria
(Beethoven's house in Heiligenstadt)

The enormuous quadrangular buildings *("Vierkant")* enclosing a central yard stand alone in the middle of each estate in the hilly country between Linz and St. Pölten.

Small, low, rural buildings still survive even in the suburbs of Vienna. They are ranged symmetrically on either side of a yard which opens on the street through an arched doorway.

Urban Settlement – In Styria, Carinthia and the Danubian countryside the most interesting examples of urban development are those based on a main road. When a town was first developed the old road was widened to form a sort of esplanade, known as the *Anger* (green). When all the land on each side of the *Anger* was built over, the resulting form was known as a *Straßenplatz* (street-square). These street-squares, shaped like spindles or regular oblong rectangles, form the heart of the town, approached by the once fortified gateways. Monuments to municipal dignity are generally to be found there: the *Pestsäule* (Plague Column) like the one set up in Vienna at the end of the 17C; also fountains, etc.

Urban development in the Lower Inn and Salzach Valleys
(Rattenberg – View from the castle)

Urban design in the Tyrol
(Kitzbühel – the Stadtplatz)

Façades are surmounted by a cornice which masks a sloping roof *(Grabendach)*. The overall effect, with its Italian echoes, forms a strong contrast with the picturesque style of Kitzbühel (opposite).
This method of roofing is best preserved in Rattenberg.

The main streets of the old cities of the Tyrol (Kitzbühel) are lined with substantial houses, often covered with external murals. The gabled roofs, side by side, form an attractive broken skyline.

48

Food and drink

Austrian cooking has drawn on the culinary traditions of the different peoples incorporated in the old Empire: German, Italian, Hungarian, Serb and Czech.

Austrian Cooking – Soup is served first, followed by the main dish, almost always consisting of meat, fried in breadcrumbs or boiled, accompanied by salad and stewed fruit (such as bilberries: *Preiselbeeren*).
Dumplings *(Knödeln)* made of liver or flour may be served instead of vegetables, as in Bavaria. Oriental flavourings give the dishes a savour which appeals to the innate Austrian taste for good living.

Meat – The most famous dish *(Wiener Schnitzel)* is fillet of veal, fried in egg and breadcrumbs, normally served with potato salad. Goulash is a highly-flavoured stew of Hungarian origin, spiced with red pepper or paprika and garnished with tomatoes, onions and potatoes. In Graz and Styria duck or chicken, fried in egg and breadcrumbs, is delicious. Game of all kinds is widely available in season.

Dessert – There is a great variety of Austrian sweets. The most famous, the Sacher cake *(Sachertorte)*, invented by Prince Metternich's chef, has a subtle and delicate flavour; it is a large chocolate cake covered with chocolate icing above a thin layer of apricot jam; the original recipe remains a secret (but see p. 386 for a version of it!) Other favourites include a jam tart *(Linzertorte)*, consisting of pastry made with almonds, filled with apricot or raspberry jam and covered with a pastry lattice; a turnover *(Strudel)* filled with apples, cherries or cream cheese and currants; plum or apricot fritters; and a sweet omelette *(Salzburger Nockerl)*.

Austrian Wine – Vineyards cover about 58 000ha – 143 000 acres in Lower Austria, in the Weinviertel, on the slopes near Vienna, in the Burgenland and Styria. White wine (81%) is much more popular than red. Annual production is of the order of 3.5 million hectolitres – 77 million gallons of which more than a third is exported.

White wines – There are many white vintages classed in importance: Grüner Veltliner (Valteline), Müller-Thurgau, Welschriesling, etc. Most vintages yield pleasant table wines which are often light and sparkling. New wine, made that year, is drunk in the typical wineshops called *Heurigen* in Vienna and *Buschenschenken* in Styria. The district of Wachau in the Danube valley produces wines with a delicate bouquet (Spitz, Dürnstein, Weißenkirchen, Krems, Langenlois). Grinzing, the most famous of Vienna's suburban wine-villages, makes a pleasant sparkling wine, Gumpoldskirchen, to the south, a stronger wine altogether.

Red wines – The grapes, especially the Blauer Portugieser and the Blaufränkisch, are of high quality. In Lower Austria the best known wines are those from Bad Vöslau, south of Vienna, from Retz (the Retz wine is known as *Spezi*, i.e. a special), from Haugsdorf and from Matzen, in the Weinviertel. In the Burgenland the wines of Pöttelsdorf, Oggau and particularly Rust, and in Styria those of Leibnitz, have a great reputation.

Schreiber/ÖSTERREICH WERBUNG

Sachertorte

Sights

Bartl/ÖSTERREICH WERBUNG

ADMONT

Steiermark – Population 3 110
Michelin map 426 fold 22 – Alt 641m - 2 103ft

The Benedictine Abbey of Admont was founded in the 11C by St Emma of Gurk *(see GURK)* and Gebhard, Archbishop of Salzburg. The spires of its church are framed by the summits of the Haller Mauern and the Großer Buchstein, the northern pillar of the Gesäuse. Matching them in the west, are the towers of Frauenberg *(see EISENERZER ALPEN)* on their hill. There is a particularly good view looking towards Admont from the Hieflau road as it runs along the Gesäuse.

The abbey buildings were completely reconstructed after a fire in 1865. Fortunately the library was spared by the flames and still has its valuable archives.

Admont Abbey Library

★★ **Stiftsbibliothek (Abbey Library)** ⊙ – The abbey library's magnificent state room stretches for 70m - 230ft, on either side of a central rotunda beneath a domed ceiling. The ceiling frescoes by Bartolomeo Altomonte (1694-1783), which depict an allegory of Theology and the various Arts and Sciences, together with the two floors of book cases and the upper gallery with its intricate wrought iron balustrade constitute a splendid Rococo ensemble of 1776, a worthy setting for the treasures the library contains. Note in particular the famous statues of the "Four Last Things" – Death, Judgement, Heaven and Hell – by **Joseph Stammel** (1695-1765), who revived the art of woodcarving, neglected in Styria since the end of the Gothic period, to its former glory in his work, most of which was donated to the abbey. The manuscripts and printed texts on display under glass are in fact a selection from the library's collection of 1 400 manuscripts and 150 000 volumes. The display is regularly rotated and follows a specific theme.

AFLENZER SEEBERGSTRASSE★

Steiermark
Michelin map 426 fold 23

This is the last really mountainous pass road in the Austrian Alps on the approaches to Vienna. The Aflenzer Seeberg (alt 1 253m - 4 111ft) or Seeberg pass makes communication easy between the Mariazell basin and the industrialised valleys of the Mur and the Mürz. The views of the imposing limestone ridges of the Hochschwab massif and the crossing of the Aflenz basin are pleasant sections on this run.

FROM BRUCK AN DER MUR TO MARIAZELL
61km - 38 miles - allow ½ day

★ **Bruck an der Mur** - *See BRUCK AN DER MUR.*
Start out from Bruck an der Mur northwards on the road to Vienna.

Leaving the industrial landscape (steelworks) of the Lower Mürz at Kapfenberg, the road winds its way through the narrow Thörlbach valley, where there are still a few wiremills and nail factories. The picturesque setting of the Thörl gateway marks the exit from this first defile.

Thörl – This little settlement, now industrial, lies in a rocky cleft. It began as a fortification barring the entrance to the Aflenz basin. Exactly in line with the valley, the ruins of the stronghold of Schachenstein stand on their steep sided spur. The castle was built in 1471. Beside the road, to the south, an oratory shelters a Calvary dating from 1530.

Of the gateway *(Törlein)* from which the village gets its name there remain, on the mountain side, an 18C building through which the roadway passed under an arch, still in existence, and a semi-circular tower with an adjacent chapel dedicated to St Barbara.

Aflenz-Kurort – Aflenz is a medium altitude, mountain air health resort, in a quiet location and very popular. In winter the chairlift to the Bürgeralm serves the sunny Schönleiten plateau, which has a ski tow and in the climbing season saves time for expeditions in the Hochschwab massif. The **church**, which is squat and rustic, belongs to the final phase of Gothic architecture in Austria. The tower has been fortified since the end of the I5C. Inside, there are Gothic statues of the twelve Apostles and rib vaulting, which emerges delicately from the side walls. The south door, with its design of little columns and string-courses superimposed on multilobed archwork, is no less curious. The relief representing the architect, at the keystone, is modern.

From Aflenz to Au the **road**★ runs along the upper banks of a green slope at the base of the last foothills of the Hochschwab. The long, low houses with wide outside galleries are typical of the area.

At **Seewiesen**, whose Gothic church is reminiscent, both in shape and setting, of the church of Heiligenblut *(qv)*, the final climb begins. To the west the Seetal, with its evenly inclined slopes, reaches its head between the ramparts of the Aflenzer Staritzen and those of the Mitteralpe (Hochschwab massif).

Brandhof – This hunting lodge was built by Archduke Johann. He was secretly married there to Anna Plochl in 1827 *(see Bad AUSSEE).*

On the north slope of the pass the route lies first along the sides, then on the floors of little valleys of Alpine pastureland. The climb to Mariazell in wide bends emphasizes the very open setting of this famous centre of pilgrimage.

★ **Mariazell** – *See MARIAZELL.*

The current Michelin Red Guide Europe offers
a selection of pleasant hotels in the cities of Vienna, Innsbruck or Salzburg ;
each entry specifies the facilities available (gardens,
tennis courts, swimming pool, car park)
and the annual opening and closing dates ;
there is also a selection of restaurants recommended for their cuisine :
well-prepared meals at moderate prices ; stars for good cooking

Burgruine AGGSTEIN★

Niederösterreich

Michelin map 426 fold 10 – 13km - 8 miles northeast of Melk – Local map under DONAUTAL

The ruins of the stronghold of Aggstein stand in the heart of the Wachau, on a choice **site**★ perched on a 520m - 1 706ft high rock overlooking the Danube from about 300m - 1 000ft.

This castle was built in the 12C. Its size and situation made it one of the most formidable and also one of the most coveted fortresses in Austria. It was destroyed by the Turks in 1529 and rebuilt and damaged several times. Today only the lofty shapes of its ruined towers and walls are left standing.

It is reached from the hamlet of Aggstein up a steep path *(2 hours Rtn on foot).* The tip of the spur on which the castle stands forms a remarkable viewpoint.

ALPBACH

Tirol – Population 2 000

Michelin map 426 fold 18 – 12km - 7 miles southeast of Rattenberg – Alt 973m - 3 192ft

In the setting of one of the quietest valleys in the Kitzbühel Alps, the mountain village of Alpbach has specialized in entertaining academics and politicians meeting here in a European Forum each year. The setting of the village and the true Tyrolean style of its chalets *(illustration p 48)* create an atmosphere favourable to unruffled discussion. Statesmen and Nobel prize winners frequently take part in round table symposia here.

Stift ALTENBURG★★

Niederösterreich

Michelin map 426 fold 11 – 7km - 4 miles southwest of Horn

Founded in 1144, this Benedictine abbey fell victim to many an assault because of its frontier location. It was sacked again in 1645, and its reconstruction was begun by a mere handful of monks who undertook to raise it from its ruins. The abbey complex was completed in the late Baroque style and is the masterpiece of **Paul Troger**, who besides painting altar panels here, was responsible for the decoration of nine cupolas. Much damage was inflicted on the abbey in both world wars, though subsequent restoration work has gone a long way to recreate its original splendour.

An avenue lined with mythological divinities leads to the entrance hall, the ceiling of which is adorned with delicate stucco.

Façade of Altenburg Abbey (detail)

Stiftskirche (Abbey church) – This is interesting in terms of both its architecture and its interior decoration. The architect responsible for the transformation of what had once been a Gothic church was Joseph Munggenast, the son-in-law and pupil of Prandtauer. The work was completed between 1730 and 1733. The **west front**, decorated with statues (St Michael, St Benedict, angels) is surmounted by a graceful bulbous belfry. It forms part of a group of buildings framing the prelates' courtyard.

The **interior**, adorned with marble, stucco and frescoes, is of noble proportions. The nave is roofed by an oval dome decorated by Paul Troger with **frescoes** whose central theme is the struggle between St Michael and the dragon. The same artist painted the Assumption above the high altar as well as a number of pictures on the side altars. The stucco work is from the workshop of **Franz Joseph Holzinger** of St. Florian; his academic style is somewhat stiff and conventional. The **organ** of 1773 is remarkable for the elegance and delicacy of its gilded woodwork.

Stiftsgebäude (Abbey buildings) ⊙ – Despite the effects of destruction and restoration, this is one of the liveliest as well as one of the most complete groupings of Baroque buildings.

The decoration of the vestibule to the library is by Johann Jakob Zeiler.

Library – This takes the form of a broad nave articulated by majestic columns between which, in place of lateral chapels, rise the shelves of books. The three domes above the room are painted, like those of the church, with frescoes by Paul Troger on the theme of Human and Divine Wisdom.

It is at Altenberg more than anywhere else that one can appreciate the Baroque concept of the library as the temple of the spirit, treated with the same architectural magnificence as the temple of God. The Benedictine motto "Ora et labora" draws a parallel between God and Spirit and opens the way for the joyful Baroque play of symmetries and intersections.

"Krypta" – With its cradle vault lit by lunettes, this vast luminous space has no equal among the abbeys of Austria. Its decor, consisting of warmly coloured frescoes painted by some of Troger's pupils, deals breezily with death, mixing macabre elements among its abundance of floral and geometric motifs.

"**Sala terrena**" – Painted all over with frescoes of limitless pictorial inventiveness, these four rooms are the epitome of Baroque extravagance but also evoke the charm and humour equally characteristic of the style. The theme of the first three rooms is water, the element which is the source of life and of purity. The fourth, or "Chinese", room is a timeless vision of the Far East.

Main staircase – Of the utmost refinement and sumptuosity, this leads to the **imperial apartments.** Here, all the decorative techniques employed come together to create an atmosphere of aristocratic solemnity – gilded capitals punctuating the play of colours of the stucco and artificial marblework, gleaming marquetry... Representing 850 years of history, the abbey's treasures (furniture, statues, documents, liturgical objects in gold and silver plate) are exhibited in the prelates' apartments (Schatzkammer in der Prälatur).

EXCURSIONS

Horn – *7km – 4 miles northeast.*
This town, built on a rocky terrace, was enclosed by a fortified wall from the 13C onward, of which a few towers still remain. In the town are some beautiful residences from the 16C and 17C, grouped around the Kirchenplatz and the Hauptplatz. They feature pretty courtyards and façades. Note also the Stadtpfarrkirche St. Georg, a Protestant church built in 1593.

Rosenburg ⊙ – *4km – 2½ miles southeast.*
At the time of the Reformation, this castle high above the river Kamp was a major Protestant stronghold. It was destroyed by a fire in 1809, but subsequently rebuilt. The inner apartments are richly decorated and furnished. There are free flight demonstrations with birds of prey.

ARLBERGGEBIET★★

Vorarlberg und Tirol
Michelin maps 426 folds 28 and 29 and 218 folds 5, 6 and 7

Between the Upper Rhine and the Inn corridor, the mountainous region of the Arlberg, with which may be grouped the Lechtal Alps and the massifs of the Verwall, the Rätikon and the Silvretta, was for a long time a formidable obstacle to communications.
The road to the Arlberg pass, which was made fit for wheeled traffic in 1825, and especially the railway tunnel, 10km - 6 miles long, completed in 1884, provide a permanent link between the Vorarlberg and the Tyrol.

The Arlberg road tunnel ⊙, 14km - 9 miles long, was opened in 1978, providing an all-the-year-round link between the two regions.

Cradle of Alpine Skiing – The teaching of Alpine skiing began at the foot of the Arlberg. In 1901 the Ski-Club Arlberg was founded and a native of Stuben, **Hannes Schneider** (1890-1955), under the direction of Victor Sohm, began to create a technique of movement on the fast slopes of the region, where styles imported from Scandinavia were often inadequate.
Schneider, with the great British sportsman **Arnold Lunn** – who in 1922 introduced slalom gates, thereby creating the Alpine slalom race, and who also introduced in 1930 the Fédération Internationale de Ski to recognize competition in downhill as well as slalom skiing – founded the **Arlberg-Kandahar Cup**, which was competed for at St. Anton for the first time in 1928.

★ARLBERG PASS

① From Bludenz to Landeck

68km - 42 miles – about 2 hours 30min – Local map overleaf

Bludenz – *See BLUDENZ.*
To drive through the Klostertal (west slope) at a leisurely pace use the old road which crosses the Innerbraz, Dalaas, Wald and Klösterle and not the Arlberg tunnel road.

Between Bludenz and Langen the road climbs in a series of steps through the **Klostertal**, a valley which takes its name from the house built in the Middle Ages by the Hospitallers of St John of Jerusalem, to provide help for travellers at a place now called the Klösterle (little monastery). It is interesting to compare the layout and rate of climb of the old road and that of the tunnel and railway, the latter being obliged to use a flanking route with a number of impressive engineering works from Bludenz onwards. The whole valley seems to depend on its role as a communications route, as is shown by the power-stations of Wald and Braz, which supply the power needed by the railway.

From Langen, where the monumental entrance to the Arlberg tunnels opens, to St. Christoph, the landscape is severe in character. Many ravines cut the thinly turfed slopes. The electricity pylons stand on concrete bases with spurs to break avalanches.

Stuben – The little settlement, nestling behind an avalanche wall on one of the most threatened sections of the road, gets its name from a room *(Stube)* where travellers could warm themselves and get some rest before a final climb.

Very high up, ahead, appear the galleries of the road to the Flexenpaß, which branches off to the left towards Rauz.

After a last climb (gradient: 1 in 10), one reaches the desolate combe of the Arlberg – Arle means mountain pine in the local dialect – and then the pass itself at 1 793m - 5 882ft.

St. Christoph am Arlberg – Founded in 1386 below the pass on the Tyrolean slope of the Arlberg, the hospice was burnt down in 1957 but has been rebuilt as a hotel with a chapel. The former statue of St Christopher, which was venerated by travellers, had to be replaced by a modern sculpture. This hospice was the nucleus of the present tiny settlement, which, since the early days of skiing, has acted as a mountain annexe of St. Anton.

The descent from St. Christoph to St. Anton is majestic. The chief attraction is the appearance of the Patteriol (alt 3 056m - 10 026ft), the boldest summit of the Verwall massif.

※※ **St. Anton am Arlberg** – *See ST. ANTON AM ARLBERG.*

The **Stanzertal** (Valley of the Rosanna), downstream from St. Anton, is one of the most attractive in the Austrian Alps. Thanks to the chalky escarpments of the Lechtal Alps to the north and to the snowfields of the Hoher Riffler to the south, the landscape is still impressive. There are also meadows dotted with little barns, and villages remarkable for the variety of their settings – Flirsch for example scattered among its fields, while Strengen lies in a ravine. When the road emerges above the Paznauntal the time has come to enjoy the picturesque setting of the Trisanna bridge.

★ **Trisannabrücke** – A metal bridge carries the railway high (86m - 282ft) above the torrent close to the medieval stronghold of Wiesberg. The bridge, which is light and slender, in no way spoils the romantic setting.

The Sanna valley, formed by the junction of the Trisanna and the Rosanna, already foreshadows the Inn valley, which is reached at Landeck. The slopes open out and perched villages begin to find room on levels left free by the forest. Note in passing the picturesque site of **Pians**, at the mouth of a tributary gorge.

Landeck – *See LANDECK.*

★ THE FLEXENPASS

② From Rauz to Warth

17km - 11 miles - allow about 45min - Local map right

Between Lech and Warth the road is generally blocked by snow from November to May.

The Flexenpaß road, which goes to the resorts of Zürs and Lech, is open all winter owing to the protective works against avalanches. It continues beyond Lech into the upper part of the valley. At Warth one can choose between returning by way of the Bregenzerwald to Lake Constance or by cutting across the chalky Tyrolean High Alps through the Upper Lech Valley towards Reutte.

The Flexenpaß road branches off the Arlberg route in its valley setting and, before beginning its climb, makes a sharp bend. From this panoramic viewpoint one can see, in line, beyond Stuben, the Klostertal and the crests of the Rätikon, characterized by the Zimba and the glacial shoulder of the Schesaplana.

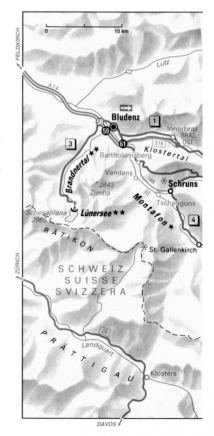

Higher up, the **ascent★** to the pass required the construction of 600m - 656yds of tunnels and avalanche galleries.
After having reached the Flexenpaß at 1 773m - 5 816ft one arrives at Zürs.

✶✶ **Zürs** – *See ZÜRS.*

✶✶✶ **Lech** – *See LECH.*

The run along the steep grassy slopes of the Upper Lech Valley continues north as far as Warth within view of the Biberkopf.

Why Kandahar? – The first downhill race on skis was organised at Montana in Switzerland on 6 January 1911 by Sir Arnold Lunn, who promoted competitive alpine skiing.
The race was sponsored by Lord Roberts of Kandahar (1832-1914), a British Field Marshal who took his title from the name of a town in Afghanistan which was captured by the Indian army during a military campaign.
This exotic title was perpetuated first by a club founded by Sir Arnold in 1924 and then by the great international event.
Skiers who are named five times among the first three in the downhill, slalom or combined event are awarded the Kandahar diamond.
Karl Schranz of Austria has gained this honour twice in his career.

★★ BRANDNER VALLEY

③ **From Bludenz to the Lünersee** *See BLUDENZ.*

★ MONTAFON

④ **From Bludenz to Partenen** *See MONTAFON.*

★★ SILVRETTA ALPINE ROAD

⑤ **From Partenen to Landeck** *See SILVRETTASTRASSE.*

The towns and sights described in this Guide are shown in black on the maps

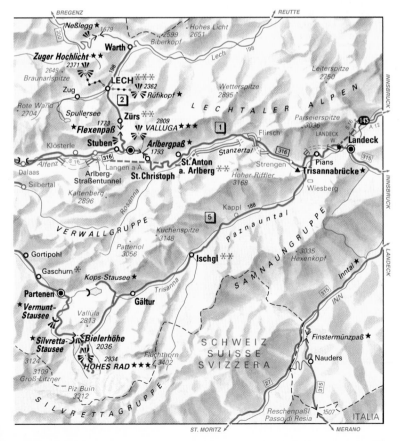

Schloß-Museum ARTSTETTEN★★

The origins of Artstetten go back to a fortified residence erected here in the 13C. Close to the Danube, and thus on the classic invasion route into the heart of Europe, this early building was much exposed to the hazards of war. The characteristic silhouette of the present castle dates only from 1912 when its pitched roofs were replaced by the present bulbous structures. Terrible fires laid waste both castle and village in 1730 and again in 1760; nevertheless, the south front dates back to 1750 and most of the rest of the building to 1691-98.

Artstetten entered the mainstream of history when, in 1823, it became the property of the Imperial family. Its effective owner at that time was the Emperor Franz I. The castle subsequently belonged to various members of the Imperial family before passing in 1861 into the ownership of Archduke Karl Ludwig, brother of Emperors Franz Joseph and Maximilian. As his summer residence for many years, Artstetten was much altered and rebuilt by the Archduke; it was he who landscaped the park, giving it its present appearance. In 1866, the unfortunate Archduke Maximilian became the owner, albeit briefly; the following year, as Emperor of Mexico, he was executed by a revolutionary firing squad. In 1890 it was the turn of Karl Ludwig's son, the heir to the Imperial throne, Archduke Franz Ferdinand, to become master of the castle. Artstetten was the final residence of Franz Ferdinand and Archduchess Sophie before their assassination at Sarajevo in 1914; the castle still belongs to their direct descendants.

ARCHDUKE FRANZ FERDINAND

Heir to the throne - The tragic death of Crown Prince Rudolf at Mayerling meant that Archduke Karl Ludwig became heir to the Imperial throne. His utter lack of interest in politics made it hard to imagine that he could ever succeed his brother, Franz Joseph. In the event, however, it was Karl Ludwig's able son, Franz Ferdinand, effectively heir already for a number of years having been entrusted with a number of official Imperial missions, who officially became next in line to the ageing Emperor in 1896, when his father died.

Franz Ferdinand had been born in 1863 in Graz and had inherited a fortune from the last Duke of Modena. In his youth there seemed to be no prospect of his ever succeeding to the throne and he therefore embarked on a military career early on.

In the service of the Empire - As a young lieutenant of 19, Franz Ferdinand trained for his chosen profession as a soldier with his regiment at Enns, where he spent five years. Later he commanded a regiment of hussars in Hungary for two years. Perceptive and far-sighted, he played the leading part in giving Austria an effective navy, and was rewarded with promotion to the rank of admiral in 1902. He was an accomplished horseman and an excellent shot, as well as a connoisseur and patron of the arts. He was also an indefatigable traveller, obtaining the Emperor's permission to make a tour of the world lasting almost a year, in the course of which he visited the USA, Japan, India and China, returning home with many new ideas and filled with reforming zeal.

Archduke Franz Ferdinand   Sophie, Princess of Hohenburg

As anxious to preserve the dynasty as the uncompromising Franz Joseph but of much more flexible mind, Franz Ferdinand strove to overcome Austria-Hungary's perennial political crises by accommodating the rising tide of nationalism among the Emperor's Slav subjects, a project doomed to failure because of the inflexibility of the Empire's privileged nations, the Germans and Hungarians.

A dynamic personality – A complex and forceful man, Franz Ferdinand enjoyed a happy family life. The two year struggle for his right to marry the woman of his choice won him the respect of the Austrian people; although she was from an old aristocratic family, Sophie Chotek was not regarded as a suitable partner for an archduke and heir to the throne, as custom demanded that he should marry only a princess. Franz Ferdinand overcame all obstacles, including the resistance of the Emperor, and Countess Chotek was made Princess of Hohenburg on 1 July 1900, her wedding day. Three children were born of the marriage. In 1918 they were exiled and their property seized but they subsequently found refuge in Vienna and at Artstetten. During the Second World War they were deported to Dachau, an experience they nevertheless survived.

Assassination at Sarajevo – On Sunday 28 June 1914, the Archduke and Princess Sophie were on an official visit to Bosnia. In spite of the tense political situation in the recently annexed province, they were welcomed in the capital, Sarajevo, by an enthusiastic crowd. As the Austrian party drove through the streets, a grenade was thrown at the Archduke's car; rolling off the folded-back hood, it exploded underneath the following vehicle, injuring a number of officers and onlookers. The Archduke ordered his chauffeur to carry on to the town hall, where speeches of welcome were made. Ordered by her husband to return to the Governor's residence, Princess Sophie insisted on staying at his side. Spurning the advice of anxious officials to wait until troops had cleared the streets, Franz Ferdinand set off again. A mistake on the part of his driver meant that the archducal car was halted for a few moments directly in front of one of the seven conspirators, the Bosnian student Gavrilo Princip. Seizing his opportunity, Princip fired two shots at almost point-blank range, killing both the Archduke and his wife. He was 51 years old, she 46. Both Princip and his fellow-conspirator who had thrown the grenade were arrested; they were condemned to 20 years imprisonment but died in gaol of tuberculosis.

The consequences of Sarajevo – The European powers had entrusted the administration of Bosnia-Herzegovina to Austria in 1878. In 1908 the province was annexed outright by the Empire in an attempt to counter "Yugoslav" agitation in both Bosnia and Croatia. The Serbian government had long stood in the way of Austrian ambitions in the Balkans; given the apparent involvement of Serbian officers in the Archduke's assassination, the time seemed ripe to bring Belgrade to heel, though the old Emperor counselled caution.

On 23 July 1914 an Austrian ultimatum was presented to Serbia and, although its basic conditions were accepted, the interlocking pattern of alliances meant that the international situation deteriorated rapidly. Russia let it be known that she supported Serbia and, after the Austrian attack on 28 July, there was no turning back; Russia mobilised on 30 July, Germany and France on 1 August and by 2 August the First World War had begun.

★★ ERZHERZOG-FRANZ-FERDINAND-MUSEUM ⊙ time: 1 hour

An important but relatively little-known chapter of history is presented in the museum under the heading "From Mayerling to Sarajevo". The castle's rooms contain various objects once in the possession of the Imperial family – personal effects, photos, furniture, weapons – associated with events leading to the outbreak of war in 1914. Though the tragic figure of Archduke Rudolf looms large, it is above all Archduke Franz Ferdinand who features in these displays, his character, his life and his manifold activities emerging in a new and sharper focus.

Bad AUSSEE⧾

Steiermark – Population 5 047

Michelin map 426 fold 21 – Local map overleaf and under SALZKAMMERGUT

Alt 659m - 2 162ft

Bad Aussee is the capital of the Styrian Salzkammergut, a region which is still deeply influenced by tradition. It is built at the confluence of two upper branches of the Traun and enjoys a peaked mountain setting. Cutting into the Bad Aussee basin, the Dachstein and the Totes Gebirge throw out a series of well defined bastions, framing picturesque lakes: the Altausseer See and the Grundlsee.

Bad Aussee, which makes equal use industrially and medically of the salt marshes and sodium-sulphate waters brought from the mines of Altaussee, offers an exceptional choice of walks and excursions.

Bad AUSSEE

The Faithful Prince – If Bad Ischl owed its fortune to Franz Joseph, the great man of Bad Aussee was Archduke Johann *(see GRAZ)*. The long contested romance of the prince with Anna Plochl, the daughter of the local postmaster, and his almost clandestine marriage at Brandhof in 1827 filled the romantic chronicles of the period, confirming the popularity of the "Prince of Styria".

At Bad Aussee itself it will therefore be no surprise to find the prince's statue in the municipal gardens (Kurpark), the medallion of the couple on the bridge over the Grundlseer Traun (Erzherzog-Johann-Brücke) and souvenirs of the Plochl family preserved in the former post office, no 37 Meranplatz.

The Upper Town – The centre of the town is the Chlumeckyplatz, formerly called the Obermarkt, a pleasant place for a stroll. The square contains a fountain and a plague column, which was reconstructed in 1876. Also on the square is the **Kammerhof** ⊘, once the office of the salt mine regulators and an impressive testimony to Late Gothic and Renaissance architecture with its marble doorway and window surrounds dating from 1536, its cartouches with cable mouldings (1624) and its coat of arms featuring the Imperial eagle above the main entrance. This historic mansion now houses a local museum, the Ausseer Kammerhofmuseum. The Hoferhaus, nearby, which in the 16C was the home of the director of the mines, has preserved mural paintings of the period. Seen on the outside are St Sebastian, St Anne's Family Group, St Florian; inside are Samson and Delilah and a hunting scene.

EXCURSIONS

★ **Grundlsee** – *5km - 3 miles to the Grundlsee resort; 10km - 6 miles to the Gössl fork. Local map below. Leave Bad Aussee on the Grundlseer Straße.*
At Seeklause (a landing-stage at the head of the lake) there is a **view**★★ of the whole Grundlsee basin, overlooked from the left by the Backenstein promontory, whose foot the road skirts after passing through the resort of **Grundlsee.**
In the distance the pale summits of the Totes Gebirge can be seen.
Turn back at the end of the lake, at the Gössl fork.
This **trip**★★ will be still more interesting if it includes a visit *(about 3 hours Rtn after leaving Bad Aussee)* to the hamlet of Gössl and from there by a 20-minute walk, to the wild **Toplitzsee**★. The views from the lake can be seen only by taking the **motorboat excursion** ⊘. Beyond the last isthmus lies the little **Kammersee** hemmed in between the walls of the Totes Gebirge.

★ **Altausseer See** – *5km - 3 miles to the north – local map below.*
The road ends at the widely dispersed resort of **Altaussee** from which one can walk round the lake *(about 3 hours)*, or undertake the popular tour of the nearby salt-mines (**Salzbergwerk** ⊘), which were used by the Germans as a place of safety for art collections during the Second World War; among them was the splendid polyptych, *Adoration of the Mystic Lamb*, from the cathedral at Ghent.

★ **Loser Panoramastraße** – *13km - 8 miles – about an hour. Leave Altaussee to the north and follow the Loser Panoramastraße signs; toll point after 3.4km - 2 miles.* This pleasant scenic road climbs to a height of 1 600m - 5 250ft.
From the mountain restaurant (Bergrestaurant) car park at the top there is an extensive view over the Lake of Altaussee, the sheer cliffs of the "Weiße Wände" ("White Walls") and, in the distance to the south, the Dachstein range and the Hunerkogel. The car park is the starting point for a number of waymarked footpaths.

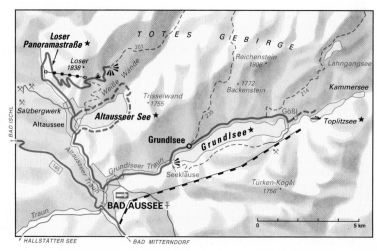

BAD

See under proper name

BADEN‡‡

Niederösterreich – Population 29 500
Michelin map 426 fold 25 – Local map under WIEN: Wienerwald

The highly reputed spa town of Baden lies in a delightful setting on the edge of the rolling hills of the Vienna woods, in the midst of vineyards and meadows. Elegant villas and Biedermeier architecture add to the town's charms. Baden has much to offer the visitor, from the restorative atmosphere of a well-equipped, modern spa resort, to the beauty of the town itself and of the surrounding area, not forgetting the wide range of leisure facilities and entertainment, culminating in the annual summer operetta festival.

Spa resort – The healing properties of Baden's hot-water springs were appreciated already in the Roman era; Emperor Marcus Aurelius described the Aquae Pannoniae as lying 18 000 double paces south of Vindobona (Vienna). Nowadays, the spa's 15 mineral springs yield 4 million litres (880 000gal UK) per day, and the spring waters reach a natural temperature of 36°C – 97°F. The spa waters are used in the treatment of rheumatic complaints, and for improving the circulation, connective tissues and blood vessels.

Famous visitors – Musicians in particular seem to have been attracted to this idyllic spot; Wolfgang Amadeus Mozart, who wrote his "Ave Verum" here, Franz Schubert and above all Ludwig van Beethoven, who visited Baden no fewer than 15 times and composed part of his "Missa Solemnis" and his Ninth Symphony here. These famous musicians were followed by the great names of waltz and operetta composition: Strauss, Lanner, Millöcker and Zeller. From 1813 to 1834, Baden was the summer residence of the Imperial court, and the "guest lists" of the spa from 1805 onwards read like a Gotha family tree. One illustrious guest, the Emperor Napoleon who stayed here with his wife Marie Louise, was particularly impressed by the Helenental river valley to the west of town.

SIGHTS

★ **Kurpark** – This fine park lies only a short distance from the centre of town and stretches as far as the Vienna woods. At the edge of the park stands the cream-coloured **Spielcasino**, successfully restored to its former magnificence. A good example of Jugendstil architecture is to be found in the **Sommerarena** (1906) with its movable glass roof, which provides a pretty backdrop for the summer operetta festival. In the afternoons, visitors to the spa can listen to concerts at the music pavilion.

★ **Spa town architecture** – During the first half of the 19C, numerous thermal establishments were built in Baden in the Classical style. Some of these are still to be found, although for the most part they are no longer used for their original purpose: the **Josefsbad**, a round, domed building in eye-catching yellow now serves as a coffee-house; the **Frauenbad** (in Frauengasse) with its pillared portico is now an

P. Koller/BILDAGENTUR BUENOS DIAS

Frauenbad, Baden

art gallery; the **Franzensbad** is a glass-making workshop. From the **Leopoldsbad** onwards, the mineral water supply still functions. On the other side of the Schwechat Joseph Kornhäusel built the **Sauerhof**, now converted into a hotel. The Kaiser-Franz-Ring, the Rainerring and the Breyerstraße feature a number of **villas** in the neo-Classical or Biedermeier styles.

Rathaus – This impressive building was constructed in 1815 by Joseph Kornhäusel, who is responsible for several other elegant buildings in town. The central block is adorned with columns and a triangular gable. In front of the Rathaus stands the richly decorated **Dreifaltigkeitssäule** by Giovanni Stanetti, erected in 1714-18 after a plague.

Beethoven-Gedenkstätte Ⓥ – *Rathausgasse 10*. The great composer came to stay here several times between 1821 and 1823.

Kaiserhaus – *Hauptplatz 17*. Emperor Franz I spent the summer in this house for thirty years. Austria's last emperor, Karl VI, also came here in 1917-1918.

St. Stephan – All that remains of the original Romanesque building is the two stumps of towers, between which a Gothic-seeming tower with a Baroque dome was added in 1697. Inside there is a dodecahedral font dating from the 14C and an altarpiece by Paul Troger depicting the Stoning of St Stephen.

EXCURSION

★ **Wienerwald** – *A tour of the Vienna woods is described under WIEN: Excursions.*

BISCHOFSHOFEN

Salzburg – Population 10 500

Michelin map 426 fold 20 – Local map under SALZACHTAL – Alt 544m - 1 785ft

It is a surprise to travellers to find, in the highly industrialized small town of Bischofshofen, one of the best preserved Gothic churches in the Austrian Alps.

Pfarrkirche – This church is the lowest of three churches (Frauenkirche and Georgskirchlein) built up a slope and linked by a narrow road, thus forming an unusual "family group" of churches. The massive tower in the middle of the church roof, above the transept crossing, is the only example of its kind in the province of Salzburg. It is a more common feature of the upper valley of the Mur (Steiermark), as Bischofshofen was the point of departure for missions to the Slavs in this region in the 9C. The transepts and tower above the transept crossing date from the 11C to the 13C. Originally, five east apsidal chapels were attached to the church. The present chancel was built in the 14C – its columns are still ringed – and the nave in the hall style of the 15C. The somewhat disparate architectural elements are unified by the skilfully constructed vaulting. On the north wall of the nave a series of murals of the 16C and 17C depict the scenes of the Passion. The side altars in the nave are adorned with excellent Gothic statuary (1480). In the north arm of the transept is the tomb, dating from the middle of the 15C, of Silvester Plieger, Bishop of Chiemsee. Opposite is a copy of the Bischofshofen **Rupertuskreuz**, a processional cross once used in Salzburg's first cathedral in the 8C which was given to the church in Bischofshofen by the Salzburg bishops in the 12C. The Baroque altar of St Anne opposite, bears a Holy Family group, dating from 1500.

In summer the nave holds the *Prangstangen*, processional staves with wool of various colours or garlands of flowers twisted round them, as still in use in neighbouring Lungau *(see the Calendar of events at the end of the guide)*.

Help us in our constant task of keeping up to date.
Send your comments and suggestions to

Michelin Tyre PLC
Tourism Department

The Edward Hyde Building
38 Clarendon Road
WATFORD Herts WD1 1SX
UK
Fax : 01923 415052

BLUDENZ

Vorarlberg – Population 14 100

Michelin map 426 fold 28 – Local map under ARLBERGGEBIET – Alt 585m - 1 119ft

At the meeting-point of five valleys (Walgau, Brandnertal, Montafon, Klostertal and Großwalsertal), the Alpine town of Bludenz is one of the busiest places in the Vorarlberg (local industries include textiles, chocolates and beer). Its crossroads location makes it a good base for tours of the surrounding area.

* **Old town** – Two towers, the upper and lower gate, and the powder magazine remain of the old fortifications. The old town centre boasts some beautiful Baroque façades and charming leafy avenues which give it a southern atmosphere. The **Pfarrkirche St. Laurentius** was completed in 1514. The altars in black marble date from 1720.

EXCURSION

** **Brandnertal** – *18 km - 11 miles along narrow roads (passing difficult other than in places provided) which rise in a gradient of 1 in 8 continuously beyond Brand, plus about 2 hours walk Rtn – local map under ARLBERGGEBIET.*
On leaving Bludenz the road offers a general view of the town and climbs through a wood cut by clearings. Beyond Bürserberg, with its pretty church, the view opens out in line with the valley to the summit of the Schesaplana, left of the dark mass of the Mottakopf, and, in the background, to a great saddle, edged with snow.
Further on the valley narrows. Through a ravine coming in on the left there is a **view**★ of the Zimba, the mini Matterhorn of the Vorarlberg. The gentle descent to the Brand basin emphasizes the picturesque **site**★ of the village.
Brand – This village was founded by immigrants from the Valais and has now become a pleasant mountain resort.
The climb brings the road to the foot of the **cirque**★★, the great natural amphitheatre whose sides bar access to the Schesaplana, then to a wild combe with slopes covered with scree. After the Schattenlagant refuge, where tourists can turn back, this combe closes in a "world's end".
Leave the car at the lower station of the cable-car.

** **Lünersee** – *Alt 1 970m - 6 463ft. 2 hours Rtn including 10min by cable-car.*
The **cable-car** ⊙ brings the visitor to the lakeside Neue Douglasshütte chalet. The Lünersee, in its barren setting of frayed crests of the Schesaplana (alt 2 965m - 9 728ft) was, in its natural state, the biggest lake in the Eastern Alps. Since 1958 a dam has raised its water level 27m - 90ft, creating a reservoir of 78 million m³ - 17 160 million gallons feeding, with a drop of 1 000m - 3 280ft, both the Lünersee power station (Lünerseewerk) above Tschagguns and the lower station at Rodund (Rodundkraftwerk).

BRAUNAU

Oberösterreich – Population 16 190

Michelin map 426 folds 6 and 7 – Alt 352m - 1 155ft

This frontier town, the birthplace of Adolph Hitler, has had the civil charter since 1260. It was not until 1779 that the town, together with the Bavarian bank of the Inn, became part of Austria. A bridge over the Inn connects Braunau with Simbach in Bavaria. The picturesque town centre and the Salzburg suburb with its numerous Gothic town houses, which survived the great fire of 1874, testify to the former wealth of Braunau, earned through the salt trade and a number of civil privileges. Vestiges of the town's original three rings of fortifications can be seen.
Park the car by the river Inn or in the Ringstraße.

Old town – The focal feature of the old town is the Stadtplatz, an elongated square which is surrounded by groups of houses dating from a wide variety of architectural periods. Particularly interesting examples of these are the **Glockengießerhaus** (Johann-Fischer-Gasse 18), built in 1385, which still has its original bell-foundry workshop, and, not far off, the **Herzogsburg**, both of which now house local museums.

St. Stephan Pfarrkirche – A massive square tower, the third highest in Austria (96m - 315ft), with a Gothic square base, abuts on the chancel which was built at the end of the 15C in the Gothic style. Built in 1906, the **high altar** is a late and rather droll example of the neo-Gothic style. The reredos echoes in some ways the authentic Gothic altar by Michael Pacher at St. Wolfgang. The side chapels contain evidence of the old patronage of the guilds, for example the remarkable **Bäckeraltar**, donated by the bakers' guild before 1490. The chapel nearest to the chancel in the south aisle contains the tomb of a Bishop of Passau who died in 1485.

BREGENZ★★

Ⓛ Vorarlberg – Population 29 000
Michelin maps 426 fold 14 and 216 fold 11
Local map under BREGENZERWALD – Alt 398m - 1 306ft
Hotels and Restaurants: see the current Michelin Red Guide Deutschland

Bregenz is the administrative capital of the Vorarlberg. It draws a considerable tourist trade from its position on the shore of Lake Constance (the Bodensee to German speakers), at the point where the "Swabian Sea" touches the mountains. With its long hours of sunshine, Bregenz remains ever-popular with visitors who are drawn to the lakeside with its wide variety of water sports facilities and especially the Bregenz Festival.

LOWER TOWN (INNENSTADT) *time: 1 hour 30min*

Lake Shore (ABY) – The main shopping streets (pedestrian zone) cluster at the foot of the former fortified city (Oberstadt or Altstadt) of the Counts of Bregenz and Montfort.

In the Middle Ages the waters of the "Bodan", as the French-speaking Swiss call it, still lapped against the base of the little lakeside chapel (Seekapelle – BY). Insulated from road traffic by the railway, the shady quays and flowerbeds of the lake shore stretch from the Seeanlagen to the passenger port. A walk along the landscaped harbour breakwater is particularly pleasant.

The **view★** (BY) from the end extends to the last hills of Upper Swabia with the island of Lindau in the foreground, with its twin belfries. To the west the Strandweg serves the beach and the festival area *(Festspiel- und Kongreßhaus)* (AY) where every summer there are lavish productions of open-air operas.

Lakeside theatre, Bregenz

★ **Vorarlberger Landesmuseum** (BY) ⊘ – The collections are particularly well displayed in the prehistory and Roman departments on the 1st floor.

The 2nd floor houses local folk costumes and examples of popular religious art. Note the portable organ dating from the beginning of the 16C.

On the 3rd floor is a display of lapidary specimens (9C ornamental plaque with interlaced motifs from Lauterach) and Romanesque and Gothic works of religious art taken from the richest churches in the province. Among these exhibits is a Crucifix from the former abbey church at Mehrerau, dating from the beginning of the 16C.

On the same floor may be seen works of mythological or religious inspiration and portraits *(Duke of Wellington)* by **Angelika Kauffmann** (1741-1807), considered a native of the Vorarlberg because of her connection with the Bregenzerwald. She lived in Rome and Venice, as well as spending 15 years in England. She was a founding member of the RA in 1768 and a follower of Reynolds.

UPPER TOWN (OBERSTADT) AND CHURCH QUARTER

time: 1 hour

With its silent squares and deserted streets, this little enclosed town is restful when the season is in full swing on the lake shore.
It can be reached by car via the Kirchstraße, the Thalbachgasse and the Amtstorstraße, on the left. Walkers will prefer to stroll up the direct way from the central crossroads of the Leutbühel by the paved ramp of the Maurachgasse as far as the Martinstor, an old fortified gateway.

Martinsturm (BY) ⊘ – This 13C tower took on its present appearance, crowned by a heavy bulbous dome, between 1599 and 1602. The chapel arranged in the base of the tower contains a massive Late Gothic altar canopy and an important series of 14C mural paintings, fairly well preserved.
The skylights in the attic provide pretty **glimpses**★ of the remains of the wall and the roofs of the old town, the lake and belfries of Lindau and, in the distance, the Appenzell Alps.

Pfarrkirche St. Gallus (BZ) – The church faces the fortified town across the Thalbach ravine.
The building is fronted by a porch-belfry. Built of sandstone in the 15C, the porch-belfry is surmounted by a scalloped Baroque gable. The church has a single 18C Baroque nave, decorated with the relative restraint which appears in the Vorarlberg churches when compared with Tyrolean and Bavarian churches of the same period.
The walnut stalls, which are in valuable marquetry, were done in about 1740 for the nearby Abbey of Mehrerau and have rounded backs decorated with effigies of saints.

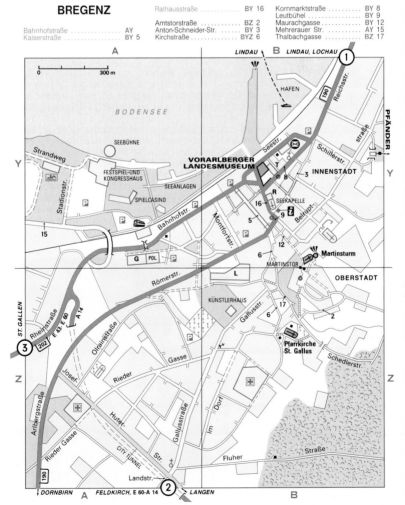

BREGENZ

Bahnhofstraße .... AY
Kaiserstraße .... BY 5

Rathausstraße .... BY 16

Amtstorstraße .... BZ 2
Anton-Schneider-Str. ...... BY 3
Kirchstraße .... BYZ 6

Kornmarktstraße .... BY 8
Leutbühel .... BY 9
Maurachgasse .... BY 12
Mehrerauer Str. .... AY 15
Thalbachgasse .... BZ 17

EXCURSION

★★ Pfänder – *11km - 7 miles by a narrow mountain road, plus 1 hour on foot Rtn. Summer fogs make it advisable to do this excursion either in the early morning or in the evening.*

Leave Bregenz on ① and the lakeside road to Lindau.

Bear right towards **Lochau**, a village on whose territory stands the 16C **Burg von Hofen**, a castle formerly owned by the von Raitenau family, known for the illustrious Archbishop of Salzburg, Wolf Dietrich. Directly after the church at Lochau turn right into the by-road to Pfänder, which when it passes over open ground gives many lovely views of the lake and of Lindau.

At the top of the climb turn to the right and leave the car 400m - 450yds further on, at the end of the authorized road. Then take the broad uphill path which, by way of the shaded Schwedenschanze terrace, leads to a television tower and the summit (alt 1 063m - 3 488ft).

The **panorama** owes a great deal of its attraction to the lake's great sheet of water and to the bird's-eye view of Bregenz. To get a better view towards the south, walk down through the woods to the "Berghaus Pfänder" beside which stands a viewing table; also nearby is an animal park (big game).

From left to right the view takes in the curving lines of the Allgäu Alps, which seem to sweep right up against the chalk cliffs (Kanisfluh) of the Bregenzerwald, the snow covered Schesaplana, the great furrow of the Rhine and, lastly, the Altmann and the Säntis, which are both situated in Switzerland. When visibility is good, one can even see the snow-capped Tödi peak (alt 3 620m - 11 877ft) in the Glarus Alps.

A **cable-car** ⓥ also joins Bregenz to the Pfänder.

BREGENZERWALD★★

Vorarlberg

Michelin maps 426 folds 14, 15, 28 and 29

The Bregenzerwald, which lies between Bregenz on the shores of Lake Constance and the Arlberg range, is not actually a forest as its name might suggest, but one of the most varied natural regions of the eastern Alps, with landscapes ranging from softly rolling hills to majestic Alpine peaks (2 600m – 7 530ft).

The fast-flowing Bregenzerach follows a broadly meandering course, at times hugging the foot of sheer cliffs and at others cutting through open valleys, before flowing along the bottom of a long, winding gorge far from any road and finally into Lake Constance. The unspoiled countryside with its agricultural tradition still intact, the typical local houses and villages, and last but not least the partly Alemannic, partly Valais population with its strong regard for the traditional local way of life make the Bregenzerwald a popular holiday destination for lovers of nature and mountain scenery.

The route described below and on the local map crosses the Brenzerwald from east to west. For a pretty tour of the Vorarlberg, take the Arlbergstraße to Rauz, and then the Flexenstraße to Warth.

Life in the Bregenzerwald – The scenery of the Bregenzerwald region to some extent brings to mind that of east Switzerland or the Allgäu, just over the German border. The local farmsteads with their wooden façades and verandas and their windows decked with brightly coloured flowers might almost have been constructed by the same builders as the farmhouses in the upper and western Allgäu.

In the **Hochtannberg** mountain villages of Schröcken and Warth, around the source of the Bregenzerach and in Damüls, which were all settled by immigrants from the

Traditional costumes from the Bregenzerwald

Tourismusbüro Bezau

Valais in the 13C and 14C, as were the Brandnertal, the Kleinwalsertal and the Große Walsertal east of Feldkirch, travellers will come across wooden chalets with exposed beams which could have come straight from the upper valley of the Rhone. The remaining 19 villages in the Bregenzerwald were settled by the Alemanni from the 10C. The beautiful traditional costumes worn by the women of the Bregenzerwald are among the oldest and least altered in the German-speaking world. Although they are worn only for special occasions in everyday modern life, they are nonetheless frequently in evidence being worn to church on Sundays or for major festivals. The remarkable variety of traditional head-dresses, which reflect the marital status of the wearer or her current activity (going to church, travelling etc.), reminds us that Bregenzerwald costumes were influenced by the Spanish early on.

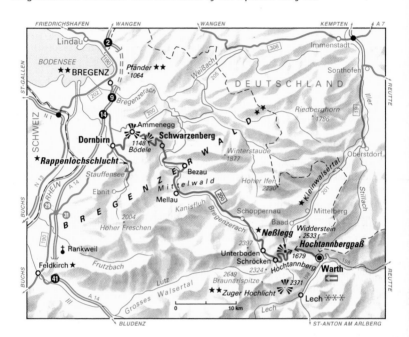

★ HOCHTANNBERGSTRASSE

From Warth to Dornbirn
65km - 40 miles - allow 3 hours as far as the Rappenloch gorge - local map above

The road between Warth and Schröcken may be closed for several days at a time between November and March because of risk of avalanches.

This run, which uses the Hochtannbergpaß threshold and the upper gorge of the Bregenzerach, follows the twists and turns of the torrent. The crossing of the Bödele pass lends a mountainous character to this last section of the trip and gives extensive views of the Rhine Valley. Between Warth and Neßlegg the road runs through the Hochtannberg pastureland.

Hochtannbergpaß – Here the road to the Hochtannberg reaches its highest point at an altitude of 1 679m - 5 508ft. This section is overlooked by the Widderstein, an outstanding peak of the Vorarlberg. According to local tradition, its rocks scraped the sides of Noah's ark.

★ **Neßlegg** – This viewpoint by the Gasthof Widderstein, at the spot where the road leaves the heart of the Hochtannberg to plunge into the wooded Schröcken tunnel, offers a general **view**★ of the cirque closing the upper valley of the Bregenzerach. From left to right one can see the Mohnenfluh, the Braunarlspitz and its snowfields, the Hochberg, the Schadonapaß gap and the Hochkünzelspitze.

From Neßlegg to Schröcken a steep and winding descent through woods gives a few glimpses of the village of **Schröcken**, clustering round its church tower. Downstream from the splendidly engineered Hochtannberg bridge, appears the hamlet of **Unterboden**, a typical specimen of Valaisian settlement. The sunken sections which follow run through the upper gorges of the Bregenzerach, within view of the Künzelspitzen escarpments.

Between Schoppernau and **Mellau** (holiday destination) the varied structure of the Kanisfluh is revealed to view; its north face forms imposing cliffs. The valley is well-populated, its scattered houses and covered bridges making a succession of pretty pictures.

Further on, the steadily widening valleys with their abundance of fruit trees are graced by the villages of **Bezau** and Schwarzenberg.

Schwarzenberg – The **village square**★ displays flower decked houses (Gasthof Hirschen), whose dark walls contrast with the bright roughcast of the church. The latter, which was rebuilt in 1757, has a roomy and well lit nave, characteristic of the local Bregenzerwald school. **Angelika Kauffmann** (1741-1807), the famous artist and herself the daughter of a painter, executed, at 16, the medallions representing the apostles, and in 1801, the picture on the high altar. You can see the bust of this local celebrity (born at Chur but whose father was a native of Schwarzenberg) against the north wall of the nave. More of her works can be seen in the Vorarlberger Landesmuseum in Bregenz and the Heimatmuseum in Schwarzenberg.

The crossing of the Bödele threshold gives, eastwards, clear **views**★ of the open basin of the Bregenzerwald and the humps of the Allgäu Alps, where the German frontier runs. In the foreground lies the long ridge of the Winterstaude. On the Rhine slope, after a long run through the forest, the **panorama**★ opens out near **Ammenegg** (Gasthaus Sonnblick). From north to southwest can be seen, in clear weather, Lake Constance, the Appenzell Alps (Säntis and Altmann) and the minor range of the Alvier.

Dornbirn – This is the economic capital and the most populous city of the Vorarlberg. The town is proud of having been able to keep its neat appearance in spite of its industry. Its annual textile fair, at the end of July, is one of the most important in Central Europe.

Beside the parish church, with its neo-Classical peristyle, is the Rotes Haus (Red House), a small wooden building dating from the 17C and well restored. With its two set back gables, it is a pleasing specimen of the traditional building style of the Alpine Rhine Valley.

★ **Rappenlochschlucht** ⊘ – *2 hours 30min return*. This is a most attractive walk up the wild gorge made by the turbulent waters of the torrent. The path leads through the Rappenloch gorge proper, partly along the cliffside and partly on overhanging walkways. It then flanks the Stauffensee, a quiet and peaceful artificial lake, before entering a second gorge, the Alpenlochschlucht, softened and shaded by beeches, oaks, hornbeams and the occasional conifer.

Return to Dornbirn.

The towns and sights described in this Guide are shown in black on the maps

BRENNERSTRASSE★

Tirol

Michelin map 426 fold 31

Local map under INNSBRUCK: Excursions

The Brenner Pass (1 374m - 4 508ft) is the lowest route across the Alps and the only one crossed by a main railway line in the open air. The motorway (**Brennerautobahn** ⊘) leading from Innsbruck to the Italian border is a toll road. It carries heavy traffic all the year round including many commercial vehicles (trucks transporting timber and wine), though it is at its busiest in summer at the time of the great German southward migration. Tourists seeking a prettier route should take the more leisurely old road (no 182) passing through the routes indicated below, or, for a better appreciation of the Alpine charms of the Sill valley, the **Ellbögener Straße**★★ *(see INNSBRUCK: Excursions)* from Innsbruck to Matrei via Vill, Igls, Patsch and Pfons *(rough and narrow road, take special care)*. Finally, excursions into the delightful tributary valleys of the Sill – the Gschnitztal and the Stubaital *(see STUBAITAL)* – are most rewarding.

Europabrücke, Brenner Pass Motorway

FROM INNSBRUCK TO THE BRENNER PASS
along Bundesstraße 182 – *37km - 23 miles – Local map under INNSBRUCK*

4km - 2.5 miles	Sonnenburgerhof: from this bend *(south of town plan of INNSBRUCK)* there is a remarkable overall view★★ of Innsbruck.
10.5km - 6.5 miles	The **Europabrücke**★, an 820m - 900yd long bridge, takes the motorway above the Sill valley at a height of 190m - 620ft.
23.5km - 14.5 miles	Upstream from Matrei is a view of the mouth of the tributary valley of Navistal, distinguishable by the churches of St. Kathrein and Tiezens.
29km - 18 miles	Stafflach: a view southeastwards, onto the snowcapped Zillertal Alps.
32km - 20 miles	On the outskirts of Gries a noticeboard recalls that this was where Charles V met his brother, the future Emperor Ferdinand I.
34km - 21 miles	Just off the road at the foot of the Luegbrücke ramp giving access to the motorway stands the little rustic St. Sigmundskapelle which has a Romanesque bell tower.

BRUCK AN DER MUR★

Steiermark – Population 15 086

Michelin map 426 fold 23 – Alt 481m - 1 578ft

Bruck lies at the confluence of the Mur and the Mürz, in the beautiful setting of the Upper Swabian massif. It is overlooked by the ruins of the old fortress of Landskron. Bruck is favoured by its situation astride important communication routes and by its proximity to the great steelworks at Leoben. It is a busy industrial town, whose factories, processing iron ore, carry memories of the rich ironmasters and traders in metal. The town's main sights are in the main square (Koloman-Wallisch-Platz) and its nearby streets.

SIGHTS *time: 1 hour*

★★ **Eiserner Brunnen** (A) – The wrought-iron wellhead was made in 1626 by a local artisan, Hans Prasser, and is considered the masterpiece of all Styria in ironwork *(illustration overleaf)*.

The forged portion stands on a stone base and is remarkably elegant in execution, particularly the canopy, which has Renaissance motifs.

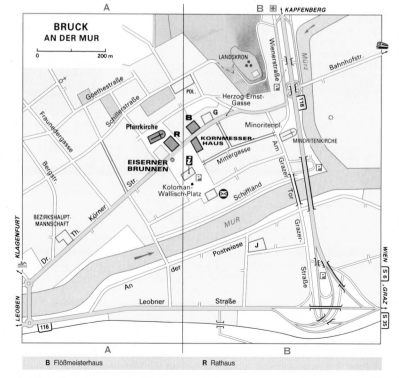

B Flößmeisterhaus	**R** Rathaus

⋆ **Kornmesserhaus** (B) – In spite of remodelling and restoration, this fine building, erected by a rich townsman, Pankraz Kornmeß, in the last years of the 15C, still has a fine air. The main façade onto the main square has a series of arcades whose decorative arches are adorned with the early rosettes characteristic of Flamboyant Gothic. The loggia which forms part of the 1st floor, already shows the influence of the Italian Renaissance.

Old Houses – There are still a good many 15C and 16C houses with arcaded courtyards. The **Rathaus** (A **R** – town hall) has a court with three storeys of arcades. The **Flößmeisterhaus** (no 5) (B **B**) a house adorned with a paired window of the Renaissance period, at the entrance to the Herzog-Ernst-Gasse, also has an interesting interior court yard.

Wrought-iron well, Bruck an der Mur

Pfarrkirche (A) – In the chancel, to the left, is a finely forged wrought-iron **sacristy door**⋆. Like the magnificent door-knocker it is believed to date from the beginning of the 16C and to come from the Kornmesserhaus.

In the north side chapel is a fine late 18C **altar of the Holy Cross** showing Christ on the Cross, between the Virgin Mary and St John.

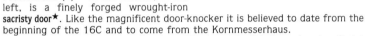

CHRISTKINDL

Oberösterreich

Michelin map 426 fold 22 – 3km - 2 miles west of Steyr

The village of Christkindl – the name means Infant Christ – has an elegant pilgrims' chapel to which a charming tradition is attached.

"Christkindl-Post" – The Austrian Postal Service sets up a special post office from the end of November to 6 January each year at Christkindl, from which one may send Christmas goodwill messages all over the world. In 1994, 1 709 000 letters were posted from Christkindl – 777 000 being dispatched abroad.

The office also undertakes to answer all letters sent by Austrian children to the Infant Jesus asking for a present (as long as a stamp is enclosed).

Chapel – The chapel, dedicated to the Infant Christ, was built in the early 18C, in the Baroque style, by Carlone. Four semicircular chapels stand round a great cupola with a fresco depicting the Assumption of the Virgin.

DACHSTEIN⋆⋆

Salzburg, Steiermark und Oberösterreich

Michelin map 426 folds 20 and 21 – Local map under SALZKAMMERGUT

The Dachstein massif (highest point 2 995m - 9 826ft) is the most characteristic example of the limestone scenery formed by the eastern Alps. Its outer ramparts guard not a world of peaks but extensive stony wastes. The number of cavities found here bears comparison with the region of the Tarn gorges in France.

⋆ NORTH FACE

To the north the Dachstein foothills, more rounded in shape, surround the Lakes of Hallstatt and Gosau. It is on this slope that recent works have opened the road to popular tourism. A cable-car serving the Dachstein ice cave terminates at the summit of the Krippenstein with its superb view. It is often used by skiers in winter, who find – besides the extensive ski slopes and touring possibilities of the plateau, served by the terminal of Gjaidalm – a few first class runs in an unusually wild landscape (descents from Krippenstein to the Schönbergalpe and if the snow permits, from Krippenstein to the end of the Traun Valley).

★★ **Hallstatt** – *See HALLSTATT.*

★★ **Ascent of the Krippenstein** ⊙ – *From Hallstatt 4km - 2.5 miles in the direction of Obertraun; then bear right 2km - 1 mile beyond the end of the lake, then 2 hours 30min Rtn on foot. Allow 2 hours 30min more to visit the Dachstein ice cave and the Mammuthöhle cave on the way to the Schönbergalpe.*
The intermediate **cable-car** station of the **Schönbergalpe** (alt 1 345m - 4 413ft) is the starting point for the visit to the Dachstein ice cave.

★ **Dachstein-Rieseneishöhle** ⊙ – *30min Rtn on foot. Warm clothing is advisable.*
Over many millions of years water hollowed out this cavity. At the end of the Ice Age the melt waters which had penetrated underground froze and scored out subterranean glaciers and ice mountains.
The Ice Cave, which is well equipped with lamps placed behind ice-draperies and hanging icicles, is toured along a circular route. King Arthur's Cathedral and the Great Ice Chapel are among the features of this underground expedition.
The tour of the **Mammuthöhle** ⊙ leads through a labyrinth of caves, tunnels, galleries etc. which make up one of the largest underground networks in Europe: total length 37km - 23 miles with a drop of 1 180m - 3 871ft. The tunnels and bare chambers are impressive in size. Particularly striking are the "Midnight Cathedral" and the "Realm of Shadows".

★★ **Krippenstein** – *From the cable-car station (hotel), 30min on foot Rtn.* A chapel stands at the top (alt 2 109m - 6 919ft) of this rounded height from where there is a **general view**★★ of the high Dachstein plateau, from which emerge the mossy heads of the final peak and also three patches of snow of which the largest is a small glacier, the Hallstätter Gletscher. To get a better **bird's-eye view**★★ of the lake at Hallstatt to the north, walk a little further to the Pioneers' Cross (Pionierkreuz). The path is marked by signs *(allow an extra 30min)* at the beginning of the Krippenstein road.

Koppenbrüllerhöhle ⊙ – *From Gasthaus Koppenrast, 3km - 2 miles upstream from Obertraun. 1 hour on foot Rtn.*
The cave, in a wooded defile of the Traun, is the only cavern in the Dachstein still in the process of natural enlargement. Crossing the cave is a torrent, which in times of flood rises into the air in the form of a waterspout with a roar which echoes the length of the valley.
Man-made galleries lead from the cave mouth to a great cleft, the Hannakluft, running in a dead straight line, where the underground waters may be seen swirling by. The Bocksee (Goat Lake) terminates the visit.

★★★ **Gosauseen** – *See GOSAUSEEN.*

★★SOUTH FACE

The towering bulk of the Dachstein massif, with its sheer rock faces rising to a height of 1 000m – 3 280ft, drops steeply down to the Alpine pastures of Ramsau. The majestic serenity of the Dachstein and the welcoming tranquillity of the mountain plateaux of Ramsau combine to form a highly original and charming landscape. The pastures, bright with Alpine flowers, the larch forests and the rocky cliffs create their own individual palette of colour, and make a particularly beautiful scene in the light of sunrise and sunset.

FROM EBEN IM PONGAU TO GRÖBMING
62km - 39 miles, not counting the detour to Stoderzinken - allow 1 day

✳ **Filzmoos** – Alt 1 057m - 3 468ft. This attractive holiday resort occupies a pretty **site**★ tucked against the western foothills of the Dachstein massif. Towering above the village is the distinctive outline of the **Bischofsmütze** (Bishop's Mitre), a 2 458m - 8 064ft tower of rock which dominates the surrounding countryside. In the winter, Filzmoos offers a small ski-slope, spread over the Roßbrand massif (1 050-1 600m – 3 445-5 249ft) and the Dachstein foothills (1 050-1 645m – 3 445-5 397ft). The ski pass is valid also for the other ski resorts which constitute the **Salzburger Sportwelt Amadé**★★ *(see alphabetical entry)*, the nearest of which are at Flachau and Altenmarkt, about 20km – 12 miles away. For cross-country skiers there is a well laid, 6km – 4 mile long track at 1 600m - 5 249ft, leading from the mountain station of the Papageno cable-car to the Roßbrand peak (hut).

South face of the Dachstein

In the summer, Filzmoos is the perfect departure point for walks in the surrounding mountains. An excursion to the **Gerzkopf**★★ summit (1 729m - 5 673ft, *4 hours Rtn on foot from Schattau*) is particularly recommended. From the summit there is a similar panorama to that from the Roßbrand peak.

★★ **Roßbrand** – Alt 1 770m - 5 807ft. After taking the Papageno cable-car, follow the ridge footpath west to the summit *(about 2 hours Rtn, easy going)*, from where there is a wide-ranging **panorama**★★ *(see RADSTADT for description)*.

Carry on towards Ramsau. After 12km - 8 miles, turn left and then take a small toll road to the right up to the foot of the Hunerkogel.

★★★ **Hunerkogel** ⊙ – Alt 2 694m - 8 839ft. *Take the cable-car to the top, allow at least 1 hour Rtn.*
From the end of the toll road (alt 1 680m - 5 512ft), the Hunerkogel can be seen looming like some impregnable fortress. The ascent of the sheer rockface by cable-car is spectacular.
From the upper station, there is a good view south of the Schladminger Tauern range and Hochgolling peak. The view takes in the mighty cliffs of the nearby summits of the Hoher Dachstein and the Koppenkarstein. To the north, the softer slopes of the Dachstein and Salzkammergut glaciers form a contrasting scene.
From the other side of the inn there is a breathtaking **view**★★★ of the successive folds of the Austrian Alps stretching away into the distance, including such peaks as those of Sportwelt Amadé, the Gasteinertal and the Hohe Tauern (Großglockner, Großvenediger).
The Dachstein glacier is equipped with about 10km – 6 miles of cross-country skiing tracks and 2 downhill ski-slopes (one for beginners and one for proficient skiers) with a drop of 400m - 1 312ft.

✳ **Ramsau am Dachstein** – Alt 1 083m - 3 553ft. At the beginning of the 20C, Ramsau was better known by the name of Ahorntal (Sycamore Valley). The houses of the resort, which is well integrated into the local landscape, occupy a sunnily exposed mountain plateau and offer numerous possibilities for accommodation (capacity about 7 000, mainly in bed-and-breakfasts, guest-houses and family hotels). Ramsau is an oasis of peace and quiet and a ramblers' paradise in every season. In winter there are still 70km - 44 miles of footpaths open to walkers.
The **cross-country ski tracks**★★★ cover over 150km - 90 miles between altitudes of 1 000-1 350m – 3 281-4 429ft and include a wide range of levels of difficulty. The nearby Hunerkogel summit also offers cross-country ski tracks at an altitude

of 2 700m - 8 858ft against a magnificent backdrop of mountain peaks.

The possibilities for downhill skiing in Ramsau are somewhat limited, but not far off are the **Schladminger Tauern**★★ *(see alphabetical entry)*, which more than amply compensate.

From Ramsau take the small mountain road towards Weißenbach, which cuts through some delightful **scenery**★. Level with Aich, at the foot of the Schladminger Tauern, the road leads into the E 651. Keen walkers can at this point make a detour up to Stoderzinken.

★★ **Walk up to Stoderzinken** – Alt 2 048m - 6 718ft. *45min driving time and 2 hours 15min on foot for the Rtn trip.*

Follow the E 651 to Gröbming and then the small, 12km - 8 mile long road signposted "Stoderzinken Alpenstraße" which has a regular gradient of 9%. Toll after 2km - 1 mile.

At the end of the road climb to the Steiner hut and from there take the untaxing footpath *(30min)* to a pretty little chapel, the **Friedenskircherl**, which seems to be hanging on the very edge of an abyss. There is a remarkable **view**★ of the Schladminger Tauern range (with the ski-slopes of Haus, Schladming and Hochwurzen in the foreground).

Turn back for a short distance, then take a challenging footpath *(at least 1 hour)* up to the Stoderzinken summit. It is recommended to wear proper climbing boots, particularly in damp weather, as the path is rocky and can be slippery. From the top, there is a marvellous **panorama**★★ of the better known peaks around Schladming and of the magnificently forested slopes of the Dachstein. For those energetic enough to walk on, it is possible to climb from here to the Brünner hut. Otherwise, turn back and return to the way you came.

DANUBE VALLEY★★

See DONAUTAL

DEUTSCHLANDSBERG

Steiermark – Population 7 620

Michelin map 426 fold 37 – 30km - 19 miles southwest of Graz

Local map under STEIRISCHE WEINSTRASSE – Alt 372m - 1 220ft

This town at the foot of the Koralpe near the Slovene border takes its name from the fortified castle of Landsberg. The prefix "deutsch" was not added until the 19C. The place is famous for its Corpus Christi celebrations in which each processional altar is magnificently bedecked with flowers.

From time immemorial wine has been made here, benefiting from the favourable climate with its 280 days of sunshine; today Deutschlandsberg is the centre for the production of the wellknown **Schilcher.**

To the north of the town stands the castle of Wildbach, where Schubert is supposed to have composed his famous Lied *"The Trout".*

Castle – *Go down the elongated main square with its brightly painted façades and follow the signs marked "Burghotel" on the right.*

Perched on one of the last vine-clad spurs of the Koralpe, the 12C keep dominates the restored castle. From the car park, the starting point for walks in the surrounding countryside, there is a fine **view**★.

DONAUTAL★★

DANUBE VALLEY – Oberösterreich und Niederösterreich

Michelin map 426 folds 6 to 13

The Danube is the longest river in Central Europe (2 826km - 1 756 miles) and the second longest in Europe, after the Volga (3 895km - 2 292 miles). It forms a natural link between Germany and southeastern Europe. It flows through or skirts ten states, and four capital cities have been built on its banks, bearing witness to its international importance. Although it provides a link between peoples, it has also often been an obstacle to their coming together.

GEOGRAPHICAL NOTES

An Alpine River – The Danube rises in the palace grounds at **Donaueschingen** in Germany (Baden-Württemberg), converging shortly afterwards with two tributaries, the Breg and the Brigach. The river almost dries up on reaching the highly fissured limestone of the Swabian Jura but then flows on between the escarpments of a picturesque ravine from Tuttlingen to Sigmaringen. Between Ulm and Vienna, the Danube takes on an Alpine character, its flow swelling almost to flood levels in early summer and drying to a mere rivulet in the winter. The variations in flow are caused by the tributaries along its south bank – the Iller, the Lech, the Isar and the Inn, which bring down melt-waters from the Bavarian and Tyrolean Alps. The volume of water in these rivers (the Inn at Passau is almost the size of the Danube itself) make the Danube a powerful river by the time it enters Austria, and able to carry a good deal of shipping. At times of spate, the alluvium transported by the river gives its waters a milky white colour.

From Vienna to the Black Sea – From the Leopoldsberg bluff, the last foothill of the Alps overlooking Vienna, one can see the first of the alluvial plains which stretch between the Alps and the Carpathians. In Hungary the Danube and its tributaries wind through reeds and marshes across the *puszta*, a grassy steppe. The altitude here is about 100m - 300ft above sea-level and the drop almost nil. From this point on, the continental climate has its effect on the river. The waters are high in May, owing to the thawing of the Carpathian snows and the spring rains. Considerable evaporation in summer nullifies the effect of the Alpine spates and causes a fall in the water level in September.

At the Iron Gates the bed of the Danube narrows until it is only about 100m - 300ft across so that the water is forced through narrow ravines: this brings a little vigour to the river, which still has some 1 000km - 600 miles to go across increasingly arid steppelands. It runs into the Black Sea through a huge delta of which the largest three arms – those of Kilia, Sulina and St George – split into innumerable branches which make the whole area look like a lake dotted with islands. Like the Dnieper and the Volga, the Danube is frozen for a period each year, which holds up navigation for more than a month. The Danube has an average daily flow of 6 000m³ - 1 319 809 gal (UK).

HISTORICAL NOTES

An Important Strategic Route – The strategic importance of the Danube goes back to Roman times. Initially an obstacle to the expansion of the Empire, it subsequently acted as a protection against barbarian incursions. Under Augustus the Romans were unable to get a footing on the north bank of the river; Trajan succeeded, subdued the Dacians, and in order to watch them more closely, built a huge stone bridge of which the ruins can be seen near the Iron Gates; Aurelius had to retire to the south bank. At the time of Attila the Danubian lands were the crossroads where the peoples mixed together to produce the complex ethnic patterns of the Balkans.

Since the Middle Ages all conquerors have regarded possession of the Danube as essential to the success of their undertakings. It was the invasion route chosen by the Turks in 1529 and 1683 *(see WIEN)*, and then by Napoleon's troops in their march on Vienna. At the time of the Treaty of Paris which ended the Crimean War in 1856, Turks and Russians attached extreme importance to the control of the islands and banks of its delta, although these could be flooded.

The Song of the Nibelungen – Originally the name Nibelungen applied to a tribe of dwarfs, whose treasure was stolen by Siegfried; later on the name was applied to the Burgundian warriors, the heroes of the best known of all German epic tales. The song was composed probably towards the end of the 12C and enjoys a fame east of the Rhine comparable with that of King Arthur in England and Roland in France. It was inspired by Scandinavian and German legends based on the annihilation of the Burgundian Kingdom by the Huns in the 5C. It tells of the splendour of the Burgundian Court at Worms and of the passions in the hearts of the heroes.

The proud Brunnhilde, wife of Gunther, King of the Burgundians **(Nibelungen)**, learns from her sister-in-law Kriemhilde that she had been won in combat by the latter's husband Siegfried and not by Gunther. Swearing a terrible revenge, she finds an accomplice in Hagen who treacherously kills Siegfried in the course of a great hunt. Fearing that Kriemhilde might use the Nibelungen treasure, her wedding present from Siegfried, to buy allies to help her avenge her husband's murder, Hagen casts the hoard into the Rhine. For thirteen long years Kriemhilde plots her revenge. She marries Etzel (Attila), King of the Huns, who invites the Nibelungen to his castle, Etzelburg, in Hungary. The Nibelungen undertake the lengthy journey down the Danube. On their arrival they realise that they have been lured into a trap; a grim struggle ensues, ending in a general massacre. Hagen is beheaded by Kriemhilde with Siegfried's sword; the secret of the whereabouts of the Nibelungen treasure dies with him.

The Danube School (early 16C) – The riverside scene from Regensburg to Vienna with its many forests has inspired a number of painters, mainly Swabians, who shared a keen sense of nature, which they conceived not simply as a setting but vibrant with hidden life which suffuses the scene depicted. Their paintings evoke secret, sometimes primeval landscapes, the abode of those legendary spirits so characteristic of the German soul.

Albrecht Altdorfer (1480-1538), a citizen of Regensburg, is the master in whose work this approach is most clearly visible. In the panels of the Passion painted for the monks of St. Florian, the *Battle of Alexander*, the *St George*, and the *Danube Valley* at Munich, Altdorfer handles contrasting light in a way so striking as to make him one of the founders of landscape painting, as well as a forerunner of Romanticism. Hans Burgkmair (1473-1531) and Jörg Breu (1475-1537) have a similar aesthetic sense. The latter worked for a long time for the Abbeys of Herzogenburg, Zwettl and Melk. **Lucas Cranach the Elder** (1472-1553), from Franconia is also reckoned among the Danubian masters. The mysterious depths of water, rocks and woods which form the backgrounds of his works show his affinity with the other painters of forest scenes.

Navigation on the Danube – Below Ulm and the confluence with the River Iller, the Danube is navigable. Clumsy craft called "Ulm boxes", as well as rafts of logs, used to float as far as Vienna. They had a draught of only about 60cm - 2ft and, being unable to go upstream, they were broken up at the end of the journey and sold as firewood.

In 1829 steamships appeared and the passenger and freight traffic grew. The Danube made trading possible between the industrial districts of the upper valley and the agricultural lands downstream. Nonetheless, international use of a river is no simple matter and free navigation remained dependent upon the vagaries of Balkan politics. The 1919 treaties, which completed the work begun in the Treaty of Paris of 1856, laid down the rules of navigation in the estuary and opened the way for the Danube becoming an international waterway. This statute has never been repealed, although its clauses have been superseded by the creation in 1948 of a new Commission for the Danube controlled solely by the riparian powers. Austria joined this new organization in 1960.

In fact, the present position is that only the Danubian powers enjoy freedom of navigation and commerce on the river. Other factors make the Danube a much less frequented river than the Rhine: large variations in flow, moving sandbanks which are dangerous to navigation and often have to be marked afresh; winter freezing; outflow into an inland sea; sparsely populated area with little industrial development.

Small sea-going ships can, at present, go up as far as Krems and 1 350 ton barges can reach Regensburg. Since 1992 the Rhine-Main-Danube connection has enabled 2 000 ton Rhine barges to go from Rotterdam to the Black Sea.

Engineering Works – For more than two centuries engineering has been going on to improve the navigability and usefulness of the river. The deepening of the riverbed near Vienna has allowed several of the arms of the river to be drained and thus removed the danger of flooding. Since 1945 the major parts of the improvement programme have been undertaken on the one hand by Austria and on the other jointly by Yugoslavia and Romania, who, between 1964 and 1971, built the immense dam of Djerdap in the Iron Gates defile.

Austria commissioned the following dams: Jochenstein on the German frontier, Aschach, Ottensheim-Wilhering, Abwinden-Asten, Ybbs-Persenbeug, Wallsee-Mitter-kirchen, Melk, Altenwörth and Greifenstein. A power station is being built at Freudenau. Altenwörth is the largest of these civil engineering projects, with an annual power output of almost 2 thousand million kWh. The power stations along the Danube produce a total of about 11 thousand million kWh per year, accounting for a quarter of Austria's national annual electricity output. To generate the same amount of energy in a traditional power station, it would be necessary to burn 2.8 million tons of fuel oil.

THE DANUBE IN AUSTRIA

The Danube is Austrian for only 360km - 224 miles from Achleiten, below Passau, to Hainburg, at the gates of Bratislava, that is, for one-eighth of its course. It is a vital artery for the economy of the country. This section of the river, wholly navigable, is used by shipping which serves Vienna, the capital, Linz, a great industrial town, and indirectly the industrial centres of Steyr and St. Pölten. Though the waters of the river are not always the colour of which *The Blue Danube* sings, especially when water levels are high, the river's banks, particularly between Grein and Krems, often have border scenery dear to the Romantics. Old fortified castles, over which the ghost of a Burgrave still watches, gracious Renaissance palaces with charming arcaded courts, and beautiful fortified churches and abbeys grace the banks of this much sung river.

① FROM PASSAU (IN GERMANY) TO LINZ

86km - 55 miles - about 3 hours - Local map overleaf

From Passau to Aschach, the route proposed below runs southeastwards along the south bank of the river. From the north bank rise the granite heights of the Mühlviertel, the last foothills of the Bohemian massif. In this section of its course the Danube crosses an area formerly filled by glaciers. With the melting of the glaciers, gravel plains formed along the valleys, while the hills were colonised by coniferous forest and grassland.

★★ **Passau** – *See Michelin Green Guide Germany.*

Leave Passau to the south, crossing the Inn. Turn immediately to the left towards the Achleiten border post.

The river soon comes into view, wide and majestic, bordered with wooded, rocky slopes, and the road, running along the valley floor, follows all its curves. At Obernzell, which can be seen on the German shore, the river opens out into a magnificent lake. This is the reservoir of the Jochenstein dam on the Danube.

Jochenstein-Kraftwerk – The Jochenstein dam, at the foot of which has been installed a power station with an annual production of now 1.6 thousand million kWh, was a joint Austro-Bavarian project.

Schloß Schönbühel and the River Danube

From Engelhartszell to Wesenufer the valley narrows. The *corniche* road, running above the first stretches of water created by the Aschach dam, gives some fine views; from time to time the outline of a castle can be seen. A little after **Wesenufer**, a pretty village with flowered balconies, the road leaves the shore of the Danube, which flows on in wide, sunken loops further north. The road climbs in a wooded gorge and reaches the picturesque valley of the Aschach, which it leaves on reaching the alluvial plain, to cross the Danube below the **Aschach-Kraftwerk**, one of the largest power stations of its kind in Europe. After Ottensheim and its dam, the road leads to Linz.

② FROM LINZ TO GREIN

67km - 42 miles – about 2 hours 30min – Local map overleaf

★ **Linz** – *See LINZ.*

Below Linz the valley opens out into a wide basin filled by the alluvial soil of the river and its tributaries, the Traun and the Enns. On this fertile soil cereals, sugarbeet and fruit trees flourish. To the north lie the slopes and wooded ridges of the Mühlviertel and of the Waldviertel.

Leave Linz to the southeast via St.-Peterstraße towards Grein.

The road goes through the impressive industrial zone of Linz with its steel works and nitrogen plant and crosses the Danube at the Steyregg bridge. A little after Steyregg, there is a last view of Linz before the road cuts across a plateau to return to the Danube plain at St. Georgen.

Take the turn towards the camp (Lager) at Mauthausen.

Mauthausen – *See MAUTHAUSEN.*

From Mauthausen to Dornach the road crosses a vast cultivated plain (sugarbeet, maize and wheat) which gradually gives way to a more wooded landscape.

Near Saxen turn right towards Burg Clam.

★ **Burg Clam** ⊙ – Dominated by its central tower, the castle's silhouette rises romantically from its leafy surroundings. The rock on which it stands has been fortified since 1149. The residential part of the castle focusses on the charmingly irregular arcaded **courtyard**★ of 1581.

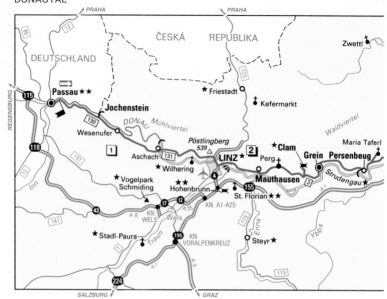

The castle houses an unusually complete pharmacy whose fittings date from 1603. There are fine examples of Vienna and Meissen work in the porcelain room and, in the dining room, some rare Louis XVI armchairs. Among the family memorabilia of the castle's owners is the breast-plate worn by Karl von Clam-Martinic at the battle of Leipzig in 1813 as well as the uniform he wore while escorting Napoleon to Elba. There are also souvenirs brought back by Heinrich von Clam-Martinic who accompanied Archduke Franz Ferdinand on a world tour in 1892-93 *(see ARTSTETTEN)*.

Return to the main road.

Below Dornach the road hugs the north bank of the river. Its waters, already held back by the dam at Ybbs-Persenbeug *(below)*, are hemmed in by rocky, wooded slopes. The approach to Grein is particularly pretty.

Grein – The charming summer holiday resort of Grein lies at the foot of a wooded bluff on which the castle is built. This commands the entrance to a picturesque valley in the Strudengau. The pretty, enclosed town square (Stadtplatz) is surrounded by turreted houses. The church contains an altarpiece by Bartolomeo Altomonte on the 18C high altar. Grein is very proud of the little **Rokokotheater** ⊙ housed in the town hall. Entirely made of wood, it was built by the townspeople at the end of the 18C and is in use every summer and autumn.

The **castle** *(30min on foot Rtn)* has four main buildings, flanked by corner turrets, which contrast with the elegance of the Renaissance inner **courtyard**★, with three tiers of arcades. A spring well, an old cistern and a virginia creeper, hanging over the arches of the ground floor arcade, make a romantic scene. Within the generous spaces of the interior is an interesting local navigation museum, the **Schiffahrtsmuseum** ⊙, with numerous models of bridges, landing stages and locks as well as works of art evoking the life of the great river in this part of Austria.

③ FROM GREIN TO KREMS

95km - 59 miles - allow a day, not including visits to Grein or Krems - local map above

Between Grein and Krems stretches the most picturesque section of the Danube valley in Austria. It is hollowed out of the granite of the Waldviertel, which forms the last foothills of the Bohemian massif.

Grein - *Description above. Time 1 hour.*

From Grein to Ybbs, the **Strudengau**★, sunken between the high wooded cliffs which overlook it from a height of over 400m - 1 300ft, often silent and shrouded in mist, provides a heroic and romantic setting. The castle ruins of Burg Struden, clinging to their rock, and then those of Burg Sarmingstein, catch the eye. The river embraces willow-covered islands, then expands into a splendid lake, formed by the Ybbs-Persenbeug dam, whose power station has an annual output of 1 358 thousand million kWh. The locks built to allow the passage of barges are particularly interesting.

Persenbeug – The castle overlooking the Danube was built in the 10C and rebuilt in the 17C. The last Austrian Emperor, Karl I, was born here in 1887.

Persenbeug, which features a Baroque town hall and elegant old houses stands at the head of a well-tilled plain formed by a meander. Between here and Melk, the valley was the scene of certain episodes in the Nibelungen epic. It was there, in the **Nibelungengau**, that the rides of Gunther and Hagen took place; it is there they collected their knights to go to Attila's court. On top of a hill in **Maria Taferl** stands a pilgrimage church with its façade designed to be seen from a distance.

★★ **Artstetten Castle and Museum** - *See Schloß-Museum ARTSTETTEN.*

At Pöchlarn, on the south bank of the river, the Babenbergs, who began the extraordinary expansion of the Austrian monarchy, settled in the 10C. It was they who, quite near, founded the Abbey of Melk, whose fine Baroque façade comes into view at Ebersdorf. Its steep promontory base, however, remains hidden for some time by trees on an island.

Take the bridge over the Danube.

★★ **Melk Abbey** - *See MELK.*

Schönbühel – From the main road through the Wachau, **Schloß Schönbühel**, built at the beginning of the 19C, can be seen standing on a rocky outcrop, on the right bank of the Danube. Its pepper-pot towers and bulbous-domed belfry, with rows of fruit trees on the hills in the background, make a charming picture. Downstream of the castle, a little way from the village, tourists following the south bank of the river can visit a former Servite convent (now a presbytery), founded in 1666 and also built on a cliff overlooking the Danube. The **church** ⊙, whose ceiling is adorned with frescoes, has a moving group behind the altar representing a *pietà*. From a terrace there is a pleasant view of the Wachau.

Take the road on the north bank towards Krems.

From Grimsing onwards the famous vineyards begin. Further on, at the highest point on the opposite shore, is the ruined fortress of Aggstein. At Willendorf a "Venus", a very primitive earthenware statue dating from about 25 000 years ago, was found in 1906. It is now kept in Vienna at the Naturhistorisches Museum.

The **Wachau**★★ owes its terraced vineyards, its orchards, its corn and tobacco to its favourable orientation and alluvial soil. Charming villages stand along the riverbanks. Ruins of fortified castles crown the crests, and rounded belfries add their note of fantasy to the countryside.

Spitz – Visitors following the main road through the Wachau would hardly suspect the presence of the little town of Spitz, hidden behind a curtain of fruit trees. It lies at the foot of terraced vineyards with only the squat shape of the parish church rising above the house roofs. Above, the ruins of the castle of Hinterhaus stand out against the wooded mountain slope. Spitz has old houses, with arcades and balconies. The Schloßgasse with its arcades is one of its most picturesque streets and leads to the 17C castle.

The **Pfarrkirche** ⊙, a Gothic building of the 15C, has a chancel out of line with the nave; the elegant chancel has network vaulting. The organ-loft is adorned with statues of Christ and the Apostles (c1420). The altarpiece (1799) by Kremser Schmidt over the Baroque altar shows the martyrdom of St Maurice.

St. Michael – This fortified church, built about 1500 in the Gothic style, is flanked, near the chevet, by a big round tower.

Weißenkirchen – *See WEISSENKIRCHEN.*

Ahead, just after Weißenkirchen, is a beautiful view of Dürnstein.

★ **Dürnstein** – *See DÜRNSTEIN.*

The slopes are lower near the towns of Stein and Krems.

★ **Krems** – *See KREMS und STEIN. Time 2 hours.*

④ FROM KREMS TO VIENNA

83km - 52 miles – allow ½ day excluding Vienna – Local map previous page

★ **Krems** – *See KREMS und STEIN.*

Cross the Danube on the great steel bridge at Stein, west of Krems.

A little after Mautern on the right, crowning a wooded hill, stands the impressive Benedictine abbey of Göttweig. Near the river are alluvial terraces on which vines and fruit trees grow, and then meadows and fields of cereals. The road runs near the river, which is divided into a number of branches at this point.

Tulln – *See TULLN.*

At Greifenstein, near the Vienna Woods, the valley narrows, and the road squeezes a passage between the river and high wooded hills.

Klosterneuburg – *See KLOSTERNEUBURG.*

The road then enters the suburbs of Vienna.

★★★ **Vienna** – *See WIEN. Time 3 days.*

⑤ FROM VIENNA TO HAINBURG

84km - 52 miles – allow ½ day excluding Vienna – Local map previous page

The chosen route follows the south bank of the river all the way. Sometimes the river splits into several arms, embracing many islands, while the valley grows much wider.

★★★ **Vienna** – *See WIEN. Time 3 days.*

Leave Vienna on road no 9, ④ on the town plan, to go through Schwechat, which is famous for its breweries.

Before skirting the buildings of the international airport of Vienna at Schwechat, one sees indistinctly on the left the outlines of the Island of Lobau where Napoleon's forces recovered their strength in 1809, after the unexpected victories of the Austrians at Eßling and Aspern.

Wildungsmauer – In spite of restorations and additions (including a 19C porch and tower), the little church of St. Nikolaus has kept its essentially Romanesque character. It originated in a fortified building going back to before the start of the 14C.

Petronell – Important Roman remains (including amphitheatres) have been found here and in neighbouring Bad Deutsch-Altenburg; this was the site of **Carnuntum**, the largest garrison on the Bernstein road and capital of the province of Pannonia. Marcus Aurelius made his headquarters here during the wars against the Marcomanni and Quadi and worked on his *Meditations*. The **Archäologischer Park Carnuntum** ⊙ contains parts of the Roman town, the great baths and some reconstructions. To the southwest of town stand the vestiges of the **Heidentor**, a building dating from 300 which once had four doorways. Further Roman artefacts are to be found in the museums of Petronell and Bad Deutsch-Altenburg.

On the south side of the approach to Petronell from the west is an unusual **Romanesque chapel**★ ⊙, circular in form, with a semi-circular chancel grafted on to its east end. The building is decorated soberly but strikingly with colonnettes and blind arcading. The carving of the Baptism of Christ in the tympanum above the entrance is perhaps an indication that the chapel was originally a baptistry.

Rohrau – Here in the 16C castle is the **Harrach'sche Gemäldegalerie** ⊙, the largest and most important private art collection in Austria with works by 17C and 18C masters from Spain, Naples and Rome, and 16C and 17C masters from Holland. One of the most famous exhibits is the gracious painting of *The Concert* (16C) by the Master of the Female Half-Portraits.

Rohrach was where the composer Haydn was born; the **Geburtshaus Joseph Haydns** ⊘ has an exhibition of the composer's original scores.

At Bad Deutsch-Altenburg cross the Danube towards Marchegg. After 9km - 5 miles turn right towards Schloßhof.

A long embankment carries the road across the floodplain of the Danube. The river itself is crossed by means of a bold piece of engineering in the form of a suspension bridge with cables hung from a single tower. The monotonous landscape of endless flat arable fields is relieved here and there by squat single-storied dwellings, a reminder that we are now in Central Europe.

Schloßhof ⊘ – This vast Baroque palace owes some of its fame to having housed the Imperial Court in the 18C. The original buildings were transformed between 1725-29 by the great Prince Eugene of Savoy (1663-1736), who also had the Belvedere built in Vienna. In his remaking of Schloßhof, Prince Eugene, who was also a distinguished patron of the arts, employed the architect Johann Lukas von Hildebrand and a workforce of 800, of whom 300 laboured to create a magnificent landscape in the French style. With its sculptures, fountains, terraces, parterres and magnificent wrought-iron gates, the garden was the envy of the prince's contemporaries. In 1760 the Empress Maria Theresa had the palace modified and added a second storey. Sumptuously furnished and decorated, Schloßhof became one of the most favoured residences of the Imperial court. Nowadays, restored, it is the scene of important annual exhibitions.

Between Bad Deutsch-Altenburg and Hainburg a range of hills comes into view, on the far bank of the Danube and its tributary the March/Morava in Slovakia; these are the Little Carpathians, the last outrunners of the great circle of mountains encircling the Hungarian plain.

Hainburg – Still with its ring of walls and fortified gateways below the remains of its castle, Hainburg had an important strategic role in the Middle Ages on the highway linking Vienna and Bratislava. The hundredfold increase in traffic between Austria and Slovakia since 1989 has brought the town a renewed importance and prosperity.

DÜRNSTEIN*

Niederösterreich – Population 1 030

Michelin map 426 fold 11 – Local map under DONAUTAL – Alt 207m - 679ft.

The little fortified town of Dürnstein stands at the foot of a ridge on which terraced vineyards are cultivated, producing a well-known wine *(details of Austrian wines in the Introduction)*. Crowned by the ruins of a fortress and still girded by its walls, it lies on a rocky ridge overlooking the Danube, forming one of the most famous scenes in the Wachau. The modern road to the Wachau avoids the old town by passing through a tunnel underneath it.

Richard the Lionheart held prisoner

It is said that during the 3rd Crusade, Richard the Lionheart, King of England, had a furious altercation with the Duke of Austria, Leopold V. At the attack against Acre in Palestine, Richard is supposed to have removed the Duke's banner from a tower, thus insulting the Duke's honour.

By chance, Richard was shipwrecked in the Adriatic on his way back to his kingdom and had to cross the land of his rival. Though disguised as a peasant, he was recognized at an inn near Vienna, arrested and handed over to Leopold, who shut him up in the fortress at Dürnstein.

In the spring of 1193, as Richard was languishing in gaol, his attention was caught by some familiar, indeed some of his own favourite, airs being played by a minstrel outside the castle walls. This turned out to be the faithful **Blondel**, who was looking for his sovereign lord. Unfortunately, Blondel's discovery of where his master was being held prisoner was to no avail, as Richard was transferred and held prisoner for nearly a year longer at the Imperial Castle of Trifels in the Rhineland Palatinate, before being granted his liberty at the price of an enormous ransom.

SIGHTS *time: 2 hours*

Hauptstraße – This, the main street, runs through the town from end to end and is bounded in the east by an old fortified gateway. It is most pleasing with its old houses, some of them 16C, with their bracketed turrets, oriels and balconies with flowers.

The wrought-iron signs of several inns – where it is a pleasure to taste the famous *Heuriger* (current year's wine) of the Wachau – will recall the story of Richard the Lionheart's imprisonment and the touching story of the faithful Blondel.

Pfarrkirche ⊙ – The Baroque **tower**★ that crowns the façade of the parish church can be seen from far off. It was designed by Matthias Steinl and Josef Munggenast. Of the former Augustine Canons' monastery, founded in the 15C and rebuilt between 1720 and 1725 in the Baroque style, one can admire the porch, with its carved columns and statues in the courtyard, surrounded by former abbey buildings.

The church is adorned with light stucco; pierced balconies run round the nave above the side altars. The woodwork of the chancel, the pulpit and the high altar makes a contrast in its richness, with the simplicity of the nave. The side chapels house paintings by Kremser Schmidt. The sacristy, also adorned with delicate stucco, shows valuable marquetry. The cloister has been altered by restorations.

Baroque church tower, Dürnstein

From the balustraded terrace at the foot of the tower of the façade, remarkable for its height and its decoration, there is a pleasant view of the Danube Valley.

Castle Ruins – *45min on foot Rtn.*
The ruins *(Burgruine)* are reached by a path which begins on the level of the ramparts east of the town and climbs among rocks. From the ruins there is a remarkable **view** of Dürnstein and the valley.

Schloß EGGENBERG★★

Steiermark

Michelin map 426 fold 38 – 3.5km - 2 miles west of Graz

A long avenue leads to the main entrance of the castle of the Princes of Eggenberg. The grounds have been turned into a deer park where peacocks, deer and wild sheep roam.

Residence of a high-ranking dignitary – Between 1625 and 1635 a princely residence for Johann Ulrich von Eggenberg was constructed round a medieval core. Von Eggenberg had been promoted to the rank of Prince of the Empire in 1623 and in the reign of Ferdinand II he was appointed to one of the most important posts, Reichfürst (Governor) of Inner Austria. The building work was entrusted to the Italian architect **Pietro de Pomis**, who had demonstrated his skills a few years earlier with his work on Ferdinand's mausoleum in Graz.

Plan – In some aspects the castle is similar to the Escorial near Madrid – huge buildings, arranged on a square ground plan and separated by corner towers, enclosing three inner courtyards and a majestic chapel. The three tiers of arches in the main courtyard are articulated by engaged columns.

Architectural theme – The exceptional originality of Schloß Eggenberg derives from the fact that the whole building is an elaborately detailed allegory of the universe. The castle teems with images and symbols of the cosmos, and the initial impression is one of identification with the four elements: the earth which supports it, the air which surrounds it, the water in the moats encircling it and the fire of its red roofs above it. The four towers stand for the four cardinal points of the compass, and mark the perimeter of a strikingly symbolical structure containing 365 windows for every day of the year, a suite of 24 state rooms for every hour of the day and night, and 52 windows letting light into these rooms and symbolising 52 Sundays, the classic religious feast days of the year.

TOUR *time: 1 hour*

★★★ **State Apartments (Prunkräume)** ⊙ – *2nd floor*. The many notable guests who have occupied these sumptuously decorated apartments include the **Emperor Leopold I** who came to Eggenberg in 1673 to celebrate his marriage to Claudia-Felizitas von Tirol.

The decoration of the 24 **state rooms** was carried out in the 17C and 18C in the Baroque style, with a rich profusion of stucco work and painting which is in turn set off by the brilliancy of the chandeliers. There are also interesting mid-18C paintings by Johann Baptist Anton Raunacher. This suite of drawing rooms and bedrooms, interspersed with a number of Chinese and Japanese cabinets which were very fashionable at the time, compose a residence of considerable charm. It is interesting to note that, although these apartments were decorated with festivities in mind, their huge dimensions do not impose the cold atmosphere that might be expected.

The spacious reception room, known as the **Room of the Planets** (Planetensaal), is the central pivot of a suite of 24 rooms, arranged in a symmetrical fashion. The walls and ceiling are decorated with paintings (completed in 1685) by the Styrian artist Hans Adam Wissenkircher. The stucco work is by Alessandro Serenio.

During the summer the Eggenberg Concerts take place here in addition to official receptions.

Abteilung für Vor- und Frühgeschichte ⊙ – The Styrian antiques collection is housed on the ground floor of the south wing.

★★★ **Strettweg Votive Chariot** – The centrepiece of the collection is a bronze chariot made 2 700 years ago in the 7C BC, a moving example of the work of the Hallstatt period. It was found in a tumulus at Strettweg, near Judenburg. Its votive role is inferred from a female figure standing in the middle of the chariot and holding out a bowl as if making an offering. The chariot is surrounded by soldiers on horseback and on foot, and the artist has captured them performing the swirling movements of a ritual

Strettweg Votive Chariot

dance. Other treasures, urns and various objects which were unearthed at the same burial mound are also on display in this room.

Abteilung für Jagdkunde ⊙ – *1st floor; access by the stairs on the left of the entrance hall.*

This museum offers a comprehensive and well-documented history of the techniques of hunting, and contains innumerable trophies, art-historical exhibits, interesting paintings and remarkable collections of old weapons.

EGGENBURG

Niederösterreich – Population 3 730
Michelin map 426 fold 11 – Alt 325m - 1 066ft

The town of Eggenburg features some beautiful medieval and Renaissance architecture and can still boast a town wall preserved almost in its entirety with three towers (the Holturm, the Wahrsagerturm and the Kanzler-Plank-Turm). The **historical town centre** is also well-preserved.

Hauptplatz – In the main square stand a 16C pillory, a Trinity column and the Gemalte Haus, a sgraffito house dating from 1547 with images from the Old Testament, based on woodcuts by Burgkmair.

Pfarrkirche St. Stephan ⊘ – Two Romanesque towers, in solid, square-cut masonry (1180), dominate the east end of the parish church. The chancel dates from the mid-14C, and the nave from the 15C. The Late Gothic hall-church with ribbed vaulting, deeply incised clustered piers and beautiful tracery windows contains some rich fittings: interesting stone pulpit (1515); delicately chased pillars (1505); and a Baroque councillors' seat with inlaid strapwork (1710).

EHRENHAUSEN

Steiermark – Population 1 170
Michelin map 426 fold 38
10km - 6 miles southeast of Leibnitz
Local map under STEIRISCHE WEINSTRASSE – Alt 261m – 856ft

Near the Slovenian frontier, a wooded bluff overlooking the south bank of the Mur and the village of Ehrenhausen was chosen by the Eggenberg family as the site of a castle and a mausoleum. The **Pfarrkirche** on the main square has a fine tower with a particularly elaborate roof. The building was remodelled in Baroque style in 1752 and given a Rococo interior.

★ **Mausoleum** ⊘ – This curious funerary monument shelters the tomb of Ruprecht of Eggenberg, who distinguished himself as a general in the struggle with the Turks at the end of the 16C. The stonework was completed in 1640 but the interior only in 1691, the work being carried out by followers of Fischer von Erlach.

The west front, adorned with carved figures, pilasters, leaf and geometrical designs, is framed between two huge statues of ancient warriors, standing on plinths ornamented with battle scenes.

The interior is striking for the number of stuccos on the central dome. The great commander lies in the crypt, accompanied by his successor, Wolfgang von Eggenberg.

Castle – The castle, standing near the square keep has preserved an elegant courtyard with Renaissance arcades in three tiers and an old well.

EHRWALD★

Tirol – Population 2 230
Michelin map 426 fold 16 – Alt 996m - 2 368ft

Ehrwald, at the west foot of the Zugspitze cliffs, is the best equipped country resort of the Zugspitze Tyrolean district (Tiroler Zugspitzgebiet), of which the basin formed by the upper Loisach valley, south of the Bavarian frontier, marks the centre. Among the many local walks, runs and tours, the classic excursion has become the ascent of the Zugspitze by way of the Zugspitzkamm cable-car.

During the skiing season the Zugspitzkamm cable-car offers trained athletes first-class ski-runs, such as the great Alpine run of nearly 23km - 14 miles (Gatterlabfahrt) which takes them from the top of the Zugspitze back to Ehrwald *(guide recommended)*.

★★★ **Ascent of the Zugspitze** ⊘ – *Allow about 1 hour, including 10min for the cable-car.*

The 4.5km - 3 mile long road leads through forests of larch and beech from Ehrwald to Obermoos and the valley station of the Tyrolean Zugspitze cable-car. It is possible to walk back along this stretch along a pretty forest footpath *(1 hour)*. Even for those not going to the top of the Zugspitze this makes a pleasant outing on foot or by car.

★★★ **Zugspitze summit** – The upper station of the cable-car, coming from Ehrwald/Obermoos, lies on Austrian territory on the western peak of the Zugspitze summit (alt 2 964m - 9 724ft).

The **panorama**★★★ to the south reveals the glacier summits of the Hohe Tauern (Großglockner and Großvenediger), the Tyrolean High Alps (Alps of the Zillertal, Stubai and Ötztal), the Ortler and the Bernina, towering over the forward bastions of the Kaisergebirge, the Dachstein and the Karwendel. Nearer, to the east, the mountains of the Arlberg (Silvretta and Rätikon) make way for a view of the Säntis in the Appenzell Alps. In the foreground can be seen the Allgäu and Ammergau mountains, part of the Bavarian Alps. To the north are the hazy Bavarian lowlands with the shimmering waters of the Ammersee and the Starnberger See.

The other facilities on the summit as well as the ski-fields of Schneeferner, where good snow conditions continue until summer (equipped with numerous ski lifts), are in Bavaria *(customs control). For more details see Michelin Green Guide to Germany.*

EISENERZ

Steiermark – Population 7 800
Michelin map 426 fold 23 – Alt 694m - 2 277ft

Eisenerz is an old mining town clustered at the foot of the large Gothic church dedicated to St Oswald, itself remarkable for fortifications recalling the Turkish threat of 1532. It is also overlooked by the strange, towering, pyramid-shaped Erzberg, known as the Iron Mountain. On its own on the southern slope of the valley is the Schichtturm bell-tower which once rang out to signal the end of miners' working shifts; the pretty baroque chapel of St Peter is also plainly visible.

★ **Erzberg** – It is only in the last two hundred years that the Erzberg has acquired its present aspect with **open-cast mines** Ⓥ and rows of associated stopes. During the Middle Ages, mining was carried out in small tunnels or isolated quarries but at the beginning of the 19C this practice gave way to a more organised system of shafts and tunnels. By 1870 the engineers felt confident enough about the uniformity of the deposits to begin systematic open excavations on the sides of the mountain. Today, as much ore is extracted in one day as was produced in a whole year during the 16C – approximately 10 000 tonnes. Forty two stopes, each 12-24m – 39-79ft deep, now form a huge stairway in the sky above Eisenerz, standing 1 465m - 4 806ft at its summit. Nearly all of the annual production of 2.3 million tonnes of ore is extracted by the open-cast system, and work continues throughout the winter. The ore goes first to blast furnaces at the foot of the mountain where the iron content is increased by 32%, and it is then upgraded at the steel works at Donawitz and Linz. All of Austria's iron ore currently comes from the Erzberg and supplies a third of the needs of the country's steel industry.

Stadtmuseum Ⓥ – This pleasant and informative museum tells the story of the art, culture and techniques of mining and the story of the town's inhabitants.

W. Geiersperger/BILDAGENTUR BUENOS DIAS

"Iron Mountain", Styria

EISENERZER ALPEN[*]

Michelin map 426 folds 22 and 23

The Eisenerz Alps, which include the astonishing Erzberg, on which the industrial power of the former Austrian Empire was based, join up to the northwest with the chalky Ennstal Alps, whose impressive walls line the Gesäuse Gorge.

A pass linking the Enns and Mur valleys, the Präbichl, rises to an altitude of 1 200m - 3 937ft. Between Hieflau and Leoben the road passes through a narrow, ryggedly picturesque defile.

GESÄUSE GORGE

[*] From Liezen to Hieflau *44km - 27 miles – about 2 hours 30min*

The **Gesäuse gorge** takes its name from the noise of its waters rushing over their rocky bed. The autumn colour of its trees makes a splendid spectacle.

Between Liezen and Admont the road winds along the Enns corridor, with its muddy floor. Soon the two onion domes of Frauenberg church on its hill come into view in the foreground. Further east in the background rise the Großer Buchstein and the Hochtor, two summits enclosing the Gesäuse gorge; its rocky entrance is visible from Admont.

From the touring route, take a narrow signposted road for 1.5km - 1 mile beginning east of the hill (on arriving at a small pass, turn sharp left).

Frauenberg – The pilgrimage church was rebuilt by the Abbots of Admont in the 17C, in an Italianate Baroque style.

The Calvary terrace at the end of a chestnut avenue forms a viewpoint overlooking the Admont basin and the steeples of the abbey church enclosed in a ring of peaks (Haller Mauern, Reichenstein and Hochtor).

Admont – *See ADMONT.*

The best **glimpse of the Gesäuse**[**] is that which, a little before the entrance to the ravine, reveals the splendid sides of the Hochtor (highest point: 2 369m - 7 770ft).

Once on the floor of the gorge the tourist will enjoy views only to the north, towards the Großer Buchstein.

Haindlkarbrücke – This bridge over a rushing tributary of the Enns offers a close **view**[*] of the formidable walls of the Hochtor, whose smallest projections are used by enthusiastic climbers.

Gstatterboden – Standing at the only point where the defile widens out is a hotel which forms the touring base of the Gesäuse massif, regarded by Viennese climbers as a high-grade climb.

Downstream, the gorge, whose cliffs are now crowned with woods, is less wild. From the steep section of the route known as the Hochsteg there is a view of the Planspitze, the final spur of the Hochtot.

Hieflau – Pop 1 370. This peaceful little place has a wooded setting at the foot of a south-facing slope.

EISENSTRASSE (IRON ROAD)

[*] From Hieflau to Leoben

50km - 31 miles - allow a day including Polster

Hieflau – *See above.*

From Hieflau to Eisenerz the Erzbach Valley has beautiful, winding gorges and offers fine panoramas of the Tamischbachturm. When you reach the basin of Eisenerz, opposite the reddish-brown **Erzberg**[*], make a small detour to see the Leopoldsteiner See.

[**] Leopoldsteiner See – This small lake with its deep green waters lies in one of the finest settings in Styria, at the foot of the rock cliffs of the Seemauer in the Hochschwab range.

Eisenerz – *See EISENERZ.*

The steep climb from Eisenerz to the Präbichl pass (alt 1 232m - 4 041ft) is overlooked by the Erzberg, with its manmade steps on this side consisting of ridges of bare rubble, and also by the lovely rock summit of the Pfaffenstein to the northwest. To enjoy a general view of the Erzberg take the chairlift up the Polster.

** **Polster** – *About 1 hour 30min Rtn from the Präbichl, including 30min by chairlift*  *and 30min on foot.*

From the summit (alt 1 910m - 6 266ft) crowned with a Calvary, there is a **view** of the Erzberg, standing out, in all its red-brown mass, against the greens of the Alpine pastures and woods and the blues of the surrounding lakes. To the north can be seen the separate sharp rock crests (Griesmauer) of the Hochschwab.

The descent from the Präbichl to Leoben, which, as far as Vordernberg, has a pleasant Alpine landscape, ends in the impressive industrial setting of the Donawitz-Leoben steelworks.

Leoben – *See LEOBEN.*

EISENSTADT

L Burgenland – Population 10 150
Michelin map 426 fold 25 – Alt 181m - 594ft.

Eisenstadt has developed on the south slope of the Leithagebirge, where the forests resemble a huge park. It is at this point that the great Central European Plain begins. The mild climate makes it possible to grow vines, peaches, apricots and almonds. The proximity of Vienna has checked the economic expansion of the town, which, however, is still the most important market in the region for wine. Since 1925 the political and administrative role of Eisenstadt, the capital of Burgenland, has somewhat revived the city. Neusiedler See, nearby, also attracts tourists to the area.

Haydn's Town – Everything here reminds one of the brilliant composer. For thirty years Joseph Haydn (1732-1809) lived sometimes at Eisenstadt, sometimes at the Esterháza palace in Hungary, in the service of Prince Miklós József Esterházy. He had been appointed assistant conductor in 1761. His job included conducting the orchestra and directing the chorus, composing music and tending to administrative work (music librarian, supervisor of instruments and chief of musical personnel). In 1766 he was promoted to musical director. Having an orchestra and a theatre at his disposal, Haydn worked without respite and achieved growing fame. His considerable work places him among the greatest names in music. *Haydn's birthplace at Rohrau see DONAUTAL* **5**.

Eisenstadt cherishes memories of the man who was to Mozart a guide, a model and a friend.

SIGHTS

Schloß Esterházy  – Eisenstadt was one of the favourite residences of this noble Magyar family, who largely contributed to the establishment of the Habsburgs' rule in Hungary. One of its princes, Mik-

Joseph Haydn

lós II, even refused the Hungarian crown which Napoleon I offered to him in 1809, preferring to continue his support of the Habsburgs.

Wishing to have a residence fit for his rank, Prince Pál Esterházy commissioned the Italian architect Carlone. On the site of a medieval fortress Carlone built, between 1663 and 1672, a great quadrilateral round the court of honour. Each of the four corner towers, at that time, was crowned by a bulbous dome.

Between 1797 and 1805 the French architect Moreau modified the building in the taste of that day. The façade to the park was given a portico in the neo-Classical style with Corinthian columns, and the entrance gateway in the main façade was surmounted by a terrace, supported by Tuscan columns. Terracotta busts, representing the ancestors of the Esterházy family and several Kings of Hungary, adorn this façade.

On the far side of the park are the former royal stables, built in 1743.

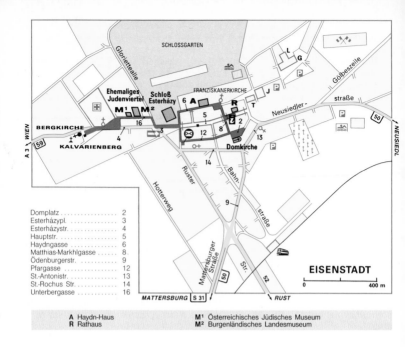

Domplatz	2
Esterházypl.	3
Esterházystr.	4
Hauptstr.	5
Haydngasse	6
Matthias-Markhlgasse	8
Ödenburgerstr.	9
Pfargasse	12
St.-Antonistr.	13
St.-Rochus Str.	14
Unterbergasse	16

EISENSTADT

0   400 m

A Haydn-Haus	**M¹** Österreichisches Jüdisches Museum
R Rathaus	**M²** Burgenländisches Landesmuseum

The château now houses local administrative offices, but the Haydn room, and the Esterházy-Museum are open to visitors. Part of the magnificent original interior décor is on show in Burg Forchtenstein.

Haydn-Saal ⊙ – *On the first floor opposite the entrance. Take the right hand staircase from the courtyard.*
The Haydn room was the great hall of state in the time of the Esterházy princes. In the noble setting of this huge hall, decorated in the 18C with stucco, monochrome and frescoes, Joseph Haydn, nearly every evening, conducted the orchestra of the princely court, often performing his own works.

Haydn-Haus ⊙ (**A**) – In Haydngasse, a quiet little street, at no 21 is the modest house in which the composer lived from 1766 to 1778. A covered passage leads to a charming little courtyard, full of flowers. A small **museum** contains interesting mementoes of the life and work of the great musician.

Level with the Franziskanerkirche turn right and follow the Hauptstraße to the town hall.

Rathaus – The town hall was built in the mid-17C in the Renaissance style. It features a highly original façade, with three oriel windows, scrolled gables and a round-arched doorway with diamond-cut stonework.

Domkirche – This Late Gothic hall-church from the 15C and 16C is dedicated to St Martin, patron saint of the Burgenland. A charming pulpit and the choir complete with organ remain of the original late Baroque interior decoration. Note the beautiful relief of the Mount of Olives, dating from before 1500.

Take the Pfarrgasse into Esterházystraße and go past the castle.

Old Jewish Quarter – Eisenstadt has evidence of a thriving Jewish community dating back to 1296. When Emperor Leopold I expelled the Jews from Vienna in 1671, many of them sought refuge in Eisenstadt. Thus, in the Unterberg district to the west of the castle, in an area delimited by the Museumsgasse, the Wolfgasse, the Unterberggasse and the Wertheimergasse, a Jewish quarter grew up, which is in a remarkably good state of preservation. The **Österreichisches Jüdisches Museum**, to be found at no 6 Unterberggasse, and the nearby Jewish cemetery are particularly interesting. The Museumsgasse is home to the **Burgenländisches Landesmuseum** ⊙, located in two picturesque old houses which are connected to one another.

Return to Esterházystraße and from there head west to Kalvarienbergplatz.

★ **Kalvarienberg und Bergkirche** – The artificial hill known as Kalvarienberg was constructed in the early 18C to provide the setting for 24 **Stations of the Cross★**, made of 260 wooden and 60 stone figures sculpted in a realistic folk style which portray the story of the Passion with dramatic intensity and Baroque flair.
Inside the Bergkirche, which was completed in 1722, the **Haydn-Mausoleum** marks the great composer's last resting place.

EXCURSION

Raiding - *46km - 29 miles - 2 hours. Leave Eisenstadt, south, on the Bundesstraße 59 A, then onto the 331. After Weppersdorf bear left towards Lackenbach to Raiding.*

Liszts Geburtshaus ⊙ - This small house where Liszt was born in 1811 was the home which went with his father's job as bailiff to the estate of the princes of Esterházy. Photos and documents are on display. The old church organ on which Liszt used to play is also here.

Höhlen EISRIESENWELT*

Salzburg

Michelin map 426 fold 20 - 6km - 4 miles northeast of Werfen
Local map under SALZACHTAL

Opening at a height of 1 664m - 5 459ft on the western cliffs of the Hochkogel (Tennengebirge), about 1 000m - 3 281ft above the Salzach valley, the **caves** of the World of the Ice Giants, with their 42km - 25 miles of galleries, are among the world's largest subterranean features. They are especially famous for the fairy-like ice decor which goes back for about 1km - half a mile and adorns the caves near the entrance.

The ice formations, which in some cases are as much as 20m - 65ft thick and whose total volume has been estimated at 30 000 m³ - more than 1 million cubic feet, have developed as a result of natural ventilation. In summer the air in the deepest cave is swept forward to the mouth and the outside world; in winter the process is reversed and cold air sweeps in so that, in spring, when water from the melting snows penetrates, it freezes immediately.

The journey up the **approach roads**★★ would be worthwhile for the views alone.

Access ⊙ - *Allow 5 hours. Take warm clothing, sturdy shoes and gloves.*
The ascent is made in 4 stages:
1. 5km - 3 miles of unsurfaced mountain road rising at a gradient of 18% which one can travel either in one's own car, or on the **bus** ⊙ (Eisriesenweltlinie) which starts from the Hauptplatz in Werfen.
2. 15min on foot from the bus terminus to the lower station of the cable-car. The path overlooks the Salzach valley and Schloß Hohenwerfen.
3. 4min in the **cable-car** ⊙ to the refuge, where tickets for the caves are sold.
4. 20min walk along a path cut out of the mountainside, which has spectacular views of the valley, the Hagengebirge, the Hochkönig and the Gasteiner Tauern, to the vast and wonderfully sited entrance to the caves.

Tour - *1 hour 15min.*
By the light of acetylene and magnesium lamps one enters the ice area of the caves, climbing up many steps to the Posselt-Halle gallery. The Hymir Halle and the Frigg Veil are both examples of fantastic ice architecture enhanced by clever lighting. The highest point (1 775m - 5 823ft) reached in the tour is at the Ice Gate (Eistor).

From then on, the path follows an amazing stratified wall of ice whose every layer is a different tone of blue or white. The "Cathedral" of Alexander von Mörk is named after the man who explored the caves assiduously and whose ashes were brought back to it. The Ice Palace marks the end of this underworld tour.

ENNS

Oberösterreich - Population 11 100

Michelin map 426 fold 9 - 20km - 12 miles east of Linz - Alt 281m - 922ft

Enns, built on the left bank of the River Enns, near its confluence with the Danube, is the oldest town in Upper Austria. The Romans, in fact, chose this site for a camp; the city, Lauriacum, that developed later was big enough to become the capital of the Roman province of Noricum *(map p 29)*. It was there that St Florian, the patron saint of Upper Austria, suffered martyrdom under Diocletian at the beginning of the 4C.

SIGHTS

Altstadt - The imposing town houses in the old town of Enns are all essentially Gothic in style, and many feature Late Gothic or Renaissance arcaded courtyards (Hauptplatz 5, 7, 10 and 14, Wiener Straße 4, 8 and 9). The **Stadtmuseum Lauriacum** (Hauptplatz 19-Z **M**), formerly the town mint, is located in one of these arcaded houses and contains a number of interesting archaeological exhibits dating from Roman times. There are some very picturesque façades around the Hauptplatz, and at Mauthausnerstraße 5 and Linzer Straße 4 and 20.

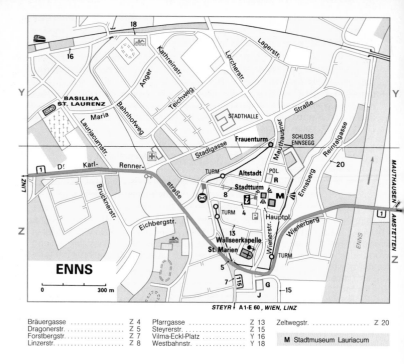

Bräuergasse	Z 4	Pfarrgasse	Z 13	Zeltwegstr.		Z 20
Dragonerstr.	Z 5	Steyrerstr.	Z 15			
Forstbergstr.	Z 7	Vilma-Eckl-Platz	Y 16	**M** Stadtmuseum Lauriacum		
Linzerstr.	Z 8	Westbahnstr.	Y 18			

Stadtturm – In the centre of the Hauptplatz stands the emblem of the town in the form of a 60m - 197ft high tower. Construction of this was begun by the townspeople in 1564, prior to obtaining building permission from the Emperor. This was granted by Maximilian II in 1565 and the tower was finished in 1568. Designed as a bell and watch-tower, it combines Late Gothic and Renaissance styles. The south side of the tower is adorned with the Imperial eagle and the Habsburg coat of arms. 157 steps lead up to the gallery, crowned with an elegantly curved domed roof. From here, there is a marvellous **view**★ of the town.

Stadtbefestigung – The town's fortifications, built 1193-94, have to a large extent survived (ramparts, moats, defensive walls, 6 watch-towers, including the Pfaffenturm, the Bäckerturm and the Frauenturm). To finance the construction of its defence system, Enns was awarded part of the ransom money England had had to pay Austria for the release of Richard the Lionheart from the fortress at Dürnstein.

Frauenturm – On the top floor is the former chapel of the Knights of St John of Jerusalem with frescoes dating from between 1320 and 1360. In the 14C, the Knights of St John here ran one of the many pilgrims' hospices along the European pilgrimage route from Danzig to Santiago de Compostela.
The key to the Frauenturm can be obtained from the tourist office in Linzer Straße.

★ **Basilika St. Laurenz** ⊙ – The basilica, which stands on the site of the ancient Roman town of Lauriacum, was built between 1285 and 1290. After the Gothic vaulting collapsed, an early Baroque cross-ribbed vault was built in 1628. Among the more interesting features of the interior decor are the tabernacle (1480), a Pietà of 1430, a Madonna from the 14C and various Late Gothic reliefs. The chancel and the crypt contain vestiges of the walls from earlier buildings on this site, dug up during archaeological excavations: Gallo-Roman temple (180), first Christian church (bishopric, 370) and early Carolingian church buildings (740).
In front of the basilica stands the octagonal **ossuary** *(Karner)* with a Gothic chapel. On the outside it is adorned with an Ecce Homo group dating from 1690, in which Pilate is depicted in the costume of a Turkish Grand Vizier.

Pfarrkirche St. Marien ⊙ – In the south of the old town stands one of the oldest Mendicant order churches in Austria. It was built by the Minorites in 1276-77, and the chancel was added in the early 14C. This is a good example of the evolution of methods for heightening and lengthening churches prevalent in Gothic religious building. The nave was converted into a double aisled hall-church in the second half of the 15C. The only ornamentation is the beautifully carved keystones. The austere architecture of the Mendicant orders forms a striking contrast to the richly ornate cathedrals built during the Middle Ages. Three Gothic arches lead into the **Wallseerkapelle**.

Wallseerkapelle – The Wallseers came to Austria with the Habsburgs and were for many years the ruling family in Enns. This chapel was added to the church in the 14C. It too is a double aisled hall-church, with a triple-aisled chancel equal in width to the nave. This original architectonic device is only found in one other place in Austria besides here. Slim columns and ribs lend the interior a sense of fragility. A remarkable painting from 1625 depicts the *Lorcher Bishops*, a view of the town with local religious dignitaries. The seated Madonna dates from the 13C, and the chancel from the 15C.

FELBERTAUERNSTRASSE★

Salzburg und Tirol

Michelin map 426 fold 33

The Felbertauern road has made a considerable difference to the lives of residents in the eastern Alps: a high level tunnel 5.2km - 3 miles long goes through the topmost crest of the Hohe Tauern between the Großglockner and Großvenediger. The panoramic road leads through the peaceful Alpine countryside of the Hohe Tauern national park, linking the eastern Tyrol (Lienz) with the northern Tyrol (Innsbruck) and connecting the beautiful wide valleys of the Isel and its tributaries (Defereggental, Virgental and Kalsertal), as well as the Mittersill with the eastern Tyrol and the valley of the Isel with that of the Puster.

Travellers to Austria may take, on one circular tour, the well known Großglockner road *(passable in summer only)* and the Felbertauern which will enable them also to see the Großvenediger snows.

Gruenert/ÖSTERREICH WERBUNG

Tauerntal

FROM LIENZ TO MITTERSILL

76km - 47 miles – about 1 hour 30min driving time, not including sightseeing and other detours

The **Felbertauerntunnel** ⊙ charges a toll.

Lienz – *See LIENZ*.

From Lienz follow the road up the long, wooded valley of the Isel, where the houses and villages are concentrated halfway up the valley slopes.

✳ **Matrei in Osttirol** – *See MATREI IN OSTTIROL. Allow 2 days to visit the village and its surroundings* (**Europa-Panoramaweg**★★, **Virgental**★).

Directly behind Matrei is Schloß Weißenstein, once the outpost of the Salzburg archbishops on the southern slopes of the Tauern.
The road now continues along the wooded slope through the **Tauerntal**★★. In the foreground the Unterer Steiner waterfall marks the mouth of the Proßegg gorge, through which the road soon passes to come to an open valley overlooked by the hanging glacier of the Kristallkopf.

Take a small mountain road to the left of the road leading the Felbertauerntunnel (toll), and follow it along the valley floor to the Matreier Tauernhaus (altitude 1 512m - 4 961ft), a mountain hotel.

★★ **Excursions in the Großvenediger massif** – *See MATREI IN OSTTIROL. Allow at least 2 hours Rtn for a brief visit, or (better) a whole day to include some sightseeing on foot.*

Drive back to the main road and go through the tunnel.

On the north face of the Tauern the road emerges from the tunnel into the upper Amertal, a rugged, more or less deserted, high altitude valley.

9km – 6 miles after the exit of the tunnel turn left towards Hintersee. After 500m park the car to the right of the road, to visit the Schößwend gorge.

★ **Schößwendklamm** – *15min on foot Rtn.*

From the other side of the road a path leads down to the Felberbach and across the river. It then leads along the river bank giving a good **view**★ of the interesting sculpture-like forms that the crystal-clear water has carved out of the rock face.

Drive on for 3km – 2 miles to the end of the road.

★ **Hintersee** – This mountain lake surrounded by spruce forest lies in the upper Felber valley, at the foot of a magnificent high mountain range, from which a number of waterfalls cascade down from a great height. To the south lies the Tauernkogel massif (altitude 2 989m - 9 806ft). Several information panels explain the geology of the area. It is possible to walk round the lake.

Turn back to Bundesstraße 108.

This stretch of road leads through Alpine meadows to **Mittersill**, a holiday resort and important road junction in the upper Salzach valley (Oberpinzgau), from where roads lead off to the Thurn *(north)* and Gerloß *(west)* passes.

FELDKIRCH★

Vorarlberg – Population 23 880
Michelin maps 426 fold 28 – Local map under BREGENZERWALD
Alt 459m - 1 506ft.

Feldkirch is the gateway to Austria for travellers coming from the west. Situated on the route through the Arlberg, about halfway between Paris and Vienna, the little fortified town nestles at the foot of Schattenburg castle, at the mouth of the last ravine of the III, but is cut off from the plain of the Rhine by the Ardetzenberg ridge.
It has preserved the symmetry of its medieval plan and the old-world charm of arcaded squares.

The "Intellectual" Town – Feldkirch's numerous educational establishments earned it the name the "intellectual" town, or "Studierstädtle". Since the Middle Ages Feldkirch has had a "Latin school"; the academic tradition is maintained by the present grammar school, for pupils who aim at higher education, and a school for teachers.
Moreover, as the constitution of the Vorarlberg did not systematically centralize all provincial administration at Bregenz, Feldkirch was able officially to remain a capital of lawyers' clerks and finance.

★OLD TOWN *time: 30min*

The triangular plan of the town dates from the 13C. It is sited in a basin and at the hub of a network of roads. Between the new town (Neustadt), to the northeast, which has become, with its hotels, the centre of tourist life, and

the suburb (Vorstadt) round the Churertor gateway in the northwest, the Marktplatz district remains the nucleus of the town. The Hirschgraben (Stags' Ditch) constitutes the most recognizable traces of the old town walls.

The late 15C **Katzenturm** (Cats' Tower) (**A**) owes its name to its defence cannon decorated with lions' heads which became known as "the cats". It is also

Marktplatz, Feldkirch

called the Fat Tower (Dicker Turm). Beside it is a small square, surrounded by picturesque houses with steep pitched roofs.

The **Churertor** (**B**) is distinguished by its stepped gable.

Marktplatz – This long, rectangular space, bordered by arcades on its long sides, has retained the charm and tranquillity of a bygone age. Here and there an inn with a painted façade, a corner tower with a bulbous dome, or a Gothic oriel window catches the eye.

To the south the view is bounded by the plain belfry and façade of the Johanniskirche. This is the former church of the monastery of the Hospitallers of St John of Jerusalem, to whom was entrusted the guarding of the way through the Arlberg.

ADDITIONAL SIGHTS

Domkirche St. Nikolaus ⊙ – The "cathedral-church" has the double nave, dear to Austrian architects of the 15C, and the fan vaulting characteristic of late Gothic religious architecture.

Over the right side altar is a **Descent from the Cross**★ painted in 1521 by Wolf Huber, an artist of the Danube school who was born at Feldkirch and who is regarded as one of the great precursors of German landscape painting.

The pulpit is surmounted by a high canopy in wrought iron.

Schattenburg – *The castle is approached by car up the Burggasse, a steep slope, or on foot by the Schloßsteig steps.*

FELDKIRCH

Bahnhofstraße	2
Burggasse	4
Domplatz	5
Fidelisstraße	7
Herrengasse	8
Johannitergasse	10
Kreuzgasse	12
Leonards-Platz	13
Montfortgasse	15
Neustadt	16
Schillerstraße	17
Schloßgraben	19
Schloßsteig	20
Schmiedgasse	22
Vorstadt	23
Wichnergasse	26
Widnau	28
Zeughausgasse	30

A Katzenturm
B Churertor

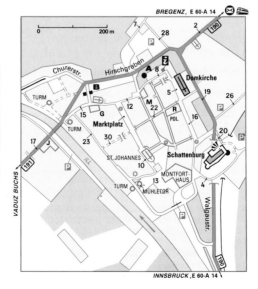

In spite of the refitting of the interior as a museum and a restaurant, this castle has, on the whole, kept its former arrangement and the defensive nature of its keep, planted on the top of a rock. The original dwelling or "Palas" is also a tower – recognizable by its tall, conical roof – with walls more than 4m - 12ft thick. The advanced defences, guarding the present approach bridge, and the ruined round tower nearby, were built about 1500, when gunpowder was already in use.

Before crossing the bridge there is a **view** of the Rhine Valley in the distance, overlooked by the Hoher Kasten (Alpstein massif, in the Appenzell district). The inner courtyard of the castle (café) is picturesque, with tiers of wooden galleries and vast roofs.

Heimatmuseum ⊙ – This local museum houses well displayed collections of religious art (especially in the former chapel), noble and bourgeois furnishings of the Gothic period, traditional peasant furniture, arms and armour, and coins and records of Old Feldkirch. It is pleasant, during the tour, to look at the changing views of Feldkirch through the windows.

EXCURSION

Rankweil – *19km - 12 miles – about 45min. Leave Feldkirch in the direction of Bregenz.*
In the suburb of Feldkirch-Altenstadt take the right fork towards Rankweil. Go up to the church *(access and description see RANKWEIL)*.
On the way back leave Rankweil on the Satteins road which climbs a low mountain range. After a winding and hilly run through small wooded valleys, the **view** opens out over the Bludenz basin and the Rätikon mountain range.
Bear right at the entrance to the village of Satteins in order to join road no 1 which returns to Feldkirch.

FERNPASSSTRASSE*

Tirol

Michelin map 426 folds 16 and 30.

The road to the Fernpaß is varied and picturesque; it is the most hilly section of the earlier route across the Alps from Augsburg to Venice, which was known in the 15C for its strategic and commercial importance, but which is nowadays principally a tourist link between the great resorts of the Bavarian Alps and Innsbruck.

This road is of vital importance to the Tyrol, since it opens the way to the upper valleys of the Lech and the Loisach, which are cut off from the Inn valley by the barrier formed by the Lechtal Alps and the Miemingergebirge. To reach these outer areas, grouped under the name **Außerfern** (the district "beyond the Fern"), follow the road from Telfs, across the plateau of Mieming, down the south slope of the Fernpaß proper, and the magnificent stretch of road from the pass to Lermoos, within view of the Wetterstein range with the Zugspitze, and finally the Zwischentoren corridor whose most dramatic feature is the Ehrenberg defile.

FROM TELFS TO FÜSSEN (IN GERMANY)
96km - 60 miles – allow half a day

From Telfs to the threshold of Holzleiten the road runs across the gentle, fairly densely inhabited slopes of the Mieming plateau, from which the well defined crests of the Miemingergebirge rise up (Hochplattig: 2 758m - 9 048ft – Griesspitzen, 2 759m - 9 052ft). Near Wildermieming views open out of the Inn valley and, in the distance upstream, the snowy heights of the Samnaungruppe. Between Barwies and Obsteig drive slowly so as not to miss the vista of the Inn valley, along a wooded ravine overlooked by the old tower of the fortified castle of Klamm and the dainty pilgrimage chapel at Locherboden.

★ **Holzleitner Sattel** – A **landscape★** of larch woods and meadows dotted with hay barns, with glimpses of the Miemingergebirge to the east and Heiterwand to the west, lends idyllic charm to this mountain col (alt 1 126m - 3 694ft).

Fernstein – On this easily defensible site is a fortified bridgehead. Below the hamlet is the **Fernsteinsee★**, a lake of green water surrounding a wooded island. On the south slope between Fernstein and Biberwier the Fernpaß road follows a tortuous path through the desolate landscapes of the Loreakopf mountain range. On the north slope the bold crests of the Miemingergebirge (Sonnenspitze) and the more massive bastion of the Wetterstein range (Zugspitze) tower beyond a dense cloak of forest.

Fernpaß – Alt 1 209m - 3 967ft. The most open **view**★ of the Sonnenspitze and the Wetterstein can be enjoyed about 1km – half a mile from the pass, on the north slope *(car park)*.
The road curves round high above the dark waters of the Blindsee, in which the surrounding pine trees are reflected. *(The best views of the lake are heading from Biberwier to the Fernpaß.)* The Weißensee, which is more accessible, is less romantic.

★ **Ehrwald** – *See EHRWALD.*

The road from Biberwier to Lermoos, skirting the Lermoos-Ehrwald basin, has wide **views**★★ of the Wetterstein and the Miemingergebirge *(details under LERMOOS).*

★ **Lermoos** – *See LERMOOS.*

To pass from the Loisach basin to that of the Lech, follow the valley named Zwischentoren ("between gates") in memory of the fortifications which once barred the road to the Fernstein and the Ehrenberg cleft. The crossing of the watershed near Lähn passes virtually unnoticed, and then the narrow bottleneck of the fortified Ehrenberg cleft is all that has to be negotiated before the road emerges into the Reutte basin.

Ehrenberger Klause – The old road on the floor of this ravine was barred by a gate, now dilapidated but formerly part of the fortifications of the Ehrenberg fortress, which from the 16C to the 18C was the key to the Tyrol against invading Bavarians, Swedes or Frenchmen. The ruins, cleared of vegetation, are visible on the wooded hillside *(left)*.
As Ehrenburg was also the seat of the administrative and judicial authorities, its name was used until 1850 to identify the present Außerfern district.

Bear right on leaving the Ehrenberg cleft.

★ **Plansee** – Initially the road runs vertiginously above a wooded ravine, at the bottom of which a small streams flows, issuing from the lake. (Pleasant views of Tannheimer Gruppe.) It then forms a lakeside quay *(6km - 4 miles)* as it runs along the uniformly wooded shore where a few hotels and campsites attract those to whom a wild setting appeals.
Looking southwest through the small strait which separates the Plansee from the Heiterwanger See one can see as far as the Thaneller mountain.

The road then continues towards Ammerwald (frontier post), Linderhof and Oberammergau.

Reutte – Reutte is the administrative and economic capital of the Außerfern. In the Untermarkt and the Obermarkt the houses are decorated with murals, balconies and window grilles. Some of the houses, notably the little building with the hooded oriel window, were painted by Johann Jakob Zeiler (1708-83), the most talented of a local dynasty of artists specialising in church decoration. Owing to its high altitude (854m - 2 802ft), Reutte is a good starting point for walkers in summer and ski enthusiasts in winter.

The road to Füssen follows the Lech valley between the Tannheimer Gruppe summits and the steep slopes of the Säuling.

★ **Füssen** – *See Michelin Green Guide Germany.*

Burg FORCHTENSTEIN

Burgenland

Michelin map 426 fold 25 – 23km - 14 miles southeast of Wiener Neustadt

The **fortress** ⓥ of Forchtenstein rears its walls and towers in wild, romantic scenery, on a bluff in the Rosaliengebirge from which there are wide-ranging views of the Hungarian Plain.
The fortress was built in the 14C by the Counts of Mattersdorf and enlarged by the Esterházy family about 1635. It contributed to the defence of Austria at the time of the Turkish invasions of 1529 and 1683, and the large collection of arms and armour which comprised the garrison's armoury, together with Turkish booty, make up the major part of the **Fürstlich Esterházysche Sammlungen**★, former royal art collections on display in the fortress.

The Michelin Motoring Atlas to Europe
*provides the motorist in Europe
with the best possible information
for route-planning and choosing where to go :
scale 1 : 1 000 000 (western Europe) and 1 : 3 000 000 (eastern Europe) ;
spiralbound and hardback versions available*

FREISTADT★

Oberösterreich – Population 6 290

Michelin map 426 fold 9 – Local map under LINZ

Alt 560m - 1 837ft

Freistadt, a former stronghold on the ancient salt route which led from the Alpine countries towards Bohemia, stands in the wild countryside of the Mühlviertel, a granite plateau covered with pasture and forest with wide horizons spreading towards the Danube and the frontier of the Czech Republic. The extensive, largely intact **town fortifications★**, including a stretch of double town wall, towers and gateways, were built in two stages, in around 1300 and 1400. They add a great deal to the charm of the town. With its main square, narrow streets and picturesque houses, Freistadt is an enchanting place to visit.

SIGHTS

★ **Hauptplatz** – This main square is rectangular and well proportioned. To the southwest stands the tower of the parish church, surmounted by a bulbous dome and a small lantern, while opposite rises the castle tower. The houses lining the Hauptplatz are for the most part fronted by porches or arcades; their façades, adorned with delicate stucco and painted in pastel shades, add a lively note to the scene. To the west, almost facing the carved fountain dedicated to the Virgin Mary, stands the **Rathaus** (R) and an old house fronted by a porch and flanked by a tower surmounted by a curious bulbous dome.

Cross the Hauptplatz and make for the castle

FREISTADT

Altenhofgasse 2
Böhmergasse 3
Heiligengeist-
gasse 4
Huterergasse 5
Pragerstrae 6
Samtgasse 9

(Schloß). On three sides the **courtyard** is overlooked by an amusing balcony with a lean-to roof. The **Schloßgasse**, a quaint and picturesque alley with flower-decked balconies and passages, ends in the Böhmergasse which leads to the Böhmertor, a former fortified gateway. Back in the old town the Waaggasse and the Salzgasse contain houses with oriel windows (*Erker*).

After glancing at the **Dechanthof** (Deanery), built in the early 18C, make for the parish church (right) before coming back to the Hauptplatz.

Stadtpfarrkirche – The first thing that strikes the eye is the elegant tower on the north side of the body of the church, a characteristic feature on the town's skyline, which was transformed into the Baroque style by Johann Michael Prunner in 1735. The four wrought-iron balconies of the tower room are particularly noticeable. The church itself is Gothic and dates back to the 13C. The triple aisled chancel, however, was not built until 1483, and is crowned with a network of ribbed vaulting. The **organ case**, adorned with statues, was built by Leonhard Freund from Passau between 1701 and 1705.

EXCURSION

Kefermarkt – *11km - 7 miles – Local map under LINZ: Excursions. Leave Freistadt southwards by the "Promenade" and take the road to Kefermarkt which follows the left bank of the Feldaist.*

The road runs through woods before reaching Kefermarkt (*see KEFERMARKT*).

FRIESACH ★

Kärnten – Population 7 070
Michelin map 426 fold 36 – Alt 637m - 2 090ft

The oldest town in Carinthia is particularly appealing with its three ruined castles, six old churches and well-preserved fortifications. The concentration of military constructions, churches and monasteries can be explained by the strategic importance of the town, which belonged to the archbishopric of Salzburg from 960 to 1803. It guarded the pass between the Mur valley and Klagenfurt and was thus a key point along the trade route between Vienna and Venice. It is not hard to imagine the eventful history of such an exposed bastion, which was besieged and set alight on numerous occasions. Despite all such drawbacks, Friesach nonetheless exerted a powerful cultural influence over the centuries.

Stadtbefestigung – The fortifications, which include the only water-filled town moat in the German-speaking world, surround the town centre with an 820m - half a mile long battlemented wall. This is executed in fine undressed masonry and stands 11m - 36ft high and about 1.5m - 5ft wide. Of the original eleven defence towers, three remain.

★ **Stadtbrunnen** – This fountain, the work of Italian sculptors in 1563, stands on the Hauptplatz, surrounded by beautiful old houses. It was originally placed in the courtyard of Keutschach's Schloß Tanzenberg, but was brought to Friesach in 1802. The octagonal fountain basin is adorned with a frieze on which scenes from Ancient Greek mythology are depicted. The bowls above are supported by atlantes and putti. The crowning glory of the fountain, a small **bronze group** dating from 1520, is of some artistic interest as it is thought to be the creation of either Peter Vischer the Younger of Nuremberg or his brother Hans.

Dominikanerklosterkirche St. Nikolaus von Myra – Friesach monastery, dating from 1217, was the first foundation of the Dominican Order in a German-speaking country. The church, the largest in Carinthia, is a triple-aisled basilica supported by pillars, characterised by an overriding simplicity of style entirely in keeping with the rules of the Mendicant Order. The church contains an interesting life-size statue of the Virgin Mary in sandstone, a fine early 14C work. The larger than life-size Crucifix on a pillar on the north side of the nave dates from 1300. The Late Gothic altar dedicated to St John made in 1510 is probably the work of a local sculptor.

Deutschordenskirche St. Blasius – The Knights of the Teutonic Order settled in Friesach from 1213 and built this church on the site of an earlier 12C building, from which the frescoes (late 12C) in the west transept come. The church owes its collection of remarkably varied and high quality Gothic wood carving to the Order's Commander Graf von Pettenegg, a keen collector of such work. Note among others the magnificent **high altar** from 1515, a work from St. Veit for the Heiligengestadekirche on Ossiach lake, and the Late Gothic Frankfurt altarpiece. The nave contains funerary plaques of members of the Order, most of whom came from Bad Mergentheim in Germany, where the Order had its headquarters until 1809.

Petersberg – *30min on foot Rtn from the Hauptplatz.*
Construction of the fortress which stands proudly on a hilltop to the west of the old town was begun in 1077 under Archbishop Gebhard. However, all that remains of the once grand, sumptuously fitted palace is one or two windows. The imposing, 30m - 98ft high, Romanesque keep now houses the **Stadt-museum** ⊙, in which the history of Friesach and the surrounding area is related. On the second floor is the old castle chapel which has preserved some of its original Romanesque painted decoration.
The old inner bailey hosts open-air theatre productions during the summer.

FROHNLEITEN

Steiermark – Population 5 060
Michelin map 426 fold 23 – Alt 438m - 1 437ft

Halfway between Bruck an der Mur and Graz, Frohnleiten is a pretty place in the heart of the Mur valley. The old town, centred on the elongated market square, contrasts with a ring of modern suburbs.
The most attractive **view**★ over the old town is from the riverside, near the bridge over the Mur, the pleasantly wooded setting acting as a foil to Frohnleiten's characteristic red-brown roofscape. A network of well-signposted paths leads the visitor through the fields, parks and woods of the peaceful surrounding countryside, while at nearby Murhof there is an 18-hole golf course to be enjoyed by casual as well as serious players.
Frohnleiten is also a good place for shopping, set in a region noted for its good food.

Hauptplatz – With its column devoted to the Virgin Mary, its fine trees and tall brightly-painted houses, the main square gives little hint of the town's troubled past. It was much abused by passing soldiery and suffered serious fires in 1528 and 1559 as well as floods in 1537, 1569 and 1572; a thunderbolt in 1763 ignited a blaze which left hardly a single house intact.

St. Georgskirche ⊙ – This interesting church is in the hamlet of **Adriach** *(1.5km - 1 mile west)*. The original unvaulted Romanesque building dates from 1050; between 1280 and 1290 it acquired a Gothic chancel, a chapel dedicated to St Joseph and a sacristy. The chapel of St Anne dates from 1500, and that of St Aloysius from 1750. The **interior** is mostly Baroque, with a pulpit of 1720, an altarpiece, a "Martyrdom of St George" and four ceiling frescoes in the nave by **Joseph Adam von Mölck** (1774).

The church's organ was built in 1590 by either Thomas Krueg or Johannes Khever Spichler, both organ-builders from the Tyrol.

GAILBERGSATTELSTRASSE
Kärnten
Michelin map 426 folds 33 and 34 – Between Oberdrauburg and Kötschach

This road links the upper valleys of the Drava (Drau) and the Gail, crossing the pass at 982m - 3 222ft.

FROM OBERDRAUBURG TO THE LESACH VALLEY
67km - 42 miles – allow half a day

The most attractive part of the route is the stretch of road which climbs the north slope in a series of hairpin bends through the larches.

Laas – The **Filialkirche St. Andreas** is a Late Gothic church (1510-18), with doorways and window frames in local red sandstone. The **vaulting★★** is particularly beautiful, with a complex and delicate network of groined ribs above the nave continuing into a pretty stellar ribbed vault above the chancel. The inventive creator of this masterpiece was Bartlmä Firtaler.

Kötschach – The small market community of **Kötschach-Mauthen**, set between the Gailtaler and Karnische Alps, is a popular medium altitude (710m - 2 329ft), mountain air health resort.

The **Pfarrkirche Unsere Liebe Frau** was converted by Bartlmä Firtaler in 1518-1527 and embodies the final, exuberantly decorative stage of the Gothic style. It has stunning **groined rib vaulting★★**, with finely executed arabesques swirling gracefully above the body of the church and ending in lilies, roses, acorns and bunches of grapes.

Beyond Kötschach, the partially modernised road should be tackled only by drivers confident of being able to negotiate 72 ravines, with steep gradients of up to 18%.

Lesachtal – The minor road up the Lesachtal, the upper valley of the Gail, joins the Puster valley via the Kartitsch-Sattel pass (alt 1 526m - 5 006ft).

Trumler/ÖSTERREICH WERBUNG

Church vaulting, Kötschach

*When driving in **Vienna**, **Innsbruck** or **Salzburg** use the detailed city maps in the Michelin Red Guide Europe which are updated each year to show*
– through-routes and by-passes
– new roads and one-way systems
– car parks

GASTEINER TAL✳✳

The Gasteiner Tal, a long, wide river valley, is one of the most attractive holiday destinations in Austria. It encompasses three main resorts (Dorfgastein at an altitude of 830m - 2 723ft, Bad Hofgastein at 860m - 2 822ft and Badgastein at 1 000m - 3 281ft), having developed into a leading thermal cure centre as early as the 15C. With its exceptional setting amidst medium and high altitude mountain peaks, it has much to offer both skiers in winter and ramblers in summer.

Thermal cures – The therapeutic effects of the thermal waters of Gastein appear to have been common knowledge for centuries; archaeologists have confirmed that the valley was inhabited by Stone Age, Celtic and Roman settlers. The growth in popularity of Badgastein as a spa resort really put on a spurt at the end of the Middle Ages, as people began to travel there from miles away to cure their rheumatic complaints.

After a temporary decline in the 17C and 18C, Badgastein renewed its development in the 19C, finally becoming the most highly sought out spa resort of the age, appreciated by politicians (including German Emperor Wilhelm I, Austrian Emperor Franz Joseph I and Bismarck), artists and writers alike (Franz Schubert, Arthur Schopenhauer).

By the beginning of the 20C, Badgastein had evolved from a somewhat lacklustre Imperial spa town into a thoroughly modern thermal resort, and it has since become the home of a balneological research institute attached to the Austrian Academy of Science, which undertakes scientific analysis of the healing powers of the Gastein springs.

The thermal springs, 17 of them in all, rise on the slopes of the Graukogel massif, and their daily output is 5 million litres (over one million UK gallons) of water at temperatures of up to 47°C – 117°F. Visitors can "take the waters" at numerous hotels and guest houses with their own thermal baths, supplied directly from the springs. The therapeutic effects of the Badgastein springs are due more to the radon, a radioactive noble gas, they contain, rather than the minerals, of which they contain very few. Depending on the particular treatment, the radon is taken into the body through bathing or inhalation. Since it is not absorbed by the body's tissue, it is soon expelled (in less than 30 minutes after bathing, or about 3 hours after inhalation). During the brief period it is in the body, radon gives off helium nuclei which give energy to the body and regenerate damaged cells. In this way it helps to soothe chronic complaints such as rheumatism, diseases of the respiratory tract (asthma), veins and circulatory system (coronary thrombosis, phlebitis), skin allergies, hormonal imbalances and problems with the autonomic nervous system. A further thermal treatment or medical cure available at Badgastein takes the form of steam baths in radioactive tunnels, in which the temperature is 37.5-41.5°C – 99.5-106.7°F. The patients are driven in on a small purpose-built railway and remain lying down to inhale the radon gas. The mild mountain climate in the sheltered valley in which Badgastein lies contributes greatly to the success of such treatments.

The hotels and guest houses of Bad Hofgastein offer the same cure facilities as Badgastein, since being connected to the Gastein springs in 1828.

✳✳ **Ski slopes** – The development of the Gasteiner Tal as a winter sports resort began in earnest after the World Ski Championships of 1958, in which the Austrian Toni Sailer won several events. The Alpine ski slopes, which have become second only to the Arlberg among Austria's most extensive and scenic skiing destinations, are spread over five different mountain sides, which can be reached by chairlifts in two stages: Fulseck (880-2 030m – 2 887-6 660ft) above Dorfgastein; Schloßalm (860-2 300m – 2 822-7 546ft) above Bad Hofgastein ; Stubnerkogel (1 100-2 250m – 3 609-7 382ft) and Graukogel (1 100-2 000m – 3 609-6 562ft) above Badgastein; and Kreuzkogel (1 588 - 2 690m – 5 210-8 825ft) above Sportgastein.

The Gastein-Super-Skischein pass gives access to 53 ski lifts (including half a dozen assorted cable-cars) and 170km – 106 miles of ski slopes for mainly intermediate abilities. The use of some form of transport, be it car or bus, to get from one place to another is unavoidable as, with the exception of Badgastein and Bad Hofgastein, there is no way of getting from one set of slopes to the other by ski and the possibilities of accommodation are widely dispersed.

From Christmas to April the upper slopes generally remain snow-covered, and snow conditions throughout the Sportgastein ski area are excellent. The relatively low altitude means that it is not always possible to ski right down into the valley (but skiers can take the cable-car down instead).

Cross-country skiers have 90km – 56 miles of track at their disposal, covering the whole valley from Dorfgastein as far as Sportgastein.

See below for further details on the various resorts.

FROM LEND TO THE TAUERNTUNNEL

41km – 26 miles including detour to Sportgastein – allow 45min driving time and at least 3 hours for brief sightseeing in Bad Hofgastein and Badgastein. In the summer, we recommend climbing to the Stubnerkogel peak, and in the winter the Kreuzkogel is not to be missed. In order fully to appreciate the magnificent scenery of the Gasteiner Tal, we recommend a stay of several days or more.

After leaving the industrial town of Lend and the Salzach valley, the road makes its way over the Klamm pass. The old road *(to the left, with 15% gradients)*, which runs along the floor of the gorge, can be avoided by taking the tunnel. At the exit to the tunnel stands the Klammstein tower.

Beyond the tunnel, the Gasteiner Tal soon widens out and takes on a less forbidding appearance with green meadows as far as the eye can see and moderately steep slopes.

✳ **Dorfgastein** – Alt 830m - 2 723ft. This pretty village located on the valley floor does not have to try too hard to convince visitors of the merits of its idyllic setting at the foot of Alpine meadows exposed to the sun, surrounded by beautiful forests. In the summer it offers plenty of fresh air and fun for all the family. In the winter, it has extensive ski slopes nearby, with a connection to the Großarl ski slopes, overlooked by the Fulseck summit (55km – 34 miles of slopes). The drop in altitude is over 1 100m – 3 609ft on both slopes, and there are good opportunities for off-piste skiing.

♨♨ **Bad Hofgastein** – Alt 860m - 2 822ft. Bad Hofgastein lies in the broadest, sunniest stretch of the valley. This smart and lively health resort has numerous hotels which offer the same spa facilities as Badgastein. Furthermore, the resort boasts modern, beautifully laid out spa gardens and a swimming pool of almost 1 000m - 10 764ft, supplied by the thermal springs.

In winter Bad Hofgastein is an excellent point of departure for exploring the network of cross-country ski tracks in the valley. For those of medium ability, there are tracks along the banks of the Gasteiner Ache towards Badgastein. More proficient cross-country skiers should try the 7km – 4 miles of track in the Anger valley. Downhill skiers of intermediate ability can choose from any number of not too steep slopes in the Schloßalm massif. A particularly good ski slope runs from the **Hohe Scharte** (peak is 2 300m - 7 546ft) dropping 1 450m - 4 757ft to the valley floor, giving marvellous **views**★★ of the Türchlwand, the Hochkönig and the Dachstein peaks. A further point in favour of the ski slopes at Bad Hofgastein is the fact that they are connected with those at Badgastein (Stubnerkogel) via the Anger valley.

Pfarrkirche – The parish church, rebuilt in several stages in the 15C and 16C, is a testimony to Bad Hofgastein's wealthy past, in the days when it was regional capital and this was the mother church of the valley. The imposing, Late Gothic body of the church is roofed with stellar and ribbed vaulting. The outside of the church walls and the niches either side of the main doorway are adorned with interesting funerary plaques of wealthy local gold- and silver-mine owners, recalling the town's heyday in the 16C and 17C.

★ **Schloßalm** ⊘ – Alt 2 050m - 6 726ft. This is reached by taking the cable-car and then the chairlift. At the top, there is a good **panorama★** of the ski slopes, beneath the Maukarspitze and Türchlwand peaks. Further south, the summits of the Stubnerkogel, Ankogel range, Graukogel and Gamskarkogel can be seen. From the second terrace of the restaurant, the view stretches as far as the Dachstein.

+++ **Badgastein** – Alt 1 013m - 3 323ft. Badgastein must rank as one of the most glitteringly beautiful spas and winter sports resorts in Austria. It is located amidst spectacular mountain **scenery★**, flanked by the Stubnerkogel to the west and the Graukogel to the east. Its large palace hotels and elegant boutiques are arranged in a horseshoe layout on the slopes of the wooded mouth of a valley. The Gasteiner Ache tumbles down over a rock face, making a waterfall in the centre of the town.

Badgastein has a wide variety of excellent modern leisure facilites: skating rink, thermal swimming baths (one of which is cut into the actual rock face), fitness centres, 9-hole golf course, tennis courts and a casino. With a resident population of 5 600, Badgastein is buzzing wih life all year round.

The local ski slopes include some fine runs down the upper section of the Stuberkogel, especially on the slopes of the Anger valley (Jungeralm, Fleichleiter). At the other end of town, the Graukogel will appeal to lovers of steep slopes.

★ **Unterer Wasserfall der Gasteiner Ache** – After gushing over the edge of a cliff, the river spreads out like a fan and tumbles noisily to the valley floor.

Go down the street past the neo-Gothic Roman Catholic church on the right and turn right into the Kaiser-Wilhelm-Promenade.

★ **Kaiser-Wilhelm-Promenade** – This promenade along the east bank of the Gasteiner Ache gives lovely **views★** of Bad Hofgastein and its surroundings lower down the valley. The slender spire of the shingled Nikolauskirche can be seen in the foreground. It is possible to extend the walk as far as the Gruner Baum hotel (swimming pool, tennis courts, mini-golf), which is about 45min from the point of departure. If pressed for time, turn left off the promenade after the Germania hotel and take the path downhill to the Nikolauskirche.

Nikolauskirche – This plain 15C church, in which religious offices are no longer held, is charming to look at. The Late Gothic stellar vaulting in the nave is supported on a central pillar. Among the vestiges of 15C and 16C frescoes on the walls is a series of scenes from the Last Judgment.

★★ **Stubnerkogel** ⊘ – Alt 2 246m - 7 369ft. *Allow 1 hour Rtn. Ascent is in a chairlift in two stages. Leave the upper station to the left and climb onto a small rise.* The **panorama★★** stretches far to the east to the Graukogel and the Ankogel glacier massif, to the south and the Kreuzkogel, to the west and the Anger valley with the glaciers of the Hohe Tauern (Großglockner, Hocharn) in the background, and to the north and the lower reaches of the Gasteiner Tal with the Hochkönig rock massif forming a natural barrier.

Turn back to the upper chairlift station and follow the ridge path as far as it goes.

Böckstein – The tiny parish church built on a hill in 1765 has a polygonal exterior and an elongated oval interior floor plan. The refined, discreet interior decor is an excellent example of the early Classical style in the Salzburg province.

★★ **Excursion to Sportgastein** – *Toll road, which is however free of charge to holders of a ski pass.*

It is not long before the peaceful, wooded mid-altitude mountain setting gives way to a much harsher, more rugged landscape. The road cuts a way between breathtaking steep rocky cliffs, going through three tunnels and passing numerous avalanche barriers. After 6km - 4 miles the road reaches Sportgastein (alt 1 588m - 5 210ft), a broad plateau set against a majestic **backdrop★** of rocky peaks and glaciers. This airy outpost of Badgastein has as yet not been the object of any major construction projects. The resort consists essentially of a large car park and a guest house.

The altitude guarantees excellent snow cover, much to the delight of cross-country (7km - 4 miles of tracks) and downhill skiers alike. A modern cable-car leads up to the Kreuzkogel summit, the highest point of the ski slopes, from where there are some exhilarating runs downhill, dropping more than 1 100m - 3 609ft, and a highly reputed off-piste run down to the toll point *(details available from the ski slope maintenance team)*.

★★★ Kreuzkogel – *Ascent by cable-car in two stages.*

Even from the level of the mountain station the **view★★** is already impressive. However, it is well worth taking the 15min walk up to the summit, marked by a cross, from where there is a marvellous **panorama★★★**. Proper mountain boots should be worn, as the snow can be quite deep in places.

To the north, Badgastein can be seen lying deep in the valley, and to the right of it are the chalk massifs of the Tennen range and the Dachstein peak. Two other prominent peaks are those of the Ankogel and the Hochalmspitze. To the south towers a formidable range of peaks on the border of Carinthia. To the west, a prolongation of the cable-car reveals the Hohe Tauern (Schareck, Großglockner and Hocharn) to view.

Travel back down to Böckstein. It is possible to carry on into Carinthia through the Tauerntunnel.

EXPLORING ON FOOT

With its varied terrain suited to walkers of all sorts of abilities, the Gasteiner Tal is one of the **best places in the whole of Austria for a ramble**. There are numerous footpaths throughout the valley, which take walkers through beautiful countryside far from any traffic.

Particularly pretty walks are possible along the **Kaiserin-Elisabeth-Promenade**, from Badgastein to Böckstein, and the **Gasteiner Hohenweg**, which runs down the mountain slope from Badgastein to Bad Hofgastein.

There are many more possibilities open to walkers in the Stubnerkogel, Graukogel, Gamskarkogel and Silberpfennig ranges, from where there are some magnificent panoramas of the surrounding mountain scenery.

It is recommended that walkers obtain a detailed map at a scale of 1: 50 000, in order to plan their route.

★★★ Zitterauer Tisch und Bockhartsee – *Allow a whole day, including a 4 hour 30min walk. Enquire at the tourist office about bus timetables between Sportgastein and Badgastein, so that travelling back to the point of departure during the afternoon will not be a problem.*

Take the cable-car up to the top of the Stubnerkogel. Turn right at the mountain station and follow the way-marked route (red and white flashes and red arrows). In just under an hour the mountain path reaches the Zitterauer Tisch (2 461m - 8 074ft). There is a marvellous **view★★★** of the whole Gasteiner Tal, especially the upper reaches of the valley. To the northeast, the view stretches as far as the Dachstein.

The path drops quickly down to Alpine pastures, before weaving a tortuous route through a bleak and craggy rocky landscape. Another good hour's walk brings you to the Miesbichlscharte (alt 2 238m - 7 343ft).

On the way down to the Unterer Bockhartsee there is a good view from a number of points of the glaciers and waterfalls of the Schareck massif as well as of the Hocharn (to the right) and the Ankogel (to the left). From the shores of the lake climb up to the hut and then down to Sportgastein. Take the bus back to Badgastein.

Palfnersee

★★ Graukogel ⊙ – *2 hours 30min on foot Rtn. Difference in altitude of about 500m - 1 640ft. This walk is recommended for good walkers wearing sturdy shoes with non-slip soles.*

Take two chairlifts one after the other up to Tonis Almgasthof (alt 1 982m - 6 503ft). A path leads from behind the guesthouse up to the Hüttenkogel summit (alt 2 231m - 7 320ft). This is marked by a cross and a viewing table. There is an incredible **panorama★★** of the Hohe Tauern (Großglockner, Hocharn, Hoher Sonnblick, Schareck) to the west, and the spectacular Reedsee, a lake surrounded by firs and larches lying at the foot of the Tischlerkarkogel and the Hölltorkogel, to the east.

Next follow the path along the ridge (extra care is needed in some of the steeper places) to the **Graukogel**. From the peak there is an even broader **view★★** as far as the Dachstein. The Palfnersee can be seen glistening immediately below.

★ Walk to the Palfnersee – *1 hour 45min on foot Rtn.*

This is an untaxing walk through some beautiful countryside. Take the chairlifts, one after the other, up to the Graukogel. From the mountain station, follow the path past the hut and continue straight on. The mountain footpath gives a good **view★** of Schareck, Hoher Sonnblick and Hocharn. It leaves the cover of the forest before climbing up to the Palfnersee (alt 2 100m – 6 890ft).

It is possible to carry on from here as far as the **Palfner pass★** (alt 2 321m - 7 615ft), from where there is a good all-round view *(allow an extra hour Rtn for this)*.

The Michelin Green Guide Italy
aims to make touring more enjoyable
by suggesting several touring programmes
which are easily adapted to personal taste

GERAS

Niederösterreich – Population 1 660
Michelin map 426 fold 11 – Alt 460m - 1 509ft

The country town of Geras is a quiet holiday resort standing at some distance from the main tourist routes. Well known in Lower Austria for its Premonstratensian abbey, Geras also has the advantage of being close to a **nature reserve** (140 hectares-345 acres); delighful forest paths enable the visitor to enjoy the well-tended woodlands and walk round the perimeters of enclosures where various animals roam freely, mainly fallow-deer, roe-deer, wild boar and wild oxen.

STIFT (ABBEY) ⊙ *tour: 1 hour*

The Premonstratensians, an order of canons regular founded in 1120 by St Norbert at Premontré, near Laon in northern France, under the rule of St Augustine, founded an abbey at Geras in 1153. The abbey buildings and the church were sacked numerous times over the course of the centuries, and little is known of their appearance during the Romanesque and Gothic periods. The abbey underwent alterations in the Baroque style as early as 1650 but many of the buildings were destroyed in a fire during 1730. In 1736 reconstruction work was entrusted to the architect Joseph Munggenast who designed the elegant building at the abbey entrance.

Stiftskirche – The main door of the abbey church is decorated with statues of St Norbert and St Augustine, the two major figures in the history of the Premonstratensian order. These beautifully-made figures were sculpted in 1655. The church has preserved its overall design from Gothic times with a central nave and aisles. The statue of the **miraculous Virgin Mary** which is venerated on the high altar survived the fire in 1730.

Marmorsaal (Marble Hall) – A fine staircase leads up to the main hall situated on the first floor of the abbey's front lodge. The almost square hall is well lit and decorated in a most refined style; it also has an air of solemnity which is in contrast to the provincial simplicity which characterises the rest of the abbey. The fireplace is beautifully decorated with stucco in various shades of black, grey and gold; above it hangs a painting of the Wedding at Cana by the noted colourist, Paul Troger. Troger was also responsible for a magnificent **fresco★** on the ceiling depicting the miracle of the loaves and fishes.

Art education centre – Since 1970, the east wing of the abbey buildings has housed an art education centre, said to be the greatest centre for creativity in Europe. About 150 courses are held here every year, covering a wide range of activities (folk art, restoration, ceramics, painting etc.).

EXCURSION

Pernegg – *12km - 8 miles southwest of Geras.*
Set amidst soothing countryside, Pernegg is home to a Premonstratensian convent for choral nuns. The **Pfarr- und Stiftskirche St. Andreas** is dwarfed by the massive square west tower. The church interior is impressive in size and features a remarkable pulpit dating from 1618 which is a richly ornate example of the Mannerist style.

Stift (Convent) – The convent, which is a daughter house of the abbey at Geras, has recently been brought back to life as a community of Thomist nuns. It is a centre for religious seminars and retreats.

GERLITZEN★★

Kärnten

Michelin map 426 fold 35 – north of Villach – Local map under WÖRTHER SEE

The foothills of the Gerlitzen (alt 1 909m - 6 562ft) dip into the waters of the Ossiach Lake (Ossiacher See) in southern Carinthia; the mountain is one of the outposts of the central rock massifs of the Alps. Its numerous mountain hotels, cable-car to Kanzel, many ski-lifts and well-exposed, sunny slopes attract skiers from Austria and much further afield.

Ascent of the Gerlitzen ⊙ – *12km - 7 miles – plus 1 hour on foot Rtn. A narrow toll-road climbs to the Gerlitzen. From Bodensdorf on the north shore of the Ossiacher See make for Tschöran, where the little mountain road to Gerlitzen starts.*
After winding through woods and pastures, the road ends at Bergerhütte, at an altitude of 1 764m - 5 787ft. Finish the climb, if necessary, by **chairlift** ⊙.

★★ **Panorama** – The circular view embraces, southwards, the three lakes at Ossiach, Wörth and Faak and, beyond the Drava valley, the long barrier of the Karawanken of which the Mittagskogel (2 143m - 7 031ft) is the most distinct peak. To the west of the Karawanken lie the Julian Alps (Triglav – alt 2 863m - 9 393ft) and the Carnic Alps. To the north, the view encompasses the mountainous district known as the Nockgebiet. The permanently snow-covered slopes of the glaciers of Hochalm and the Ankogel (in the Hohe Tauern range) glitter in the northwest.

GERLOSSTRASSE★

Tirol und Salzburg

Michelin map 426 folds 32 and 33

The Gerlos pass links the Zillertal, a prosperous valley, with the Oberpinzgau (Upper Pinzgau), a long basin through which the Upper Salzach flows, taking in many torrents which tumble down from the glaciated summits, visible here and there, of the Hohe Tauern (Großvenediger massif). A visit to the well-known Krimml falls is worth the trip.

FROM ZELL AM ZILLER TO MITTERSILL

67km - 42 miles – about 2 hours, not counting the walks to the Zittau refuge and the Krimml falls
The road on the west side of the pass (Zillertal slope), downstream from Gerlos, has narrow sections. Upstream from Gerlos and on the road descending to Krimml, a toll is payable at the pass ⊙.

Zell am Ziller – *See ZILLERTAL.*
On leaving Zell am Ziller the road climbs quickly in hairpin bends up the Hainzenberg slope. It soon leaves behind the pretty pilgrims' chapel of **Maria Rast** (1739) which guards the Zillertal. It then approaches the hanging Gerlos valley.

✳ **Gerlos** – At an altitude of 1 250m - 4 101ft, this village tucked in a tributary valley of the Ziller is a favourite destination for skiers in the winter. Excellent ski slopes offer numerous possibilities to downhill skiers, while cross-country skiers are equally well-catered for. Summer holiday makers can choose between rambling and climbing, or, if they prefer, water sports on the **Durlaßbodensee**.
The climb from Gerlos to the Gerlos pass begins with the road making a wide curve at the foot of the Durlaßboden earth dam. A second bend takes the road up the mountainside above the artificial lake which drowned the Wildgerlostal. The snow-covered cliffs of the Reichenspitze, which bar this high valley, and the Wildkarspitze, in the foreground on the left, come into view from time to time. The road leaves to one side the Königsleiten and its chairlift, continues up to the actual Gerlos pass (alt 1 507m - 4 944ft) to reach the Filzsteinalpe, its highest point (alt 1 628m - 5 341ft – *car park*).

★★ **Climb to the Zittauer Hütte** – *This taxing walk is recommended only for those with a good level of fitness and endurance; allow 3 hours for the climb up and 2 hours 15min for the climb down (900m - 2 953ft difference in altitude). Proper walking boots are essential.*

Shortly before the toll station, turn left and take the first road on the right. Drive on for about 5km - 3 miles to the end of the road and leave the car in the car park (fee charged) of the Gasthaus Finkau (alt 1 424m - 4 672ft).

The path leads up through woodland and then across pretty Alpine pastures alongside the Wilder Gerlos, a gushing mountain stream which takes its source from the mountain glacier of the same name. The Zittau refuge can be glimpsed against a backdrop of rocky cliffs higher up.

A 1 hour 45min climb brings walkers to a refuge which marks the beginning of the core area of the Hohe Tauern national park. The climb continues up a narrow footpath, which becomes increasingly steep, and which at times follows steps cut into the rockface itself.

On arrival at the Zittau refuge, there is a breathtaking view of the surrounding magnificent **Alpine peaks★★**. The **Untere Gerlossee** can be seen shimmering blue at the foot of the glittering glaciated peaks of the Wildgerlos and the Reichenspitze. Further below lie the two lakes of Durchlaßboden and Finkau.

The rapid **descent★** down the Krimml slope first reveals the full length of the Upper Pinzgau cleft and then the two main falls of the Krimml. The road, cut into the steep rock mountainsides or avoiding these by way of bridges, finds better terrain in the Blaubach ravine (a series of hairpin bends). On leaving the valley, one sees the most remarkable sight; the landlocked lake of the Burgwandkehre encircling a rounded hillock, the Trattenköpfl.

★ **Trattenköpfl** – Alt 1 166m - 3 824ft. A close **view★** of the lower Krimml falls may be had from the car parks at the entrance to the tunnel.

★★ **Krimml Waterfalls** – *See KRIMMLER WASSERFÄLLE.*

From Wald to Mittersill, the Oberpinzgau affords good examples of balconied houses and fences constructed of interwoven laths *(illustration p 47)*. Near Rasthaus Venedigerblick on the road between Rosental and Neukirchen, there is a quick glimpse of the dazzling summits of the Kleinvenediger and the Großvenediger.

Neukirchen am Großvenediger – Holiday resort.

The road arrives at Mittersill, an important crossroads *(see FELBERTAUERN-STRASSE and KITZBÜHEL)*.

Bad GLEICHENBERG ✝

Steiermark – Population 1 920

Michelin map 426 fold 38 – Alt 317m - 1 040ft

The spa of Bad Gleichenberg, not far from the Hungarian and Slovenian frontiers, is restful and favoured by a mild climate.

In 1834, the Count of Wickenburg, from the Rhineland like his contemporary Metternich, was introduced to the healing properties of the Gleichenberg springs. Being a shrewd businessman as well as the local governor, he did not need long to transform the town into an elegant spa resort. By the end of the 19C, Bad Gleichenberg was the most highly reputed spa resort in Austria.

The town, set amidst countryside more reminiscent of a landscaped garden, still boasts some beautiful Biedermeier style villas and town houses. A large 20ha - 50 acre park adds to the effect of the town's natural surroundings. The spa is sought out by sufferers of a variety of complaints, such as diseases of the heart, lungs and circulatory tract, stomach or digestive problems, rheumatism or ezcema. However, it is not only the sick who appreciate the pleasant atmosphere here; after Graz and Mariazell, Bad Gleichenberg is the most popular holiday destination in Styria.

The current Michelin Red Guide Europe offers
a selection of pleasant hotels in the cities of Vienna Innsbruck or Salzburg;
each entry specifies the facilities available (gardens,
tennis courts, swimming pool, car park)
and the annual opening and closing dates ;
there is also a selection of restaurants recommended for their cuisine :
well-prepared meals at moderate prices ; stars for good cooking

GMÜND

Kärnten – Population 2 607
Michelin map 426 fold 34

At one time, under the Archbishops of Salzburg, Gmünd controlled the traffic on the main road between Nuremberg and Venice which was then an important route for both strategic and commercial reasons, passing through the Radstädter Tauern mountains and skirting the Katschberg.

Gmünd has remained a walled town to this day, and still has a fortified gate at either end of the lively and typical Straßenplatz (p 48). The most striking buildings are two large castles. The older of the two dates from the 15C-17C and has preserved its military appearance; its walls, which were badly damaged by fire in 1886, still tower above the roofs of the town. Since 1992, it has been used as an art and cultural centre. The "New Castle" (Neues Schloß) forms part of the northern entrance to Gmünd, and was built in 1651 by Count Christoph Lodron, brother of Paris Lodron (qv). A fine façade with two tall staircase towers faces the park, which is now a public garden.

Porsche Museum

Porsche-Automuseum Helmut Pfeifhofer ⊙ – This, the only private Porsche museum in Europe, is a reminder that in 1944 the world-famous engineer Ferdinand Porsche moved to Gmünd where he established his main workshop; the company's Head Office was also located there until 1950. Over two dozen exhibits are on show, together with several prototypes of military and sports vehicles, as well as lifesize wooden models of the first Porsche car bodies.

GMUNDEN★

Obersterörreich – Population 12 720
Michelin map 426 fold 21 – Local map under SALZKAMMERGUT
Alt 440m - 1 444ft

In Gmunden, a country resort in the Salzkammergut much sought after by Romantic or Biedermeier (qv) artists and poets, the delighted visitor will find a colourful little town with one of the best equipped lake beaches on the north slope of the Alps, and wonderful views of the Traunsee. Lake cruises ⊙ can be made on the restored paddlesteamer Gisela which welcomed Emperor Franz-Joseph aboard in 1872. Gmunden has been famous for the manufacture of artistic pottery since the 15C.

★ **Esplanade** – This walk along the lake shore extends for 2km - 1 mile – first among flowerbeds, then beneath chestnut trees. It leads from the Rathausplatz (main square), which is marked by the town hall, a Renaissance building, with a porcelain tiled clocktower, to the yacht harbour and the beach (Strandbad). In the opposite direction the walk can be pleasantly continued by crossing the river and following it as far as the war memorial (Kriegerdenkmal) or downstream along the Traun River (2km - 1 mile).

Schloß Ort, Gmunden

Southwards, the **view★** takes in the crests of the Erlakogel, which resemble the form of a recumbent woman and are known as the Sleeping Greek (schlafende Griechin).

★ **Schloß Ort** – Built on a little island linked to the mainland by a breakwater, this **Seeschloß** (Lake Château) forms the typical souvenir picture of Gmunden. Through a doorway in the bulbous tower you can reach the charming inner court, lined on two sides by arcaded galleries superimposed in the style of the 16C.

Archduke Salvator, the nephew of the Emperor Franz Joseph, acquired the estate in 1878. Tired of court life, he lived under the assumed name of **Johann Ort** until he disappeared, in conditions which have never been explained, on a cruise off the coast of South America.

★ **Kammerhofmuseum** ⊘ – The museum takes its name from the salt mines administration building in which it is housed and has a wide range of exhibits on Gmunden and the surrounding area. The grand ceramics hall is particularly impressive. There are numerous memorabilia of Brahms (his studio, piano, cutlery...) and of the great 19C Austrian dramatist, Friedrich Hebbel, who died in Vienna in 1863.

EXCURSIONS

★ **Gmundnerberg** – *9km - 5miles southwest – Alt 833m - 2 733ft. Leave Gmunden by the Esplanade and the Bad Ischl road.*

In **Altmünster**, a holiday destination, bear right. The road ends in a run along the crest *(after a sanatorium)* which has **views★** to the south over the whole of the Traunsee basin. The west bank of the lake is flat and populated, the east steeply sloped. The Sleeping Greek *(see above)* can be recognized.

★ **Almtal (Alm Valley)** – *37km - 23 miles return – half a day. Leave Gmunden to the east on the B120.*

Scharnstein – Strung out along the main road, the village has a much-restored castle dating from 1584 which houses two unusual museums.

The exhibits displayed in the 21 rooms of the **Österreichisches Kriminalmuseum** (Austrian Crime Museum) ⊘ trace the fight against crime from medieval instruments of bodily restraint to political violence and contemporary terrorism. Weapons and devices used by wrong-doers are on show, as are the tools of the executioner's trade, notably a guillotine. No one can fail to be affected by such spectacles and the museum is consequently a place more for adults than children.

The extraordinary **Reptilienzoo** (Reptile Zoo) ⊘ occupies the cellars underneath the Museum of Crime. In its glass cages are over a hundred poisonous animals from all over the world (snakes, scorpions, giant spiders), just a hair's breadth away from onlookers.

Follow signs towards Grünau im Almtal.

Beyond Grünau the road rises gently through a wooded mountain landscape, particularly attractive in autumn.

★ **Cumberland Wildpark** ⓥ – *In Grünau.* This wildlife park, covering an area of 60ha - 148 acres, is set in pleasant wooded mountain countryside. Footpaths run for miles alongside a stream, or skirting some of the numerous lakes, enabling visitors to admire the resident wildlife in the most natural setting possible. The wildlife park is a research centre for the Konrad-Lorenz-Institut, named after the famous Austrian zoologist and animal behaviourist (1903-1989).

Continue up the valley as far as Seehaus.

After the peaceful little village of Habernau the road turns south and terminates on the forested banks of the Almsee. The waters of the romantic **lake** reflect the great natural amphitheatre closing off the valley. Signposted footpaths invite the visitor to further exploration of these splendid landscapes.

Konrad Lorenz

Konrad Lorenz (1903-1989) is widely regarded as the one of the founders of modern ethology, or the comparative study of different types of animal behaviour across unrelated species. Lorenz was interested in particular in the behavioural processes of birds, and soon after finishing his medical studies in Vienna (Ph.D. in zoology, 1933) he won international attention for his observations of the early learning behaviour of young ducks and geese. He discovered that by imitating the quacking of a mother duck in front of newly hatched ducklings, for example, he could make them adopt him as their "mother figure" and follow him in a line as they instinctively would their parent. Lorenz developed his early work on how instinctive behaviours are stimulated to include the study of the evolution of behavioural patterns in a species and how this is affected by environmental factors. He argued that animals are genetically programmed to adapt their behaviour from generation to generation, as they learn the lessons necessary for the survival of their species.

Later on in his career, Lorenz applied his train of thought to human behaviour, in particular aggression, suggesting that since humans did not share the need of lower mammals to fight for survival, their innate aggressive tendencies might be adapted into more sociably acceptable behaviour patterns by a proper study of and provision for their basic human needs.

In 1973, Lorenz shared the Nobel Prize for Medecine with fellow ethologists Karl von Frisch and Nikolaas Tinbergen.

GOSAUSEEN★★★

Oberösterreich

Michelin map 426 fold M 6 – Local map under SALZKAMMERGUT

The Gosau lakes lie amidst craggy mountain scenery in the northwest of the Dachstein range, forming one of the unique features of the Austrian Alps. From June to October, they are a popular destination for nature-lovers.

★★★ **Vorderer Gosausee** – Alt 933m - 3 061ft. The shores of the lake can be reached from the car park, beyond which the road is closed to traffic. There is an unforgettable **view**★★ of the Hoher Dachstein limestone range (alt 2 995m - 9 826ft) with its small glaciers. The play of light on the scene is particularly effective very early or very late in the day, when the glaciers and rockfaces are bathed in light while the valley lies in shadow.

A **tour of the lake**★★★ is an absolute must. This easy walk *(allow about an hour)* gives a marvellous view of the craggy peaks of the Gosau ridge. The mountains and surrounding forest are reflected in the still, clear waters of the lake, making a fairy-tale scene.

★★ **Walk to the Hinterer Gosausee** – *From the far (southeast) end of the Vorderer Gosausee, allow 1 hour 45min there and back. This walk is recommended for ramblers with a good level of fitness.*

The path through the undergrowth soon becomes steeper. On reaching the densely wooded shores of the **Hinterer See**★★ (alt 1 154m - 3 786ft), take the right shore as far as the Hinterer-See-Alm.

Keen walkers can continue as far as the **Adameck-Hütte** (alt 2 196m - 7 205ft), although it is necessary to be in good physical shape for this. We recommend an early morning departure. Allow 2 hours 30min for the climb from Hinterer See (the footpath begins just before the Hinterer-See-Alm). From the Adamseck-Hütte it is well worth making a 20min detour to the edge of the Gosau glacier. From the car park, the entire walk takes about 8 hours, in other words a day's hard walking, or two days including an overnight stay in the refuge.

Hinterer Gosausee

109

GRAZ★★

Ⓛ Steiermark – Population 243 405
Michelin map 426 fold 38 – Alt 365m - 1 194ft

The capital of Styria is in the valley of the Mur, bounded to the west by the last foothills of the Alps and to the north and east by the Styrian hills. Because of this attractive setting and its extensive parks Graz is sometimes called the Garden City. Its basically continental climate is softened by Mediterranean influences. With its tiled roofs bearing the patina of age, the old city centre has an undeniable charm, a pleasing synthesis of Germanic sobriety and Italian grace.

In recent times, Graz has become an industrial, administrative, cultural and educational metropolis, Austria's second city. The industrial suburbs which have grown up since the end of the Second World War manufacture all kinds of products, from railway rolling stock to beer and shoes; the city employs some 130 000 people. The three universities of Graz have 40 000 students between them; as well as Austria's second most prestigious opera house, there is a theatre and even a casino. Graz hosts the international festival known as the **"Styrian Autumn"** (Steirischer Herbst), which is mostly devoted to avant-garde art, and the **"Styriarte"**, a summer festival of ancient music *(see the Calendar of events at the end of the guide)*.

OUT AND ABOUT IN GRAZ

Tourist information

Grazer Tourismus GmbH, Herrengasse 16, A-8010 Graz. Opening times: May to October Monday to Friday 9am to 7pm, Saturdays 9am to 6pm, Sundays 10am to 3pm, ☎ 03 16/ 83 52 41 11.

Informationsbüro (Hauptbahnhof), Bahnsteig 1. Opening times: Monday to Friday 9am to 7pm, Saturdays 9am to 5pm, Sundays and public holidays 9am to 4pm, ☎ 03 16/ 91 68 37.

Fremdenverkehrsbüro und Kongreßstelle der Stadt Graz, Hans-Sachs-Gasse 10, ☎ 03 16/ 83 52 41 19.

Public transport

Tourist day-tickets, valid for 24 hours, are available. A leaflet for visitors on public transport in Graz, *Einsteigen leicht gemacht,* can be obtained from the Graz tourist information office. The tourist information centre on Jakomini-platz is open Monday to Friday 9.30am to 6.30pm, Saturdays 9am to 1pm (5.30pm on the first Saturday of the month).

Post offices

Main post office : Hauptpostamt, Neutorgasse 46.
Station post office : Bahnhofspostamt, Bahnhofgürtel 48-50

Markets
Farm produce
Kaiser-Josef-Platz and Lendplatz, Monday to Saturday 7am to 12.30pm
Hauptplatz and Jakominiplatz Monday to Friday 7am to 6pm, Saturdays 7am to 12.30pm
Flea market
Karmeliterplatz, 3rd Saturday in the month

HISTORICAL NOTES

The Romans arrived in Styria in 16 BC but preferred to settle at Flavia Solva (Leibnitz) to the south rather than on the site of Graz which was liable to flood. In the 10C, a settlement was founded at the foot of the Schloßberg, probably the work of Slav colonists who built the little frontier castle on the Schloßberg itself from which the town took its name (*gradec* = Slavonic diminutive for "castle"). In the first half of the 12C a market was founded where the Sackstraße runs today. From 1189 Graz enjoyed the status of "civitas"; a manor house, a church and an administrative centre stood at the foot of the Schloßberg. For a while, until the line died out in 1246, the town was governed by the Babenberg family; there followed a short period of domination by the kings of Hungary and Bohemia.

An Imperial city – In 1379 the Leopoldine branch of the Habsburgs chose Graz as their residence. In 1440, the Styrian prince Friedrich III, who by preference resided in the city, was elected King of Germany, then, in 1452, crowned Holy Roman Emperor. It was he who made Graz an Imperial city and it is from this time that the cathedral dates, as does the "castle" near the Burgtor (though all that remains of it is the double staircase). Here and there on the city walls can be seen the initials of his device "AEIOU" *(see Historical notes in Introduction)*.

A bastion of Christianity – In 1480 an army of 20 000 Turks overran Styria and devastated the area. Fifty years later, Suleiman the Magnificent sacked the whole of the Mur valley and eastern Styria; the Turkish threat hung over the province until 1683. It was because of such dangers that Graz had provided itself with ramparts as early as the 13C. In 1543 the defences including the Schloßberg fortress were strengthened on the orders of Emperor Ferdinand I by the Italian **Domenico dell'Allio**, who was also architect of the Landhaus. The measures taken to ward off attack were thoroughgoing; a huge arsenal of arms and munitions was built up, the raw material coming from Styria's **"Iron Mountain"** *(see EISENERZ)*. This was then fashioned into swordblades, halberds, breast-plates and fire-arms by a legion of armourers, gunsmiths, blacksmiths and furbishers.

Whenever invasion seemed imminent, the arms were distributed to volunteers chosen from the local population to reinforce the professional troops. The construction of the Zeughaus (Arsenal) next to the Landhaus in 1642 made it possible to bring together arms and munitions which until then had been distributed around the city, in sheds near the city gates, beneath sentry-walks or in the cellars of the Landhaus.

Following the Habsburg partition of the country in 1564, Graz became the capital of a vast area known as **Inner Austria**, comprising Styria, Carinthia, Gorizia, Carniola and Istria. The splendid court of Archduke Karl II, a true prince of the Renaissance, brought many cultural and artistic benefits to the city; many of its monuments date from this time, as does the Spanische Reitschule *(see WIEN).*

The Reformation – By 1568 three-quarters of the population had embraced Protestantism. In this year a school and seminary were founded, where the present Paradeishof stands (CZ **26**), and it was here that the German astronomer Kepler taught between 1594-98.

In 1571 Archduke Karl II called in the Jesuits to implement the Counter-Reformation; they founded a college (in the Bürgergasse) and a school (Hofgasse), and remodelled the interior of the Hofkirche (court church, now the cathedral) in the taste of the time. In 1585 the Archduke founded **Graz University**, which became the intellectual hub of Inner Austria.

The city's fortunes took another turn in 1619 when Karl II's son, Archduke Ferdinand II, was elected Holy Roman Emperor. Ferdinand moved the court to Vienna, and Graz, no longer an Imperial residence, lost much of its dynamism. In the 18C, following the reforms of Maria-Theresa, the city had to forgo many of its privileges; later, under Joseph II, the University was downgraded to a grammar school. Graz's days of splendour came to a definite end; this is why the city has so few buildings dating from the late Baroque period.

A Prince beloved by his people, Archduke Johann – The Habsburg Archduke Johann enjoyed great personal popularity in Styria and his memory is still honoured today. Born in the Palazzo Pitti in Florence, he was the thirteenth child of one of Maria Theresa's sons, the Grand Duke of Tuscany, the future Emperor Leopold II. Entrusted with high command in the army, Johann took part in the campaigns against Napoleon. On settling in Graz, he devoted himself to studies of all kinds, roaming through Styria and Carinthia in the company of naturalists, archaeologists and painters.

His romantic marriage to Anna Plochl, a postmaster's daughter from Bad Aussee, together with any number of public enterprises, did nothing to diminish his popularity. He founded model farms, presided over the construction of the railway from Graz to Mürzzuschlag (1848) and promoted the prosperity of the Eisenerz area. In Graz itself, the Technische Hochschule is proof of his progressive spirit, as is the Joanneum Landesmuseum, Austria's oldest museum, founded in 1811 and today boasting 14 departments dispersed among 8 different institutions.

★★ OLD GRAZ *time: 3 hours excluding Zeughaus*

This is one of the most extensive historic city centres in the German-speaking world. Dominated by the Schloßberg and bordered on the west by the river, its 18C and 19C façades conceal much older buildings with quiet arcaded courtyards – at least fifty of them – some grand, some intimate, the grandest, but not the oldest, being that of the Landhaus.

★ **Hauptplatz** (CZ). – The heart of Graz, this is the liveliest of squares. The city trams come and go incessantly, disgorging ever more people to join the motley crowd thronging the market stalls. Behind the brightly-painted 17C-19C façades are buildings of much older, medieval date, often stretching right back towards the rear of the plot they occupy. At the corner of the Sporgasse stands the arcaded **Haus Luegg** (CZ **A**) with its luxuriant 17C stucco work. The city's oldest pharmacy is at no 4; dating from 1535, it still has some of its original fittings. The **Erzherzog-Johann-Brunnen** (fountain) of 1878 lords it over the square, relegating the statue of the Emperor to second place (on Freiheitsplatz – DY **10**), a reminder of the affection in which their benefactor was held by the local people. The four female figures gracing the fountain are allegories of the four rivers flowing through Styria at the time of the monarchy, though the boundary revisions of 1918 left the province with only two of them (the Mur and the Enns).

From the pavement in front of the city hall (raised to its present level in 1893) there is a view of the wooded spur of the Schloßberg keeping watch over the city, with, at its far end, the familiar outline of the Uhrturm (Clock Tower), the emblem of Graz.

The Landhaus is reached via the broad and busy **Herrengasse** (DZ) with its elegant shops and offices. The **Gemaltes Haus** (painted house, at no 3) was residence of the archdukes until the building of the castle in 1450. The murals on historic (notably Roman) themes date from 1742, when they replaced the original decoration by Pietro de Pomis, architect of the mausoleum.

Courtyard of the Landhaus

★★ **Landhaus** (DZ) – This, the former seat of the Styrian Diet, is a remarkable Renaissance palace built 1557-65 by Domenico dell' Allio, the military architect who had just completed the total reconstruction of the Schloßberg fortress for Emperor Ferdinand I. Today the Landhaus still serves as the meeting place for the Landtag, the Styrian provincial parliament.

The severity of the Herrengasse façade contrasts with the southern elegance of the courtyard with its three storeys of arcades, flower-bedecked balconies, staircase wells and loggias. The stairway gracing the chapel in the northwest

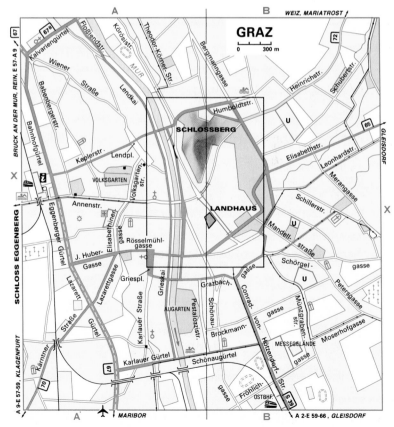

corner of the courtyard was built by another Italian, Bartolomeo di Bosio. The old wellhead, the work of local craftsmen, has a fine bronze dais with amoretti and female figures. It was once coloured.

The courtyard forms an enchanting setting for the various performances given here in summer.

A few paces along the Stempfergasse (DZ 30) reveal the best view of the façade of the Landhaus, with its middle bay emphasised by a little copper bell-turret. The lower parts of the columns of the twin windows rise from a sculpted ring, a motif much favoured by Domenico dell'Allio. The façade next to the Landhaus is that of the arsenal.

★★★ **Zeughaus (Arsenal)** (DZ) ⊙ – With its portal foreshadowing the appearance of the German Baroque, the real function of this solid-looking building – an arms depot – is betrayed by the statues of Mars and Minerva. In its day it was one of the many arsenals in the world, but it is the only one to have been preserved in its original state with its contents intact.

The arsenal was built in 1642. By the beginning of the 18C the Turkish threat had finally disappeared and it was decided to store the standing army's equipment in Vienna. The question of what to do with the now obsolete material at Graz was settled when Maria-Theresa allowed the Styrians to keep it here in recognition of the services rendered by the local militias. To enter the arsenal is to leave behind the contemporary bustle of the Herrengasse and to be transported back into the world of four centuries ago; it is as if cavalrymen and footsoldiers could appear at any moment, fresh from being mustered in the courtyard of the Landhaus, to fit themselves out from the array of neatly laid-out material, and set off to harrass the Infidel.

The four storeys of the arsenal contain more than 32 000 arms of all imaginable kinds; cold steel, arms on poles and fire-arms – arquebuses, pistols and muskets with their powder horn – heavy armour for knights and soldiers, breastplates and harnesses for use in battle or jousting.

Several items are particularly striking, like the armour for a horse, hammered out at Innsbruck in 1505 by the Imperial armourer Conrad Seusenhofer. There is also a complete set of ornate parade armour made in 1560 by the master armourer Michael Witz the Younger from Innsbruck, richly engraved and embossed jousting suits from the workshops at Nuremberg and fine inlaid pistols and sporting guns of the 16C and 17C.

From the top storey of the arsenal the view takes in the Landhaus courtyard and, over the rooftops, the Schloßberg and clock tower. On coming out into the Herrengasse again, note the parish church to the right.

Stadtpfarrkirche zum Heiligen Blut (DZ) – The original Gothic church building was remodelled in the Baroque taste, then re-Gothicised between 1875-82. Its Baroque **bell-tower**, the city's finest, was built entirely out of wood in 1780-81 by the architect Josef Stengg and the master carpenter Franz Windisch. It is topped by a three-barred cross, a reminder of its consecration by the Pope.

Inside, on the altar in the south aisle, is an Assumption of the Virgin attributed to Tintoretto. The stained glass of the chancel, the work of the Salzburg artist Albert Birkle in 1953, has an unusual feature; in the left-hand window, the fourth panel from the bottom on the right has a Hitler and a Mussolini taking part in the flagellation of Christ.

There is an organ concert in the church every Thursday evening in summer.

Go into the Altstadtpassage (DZ 3) by No 7 Herrengasse.

The first courtyard has arcaded and vaulted galleries dating from 1648.

A little further on, to the right, are a number of courtyards of which one is reminiscent of the Landhaus.

The passageway comes out onto the **Mehlplatz** (DZ 22). Here there are two splendid façades, Baroque on the left, Rococo on the right. The former (no 1) was once a music school run by the parents of Robert Stolz, composer of operettas.

Go right into the **Glockenspielplatz** (Carillon Square – *performance at 11am, 3pm and 6pm* – DZ 12). Dancing figures in local costume appear at each carillon performance in the pediment of an imposing house with a bell-turret.

Leave the Glockenspielplatz via the narrow passageway called Abraham-a-Santa-Clara-Gasse (DZ 2), then turn left for a view of no 1 Burgergasse (DZ), the sombre palazzo-like building which once served as a boarding-house for aristocratic pupils of the Jesuits. The building's history seems to be summed up by its Baroque doorway; two angels support a cartouche with the effigy of Archduke Karl II who was responsible for bringing the Jesuits to Graz, while the cartouche itself is framed by allegories representing the Roman Catholic Church and Science.

To the right, a stairway leads to the city's most unusual building, the Mausoleum.

★★ **Mausoleum** (DZ) ⊘ – The great west stairway gives the best view of this extraordinary edifice which combines the Mannerist phase of the Austrian Baroque and the theatricality of the great contemporary churches of Rome. The commission for an Imperial mausoleum was given by Emperor Ferdinand II to an Italian architect, Pietro de Pomis, who worked on the project between 1614-33, and it was another Italian, Pietro Valnegro, who completed the exterior in 1636 with the building of the tower of the apse.

The space available to de Pomis was very limited and it was an architectural tour de force on his part to have designed a façade of such harmony and dignity with no hint of coldness or ostentation. His success in integrating the four pediments which help articulate the façade is particularly subtle, as is his handling of conventional proportion to offset the effect of the façade being seen from the foot of the great stairway. Responsibility for the exuberant stucco-work and frescoes

Mausoleum of Emperor Ferdinand II, Graz

of the interior was given to Johann Bernhard Fischer von Erlach (qv), one of the city's most famous men. A particularly fine oval dome surmounts the funerary crypt with the red marble sarcophagus of Karl II and Maria of Bavaria, the Emperor's parents. Only Karl's Archduchess lies here, the Emperor himself being buried at Seckau abbey. The tomb of Emperor Ferdinand II is to the right of the altar.

★ **Domkirche (Cathedral)** (DZ) – Before becoming the cathedral in 1786, this vast and luminous edifice served as church to the Imperial court. It was built between 1438-64 by Emperor Friedrich III, whose coat of arms adorns the main entrance. On the southwest corner of the entrance is a series of **frescoes** (1485); as well as including the earliest known depiction of the city, they show the various troubles visited on Graz in the year 1480 (Turks, plague, and swarms of locusts). Inside, the Baroque decor mostly dates from the time when the church was handed over to the Jesuits (1577 onwards).

The church's **interior** has most attractive reticulated vaulting. Of the original decor perhaps the most striking features are the two frescoes of St Christopher (late 15C), discovered in the course of restoration work at the beginning of this century. They recall an old belief according to which one would not die on a day on which one had looked at the Saint's image.

The long chancel has a Baroque altar of particularly harmonious design. Near the entrance to the chancel are two magnificent **reliquary chests**★★★. Brought here by the Jesuits, they are works of great sophistication and were once the marriage chests of Paula di Gonzaga, Duchess of Mantua. Made of ebony and decorated with reliefs in bone and ivory, they date from around 1470 and are in the style of Mantegna. Their subject-matter goes back to the "Triumphs" of Petrarch, moral and allegorical poems dealing with the various stages of life from the standpoint of a calm acceptance of death.

The organ with its 5 158 pipes dates from 1978.

Leave the cathedral by the north entrance.

Cross the street by the **Burgtor** (Castle Gate) (DZ) and go through the impressive stone gateway commanding the first courtyard of the 15C castle. The left doorway, before the covered way, gives access to the buildings of the provincial government (Landesregierung) and the **Treppenturm**.

★★ **Treppenturm (Staircase Tower)** (DY B) – This highly unusual architectural feature with its double stairway (Doppelwendeltreppe) wound around twin axes, is all that remains of the former residence of Friedrich III. The tower was added in 1499 by his son Maximilian I and is a notable technical achievement.

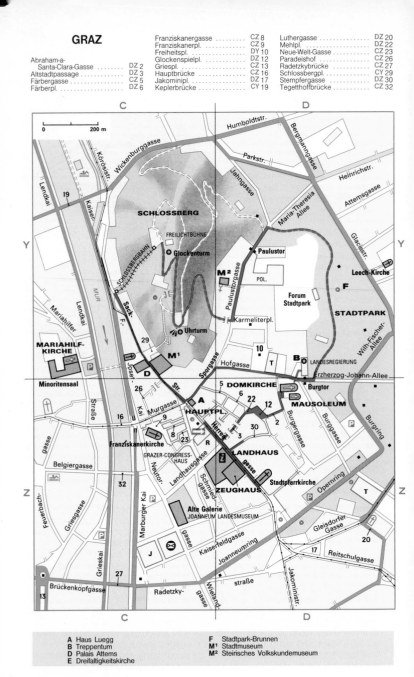

GRAZ

Abraham-a-
Santa-Clara-Gasse .... DZ 2
Altstadtpassage .... DZ 3
Färbergasse .... CZ 5
Färberpl. .... DZ 6

Franziskanergasse .... CZ 8
Franziskanerpl. .... CZ 9
Freiheitspl. .... DY 10
Glockenspielpl. .... DZ 12
Griespl. .... CZ 13
Hauptbrücke .... CZ 16
Jakominipl. .... DZ 17
Keplerbrücke .... CY 19

Luthergasse .... DZ 20
Mehlpl. .... DZ 22
Neue-Welt-Gasse .... CZ 23
Paradeishof .... CZ 26
Radetzkybrücke .... CZ 27
Schlossbergpl. .... CY 29
Stempfergasse .... DZ 30
Tegetthoffbrücke .... CZ 32

A Haus Luegg
B Treppentum
D Palais Attems
E Dreifaltigkeitskirche

F   Stadtpark-Brunnen
M¹ Stadtmuseum
M² Steirisches Volkskundemuseum

Freiheitsplatz (^{DY} 10) – In the centre of the square stands the statue of Franz II, the last Holy Roman Emperor and elder brother of Archduke Johann. Closing the square is a large red building with a neo-Classical pediment; this is the city residence of the abbots of St Lambrecht *(qv)*. The figure chased by wolves in the half-relief of the pediment is the building's architect, a droll reference to his problems in getting the commission in the face of competition from a rival, an architect named Wolf.

Just before the Sporgasse, on the left, is the old **Hofbäckerei** (Imperial Bakery) with its fine shop front. The bright and busy **Sporgasse** (CY) winds down to the Hauptplatz; no 22 is the House of the Teutonic Knights; it has an arcaded courtyard in Gothic style. The narrow façade of no 3 is an interesting example of Jugendstil (Art Nouveau).

Turn right into Sackstraße.

Sackstraße (CYZ). – This was once a cul-de-sac (Sack) ending in a city gateway whose site is now occupied by the Palais Attems (no 17). The road was lengthened on two occasions in the course of extending the city walls. Because of its proximity to the river, it became the heart of an artisans' district with a great variety of trades: millers, tanners, parchment-makers... After 1650, the oldest part of the street became known as "Lords Lane" because of the aristocratic mansions which can still be seen here.

The Krebsenkeller at no 12 has a **Renaissance courtyard**★ with double windows and arcaded loggias, giving an Italian feel and at the same time an air of secrecy to the ensemble. The **Palais Herberstein** at no 16, once a grand mansion which now houses the Neue Galerie (19C and 20C art), boasts a monumental staircase as evidence of its past splendour.

The Palais Khuenberg at no 18 houses the **Stadtmuseum (M¹)** ⊙. The exhibits include models of the Landhaus, the Mausoleum, and of the city as a whole as it appeared around 1800. There is also an analytical diagram of the three plagues depicted in the frescoes of the southwest corner of the cathedral. On 18 December 1863 the palace was the birthplace of Archduke Franz Ferdinand, who later became heir to the Imperial throne.

Palais Attems (D) – Opposite the Stadtmuseum, this is without doubt the finest of all the city's Baroque palaces. Its **façades**★★ repay close inspection, with their profuse decoration of pilasters, mouldings and curvilinear window pediments. The palace was built between 1702-16 for Count Attems on a site previously occupied by six town houses.

The nearby city gate was demolished at the same time, having outlived its usefulness.

Dreifaltigkeitskirche (E) – Built in 1704, the church seems to be watching over its neighbour, the Palais Attems. It reveals its calm and harmonious façade with its scrolled pediment in an almost shy way, notwithstanding the abundance of iconography referring to the Trinity, to which the church is dedicated.

The view from the church door shows the Schloßbergplatz (**CY 29**) from which some 260 steep steps climb up to the Schloßberg itself.

★ **Medieval Quarter** – Towards the end of the Middle Ages, a cattle market was held between the river and the ramparts, where the Franziskanerplatz (**CZ 9**) and the Neutorgasse (**CZ**) are now. The strange name (Kälbernes Viertel = Calf Town) still used by locals for the area around the Franciscan church recalls these times. In 1620, the area was brought within the ramparts when the city's defences were being strengthened.

The quarter has kept much of its charm, and a stroll through its narrow **streets**★ with their Italian atmosphere is most enjoyable, particularly the pretty Neue-Welt-Gasse (**CZ 23**) and the Franziskanergasse (**CZ 8**), both piled high with the wares of fruiterers and greengrocers.

Franziskanerkirche (**CZ**) – Traders set up their stalls against the walls of this church, which was re-roofed after the Second World War and given modern glass which lights the interior in a most attractive way. It was in 1240 that the Minorites installed their convent here, which subsequently passed into the ownership of the Franciscans. The oldest part of the church, the Jakobs-kapelle, dates back to 1330.

★ **PARKS** *time: 2 hours*

★ **Schloßberg** (CY) ⊙ – *Reached by funicular (Schloßbergbahn), from the northern end of the Sackstraße, or via the steps leading from the Schloßbergplatz (CY 29).* Overlooking the city from a height of 123m – more than 400ft, the impregnable hilltop bristled with redoubts and fortifications right up to the Napoleonic

A. Zane

Uhrturm, Graz

wars. In 1809 Graz was occupied by French troops led by General MacDonald, though the fortress withstood all assaults. Much to the chagrin of the townsfolk, one of the provisions of the Treaty of Schonbrunn in 1809 involved the dismantling of the Schloßberg. Nevertheless, they succeeded in acquiring the **Uhrturm** (Clock Tower) and the **Glockenturm** (Bell Tower) with its four-and-a-half ton bell "Lisl", the biggest in town. The rest of the fortress was duly demolished. Later in the 19C the process of converting the Schloßberg into a park was begun. Today it forms a series of pleasantly shaded gardens and terraces for strolling and sitting, while its nearly-tame squirrels are the delight of local children.

Near the bell tower is an open air theatre (Freilichtbuhne) with a sliding roof. Beyond, a wide chestnut avenue descends to the clock tower rising from its massed beds of flowers. The dial is unusual; for a long time it had a single hand, 5.4m – 8ft long, which showed the hours. The smaller, minute hand (2.7m – 9ft long) was added later, a strange inversion of normal practice.

Go down the steps leading to the Herberstein gardens. From the terrace there are fine **views**★★ over the city and the valley of the Mur. In the distance to the southwest, beyond the reddish-brown roofs of Graz, can be seen the outlines of the Styrian Prealps.

Climb back up to the clock tower and then go down the first path on the right which leads to the Karmeliterplatz. Here there is a Trinity Column, erected in 1680 in thanksgiving for relief from the plague.

Go up the Paulustorgasse.

Steiermärkisches Landesmuseum Abt. Volkskunde (DY M²) ⊘ – The local folklore museum forms part of the Joanneum *(below)* and has been housed since 1913 in this former Capuchin monastery. It is devoted to the province's folklore and has some particularly interesting reconstructions of house interiors.

On the rise beyond the museum is one of the "Heimatwerk" shops offering contemporary local crafts.

Paulustor (DY) – Together with the Burgtor, this is all that remains of the city walls. Built towards the end of the 16C, it displays the coats of arms, in marble, of Ferdinand II of Austria and of Maria Anna of Bavaria.

★ **Stadtpark (**DY**)** – This is an "English-style" park, laid out informally in the second half of the 19C along the line of the old walls. It runs in a broad band for a distance of 1 200m – some ¾ mile to the east and southeast of the old city centre. In the middle of the park is the **Forum Stadtpark**, a meeting-place of avant-garde artists since 1960. In front of the building stands the **Stadtpark-Brunnen (F)**, a fountain in a luxuriant set- ting of fine old trees, shrubs and flower-beds. The foun- tain is the work of crafts- man Antoine Durenne. Two similar, but smaller, foun- tains made thirty years be- fore their counterpart in Graz adorn the Place de la Concorde in Paris.

Go south through the Stadtpark to the Burgtor. Take Hofgasse, then Spor- gasse. Turn left into Fär- bergasse and carry on across Färberplatz and along Prokopigasse. Level with Mehlplatz turn right into Altstadtpassage, which leads into Herren- gasse. It is not far from here to Hauptplatz.

ADDITIONAL SIGHTS

★ **Mariahilf-Kirche** (CY) – One of the finest of the city's churches, with ele- gant twin towers and im- peccably proportioned Ba- roque façade, this was the province's most popular place of pilgrimage after Mariazell.

Mariahilf-Kirche, Graz

GEORG MILKES

It was begun in 1607-11 by Pietro de Pomis, architect of the Mausoleum and Schloß Eggenberg, who was buried here on his death in 1633. The late Baroque towers of 1742-44 are the work of Josef Hueber. Renaissance in structure, the interior gives an overall impression of harmony and repose. The door on the left of the façade leads to the cloisters, beyond which is a further courtyard with a little building in the style of the Renaissance, albeit designed as late as the end of the 17C; its first floor is given over entirely to the **Minoritensaal** ⊙, one of the city's main concert halls. The charming walnut rostrum of this former ceremonial refectory forms part of the design of the entrance doorway.

Alte Galerie des Steiermärkischen Landesmuseums Joanneum (CDZ) ⊙ – The art gallery occupies the ground and second floors of the building. The **medieval art★** section is particularly interesting, with works by Austrian masters of the 12C to 16C. On the **ground floor**: stained glass, the "Admont Madonna" from 1320, two Admont Pietàs from 1400 and 1420, a Virgin Mary in Glory from 1420, a votive painting of St Lambrecht from 1430, a *Martyrdom of St Thomas à Beckett* by Michael Pacher from 1470/1480, a large Mariazell altarpiece from 1518-22.

2nd floor: Renaissance, Mannerist and Baroque art: works by Jan Brueghel the Elder, Pieter Brueghel the Younger, Lucas Cranach the Elder, a *Naked Warrior* by Godl/Magt, paintings by Sofonisba Anguissola, Luca Cambiaso, Dosso and Battista Dossi. Austrian and German Baroque artists such as Johann Heinrich Schönfeld, Johann Michael Rottmayr, Josef Stammel, Franz Anton Maulbertsch, Paul Troger and Franz Christoph Janneck. There is also a sizeable collection of Baroque sketches in oil (bozzetti).
The museum also organises special exhibitions of its graphics collection.

Leechkirche (DY) – The university church of Maria am Leech is the oldest religious building in Graz. It was built 1275-93 by the Teutonic Order and bears a certain resemblance to the Sainte-Chapelle in Paris. The early Gothic, many-layered **west front★** is crowned by a Virgin and Child on the tympanum, a work in late Romanesque angular style. The **stained glass★**, which dates from 1330 and depicts various saints and the story of Christ's Passion, is of particular interest.
Excavation work in the church has revealed that this was a burial place in the 9-8C BC for the urnfield culture. This tradition was also followed in the Hallstatt period (7C BC). In the 11C or early 12C, there was a round building on this site, but it is unclear what its function was.

EXCURSIONS

★★ **Schloß Eggenberg** (AX) – *3.5km - 2 miles west. See Schloß EGGENBERG.*

★★ **Österreichisches Freilichtmuseum** (Austrian Open Air Museum) ⊙ – *15km - 9 ½ miles northwest via the Bruck-an-der-Mur road* (AX). *Leave the motorway at Gratkorn, cross the Mur, turn right after the railway and continue for 3km - 2 miles. Description under MURTAL.*

★ **Stift Rein** (AX) – *15km - 9 ½ miles northwest.*
Founded in 1129 by monks from the abbey at Ebrach in Germany, Rein is the oldest Cistercian abbey in Austria. Its buildings, dominated by the elegant Baroque tower, stand out against a background of wooded hills, including the 1 000 - 3 281ft high Ploschkogel.
The abbey's Cistercian monks played an important cultural and commercial role in the early development of this part of Styria. Devastated by the Turks, it was fortified in the 15C, then remodelled in the Baroque style in the 18C.

★★ **Stiftskirche** ⊙ – It was a master-builder from Graz, one Johann Georg Stengg, who presided over the transformation of the old Romanesque abbey church, which now has the rank of minor papal basilica. The alignment of the building was changed for reasons of convenience. A new façade, curvilinear in the extreme, resembles a violin in its subtle play of convex and concave forms. A characteristic Baroque trick is the organ topping the main pediment.
The interior, bathed in light, is a stage as much as a church, a splendid setting for the drama of the Mass, best viewed from the grand balconies swelling out from above the side chapels of the nave. *Trompe-l'œil* effects abound in the exuberant and brightly-coloured decor, the work of Josef Adam Mölck, contributing further to a theatricality hardly to be expected among the followers of St Bernard.
The painting on the main altar is by Kremser Schmidt *(qv)*.

Wallfahrtskirche Mariatrost – *7km - 4 miles east via road no 72* (BX). Austria has many of these great pilgrimage churches dedicated to the Virgin Mary standing on a prominent site just outside the city limits. Salzburg is proud of the sanctuary of Maria Plain, Linz is overlooked by Pöstlingberg, Klagenfurt venerates Maria Saal. Graz has Mariatrost, strikingly sited in its leafy suburban setting, easily identifiable by its twin towers resembling organ pipes. This was among the most ambitious of Baroque architectural projects, its aim the exaltation of the Virgin Mary, comforter of humanity. Building began in 1714 under the direction of the architects Stengg, first Andreas, then Johann Georg. Inside, there are murals – much restored – painted between 1735-54 by Lukas von Schramm and Johann Baptist Scheidt, a pulpit by Veit Koniger, and a fine organ, a work from Vorarlberg dating from 1993. An unusual feature is the painting of the **Black Virgin of Czestochowa** in Poland, supported by a pair of angels between the two eastern windows beneath the dome.

Schloß GREILLENSTEIN*

Niederösterreich

Michelin map 426 west of fold 11 – 1km - ½ mile north of Fuglau

Greillenstein castle, with its austere façades and innumerable windows, stands in a wild stretch of country in Waldviertel, to the north of the forests in the River Kamp valley.

The huge castle is laid out according to a square ground plan around a main courtyard relieved by a two-tiered arcaded gallery facing south. The Renaissance building was built between 1570 and 1590 on the ruins of an earlier fortress. A tall entrance tower crowned with four corner turrets dominates the castle. As Greillenstein has always been owned by the same family, many of the castle's original interior fittings have been preserved.

Museum Schloß Greillenstein

Schloß Greillenstein

TOUR ⏱ time: 45min

The castle's perimeter – a balustrade with obelisks and fine sculptures – dates from the 17C and depicts an entire fable: how a raging lion is transformed into the most gentle of beasts, mirroring the triumph of good over evil. A splendid entrance gateway with rusticated columns and a projecting pediment leads into the attractive inner courtyard.

The courtyard balustrade and the six monumental vases were sculpted in stone after sketches by J B Fischer von Erlach. Note the variety of the chimneys, none of which is like another.

Registrar's Office – From the 16C onwards Greillenstein had jurisdiction over an area covering fourteen local villages; the main administrative, fiscal and judicial matters were settled at the castle. The filing cabinets and pigeon holes containing contemporary documents have been preserved.

Courtroom – This baronial courtroom has been preserved in its original state, including the bar where the oath was taken. Minor local cases were heard here. In 1634 Ferdinand II granted Greillenstein the powers of a higher court. In theory this enabled more serious cases to be heard, even those involving the death sentence, although this never actually happened.

Chapel – The chapel is well lit and roofed with a network of delicate pointed vaulting. The **Renaissance altar★** is of an elegant and original design; the entablature, supported on four columns of imitation marble framing a painting of the crucifixion, gives the sanctuary an unusual solemnity.
When the Kuefstein family, the owners of Greillenstein castle, converted from Protestantism to the Catholic faith, they kept the Protestant altar (1603) and placed it to the right of the new altar.

Turkish Room – This room contains a number of souvenirs of a member of the Kuefstein family who was appointed Ambassador to Turkey in 1628. During his two-year stay he succeeded in signing a peace treaty which established a ceasefire lasting 25 years.

GROSSGLOCKNER-HOCHALPENSTRASSE★★★

Salzburg und Kärnten

Michelin map 426 folds 19 and 33

Like the Iseran pass in France and the Susten pass in Switzerland, the Großglockner route *(1)*, opened in 1935, heralded the age of modern Alpine roads designed specifically for motor traffic.

The promotion of tourism loomed large in the concept of this great highway, notably in the construction of two spurs; the first of these leads to the summit of the Edelweiß-Spitze, the second to the Franz-Josephs-Höhe with its view of the dazzling Pasterze glacier at the foot of the highest peak in the Austrian Alps, the Großglockner mountain itself (3 797m - 12 457ft). The first known description of the Großglockner, by the scientist Balthasar Haquet, dates from 1779. Celebrated in myth and legend, the mountain has long attracted crowds of visitors and climbers. The modern road follows in part the course of a much older track.

The area around the Großglockner is an integral part of the **Hohe Tauern National Park** ⊙, 1 800km² - 695sq miles in extent, designated particularly to protect the Alpine flora and fauna.

---

(1) For more detailed information consult the official map-guide Freytag "Großglockner-Hochalpenstraßen" (in German) at a scale of 1:50 000.

The Großglockner

VIENNASLIDE

FROM ZELL AM SEE TO HEILIGENBLUT
75km - 47 miles – day trip with 2 hours 30min driving time.

The Großglockner toll road ⊘ is generally blocked by snow from early November to the beginning of May (the Edelweiß-Spitze and Franz-Josephs-Höhe are often snowed in longer). Avoid arriving at the Franz-Josephs-Höhe at midday as the car parks may be full and there may be a tailback of waiting cars on the road going up.

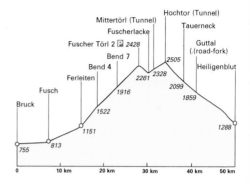

★ **Zell am See** – *See ZELL AM SEE.*

South of Zell am See the road to the Großglockner properly speaking begins at Bruck. It plunges into the **Fuschertal**, a valley whose austere setting and scanty sunshine have not encouraged people to settle there. In the east stand the dark foothills of the Schwarzkopf.

Between Fusch and Ferleiten the route, which is already more hilly, includes a short *corniche* section above a little wooded gorge, the **Bärenschlucht.** Beyond the gorge one begins to see the summits across the end of the valley, particularly the fine **Sonnenwelleck** group, rocky and jagged, and the Fuscherkarkopf, rounded and snow covered, standing to the right of the gap made by the Untere Pfandlscharte (alt 2 663m - 8 737ft).

Stop at a small dam on the right.

Further upstream the Walcherbach falls tumble down the opposite slope.
From Ferleiten to the Fuscher Törl the route continues with several hairpin bends along the east side of the valley. Here it has to climb some 1 300m - 4 200ft – and flat sections are few. The first few miles (hairpin bends nos 1 to 4) are on the level of the Großes Wiesbachhorn and the "3 000m"-"10 000ft" peaks nearby. Above the Piffkar ravine (alt 1 620m - 5 315ft) the views★★ are magnificent towards the Sonnenwelleck group and the Fuscherkarkopf, at the foot of which lies a great natural amphitheatre, streaked with waterfalls, the Käfertal. The view from the Hochmais car park (alt 1 850m - 6 070ft – *information panel 100m above the road)* is particularly impressive. The last larches disappear and the road continues as a *corniche* as far as the bridges of Naßfeld. From here it climbs to the pass across the basins of Naßfeld and passes through a rocky wasteland known as the Witches' Kitchen (Hexenküche). About a mile before the pass there is a botanical nature trail and an information centre on the Hohe Tauern national park (slide show).

Continue to the summit of the Edelweißspitze.

★★ **Edelweißspitze** – Alt 2 577m - 8 455ft. *Coaches are forbidden.* From the observation tower erected on this lookout-peak, the panorama is made especially attractive by the heights enclosing the Fuschertal to the west, the Brennkogel across to the Großes Wiesbachhorn. The peak of the Großglockner can be seen just behind the Sonnenwelleck. To the east, the Goldberg group is more conspicuous for its covering of snow than for its height. Due north the Fuschertal gap opens up a view of the Zell lake, the chalky massifs of the Loforer and the Leoganger Steinberge, and still further to the right, the Steinernes Meer.

★ **Fuscher Törl** – Alt 2 428m - 7 964ft. The road builders used this "little gate" (Törlein) to form a panoramic bend. Leave the car in the Fuscher Törl 2 car park.

The road between the Fuscher Törl and the Hochtor tunnel passes through a somewhat sinister and stony landscape. As the roadway could not pass directly from the Fusch to the Möll valleys – the passes here being blocked by glaciers – the engineers overcame the difficulty by suspending the road above the Seidelwinkl valley, one of the branches of the adjacent Rauris valley. The views are impressive looking east towards the jagged heights of the Goldberg.

Hochtor – The road reaches its highest point 2 505m - 8 218ft – at the north end of the tunnel pierced under the pass (alt 2 575m - 8 448ft). From the south exit there is an open view of the Schober massif.

The winding descent from the Hochtor passes through Alpine pastures within view of the Schober massif, which forms a crown round the Gößnitz valley. At the Tauerneck bend the sharp peak of the Großglockner rises behind the Wasserradkopf foothills and there is a view down into the Heiligenblut basin. From the Guttal ravine, turn right into the "Glacier Road" (Gletscherstraße).

Schöneck - Alt 1 958m - 6 424ft. An excellent bird's-eye view of Heiligenblut. As the Großglockner gets nearer, the **view★★**, soon extending to the tongue of the Pasterze glacier, becomes magnificent. To reach the terrace of the Franz-Josephs-Höhe one must tackle another series of hairpin bends in the Sturmalpe combe.

The artificial Lake Margaritze is retained below the tongue of the glacier by two dams bedded on a rock bar. The reservoir is part of the Glockner-Kaprun, an impressively vast, hydroelectric scheme.

★★★ **Franz-Josephs-Höhe** - On this spur is a large mountain mansion, the Kaiser Franz-Josephs-Haus, to which the Heiligenblut mountaineering school is transferred in summer. This is an institution whose course of training for beginners ends with a climb up the Großglockner.

The "Glacier Road" ends here in a long panoramic terrace, partly hewn in the rock. Go along it, if possible, to the last platform, the Freiwandeck, at an altitude of 2 369m - 7 772ft. At the foot of the Großglockner, buttressed by shining ice and sharp ridges, the magnificent 10km – 6 mile flow of the Pasterze glacier begins. Upstream, at the foot of the Johannisberg icecap, a spur has produced the effect of an eddy, creating a semblance of fluidity.

Pasterzengletscher ⊘ - The descent from Freiwandeck to the glacier is made by funicular (Gletscherbahn).

★★ **Wasserfallwinkel** - Alt 2 548m - 8 360ft. *From Freiwandeck 1 hour 30min Rtn; follow the signs "Zur Hofmanns- und Oberwalder Hütte".* The Gamsgrubenweg, a path, above the Pasterze, leads to the viewpoint.

★★★ **Walk to the Oberwalder Hütte** - *1 hour 15min there and back from the waterfall. This hike is recommended to fit, experienced walkers with sturdy shoes and a good sense of direction, and it should only be undertaken in dry weather.*

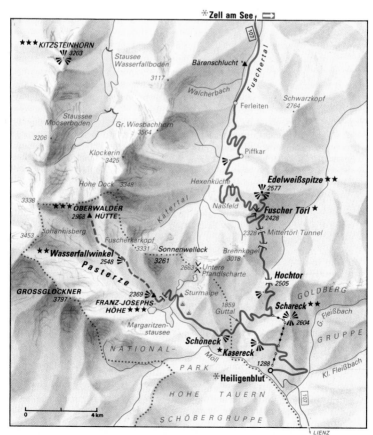

The somewhat steep path leads to the edge of the Bockkar glacier. Turn left along the glacier, cross the waterfall over a small bridge and then *(care is needed)* climb a rocky corridor between two glacier tongues. Carry on to the end of the corridor *(without walking on the glacier itself, which is dangerous)*. There is a magnificent **Alpine panorama**★★★ with a view of the Oberwald refuge on a rocky spur further uphill.

Turn about; at the Guttal fork, go down towards Heiligenblut, opposite the wooded opening of the Gössnitztal. The wooded valley ends in a cascade.

★ **Kasereck** – Alt 1 913m - 6 276ft. Halt on this grassy spur, which has **views**★ of the Großglockner and the Heiligenblut basin.

Near the chalets are grain driers in the form of grilles *(illustration p 47)*. The last hairpin bend, curving above the Fleiß valley, reveals the Sonnblick (alt 3 105m - 10 187ft). Here is the famous view of the church of Heiligenblut, a stone spike standing out against the background of the far-off Großglockner.

★ **Heiligenblut** – *See HEILIGENBLUT.*

GURGLTAL★★

Tirol

Michelin map 426 fold 30 – Local map under ÖTZTAL

The Gurgl valley, which branches off the **upper valley of the Ötz**★★, must number among the most remarkable holiday destinations in the Austrian Tyrol. Its exceptionally beautiful **setting**★★ makes it a favourite location for ramblers and hikers.

Accommodation – There are three possibilities (primarily hotels and guest-houses in the upper comfort quality range): **Untergurgl** (alt 1 793m - 5 883ft); **Obergurgl**✳ (alt 1 930m - 6 332ft), which is particularly pretty with its **view**★ of the glaciated peaks of the Schalfkogel; and the popular winter sports resort **Hochgurgl**✳ (alt 2 150m - 7 054ft).

Ski slopes – These cover 110km – 68 miles of pistes of varying degrees of difficulty at altitudes ranging from 1 800 to 3 082m (5 906 to 10 112ft). They are equipped with 23 ski lifts. The high altitude guarantees snow cover from Christmas to April. The greatest disadvantage of the ski resort is the lack of connections for skiers between Hochgurgl and Obergurgl. The possibilities for cross-country skiers are limited.

★★ **Hohe Mut** ⊙ – Alt 2 653m - 8 704ft. *Allow 1 hour there and back. Take the chairlift up in two stages.*
There is a splendid **panorama**★★ of the Rotmoosferner and Gaisbergferner glaciers to the southeast and of the Manigenbach to the west.

Listed below are several easy walks, which can be combined to make up a pleasant day's outing.

★★ **Walk from the Hohe Mut to the Schönwieshütte** – *400m - 1 312ft drop in altitude.* Those in a hurry can walk straight to the Schönwies refuge in about an hour. It is preferable, however, to follow along the foot of the cliff to the foot of the **Rotmoosferner glacier**★★ and then carry on along the banks of the Gebirgsbach in the valley floor. The path leads through a majestic, captivating **Alpine setting**, dominated by the Liebenerspitze (alt 3 400m - 11 155ft) and Seelenkogel (alt 3 470m - 11 385ft) summits. From the refuge there is a view of the Gamples-kogel peak.
For those who do not wish to take the chairlift to the top of the Hohe Mut can reach the refuge in about an hour along a wide footpath from Obergurgl.

★ **Around the Schönwieshütte** – *Allow 1 hour 30min there and back.* Two easy detours are recommended from the refuge. Go towards the Langtalereckhütte as far as the so-called **Gurgler Alm** (alt 2 252m - 7 388ft), from where there is a **view**★ of the three glaciers higher up with the Schalfkogel (alt 3 540m - 11 614ft) in centre picture.
Return the way you came and turn left shortly before the refuge towards the Schönwieskopf (alt 2 324m - 7 625ft). From the summit, a wide **panorama**★ stretches away over the valley.

★ **Walk from the Schönwieshütte through the Zirbenwald to Obergurgl** – *1 hour 15min on foot, dropping 330m – 1 083ft in altitude. This is a pleasant walk through pretty countryside, with numerous inviting benches along the route.*
From the refuge take a wide footpath towards Obergurgl. Shortly after setting out turn left and take a steep path downhill, waymarked in blue. Next, the path leads past the impressive **Rotmoos waterfall**★. Take the left fork, following a path which leads into the woods and along the valley floor. It is not unusual to catch sight of chamois in this area. There is a good view of Obergurgl and Hochgurgl at the end of the path.

GURK★

Kärnten – Population 1 434
Michelin map 426 fold 36 – Alt 662m - 2 172ft

The cathedral of Gurk, in a cultivated valley in the north of Carinthia, was the seat of a chapter until the see of the province was transferred to Klagenfurt in 1787; it remained almost forgotten through the first half of the 19C. Then archaeologists and ecclesiastical authorities took steps to make it well known and have succeeded in drawing crowds to the church, a masterpiece of Romanesque architecture in Austria. The church furnishings are a revelation of Baroque inspired by the Counter-Reformation.

★★ CATHEDRAL (DOM) *time: 1 hour*

The onion-domed cathedral, which was built from 1140 to 1200 by Prince-Bishop Roman I, Councillor to Frederick Barbarossa, is a symmetrical building with a triple nave and a non-protruding transept. It occupies the site of the first monastery at Gurk, founded in the 11C by the Countess Emma of Friesach-Zeltschach (died in 1045; canonized in 1938 – St Emma), who is still venerated in Carinthia.

After a general view of the façade, severe in style and with two towers, skirt the south side, going through the churchyard.

The careful setting of the stones, with their golden yellow patina, the elegant arched cornice, running along the wall, and the simple style of the chevet, with the shallow apses, are characteristic of the building.

Return to the front porch.

Porch – The porch has had no exterior outlet since the Gothic period, when it was closed by a wall which features stained glass windows (restored) dating from 1340. In the porch are Gothic mural paintings of scenes from the Old and New Testaments, similar in style to the school of Giotto. The Romanesque doorway, with deep splaying, shows elaborate decorative foliage on the pilasters, vaulting and capitals. The panels themselves still have, in the upper third of their surface, medallions carved and painted in 1220.

Interior ⊘ – Some discord is noticeable between the Romanesque structure of the main building, its vaulting with Gothic network and the Baroque furnishings and adornments. The altarpieces of the altars enclose the main and smaller apses. Before examining the furniture and decoration of the church, of which the main features are illustrated on this page, turn and look at the architecture of the narrow vestibule (Innere Vorhalle): the semicircular engaged pilasters have fine Romanesque capitals with palm branches and foliage.

(1) Reliquary of St Emma: an elegant work, in the form of a tree, covered with precious stones.

(2) Samson doorway (Samson slaying the lion): the finest piece of Romanesque sculpture (1180) in Gurk.

(3) and (8) **Carved panels★** (16C) vividly depicting scenes from the life of St Emma.

(4) A gigantic picture – as tradition required – of St Christopher (1250).

(5) **High Altar★★** (1626-1632) with full size, strikingly realistic figures (72 statues, 82 angels' heads), a masterpiece by Michael Hönel from Pirna in Saxony. During Lent the altar is shrouded by a **Fastentuch** (Lenten veil). This is a curtain, intended to deprive believers of the view of the high altar during this time of penance. The curtain at Gurk is a rare example of one entirely decorated with paintings (scenes from the Old and New Testaments).

(6) Stalls (1680): these are the work of a local artisan. They are decoratively carved with the same happy inspiration as the "best" furniture in the peasants' houses.

(7) The 24 Elders of the Apocalypse and the Conversion of St Paul: Gothic murals (1380).

(8) See (3) above.

(9) Altar of the Holy Cross (1740), with a *pietà* in lead by Georg Raphaël Donner, his last piece of work.

(10) **Pulpit★** (Baroque, 1740), one of the most inspired works of the Counter-Reformation, on the triumph of the Church and of Truth (note especially the carvings of the sounding-board). The lead reliefs are the work of Georg Raphael Donner.

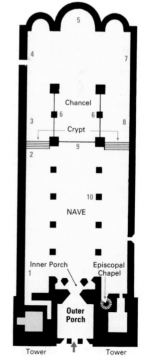

★ **Crypt** ⊙ – A subdued half-light greets visitors to the crypt, which was completed in 1174. This masterpiece of the Romanesque style is supported on 100 marble pillars which seem to form a mysterious underground forest. The stone sarcophagus of St Emma rests on three marble heads and is protected by a Baroque canopy made of red marble.

Episcopal Chapel ⊙ – The chapel is built into the gallery behind the façade and displays an impressive series of Romanesque **murals**★★ in a lively angular style. The general theme, which gives the key to the symbolic meaning of the various scenes, will be found in the Latin inscription over the altar niche: "Here shines in splendour the throne of the great King and of the Lamb." On the walls may be seen the throne of Solomon opposite the Transfiguration of Christ. The vaults of the chapel, one depicting the Garden of Eden, the other a celestial Jerusalem, show an admirable adaptation of ornament to architecture.

Before leaving Gurk look at the large group of 15C and 17C priory buildings once occupied by the cathedral canons.

Bad HALL✠

Oberösterreich – Population 4 060

Michelin map 426 folds 21 – 19km · 12 miles west of Steyr – Alt 388m · 1 273ft

Iodized springs, which are among the most concentrated in Central Europe, and up-to-date equipment for the treatment of diseases of the eyes, heart, and circulatory disorders, make Bad Hall a much sought after spa resort. The thermal park, with paths bordered with fine trees and lawns adorned with clumps of flowers, is well laid out, covering 36ha-89 acres. Generous sports facilities (golf, tennis, themal baths) add to the resort's appeal.

Pfarrkirchen ⊙ – *1km - 1/2 mile southwest.* The **parish church**★ in this village is one of the most attractive of its kind in Austria. Its interior decoration in a charming Rococo style was carried out in around 1744. The frescoes on the vaulting, enhanced by delicate stucco work, make a picture of great harmony glorifying the mystery of the Holy Blood. The pulpit, the organ-loft and the high altar are richly adorned with paintings of cherubs and statues. They are well proportioned and fit perfectly into an ensemble dominated by pastel shades.

HALL IN TIROL★

Tirol – Population 12 622

Michelin map 426 fold 31 – Local map under INNSBRUCK – Alt 581m · 1 906ft

Hall in Tirol was the salt town of the Inn valley. During the Middle Ages, like the mining towns of the Salzkammergut in Upper Austria or the archbishops in Salzburg, it played a leading part in the economic life of the country and was especially cherished by the princes of the Tyrol. From 1303 onwards these granted it liberal constitutional rights and, by comparison with their austere court at Innsbruck, regarded it as a centre for pleasure and amusement.

However, the time is past when Hall marked the starting point of a large volume of river traffic on the Inn and the end of their journey upstream for the rafts of logs which stoked the salt boilers. Hall is still wrapped in the charm of the Middle Ages. This erstwhile mint town with its picturesque old town centre nonetheless keeps firmly in touch with the present; it is a highly active cultural and economic centre.

★ **General View** – An excellent general view of the town may be had from the opposite bank of the Inn *(under the motorway and up the minor road to Tulfes).* In front of the three belfries of the Upper Town can be seen the remains of the former castle, Burg Hasegg, and the **Münzerturm** (Mint Tower) with its curious polygonal crown.

★ **UPPER TOWN** (OBERE STADT) *time: 1 hour*

No traffic is allowed in the Upper Town on Saturday mornings.

Start from the Unterer Stadtplatz (**24**), *an open space formed by the road from Innsbruck to Vienna. Take the Langer Graben up to the Oberer Stadtplatz.*

Oberer Stadtplatz – This irregular open space is surrounded by interest-ing buildings. Several picturesque streets, lined with façades with oriels on several floors grouped together behind grilles, also radiate from the square.

★ **Stadtpfarrkirche** (**A**) – The parish church was built at the end of the 13C, but by the early 14C it was already in need of enlargement. The chancel dates from this period. During 1420 to 1437, Hanns Sewer, the master-builder from Hall, began an ambitious project to extend the building. He faced a hard task, however, as the church, like the rest of the town, stands on an enormous conical pile of

HALL IN TIROL

Agramsgasse 2
Eugenstraße 4
Krippgasse 5
Langer Graben 7
Milserstraße 8
Quarinonigasse 12
Rosengasse 13
Salvatorgasse 14
Scheidensteinstraße ... 15
Schulgasse 16
Schweighofstiege 17
Speckbacherstraße ... 18
Stiftsplatz 20
Unterer Stadtplatz ... 24
Walpachgasse 25

A Stadtpfarrkirche
B Rathaus

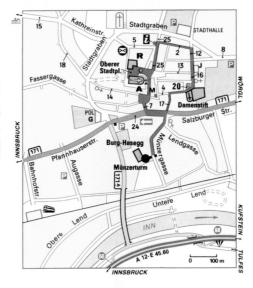

debris, which drops sheer away from the south side of the church. As a result, it was only possible to extend the building to the north, which accounts for the asymmetry which strikes visitors entering the generously proportioned hall-church with its triple nave.

In the 18C, the influence of the Baroque made itself felt on the church **interior,** which boasts ceiling paintings by Josef Adam Mölk and a high altar adorned with a painting by Quellini, a pupil of Rubens. The **Waldaufkapelle** (late 15C) in the north transept houses a Late Gothic figure of the Virgin Mary from the workshop of Michael Pacher.

Rathaus (R) – The town hall is distinguished by its large hipped roof. Once the town fortress – note the tin-clad wall – it consists of two main parts: that to the east with the great stone doorway, which dates from the Renaissance; that to the west is the royal residence, which was donated to the town by Duke Leopold IV in 1406. The council chamber is particularly handsome, with a beamed ceiling dating from 1451.

Walk up the Wallpachgasse (25) for a clear view of the Bettelwurfkette mountains (Karwendel massif).

Follow the Agramgasse (2), the Quarinongasse (12) and the Schulgasse (16) to the Stiftsplatz.

Stiftsplatz (20) – Contrasting with the fantasy of the medieval town, the classical arrangement of this square is entirely harmonious, bounded as it is on the east by the sober façades of the former college and church of the Jesuits (transformed into a concert hall), and on the south by those of the Damenstift (former convent for noble ladies).

Damenstift – Archduchess Magdalena, the sister of Archduke Ferdinand II, founded this ladies' abbey in 1567-69. The stucco work and main doorway date from 1691. The **west front★** with its four full-length fluted pilasters is a fine example of the transition from the Renaissance to the Baroque style.

Return to the Unterer Stadtplatz via the Eugenstraße (4) and the Schweigerhofstiege steps (17) to the left. Follow the Münzergasse to Burg Hasegg.

Burg Hasegg ⊙ – Dominated by its famous tower, the castle originated as a strongpoint controlling river traffic. It took on its historical importance in 1567, when the rulers of Tyrol transferred their mint here. The most famous coin produced in Hall was the **Haller Silbertaler** (silver dollar), accepted all over Europe until the early 19C. In 1975 the **mint** started production again; it is open to the public.

Also in the castle is the **Stadtmuseum** ⊙ with a rich collection of exhibits on the history of the town.

From the top of the **Münzerturm** *(200 steps)* there is a splendid view of the town and the impressive mountain range to the north with the Bettelwurf peak (alt 2 726m - 8 944ft).

Return to the Unterer Stadtplatz.

The key on the inside front cover explains the abbreviations and symbols used in the text or on the maps

HALLEIN

Salzburg – Population 20 000

Michelin map 426 fold 20 – Local map under SALZKAMMERGUT

Alt 461m-1 513ft

The history of Hallein has been much influenced by that "white gold-dust", salt. Everyday life is concentrated nowadays in Hallein's squares and the attractive pedestrian zone at the heart of the town. However, lovingly restored old houses, sleepy alleyways and other romantic spots are still to be found in the picturesque old town. Hallein is the economic centre for the whole of the region, and a major focal point for local cultural, economic and leisure activities.

High above Hallein lies the spa resort of **Bad Dürrnberg**, site of important prehistoric archaeological finds.

Located in the upper town on the north side of the parish church are the home and tomb of **Franz-Xaver Gruber** (1787-1863), the composer of the famous carol *Stille Nacht, Heilige Nacht (Silent night, Holy night)*.

Salzbergwerk Dürrnberg ⊙ – From the upper station of the cable-car to the salt mines, make for the entrance of the mines, towards Bad Dürrnberg. On the way, you will pass the pilgrimage church of Mariä Himmelfahrt, built from local pink marble in the early 17C by Italian master-builders under Archbishop Wolf Dietrich. Between the church and the salt mines lies the only Celtic open-air museum in Europe. It includes a reconstructed Celtic village and a royal grave. The tour of the oldest mine in the world open to the public entails a trip in the mine train, and a walk along a footpath through several galleries. A double toboggan (Doppelrutschen) leads down into the depths of the mountain. The visit ends with a raft trip across the floodlit underground salt lake.

Salzbergwerk Dürrnberg

Dürrnberg salt mines

The mountains in Austria provide many miles of Alpine skiing or cross-country skiing suitable for all levels of expertise.

To choose an Austrian ski resort, consult the map of places to stay on pages 12 and 13 and the table in the Practical information section.

The Calendar of events in the Practical information section gives details (date, place and description) of the most popular sporting and cultural events in Austria.

HALLSTATT★★

Oberösterreich – Population 1 131

Michelin map 426 fold 21 – Local map under SALZKAMMERGUT

Alt 511m-1 677ft

The village of Hallstatt clings to the steep slope of a foothill of the Dachstein and takes its name from the **lake★★**, the Hallstätter See, into whose dark waters the slope dips. Hallstatt provides a picture of romantic Austria with streets so narrow and so steep that it has become customary to make the popular Corpus Christi procession on the lake in boats.

A Cradle of Civilization – The salt mines in the neighbouring mountains have been exploited since the Neolithic Era. Although mining began in 3000 BC on a local scale, during the first millenium it developed into a European enterprise; there is proof that the salt was distributed by the trade routes as far as the Baltic in the north and the Mediterranean in the south. It was their iron and bronze tools that enabled the miners of Hallstatt to become masters of the art of salt extraction. So many traces of salt mining have been found in the vicinity of Hallstatt (excavation of 2 000 graves) that the name has been given to the **Hallstatt Period** (1000-500 BC), which was marked by the development of iron metallurgy and Celtic immigration into Gaul. Hallstatt artefacts are displayed in the local prehistoric museum, **Prähistorisches Museum** ⊙, in the natural history museum in Vienna and in the collection of antiquities at Schloß Eggenberg near Graz.

The salt mines, **Salzbergwerk** ⊙ are still being worked in the Salzburg hanging valley, where the excavations took place, and the galleries may be visited. *Allow 3 hours for this excursion taking the funicular from Lahn.*

Hallstatt

SIGHTS *time: 1 hour*

Leave the car on one of the **viewing terraces**★ constructed above the town at the halfway point on the underground one-way bypass (the north-south terrace is open-air; the south-north terrace is covered). Go down the steps marked "Abgang zur Stadt" and turn left into the pretty street leading up to the church (Kirchenweg).

Pfarrkirche - In the romantic **setting**★★ of its churchyard bordering the lake, this massive building of the late 15C is flanked by a squat tower whose peculiar roof, with its overhanging eaves, suggests some Chinese building, in contrast with the pointed steeple of the Protestant church built on the lakeshore in the 19C.
Inside, the hall-type nave and chancel are double, with star vaulting, bearing witness to the taste for twin naves which became fashionable in the mountain districts of Austria at the end of the Gothic period. The large **altarpiece**★ on the high altar, presented by a rich *Salzfertiger* (salt merchant), represents the Virgin between St Barbara and St Catherine *(centre panel)*. It was painted between 1505 and 1515.

St. Michaelskapelle - *North of the church, beyond the tiny cemetery.* The lower storey of this Gothic church houses the parish charnelhouse, in use since 1600 as the cemetery is so small. Of the 1 200 skulls contained here, 700 are inscribed with the date of death, the age, the profession etc. of their previous occupants and painted with motifs such as roses, laurel, ivy or oak leaves.
Return and go down the Kirchenweg; turn right after the covered passage.

Heimatmuseum ⊘ - The local museum is in a picturesque house abutting on the rock and contains collections of folklore and history.
Return to the lower town in order to take a walk along the lakeshore; and then to the car by way of the Kirchenweg and the stairs leading to the viewpoint terraces.

HEILIGENBLUT ✻

Kärnten – Population 1 334

Michelin map 426 fold 33 – Local map under GROSSGLOCKNER – Alt 1 288m - 4 226ft

Heiligenblut, at the foot of the south slope of the Großglockner, is a welcome return to civilization for the tourist who has just traversed the lonely upper mountains. The **site**★ of the church is picturesque; the slim building with its steeple in silhouette against the Großglockner. Owing to the town's proximity to the Franz-Josephs-Höhe training school *(see GROSSGLOCKNER)*, it has become a mountaineering centre.

✻ **Ski slopes** - These stretch between the Schareck, Gjaidtroghöhe and Viehbühel peaks at altitudes from 1 300m to 2 900m (4 265ft to 7 431ft). Keen skiers will find 12 ski lifts and 55km - 34 miles of pistes of an average level of difficulty, well laid out through the rugged, treeless Alpine landscape. In spite of the high altitude, snow conditions can begin to deteriorate from as early as March. A big advantage of this resort is that skiers can almost lose themselves in the snowy expanses, giving themselves the impression of skiing along some private piste.

Church ⊙ - The church was built between 1430 and 1483 by the monks of Admont, to perpetuate their devotion to a relic of the Holy Blood (Heiliges Blut). The chancel stands on a twin-aisled crypt containing the tomb of Briccius, an officer of the Imperial Court of Byzantium, who is said to have brought the precious substance there in the 10C. This and the nave, whose pillars without capitals reveal that it was built at a later date, are roofed, in the late Gothic tradition, with network and star vaulting. The side galleries of the nave were necessary to accommodate crowds of pilgrims.

Outstanding among the church's furnishings are the great **altarpiece** on the high altar (1520), attributed to the school of Michael Pacher, and the ornately sculpted Gothic canopy (1496) carved in pale standstone.

★★ **Schareck** ⊙ - Alt 2 604m - 8 543ft. *Cable-car ascent in two stages, then 10min on foot to the summit (marked by a cross).*

The impressive **panorama**★★ stretches over the pyramidal Schildberg and the Großglockner range to the west, and to the east the Gjaidtrog, the highest point of the ski slopes, with the Hocharn to its left.

Schloß HERBERSTEIN ★

Steiermark

Michelin map 426 folds 24, 38

The castle complex of Herberstein is one of the largest architectural feats in Styria. It is perched on a rocky spur, surrounded on three sides by the course of the Feistritz, in the middle of a rugged gorge.

Its origins date back to over 700 years ago. After the initial building was completed in the 13C, numerous modifications and extensions were carried out until the 17C, resulting in the final magnificent palace compound with its elaborate layout. The Gothic, Renaissance and Baroque styles have left their mark on the building in the form of architectural features typical of each period. In this way, Herberstein retraces very vividly cultural evolution from the early Middle Ages up to modern times. The history of the Herberstein family, which has occupied the castle without a break from 1290 to the present, is intricately linked with that of the building itself.

TOUR *1 hour*

The walk from the car park to the castle *(15min on foot, or take the transport provided, "Herberstein-Erlebnisexpress")* provides a good view of the church and presbytery in St. Johann-bei-Herberstein, formerly part of an Augustinian abbey.

Courtyard - This is perhaps the most Italian of the arcaded courtyards in Styria. With its slim columns and crowning balustrade it is entitled to its exotic name, the Florentine courtyard. In the past jousting was held here.

Interior ⊙ - The twelve furnished rooms display many historical and family souvenirs; they also house annual exhibitions.

Tierpark ⊙ - The animal park continues an old tradition, since the castle grounds used to be a game reserve.

A natural setting of rocky outcrops, ancient trees and terraced hillsides provides the perfect habitat for 600 kinds of animal from five continents. All that separates visitors from some of the animals, such as bison, Przewalski's horses and Hartmann's mountain zebras, is a ditch. From time to time the footpaths lead straight through the enclosure.

Stift HERZOGENBURG ★

Niederösterreich

Michelin map 426 fold 11 - 12km - 7 miles north of St. Pölten

The Augustinian Canons' Monastery at Herzogenburg, founded at the beginning of the 12C by Bishop Ulrich of Passau, has enjoyed a prosperity to which the collections of works of art and manuscripts bear witness. The church and monastery buildings were virtually rebuilt in the Baroque style in the 18C.

TOUR ⊙ *time: 1 hour*

Church - Franz Munggenast was in charge of the building of the church. The tower is crowned with the most unusual motif of a cushion bearing a replica of a ducal headdress, attributed to Fischer von Erlach. Inside the church, the paintings and stucco go well with the church's Baroque architecture. A series of domes rests on columns surmounted with Corinthian capitals. All the vaulting is painted with frescoes, as are the altarpieces on the side altars, by Bartolomeo Altomonte. The pictures on the high altar, painted by Daniel Gran, show great skill in the art of composition: the Virgin and Child are flanked by the patron saints of the monastery, St George and St Stephen.

Monastic buildings – These buildings were designed by Jakob Prandtauer who oversaw construction work until his death in 1726. The central section of the east wing, the work of Fischer von Erlach, is of particular interest. The vaulting of the main hall (Festsaal) is adorned with a huge allegorical composition by Altomonte to the glory of the Prince-Bishops of Passau. Decorated with pictures, frescoes and *grisailles* (paintings in tones of grey), the library contains more than 80 000 works. One room, exposing Gothic art, contains a collection of 16C **paintings on wood**★, belonging to the Danubian School, among which are four panels by Jörg Breu representing scenes from the Passion on the outside and the Life of the Virgin inside.

Burg HOCHOSTERWITZ★

Kärnten

Michelin map 426 fold 36

9km - 6 miles east of St. Veit an der Glan – Local map under ST. VEIT AN DER GLAN

The castle of Hochosterwitz, standing on a height in the St. Veit basin on the edge of the Zollfeld, the cradle of Carinthia *(see MARIA SAAL)*, has remained the property of the Khevenhüller family since 1571. It is worth seeing chiefly for its **site**★★, like an eagle's eyrie. The ramp leading up to it, fortified with extraordinary care in view of the Turkish threat, is no less interesting.

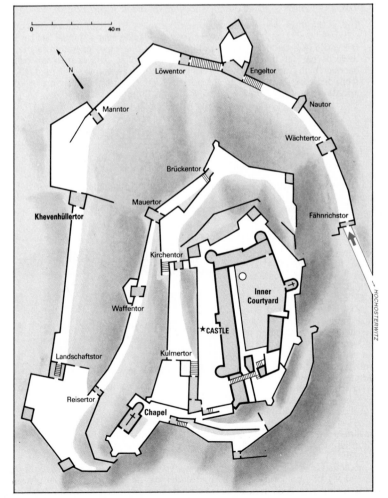

Burg HOCHOSTERWITZ

TOUR ⓥ *time: about 1 hour on foot Rtn, or else use the lift*

Drive through the hamlet of Hochosterwitz at the foot of the rock and take the by-road up to the castle. Leave the car in the car park. The battlemented castle is approached by a ramp constructed between 1570 and 1586 by Georg Khevenhüller (1534-1587), Governor of Carinthia.

There are fourteen gateways along the way; the natural gaps in the ravine were used to form centres of resistance isolated behind drawbridges. The largest gateway is the 7th, known as the Khevenhüllertor (1582), surmounted by a lion's head and a bust of Georg Khevenhüller. At the end of the climb, with many **views** of the hilly St. Veit area, from which the Ulrichberg mound emerges, one passes the castle chapel (Burgkapelle) and reaches the **inner courtard** (Innerer Burghof), now a rustic café-restaurant. Certain rooms of the castle are open to visitors. Exhibited are collections of arms and armour belonging to the Khevenhüller family.

NB This guide adopts German alphabetical order, in which the vowels ä, ö, and ü are classified under ae, oe and ue respectively.

HÖLLENTAL★★

Niederösterreich

Michelin map 426 fold 24 – northwest of Gloggnitz

Höllental, or Hell's Valley, is the name given to the gap made by the Schwarza River between the two chalky massifs of the Schneeberg and the Raxalpe.

FROM SCHWARZAU TO HIRSCHWANG
18km - 11 miles - about 30min - local map under SCHNEEBERG

This is the most picturesque section of the valley. The road follows the course of the Schwarza, a torrent with green waters leaping over a shingle bed cut into the rocks. A little after Schwarzau im Gebirge fine views open out on the left towards part of the Schneeberg massif. The valley gets deeper and deeper between high craggy slopes. Fir trees cling to the greyish rocks; the road crosses from one bank of the river to the other. At Hirschwang the valley grows wider and its sides lower, marking the end of the "infernal" section.

Schloß-Museum HOHENBRUNN★★

Oberösterreich

Michelin map 426 fold 9 – 1.5km - 1 mile west of Markt St. Florian

Too large for a hunting lodge and too open to the surrounding country ever to have made any pretence at defence, Schloß Hohenbrunn, with its many windows and handsome arcades, is set like a Palladian villa in an attractive natural setting.

It was built between 1722 and 1732 for a prior at the abbey of St. Florian on a piece of land which he had inherited from his family. The buildings, erected on a square plan round a central courtyard, were designed by one of Austria's most celebrated Baroque architects, the Tyrolean **Jakob Prandtauer**. Hohenbrunn is in fact the only castle that can be attributed with any certainty to Prandtauer, to whom the abbeys at Melk and Herzogenburg are attributed. He also put the final touches to the abbey of St. Florian

Schloß Hohenbrunn

and, after his death, the work was completed by Jakob Steinhueber, a foreman working at the abbey. The castle owes its name (Hoher Brunnen = high fountain) to a pumping appliance originally installed in a tower flanking the south façade.

The castle was in a state of considerable disrepair in 1963 when it was bought from the abbey of St. Florian and restored under the auspices of the local provincial authority. Since 1967 it has housed an interesting hunting museum.

★★ JAGDMUSEUM ⊙ *time: 1 hour*

The exhibition of numerous weapons, models, plaster casts of footprints and stuffed animals provides a fascinating and informative exploration of hunting in Upper Austria. Objects of historic interest include the hunting clothes of Emperor Franz Joseph I and an extraordinary rifle (3.12m - 10ft 3in long) belonging to the Archduke Karl Salvator. The **porcelain collection** is unparalleled in Europe.

A tour of the museum provides an opportunity to visit most of the castle. Even the non-specialist visitor will find interest in the exhibits which in no way detract from the elegant but rural character of the castle interior.

HOHENTAUERNPASSSTRASSE★

Steiermark

Michelin map 426 folds 22 and 36

The Hohentauern pass (alt 1 265m - 4 150ft), known still as the Triebener Tauern or **Rottenmanner Tauern**, leads to a narrow road locally called the **Tauernstraße** (the Tauern Road). This was used long ago by the Romans as a link between Juvavum (Salzburg) and Virunum (near Klagenfurt). *See map of Roman provinces in the Introduction: Historical table and notes.*

The freshness and transquillity of the Pölstal makes this difficult mountainous section worthwhile. Near the Möderbrugg the valley is dotted with dilapidated mining or industrial buildings, survivals of a vanished industry based on silver mining and silver and metal work by artisans. Compared with the Pölstal, the crossing of the Schober pass by the main road from Trieben to Leoben is a mere formality.

FROM JUDENBURG TO LIEZEN *73km - 45 miles - about 3 hours*

The steep gradients on the north slope of the pass call for great care. It is best to travel from Judenburg to Liezen in order to take this section downhill.

Judenburg - *See PACK- und STUBALPENSTRASSE.*

Branching off from the Vienna-Klagenfurt road, 6km - 4 miles from Judenburg, the Trieben road crosses to the north bank of the Mur. It climbs briefly on the last slopes of the Falkenberg - there are pretty views upstream of the wide valley overlooked by the Bocksruck - to enter the Pölsbach valley over the slight shelf of the Pölshals. To the rear, the ruins of Reifenstein *(right)* dominate the industrial settlement of Pöls (cellulose industry). Ahead, far off, the jagged crests of the Hochschwung loom on the horizon.

Unterzeiring - The buildings of a former fortified priory attached to Admont and the crumbling castle ruins of Burg Hanfelden lend distinction to this village.

Oberzeiring - *1.5km - 1 mile off the Hohentauern road (take the fork signposted Unterzeiring).*

This is an old mining village with a disused silver mine, **Silberbergwerk** ⊙, open to the public *(Schaubergwerk).*

Möderbrugg - Several artificial water falls, here enclosed in old wooden troughs, recall the time when the noise of the little hammers used for iron-beating was heard in the village.

Huge squat barns are visible one above the other, on the slopes of the Pölstal. After the tiny resort of St. Johann am Tauern the climb becomes steeper. To the left rises the Großer Bösenstein, from the foot of which the Polster pass rises in a smooth curve. At last one reaches the upper combe of the pass, a quiet setting for the little resort of Hohentauern.

On the north slope of the mountain the road plunges into the Wolfsgraben, a dark gorge of the Triebenbach, to emerge finally on the mountainside above Trieben. The Paltental unfolds between Trieben and Selzthal. The valley is used by the main road from Graz to Salzburg.

Rottenmann - This little town was once enriched by the traffic in salt. It still has its *Straßenplatz (qv)*, its priory near the church, some traces of town walls (behind the church on the mountainside), and makes a pleasant halt.

The high perched shape of the fortress of Strechau, formerly a refuge for Protestants in Upper Styria, lends attraction to the drive from Rottenmann to Selzthal. At Liezen there are extensive views of the Enns gap and, from the bridge over the torrent, the Großer Grimming (alt 2 351m - 7 713ft), an outcrop of the Dachstein (southwest).

The key on the inside front cover explains the abbreviations and symbols used in the text or on the maps

INNSBRUCK★★

L Tirol – Population 116 100
Michelin map 426 fold 31
Local maps under Excursions below and SEEFELDER SATTELSTRASSEN
Alt 574m - 1 883ft

Innsbruck (literally, Bridge over the Inn) is at the junction of the Inn valley and the Sill gap, on the busy road which runs, parallel with the equally busy railway line, towards Italy. Several million cars a year are driven along it towards the Brenner pass and the south. Innsbruck is the cultural and tourist capital of the Tyrol and, besides Grenoble and Bolzano, the only town of more than 100 000 inhabitants within the Alpine range.

The view along the Maria-Theresien-Straße towards the steep slopes of the Nordkette (Karwendel mountain range) combines townscape and landscape to form a **picture★★** which has a leading place in the illustrations of glossy tourist literature on Europe.

Many aspects of local behaviour show how closely man is linked with mountain life. At Innsbruck itself, though the altitude is less than 600m - 2 000ft it is not unusual, in winter, to see employees and students devoting their midday break to the ski-runs starting from Seegrube, the halfway station of the Nordkette cable-car. The 1964 Winter Olympic Games marked a decisive development in the tourist amenities of Innsbruck: a ski-jump was constructed at Bergisel, an ice-stadium erected (indoor ice-rink) and an airport built. The superior quality of this equipment brought to the city the 1976 Winter Olympic Games – the already existing installations were improved and new equipment was built (speed skating track).

The city is almost overrun by tourists in the summer but benefits from the historic centre having been made into a pedestrianised zone. The relative lack of industry here has enabled Innsbruck to keep its charming provincial character, once the main thoroughfares are left behind.

HISTORICAL NOTES

The Tyrol came into existence as a state in the 12C, on the southern slopes of the Alps, an area which is now part of Italy but was then under the jurisdiction of the Counts of Tyrol whose seat was above Merano.

In the 14C the Tyrol came under the Habsburgs. Power weighed in favour of the territories in the Inn valley, on the northern slopes of the mountain chain, and Innsbruck, now the capital, enjoyed a long heyday, particularly during the reign of Maximilian I.

"The Last Knight" – **Maximilian of Habsburg**, who was especially fond of the Tyrol, was invested with Imperial rank in 1493. A great hunter, he believed that this sport was of prime importance for princes, since it enabled them to make contact with their more humble subjects.

"Max" married, as his first wife, Maria of Burgundy, the daughter of Charles the Bold, and by the increase of territorial power which their union brought him, justified the couplet so often applied to the Habsburg monarchy in later days:

"Bella gerant alii, tu, felix Austria, nube
Nam quae Mars aliis, dat tibi regna Venus."
i.e." Let others war, thou, happy Austria, wed;
What some owe Mars, from Venus take instead."

It was in the parish church of St. Jakob in Innsbruck that the second marriage of the Emperor, with Bianca Maria Sforza, took place in 1494.

Soon afterwards the Emperor had the famous **Goldenes Dachl** erected. This depicted him with his two wives and became the town's emblem. In fact his attachment went further than this; he chose Innsbruck as his burial-place and ordered the sumptuous Hofkirche as his mausoleum. This building, however, never received the remains of the Emperor, as the town gates were closed against him by the burghers, who were exasperated at the debts left by the noblemen in his suite. He died in 1519 at Wels and was buried at Wiener Neustadt, his birthplace.

From Laughter to Tears (18C) – Innsbruck also enjoyed a period of splendour under the reign of Maria Theresa. In 1750 the famous picture of the *Madonna* by Lucas Cranach – withdrawn from the former church of St. Jakob which was badly damaged by an earthquake – was reinstalled in the rebuilt parish church. The Empress knelt in the state car which carried the picture. At the end of the procession was a boy of nine, proudly wearing Hungarian national dress. He was the future Joseph II.

In 1765 the town was enlivened by new celebrations, dynastic this time. The Imperial family was celebrating the marriage of Leopold, Grand Duke of Tuscany, with the Infanta of Spain, Maria Ludovica. A triumphal arch was erected at the head of Maria-Theresien-Straße. Then the Emperor Franz suddenly died. That is why the triumphal arch, which dates from these events, is devoted equally to earthly glories and to funeral trappings.

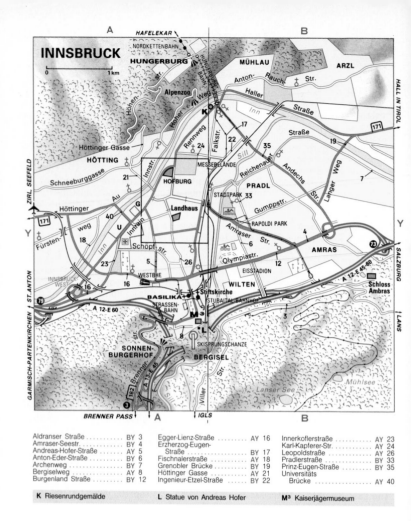

INNSBRUCK

0   1 km

Aldranser Straße	BY 3	Egger-Lienz-Straße	AY 16	Innerkoflerstraße	AY 23
Amraser-Seestr.	BY 4	Erzherzog-Eugen-		Karl-Kapferer-Str.	AY 24
Andreas-Hofer-Straße	AY 5	Straße	BY 17	Leopoldstraße	AY 26
Anton-Eder-Straße	BY 6	Fischnalerstraße	AY 18	Pradlerstraße	BY 33
Archenweg	BY 7	Grenobler Brücke	BY 19	Prinz-Eugen-Straße	BY 35
Bergiselweg	AY 8	Höttinger Gasse	AY 21	Universitäts	
Burgenland Straße	BY 12	Ingenieur-Etzel-Straße	BY 22	Brücke	AY 40

K Riesenrundgemälde   **L** Statue von Andreas Hofer   **M³** Kaiserjägermuseum

GENERAL VIEW

In the town itself the belfry (Stadtturm - *see below*) can be used as an observatory. To get a general view go up to the **Hungerburg★** (AY), either by car via the Alte Innbrücke (Old Bridge over the Inn), the Höttinger Gasse, the Hötting church and the Höhenstraße, or by **funicular** ⊙ (Hungerburgbahn). From the terrace there is a view of the whole town and the majestic peaks of the Serles and Nockspitze marking the entrance to the tranquil Stubaital to the south. Travellers descending by car from the Brenner by road no 182 will look for the view at Sonnenburgerhof on one of the last bends in the road; from this corner by the tram crossing there is a remarkable **view★★** of the whole of Innsbruck.

OLD INNSBRUCK *time: 4 hours*

Leave from the Annasäule, a column in Maria-Theresien-Straße.

★ **Maria-Theresien-Straße** (CZ) – This lively "street-square" has an imposing **vista★★** of the Nordkette, with its rocky crown rising to an altitude of 2 334m - 7 657ft. The foreground is punctuated by the bulbous towers of the Spitalskirche and the belfry. A variety of attractive old houses are to be found in this street, such as the Palais Lodron at no 11, the Palais Troyer-Spaur (1681-83) at no 39, the late 17C, baroque style Palais Trapp-Wolkenstein at no 38 and the Palais Sarntheim at no 59. The tall, white Annasäule against the greenish ochre background of the façades of the houses, is a favourite subject for amateur photographers.

Annasäule (CZ A) – This monumental column, set up in 1706, commemorates 26 July 1703 – the birthday of St Anne – when the Bavarian invaders retreated during the War of the Spanish Succession (1703). The Virgin Mary has the place of honour on the top of the slim column, St Anne appearing only on the base beside St George, once the protector of the Tyrol, together with Sts Vigilius and Cassianus, who are the patron saints of Trent and Bressanone and whose dioceses formed the basis of the territorial unity of the region.

Prolonging the Maria-Theresien-Straße is the Herzog-Friedrich-Straße, a busy street, whose arcades contain shops. In the centre of the street stands the Goldenes Dachl.

Stadtturm (Belfry) (CZ B)⊙ – The belfry stands beside the old town hall. The tower has a square base from which rises an octagonal Renaissance structure, bristling with turrets and crowned with a dome and a small lantern. A staircase leads to a viewing platform from which there is a fine **panorama**★ over the city.

★ **Goldenes Dachl (Little Golden Roof) (CZ)** – This charming, ornate structure, finished was 1500, was added to the style-less building which took the place of the former ducal palace. According to a tradition, which the most cultivated Tyrolese are sorry to see denied by irrefutable evidence, it was Friedrich the Penniless, Duke of the Tyrol (1406-1439), who, wishing to put an end to the jokes about his poverty, had the little roof of the structure, in full view of passers-by, covered with golden coins. As a matter of fact, the work dates from the reign of Maximilian and symbolizes the power of the Habsburgs. The whole thing, Gothic in style with its decoration growing richer as it rises towards the roof, bears witness to the growing influence of the Renaissance.

The balustrade on the 1st floor is adorned with a frieze of delicately carved coats of arms, representing, from left to right, Styria (set back), Austria, Hungary, the Holy Roman Empire (a double-headed eagle), the kingdom of Germany (a single-headed eagle and a golden fleece), Philip the Fair (Maximilian's son), the Sforzas of Milan and the Tyrol (set back).

The 2nd storey looks like a lavishly decorated loggia. The designs on the balustrade, by the same hand as those on the 1st floor, include, in the centre, two pictures of Maximilian. On the left, the Emperor turns towards his second wife, Bianca Maria Sforza, who can be recognized by her long hair and her Italian headdress. The portrait of Maria, Maximilian's first wife, wearing

Goldenes Dachl, Innsbruck

the Burgundian headdress, completes the trio. On the right, Maximilian stands between his councillor (on the right) and his jester (on the left). The side panels each represent a couple of acrobatic dancers. The ensemble, the amusing work of a Swabian sculptor Niklas Türing the Elder who was for a long time unknown, was used as the royal lodge during popular festivals and when tournaments were held. All the original carvings, owing to their damaged condition, have been replaced by copies but the originals can be inspected in the Tiroler Landesmuseum Ferdinandeum *(see below)*.

★ **Helblinghaus (CZ)** – *Photograph p 134.* This house at the opposite corner of the Herzog-Friedrich-Straße was given a Rococo facing in the 18C, displaying lavishly decorated window frames and a highly decorated pediment. The arrangement of the windows in convex bows – a remedy for the lack of sunlight in the narrow streets of old cities – is still often seen in southern Germany. Further to the left, towards the quays on the river, is the historic inn named the Goldener Adler (Golden Eagle) (**E**). It is proud of the guests it has received since the 16C and displays their names on a marble plaque outside.

Return along Maria-Theresien-Straße, to take Pfarrgasse, which leads to the Domplatz.

Dom zu St. Jakob (CZ)⊙ – The cathedral building, which was rebuilt at the beginning of the 18C, remains essentially the church of the Roman Catholic Old Tyrol.

The **interior**, in the Baroque style, is roofed with domes – three on the nave and a dome with a lantern on the chancel – decorated in 1722 by a famous pair of artists from Munich, Cosmas Damian Asam (painter) and his brother Egid Quirin Asam (stucco worker); their compositions, with clever effects of perspective, glorify the Trinity and the intercessions of St James. Above the high altar the picture of *Our Lady of Succour* (Mariahilf), painted by Lucas Cranach the Elder and presented by the Elector of Saxony to the Archduke Leopold of the Tyrol, who took it with him on all his travels, is an object of deep devotion. In the north transept is the canopied tomb of the Archduke Maximilian (who must not be confused with the Emperor of Austria), a Grand Master of the Teutonic Order, who died in 1618. This tomb, which was restored to its original state in 1950, adds to the furnishings of the church a note of gravity which contrasts with the decorative exuberance of the pulpit and organ.

Round the cathedral of St. Jakob is the colourful old town with its ancient, balconied houses with picturesque signs, reliefs, stuccowork and frescoes.

Turn back. At the Goldenes Dachl, turn left into the narrow Hofgasse, then, after a covered alley, left again into Rennweg, which skirts the Hofburg.

★ **Hofburg** (CZ) ⊘ – On the site where the Habsburg princes of the Tyrolean branch of the family (Leopold III, Friedrich IV the Penniless and Sigismund the Rich) had little by little had a large and rather disjointed building constructed, Maximilian I had a castle of the present dimensions built, which was modified under Maria Theresa between 1766 and 1770. The long façade, flanked by two domed towers, was finished in 1770 and is a typical example of the evolution of Baroque civil architecture in Innsbruck.

Inside, the state rooms, which may be visited, are devoted to the glories of the Tyrol and of the Habsburg monarchy, especially the **Riesensaal**★★ (Giants' Hall). This state room, lined with stucco panels with a porcelain finish, is about 31.5m - 100ft long. The ceiling fresco was painted by Franz-Anton Maulpertsch in 1776. The main theme is the triumph of the House of Habsburg-Lorraine, personified by two women holding their hands out to one another (note among the symbols the green shoot sprouting from a dead tree trunk).

On the walls are full-length portraits of Maria Theresa's children following the Imperial couple in procession. Numerous other portraits include those of Louis XVI and Marie-Antoinette.

Return to the Rennweg and enter the Hofkirche (enter through the Tiroler Volkskunstmuseum to the left of the church).

Hofkirche (CZ) ⊘ – This church was built by Ferdinand I *(see genealogical tree in the Introduction: Historical table and notes)* who finally implemented the projects of his grandfather Maximilian I. The nave with its three aisles, all equal in size, built to contain Maximilian's mausoleum, is still Gothic in style, although masked in part by Renaissance (tower, entrance porch, capitals) and Baroque additions (stuccowork).

On the gallery are placed the 23 statuettes of the protecting saints of the Habsburg family. The comparative grace of these effigies contrasts with the sombre colossi who actually stand guard over the tomb.

★★ **Maximilian's Mausoleum** (Grabmal Kaiser Maximilians I) – This tomb is the most important specimen left to us of German Renaissance sculpture. The Emperor intended it to glorify the splendours of his reign and also to record the flawless legitimacy of the Holy Roman Emperors as the heirs of the Caesars.

The original plan was grandiose but not beyond the bounds of possibility, for Innsbruck at that time enjoyed international renown for its bell founders and armour makers. The plan included, in particular, 40 large statues, 100 small

On the banks of the Inn

bronzes of saints and 34 busts of Roman emperors. In spite of a century of work this programme was not fully completed when, in 1584, the casting of the kneeling statue of Maximilian, which crowns the structure, marked the end of the work.

The 28 impressive, larger-than-life-size statues of the "black fellows", as the people of Innsbruck call them, all in bronze save two which are in copper, stand on guard over the empty tomb. A torch could be set in the right hand of each during funeral services. The choice of figures is sometimes unexpected: it takes into account the ties of blood and marriage. Here are the royal families of Habsburg, Burgundy and Austria, but also the purely sentimental lineage of heroes of chivalry or precursors of medieval Christianity: King Arthur, Theodoric of Verona and Clovis. The contribution of Albrecht Dürer undoubtedly raises the artistic level of the group, with the statues of King Arthur - a British-looking type in armour ! - and of Theodoric, a supple and vigorous work. These figures are of inestimable value to those interested in the history of fashion. The tomb itself is surrounded by a splendid Renaissance grille in which, according to the Tyrolean taste of the period *(see STAMS)*, wrought iron and embossed sheet-metal are combined. It is surmounted

Mausoleum of Maximilian I

Wiesenhofer/ÖSTERREICH WERBUNG

by the kneeling statue of Maximilian and supported at the four corners by statues of the cardinal virtues, all carved by **Alexandre Colin** of Mechelen (Malines) in Flanders (1527-1612). Reliefs in marble, all except three panels, by this same Alexandre Colin, cover the sides of the structure, depicting great events of the reign (battles, weddings, etc.).

After going round the tomb do not neglect the Renaissance furnishings of the chancel and church and, on the north side, the gallery known as the Princes' Chancel and the 1567 stalls.

The Hofkirche has also played the part of the national church of the Tyrol since the revolt in 1809. It contains the tomb and memorial of **Andreas Hofer** (1767-1810), hero of the Tyrolean uprising against Napoleon near the exit.

★★ **Silberne Kapelle** ⊘ - This separate chapel, built by Archduke Ferdinand of Tyrol *(see genealogical tree in Introduction and under Schloß Ambras below)* so that he might rest beside his wife who was a commoner, was finished in 1587.

It owes its name to the large embossed silver Madonna, surrounded by designs representing the symbols of the Litanies, which are to be seen on the altarpiece of rare wood. The first bay, near the entrance on the left, contains the tomb of Philippine Welser, the beloved wife of Ferdinand, and is one of the most highly finished works of the Flemish master Alexandre Colin *(see above)* in his maturity. Nearer to the altar, the funeral statue of Ferdinand, by the same sculptor, depicts the deceased in full armour. His own armour is displayed separately on a console, in a kneeling position, facing the altar. A small 16C cedarwood organ, of Italian origin, completes the artistic reliquary formed by the chapel.

★★ **Tiroler Volkskunstmuseum** (CDZ) ⊘ - The ground floor of this museum displays a collection of Tyrolean Christmas crib scenes from their origins to the present. The upper floors contain, most notably, beautiful panelled rooms with stoves which come from the houses of a variety of classes: nobility, merchants and farmers. Those on the first floor feature essentially Gothic style decoration, while those on the second floor date from the Renaissance and Baroque.

On the first floor are models of various Tyrolean farmhouses, along with skilfully decorated furniture, farming implements, tools, wood carvings from the Grödner Tal region, musical instruments and games. There are some interesting examples of masks and costumes worn during carnival season in Imst and the area around Innsbruck. On the second floor there is a valuable collection of

Ad-Pichler-Platz .... CZ 2
Bozner Platz .... DZ 10
Burggraben .... CZ 14

Domplatz .... CZ 15
Herzog-Friedrich-
  Straße .... CZ 20
Ingenieur-Etzel-
  Straße .... DZ 22
Landhausplatz .... CZ 25

Leopoldstraße .... CZ 26
Meinhardstr. .... DZ 28
Meraner Straße .... DZ 30
Pfarrgasse .... CZ 32
Stiftgasse .... CZ 37
Südbahnstraße .... DZ 38

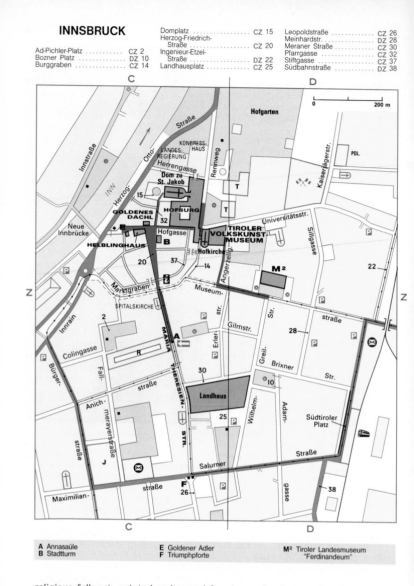

A Annasäule
B Stadtturm

E Goldener Adler
F Triumphpforte

M² Tiroler Landesmuseum
   "Ferdinandeum"

religious folk art, painted and carved farmhouse furniture and costumes worn by the farming community during festivals. The exhibits on display come from the old Tyrol, which included what is now the Trentino region and the Ladin valleys around the Dolomites.

Take the Angerzellgasse into Museumsstraße to get to the "Ferdinandeum"

★ **Tiroler Landesmuseum "Ferdinandeum"** (DZ **M²**) ⊙ – This museum is devoted essentially to the development of the fine arts in the Tyrol. Tyrolean Gothic art predominates. Many of the works displayed also have historical value: the 1370 chapel altar of Schloß Tirol, the original bas-reliefs of the Goldenes Dachl, etc. There is also a good collection of Dutch masters. A further room contains a relief model of the Tyrol at a scale of 1: 20 000.

ADDITIONAL SIGHTS

City centre *plans above and p 136*

Hofgarten (DZ) – This public garden with shady lakes and fine weeping willows offers the visitor to Innsbruck welcome relaxation. Evening concerts are held in the gardens in summer.

Landhaus (DZ) – The Landhaus, an excellent specimen of Baroque civil architecture, was built from 1725 to 1728 by Georg-Anton von Gumpp to house the Diet and the provincial government. The grand staircase is adorned with stucco and displays statues and busts of antique gods. Note the ceiling design: the eagle of the Tyrol holding the map of the province.

Triumphpforte (CZ **F**) – The triumphal arch commemorates the days of rejoicing and mourning which marked the year 1765 (marriage of Archduke Leopold) for the Tyrol.

On the south side, the monument is crowned by a medallion of Franz I and Maria Theresa, while statues of the betrothed couple can be seen on the left side (on the right are the sisters of the Infanta).

The north face of the monument bears symbols of mourning (medallion of Franz I being displayed by the Angel of Death, and a woman mourning the Emperor's sudden demise).

Riesenrundgemälde (Bergisel Panorama) (ABY **K**) ⊘ – *Beside the Hungerburg funicular station.*

This huge circular oil painting depicting the Battle of Bergisel *(see below)* was painted in honour of Andreas Hofer, hero of the Tyrolean uprising against Napoleon. Such panoramas were all the rage in the 19C. It is an amazing technical achievement (10m - 33ft high by 100m - 330ft long) which transports the spectator to the heart of the action by a successful use of perspective.

Alpenzoo (AY) ⊘ – The pleasure of a visit to this Alpine zoo is further enhanced by the beauty of the site it occupies on a south-facing slope with a far-reaching view of the Inn valley plain. The zoo gives visitors an overview of the animal world, both past and present, found in the Alpine region. Over 2 000 animals from 150 species, including mammals, birds, reptiles, amphibians and fish, are on display.

Innsbruck-Wilten, Bergisel and Amras *plan p 136*

The Wilten quarter is where the River Sill, running down from the Brenner, emerges from its final gorge to flow towards the alluvial delta. This was the site of the Roman town of Veldidena. To the south it abuts on Bergisel, a wooded eminence which became a sacred spot in the Tyrol after the battles on its slopes between Napoleon's troops and the Tyrolese insurgents under Andreas Hofer in 1809.

Wilten: Stiftskirche (ABY) ⊘ – The Abbey of Wilten, entrusted to the Premonstratensians in 1128, is the institution most closely connected with the origins of modern Innsbruck. In fact the monks of St Norbert owned all the land south of the Inn. It was only by an agreement made in 1180 between their provost and the Counts of Andech, who represented the civil power at the time, that the primitive settlement on the north bank was moved to the present "old town" (the Hofburg quarter).

The church, which can be recognized from a distance by its yellowish red roughcast, is a Baroque building of the 17C, restored after damage in 1944. The façade, transformed in 1716 by the same architect who designed the Landhaus *(see above)*, is deeply convex on each side of the doorway, which is guarded by two stone giants wearing the warrior costumes of classical tragedy. They represent Aymon, on the left, and Thyrsus, on the right.

In the narthex, enclosed by a magnificent **grille★** dating from 1707, with luxuriant adornments of foliage, is another statue, also in wood with more naive carvings (c1500). This is the giant Aymon who came from the Rhine Valley; according to tradition he founded the abbey as an act of expiation for his murder of the local giant, Thyrsus. He also rid the nearby Sill gorge of a tiresome dragon for good measure.

The building proper has a certain distinction with its series of altarpieces in black wood, relieved with gold, but many of the paintings and stuccowork adorning the vaulting had to be restored. Above the high altar, note the work known as *Solomon's Throne* (1665), a sort of gallery on a reduced scale, framed between columns and lions, which draws the eye in towards the focal point of Christ seated on a throne.

★ Wilten: Basilika (AY) ⊘ – In order to perpetuate devotion to Our Lady of the Four Columns, who had been the object of a popular pilgrimage at Innsbruck since the Middle Ages, the Premonstratensians of the nearby monastery had the parish church of Wilten completely restored between 1751 and 1756. The church was raised to the status of a basilica in 1957.

The building's sumptuous **interior** bears witness to the skill of the artists of the Rococo period, and especially of a team of decorators formed by a stucco-moulder, Franz-Xaver Feichtmayr, of the Wessobrunn School, and a painter from Augsburg, Matthäus Günther. Stucco work in the form of flowers, scrolls and angels is arranged most successfully in the escutcheons. The fine paintings on the vaulting depict the Virgin as an advocate (chancel) and the Biblical figures, Esther and Judith (nave). The statue of the Virgin Mary, particularly venerated by pilgrims, is enthroned by a glory at the high altar, under a baldaquin supported on marble columns.

Bergisel (ABY) – *Reached by car via the Brennerstraße, the Bergiselweg and the avenue leading into the park.* This wooded hill has been laid out as pleasant walks and many city people come to it in search of rest or pleasure. The ski-jump in the background recalls the 1964 and 1976 Winter Olympic Games. Several monuments, especially the statue of Andreas Hofer (AY L), commemorate the fighting in 1809; the "panorama" depicting the fighting is on the far side of the town *(see above)*.

The **Kaiserjägermuseum** (Memorial to the Imperial Light Infantry) (AY **M³**) ⊙ contains mementos of the 1809 uprising and of the Tyrolean crack corps (arms, uniforms and paintings), which was disbanded in 1919.

From the various rooms, and especially from the moving 1914-1918 war memorial on the ground floor, there are **views★** of the town of Innsbruck and the mountain barrier of the Nordkette.

Schloß Ambras (BY) ⊙ – *From the centre of Innsbruck take Olympiastraße east; by the skating rink turn right; after passing under the motorway turn left into the Aldrans road; after 500m - 550yds turn left to Schloß Ambras.*

Extensive rebuilding has gone on since the end of the 16C, in both parts of the castle: the "lower castle", which includes the present entrance lodge, and the "upper castle", a former medieval fortress, much remodelled. This was the favourite residence of the Archduke Ferdinand (1529-1595), Regent of the Tyrol, and the beautiful Philippine Welser, his first and morganatic wife, whose memory the people of Innsbruck still revere in the Silberne Kapelle *(see above)*. Ferdinand, a keen collector, had accumulated in the various rooms a huge and varied treasury of *objets d'art* – especially armour and portraits.

During the years that followed, parts of the collection were dismantled by the Habsburgs and moved to their home in Vienna. Archduke Franz Ferdinand *(qv)*, who was later to die so tragically at Sarajevo, stayed on a number of occasions at Ambras and was responsible for some of the changes.

In the lower castle is the gallery of **Arms and Armour★** (Rüstungssäle) with its exhibits of jousting equipment. In one room (Kunst- und Wunderkammer) there is a Cabinet of Curiosities with displays of minerals, animals, robots, objects used in the celebration of Bacchic ceremonies... On the way to the upper castle is the huge **Spanish Room** (Spanischer Saal) with its splendid Renaissance inlaid ceiling.

Hochschloß – In the upper castle there is a gallery of Habsburg portraits (15C-18C). The furniture and frescoes complete the Renaissance furnishings of the castle.

Unterschloß – The lower castle contains arms from the 16C and 17C, and a curiosities room with exhibits from the 16C.

EXCURSIONS

★★ **Hafelekar** ⊙ – Alt 2 334m - 7 657ft – *Local map opposite – 2 hour trip using the cable-car from the Hungerburg.*

A magnificent viewpoint overlooks the Inn Valley and the Stubai Alps (south), and the chalky heights of the Karwendel (north).

★★ **Tour of the Mittelgebirge** – *67km - 42 miles – about 4 hours – local map opposite. The Ellbögener Straße is a narrow corniche road with hairpin bends and a gradient up to 1 in 7 in places (not recommended for caravans). Leave Innsbruck by the Hall in Tirol road* (BY – plan p 136).

★ **Hall in Tirol** – *See HALL IN TIROL.*

The road to Tulfes crosses the Inn, goes under the motorway and, as it climbs, gives attractive open views of the town of Hall, its three church towers and the Bettelwurf range in the Karwendel massif. 2km - 1 mile from the bridge, after a rotunda-chapel on the right, turn left into the downhill road leading to the isolated church of Volders.

Volders – *See VOLDERS.*

Turn back, and again take the road on the left to Tulfes, which soon emerges on the plateau where the attractive villages of Tulfes, Rinn, Sistrans and Lans appear, facing the Nordkette.

★ **Igls** – Pop 1 678. This winter sports resort, of long-established repute, has taken on new life since the 1976 Olympic Games, with the building of a rather daring toboggan and bob-sleigh run. It enjoys a terrace setting and the resinous scents of the forest. Its sporting facilities indicate the proximity of a large town and the favour of a wealthy clientele. The Patscherkofel cable-car and the chairlift which continues to the summit have made more summer and winter excursions possible on the nearby wooded slopes. These face north and make good snowfields.

The **Ellbögener Straße★★**, which was once used for carting salt, overlooks the Sill and the Brenner motorway which is carried over the river by the famous Europa Bridge. The approach to Patsch offers a **view★** along the length of the Stubaital,

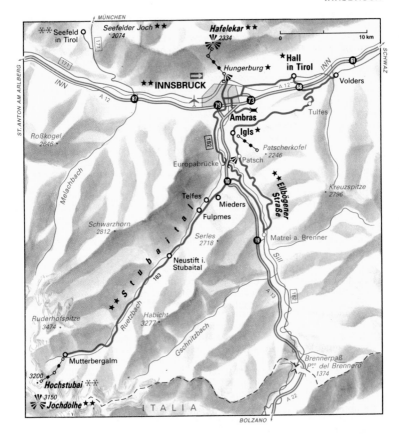

which opens out at the foot of the sharp pyramid of the Serles with the more massive snow-capped summit of the Habicht in the middle distance. After St. Peter, a village clinging to a promontory, the slope is steeper and the run becomes hilly. On rejoining the Brenner road at Matrei, bear right towards Innsbruck. *See under BRENNERSTRASSE for the sights on the Brenner road, between Matrei and Innsbruck.*

★★ **Stubaital** – *44km - 27 miles as far as Mutterbergalm – about 2 hours. Leave Innsbruck on the Brennerstraße (*AY *plan p 136); after 15km - 9 miles bear right towards Schönberg. For description of valley, see STUBAITAL.*

INNTAL★

Tirol

Michelin map 426 folds 29 and 30

Since the southern frontier of Austria was brought back, in 1919, to the crest line of the Alps, the Inn valley has become the backbone of the Tyrol. For 185km - 115 miles, from the Finstermünz ravine to the Kufstein gap, the scenery is typical of the longitudinal furrows of the Alps, where the last phases of the Ice Age made characteristic changes in the relief, as in the **Mittelgebirge** (Pre-Alpine) area round Innsbruck, where spacious plateaux form ideal sites for villages.

Below Landeck the Inn valley emphasizes the meeting of the pale cliffs of the limestone Alps (north) and the more solid dark rocks of the crystalline central massifs (south). In the latter, dark coloured rocks of a heavier shape predominate. The Sellraintal, a tributary valley which joins the Inn valley opposite the promontory of the Martinswand, between Zirl and Innsbruck, marks the traditional boundary between the upper and lower valleys of the Inn (Oberinntal and Unterinntal).

Owing to the sheltered climate of the valley – sometimes oppressive in summer – and the influence of the wind *(Föhn – qv)*, funnelled by secondary valleys oriented due south, it is possible to grow cereals and even peaches, apricots and corn.

The itinerary below describes the Austrian part of the deep and splendidly forested upper valley of the Inn **(Oberinntal)**.

FROM NAUDERS TO IMST *104km - 65 miles - allow half a day*

When following this route from north to south, at Kajetansbrücke bear left to enter the Finstermünz pass or bear right to enter the Engadine in Switzerland.

Leaving the **Nauders** (holiday destination) basin, where there are still crops at over 1 300m - 4 000ft, as in the nearby valley of the Alto Adige (Val Venosta or Vintschgau), the road plunges into the Finstermünz pass.

★ **Finstermünzpaß** – This grim gorge forms the natural frontier between the Tyrolean Inn valley and the Lower Engadine and the Alto Adige.

Though the Engadine road follows the floor of the gorge throughout, the road from Nauders plunges into it through a rocky gap guarded by an old fort and, at the narrowest section of the Inn gorge, provides glimpses of the fortified bridge of Altfinstermünz, which commanded this section before the present road was made (1850-1854).

Downstream from the hamlet of Hochfinstermünz the **corniche road★** clings to the cliffs of the right bank. Stop at the overhanging **viewpoint★** marked by a single pine, for a view down into the valley, opposite the tributary gorge, which is the lower end of the Romansh Samnaun valley in Switzerland.

The floor of the valley is reached at the Kajetansbrücke (St Gaëtano) bridge.

Pfunds – Holiday destination.

Near the "Dreiländereck" (the point where the Swiss, Italian and Austrian borders meet), stand the twin towns of Pfunds-Stuben and Pfunds-Dorf separated by the Inn. They owe their charm to their Rhaeto-Romansh houses like those in the neighbouring Engadine with prominent oriels and deeply recessed little windows.

On leaving Stuben, bear left at the fork, into the old Landeck road, passing through Birkach. From the end of the valley below Stuben, one can recognize the Schmalzkopf group (south) and on the opposite slope, the more prominent peak of Piz Mundin (alt 3 146m-10 322ft). Between Ried im Oberinntal and Prutz stand the ruins of Laudeck on a rock, flanked by the little white bell tower of Ladis. Near Prutz the jagged skyline of the Kauner Grat can be seen rising above the end of the tributary valley of the Kaunertal.

★★★ **Kaunertal** – *21km - 13 miles from Prutz. See KAUNERTAL.* From the Gepatsch dam (alt 1 767m - 5 796ft) there is a sweeping view over the Weißseespitze mountain range. A **panoramic road** runs along the east bank of the Gepatsch reservoir and climbs tortuously up throught the pine trees to the foot of the Weißseeferner (alt 2 750m - 9 022ft).

The trip from Prutz to Landeck includes long sections of rocky *corniche* above the Inn, which is crossed by two bold, covered bridges.

Pontlatzerbrücke – At the bridgehead on the left bank a memorial crowned with an eagle commemorates the battles in which the Tyrolese checked the Bavarians in 1703 (War of the Spanish Succession) and, in 1809, a French force marching on Finstermünz.

Landeck - *See LANDECK.*

From Landeck to Imst the valley is narrow and wooded. From the bridge at Zams there is a magnificent view of the slender ruins of Schrofenstein, clinging to the flank of the Brandkopf. In the forest, further downstream, the tiny village of Zamserberg nestles below the ruins of the Kronburg.

At last the road emerges into the wide Imst basin, cut at either end by wooded gorges, in sight of the jagged crests of the Stubaier Alps (east).

Imst - The upper town (Oberstadt), which is the more attractive with its houses with rounded window grilles and pretty fountains surmounted by old statues (St Sebastian), nestles round the imposing parish church (Pfarrkirche) of Gothic origin, rebuilt after a fire in 1822 but preserving its Gothic doorways and, outside, the traditional giant-sized statue of St Christopher.

H. Wiesenhofer/ÖSTERREICH WERBUNG

Carnival time at Imst

The well known Imst carnival, with its procession of ghosts *(Schemenlaufen)*, takes place only every 4th or 5th year *(see the Calendar of events at the end of the guide)*. Those who are interested may see the masks and dresses used on this occasion in the Heimatmuseum.

The term "Alpine plant" is usually reserved for plants which grow above the tree line (see the chapter on flora in the Introduction). Their early flowering is due to the brevity of the growing season (June-August) and their intense colours are caused by the strong ultra-violet light on the mountain peaks. Relatively few of the flowering plants catalogued in the Alps are native species. Most of them originated elsewhere: on the plains or lower slopes (very hardy plants), in the Mediterranean, Asia or the Arctic.

ISCHGL★★

Tirol – Population 1 280

Michelin map 426 fold 29 – Local map under ARLBERGGEBIET

Ischgl undoubtedly ranks among the most beautiful of Austria's winter sports resorts. Its setting on the **Silvrettastraße★★** *(qv)*, at 1 377m - 4 518ft above sea level, draws holiday makers from all over the world. Another particular point in the resort's favour is the amount of accommodation on offer, with 8 000 guest beds in hotels in the upper class comfort category. Possibilities for whiling away one's leisure hours include the Silvretta Center which contains an indoor swimming pool, a sauna, 8 tennis courts, a billiards room and a bowling alley.

In summertime, Ischgl is transformed into a peaceful holiday resort, quite unlike its winter alter-ego. It is an ideal stopover for those exploring the Arlberg region.

★★ **Alpine ski slopes** – The ski slopes at Ischgl and the neighbouring Swiss resort of Samnaun★ (alt 1 840m - 6 037ft) belong to the Silvretta-Skiarena (alt 1 400-2 900m – 4 593-9 514ft) which has 200km - 124 miles of pistes and 40 skilifts. Almost the entire site lies over 2 000m - 6 562ft above sea level, with the result that snow cover remains excellent until well into April. Only on the lowest sections of the slopes is the snow occasionally icy. Connections between the mountain slopes are good, enabling skiers to get maximum benefit from the variety of pistes which cover this vast resort.

Several of the ski slopes have really made a name for themselves, in particular the magnificent descents from the Palinkopf peak to Samnaun and the Gampenalp. For less high-powered skiing, the best slopes are those towards Switzerland and the Velillscharte.

For **cross-country skiers** there is a ski track towards Galtür *(see SILVRETTASTRASSE)*, from where there are more possibilities available.

Ischgl

★ **Pardatschgrat** 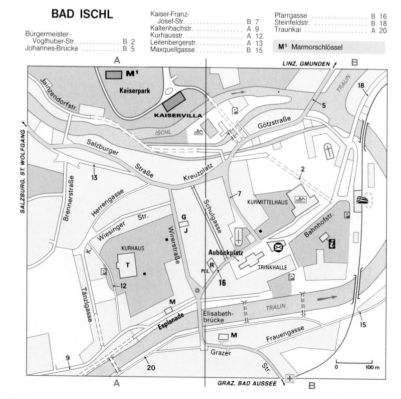⊙ – Alt 2 624m - 8 609ft. *Take the cable-car up in two stages.* There is a particularly pretty view of the Paznaun valley if you sit facing the way the cable-car is going. The houses of Ischgl lie scattered at the foot of the Seeköpfe and Küchlspitze (alt 3 147m - 10 325ft) peaks. From the station at the top there is a good view of the ski slopes surrounded by the Vesulspitze, Bürkelkopf, Flimspitze and Piz Rots summits. Directly to the south lies the Fimbatal, dwarfed by the Fluchthorn massif.

Readers should note that an almost identical view can be enjoyed from the Idalp summit (alt 2 311m - 7 582ft), which is reached by the Silvretta-Seilbahn (cable-car).

★★ **Trida Sattel** – Alt 2 488m - 8 163ft. *Take the cable-car up from Samnaun or follow the ski tracks from Ischgl.* From the terrace of the mountain restaurant, the **view**★★ extends southwards over the sheer Stammerspitze, Muttler and Piz Mundin peaks, and to the southeast over the Ötztaler alps. To the north lie the ski slopes across the Swiss border, at the foot of the Bürkelkopf.

An even more far-ranging **panorama**★★ can be enjoyed from the Visnitzbahn and Mullerbahn chairlifts.

Bad ISCHL⚕

Oberösterreich – Population 13 027

Michelin map 426 fold 21 – Local map under SALZKAMMERGUT – Alt 469m - 1 539ft

Bad Ischl is in the heart of the Salzkammergut and is the watering-place in Austria where the reign of Franz Joseph has left the greatest marks of luxury, having been for seventy years one of the most brilliant centres of fashionable life in Europe. The therapeutic properties of its saline waters were brought to public notice about 1820 by a Viennese practitioner, Dr Wirer, and were confirmed by some historic cures, such as those which justified the nickname "Princes of the Salt", given to the children of the Archduchess Sophia born here and also to Franz Joseph.

By establishing his summer quarters at Ischl, near his favourite hunting grounds, Franz Joseph turned the spa into a holiday resort which attracted many crowned heads, fahionable composers such as Anton Bruckner, Johann Strauss, Emmerich Kálmán, Karl Millöcker and Franz Lehár (whose villa is now a museum), painters such as Ferdinand Waldmüller and Rudolf von Alt; Lenau and Nestroy from the world of poetry and the theatre. With the disappearance of court life, the spa

BAD ISCHL

Bürgermeister-Voglhuber-Str.	B 2
Johannes-Brücke	B 5
Kaiser-Franz-Josef-Str.	B 7
Kaltenbachstr.	A 9
Kurhausstr.	A 12
Leitenbergerstr.	A 13
Maxquellgasse	B 15
Pfarrgasse	B 16
Steinfeldstr.	B 18
Traunkai	A 20

M¹ Marmorschlössel

has concentrated its efforts on the renewal of its facilities, in rebuilding the medical establishment (Kurmittelhaus) and in modernizing the majestic Kurhaus or casino.

An Alpine resort – The parks and *Biedermeier* style buildings cluster in a setting of densely wooded mountains, on the inside of a loop at the confluence of the rivers Traun and Ischl. The **Auböckplatz (B)**, bordered by the drinking-hall *(Trinkhalle)*, a former pumproom (1831), and the parish church, reconstructed at the end of the reign of Maria Theresa, is the traditional centre of town life. The Auböckplatz is linked to the Elisabethbrücke, a bridge spanning the Traun, by the **Pfarrgasse (B 16)**, the main shopping street of Ischl, which retains such survivals from 19C spa life as the Zauner Café and pastry shop. The Pfarrgasse ends at the **Esplanade (A)**, a shady walk beside the Traun, which was once the domain of the rich *Salzfertiger* (salt refiners) who were responsible for storing salt for the Treasury before it was sent downstream. One of their dwellings, the Seeauer House (no 10), with a Rococo façade and triple gables, has kept its original character. The parents of Franz Joseph stayed there between 1844 and 1877; Franz Joseph and his "Sissi" lived there in 1853. Later it became a hotel and now it houses the local museum.

★ KAISERVILLA (A) ⊙
time: 1 hour

The Imperial villa stands to the north of the town, on the left bank of the Ischl, in a magnificent landscape garden, the **Kaiserpark**. It was given to the Imperial couple as a wedding present by the Archduchess Sophia. Though it has Classical colonnades, the house reveals the simple character of Franz Joseph by the importance given to hunting, of which he was an ardent devotee, and the sovereign disregard of modern comfort and amenities to be found in his private apartments (the study and the bedroom). One of the more moving parts of the tour is the visit to the Grey Saloon, off which lie the Empress' oratory and

Sissi, with Romy Schneider and Karlheinz Böhm

her private cabinet. This is exactly as it was left by "Sissi" on 16 July 1898 on the eve of her departure for Geneva – a journey from which she never returned. It was in the Kaiservilla that Franz Joseph signed the fateful declaration of war with Serbia on 1 August 1914.

Marmorschlössel (M¹) – In the park is the little "marble castle", a favourite retreat of the Empress Elisabeth, who made it in some degree her Trianon; it now houses a photography museum, **Photomuseum** ⊙.

KAISERGEBIRGE★★

Tirol

Michelin map 426 folds 17, 18 and 19

The limestone massif of the Kaisergebirge is surrounded by the continuous belt of valleys in which Kufstein, Walchsee, Kössen, Griesenau, St. Johann in Tirol and Ellmau stand. It is well known for its mountaineering routes and is one of the most detached of the Northern Limestone Alps. This fact enables the peaks of its outer limits to be easily distinguished.

The Kaiser has two ridge peaks: to the south, the highest, the **Wilder** (wild) **Kaiser** (alt 2 344m - 7 690ft) is distinguished by steep cliff walls which can be seen from Kitzbühel and even better from Ellmau; to the north, the less jagged **Zahmer** (tame) **Kaiser** rises from foothills of sweeping Alpine pastures.

WILDER KAISER

① From Lofer to Kufstein

68km - 42 miles - about 3 hours - local map below

The starting point of the trip is the Saalach valley, at the foot of the Loferer Steinberge, a fine limestone massif. Before the Wilder Kaiser comes into view there are pretty scenes of mountain life in the Strub valley.

★ **Lofer** - *See LOFER.*

West of Lofer the eye is caught by the summits of the Loferer Steinberge. The valley narrows to the width of the wooded ravine known as the Paß Strub (memorial commemorating the fighting by Tyrolean rebels in 1800, 1805 and 1809), where the torrent swirls and foams.

Beyond the Paß Strub the drive through the Strub valley provides more views of the Loferer Steinberge.

West of the Paß Strub the itinerary leaves the modern road, no 312, to follow the old road serving the hamlet of Strub and the village of Waidring.

Strub - Although somewhat decrepit, even the oldest houses have kept their Tyrolean character and style.

Waidring - Population 1 494. A group of houses with flower-decked balconies, little belfries and shingle roofs, weighed down with stones, make a charming picture round a square with a fountain.

The parish church features beautiful stucco work and pastels in the Rococo style.

The approach to Erpfendorf from the east reveals the heart of the Leukental, a valley marked by the church towers of Erpfendorf and Kirchdorf.

Erpfendorf - Population 840. The church, finished in 1957, is the work of Clemens Holzmeister, a master of contemporary religious architecture in Austria and designer of the new building for the Salzburg Festival.

The belfry, entrance porch and corbelled baptistry chapel, which resembles an oriel, partially hide the façade.

The interior decoration consists of stained-glass windows, mosaics in the chancel and woodwork (a rood beam depicting the Crucifixion).

The route through the Leukental, when passing Kirchdorf and on arriving at St. Johann, provides fine views of the Wilder Kaiser.

St. Johann in Tirol - *See ST. JOHANN IN TIROL.*

It is the section from St. Johann to Ellmau which offers the most distinct views of the south wall of the Wilder Kaiser, with the Treffauer as its outwork.

Spital - This 13C hospice, surrounded by the buildings of an agricultural school and standing alone in the St. Johann basin, is marked by two century-old lime trees. It was decorated in 1744 by the painter Simon-Benedikt Faistenberger, a native of Kitzbühel. The window behind the high altar is the only authentic 15C specimen of stained glass still extant in the Tyrol. The hospice also has the province's oldest bell.

Ellmau - Population 2 400. A little chapel with a bulbous belfry marks the attractive site of the village facing the Kaisergebirge.

Turn right into the Scheffau road to the Hintersteinersee.

Hintersteinersee - The crystal clear waters of this mountain lake reflect the rocky crags of the Wilder Kaiser.

Take the road down to Scheffau and on to Söll.

Söll – This charming little town, lying at the foot of the Hohe Salve with its characteristic rounded peak, is grouped round a Gothic church to which Baroque elements were added in 1760. Söll is one of the most popular holiday destinations in the region.

★★ **Hohe Salve** – Alt 1 829m - 6 000ft. *Cable-car and chairlift.* From the summit with its chapel there is a marvellous **panorama**★★ to the south, taking in the Brixen valley, the Kitzbüheler Alps (Großer Rettenstein) and further off in the distance the Hohe Tauern (Großvenediger) and the Zillertaler Alps. To the north, the horizon is dominated by the jagged rocky peaks of the Wilder Kaiser.

✲ **Skiwelt Wilder Kaiser-Brixental** – This skiing area encompasses 8 winter sports resorts from the Wilder Kaiser (Going, Ellmau, Scheffau, Söll, Itter) and the Brixen valley (Brixen, Westendorf, Hopfgarten). It is virtually possible to ski across the entire area with its 250km - 155 miles of ski-runs and 90 skilifts without needing to take off your skis, although some of the connections between individual mountains can be a little arduous. This large skiing area set amidst medium-altitude mountains is ideal for skiers who prefer a more gentle and relaxed style of skiing. There are numerous untaxing ski-runs through the forest. More experienced skiers will be drawn to the black run on the Hohe Salve.

For easiest access to the skining area, the resorts of Scheffau, Söll and the pretty town of Brixen are particularly to be recommended.

For those interested in cross-country skiing, there are 110km - 68 miles of ski-tracks divided between the various resorts, of which 30km - 19 miles each are concentrated around Söll and Hopfgarten.

Kufstein – *Via road 173 ("Eibergstraße") and the Weißbach gorge. See KUFSTEIN.*

ZAHMER KAISER

② From Kufstein to St. Johann in Tirol

61km - 38 miles – allow half a day excluding walks – local map below

Skirting the Kaisergebirge to the north, the road continues first at the foot of the slopes of the Zahmer Kaiser and then through a harsher landscape towards the Wilder Kaiser mountain walls. It passes through villages like Ebbs or Walchsee where the comfortable houses are reminders of the proximity of Bavaria.

Kufstein – *See KUFSTEIN.*

North of Kufstein the Kaisergebirge massif ends above the alluvial plain of the Inn in great precipices cut through by the terminal gorge of the Sparchenbach, a torrent whose valley – the Kaisertal – runs into the heart of the massif. Leaving

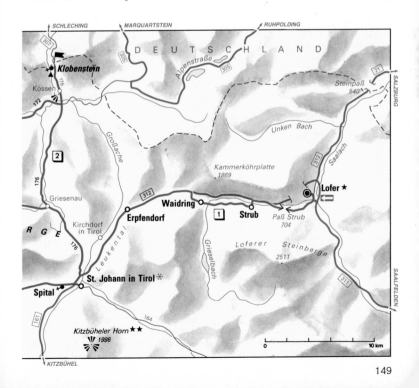

the foot of these cliffs, the road provides an extensive view of the Ebbs plain, dominated by the pilgrim church of St. Nikolaus, which is perched on a wooded foothill.

Between Durchholzen and the Walchsee the corridor opens out into an attractive valley, partly drowned by the lake and overlooked by a few peaks of the Zahmer Kaiser.

Walchsee - Population 1 321. The lake (of the same name as the village) is used for water sports. In the village are some fine houses with painted façades.

Turn left into road no 176.

Klobensteinschlucht - *Allow 15min on foot Rtn to visit the gorge (Austrian customs control). Access and description under KLOBENSTEINPASS.*

South of Kössen the road rises, opening up a more extensive view which now reaches ahead to the rocky Wilder Kaiser.

From a clearing containing the inn at Griesenau, one of the mountaineering centres of the massif, one can enjoy vistas of the Ackerlspitze cliffs.

In Griesenau turn right into the toll road ⊙.

Scenery in the Kaisergebirge

★ **Stripsenkopf** - *4 hours on foot Rtn.* From the Griesener Alps, terminus of the motor road, one climbs to the Stripsenjoch pass (mountain hotel) and then, turning northwards, to the summit of the Stripsenkopf (alt 1 807m - 5 928ft). There is a closeup **view**★ of the magnificent north walls of the Wilder Kaiser.

The final part of the road is particularly attractive. After the romantic Ruppertsau clearing, the horizon broadens. The road ends in a pretty **panoramic descent**★ through the meadows above the Leukental and the depression of St. Johann in Tirol, facing the knolls of the Kitzbüheler Alps.

St. Johann in Tirol - *See ST. JOHANN IN TIROL.*

KAPRUN ✳

Salzburg – Population 2 800
Michelin map 426 fold 33 – Alt 786m - 2 579ft

This peaceful town at the foot of the Großglockner road owes its development to the construction of a hydroelectric power station upstream of it in the Kapruner valley between 1938 and 1951.

From 1965, the linking of the Schmieding glacier with the flank of the Kitzsteinhorn has made it possible to ski all year round. As a result, Kaprun has gradually made a name for itself as one of the leading summer ski resorts in Europe. The resort can also boast numerous leisure facilities (18-hole golf course, swimming pool etc.) and took on a new dimension by linking itself with **Zell am See**★ *(qv)*. These two towns, separated by a distance of only 7km - 4 miles, have evolved into a huge sport and relaxation complex under the name of **Europa-Sportregion**. However, the village of Kaprun itself, at the mouth of the valley, is quite a distance away from the ski slopes *(some form of transport is necessary).*

During the summer the Kapruner valley, famed for its magnificent mountain setting, has numerous interesting footpaths to offer the visitor. The **Alexander-Einziger-Weg** from the Alpincenter (upper section of the Kitzsteinhorn) to the summit of the Maiskogel is well worth a detour *(beforehand, enquire at the tourist office about bus times to the Kitzsteinhorn car park)*.

★★ KAPRUNERTAL

Allow a day (at least 2 hours 30min for the Kitzsteinhorn and at least 4 hours for the reservoirs, which are only accessible between late May and mid-October).
The Kapruner valley lies between the ice-capped summits of the Hohe Tauern and the green-shimmering waters of the **reservoirs★★**, lying one above the other, attached to the hydroelectric power scheme. The Glockner-Kaprun power station is one of the most pioneering and successful achievements of Austrian technology. Located 2km - 1 mile upstream of the town, the **Kapruner Kraftwerk** ⊙ (output: 220 000kW) is the lower station of the power complex. The road becomes noticeably steeper at this point, while the valley tucked between sheer cliffs appears ever more barren. Further up ahead looms the wall of the Limberg dam. *Park the car at the foot of the Kitzsteinhorn skilift.*

★★★ **Kitzsteinhorn** ⊙ – *Rather than taking the funicular, which travels underground thus not giving a view of the surrounding landscape, take the cable-car.*
The **trip★★** between two particularly sheer rock faces is most impressive. Finally, the cable-car reaches Langwied station (alt 2 000m - 6 562ft), which is the departure point for the ski slopes during winter.
Take the Langwiedbahn up as far as the upper section and the **Alpincenter** station (alt 2 452m - 8 045ft, restaurant). There is a beautiful view of the Kitzsteinhorn massif and the summer ski slopes.
The connecting cable-car climbs to 3 029m - 9 938ft above sea level, reaching a snow-covered mountain ridge just below the summit (alt 3 203m - 10 503ft, accessible only to mountaineers). From the upper station climb to the second level of the viewing terrace. Straight ahead stands the Großvenediger, dominating the whole **panorama★★★**. To the left are the Granatspitze and the Stubacher Sonnblick, and to the right tower the peaks of the Zillertal, Kitzbüheler Alps, Zell am See with its lake and numerous limestone ridges from the Wilder Kaiser as far as the Hochkönig. On a clear day the view stretches as far as the Zugspitze on the other side of the Karwendel range.
Go down three floors and follow the tunnel for 360m to the "Glocknerkranzl" terrace. From this terrace there is an impressive **view★★** of the Großglockner, flanked by the Bärenkopf and Hoher Riffel peaks.

※※ **Kitzsteinhorn ski slopes** – These are open all year round. Admittedly, the total area covered is relatively modest (15 skilifts and 35km - 22 miles of ski-runs), but it offers fantastic snow conditions in a spectacular setting between 2 000m and 3 000m (6 562-9 843ft) above sea level. The facilities are among the most modern and comfortable anywhere in Austria. The ski-runs are suitable for all levels of ability, with a slight preponderance of easier runs.
Return to the lift and travel down to the Kesselfall-Alpenhaus car park.

★★ **Hydroelectric dams** – A bus runs to the lower station of the Lärchwand funicular. During the ascent there is a good view of the valley through which you have just travelled, and also of Kaprun. At the upper station, the wall of the Limberg dam comes into view, with the Wiesbachhorn, the Bärenkopf and the Klockerin peaks in the background.

Limbergsperre – The Limberg dam (alt 1 672m - 5 486ft) is an arch gravity dam measuring 120m - 394ft high by 357m - 1 171ft along the top of the dam wall. The power station at the foot of the dam wall receives water from the Mooserbodenspeicher reservoir opposite and expels it into the Wasserfallboden reservoir behind the dam.
From the upper station, take a bus which travels along the Mooserbodenstraße, 1 700m – about a mile of which cuts through tunnels, to the Mooser dam. During the drive, there is a good view, initially close at hand and then from above, of the **Wasserfallboden reservoir★** in its marvellous isolated mountain setting.

★ **Mooser- und Drossensperre** – Alt 2 036m - 6 680ft. Both valley exits of the Mooserboden are blocked by arch gravity dams lying to the east and west of the so-called Höhenburg. The **Mooserboden reservoir★★**, lying amidst spectacular Alpine scenery at the foot of the ice-clad Hohe Tauern, makes an indelible impression on visitors.
Crossing the first dam, there is a wonderful **view★★** down onto the green waters of the Wasserfallboden, against a mountain backdrop formed by the Leoganger Steinberge and the Steinernes Meer.
A 12km - 8 mile long gallery carries melt-water from the Pasterzen glacier and water from the Leiterbach, collected daily in the Margaritze overflow reservoir at the foot of the Großglockner, to the Mooserboden.

KARWENDELGEBIRGE★

Tirol und Bayern (Germany)

Michelin map 426 fold 17 – north of Innsbruck

The limestone massif of the Karwendel (highest point: the Birkkarspitze, 2 749m - 9 019ft), whose first section, the Nordkette, lies north of Innsbruck, can also be seen as an impressive feature from Mittenwald or from the road to the Achensee. Only an excursion into the Rißbach valley with a possible detour through Bavaria will enable the motorist to get near the greyish, pitted cliffs, the *Kar* which give these mountains their character. If time is scarce, it is worth driving as far as the Achensee, the largest lake in the Tyrol.

FROM THE INN VALLEY TO THE SYLVENSTEIN DAM (GERMANY)

39km - 24 miles – about 2 hours 30min – Local map below

This transverse route through the Achenpaß defile in the northern Alps links the Inn valley to the upper Isar valley or the Tegernsee *(see Michelin Green Guide Germany)*. Customs control on leaving Achenwald.

Beginning at the Inn valley *(exit on motorway "Wiesing-Achensee")*, the panoramic road climbs up in full view of the mouth of the Zillertal.

★★ **Kanzelkehre** – This terraced viewpoint is laid out on a curve. The **view**★★ looks down on the Inn valley and the lower Ziller valley, which is dotted with very sharp steeples (Wiesing in the foreground). The scale of these valleys, with their attractive landscapes fashioned by hand over many centuries, is more impressive than the surrounding mountains.

The Rofangebirge mountain peaks tower up to the north.

Eben – The church of this Lilliputian village contains the chalice of St Notburga, who was much venerated in Bavaria and the Tyrol as the patroness of servants.

Erfurter Hütte ⊙ – Alt 1 834m - 6 033ft. *Access by cable-car.*
This hut, the departure point for climbing expeditions to scale the Rofangebirge massif, is set in a magnificent panorama above the Achensee and the Karwendel.

★★ **Achensee** – Geographers will be interested in the local anomaly of the parting of the waters between the Isar (to the north) and Inn (to the south) basins. The lake empties through the Achenbach, a tributary of the Isar, though the sheet of water lies in a hanging valley over the trench formed by the Inn. A morainic barrier, created by the former Inn glacier, explains this phenomenon. Engineers have taken advantage of the site by tapping the waters of the Achensee for the benefit of the electrical power station about 350m - 1 150ft lower down, near Jenbach, in the Inn valley.

The road, forming a corniche, offers the finest **view**★★ of the Karwendel summits, which rise massively round Pertisau on the opposite shore.

To drive along the edge of the lake, turn round at the village of Achensee and use the old road (one way: north-south).

Sylvenstein-Staudamm – *This dam is described in the Michelin Green Guide Germany.*

FROM THE SYLVENSTEIN DAM TO ENG

37km - 23 miles – about 1 hour 30min – Local map above

The road, for which a toll ⊙ is charged, is narrow and winding and cannot be used from December to May. Customs post.

Sylvenstein-Staudamm – *This dam is described in the Michelin Green Guide Germany.*

On leaving the banks of the artificial lake, and reaching Vorderriß, turn left into the deep Rißbach valley.

Hinterriß – The hunting lodge built in the 19C for the Duke of Coburg-Gotha is a favourite holiday resort of the Belgian royal family.

Use binoculars to scan the slopes and steep cliffs overlooking the road, to see some of the 5 000 chamois which still live on the massif.

Eng – The road ends here, in the **Großer Ahornboden★**, a grassland where the maples glow with magnificent colours in the autumn in an otherwise severe landscape. The walls of the Spritzkarspitze (alt 2 605m - 8 547ft) and the Grubenkarspitze (alt 2 661m - 8 727ft) form a natural amphitheatre marking the end to the valley.

KATSCHBERGSTRASSE

Salzburg und Kärnten

Michelin map 426 folds 34 and 35

The old Katschberg road linking the Lungau with the lakes of Carinthia runs along the Lieser valley south of the Tauern. For those who prefer, the Tauern motorway tunnel avoids the long climb over the pass (alt 1 641m - 5 384ft).

FROM ST. MICHAEL IM LUNGAU
TO SPITTAL AN DER DRAU

43km - 27 miles – about 3 hours

The Katschberg tunnel is liable to **toll**⊘.

St. Michael im Lungau – *See RADSTÄDTER TAUERNSTRASSE.*

South of the tunnel, just before Rennweg, the view opens up into the upper Lieser valley, with the village of St. Peter in the foreground. Below Rennweg, the road follows every twist and turn of the foaming Lieser.

Gmünd – *See GMÜND.*

The valley, more and more narrow and winding, eventually becomes a regular ravine. On this torrent-like section of the Lieser, kayak championships often take place.
After passing to the west of the **Millstätter See** lake *(Millstatt: 6km - 4 miles)* the road reaches Spittal an der Drau in the Drava valley.

Spittal an der Drau – *See SPITTAL AN DER DRAU.*

KAUNERTAL★★★

Tirol

Michelin map 426 fold 3

This long valley, through which one of Europe's highest-altitude roads leads (highest point: 2 750m - 9 022ft), is the ideal place for a day trip with its magnificent mountain scenery and large reservoir. Skiing is possible all year round on the Weißseeferner glacier.

*Ideally you should set off early in the morning. A visit of the valley in its entirety involves first a drive to the Weißseeferner glacier, then a walk to the Karlesspitze summit, then a hike to the Gepatschferner glacier and along the road to Piller. From here, it is possible to follow the **Pitz valley★★★** which runs parallel to the Kauner valley. Allow 6 hours not including rests.*

★★FROM PRUTZ TO THE WEISSSEEFERNER GLACIER

40km - 25 miles – 1 hour

In Prutz, turn left off the Bundesstraße 315 towards Switzerland and Italy. The road runs alongside the river Faggenbach in a deeply incised, green valley at the foot of the Köpfle (alt 2 834m - 9 298ft) and Peischl Kogel (alt 2 913m - 9 557ft) peaks.
After 12km - 8 miles, the road passes through the village of Feichten. From here on a toll is payable. The valley becomes considerably wider, and there are fleeting glimpses of the Gletscherkessel lying in the distance. After 10km - 6 miles of steep climb through a beautiful forest, the road brings you to the Gepatsch reservoir *(car park)*, the largest in west Austria. There is a very pretty **view★** of the lake and the Weißseespitze (alt 3 526m - 11 568ft). The road runs along the left bank of the lake for 6km - 4 miles, sprayed by numerous **waterfalls★** as it goes. The best view of the long lake with its border of pine trees is to be had after the Faggenbach bridge.

From bend 12, there are impressive views of the splendid tongue of the Gepatsch glacier. The lookout point in bend 7 gives a magnificent **view★★** as far as the Weißseespitze, the Fluchtkogel (alt 3 497m - 11 473ft) and the Hochvernagtspitze (alt 3 535m - 11 598ft).

The surrounding landscape becomes ever more rocky, as vegetation thins out. There is a **view★** to the right of the picturesque Krummgampen valley with its reddish cliffs. Shortly after this, the Weißsee comes into sight on the left. The final, steep stretch of road leads to the edge of the Weißseeferner glacier, where the road comes to an end (alt 2 750m - 9 022ft). From this point, a chairlift and four T-bar lifts provide access to a small summer ski area (highest altitude: 3 160m - 10 367ft).

★★★ ASCENT TO THE KARLESSPITZE

★★★ Wiesejaggl-Sessellift (Chairlift) ⊙ – Alt 3 010m - 9 875ft. *45min there and back.* During the ascent in the chairlift and on the summit itself, visitors find themselves surrounded by magnificent **mountain scenery★★★**. Besides those peaks already mentioned, the view encompasses those of Ölgruben and Bligg.

★★ Walk to Klettersteig Panoramablick – Alt 3 160m - 10 367ft. *1 hour there and back from the upper station of the chairlift. The path leads through snow (mountain boots, sunglasses and warm clothing are essential). The walk is not particularly difficult, but it is quite taxing, as the path is very steep.*
This excursion offers even inexperienced hikers the rare opportunity of seeing a glacier at close hand without running any risks. The walk leads to a pass at the foot of the **Karlesspitze**, from where there is a **view★** to the south over the Dolomites and to the southwest over the Swiss Alps.
Return to the car and drive back down to the Faggenbach bridge (car park).

★★ HIKE TO THE GEPATSCHFERNER GLACIER

1 hour 15min there and back from the bridge

The path runs along the right bank of the river. After about one hundred yards, it brings you to a huge waterfall. There follows a very steep climb through pretty countryside, in which the reddish colour of the cliffs dominates. Numerous Alpine flowers bloom along the way. Finally the path reaches a point near the Gepatschferner glacier, which is the largest in Austria. There is a fine **view★★** of the S-shaped tongue of the glacier. The rocky cirque is closed off by the Rauher Kopf and Schwarze Wand peaks.

★ PILLERPASS-STRASSE

20km - 12 miles as far as Wenns – allow 1 hour

A drive along this road leading through a pretty medium-altitude mountain landscape is an ideal way to round off a sightseeing trip to the Kauner valley. 9km - 6 miles after the toll booths, turn right and drive up to the holiday resorts of Kauns and then Kaunerberg. Nearby, there are good **views★** of the lower stretch of the Kauner valley.
Carry on towards Piller *(take a left turn 500yds or so after entering Kaunerberg)*. Having gone through Weiler Puschlin, the road brings you to the pass, at an altitude of 1 559m - 5 115ft. The road then winds its way tortuously through extensive forest, across the Venet massif, before passing through the village of Piller and finally running into the **Pitz valley★★★** *(see PITZTAL)* at the level of Wenns.

KEFERMARKT

Oberösterreich – Population 1 744

Michelin map 426 fold 9 – 10km - 6 miles south of Freistadt
Local map under LINZ: Excursions – Alt 512m - 1 680ft

Kefermarkt stands on the left bank of the Feldaist, in a restful, hilly landscape marking the transition between the Mühlviertel *(see LINZ: Excursions)* and the Waldviertel.

St. Wolfgangskirche ⊙ – This Gothic church contains a remarkable altarpiece of carved wood, which ranks among the finest of its kind. Author Adalbert Stifter, under whose direction the altarpiece was restored between 1852 - 1855, mentioned it in his great novel *Nachsommer* (1857, "Indian Summer").

★★ Altarpiece – The altarpiece is in the chancel, behind the high altar. It is outstanding for its monumental size - it is more than 13m - 40ft high – the beauty of its proportions and the carved decoration, which show the exceptional skill of the artist. The altarpiece was made at the end of the 15C by an unknown sculptor and was probably painted. Today all its carved portions, in high or low relief, are in the natural limewood.

Under richly carved canopies three figures – St Wolfgang, flanked by St Peter and St Christopher – occupy the central panel. The skill of the draping and the expression of the faces recall the admirable composition of the altarpiece of St Wolfgang in the Salzkammergut, a masterpiece by Michael Pacher.

On the shutters flanking the central panel are depicted the Annunciation and the Birth of Christ *(above)* and the Adoration of the Magi and the Dormition of the Virgin *(below)*.

Adalbert Stifter spent his childhood in the Bohemian Forest and seems to have developed there the sensitivity to nature which was to characterize his writings. He trained as a scientist, before becoming a private teacher in Vienna. His artistic activity at first took the form of landscape painting, until in his thirties he turned to short story writing. In the preface to his collection of stories entitled *Bunte Steine* (Coloured Stones, 1953), Stifter outlined his theory of the "sanftes Gesetz" (gentle law) which he perceived as underlying all processes. This belief shapes all his work, in which he typically rejects violence, emphasising the importance of natural growth and development. The young man's gradual maturing and awakening to knowledge, as described in *Der Nachsommer*, represents the culmination of Stifter's ideal.

The Michelin Map to use with this Guide is: 426

KITZBÜHEL✳✳

Tirol – Population 7 872
Michelin map 426 folds 18 and 19 – Alt 762m - 2 500ft

Kitzbühel is one of the oldest and most exclusive holiday resorts in the Austrian Alps. The valley in which it lies would appear to have been inhabited long before recorded time. The village itself developed thanks to its favourable geographical location on the main route from Venice to Munich. Its economic growth was further assured by rich local mining deposits. In 1255 it became a market town, and in 1271 a fully fledged town.

Until the end of the 19C, Kitzbühel developed peacefully, untouched by the destruction of war. At that time, the town's inhabitants sent for a delivery of skis from Norway, so that they could try the sport out on the slopes of the Kitzbüheler Horn. However, it was not until 1931 that the Hahnenkamm opposite was opened to skiers in its turn.

The village rapidly developed its tourist industry, drawing holiday makers from all over Europe, especially from Great Britain and Germany. The seal was put on its reputation with the construction of one of the most famous and testing World Cup downhill ski runs – the **Streif**.

In spite of this evolution, Kitzbühel retains some of the atmosphere of the fortified medieval village it once was. Its original site, on a terrace enclosed by two torrents gushing down from the Hahnenkamm, can still be discerned, despite the ever expanding suburbs. The nucleus of the town is formed by two pedestrian streets, the "Vorderstadt" and the "Hinterstadt", which are lined by elegant gabled Tyrolean houses. Numerous smart boutiques make this a tempting place to while away time window-shopping.

Kitzbühel can accommodate up to 7 200 visitors, mainly in hotels and guesthouses. Besides skiing, there are plenty of other sport and leisure activities on offer: ice-skating, curling, swimming (indoor pool with a health centre), casino.

The resort is popular with those on summer vacation as well. It has made quite a name for itself as the hub of Austria's tennis circuit (international tournaments are hosted here) and as one of the country's leading golf venues (two nine-hole and one eighteen-hole courses). Furthermore, it can boast a hang- and paragliding school and several riding centres. However, the main leisure activity during summer months is hiking, along some of the 200km - 124 miles of waymarked footpaths, which principally run along the ski slopes. These paths are suitable for those in search of an untaxing ramble, picturesque scenery and spectacular views *(lifts have been installed, as an alternative to walking, to give access to some of the best viewpoints)*.

Kitzbühel Alps – Between the Wörgl-Saalfelden gap and the Upper Valley of the Salzach, the smoothly rounded Kitzbühel Alps reach an altitude of 2 362m - 7 749ft at the Großer Rettenstein. Known locally as Grasberge (grass mountains), they form a charming and tranquil pastoral landscape.

KITZBÜHEL

The contrasting shapes and colours of the surrounding massifs – the jagged walls of the Wilder Kaiser in the north and the enormous ridge of the Hohe Tauern in the south – make the Kitzbühel Alps much sought after for the quality of their views.

⁂ **Ski slopes** – These are spread over four separate areas: Hahnenkamm-Steinbergkogel-Pengelstein (alt 750-1 970m – 2 461-6 463ft), Kitzbüheler Horn (alt 750-2 000m – 2 461-6 562ft), Stuckkogel (alt 900-1 580m – 2 953-5 184ft) and Paß Thorn (alt 930-1 980m – 3 051-6 496ft). Buses transport skiers to each mountain. There are 64 ski lifts leading to 55 ski-runs covering a total distance of 158km - 98 miles. In con-

Kitzbühel in the snow

trast to the sporty image that the resort has acquired through the international competitions held here, the ski slopes are principally suited to more gentle skiing, with long, pleasant runs through pine forests ranging from relatively easy (Pengelstein, Kaser) to middlingly difficult (Fleck, Oxalm-Nord). Only about 12km - 8 miles of ski-runs cover steeper terrain, mainly in the area of the Steinbergkogel peak. Because of the resort's relatively low altitude, snow does tend to disappear from some of the slopes as early as March, however.

To avoid the long queues at the Hahnenkamm massif, day-trippers would be better off travelling to the neighbouring Kirchberg peak, where the Fleckalm cable-car gives access to the heart of the mountain range in 15 minutes. The flank of the Kitzbüheler Horn opposite, which is equipped with modern skilifts, is not to be missed, especially when snow conditions are good, as it is then possible to ski right down into the valley.

SIGHTS

Pfarrkirche (A) – Like the neighbouring Liebfrauenkirche the church is set off by its raised site. The slender tower flanks a 15C Gothic triple nave, whose large overhanging roof, covered with shingles, gives it a distinctive mountain style. The nave is short but not without grace. The talent of a local family, the **Faistenbergers**, who were all well known artists in the 17C and 18C, is represented by the high altar, by Benedikt Faistenberger (1621-1693) and the painted ceiling of the Chapel of St Rosa of Lima by his grandson, Simon-Benedikt (1695-1759).

Liebfrauenkirche (B) – This church is distinguished by a massive square tower. Inside, there is a Coronation of the Virgin painted on the vaulting by Simon-Benedikt Faistenberger in 1739 and a Rococo grille (1778).

A 17C painting of Our Lady of Succour (Maria-Hilf) after Cranach the Elder reminds us of the important role this church played as a place of pilgrimage until the 19C.

Heimatmuseum (M) ⊙ – This local museum collection will be instructive to tourists interested in the origins of the town, which belonged to Bavaria for nearly 1 000 years.

EXCURSIONS

★★ **Kitzbüheler Horn** ⊙ – Alt 1 996m - 6 549ft. *Allow 1 hour 30min there and back. Take the cable-car up (in two stages).*
There is a fabulous **panorama**★★ of the jagged peaks of the Kaisergebirge to the northwest, the Kitzbühel ski slopes at the foot of the Rettenstein to the southwest and the Hohe Tauern with the Großvenediger and Großglockner summits to the south.
Return to the upper cable-car station, from where the limestone massif of the Loferer Steinberge can be seen lying to the east.

In the summer, the Kitzbü-heler Horn is a departure point for an interesting **ramble to the Bichlalm** (alt 1 670m - 5 479ft. *Allow 3 hours. Stout footwear essential).* From here, take the chairlift back down into the valley, and then the bus back to town *(enquire in advance about timetables at the tourist office).*

* **Ehrenbachhütte** (Hahnen-kamm-Massiv) – Alt 1 802m - 5 912ft. *Take the cable-car up from Klausen (near Kirchberg), 45min there and back.*
There is a good **view**★ of the Wilder Kaiser, the Hohe Salve, the Kitzbüheler Horn and the Großer Rettenstein peaks.
In the winter, it is possible to ski up to the **Steinberg-kogel** summit (alt 1 975m - 6 480ft), from where there is a wide-ranging **pano-rama**★★ (Hohe Tauern, Leo-ganger Steinberge).
In the summer, ramblers

KITZBÜHEL

Bichlstraße	2
Franz-Reich-Str.	4
Graggaugasse	5

KLAGENFURT Note

A Pfarrkirche   **B** Liebfrauenkirche   **M** Heimatmuseum

can walk from the upper cable-car station to the Jufenkamm ridge, and then follow the path along the ridge south to the Pengelstein mountain refuge and on to the **Schwarzkogel**★ summit (alt 2 030m - 6 660ft).

Schwarzsee – *5km - 3 miles on the Kirchberg road and the lake road to the right (level-crossing). It is, however, more agreeable to walk all the way via the Liebfrauenkirche and the Lebenberg road (northwest of the town plan).*
This lake offers the opportunity of bathing within view of the Kaisergebirge.

Paß Thurn – Alt 1 273m - 4 176ft. *20km - 12 miles south. Leave Kitzbühel on the road to Mittersill.* The best-arranged **viewing point**★ for cars to halt at is about 1 800m - 5 904ft beyond the crest, on the Oberpinzgau slope, level with the "Tauernblick Buffet". From this point there is an end view of the Hollersbachtal, which runs south towards the main crest of the Hohe Tauern range.
The slopes overlooking the pass are the skiing fields of the resort of Mittersill.

KLAGENFURT

L Kärnten – Population 90 000

Michelin map 426 fold 36 – Local map under WÖRTHER SEE – Alt 446m - 1 463ft

A site on the banks of the warmest Alpine lake in Europe and a mild southern climate have ensured that Klagenfurt remain highly favoured as a holiday destination over the centuries. The old town centre reflects about 800 years of the town's history. In the 16C and 17C Italian architects designed the town's geometric layout, with broad streets running in a grid pattern. They were also responsible for more than 50 beautiful arcaded courtyards, most of which have been restored and are now accessible to the public. Klagenfurt has received the Europa-Nostra award no less than three times in recognition of its efforts to preserve its historical town centre. For over 400 years the town and nearby lake, Wörther See, have been linked by a canal. The Lendkanal flows directly into the lake, past green banks dense with plantlife and beautiful villas dating from the turn of the century.
The heart of the modern town is marked by the Neuer Platz and the Lindwurm-brunnen, a fountain adorned with the town's emblem – a fearsome dragon.

SIGHTS

* **Landesmuseum** (Z **M¹**) ⊙ – The lawns around the local government and museum buildings are used for an open-air display **(Parkmuseum)** of Roman stone monuments from the different excavations which have been carried out in Carinthia. Note especially the reconstruction of a Celtic fountain.
In the museum proper, which is devoted to the evolution of the province through the ages, special displays have been made of mineralogy and prehistoric and Roman antiquity.

...e diagrams of mines, a magnificent relief map of the Großglockner ...sif and the glaciary basin of the Pasterze, and a fossilized rhinoceros skull the Lindwurmschädel – found in the Zollfeld in 1335 and said to have inspired the designer of the Lindwurm fountain *(see above)*. A large mosaic with mythological designs is a reminder of the former Roman capital, Virunum. Numerous **works of religious art**★, notably the impressive altarpiece of St Veit, mark the contribution of the 15C and 16C.

★ **Diözesanmuseum** (Z M²) ⊘ – The museum aims to give a good general picture of religious art in Carinthia from the 12C to the 18C; it displays examples of all the arts: jewellery, tapestry and embroidery, sculpture, painting, stained glass. Next to immensely appealing specimens of folk art, there are outstanding **works of art**★★ like the rare 12C **processional cross** (ironwork with traces of gilding) or the fine **Magdalen window** dating from 1170, the oldest of its kind in Austria but of strikingly modern design.

Alter Platz (Y) – This wide street and square which retains a certain nobility from the surrounding 16C mansions with their Baroque façades and flowered courtyards is in the heart of the old town. A few narrow, crooked streets leading off it afford vistas of the nearby towers and belfries. It is best to approach the courtyard of the Landhaus through the Alter Platz.

Landhaus (Y) – Originally the arsenal, then the state headquarters of Carinthia, this building now serves to house the departments and assemblies of the regional government. Finished in 1590, it owes the design of its inner court – especially in the Renaissance group formed by the two-storey gallery and two staircases – largely to an architect from Lugano, Antonio Verda.

Großer Wappensaal, Landhaus, Klagenfurt

Großer Wappensaal ⊘ – The state hall on the 1st floor of the central block was decorated by Josef-Ferdinand Fromiller (1693-1760). This Carinthian master of Baroque painting depicted on the ceiling, in the middle of a zenithal perspective formed by *trompe l'œil* (false perspective) galleries, a scene showing members of the States of Carinthia paying homage to the Emperor Karl VI (1728). The walls and window embrasures bear 665 heraldic shields representing the coats of arms of noblemen who sat in the States (Parliament) between 1591 and 1848.

Bergbaumuseum (Y) ⊘ – *Access via the Botanical Gardens.*
The old air-raid galleries in the Klagenfurt Kreuzbergl are now home to the oldest museum on mining in Carinthia. A variety of rare and valuable exhibits illustrate local mining history. Mine locomotives, tools etc. testify to the harsh and dangerous daily toil of the miners. Mineral samples from a number of historical mines are an indication of the reason Carinthia was regarded as one of the richest mining regions in the world during the Middle Ages.
The best and largest mineral samples from Carinthia are also on display, such as an enormous chunk of cairngorm weighing about 200kg - 440lb and measuring 1m - 3ft in height. A display of fossils charts geological eras spanning a period of over 500 million years.

KLAGENFURT

August Jaksch
   Straße .... Z 2
Benediktinerplatz .... Z 3
Feldm-Conrad-Platz .... Y 4

Heiligengeistplatz .... Y 6
Herrengasse .... Y 7
Kramergasse .... Y 9
Pernhartgasse .... Y 10
Purtscherstraße .... Y 12
St. Veiter Straße .... Y 13
Theaterplatz .... Y 15

Wienergasse .... Y 17
Wiesbadener
   Straße .... Y 18

M¹ Landesmuseum
M² Diözesanmuseum

(town plan of Klagenfurt)

EXCURSIONS

Minimundus ⓥ – *3km - 2 miles west of Klagenfurt. Leave via the Villacher Straße* (YZ).
More than 160 scale models (1:25) of world monuments, from Big Ben to the Eiffel Tower, are displayed in a park-like setting.

St. Kanzian Lakes – *20km - 12 miles east of Klagenfurt. Leave by road no 70, the Völkermarkter Straße* (Y).
This well-wooded lake district offers swimming and windsurfing as well as tennis and riding and an extensive network of signposted footpaths.
The Klopeinersee has a built-up lakeside with all kinds of water-based activities reached by private as well as public roads. The Turnersee and Kleinsee are quiet by comparison.
The road from Klagenfurt to St. Kanzian runs on a bridge over the Völkermarkter Stausee, an artificial lake formed by damming the Drava *(bathing forbidden)*.

GREEN TOURIST GUIDES

Architecture, Art
Geography, History
Picturesque routes
Touring programmes
Town and site plans

159

KLEINWALSERTAL*

Vorarlberg und Bayern (Germany) – Population 5 300
Michelin map 426 fold 15 – Local map under BREGENZERWALD
Alt of resorts: 1 088m - 3 570ft to 1 244m - 4 081ft

The Kleinwalsertal, which forms a tiny mountain area of about 100sq km - 38sq miles, is a region isolated from the rest of Austria by the peaks of the Allgäu Alps and is thus exclusively oriented towards Germany - whether it be economically or through tourism.

Walser Colonization - The upper valley of the Breitach was settled in the 13C by emigrants of Germanic origin from the Upper Valais - the Walser. As in other regions of the Vorarlberg (Großes Walsertal and Hochtannberg) cleared by these hardy workers, the small dark timber houses sprinkled about the slopes follow the traditions of their hardy individualism. Until the modern road (1930) was built, the inhabitants were able to live their patriarchal way of life and wear their curious costumes; today, however, these are worn mostly at weddings and in the Corpus Christi procession.

A unique administration - The Walser settlers passed under the sovereignty of the Habsburgs in 1453, so that they found themselves Austrian when the national frontiers were fixed. Cut off from the rest of Vorarlberg and oriented solely towards Germany in the commercial field, the district has had a special status since 1891 (exempt from customs duty).

Although under Austrian sovereignty, the Kleinwalsertal is now economically part of Germany. The postal vans which serve Mittelberg from Oberstdorf are German; locally issued postage stamps are Austrian (but can be paid for with Deutschmarks). German currency is the only means of payment for commercial transactions, including hotel bills and in the casino at Riezlern.

FROM OBERSTDORF (GERMANY) TO MITTELBERG

16km - 10 miles – about 1 hour

** **Oberstdorf** - *See Michelin Green Guide Germany.*
Leave Oberstdorf on the Upper Breitach Valley road (B 19).

The parish church steeples stand out against the limestone on Allgäu Alps. The Widderstein *(for the legend attached to it see BREGENZERWALD)* is visible in the distance behind **Hirschegg** and so are the three rocky crests of the Schafalpenköpfe to the east of Mittelberg.

Beyond **Mittelberg,** the valley's commercial centre, there is an authentic Valaisian hamlet, **Bödmen,** with its traditional chalets.

KLOBENSTEINPASS

Tirol
Michelin map 426 fold 18 – On the Ache, north of Kitzbühel
Local map under KAISERGEBIRGE

The Ache, a voluminous torrent flowing down from the Kitzbühel Alps, makes for the Chiemsee under various names (Kitzbüheler Ache, Kössener Ache, Tiroler Ache). After **Kössen** it plunges into a ravine, which forms a natural frontier between the Tyrol and Bavaria.

The road using this picturesque section runs from Kössen to Schleching (Bavaria); in the steep part of the ravine it overlooks two curious pilgrim's chapels clinging to the slope.

Chapels - *15min on foot Rtn by a downhill road branching off the route at the south entrance to the tunnel (the Austrian side) which marks the frontier with Germany.*

The two adjoining chapels are built between blocks of rock in a curious way. The larger chapel contains a black Madonna, a replica of the statue of Our Lady of Loretto. The smaller one features a cleft like a sword-cut through the rocks, which was once its only entrance.

KLOSTERNEUBURG

Niederösterreich – Population 30 500
Michelin map 426 fold 12 – Local map under WIEN: Wienerwald

In 1106, on marrying Agnes, the daughter of the Salian emperor, Babenberg Margrave Leopold III moved his court from Melk to Klosterneuburg. He had his stronghold built on a hill that had probably been settled by the Romans. In 1133, he founded an abbey there run - as it still is - by Augustinian canons.

In 1296 Klosterneuburg was granted its town charter. Blessed over the centuries by periods of prosperity, it developed into the lively town it is today.

ABBEY (STIFT) ⊘ *guided tour: about 1 hour*

Stiftsbau (Abbey building) - Under Emperor Karl VI, father of Maria Theresa, the impressive abbey building complete with domes took on its present appearance. The aim of the original plans was to emulate the monastery at Escorial. As a counterbalance to the abbey church, intended to embody spiritual strength, the abbey was supposed to emanate worldly power. However, these ambitious projects were only ever realised in part, with the initial completion of an eighth being augmented by further construction in the 19C, taking the total to a quarter of the original design. The architect was Donato Felice d'Allio, who firmly left his own mark on the building, despite the fact that the influence of Fischer von Erlach makes itself felt.

The Imperial staircase, generous in dimension but somewhat impoverished in ornamental detail, leads up to the **Imperial apartments**, some of which contain valuable furnishings. Note in particular the Gobelins room, adorned with priceless tapestries which were woven in Brussels at the beginning of the 18C and which depict scenes from the life of Telemachus. The cupola of the oval marble room is decorated with a fresco by Daniel Gran, portraying the *Apotheosis of the House of Habsburg*.

Above the Imperial apartments is the **abbey museum**, which contains a paintings gallery and a collection of Gothic and Baroque sculpture.

Cross the Stiftsplatz to get to the abbey church. Spare a glance in passing at the Gothic column dating from 1381.

Stiftskirche (Abbey church) - This Romanesque basilica with three aisles dates from 1114-1236, but has been modified a number of times over the centuries, most particularly in 1634 when it was converted into a Baroque style building by Johann Baptiste Carlone and Andrea de Retti. The **church interior★** is Baroque throughout, the final work on the project having been completed in 1730. On entering the church it is immediately obvious that great artists have been at work here, and that they have successfully worked as a team to produce a remarkable and harmonious result. The frescoes in the nave were executed by Georg Greiner *c*1689. Shortly after this, the six side altars decorated with sculptures by the Späz brothers made their appearance. The high altar itself is the creation of Matthias Steinl, as is the sounding board above the marble pulpit and more especially the beautiful **choir stalls**. The altar painting is by Johann Georg Schmidt, while the ceiling frescoes above the chancel, depicting the *Assumption of the Blessed Virgin Mary*, are by Johann Michael Rottmayr.

Kreuzgang (Cloisters) - These date from the 13C and 14C and are a fine example of early Gothic architecture with Burgundian influence. The old pump house contains a remarkable seven-armed **bronze candelabra**, a Veronese work dating from the 12C, symbolising the Tree of Jesse.

The Leopoldskapelle contains some wonderfully luminous **stained glass** dating from the 14C. The chapel also houses the tomb of Leopold III, who was canonised in 1485. His bones are kept in a reliquary above the famous Verdun altarpiece.

★★ Verdun altarpiece - This is the master-work of Nicolas de Verdun, a talented goldsmith and enamel-worker from Lorraine, to whom we also owe parts of the Shrine of the Magi in Cologne Cathedral. He won the commission in 1181. With its 45 champlevé enamelled and gilded panels the work can surely be described as a perfect masterpiece. After a fire in

Detail of the Verdun Altarpiece, Klosterneuburg Abbey

161

the church – legend has it that the blazing altar was extinguished with wine – in 1330, six of the panels had to be reworked; at the same time they were inserted into their present frame, a hinged altarpiece (triptych) which depicts scenes from the Old (upper and lower panels) and New (central panel) Testaments.

ADDITIONAL SIGHT

Martinstraße – This narrow, slightly sloping street is a picture of idyllic calm. It is lined by pretty town houses, including the Kremsmünsterer Hof (no 12) and the Martinschloß (no 34). The street leads up to the **Martinskirche**, the oldest church in Klosterneuburg, which boasts some sumptuous Baroque fittings.

KREMS und STEIN★

Niederösterreich – Population 23 123

Michelin map 426 fold 11 – Local map under DONAUTAL – Alt 221m - 725ft

At the eastern end of the Wachau, **Krems** stands on the left bank of the Danube at the foot of terraced loess hills covered with vineyards famed for their wine. This large settlement in fact consists of three towns in one, along with **Stein** and **Und**, giving rise to the Austrian joke: "Krems, Und (and) Stein are three towns".
Krems was for a long time the home of the painter Martin Johann Schmidt (1718-1801), known as **Kremser Schmidt**, who was responsible for much work in the churches and abbeys of Austria.

Stein

Becker/ÖSTERREICH WERBUNG

SIGHTS

Krems

★ **Piaristenkirche** (BZ) – Dominating the old town, this is an unusual church with an elevated chancel and a triple hall nave. Both chancel and nave have fine network vaulting. The seven huge windows making up almost the whole of the south wall flood the interior with light as in no other church in Austria.
The chancel was completed in 1457 and the nave between 1511-15, manifestly inspired by the Stephansdom in Vienna.
The Jesuits were given the church in 1616 and it is they who were responsible for the chapel dedicated to St Francis Xavier of 1640. The fresco at the entrance showing the death of the saint at the gates of China is the work of Kremser Schmidt *(see above)*, as is the majestic Assumption forming the centrepiece of the **high altar** of 1756. A further six paintings by this artist adorn the body of the church. Notable too are the **choir-stalls**, still in the style of the Renaissance although dating from well into the 17C.

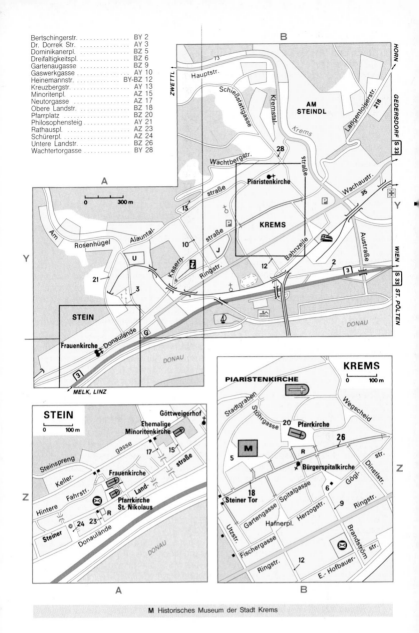

Bertschingerstr.	BY 2
Dr. Dorrek Str.	AY 3
Dominikanerpl.	BZ 5
Dreifaltigkeitspl.	BZ 6
Gartenaugasse	BZ 9
Gaswerkgasse	AY 10
Heinemannstr.	BY-BZ 12
Kreuzbergstr.	AY 13
Minoritenpl.	AZ 15
Neutorgasse	AZ 17
Obere Landstr.	BZ 18
Pfarrplatz	BZ 20
Philosophensteig	AY 21
Rathauspl.	AZ 23
Schürerpl.	AZ 24
Untere Landstr.	BZ 26
Wachtertorgasse	BY 28

M Historisches Museum der Stadt Krems

In 1776 Maria-Theresa put the church and the adjoining college in the charge of a congregation of Piarists, an educational Order who still officiate today.

Pfarrkirche (BZ) – This early Baroque church, completed in 1630 under Italian architect Cyprian Biasino, is somewhat overloaded inside with statues and gilding.
The vaulting of the nave and chancel is adorned with frescoes painted at the end of the 18C by Martin Johann Schmidt.

Historisches Museum der Stadt Krems (BZ M) ⊙ – The historical museum is located in the former Dominican monastery *(restored)*. The influence of the friars on the 13C and 14C Gothic church is manifested by its austere appearance. It houses a gallery of paintings devoted to Martin-Johann Schmidt (1718-1801).
The cloister is surrounded by conventual buildings. Its eastern gallery has Gothic blind arcades shielded under small gables. A collection of historical and artistic documents can be found in the chapter-house, warming room and other rooms.
There is also a **Wine Museum** (Weinbaumuseum) which displays everything connected with wine growing and wine in the Danube Valley.

Obere und Untere Landstraße (BZ **18, 26**) – This is the main artery of old Krems, approached from the west through the **Steiner Tor**, a monumental gateway dating from 1480 surmounted by a baroque octagonal lantern and flanked by a pair of towers with pepper-pot roofs. The main street itself has many old houses with Renaissance or Baroque façades.

Burgerspitalkirche (BZ) – This elegant Gothic chapel is all that remains of the old town hospice built here in the 15C. The peaceful atmosphere of the interior with its single rib-vaulted nave is conducive to contemplation. The high altar is flanked by two superb gilded wooden statues, the work of Matthias Schwanthaler.

Stein

Stein extends along a narrow strip of river bank parallel to the Danube and is bordered by terraced vineyards to the north. This site, together with some extraordinarily old buildings, contributes greatly to the town's charm. Some of the original town wall and a number of houses have survived from the Middle Ages and Renaissance period. It is thus a rare treat to stroll along the main street, the Steiner Landstraße, and through some of the narrower alleys climbing the hillside.

★ **Old houses** – Along the **Steiner Landstraße**, which is delimited by Krems to the east and the Linzer Tor gateway to the west, and which opens out here and there into small squares, stand several very well-preserved elegant town houses and cathedral courtyards. Most of these are two or three storeys high and reflect the wealth of this rich commercial town. The houses to the west of the street, between the Pfarrkirche and the Reisperbach, boast some particularly sumptuous façades.

Pfarrkirche St. Nikolaus – The parish church stands in the centre of town and, along with the **Frauenkirche** behind it, dominates the town's skyline. The mighty west tower with its delicate, curved Baroque dome is particularly eye-catching. Inside the church are a ceiling fresco and altar paintings by Kremser Schmidt.

Ehemalige Minoritenkirche – This triple-aisled basilica with pillars was consecrated in 1264. Its tower dates from 1444. The 14C frescoes are particularly interesting. Those in the chancel depict the Virgin Mary enthroned with donors.

Göttweigerhof – *Göttweigerhofgasse 7.* This complex, already described as a court in 1286, ceased to belong to Göttweig abbey in 1839. The **chapel** is decorated with early Gothic **frescoes**, which were painted between 1305 and 1310 and which rank among the most interesting of their kind in Austria.

EXCURSIONS

★ **Kremstal** – *16km - 10 miles. Leave Krems on the Kremstalstraße and the road to Zwettl* (AY).
As soon as it leaves the town, the road joins the Krems River and runs along its left then right bank through a pleasant landscape of loess hills where vines and fruit trees – peaches, plums and apricots – are grown on terraces.
Soon the church and ruined castle of **Rehberg** perched on a rocky spike come into view and then the Gothic tower of **Imbach** church.
Soon after Imbach appears the proud shape of the ruined fortress of **Senftenberg**, crowning a bluff. Beyond the attractive village of Senftenberg, the valley narrows between rock outcrops and becomes wild and solitary.
Turn back to Krems at Untermeisling.

Stift Göttweig ⊙ – *6km - 4 miles south of Krems on the road to St. Pölten* (BY). The massive, pale-coloured abbey buildings with their corner turrets and onion domes rise four-square from the surrounding countryside on the side of a hill, making an unforgettable sight. The striking architecture of this Benedictine foundation has earned it the humorous local nickname "Austria's Monte Cassino" (after the Italian abbey where the Benedictine Order originated).
In 1094, the first Benedictine monks arrived at the Augustinian canonry founded by St Altmann in 1083. After the great fire of 1718, work was begun on reconstructing the Baroque abbey following plans by Johann Lukas von Hildebrandt; however, the project was to remain unfinished.
The abbey church's **façade★**, with its two squat corner towers, the narthex, the four Tuscan columns and a balustrade running above, could perhaps be less heavy, but its expansive theatricality is nonetheless satisfying. The church interior is richly decorated with elaborate stucco work. The mighty high altar (1639) and pulpit are the work of Dutch master Hermann Schmidt. Note the organ case which dates from 1703.
The western wing of the abbey houses the monumental **Imperial staircase★** with a ceiling fresco by Paul Troger (1739) depicting the *Apotheosis of Karl VI*. The stairwell, completed by Franz Anton Pilgram in 1739 and a masterpiece of elegance and spaciousness, rises up three storeys.

KREMSMÜNSTER

The impressive Benedictine Abbey of Kremsmünster stands among the hills rising between the foothills of the Alps and the Danube, on a bluff which overlooks the Krems valley. The tourist coming from the east suddenly sees the tall façade of the monastery buildings, from which emerge the two domed towers of the abbey church and, on its right, the "mathematical tower". Of all the abbey's features, the monumental fish-pond should be visited. The abbey was founded in the second half of the 8C and was the work of Tassilo III, Duke of Bavaria. According to legend, Gunther, the son of Tassilo, was mortally wounded by a wild boar when hunting in the forests which then covered the domain. Tassilo decided to create a religious community on this spot in memory of his son. The present appearance of the abbey church and its monastery buildings dates from the 17C and 18C. Great architects – Carlo Antonio Carlone, Jakob Prandtauer – and talented painters – Altomonte, Kremser Schmidt – participated in the transformation of the abbey into the Baroque style.

ABBEY (STIFT) ⊘ *2 hours 30min for a complete tour*

Park the car in the outer court of the abbey. Tickets on sale in the abbey shop in the first courtyard, near the fish-pond.

★ **Fischbehälter** – The **fish-pond** was built by Carlone and enlarged by Prandtauer between 1690 and 1717. It brings an unexpected note to the abbey buildings with its five basins, surrounded by arcades and adorned with statues (Samson, David, Neptune, Triton, Jonas and St Peter) spouting water, which suggest the elegance of the Italian Renaissance. It was restored in 1971, with the exception of the ceiling frescoes which had been too affected by damp to be treated.

Stiftskirche (Abbey church) – Only the twin towers suggest that this is in fact a church. The basilica, essentially transitional Romanesque-Gothic, was transformed into the Baroque style by Carlo Carlone after 1680. The ceiling frescoes by the three Grabenberger brothers are set amidst richly sculpted stucco work. Sumptuously framed pictures stand on 12 altars. The really unusual feature of the church is however the 24 **marble angels** on either side of these, 16 particularly finely sculpted ones of which were the work of Michael Zürn the Younger between 1682 and 1686.

Stiftsgebäude (Abbey Buildings) – The **Kaisersaal** (Emperors' Hall) owes its name to portraits of the Holy Roman Emperors (from Rudolf of Habsburg to Karl VI). The pictures were painted at the end of the 17C by Altomonte. Ceiling frescoes and stucco mouldings of great delicacy adorn this state hall. On the 2nd floor are several rooms containing **collections** of paintings. A *Crucifixion* in the second room, in Flemish Renaissance style, attracts special attention.

Displayed with a great deal of pride is the **Tassilo chalice**★★★, presented to the monks by the Duke at the end of the 8C. This piece of goldsmith's work, the oldest known in the Austro-Bavarian lands, is of copper gilt, inlaid with niellated silver plaques; the decorative designs and characters – Christ and saints – show the influence of the earliest Christian art – the Anglo-Irish.

The unusually extensive **library**★ (65m - 213ft long) contains a total of 165 000 volumes; it recalls the old Benedictine adage that a bookless abbey is like a fortress without an armoury.

★ **Mathematischer Turm** – The "mathematical tower", or observatory, is about 50m - 164ft high. It contains extensive collections relating to paleontology, physics, mineralogy, zoology, anthropology and astronomy. Though built in 1758 it has a decidedly modern appearance. From the top the view stretches as far as the Alps.

Tassilo chalice

EXCURSION

Fahrzeugmuseum (Motor Museum) ⊙ – *10km - 6 miles west via the Bad Hall road. Time 1 hour*. Occupying four floors of **Schloß Kremsegg**, this is a collection of some 100 vehicles from the early days of motoring to the 1960s. Mercedes are particularly well represented, with some 30 vehicles on display, including the famous "Pullman 600".

KRIMMLER WASSERFÄLLE★★★

Salzburg

Michelin map 426 fold 32

The Krimml falls, one of the finest cascades in the Alps, foam and tumble their way over the rocky sides of the wooded amphitheatre at the end of the Salzach valley. They are a magnificent sight, especially in the midday sun when the spray glitters with rainbow colours. The Krimmler Ache, which rises from the glacier of that name at an altitude of 3 000m - 9 843ft, drops down 380m - 1 247ft to the valley in three waterfalls. A rather steep but shaded footpath leads to the falls, which are the most popular natural tourist sight between Innsbruck and Salzburg.

TOUR ⊙ *3 hours walk there and back to see the waterfall in its entirety.*

Keen walkers might like to take a whole day over the excursion, or even two days with an overnight stay at the mountain refuge.

Leave the car in the car park at the bottom of the Krimml valley on the Gerlospaß road (to avoid the toll on the Gerlospaß road, go into Krimml and leave the car in the town).

Pass under the road and take the wide path which leads to the foot of the cascades and then climbs through the woods in hairpin bends. Minor paths branch off to viewpoints overlooking the two lower falls. At the top of the climb *(1 hour 15min)* the path emerges onto an Alpine pasture beside the Berggasthof Schönangerl (alt 1 300m - 4 265ft). Take the path, which becomes increasingly steep, to see the upper, much more powerful, waterfall (alt 1 470m - 4 823ft; *30min walk*).

After this, the landscape changes dramatically, with peaceful, gently sloping Alpine meadows stretching away as far as the eye can see. Keen ramblers can walk along the banks of the Krimmler Ache to the Krimmler Tauernhaus (alt 1 631m - 5 351ft; *2 hour walk*) and on to the Warnsdorfer Hütte mountain refuge (alt 2 336m - 7 664ft; *5 hour walk*) at the foot of the Krimml glacier.

KUFSTEIN

Tirol – Population 13 125

Michelin map 426 fold 18 – Local map under KAISERGEBIRGE – Alt 499-1 637ft

Kufstein is the last Austrian town in the Inn valley. It is grouped at the foot of a rocky height and crowned with a fortress, which gives some idea of the unfriendly relations between Bavaria and Austria in past centuries.

HISTORICAL NOTES

A much-coveted town – As a frontier town commanding a route of great strategic importance, Kufstein was frequently the subject of bitter dispute between Bavaria and the Tyrol.

A fortress was first mentioned here in 1205. By 1393 the town was granted a charter by Duke Stephen III of Bavaria, which raised it to the rank of borough. In 1504 Emperor Maximilian took possession of the town and incorporated it permanently into the Tyrol. In 1703, under the threat of Bavarian attack, the town was almost completely burnt down by the commander of the fortress who wished to have a clear field of fire. It was here, in 1809, that Andreas Hofer, hero of the rising against Napoleon, gave battle against the Franco-Bavarian coalition.

Today's Kufstein is a busy and attractive place, benefiting from its frontier position on the mainline railway and its proximity to the Brenner autobahn. Nearby are the popular Kaisergebirge, linked to the town by the "Wilder Kaiser" (Y) chair-lift.

Kufstein is known as "the town of the five lakes", which are most popular for day-trips (Hechtsee, Langsee, Pfrillsee, Egelsee and Stimmersee).

General view – To appreciate the site★ of the castle, climb the Heldenhügel (z), a wooded rise topped by a statue of Andreas Hofer (Andreas-Hofer-Denkmal).

FORTRESS (FESTUNG) (Z) *30min return on foot.*

Like its prestigious neighbour Salzburg, Kufstein owes much of its character to the acropolis which dominates the town.

Starting from the Unterer Stadtplatz, leave the church, and make for the Neuhof *(left)* which contains the auditorium for the Heldenorgel. Pass through the walls by a covered stairway beneath the Bürgerturm (Burghers' Tower).

Other possible access: take the lift at the foot of the rock along the Inn-Promenade. Go straight ahead (the entrance to the buildings – see below – is on the left) through a new gateway and over a bridge to the Wallachenbastion, which forms a **viewpoint★** overlooking the River Inn and the wooded Pendling, a small mountain range.

There is a view across the Inn of the Kitzbühel Alps, to the left, and in clear weather as far as the snows of the Stubai Alps, southwest of Innsbruck.

Heimatmuseum ⊘ – The local museum houses an array of objects collected by the local geography society. The rooms devoted to illustrations of the fortress through the ages are the most interesting feature.

★ Kaiserturm ⊘ – This colossal tower, completed in 1522, rears up, with walls up to 4.50m - 25ft thick, on the highest point of the rock.

The interior is arranged round a huge central pillar, encircled by a vaulted gallery. The design can be clearly seen from the 2nd floor, at the beginning the tour. On the 3rd floor thirteen cells are reminders of the captives imprisoned at Kufstein, when the castle was a state prison from 1814 to 1867. The tour continues through bastions, casemates and cellars.

Tiefer Brunnen – This well was bored in the rock at the time of the Emperor Maximilian and is over 68m - 200ft deep.

KUFSTEIN

Hans-Reisch-Str.	Z 2	Langkampfener Str.	Y 10	Otto-Lasne-Str.	Y 23
Innbrücke	Z 4	Madersperger Str.	Z 12	Römerhofgasse	Z 24
Innpromenade	Z 5	Marktgasse	Z 14	Stuttgarter Str.	Y 26
Kaiserbergstr.	Y 7	Maximilianstr.	Z 15	Thierseestr.	Y 27
		Neuhof	Z 18	Unterer	
		Oberer		Stadtplatz	Z 29
		Stadtplatz	Z 19	Willy-Graft-Str.	Y 30

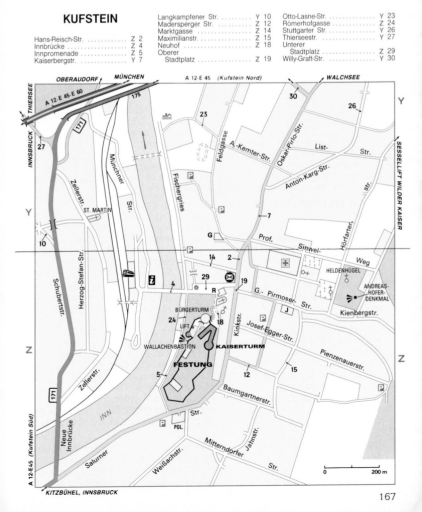

Heldenorgel ⊙ – This instrument, known as the "Heroes' organ", was first played in public in 1931. It was built in the top storey of the Bürgerturm to commemorate the German and Austrian dead from the First World War. The recitals can be heard for several miles round the town in still weather. Indisputably the largest instrument of its kind in the world, since 1971 the organ has been able to boast 4 307 pipes and 46 registers. The organist's keyboard and the gallery for the audience are at the foot of the rock.

EXCURSION

★ **Ursprungpaßstraße** – *26km - 16 miles from Kufstein to Bayrischzell (Germany).*
This trip can be the beginning of a tour in the Bavarian Alps (customs formalities); description of the Deutsche Alpenstraße (German Alpine Road) in Michelin Green Guide Germany. Leave Kufstein on the Bayrischzell road, northwest of the plan.

The road rises rapidly into the woods and on leaving the Inn valley loses sight of the fortress.

Thiersee – Population 2 263. The Pendling spur dominates the scene of a small lake at the foot of a terraced village. A passion play is performed here every six years.

A succession of combes and gorges leads to the Ursprung pass (alt 849m - 2 785ft). After the pass the road begins the final descent to Bayrischzell.

LAMBACH

Oberösterreich – Population 3 165

Michelin map 426 fold 21 – 15km - 9 miles southwest of Wels – Alt 349m - 1 145ft

In the Middle Ages when the River Traun was not navigable above the Traunsee *(qv)*, Lambach on the north bank became the point where salt carried overland in sacks from Hallstatt was loaded on to boats for Vienna and Bohemia. To this economic function was added the prestige and fame of a Benedictine abbey founded in the 11C.

ABBEY (STIFT) *time: 1 hour 30min*

In the west front is a richly decorated doorway built by Jakob Auer in 1693. Four marble columns support an entablature surmounted by statues: the Virgin, holding the Infant Jesus in her arms, between St Adalbero, the founder of the abbey, and St Kilian. It was in 1056 that Adalbero, Count of Lambach and Wels and Bishop of Würzburg, decided to convert the castle at Lambach into a Benedictine abbey. Evicted from his see on several occasions by the German Emperor Henry IV in the course of his Investiture struggle with Pope Gregory VII, Adalbero undertook a number of journeys in the Papal States. It was no doubt during these travels that he acquired his taste for the kind of Byzantine frescoes then to be seen in Lombardy and the Veneto.

Stiftskirche (Abbey Church) ⊙ – In the 17C the abbey was rebuilt according to Baroque precepts. The Romanesque chancel and transept, at the west end of the church were abandoned in order to reorientate the church to face the east. The chancel was demolished but the transept was retained, outside the new edifice, in order to support the extra load of the towers (estimated at 900 tons). The walls were doubled in thickness too, thereby covering up the frescoes for more than two centuries and guaranteeing their preservation.

★★ **Romanesque frescoes (11C)** – Uncovered and restored in 1967, they are the only ones of their kind in the whole of Austria. It is likely that they were completed for the consecration of the abbey in the year of Adalberto's death (1090).
Both in terms of style and subject-matter, the frescoes owe more to Byzantium than to Western Europe. Among the great variety of figures one particular scene in the central dome stands out, the **Virgin Mary and Infant Jesus accompanied by two Midwives**. This unusual subject is perhaps intended as an affirmation of Christ's truly human birth. To the left, the Three Wise Men bring their gifts. More difficult to distinguish is the subject-matter in the south dome; this represents the city of Jerusalem and Herod interrogating the Wise Men. The fact that a number of scenes are based on the life of Herod is not without relevance to the contemporary quarrel between secular power (the Emperor) and spiritual power (the Pope). In terms of technique, most of the work is "a fresco" with occasional touches of "secco".

Klostergebäude (Abbey buildings) – The abbey is composed of three complexes, the first to the north of the church around the cloisters, the second – horse-shoe-shaped – around the abbey courtyard, and the third around the rectangular abbey garden. In the west wing of this section, called the "New

Convent", there is the Baroque **abbey library** with frescoes by Melchior Seidl. The north wing houses the **refectory** on the ground floor, a well-proportioned room with outstanding stucco decoration by Diego Francesco Carlone and frescoes by Wolfgang Andreas Heindl. The **dispensary** on the floor above also contains some beautiful stucco work.

★ **Kleines Theatre** – The abbey has its own theatre, the only one of its kind to have survived in Austria. The stage dates from 1769. On 23 April 1770, while on her way to marry the future Louis XVI, **Marie-Antoinette** of Austria stayed at the abbey with her mother and their retinue. An improvised play, "The Marriage Contract", was staged for their entertainment; it made the 15-year-old Marie Antoinette laugh so much that she had to be reminded that such behaviour was not appropriate for a future queen of France.

Another famous name associated with the abbey is that of **Mozart**, who is supposed to have written the **Lambacher Symphony** while staying here.

ADDITIONAL SIGHT

★ **Pfarr- und Wallfahrtskirche Stadl-Paura** – *2km - 1 mile. Leave Lambach to the south. Cross the River Traun and turn right after 500m towards the mound on which the church is built.*

The **Dreifaltigkeitskirche** was built as the result of a vow. In 1713, when the whole land was being ravaged by plague, Abbot Maximilian Pagl swore to build a church dedicated to the Holy Trinity as soon as the country had been delivered from its torments. Between 1714 and 1725 he constructed one of Austria's most unusual Baroque monuments.

Everything in the building, designed by the Linz architect Johann Michael Prunner, is a symbol; faith in the Trinity is expressed in the plan itself, the circular nave being inscribed within an equilateral triangle formed by the three chancels. This architectural conceit, mixing logic with theatre, is continued throughout, regardless of liturgical convenience, and hence there are 3 façades, 3 portals, 3 altars, 3 miniature organs and 3 sacristies. The frescoes in the dome and the altarpieces are by Carlo Carlone, Martin Altomonte and Domenico Parodi.

Dreifaltigkeitskirche, Stadl-Paura

LANDECK

Tirol – Population 7 325

Michelin map 426 fold 29 – Local map ARLBERGGEBIET – Alt 816m - 2 677ft

This tourist destination at the junction of the Arlberg road and the Inn valley is an important communications centre. Its massive fortified castle (13C) and a series of feudal strongpoints perched like eagles' nests in the near neighbourhood bear witness to the strategic importance of this section of the valley.

The pretty Tyrolean villages in the neighbourhood, Stanz, Grins, Tobadill, Fliess, etc., each on its natural terrace, are worth visiting.

Pfarrkirche – This church on a terrace at the foot of the castle is one of the most carefully planned Gothic buildings in the Tyrol. Inside, the Flamboyant fenestration and particularly the network vaulting indicate the later period, the end of the 15C.

The high point of the church's decoration is the "Schrofenstein" altarpiece at the high altar, representing the Adoration of the Magi. The work dates from the beginning of the 16C, except for the side panels and the crown, which are modern. The unusually high predella shows, in the centre, the sainted King Oswald, holding his sceptre and a sacred vase. The donors kneel on either side. These lifelike coloured statuettes reproduce the features of Oswald von Schrofenstein, whose ruined castle can still be seen nearby *(see INNTAL)*, and of Praxedis von Wolkenstein.

LECH✷✷✷

Vorarlberg – Population 1 270

Michelin map 426 fold 29 – Local map under ARLBERGGEBIET – Alt 1 447m - 4 747ft

Lech is indisputably the prettiest holiday destination in the Austrian Alps and one of the few resorts in the northern Alps to have made a name for itself as an international winter sports venue worthy of inclusion in the same league as St Moritz, Davos and Zermatt in Switzerland, or Courchevel, Méribel, Val Thorens, Val d'Isère and Chamonix in France.

Lech has won its reputation thanks in part to its merging with the neighbouring resorts of **Zürs**✷✷ and **St. Anton**✷✷ *(qv)*, to create a skiing area capable of meeting the most demanding standards, but most of all because of its insistence on quality above quantity. Here, biggest is not allowed to be best, and tourist facilities have been built very much with the welfare of the natural environment in mind.

For this reason, guest capacity is only about 7 000, or three to six times smaller than the demand in the other major European winter sports resorts listed above. Accommodation is furthermore quite dispersed, consisting mainly of hotels and family guesthouses in the luxury category. Après-ski catering in Lech emphasises the art of living, with exclusive boutiques, elegant cafés, gourmet restaurants and cultural activities. Sports facilities are varied and of a high quality: indoor swimming pools, ice-rinks, fitness centres and tennis and squash courts.

During winter Lech gives off an air of stylish chic while at the same time remaining effortlessly laid back. The village, which has been a meeting place for Europe's aristocracy for decades, also draws a loyal clientele of families and habitués. *Because of the limited capacity for accommodation, it is necessary to reserve a long time in advance for the seasons around Christmas and in February/March.*

Lech also has plenty to offer in the summer months, when life takes on a much calmer pace and prices are noticeably more reasonable. Although there are no particularly breath-taking panoramas, the soft green meadows of the surrounding countryside are most restorative. The area lends itself especially to rambling *(see Excursions below)* and mountain biking, most popularly in the Formarin, Ferwall and Moos valleys. One of Lech's major attractions is the $1\ 200m^2$ - $12\ 917ft^2$ open-air swimming pool in a pretty woodland setting. Anglers can choose between lakes such as the Formarinsee, Spullsee, Zürssee or Zugweiher *(details of fishing permits available from tourist office).*

HISTORICAL NOTES

The village of Lech was founded by the Valais towards the end of the 12C. For goods in kind, the Barons of Rettenburg in the Allgäu let them clear and cultivate the upper valley of the Lech. Since the predominant plantlife was pine trees (*Tannen* in German), the Valais called the town Tannberg am Lech ("pine mountain by the Lech"). In time this was shortened to Lech, after the river which rises 14km - 9 miles west of the town.

The Lech valley developed into one of the most densely populated areas in the northern Alps. Access routes to the valley were constantly under the threat of avalanches, with the result that the Valais remained effectively cut off from the outside world throughout the long winters. The harsh climate at this altitude made

Lech

any kind of crop-farming or tree plantation impossible, so local people earned their living exclusively from dairy-farming and stock-raising. To encourage them to settle in the region permanently, despite the difficult living conditions, they were granted certain rights and privileges, for example their own court of law, which held session in the Weißes Haus. This historical building is still standing.

Thanks to its sheltered location, Lech can look back on a relatively peaceful past. Its development was interrupted only by two outbreaks of the plague, in 1574 and 1635, and then by the Napoleonic Wars.

The completion of the Arlberg and Flexen pass road in 1900 heralded the dawn of a new age. From now on, Lech was accessible also during the winter months, and it gradually evolved into a tourist destination. Pioneers of the sport of skiing followed, coming from the region of Lake Constance mainly to Zürs. But Lech was quick to catch up, and the first skilift began operating in 1939. After the Second World War, the town's economic growth put on an incredible spurt. The vast Arlberg snowfields drew winter sports enthusiasts from all over the world. Lech nonetheless managed to adapt to these changes without too much upheaval and whilst preserving its natural environment.

★ SITE

The town of Lech, covering an area of 90km²-35sq miles, lies on a mountain plateau (alt 1 444-1 717m – 4 738-5 633ft). Limestone peaks (the Mohnenfluh and Braunarlspitze to the north, Rote Wand to the west, Schafberg and Omeshorn to the south and Rüfispitze to the east) tower above the lush Alpine pastures and woodland which grows at up to 1 800m - 5 906ft above sea level. Although difficult access roads and the sheer cliff faces of Omeshorn and Rüfikopf lend the area an undeniably mountainous aspect, the mountains around Lech are not in fact that high. None of the surrounding peaks is taller than 2 700m - 8 858ft, and there is not a single glacier in sight.

HOLIDAY RESORT

The town of Lech is spread along the banks of the river of that name. Lech town centre lies on the intersection of the river valley with the valley in which Zürs is situated. With the exception of the Gothic **church** (14C), and one or two farmhouses from the days of the Valais (Haus Anger no 19) and of the court in the Weißes Haus (16C) opposite the Hotel Krone, Lech retains little physical evidence of its past.

Further uphill the resort of **Oberlech** (alt 1 700m - 5 577ft), consisting exclusively of hotels, stands on a slope of the Kriegerhorn. This spot is blessed with plenty of sunshine and offers excellent snow conditions and a sweeping view. In winter Oberlech is only accessible via a cable-car.

For holiday makers seeking respite from the hubbub of the ski slopes and other holiday makers, the hamlets of **Zug** to the west and Stubenbach to the east offer a calmer alternative.

SKI SLOPES

The **Arlberg ski slopes**✵✵✵, which encompass from north to south the resorts of Lech, Zürs, Stuben and St. Anton am Arlberg, are the largest and most varied in Austria. They include over 200km - 124 miles of maintained and 220km - 137 miles of unmaintained ski-runs, to which 88 ski-lifts give access. It is possible to ski from Lech to Zürs and back, and likewise from Stuben and St. Anton. To get from Zürs to Stuben or St. Anton, however, it is necessary to take the bus.

The **skiing area**✵ attached to Lech extends over two mountains. Most of the ski-runs are to be found on the Kriegerhorn and the Zuger Hochlicht (alt 1 450-2 377m – 4 757-7 799ft). The guaranteed snow cover and the gentle slopes make skiing here an enjoyable and relaxing experience. The Mohnenmähderpiste (very easy) and the Steinmähderpiste (for those of average ability) are definitely worth a try. Experienced skiers will prefer the Rüfikopf opposite (alt 1 450-2 362m - 4 757-7 749ft). This is the departure point for two off-piste runs (the Langerzug and the Tannegg), which can be tackled with an accompanying ski instructor.

Holiday makers should also enquire about the ski slopes at Zürs and St. Anton *(qv)*, which also have plenty to offer by way of enjoyment.

VIEWS FROM THE PEAKS

★★ **Zuger Hochlicht** – Alt 2 377m - 7 799ft. *In winter accessible to skiers only, allowing 1 hour 30min there and back. Take the Schlegelkopf and then the Kriegerhorn chairlifts, followed by the Mohnenfluh cable-car. In the summer, it is possible to to take the* **Petersboden chairlift** ⊘ *from Oberlech, and then do the tour of the Zuger Hochlicht round via the Mohnenfluhsattel gap and on to Butzensee lake (2 hours 15min there and back on foot).*

From the Kriegerhorn (alt 2 173m - 7 129ft) there is a broad view of the Zuger valley against a backdrop of the Rote Wand cliffs, to the west, and of the Zuger Hochlicht ski slopes, framed between the peaks of Braunarlspitze and Mohnenfluh, to the north. To the south lies Zürs in its valley, at the foot of the majestic Rüfispitze and the precipitous Roggspitze.

The Zuger Hochlicht reveals a beautiful **panorama★★** of the Arlberg region, the Lechtal Alps and the Rätikon (especially the eye-catching peak known as the Drei Türme, or "three towers"). There is an all-round panorama from the peak itself, reached in a few minutes from the far left end of the cable-car station. The Hochtannberg pass road can be seen further below.

★ **Rüfikopf** ⊙ – Alt 2 362m - 7 749ft. *Take the cable-car.* There is a beautiful overall view from this summit of the holiday resort and Lech ski slopes, at the foot of the rocky Mohnenfluh and Braunarlspitze peaks. The Rüfikopf is a good departure point for a ski trip to Zürs.

EXCURSIONS

★ **Spullersee** – *Take the bus to the lake (from the stop in front of the post office; enquire at the tourist office for timetable). Allow 30min. Cars can be parked in Anger underground car park (free during summer) opposite the post office. Before 9am and after 3pm, motorists can drive to the lake in their own car; there is a toll levied on this stretch of road.*

This beautiful **drive★** leads through charming, green countryside. Level with the toll booth, there is a municipal swimming pool set in the woods. Then the road passes through the pretty village of Zug, with Alpine pastures, through which the Spullerbach winds a course, stretching on either side in between clumps of fir and larch.

Finally after a very steep climb the road reaches the **Spullersee★**, which lies in a spectacular setting in a natural amphitheatre 1 827m - 5 994ft above sea level. The major summits are the Plattnitzer Spitze and Rohnspitze to the south, the Wildgrubenspitze to the east and the Spuller Schafberg (alt 2 679m - 8 789ft) and Pfaffeneck to the north.

★ **Formarinsee** – *Take the bus to the lake. The first half of the trip is identical to that described above. Allow 30min for the bus ride and then 10min walk downhill on a good footpath.* The Formarinsee (alt 1 789m - 5 869ft) lies at the foot of the Rote Wand (alt 2 704m - 8 871ft).

The Lechtal Alps have 200km - 124 miles of waymarked footpaths, offering numerous possibilities to walkers and ramblers.

★★ **Walk from the Formarinsee to the Spullersee** – *Allow 4 hours for this quite taxing walk, parts of which should be tackled with care. Difference in altitude is about 600m - 1 969ft. Climbing boots are essential. This excursion is dangerous in mist or fog, or if the ground is damp.*

Take the bus which goes to the Formarinsee. On arrival at 1 871m - 6 138ft, instead of walking down to the lake, take the footpath climbing gently up to the left *(waymarked in yellow)*. The path, dotted with Alpine roses, leads right along the edge of the cliff, offering lovely views of the Formarinsee below before reaching the **Freiburger Hütte** (mountain refuge).

From here take path no 601 towards the Ravensburger Hütte *(waymarked in red)*. After half an hour's easy climb towards the Formaletsch range the path crosses a picturesque limestone plateau, a real sea of rocks, known aptly enough as **Steinernes Meer** *(Take care! Do not leave the waymarked path.)*

The path becomes clearer again and climbs steeply and tortuously up to the **Gehrengrat**, where chamois and ibex are frequently to be seen. There is a good view of the Verwall range, the Kloster valley and the Rätikon. A very steep path leads from the summit down to the Spullersee *(allow 1 hour 30min; follow signs to Ravensburger Hütte, or "RH")*. On reaching the lake, turn left. In 5 minutes, the path comes to the bus stop for the return trip to Lech.

Oberes LECHTAL

Vorarlberg und Tirol

Michelin map 426 folds 15, 16 and 29

Upstream from Reutte the Lech valley hollows out a remarkably uniform furrow for 60km - 37 miles between the Allgäu and Lechtal Alps, and parallel to the Inn valley. The relatively under-used road between Reutte and Warth forms an interesting touring route. In the course of a journey through Austria it affords a peaceful interval which some will be glad to prolong.

FROM REUTTE TO WARTH

61km - 38 miles – 2 hours

The road between Steeg and Warth can be closed (not more than 3 days) owing to avalanches. On the whole, it is not usually possible to drive between Warth and Lech in winter.

Reutte - *See FERNPASSSTRASSE.*

Upstream from Reutte the landscape remains austere, largely owing to the wanderings of the torrent, which has spread great beds of gravel - at best wooded with conifers, or else bare of plant life – leaving no terraces or localised areas of flat land suitable for settlement. After Stanzach, however, the countryside is greener and more pastoral, and the back drop of mountains gains in majesty with the appearance, to the northwest, of the magnificent steep crests of the Allgäu Alps.

Elbigenalp - Population 710. The prettiest painted houses in the village of Elbigenalp often belong to local people who had at one time worked in Holland or Germany where they became wealthy in some prosperous business. A small professional school perpetuates the Tyrolean tradition of wood-carving. The church, rebuilt in the 17C, stands apart in the fields in an enclosure. Its sharp pointed spire attracts the visitor to the most remarkable building in the Upper Lech, especially since the restoration of the Baroque interior (1969). Alongside the main church is the small 15C Martinskapelle, in which the crypt once served as a charnelhouse. This is decorated with a series of painted panels representing The Dance of Death. This popular 19C work was done by Anton Falger (1791-1876), the valley's chronicler.

Above Steeg the road climbs through a succession of narrow passes above the Lech before suddenly rising through a broken scenery of rocks and woods to overlook the steep slopes below which runs the torrent. The road then emerges into the Alpine pastures of Lechleiten, facing the Karhorn, before reaching Warth.

When driving in Great Britain
use the Michelin Motoring Atlas Great Britain
Scale 1 : 300 000

LEOBEN

Steiermark – Population 32 010

Michelin map 426 fold 23 – Alt 541m - 1 775ft

Leoben, seat of the Montanuniversität, a famous metallurgy and mining university, has been centre of the Styrian metal industry since the Middle Ages. The proximity of the Erzberg with its iron deposits *(see EISENERZ)* has encouraged the development of the metallurgical industry in Donawitz to the northwest. Leoben's industrial suburbs form a striking contrast to their Alpine surroundings.

It was in Leoben that Napoleon signed a peace treaty with Austria on 18 April 1797, as a preliminary to the Treaty of Campo-Formio.

Old town - Gracious houses around the **Hauptplatz**, such as the house on the corner with Homanngasse or the Hacklhaus dating from 1680, testify still to the wealth of the iron merchants of yesteryear. More beautiful old houses can be seen in the Dominikanergasse and, especially, the Homanngasse. The column in memory of the plague *(Pestsäule)*, which features a sculpture group of the Trinity, was put up in 1717. The old town wall, in many places in ruins or incorporated into other buildings, is best preserved where it runs alongside the river Mur.

Kirche Maria am Waasen - West of the town, near the bridge over the Mur, the Gothic church of Maria am Waasen has 15C stained-glass windows in the chancel; they depict the Apostles, the Coronation of the Virgin and scenes from the Life and Passion of Christ.

173

LERMOOS*

Tirol – Population 950
Michelin map 426 fold 16 – Alt 1 004m - 3 294ft

Together with Ehrwald and Biberwier, Leermoos occupies an exceptional **site★★** in the upper valley of the Loisach, a central point in the Northern Limestone Alps. The little resort faces the escarpments of the Zugspitze, which is separated from the bold pyramid of the Sonnenspitze (Miemingergebirge) by the Gaistal gap. One can hardly find a better point from which to admire this group of peaks. Lermoos is therefore one of the best resorts for mountain views in Austria. It is also well equipped for winter sports.

Pfarrkirche zur hl. Katharina – This church is an example of the southern German Baroque style, manifested in the staggered spatial layout. The ceiling and cupola are decorated with *trompe-l'œil* paintings by Italian artist Giuseppe Gru in 1784. The Rococo statues of St George and St John of Nepomuk, and the gilded splendour of the pulpit are of particularly high quality.

Lermoos and the Wetterstein mountains

LIENZ

Tirol – Population 11 700
Michelin map 426 fold 33 – Alt 678m - 2 224ft

Lienz lies in the shadow of the Dolomites, whose slopes, wrinkled with ravines and divided into many facets, thus justify their popular nickname of *Unholde* – the unfriendly. The town is the southern terminus of the road to the Großglockner and the Felbertauern. It is also the chief town in the Osttirol district of Austria, which has been cut off from the central part of the province of Tirol *(see map on p 3)* and from Innsbruck, the provincial capital, since the transfer of the Pustertal (Val Pusteria) to Italy in 1919. Only in 1967 with the opening of the Felbertauern tunnel was the situation changed. About 15km - 9 miles downstream, between Nikolsdorf and Oberdrauburg, the small ravine of the Drava known as the Tiroler Tor (gate of the Tyrol) has marked the natural frontier with Carinthia since the 16C.

SIGHTS

Schloß Bruck und Osttiroler Heimatmuseum ⊙ – This castle is a former fortress of the Counts of Görz (now Gorizia) whose estates, extending from the Tauern to Istria, enabled the Habsburgs, who inherited them in 1500, to practise their policy of expansion towards the Adriatic. The castle now houses the museum of the East Tyrol, which is devoted among other things to local antiquities, folklore and handiwork. The Knights' Hall (Rittersaal) shows how the castle looked in medieval times with its bare beams and rafters, on which are traces of colouring. The two-storey chapel shelters, under its 15C Gothic vaulting, some mural paintings (1495) and an altarpiece from Michael Pacher's school.

The large **Albin-Egger-Lienz gallery** gives a comprehensive review of the work of this painter (1868-1926), who was often inspired by the Tyrol and its inhabitants. His violent and unadorned expressionism recalls the manner of the Swiss painter Ferdinand Hodler. The museum also exhibits, in another interesting gallery, the work of other contemporary artists.

LIENZ

Albin-Eggerstraße 2
Andrä-Kranzgasse 3
Gratendorferstraße 4
Haugerplatz 6
Hauptplatz 7
Johannesplatz 8
Messinggasse 10
Patriasdorferstraße 12
Rosengasse 13
St. Michaelsgasse 16
Schweizergasse 17
Südtirolerplatz 18

The fragments of stonework collected in the section on Roman archaeology come mostly from the excavations at Aguntum and Lavant-Kirchbichl, which specialists may see east of the town, on either side of the Drava.

Pfarrkirche St. Andrä – This church has a late Gothic nave and an 18C chancel. During its restoration in 1968 mural paintings of the 14C, 15C and 17C were discovered. Under the gallery are the magnificent 16C **tombstones**★, in Salzburg marble, of Count Leonard, the last of the Görz-Tirol line, and his successor, Michael von Wolkenstein (with his wife, Barbara von Thun).

Within the graveyard, which was once fortified, stands a monument to the war dead by Holzmeister. The memorial chapel contains the tomb of Albin Egger-Lienz, who helped to design this unusual churchyard.

EXCURSION

★★ **Tauerntal** – *45km - 28 miles – plus 2 hours on foot Rtn – Description under FELBERTAUERNSTRASSE.*

From Lienz take the Felbertauern road; at the Matreier Tauernhaus follow the excursion to the Großvenediger.

For a full day excursion in the high mountains (205km - 127 miles), leave Lienz early. From Mittersill on the north side of the Felbertauerntunnel take the Salzbach valley east to Bruck. Return south to Lienz via the Großglockner-Hochalpenstraße.

MICHELIN GUIDES

The Red Guides (hotels and restaurants)
Benelux – Deutschland – España Portugal – Europe – France – Great Britain and Ireland – Italia – Switzerland

The Green Guides (fine art, historic monuments, scenic routes)
Austria – Belgium and Luxembourg – Brussels – California – Canada – Chicago – England: The West Country – Europe – Florida – France – Germany – Great Britain – Greece – Ireland – Italy – London – Mexico – Netherlands – New England – New York City – Portugal – Quebec – Rome – San Francisco – Scandinavia-Finland – Scotland – Spain – Switzerland – Tuscany – Venice – Wales – Washington DC

and the collection of regional guides to France

Hauptplatz, Linz

LINZ★

L Oberösterreich – Population 197 960

Michelin map 426 fold 9 – Local map under DONAUTAL – Alt 266m – 873ft

Linz, the capital of Upper Austria, is built on both banks of the Danube, at a point where the valley opens out after a narrow section. Three modern bridges link the city with its suburb of Urfahr, on the left bank.

As a bridgehead, Linz owes a good deal of its prosperity to the Danube. Today it is a rapidly-growing industrial city, whose symbol is the **Neues Rathaus** (Z R). Opened in 1985, this ultra-modern city hall stands on the north bank of the river near the Niebelungen bridge.

A Daughter of the Danube – The Romans had already recognized the importance of this crossroads site, which commands both the Danube valley and the former salt road, which extended from Hallstatt in the Traun valley to Bohemia. From the Middle Ages onwards, shipping on the Danube contributed to the growth of the town, which was well fitted to take a leading role in river traffic, owing to its wood and iron industries. Today, large scale engineering works have made the port of Linz the biggest on the middle Danube.

Famous talents – The German astronomer **Johannes Kepler** (1571-1630) lived in Linz and it was here that he wrote his best-known work *Harmonica Mundi*. Closer to our time, the Austrian writer **Adalbert Stifter** (1805-68), considered by Nietzsche to be one of the great masters of 19C German prose, was Director of the city's schools. Linz was a staging-post for Mozart in the course of his many tours; in 1782 his "Linz Symphony" was hurriedly written here for a concert he was due to give at the city theatre". Beethoven too composed a symphony in Linz, his Eighth, but more than any other composer, the city cherishes the memory of **Anton Bruckner** *(qv)* who was cathedral organist here for 12 years.

Linz keeps its musical traditions alive through its international festival of classical music, the Bruckner Festival *(See the Calendar of events at the end of the guide)*.

An Industrial Capital – The coming of railways – the first train in Austria ran between Linz and Budweis (České Budějovice) in 1832 – facilitated the installation of engineering and textile industries between the old town and the confluence of the Danube and the Traun. This enabled Linz to expand and absorb Scharlinz, Bergern and Kleinmünchen, which are now part of its southern suburbs.

Since the end of the Second World War industrial development has accelerated with emphasis on chemicals and other heavy industries.

Nowadays, the company VÖEST-ALPINE, in the field of steel, assembly and construction of industrial machinery, and ÖMV industrial chemistry sites (Chemie Linz and Agrolinz Melamin) alone between them employ almost 20 000 people. Their equipment and production processes are among the most modern in Austria and this, plus the fact that both industrial groups concentrate their efforts on production for export, means that they are of great economic importance to Linz and the region.

GENERAL VIEW

We recommend that you approach Linz along the Danube, preferably from the west. Howerer, it is from the Pöstlingberg hill (alt 537m - 1 762ft) that the most interesting general view of the town can be enjoyed.

★ **Pöstlingberg** (X) ⊘ – *4.5km - 3 miles northwest. On the left bank of the Danube beyond the north end of the Nibelungenbrücke turn left into Rudolfstraße, then right into Hagenstraße. After a level crossing the road climbs quickly. Turn right by the oratory. Leave the car in the car park below the church.*

From a flower-decked terrace below the pilgrimage church there is an extensive view★ down from nearly 300m - 1 000ft into the Danube valley, where Linz is spread out along the south bank in a basin encircled by hills; on the north bank lies the built-up area of Urfahr. It is easy to make out the city centre with its shopping avenues and the extensive industrial suburbs with their factory chimneys. Southwards, serving as a backcloth to this fine urban panorama, rise the foothills of the Alps.

★ **OLD LINZ** (Z) *time: 1 hour 30min*

Leave from the Hauptplatz. Follow the route marked on the town plan.

Hauptplatz – This large square is more striking as a whole than for the beauty of the individual buildings round it. In the centre stands the Trinity column *(Dreifaltigkeitssäule)*, erected in 1723 by order of the States of Upper Austria (provincial assembly) and the local council and population to commemorate the escape of the town from plague, fire and Turkish invasion. With its statues and cherubs in white marble, and the group representing the Holy Trinity at the top, it is a fine example of the Baroque columns which were set up in many towns of the Empire at that period.

Leave the square along the Domgasse (5) to the southeast.

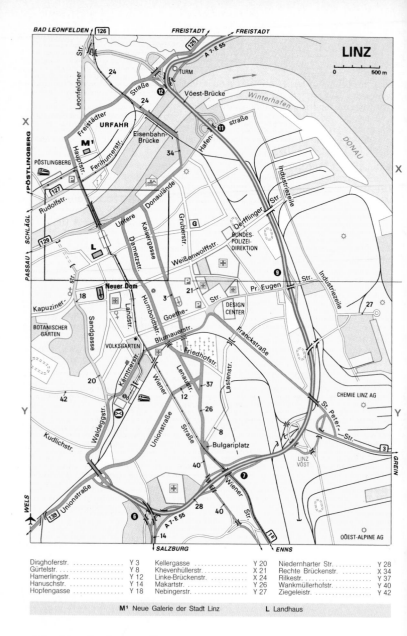

Dinghoferstr.	Y 3	Kellergasse	Y 20	Niednerharter Str.	Y 28
Gürtelstr.	Y 8	Khevenhüllerstr.	X 21	Rechte Brückenstr.	X 34
Hamerlingstr.	Y 12	Linke-Brückenstr.	X 24	Rilkestr.	Y 37
Hanuschstr.	Y 14	Makartstr.	Y 26	Wankmüllerhofstr.	Y 40
Hopfengasse	Y 18	Nebingerstr.	Y 27	Ziegeleistr.	Y 42

M¹ Neue Galerie der Stadt Linz	**L** Landhaus

Alter Dom St. Ignatius ⊙ – This church was built for the Jesuits in the second half of the 17C. Designed by Pietro Francesco Carleone, it is the city's most important Baroque church, which served as diocesan cathedral from 1785 to 1909. The plain façade is in striking contrast to the interior, where stucco, pink marble columns, an elaborately carved pulpit and choir stalls and a high altar adorned with marble statues make up a highly elaborate décor.

A medallion to the left of the entrance recalls Bruckner's twelve year service as organist here, during which time he had the organ – originally from Engelszell abbey - rebuilt according to his specifications.

Turn right into the Graben (Moat); continue into the Promenade (30); turn right to the Landhaus.

Landhaus (**L**) – This building, which is the headquarters of the provincial government, was erected in the second half of the 16C. The inner court is lined on two sides with arcades and has an octagonal fountain in its centre. On the base of the fountain, seven figures representing the planets recall that the great astronomer and mathematician Kepler taught between 1612 and 1626 at the regional secondary school, which was then in the Landhaus.

LINZ

Altstadt	Z 2
Domgasse	Z 5
Elisabethstr.	Z 6
Hagenstr.	Z 10
Hofgasse	Z 15
Honauerstr.	Z 17
Klosterstr.	Z 22
Promenade	Z 30
Rathausgasse	Z 32
Rechte-Donaustr.	Z 35
Schmidttorstr.	Z 38
Theatergasse	Z 39

(map of Linz)

D Minoritenkirche	**M²** Stadtmuseum Nordico
L Landhaus	**R** Neues Rathaus

The north door, opening onto the Klosterstraße (**22**), is a fine work in the Renaissance style. The windows of the room over the passage are in harmony with the architecture of the doorway.

Minoritenkirche (D) ⊘ – The Gothic church, founded in the 13C by the Minorite Brothers or Franciscans, was remodelled in the Rococo style in the 18C.
Interest lies in its decoration. The altarpiece on the high altar by Bartolomeo Altomonte represents the Annunciation; the altarpieces on the six side altars were executed by Kremser Schmidt *(qv)*.

Take the Altstadt north.

Schloß – The oldest part of the palace, which was the residence of the Emperor Friedrich III, dates from the end of the 15C.
It houses the art and historical collections of the provincial museum.

★ **Oberösterreichisches Landesmuseum** ⊘ – On the 1st floor, the history of art in Upper Austria is traced from the Middle Ages to the Rococo period. There is a large collection of weapons. On the 2nd floor are to be found collections of popular art and folklore. Reconstitutions of Gothic and Renaissance interiors are also on view as well as a 19C painting gallery.
Cross the many courtyards in the palace to descend to a terrace from which there is a pleasant view of the Danube, the Pöstlingberg hill and the first hills of the Mühlviertel.

Martinskirche – The chapel's nondescript exterior belies a building of ancient origin. Archaeological investigations have shown that the present structure is the result of the remodelling of the Palatine hall of a royal residence of Carolingian times, which itself was built on Roman foundations. The chancel is Gothic.

Return to the Hauptplatz via the quayside (Obere Donaulände).

ADDITIONAL SIGHTS

★ **Priesterseminarkirche** (Z) – The little seminary church was built early in the 18C for the Teutonic Order to the plans of the well-known architect

Linz headdress

Johann-Lukas von Hildebrandt. Dedicated to the Holy Cross, it is a tour-de-force on the part of its designers, who have succeeded in investing a small building with great majesty. The exterior is highly ornate. The vaulting is adorned with graceful stucco-work by Paolo d'Allio, while over the high altar is a moving Crucifixion from the brush of Altomonte.

Neuer Dom (Y) – More impressive than its style, conventional neo-Gothic, is the sheer size of this vast building, the largest church in Austria, able to hold a congregation of 20 000. Its designer was Vincent Statz, then resident architect at Cologne Cathedral. The only constraint imposed on him was that the spire should not be taller than that of the Stephansdon in Vienna; at 134m - 440ft, the new cathedral's spire is 3m - 10ft lower than its venerable counterpart.

The foundation stone was laid in 1862 and the great edifice completed in 1924. Cathedral status was conferred on it in 1909. The stained-glass windows are particularly interesting.

Neue Galerie der Stadt Linz – Wolfgang-Gurlitt-Museum (X M¹) ⊘ – *In Urfahr on the north bank of the river.*
The museum is devoted to European painting and graphic arts of the 19C and 20C (Kokoschka, Klimt, Schiele, Kubin, Hrdlicka, Rainer, Appel).

Stadtmuseum Nordico (Z M²) ⊘ – The name of the building goes back to 1675 when it was used by the Jesuits for the education of young people from northern Europe, though originally it belonged to Kremsmünster Abbey.

The museum's collections, displayed on the 1st floor, are devoted to the history of the city since ancient times. The top floor is used for temporary exhibitions.

EXCURSIONS

★★ Stift St. Florian – *18 km - 11 miles - plus 1 hour 30min sightseeing - local map right. Leave Linz on ③, road no 1, going southeast towards Enns* (Y). *In Asten turn right under the motorway to St. Florian. The village is overlooked by its great abbey (description under Stift ST. FLORIAN).*

Mühlviertel – *Round tour of 90 km - 56 miles - about 4 hours - local map right.*
The Mühlviertel, the district of the Mühl, a small river which flows into the Danube above Linz, is a hilly upland stretching between the Danube and the Czech frontier and varying

in height between 600 and 1 000m - 2 000 to 3 000ft. The underlying rock is granite, which has been quarried extensively along the steep bank of the river, as at Mauthausen. The region beyond has wide valleys covered with a dark green carpet of forests contrasting, in its melancholy, with the Danube valley, where the towns are more frequent.

Leave Linz on the road (no 126) north to Bad Leonfelden.

As soon as it leaves Linz the road enters a little verdant gorge and begins to climb gently, sometimes among rocks, sometimes among orchards. Firs take the place of fruit trees and become denser after Glasau. The wild nature of the hills, where meadows alternate with fir forests, grows more marked near Bad Leonfelden. About 500m north of the town bear right towards Freistadt. The well-engineered road runs through quiet countryside.

★ Freistadt – *See FREISTADT.*

Directly after leaving Freistadt, leave the Linz road and cross to the east bank of the Feldaist.

The road runs through woods before reaching Kefermarkt.

Kefermarkt – *See KEFERMARKT.*

At the main crossroads in Kefermarkt turn right towards the railway station; cross the track and the Feldaist. After 7km - 4 miles turn left into the main road, no 125, connecting Freistadt and Linz.

LOFER★

Salzburg – Population 1 690
Michelin map 426 fold 19
Local map under KAISERGEBIRGE – Alt 625m - 2 051ft

The village of Lofer with the delicately chiselled, snow-flecked cliffs of the Loferer Steinberge in the background, makes a delightful **picture★★**. The church tower stands out with its two onion roofs before a natural amphitheatre which, between the massive wooded foothills of the Ochsenhorn (2 511m - 8 238ft – at its highest point) and the Breithorn, opens on a view of the summit of the Großes Reifhorn.

From one end to the other of the village's twisting main street, may be seen the comfortable and well cared for houses adorned with rounded oriel windows of Bavarian type. The peasant houses on the outskirts of the village are often bedecked with a climbing pear – the local tree.
Lofer is the starting point for many excursions among the Alpine pastures; the most popular are to the Au meadows (Auerwiesen), the Loferer Alm and the pilgrimage church of Maria Kirchental.

EXCURSION

Wallfahrtskirche Maria Kirchental ⊙ – *4km - 2 ½ miles south of Lofer. At St. Martin bei Lofer take the narrow toll road to the right.*
A destination for pilgrims from all over the province, the church was built in 1694-1701 to the plans by the famous Johann Bernhard Fischer von Erlach *(qv)*. Its rustic yet graceful architecture recalls the cathedral at Salzburg (1655) or, even more, the Salzburgers' favourite sanctuary, Maria Plain.
Consecrated in 1701 by the Bishop of Seckau, the church was steadily decorated and furnished over a period of more than a century as the offerings of the pilgrims mounted up. It is nicknamed, not without a touch of humour, the "Pinzgau Cathedral" *(for the Pinzgau see SALZACHTAL)*.
The church's wooded and mountainous setting contributes to its charm and peaceful atmosphere.

MALLNITZ✳

Kärnten – Population 1 014
Michelin map 426 fold 34 – Alt 1 190m - 3 904ft

At the foot of the Goldberg, the Ankogel and the Hochalmspitze, the last 3 000m - 10 000ft high summits in the Eastern Alps, the magnificent length of Mallnitz extends over an area of 110sq km - 42.5sq miles within the Hohe Tauern National Park.
During the summer Mallnitz is the point of departure for first class **hikes and Alpine tours**. A magnificent route, although quite long *(8 hours on foot)* is the Göttinger Weg, which leads from the second section of the Ankogel railway up to the **Hagener Hütte** mountain lodge and then down to the mountain inn of Jamnig, from where the bus takes you back to Mallnitz. Another lovely hike leads to the Arthur-von-Schmidt-Hütte mountain lodge on **Dösner See** lake *(4 hour 30min return trip)*. For less serious walkers, we recommend the easier route to the Stappitzer See lake *(20min return trip from the Hotel "Alpenrose" at the end of the road)*.
During the winter, the chairlift serves a **skiing area** which is restricted to a 15km - 9 mile piste, but which does however provide plenty of opportunities for off-piste skiing and ski tours. The 1 400m - 4 593ft difference in altitude is enticing. Excellent snow conditions attract skiers late into the winter season, above all from the second section upwards.
Mallnitz has 4 cross country skiing courses totalling 25km - 15.5 miles.

★★ **Ankogelbahn** ⊘ – In two sections. From the last mountain station, you can get to Hannover Hütte mountain lodge (alt 2 722m - 8 930ft) in 10 minutes on foot. A beautiful **panorama**★★ opens up from here to the east, looking out over the Ankogel and the Hochalmspitze peak, to the west over the Hohe Sonnblick and the Schareck, to the south over the Seebach valley at the foot of the Maresenspitze peak.

From the terrace of the mountain station, mountaineers habitually prepare themselves to conquer the Ankogel (alt 3 246m - 10 649ft), although it is only recommended to experienced Alpine climbers.

MALTATAL★★

Kärnten

Michelin map 426 fold 34

30km - 18.6 miles of road leads to this magnificent valley, which is one of the most beautiful excursion destinations in Carinthia and extends from Gmünd *(see GMÜND)* to the foothills of the Hohe Tauern National Park.

It became especially famous after the Kölnbrein dam and the reservoir were built, but it owes its attraction above all to its highly diverse landscape (green forests in the lower part and the wonderful glacier panorama of the Ankogel massif and the Hochalmspitze peak in the upper part).

This is a conservation area and is particularly suitable as a point of departure for both **medium and high altitude Alpine hikes**.

The village of **Malta** at 840m - 2 755ft above sea level is an entrancing holiday spot. Its church, which dates from the 15C, houses Baroque altar furniture from the 18C and frescoes from the 14C and 15C.

★★ **Hochalmstraße** ⊘ – Above Malta, a toll is payable to drive the last 18km - 11.2 miles to the dam. The regular gradient of this excellently laid out road is a maximum of 13%, leading over 9 bridges and through 7 tunnels, including one especially impressive one, which is designed as a hairpin bend. Single line traffic alternates at two narrow points. A particular attraction of the road is its luxurious vegetation (spruce, larch, alder and birch) and the waterfalls, which tumble down from the surrounding peaks into the valley.

★ **Kölnbreinsperre** – The road ends here at 1 900m - 6 233ft above sea level. The dam is 200m - 656ft high, 41m - 134ft thick at the base and a total of 626m - 2 054ft wide, making it the largest dam in Austria. The reservoir covers

Kölnbrein dam

an area of 225ha - 556 acres, and its volume is 200 million m³ – 7 063 million ft³. Apart from its phenomenal technical capacity, the aesthetic design of this concrete colossus with its flowing, parabolic shape, is well worth seeing.

A futuristically striking mountain hotel is located close to the dam.

It is the point of departure for some wonderful walks. The hike along the lake (also suitable for inexperienced hikers), which provides a wonderful view over the **surrounding Alpine landscape**★★, should not be missed. Visitors with more stamina should climb the Arlscharte.

★★ **Hike to the Arlscharte and the Arlhöhe** – *3 hour 45min return trip on foot from the dam.* Go towards the "Osnabrücker Hütte" mountain lodge. The trail leads along the northern bank of the lake and soon proffers a magnificent view over the Ankogel glaciers. After walking for three quarters of an hour, you will reach a memorial to a tragic accident which occurred during the building of the dam.

Turn to the right and walk on up the relatively steep Alpine flower trail. After ten minutes, the trail divides; turn left (the right hand trail leads to the Jägersteighütte mountain lodge). The trail, which is marked in red and white, climbs fairly steeply to the peak, which takes three quarters of an hour to reach. From the peak, the view extends over Pfringersee lake below and over the Schödertal valley. Opposite there is a **view**★★ over the two artificial lakes, over which tower the Kölnbreinspitze peak and its small glacier on the left and the impressive massif of the Hochalmspitze peak on the right.

Walk a few metres towards Pfringersee, then turn left and follow a waymarked trail *(red cross on a white background)*, which leads to an elevated point and then follows a kind of ridge trail. After 20 minutes you will reach the **Arlhöhe** (alt 2 326m - 7 631ft), where you will find an orientation map. Magnificent **panorama**★★ over the artificial lake, over the furthest end of which tower the gleaming glacier of the Hochalmspitze and the rocky mass of the Schwarzhorn. Further to the right rise the Tischlerspitze peak and the Tischlerkarkopf (glaciers in the Ankogel range). In the north the Zwölferkogel dominates the deep Schödertal valley. Return to the dam along the same trail.

★ **Excursion to the Gößkarspeicher** – *Return trip involving a 1 hour drive and 45min on foot.* Halfway between Malta and the toll station, turn to the left towards the Gießener Hütte mountain lodge, along a little 12km - 7.5 mile long mountain road which is quite steep (800m - 2 625ft difference in altitude), which is best travelled during the morning.

Since no cars are allowed along the last section, continue on foot to the Gößkar reservoir *(15min climb)*. Beautiful **wooded area**★, over which tower by the Großer Gößspitze and the Dösnerspitze peaks.

Walk right along the left bank of the lake. Fantastic **view**★ over the Hochalmspitze peak and its glacier, from which waterfalls simply thunder down.

Return to the reservoir, continue to its end and then turn to the right along the meadow (through a fence) until you reach a wide, moderately steep trail. **View**★ over the rocky peaks of the Riekenkopf and the Pfaffenberger Nocken. Walkers return from here to the car park, whilst hikers can climb up to the Gießener Hütte mountain lodge, from where the climb to the legendary Hochalm peak commences.

MARIA SAAL ★

Kärnten – Population 3 220

Michelin map 426 fold 36 – 7km - 4 miles north of Klagenfurt – Alt 504m - 1 654ft

The pilgrimage church of Maria Saal is the building nearest to the former Roman city of Virunum, capital of Norica *(map of Roman provinces p 29)*. The city's ruins are scattered over the Zollfeld plain, between Klagenfurt and St. Veit.

In the 8C to 9C, following the Barbarian invasions, Carantania (as Carinthia was then known) was the centre from which the reconversion of the province to Christianity began. The church of Maria Saal, recorded for the first time in the middle of the 8C, is the oldest in Carinthia.

★★CHURCH (KIRCHE) *time: 30min*

The present Gothic building is protected by a fortified enclosure, which once also included the churchyard and recalls how exposed the Zollfeld was to the Turkish hordes up to the 17C.

The existing church was built as a single project in the middle of the 15C.

Among the buildings around the church note especially the octagonal **ossuary** with two tiers of galleries. Originally a Romanesque structure, it was converted in the 15C into a copy of the Holy Sepulchre in Jerusalem by a brotherhood of the Holy Sepulchre; the galleries date from this time.

Baroque organ, Church of Maria Saal

Exterior – With its twin towers of volcanic stone, decorated with delicate blind arcades, and its vast roof of greenish stone slabs, the church makes a striking impression.

Many stone fragments are sealed into the south wall. The low reliefs from the Roman era include the triumph of Achilles, who is dragging the corpse of Hector, and a fragment representing a **Roman mail wagon**★. The splendid tombstone of the Keutschach family, a work executed in Salzburg in 1510 for Archbishop Leonard von Keutschach has the Coronation of the Virgin as its central subject.

Interior – The interior of the church, remarkable for its unity, shows the design associated with late Gothic. In the main nave, the spaces in the network vaulting are decorated with figures emerging from chalices of flowers, representing the genealogy of Christ (1490).

The furnishings are of great value. In the north aisle, the **altar to St Modestus**★ combines a Carolingian table with a Romanesque sarcophagus, brought here some time ago to hold the sacred relics of the bishop. The chapel situated to the north contains the Arndorf altarpiece (c1520), depicting the Coronation of Our Lady. The **statue of the Virgin** on the high altar (1425), with its serene and rather sleepy face, is an object of devotion for pilgrims. The chapel to the south is occupied by the St George altarpiece (1526), on which the severity of expression of the main painting contrasts with the lighter, more popular appeal of those on the reverse side.

Johann Martin Jäger's Baroque **organ** of 1735, glittering with gilding, is known for its volume and brilliance of tone. One of the church bells, called Maria Saalerin, was cast in 1687 from the bronze of captured Turkish guns.

ADDITIONAL SIGHT

★ **Kärntner Freilichtmuseum** ⊘ – *Just north of the town centre. Time: 45min.* Covering an area of 4 hectares – 10 acres, this open-air museum of vernacular building was opened in 1972. Some 30 old structures have been dismantled and then reassembled here in a wooded valley setting. They include farmhouses, stables, barns and a variety of outbuildings, mostly timber-built; part of one of them dates back to the 17C. By preserving exhibits representative of rural activities, the museum goes to the heart of country life in Carinthia in past centuries, particularly in the interiors and furnishings.

Sawmill – Beside the sawmen's lodging-house (18C) stands the fascinating "long sawmill" (19C), powered by a water-wheel. All over Europe, the sawman's trade involved length-wise sawing of different kinds of tree into beams and planks. This work was carried out by hand until the early 20C, the long saw being moved up and down by a pair of sawmen. In a region where timber and its products were all-important, this sawmill is an example of astute early mechanisation designed to minimise the sawman's toil.

The museum also has mills (nos 25 and 28) and a lime-kiln (no 24), the latter still in seasonal use in southern Carinthia after the last war. Apiaries and drying-racks (nos 29-35) also used to be common features in the countryside of the south of the province, just as they still are in neighbouring Slovenia.

MARIASTEIN

Tirol – Population 170
Michelin map 426 fold 18 – 10km · 6 miles north of Wörgl – Alt 563m · 1 847ft.

Schloß Mariastein draws pilgrims and tourists to a quiet little valley with fir covered slopes, which lies parallel to the Inn.

Leave the car in the valley just before the final steep climb to the castle.

Castle and Chapels – The massive defensive tower of "Stein" was built on a huge eroded rock in the 14C. Its Lady Chapel later made it an object of Marian pilgrimage, and ultimately the religious eclipsed the military function of the tower.

Enter the castle court and climb the tower staircase. The Knights' Hall (Rittersaal) on the 2nd floor houses the **Schloßmuseum** ⊙; the exhibits include the crown and sceptre of the Tyrolean counts. The upper storeys contain two chapels, one above the other. The **Kreuzkapelle** (Chapel of the Cross) still has a Gothic interior dating from 1550. Above is the **Gnadenkapelle** (Chapel of Miracles) which has recovered its Baroque harmony and good lighting, owing to the heightening of the windows and the removal of the second-rate decoration which changed its character in the 19C. The Virgin is venerated in a gracefully-draped statue dating from 1450.

Before leaving the little valley go up the slopes facing the castle to see it outlined against the crests of the Kaisergebirge on the horizon.

MARIAZELL★

Steiermark – Population 1 930
Michelin map 426 fold 23 – Alt 868m · 2 848ft

Mariazell is the most popular place of pilgrimage in Austria. It occupies a charming **site★** on the gentle slopes of an escarpment, out of reach of morning mists (fine cloud effects in still weather) and dipping towards a verdant Alpine basin. This extreme eastern end of the Alps, very jagged in outline, includes wild areas (massifs of the Hochschwab and the Ötscher, the Salza valley, etc.) in spite of its modest altitude. A good impression of the region can be obtained by climbing to the **Bürgeralpe**, served by frequent **cable-cars** ⊙ from the centre of the town.

Pilgrimage – The Habsburg cult of the Virgin of Mariazell and the continued devotion of the people enabled the church to celebrate its eighth centenary in 1957. It was in 1157 that Benedictines from St. Lambrecht abbey *(qv)* founded a priory here. As early as the beginning of the 14C the first rescripts of indulgences appeared here, testifying to the attraction of the church for crowds of Christians. In 1377 Louis I of Anjou, King of Hungary, won a victory over the Turks which he attributed to the Virgin of Mariazell. From that time on, the worship of the Virgin of Mariazell symbolized more and more the spiritual forces which guaranteed the cohesion of the Austrian Empire. Even today many former subjects of the Empire, from countries like the Czech and Slovak Republics, Hungary and ex-Yugoslavia, make the pilgrimage in large groups. The most solemn ceremonies are on 15 August and 8 September. For the rest of the summer the largest crowds assemble on Saturday evenings, when a great torchlight procession takes place.

★BASILICA *time: 30min*

In the 17C the growing number of pilgrims made it necessary to enlarge the original Gothic building which dated back to the 14C. The architect, **Domenico Sciassia** was given the task (1644 to 1704). He kept the nave but demolished the chancel to replace it by two vast bays, one of which was roofed by a dome. When he remade the façade, he left the Gothic porch intact between the two new and much squatter bulb-topped towers. This unusual combination has become the emblem of this pilgrim city. The main doorway still has its carved Gothic tympanum, whose lower register is devoted to the history of the pilgrimage.

Enter the church. The brilliant structure of the Gnadenkapelle marks the transition from the Baroquised Gothic main building to the after-nave, which is 17C.

West Nave – This is nothing other than the former Gothic building, whose slim design can still be distinguished in spite of the Baroque shell and the width gained by including the former buttresses inside the building. By means of this last device, Sciassia made room along the aisles for a series of side-chapels, and on the first storey for a gallery whose large windows give an exceptional degree of light. To appreciate fully the details of the Baroque decoration – stucco and paintings – one should walk along these galleries.

The chapel in the north aisle dedicated to St Ladislas, King of Hungary, until recently housed the mortal remains of Cardinal Mindszenty, Primate of Hungary, now transferred to Esztergom in that country.

Gnadenkapelle (Chapel of Miracles) – The chapel, built on a trapezoidal plan in the centre of the church, shelters a Romanesque statue, always in full regalia, of the Virgin of Mariazell. She stands beneath a valuable silver baldaquin resting on twelve columns designed by J E Fischer von Erlach the Younger (1727). The enclosing grille, also of silver, was ordered by Maria Theresa from Viennese silversmiths in 1756.

East Nave – This truly monumental piece of Baroque architecture is superbly proportioned. It forms a second, inner nave, beyond a false transept. The first bay is lit by an oval lantern-dome which harmonises with the extended shape of the whole church. The second square bay, which closes the perspective, contains the majestic high altar by J B Fischer von Erlach, which was completed in 1704 and inspired by the commemorative arches of antiquity. The statues of the Crucifixion group, like those of the great angels guarding the Gnadenkapelle are copies of the solid silver statues which were melted down to meet the needs of the Austrian treasury during the Napoleonic wars.

Schatzkammer (Treasury) ⊙ – The display includes a remarkable brocade chasuble, (c1500) with high relief embroidery of saints under canopies, and various robes for attiring the Virgin of Mariazell. Ex-votos from the 15C to 20C can also be seen.

EXCURSION

★ **Erlaufsee** – *Round tour of 20km - 12 miles – about 2 hours 30min. Leave Mariazell on the road to Bruck an der Mur. On reaching the valley floor turn right into the Lunz road.*

Marienwasserfall – *Access to the waterfall is by the inn of that name.* This small cascade flows like a shimmering veil in a rocky niche.

Go back to the car. At a junction of three roads, bear right.

Erlaufsee – The road emerges from the woods and runs along the south shore of the lake. The scene is dominated to the northwest by the summit of the Gemeindealpe.

At the end of the lake, turn left towards Mitterbach and stop at the chairlift station (Alpensesselbahn) for the Gemeindealpe.

★ **Gemeindealpe** – Alt 1 626m - 5 335ft – *About 1 hour 30min Rtn, including 1 hour by chairlift.*
From this height one can enjoy a general **view** of the Ötscher massif, overlooking a mountainous area cut across by the furrows of the Ötschergraben and the Tormäuer. In the opposite direction the water of the Erlaufsee lies in the foreground of the Mariazell basin. In clear weather the bastions of the Dachstein (southwest) are visible.

Return to the lower station and make for Mitterbach and from there to Mariazell by the direct road.

MATREI IN OSTTIROL ✳

Tirol – Population 4 500
Michelin map 426 fold 33

The popular holiday resort of Matrei in East Tyrol lies at an altitude of 1 000m - 3 281ft in beautiful and diverse surroundings at the junction of the Tauerntal, Virgental and Iseltal valleys, and boasts the third largest municipal area of Austria. Thanks to the natural barriers provided by the Hohe Tauern in the north, the region boasts an especially pleasant climate. The village itself lies in a restful low mountainous area and is framed by the highest and most beautiful peaks in Austria (Großglockner in the east and Großvenediger in the west). Thanks to its extraordinary position it has become a well known point of departure for **hikes**★★★ into the Eastern Alps.

During the winter the **skiing area**✳ offers satisfactory conditions for skiers. 3 chairlifts and 3 T-bar lifts lead to 30km - 18 ½ miles of pistes of between 1 000 and 2 400m - 3 280 and 7 874ft in length, some with artificial snow. It is a particularly attractive resort for lovers of long distance skiing and ski tours, with 24km - 14.9 miles of long pistes and vast off-piste areas.

SIGHTS

Pfarrkirche St. Alban – Only the church tower bears witness to the original Gothic style of the building. It was converted to Baroque style at the end of the 18C (ceilings painted with frescoes, altar furnishings).

St. Nikolauskirche – *Approach by car. From the main square in Matrei, drive over the bridge to Linzer Straße, then turn into the second small street on the left (Bichler Straße). Drive to the end of the street and leave the village. The road leads over a bridge and then right past a wooden well. Turn right at both the next sets of crossroads. The road is no longer tarmac, but is quite drivable. Turn right into the next small road, which leads to the church which is situated in a beautiful location above Matrei.*

St. Nikolaus is a Romanesque building dating from the second half of the 12C, and is unquestionably one of the most interesting churches in the Tyrol. Inside, the narthex and the dome are worth seeing. These were converted to the Gothic style in around 1470. The choir, a special feature, is situated in a tower and is two storeys high, decorated with important 13C **frescoes**★. The lower storey represents scenes from the creation (Adam and Eve are noteworthy). The upper storey is reached via a double staircase and is even more interesting. The frescoes show the 4 elements, which carry the 12 Apostles and the Evangelists. Note the three beautiful sculptures from the 15C, of St Nicholas, St Alban and the Virgin and Child.

Y. Bontoux

Detail of the 13C frescoes in St. Nikolauskirche

EXCURSIONS

★★ **Goldriedbahn and the Europa-Panoramaweg** –
In the summer it is worth buying a ticket which includes the valley trip with the Glocknerblick chairlift and the return trip to Matrei in the bus *(ask for times at the tourist information office).* You should plan an entire day for the interesting trip to Kals-Matrei pass and to Großdorf *(1 hour 45min of which is an easy walk).* Hikers will want to climb up to the Blauspitze peak.

★★ **Goldriedbahn** – Alt 2 150m - 7 054ft. *40min trip in 2 sections.* Magnificent **view**★★ over the steep rocky mass of the Kendlspitze peak, the Virgental valley, the Kristallkopf and the Großglockner.

★★ **Walk to the Kals-Matrei-Törlhaus** – Take the so-called Europa Panoramaweg trail at the mountain station of the chairlift. 60 "ten thousand footers" can be seen from this easy trail. After 25 minutes you reach the highest point on the trail (alt 2 259m - 7 411ft), which boasts a magnificent **view**★★ over the Großvenediger in the north west. The trail to the Törlhaus which is bordered with willow herb runs along opposite the glaciers of the Großglockner through a larch forest. The Kalsertal valley, and on the right the Schober group, can be seen from the pass.

★★ **Hike to the Blauspitze** – *2 hour 45min return trip from the Kals-Matrei pass. Recommended excursion for experienced hikers. Climbing boots are essential for climbing up to the peak.*
Take the ridge trail towards Sudetenhütte mountain lodge. Turn right after almost an hour *(trail waymarked with red crosses).* Care is needed at the end of the well secured (roped) section. A magnificent **panorama**★★, especially over the glaciers of the Großglockner, can be enjoyed from the first peak. The impressive ridge trail to the cross is only recommended to experienced mountaineers who have a good head for heights.

★★ **Kalsertal** – Climb down from the Kals-Matrei pass on the other side. In an hour you will reach the mountain station of the Glocknerblickbahn railway. Take the train down into the valley. The trip to Großdorf offers a magnificent **view**★ over the valley. Then walk to Kapellenplatz and take the bus back into Matrei. It is best to sit on the left in the bus so that you can see the impressive valley sides. On the final bends into Iseltal, you will capture a brief **view**★ over the Dolomites to the south.

Großvenediger seen from the Grüner See

★★ **Excursions into the Großvenediger Massif** – *The approach is described under FELBER-TAUERNSTRASSE.* Many beautiful hiking and Alpine routes are located in this massif.

★★ **Walk to Innergschlöß** – *2 hours return trip on foot. It is possible to make the trip in horse-drawn transport (1 hour 30min return trip).* It takes 45min to get to Außergschlöß (alt 1 695m - 5 561ft). The romantic scenery surrounding the chalet in the midst of boulders and larches almost pales into insignificance at the sight of the majestic Großvenediger with its cowl of glaciers (alt 3 674m - 12 054ft), which rises up at the right hand end of a chain of mountains. An almost flat trail leads to the strange chapel of Außergschlöß, canopied by a mighty rock face, to Innergschlöß *(inn)*, and into the domain of the experienced hiker and the mountaineer.

★ **Bergbahn Venedigerblick mountain railway** – Alt 2 000m - 6 562ft. *15min ascent.* **View**★ over the Großvenediger and the Tauern valley.
Hikers with plenty of stamina will reach the magnificent Drei-Seen-Weg trail from the mountain station of the chairlift. Less agile visitors should content themselves with the walk to the Zirbenkreuz (cross).

★★ **Drei-Seen circuit** – You should climb at least up to the Meßeling pass *(3 hour 15min return trip and a 563m - 1 847ft difference in altitude).* The entire circuit is described below *(5 hours 15min on foot). Climbing boots are recommended.* First of all follow the pleasant trail along the Meßelingbach which is well marked in red and white. After 45min you will reach the Grüner See, or Green Lake, which lies in a magnificent **setting**★★ of Alpine pastures, and which looks out over the glaciers of the Großvenediger in the west and the threatening rocky sides of the Teufelsspitze peak in the east.
The higher you climb, the greener the surface of the lake sparkles. After a further 15min you will reach the Schwarzer See, or Black Lake, and can walk along its left bank, followed by the Grauer See, or Grey Lake, 30min later. Continue towards St. Pöltner Hütte mountain lodge. After 10 minutes you will reach the Meßelingscharte (alt 2 563m - 8 409ft), which already boasts a remarkable **view**★★.
Fit hikers with a good head for heights and who are wearing sturdy footwear can climb up to the Meßelingkogel (alt 2 694m - 8 838ft – *45min return trip).* Enjoy a unique **panorama**★★★ over the three lakes from the peak, with the Großglockner (in the background), the Tauerntal valley and the huge glaciers of the Großvenediger. Lower down it is possible to pick out Wildensee and Löbensee lakes.
Continue from the Meßelingscharte along the mountainside towards **St. Pöltner Hütte** mountain lodge *(50min on foot).* After 20min you will be able to easily climb up the Alte Tauern with the aid of the rope fixed to the wall. The view from the peak, with the beautiful gentian meadows, looks out across the Tauernsee and Langsee lakes, over which tower the Hochgasse and Höndl. Then climb down to the mountain lodge (alt 2 481m - 8 140ft) at the foot of the peaked Tauernkogel.
Turn back to the bottom of the valley towards Außergschlöß. In just under an hour you will reach a small bridge over the Tauernbach above the Zirbenkreuz.

Anyone who is feeling tired can turn back to the car park at this point. We recommend that hikers with more stamina should climb up to Außergschlöß *(allow a good 30min for the climb)*. The trail through magnificent larch forest is rewarded at the end with a **view★★** over the Tauerntal valley and a waterfall which comes from Dichtensee lake.

★ **Hike to the Zirbenkreuz** – *1 hour 45min on foot, 600m - 1 969ft difference in altitude down the mountain.* From the mountain station of the Venedigerblickbahn railway, the trail leads along the mountainside and finally climbs up to a bridge and then to the cross. It is possible to return to the car park at this point. We recommend however that hikers with more stamina should climb up to Außergschlöß *(see above)*. This hike can be combined with the hike to Innergeschlöß.

★ **Virgental** – *18km - 11 miles drive from Matrei to Ströden.* This beautiful valley to the south of the glacier of the Großvenediger is an interesting excursion destination for all summer visitors in the Matrei area. The dense forests in the lower part and the Alpine mountain scenery in the upper part are impressive. Prägraten (alt 1 310m - 4 298ft) is the most beautiful holiday resort in the valley.
The Umbal falls at the end of the road are well worth a visit.

Burg MAUTERNDORF ★

Salzburg

Michelin map 426 fold 35

The castle overlooks an ancient route, once used by the Romans, which now links the Hohe Tauern mountains and Salzburg. There is evidence that there was a customs post *(Mautstelle)* here as early as 1002. The holiday resort of Mauterndorf (population 1 685) owes much of its dignity to a number of substantial buildings, many of them embellished with bay windows and stepped gables.
The first castle was built by the Archbishops of Salzburg in the middle of the 13C to enable them to keep a close eye on their possessions in the Laugau; it was not until 1339 that the castle chapel was built and the frescoes painted.
Prince-Archbishop Leonhard von Keutschach was particularly fond of the castle. In 1494 he added a room above the chapel; visitors may see the mural decorations and the bed recess.

"The Prince-Archbishop's Turnip" – The story goes that Leonhard von Keutschach led a lively student life as a young man, rarely heeding his family's advice. One day, on a visit to Pinzgau, he was walking in a turnip field with his uncle Wolf zu Alm, who soundly berated him on the subject of his studies. Piqued by the young man's impertinent reply, the uncle flew into a rage and threw a turnip at him saying, "If you don't mend your ways, I will never receive you again!" The turnip changed Leonhard's life; he applied himself to his studies and later became Prince-Archbishop of Salzburg. In gratitude, he had a turnip included in his coat of arms, which appears in various places at Mauterndorf.

TOUR *time: 1 hour*

The exterior of the **keep** in the main courtyard is well worth examining. A security device, typical of medieval keeps, controlled the entrance. The only access was through a door which was always in view, about 8m - 26ft above ground level (left of the fresco of St Christopher). This door was approached by means of a wooden gallery against the wall linking the keep to a separate building. In the event of an attack, this vulnerable link could be quickly removed and the keep isolated. The existence of a late 15C **fresco of St Christopher**, patron saint of travellers, strongly suggests that in the Middle Ages the main road passed through the castle courtyard, thus facilitating the collection of toll charges. Most of the present buildings date from the spate of construction from 1546-1559, although there was also some major, albeit respectful, restoration work carried out in 1896. Since 1968 the castle has been owned by the Land (Province) of Salzburg; it houses an interesting museum of local arts and traditions, the **Lungauer Landschaftsmuseum** ⊙

If you intend combining a tour of Austria
with a visit to one of the neighbouring countries,
remember to take the appropriate Michelin Green Guide
to Germany, Switzerland or Italy,
or take the Michelin Green Guide Europe

MAUTHAUSEN

Oberösterreich – Population 4 350
Michelin map 426 fold 9 – 25km - 16 miles east of Linz
Local map under DONAUTAL – Alt 250m - 820ft

Mauthausen's provincial-style houses run down almost to the banks of the Danube. The sleepy little town has a traditional market place with a stone fountain playing under the shade of two great plane-trees. On the way in from the east stands the **Heinrichskapelle**, the Gothic chancel of a church built around 1400 and subsequently demolished. With its walls rising from the waters of the Danube, the old fortress of **Schloß Pragstein** now plays a peaceful role as local museum and school of music.

Until 1938, when Austria was annexed to Hitler's German Reich, Mauthausen was known only for its granite quarries, which supplied most of the paving-stones for Vienna. One of the quarries was used as a Nazi concentration camp, which made the name of Mauthausen one of the most sinister under their rule. In 1949 the Austrian Government declared the camp to be a historic monument. By that time many of the buildings had been destroyed.

Konzentrationslager (Concentration Camp) ⓥ – From 1938 until 5 May 1945 about 200 000 people were imprisoned at Mauthausen and its 49 subsidiary camps, over 100 000 of whom died. Some of the huts and rooms in which the prisoners suffered and died still stand. One of the buildings has been turned into a museum with photographs and other documentary material on the horrors perpetrated in this sinister place. Outside the camp limits are the memorials set up by countries whose people perished here. Below the plateau is the "Todesstiege" (Staircase of Death), leading to the quarry.

With this Green Guide
*use the **Michelin Map** no 426 at a scale of 1 : 400 000 (1cm : 4km)*
This map provides both motoring and tourist information

MAYERLING

Niederösterreich
Michelin map 426 fold 25 – 36km - 22 miles southwest of Vienna
Local map under WIEN: Excursions; Wienerwald

A Carmelite convent built by order of the Emperor Franz Joseph marks the site of the hunting-lodge in which a drama that shook the world took place.

A Tragic Love Story – The secrecy with which the Imperial family surrounded the tragic affair gave rise to the most fanciful theories. Nonetheless, with the help of recently discovered documents, most of the drama can be recreated. In 1888 the Archduke Rudolf, only son of the Emperor Franz Joseph and Empress Elisabeth and heir to the throne of Austria-Hungary, was thirty years old. His support for the parliamentary opposition in Hungary together with his liberal ideas frightened the aristocracy. His lack of faith angered the Church; and his dissolute life, worsened by his unfortunate marital obligations, created estranged relations with his family. His last "conquest" was made at a ball at the German Embassy, where he made the acquaintance of a girl of seventeen, Maria Vetsera. He fell in love with her and his love was returned. Hearing of this liaison, the Emperor decided to put an end to the scandal. In the afternoon of 28 January 1889 he had a stormy interview with his son during which he told him of the refusal of Pope Leo XIII to annul his marriage; he also demanded that

Archduke Rudolf

190

he reveal the names of the Hungarian conspirators. Refusing to betray his friends and weary of a situation full of unsolved problems, Rudolf, already depressed, decided to commit suicide with his loved one. The following

> Almost a century later, this tragic story continued to arouse a certain fascination. Sir Kenneth Macmillan choreographed the ballet *Mayerling* to music by Liszt for the Royal Ballet of London, which first performed it in 1978.

day, he did not appear at dinner but isolated himself in the hunting lodge at Mayerling with Maria. On 30 January they were found dead. Maria was the first to die. Rudolf then wrote to his mother, his wife, and his very old friend Maria Caspar (Mizzie), and at dawn shot himself.

MELK★★

Niederösterreich – Population 5 070

Michelin map 426 fold 10 – Local map under DONAUTAL – Alt 213m - 699ft

The Abbey of Melk, which crowns a rocky bluff overlooking the Danube from more than 50m - 150ft, is the apogee of Baroque architecture in Austria.

The Cradle of Lower Austria - The princely family of Babenberg, who were natives of Bavaria, established their rule on the site of a Roman stronghold at Melk, fixing their seat there at the end of the 10C. Recalling the fate of the Nibelungen – Melk is said to be the Medelike of the famous story - the Babenbergs continued down the Danube valley and established their court first at Tulln, then at Vienna.

At the end of the 11C, Leopold III von Babenberg handed over his castle to the Benedictines, who converted it into a fortified abbey. The spiritual and intellectual renown of Melk spread through the whole of Lower Austria.

Days of Storm and Days of Glory - The spread of the Reformation hindered the development of monastic life. The Turkish invasion in 1683 sowed ruin and chaos beyond Vienna, and many of the monastery estates were ravaged. The abbey itself was gutted by fire but was entirely rebuilt from 1702 onwards in its present form. In 1805 and 1809, during his successful campaign against Austria, Napoleon I stayed at Melk and established his general headquarters there. As it has succeeded in conserving its art treasures, the abbey is able to play an important role in the aesthetic education of the Austrian public.

TOUR ⊙ *time: 1 hour*

High above Melk's high street (Hauptstraße) lined with fine town houses, stands the south façade of the abbey, extending for some 240m - 787ft.

*The abbey can be reached directly on foot from the Stiftsweg (**16**). The road approach is from the east end of the town; follow signs marked "* ℗ *Stift Melk".*

In 1702 Abbot Dietmayr laid the first stone in the rebuilding of the monastery. The architect, Jakob Prandtauer, managed to make the best of the difficult trapeze shaped site and to create a structure perfectly suited to the situation. After his death in 1726 the work was completed with the help of his plans by his pupil, Franz Munggenast.

MELK

Abbe-Stadler-Gasse	2
Abt-B.-Dietmayr-Straße	3
Bahngasse	5
Fischergasse	6
Fisolengasse	7
Hauptplatz	9
Hubbrücke	10
Josef-Büchl-Straße	12
Kaiblingergasse	13
Kirchenplatz	14
Kremser Straße	16
Nibelungenlände	17
Pischingerstraße	19
Prinzlstraße	20
Rathausplatz	21
Roseggerstraße	23
Stadtgraben	24
Stiftsweg	26

The outer gateway, giving access to the first courtyard, is framed by the statues of St Leopold and St Coloman, the abbey's patrons, and flanked by two bastions built in the 17C and 18C. On the inner gate is the abbey coat of arms. Directly beyond a vestibule with a painted ceiling depicting St Benedict, the founder of the Order, is the **Prälatenhof** (Prelates' Courtyard), a fine group of buildings, its walls adorned with statues representing the prophets. The dome of the abbey church may be seen beyond the fountain.

Kaisergang – The Emperors' gallery, which is 196m - 644ft long, provided access to the chambers reserved for important visitors. It was decorated with paintings of the kings and regents of Austria, the place of honour being taken by the Empress Maria Theresa and her husband, François of Lorraine. Several rooms (west of the staircase) have been converted into museum galleries. The galleries contain old engravings of the abbey, a Gothic altarpiece (by Jörg Breu) from the former abbey and liturgical ornaments.

Marmorsaal – This hall, preceded by a vestibule adorned with portraits of the founder of the abbey and its architect, impresses the visitor less by the lavishness of its decoration than by the strength of its design which is dominated by a series of pilasters covered in a reddish brown stucco in imitation of marble *(Marmor)*. The allegorical painting on the ceiling "Reason guiding Humanity from the darkness of obscurity towards the light of civilization and culture" was done in 1732 by Paul Troger, whose blue tones are famous.

Terrace – This is situated at the very tip of the rocky spur, over the elegant portico linking the symmetrically designed Marble Hall and Library. It affords a fine view of the Danube and the façade of the abbey church.

Bibliothek (Library) – Like the "marble" hall, the library is two storeys high and has a fine ceiling painted by Troger. It contains 80 000 books and 2 000 manuscripts. The gilded wood statues at the entrances represent the four faculties; the woodwork and gilding of the interior add to the splendour.

★★★ **Stiftskirche** – The abbey church is surrounded by the abbey buildings but dominates the group with the symmetrical towers of its west front and its great octagonal dome.

The interior gives a great impression of lightness, which is due to the many windows, the sweep of great fluted pilasters and to a judicious use of colours, in which brownish-red, grey, orange and golden tones are mingled. The lavish decoration includes frescoes, gold ornaments and marble.

The vaulting of the nave, the dome and the altars are crowded with figures. In the dome, which is 65m - 213ft high, are enthroned God the Father, Christ, the Evangelists and the Doctors of the Church. On the nave vaulting St Benedict is

Abbey of Melk

triumphantly received into Heaven. All these paintings are by Johann Michael Rottmayr, as well as those on the side altars depicting the Adoration of the Magi, St Michael and the Baptism of Christ. Paul Troger did the paintings on the other side altars, among them St Nicholas and St Sebastian, while the Italian painter Hippolyto Sconzani was responsible for the wall paintings.

In the midst of these riches the eye is caught by the high altar. In the centre of the group of statues, the two Princes of the Apostles, St Peter and St Paul, to whom the church is consecrated, take leave of one another before their martyrdom.

EXCURSIONS

Schloß Schallaburg ⊙ – *6km - 4 miles south of Melk towards Anzendorf. Time: 1 hour.*
The castle has substantial Romanesque remains and a Gothic chapel but it is the great arcaded 16C **Renaissance courtyard★** which makes the most striking impression, as if it had been moved by magic from faraway Rome to its present Alpine surroundings.

The Austrian predilection for arcaded courtyards is repeated here with an extraordinary profusion of terracotta ornamentation. Statues, atlantes, caryatids, floral motifs, cartouches and ornamental keystones are boldly and harmoniously combined to form a masterly composition in the Antique taste of the period.

Today, Schallaburg is an educational and cultural centre for the *Land* of Lower Austria, used every summer for prestigious exhibitions.

MILLSTATT★

Kärnten – Population 3 200
Michelin map 426 folds 34 and 35 – Alt 604m - 1 982ft

Owing to its favourable climate and a pleasant beach by the lake of the same name (the water reaches 26°C - 82°F in summer), Millstatt has become a very popular resort. The lake (12km - 8 miles long, 1km - half a mile wide) reflects the distant peaks of the Kreuzeck and Reißeck (northwest), outcrops of the Tauern range. The mountain setting and the peaceful, wooded shore on the south side of the lake provide a tranquil backdrop for this long narrow stretch of water.

As cultural centre of the Carinthian uplands, Millstatt hosts a series of music concerts, the Internationale Musikwochen, between May and October.

ABBEY (STIFT)

time: 1 hour

The main door and cloisters of this ancient abbey are one of the glories of Romanesque art in Austria. It is interesting to see how the buildings and works of art are connected with the three stages in the history of the abbey, which was a Benedictine monastery of the congregation of Hirsau (1080-1469), a priory of the military Order of St George (1469-1598) and a Jesuit house (1598-1773). Since 1773 the monastery buildings have not been used for religious purposes.

From the car park in the town centre go though an archway into the abbey courtyard.

A mansion has replaced the 15C castle of the Grand Master of the Knights of St George.

Abbey cloisters at Millstadt

★ **Stiftshof (Abbey courtyard)** – The 1 000 year old "Judgement" lime tree, and two tiers of galleries with Italian arches form a colourful scene. The elegance of this 16C architecture reveals the riches of the Order of St George, which was founded by the Emperor Friedrich III, to assist in the defence of Christianity against the Turks.

Kreuzgang (Cloisters) ⊘ – *Enter from the east side of the courtyard.* The cloisters were endowed with Gothic vaulting by the Knights of St George at the beginning of the 12C. They still possess the Romanesque blind arcades with slim marble columns and the capitals decorated with animals or symbolic plants. In the east gallery, which is the most open, may be seen the design, often reproduced in tourist literature, of a gnome and a lion each supporting a slim column. In front of a former communicating door into the church are two detached columns, each resting on a sculptural group representing a woman (the Church) taming a monstrous male figure (the pagan world).
The cloisters lead to the small abbey museum (Stiftsmuseum).
Return to the abbey courtyard to go up to the church.

Stiftskirche – The porch contains a magnificent marble **Romanesque west door★★**, whose decorative designs in the covings – rolls, braids – are preserved in all their delicacy. Masks and animals along the ends of the small columns represent the struggle between good and evil. The tympanum shows Abbot Heinrich II (1166-1177) paying homage to Christ in his abbey church.

Interior – The interior owes its network vaulting, with historiated keystones, to the Knights of St George and its furnishings, as well as the statues in the main nave (saints of the Society), to the Jesuits. Two side chapels, facing one another, contain (on the left) the Tombstone of Grand Master Siebenhirter (d 1508), and (on the right) that of Grand Master Geumann (d 1533).

Oberes MÖLLTAL★

Kärnten

Michelin map 426 fold 33

The winding valley of the Möll, a tributary of the Drava, forms an important communication route. First of all, downstream from Heiligenblut it provides an exit for the Großglockner road; in the lower section, between Winklern and Möllbrücke, a road has been built to divert the large volume of traffic between the Dolomites, Lienz and the Carinthian lakes from the more southerly Drava valley.

FROM HEILIGENBLUT TO LIENZ

38km - 24 miles - allow half a day

★ **Heiligenblut** – *See HEILIGENBLUT.*

South of Heiligenblut the road passes through the gap made by the Möll in the Zlapp "bolt", then drops rapidly to a lower level in the valley. The peak of the Großglockner is now out of sight.
The valley of the Möll, quiet and green, is dotted with houses of dark wood lending a touch of mountain scenery to this section. In the meadows are crop drying racks *(illustrated and explained p 47).*

Döllach – Population 1 550. *Facilities at Großkirchheim.* The town was formerly a gold and silver mining centre.

Below Mörtschach there is a first glimpse, to the south, of the cliffs and pinnacles of the Dolomites at Lienz.
At Winklern the Möll valley turns abruptly east between wooded slopes. The road to the **Iselsberg pass** (alt 1 204m - 3 950ft) branches off to the southwest. The **descent★★** from Iselsberg to Lienz, on which the first two loops invite a halt (Gasthaus Dolomitenblick), is magnificently designed within view of the Lienz Dolomites. These have innumerable facets on their surface whose grey tone is warmed by the least ray of sunshine. Far below, the deep upper valley of the Drava curves southwestwards past Lienz.

Lienz – *See LIENZ.*

*Every year
the Michelin Red Guide Europe
presents a wealth of up-to-date information in a compact
form ; it is the ideal companion for a holiday or a business trip*

MÖLLTALER GLETSCHER★★

Kärnten

Michelin map 426 fold 34

21km - 13 miles from Flattach to Eissebahn – *Toll after 9km - 5 ½ miles (buy a return ticket for the mountain railway). Allow a 2 hour 45min return trip for the excursion, including 1 hour 15min travelling time.*

Long Alpine lakes, which are used to generate hydro-electricity, lie along this especially picturesque route, together with the Mölltaler glacier, on which it is possible to ski the whole year round.

The **road★★** climbs steadily (up to 15% gradient), the impressive difference in altitude is 1 500m - 4 921ft (from 830 to 2 300m – from 2 625 to 7 546ft).

The first 12km - 8 miles lead through untouched forest. Waterfalls spurt out of steep rocky cliffs.

After the last tunnel, 3km - 2 miles above the toll station, the valley widens and Alpine pasture replaces the forest. The view extends right over a grandiose **Alpine basin★★**. The road leads through several avalanche protection terraces, and there is soon a magnificent **view★★** over the Wurten reservoir below.

Immediately after the Stübeler See lake, park at the valley station of the mountain railway.

★★ **Eissebahn** – Alt 2 798m - 9 180ft. The complex, which also includes a further 3 ski lifts, leads to a small skiing area which is particularly popular thanks to the certainty of snow in winter and to its beautiful setting. During the trip you will see *(on the left)* the Weißseekopf and the Schwarzseekopf, which overhang two large lakes separated by the Hochwurten dam.

The **Schareck glacier** begins at the mountain station. Skiers can get almost up to the peak (alt 3 122m - 1 024ft) with a T-bar lift, where an even wider panorama can be enjoyed. After 15 July, the snow conditions are however generally only moderate.

Go past the inn and you will see opposite the huge mass of the **Hocharn glacier** (alt 3 254m - 10 676ft) and on the left the **Hohe Sonnenblick** (alt 3 105m - 10 187ft). Using binoculars it is possible to see the weather station at the peak and also the numerous roped parties of mountaineers climbing the glacier.

Hikers can climb down to the car park on the glacier trail in 1 hour 15min. The trail runs past the Hochwurten dam and Weißersee lake.

MÖRBISCH★★

Burgenland – Population 2 360

Michelin map 426 fold 26 – 21km - 13 miles southeast of Eisenstadt – Alt 118m - 387ft

Mörbisch is the last village on the western shore of Neusiedler lake before the Hungarian frontier. A well known white wine is produced in the neighbourhood. The village is charming, with colourful and picturesque alleys at right angles on either side of the main street.

The houses are whitewashed and nearly all have an outdoor staircase, surmounted by a porch. Doors and shutters painted in bright colours, bunches of maize hanging on the walls and generously flower-decked balconies and windows strike a cheerful note and form a delightful picture.

A road east of the village leads across marshes and reed-beds to a small bathing centre *(charge)* on Neusiedler lake, as well as to the site of the Mörbisch Summer Festival *(see the Calendar of events at the end of the guide).*

MONDSEE

Oberösterreich – Population 2 938

Michelin map 426 fold 20 – Local map under SALZKAMMERGUT

Alt 493m - 1 617ft

Up to 1791 the history of Mondsee is intermingled with that of its Benedictine abbey. Nowadays many tourists are attracted to this township, which bears the same name as the nearby lake whose shady banks are approached from the town along an avenue of lime trees.

The **Mondsee★**, a lake shaped like a crescent at the foot of the cliffs of the Drachenwand and the Schafberg, is the most temperate in the Salzkammergut. The lake has become even better known since the section of the Salzburg-Vienna **motorway★** along its north shore was opened.

The neighbouring region still produces one of the rare strongly-flavoured Austrian cheeses, known as Mondsee.

Mondsee seen from the Schafberg

SIGHTS

★ **Pfarrkirche** – This late 15C church once belonged to an abbey, whose former buildings stand on the left of the square. The present façade, with its Baroque helmeted towers, was remodelled in 1740.

The interior escaped the Baroque influences of the 17C – as the monastery was in financial difficulties – and has preserved its Gothic network vaulting. **Meinrad Guggenbichler** (1649-1723) who is known in Austria's art history as the Sculptor of Mondsee, endowed the different halls with furnishings (7 of the 13 altars) which give a great unity of style. The altar of the Holy Sacrament, on the lower left hand side, with its twisted columns supported by cherubs is one of his most characteristic works. The altar to St Sebastian (facing the other altar) is well known with its statue of St Roch. In the choir can be seen the gate to the sacristy once again in its original colouring. The seven charming little statues surmounting the arch are, like this masterpiece of ironwork, late 15C.

Heimat- und Pfahlbaumuseum ⊘ – Installed in various parts of the former abbey, the museum presents local antiquities (one phase of the Neolithic Era being known as the "Mondsee Culture") and traditions.

A photographic sequence illustrates the making of *Einbaum* boats, cut from a single tree, of which some were in use until recently. In the upstairs part of the church, under the Gothic arches of the monks' library, the history of the abbey and the showing of manuscripts (reproductions) is featured. Also exhibited are works of Meinrad Guggenbichler and religious works of art from the abbey.

Freilichtmuseum Mondseer Rauchhaus ⊘ – *Access via the motorway in the direction of Salzburg-Vienna (the second parking area after the Mondsee exit).*

The smokehouse is a primitive wooden chalet (mentioned in records going back to the 15C), built in the local style and surrounded by outbuildings, moved here from its original site. The most noticeable feature is the old-fashioned but logical placing of the vaulted hearth which lacks a chimney. The escaping smoke formed a rising cloud which spread out to dry the farm crops in the attics without inconveniencing the inhabitants. One or two annexes bear witness to the work of local farmers: home, silo, mill, drying sheds for linen and fruit.

Maria-Hilf-Kapelle – *Access via the motorway: see above.* This 15C chapel which has been remodelled in the Baroque style is charmingly situated on a bluff overlooking the lake.

MONTAFON ★

Vorarlberg
Michelin map 426 folds 28 and 29 – Local map under ARLBERGGEBIET

Montafon is a charming, densely populated valley. Thanks to the protection of the surrounding mountains and the positive effects of the Föhn, a warm, dry southerly wind, it is possible to grow fruit in the valley basin up to quite a high altitude, whilst the local breed of red brown cows thrives on the Alpine meadows higher up still.

Although the language spoken here is German, the harsh sounds of the local names and the building style (timber-clad stone houses with arched doors) point to the influence of the old Rhaeto-Romanic culture, which is still alive in Engadin, on the south side of the Silvretta range.

The Montafon region has fundamentally altered as a result of modern civilization and above all through the development of winter sports and electricity production (Rodund power station at Vandans). It has been popular for some time as a relaxing holiday area offering a broad range of activities (downhill and cross-country skiing, hiking). The famous **Silvrettastraße**★★ *(qv)* mountain road also runs through the Montafon.

FROM BLUDENZ TO PARTENEN

40km - 25 miles – allow at least 1 day

Bludenz – *See BLUDENZ.*

Turn left in St. Anton in Montafon towards Bartholomäberg. The small mountain road takes you along a spectacular route high above the valley floor.

Bartholomäbergkirche – From the church itself there is an impressive **panorama**★ of the village of Vandans at the foot of the sharp Zimba peak (alt 2 643m - 8 671ft) and of the villages of Schruns and Tschagguns, over which tower the lofty summits of Schesaplana (alt 2 965m - 8 842ft) and Drusenfluh, the **Drei Türme** (a rocky massif in the form of three towers standing one behind the other) and by the Sulzfluh.

The **Baroque interior decoration** of the church is one of the most beautiful art treasures of Vorarlberg. The

Drei Türme mountains

high altar and the pulpit are the work of Georg Senn (1737). The organ, which dates from 1792, is one of the finest instruments in Austria. The triptych dedicated to St Anne (1525) on the right hand side of the nave is especially interesting.

Continue towards Innerberg. After about a kilometre – half a mile, there is a magnificent **view**★ to the right over St. Gallenkirch at the foot of the Valiseraspitze peak, and opposite over the Kreuzjoch massif, as well as the Silbertal valley and the Verwall range.

In Innerberg (alt 1 161m - 3 809ft), turn right towards Silbertal. Turn left on the main road at the bottom of the valley and park at the foot of the Kristbergbahn railway.

★ **Kristbergbahn** ⊙ – The Kristberg inn (alt 1 430m - 4 691ft), with a chapel nearby, can be reached in 5min from the mountain station. It affords an especially beautiful **all-round view**★ over the Montafon.

Hikers can climb up to the Kristbergsattel and then follow the ridge path to the left as far as the **Ganzaleita** viewpoint (alt 1 610m - 5 282ft), from where the view encompasses the Lechtaler Alps and the Rote Wand.

At the Litz, a mountain torrent, continue towards Schruns. The route takes you through an unspoiled **natural landscape**★ which boasts luxurious vegetation.

✤ **Schruns** – Alt 690m - 2 264ft, population 3 800. This holiday resort and local capital of the Montafon is located in a broad section of the valley and has good accommodation and leisure facilities (swimming pool, 21 tennis courts). In the summer it is an ideal point of departure for hikes in the medium altitude mountains. In the winter, the **skiing area**✤ (35km - 22 miles of piste) is especially suitable for beginners and for relaxed skiing. Plenty of easy ski-runs in the foothills of Kreuzjoch and Fredakopf offer excellent skiing conditions. Good skiers can try their hand at the off-piste section at Sennihang. The attraction of the area lies in its considerable differences in height (700-2 400m - 2 296-7 074ft), which result in landscapes ranging from Alpine scenery devoid of vegetation to wooded areas beneath the Kapell. However, due to the low altitude of Schruns, it is frequently not possible to ski back to the town, and skiers must take the cable-car from Kropfen (alt 1 335m - 4 380ft) down into the valley.

Ski passes are available to tourists (three days or more), which are valid for the entire Montafon valley with its 73 ski lifts and 210km - 130 miles of piste. Buses run regularly between the individual locations (Tschagguns-Vandans, Schruns, Kristberg, Gargellen, St. Gallenkirch and Gaschurn). **Cross-country skiers** are restricted around Schruns to 13km - 8 miles of easy tracks. The surrounding locations provide more opportunities: 11km - 7 miles of more demanding cross-country tracks on the Kristberg at between 1 450m - 4 757ft and 1 550m - 5 085ft in altitude, 6km - 4 miles in Tschagguns and 8km - 5 miles in Vandans, as well as the extensive cross-country skiing area in the Hochmontafon *(see below)*.

★ **Sennigrat** ⊙ – *1 hour return trip.* First take the Hochjochbahn train *(charge for parking)* or the Zamangbahn train *(free parking)* to the **Kapell** (alt 1 850m - 6 069ft). Enjoy the view down into the valley and the many scattered chalets of Schruns. Then take the chairlift up to the Sennigrat (alt 2 210m - 7 250ft). Here the **panorama**★ takes in the Kreuzjoch area, the Madrisa massif above the Gargellental valley, and the Rätikon (Sulzfluh, Drei Türme, Schesaplana) with Silbertal and Arlberg in the background.

★★ **Hike to the Kreuzjoch and the Zamangspitze** – *4 hours on foot for the return trip. Plenty of opportunity to shorten the route: for walkers, just go as far as the mountain lodge and the lake path (just under 2 hours). Climbing boots are recommended.*

The Wormser Hütte mountain lodge (alt 2 305m - 7 562ft) can be reached in 20min. From the lodge, follow a ridge path to the Kreuzjoch (the Kreuz or cross itself is at an altitude of 2 395m - 7 857ft) and then on to the Zamangspitze peak (alt 2 386m - 7 828ft), from where a **panorama**★★ opens up over the Silvretta massif and the Hochmontafon. Return to the lodge along the same route and continue along the lake path past **Herzsee** and **Schwarzsee** lakes back to the Kapell, returning to Schruns in the cable-car.

Behind Schruns the road winds up the Hochmontafon. It leads through **St. Gallenkirch**✤ (alt 900m - 2 953ft) and **Gaschurn**✤ (alt 1 000m - 3 281ft) and finally, after Partenen, to the **Silvrettastraße**★★ *(qv)*.

✤ **Silvretta Nova skiing area** – The villages of St. Gallenkirch and Gaschurn have joined together to create an extensive, varied skiing area with 33 ski lifts and 100km - 62 miles of piste between 900m and 2 300m - 2 953ft and 7 546ft in altitude. Good skiers use the black Buckelpiste and the ski-run into the valley from the Schwarzköpfle, and, on powdered snow, the Ziglamstrecke run at the foot of the mountain peak, which provides a remarkable **view**★★ over the Silvretta group. The pistes from the Gampabing lift are suitable for skiers of average ability. **Gargellen**, the highest village in the Montafon (alt 1 423m - 4 668ft), 8km - 5 miles up the valley from St. Gallenkirch, offers interesting Alpine ski pistes. For cross-country skiers there are connected ski-runs in the floor of the valley between St. Gallenkirch and Partenen. In addition, a 15km - 9 mile cross-country track, which runs around the Silvretta reservoir at an altitude of 2 030m - 6 660ft, can be reached with the funicular railway and the bus.

★★ **Valisera Kabinenbahn cable-car** ⊙ – Alt 2 100m - 6 890ft. *Around 45min return trip from St. Gallenkirch.* There are some beautiful views over St. Gallenkirch and Schruns during the first extremely steep and wooded section. From the mountain station the view extends over the rocky peak of the Reutehorn, which dominates the Gargellental valley. During the second section there is a good view over the skiing area. Opposite the top station lie Heimspitze and Valiseraspitze peaks. To the south east, the Silvretta group is visible, and to the north the Zamangspitze peak and the Verwall range can be seen. The Bella Nova restaurant is just a few steps away, and provides a view over the magnificent Gargellental valley.

★ **Versettla Kabinenbahn cable-car** – Alt 2 010m - 6 594ft. *45min return trip from Gaschurn.* Descend to the Höhenrestaurant from the mountain station. **View**★ over the Silvretta range (Piz Buin, Großer Litzner, Großes Seehorn) and the whole of the Silvretta Nova skiing area. A broader panorama can be enjoyed from Burg and Versettla *(take the Burg skilift in the winter, and the Versettlaweg path in the summer)*.

MURAU

Steiermark – Population 2 630
Michelin map 426 fold 35 – Alt 829m - 2 720ft

Charmingly situated in the upper Mur valley, the small town of Murau was already celebrated at the end of the 19C for its clean air and pleasant climate. Owing to the protection of the Niedere Tauern hills, rainfall is very moderate.

SIGHTS

Old Town – The castle at Murau was built by Ulrich von Liechtenstein; outside the castle walls he established a market which was to play an important local role during the Middle Ages.

The historic town centre, on the north bank of the River Mur, with its narrow streets and innumerable shops, is endowed with undeniable charm. The Raffaltplatz, shaded by chestnut trees and ringed by houses with smart, multi-coloured façades, suggests a certain Italian influence.

The parish church of St. Matthäus can be reached from Anna-Neumann-straße or Schillerplatz by narrow pedestrian alleys and a covered flight of steps.

Murau

S. Bohviac/BILDAGENTUR BUENOS DIAS

★ **Stadtpfarrkirche St. Matthäus** – The church, which stands on a hillside below the castle, was dedicated to St Matthew on completion of the chancel in 1296. The Gothic character of the building, with its majestic nave and splendid decorations, was not destroyed by alterations carried out in the first half of the 17C. There are several beautiful **frescoes** dating from the 14C-16C, including a 14C St Anthony and his pig in the south transept, an entombment of Christ (1377) and an Annunciation on the south wall of the nave. The north transept was decorated in the late 16C – early 17C with a large number of small paintings (executed on dry plaster) depicting epitaphs on deceased members of the House of Liechtenstein. The magnificent **Baroque high altar★** (1655) was created by local artists who placed at its centre a Gothic crucifixion (1500); the sky-blue tabernacle is complemented by wood and gilt work. The heavy pulpit was sculpted in the late Baroque style in 1777 by an artist from Freisach.

Schloß – *Access on foot by the long wooden staircase to the north of the church. Only the interior courtyard is open to visitors.*
The first castle was built by Ulrich von Liechtenstein in 1232; all that remains of it are the cellars and a well 48m - 157ft deep. It occupied a commanding position in the Mur valley, at a point where the river becomes wider, and guaranteed the autonomy of a region in which prosperity was derived from iron ore and salt as well as commerce.
The present castle was built between 1628 and 1643 by Count Georg-Ludwig von Schwarzenberg; the tall façades of the courtyard rest on cloister galleries, the arcades of which are supported by stout twin pillars. The austerity of the façades of the inner court is tempered by the elegant chapel door and by round-headed windows and oculi.

★ **Leonardikapelle** – *1km - half a mile south of the old town. Take the road to the Frauenalpe; after 300m turn right into Leonhardweg, a footpath which leads to the chapel.*

This Gothic building was already a place of pilgrimage in 1439. During the walk up to the chapel, there is the opportunity to pause by the side of the **pond★** a wild and peaceful spot. The pleasant walk round the pond *(20min)* provides romantic views of the chapel surrounded by greenery.

EXCURSIONS

Mur Valley by train (Murtalbahn ⊙) – *74km - 46 miles Rtn – about 5 hours.* This picturesque excursion is made by **steam train** along the Murau-Tamsweg line.

Oberwölz – *Leave Murau on Bundesstraße 96 going east; in Niederwölz take the road to Oberwölz. See OBERWÖLZ.*

MURTAL

Steiermark

Michelin map 426 folds 23, 37 and 38

The route from Graz to Leoben runs up the deeply wooded Mur valley for 70km - 43 miles. This is only about one-seventh of the course of the river, which rises in the Radstädter Tauern, in the Salzburg district, and ends in Hungary, 483km - 300 miles away, where it joins the Drava, a tributary of the Danube.

An Industrial Corridor – In a mountainous and wooded region like Styria, valleys are of great economic importance. The commercial exploitation of the forests in the Mur valley supports the many saw and papermills. The mining of magnesite, which is exported to all parts of the world and is used on the spot to make firebricks for furnaces, has also contributed to the prosperity of the region.
Between Graz and Bruck an der Mur, three power stations use the waters of the river to produce electricity.

FROM GRAZ TO LEOBEN *70km - 43 miles*

★★ **Graz** – *See GRAZ.*

Leave Graz on the road to Bruck an der Mur (AX).

Once the road has crossed to the east bank wooded hills appear and then rock outcrops.

Österreichisches Freilichtmuseum (Austrian Open-air Museum) ⊙ – *In Stübing.* This museum of Austrian traditional rural architecture occupies an area of 50ha – 120 acres in a tributary valley of the Mur. About 80 farmhouses with their annexes have been reconstructed on this site and aligned east to west to correspond with the geography of the country.
The first group of buildings is from Burgenland in eastern Austria, showing the thatched roofs characteristic of that region. This is followed by a number of traditional structures from the eastern Alps: 18C Styrian houses in which the "smoke room" with its twin fireplaces served as a kitchen, the living-room and bedroom in one; and a Carinthian farmstead with its buildings grouped around a central courtyard. Then there is a massive farmstead from the Danube valley on a quadrangular plan in which living quarters, stables and barns form a single block, and next to it a typical farmhouse from the Waldviertel. An almost Alpine landscape forms the setting for the group of houses from the Tyrol. The final exhibit is a fine house from the Bregenzerwald near the Swiss border.
The universal use of timber as a building material is striking. Both houses and farm buildings have been fitted out with appropriate furnishings and equipment: from cribs to spinning wheels, decorated chests, tools and implements. The piety of rural communities is evoked by numerous religious images and sculptures. The museum takes as its emblem a rose carved in wood bearing the date 1721. Also represented are some of the old rural industries, including a sawmill, smithies, various mills etc.
New exhibits are regularly being added to the museum's collection, but it already presents an excellent picture of the country's rural heritage.
North of Peggau, a large industrial town covered in dust from its cement factories, beside the road (right) rises an impressive limestone cliff. In the mountain behind lies the Lurgrotte, an underground network of galleries which links the valley of the Mur with the small valley of the Semriach to the east.

★ **Lurgrotte (Peggau entrance)** ⊙ – The walk beside the underground river reveals several concretions such as the stalactite of the "Prince", which stands at the end of the walk. *It is possible to continue to Blocksberg.*

The valley, often bordered by rocky slopes, becomes greener and more picturesque.

There is an attractive view from the bridge by-passing the town of Frohnleiten, whose houses cluster at the foot of the church on the steep bank of the River Mur. The long leats, which supply the Laufnitzdorf and Pernegg power stations, have created new stretches of water parallel to the river.

★ **Bruck an der Mur** – *See BRUCK AN DER MUR.*

West of Bruck the road follows the south bank of the Mur, which runs in a west-to-east direction. To the left you see the summit of the Brucker Hochalpe, a limestone massif which reaches an altitude of 1 643m - 5 390ft. The valley now widens and becomes more and more industrial until it reaches Leoben.

Leoben – *See LEOBEN.*

NEUSIEDLER SEE★

Burgenland

Michelin map 426 fold 26

The Neusiedler See is the only example in Central Europe of a steppe-type lake. It has a melancholy aspect and is one of the great curiosities of the Burgenland *(general information on this "Land" p 32).*

A Capricious Lake – The lake has an area of 320km^2 - 124sq miles, of which most belongs to Austria, though Hungary holds the southern basin (1/5 of the total surface). Its waters are warm and salty and it is almost completely surrounded by a thick belt of reeds. It is nowhere more than about 2m - 7ft deep and is fed from underground lakes. The only tributary of any size, the Wulka, is an almost negligible factor as the volume of normal evaporation is four times the quantity of water that flows in. There is no permanent outflow. When a strong wind blows for some time in the same direction, the waters are driven towards one shore, while the level on the near shore drops perceptibly. When the wind drops, the lake returns to its normal level and appearance.

A Bone of Contention – It even happens that the waters disappear altogether (the last time was 1868-1872). For the lakeside dwellers this is a wonderful chance to enlarge their estates. Each refers to documents used by his family in similar circumstances; disputes break out and lawsuits are begun until such time as the lake reappears as mysteriously as it vanished.

H.W. Partaj/BILDAGENTUR BUENOS DIAS

Reed banks on the Neusiedler See

A Paradise for Birds – In the inextricable thickets formed by the reeds, an extraordinary aquatic fauna lives. More than 250 varieties of wildfowl have settled by the lake: herons, waterhens, wild duck and geese, gulls, teals, storks, bustards, egrets, etc.

National park – Since 1992, the lake has been incorporated into the Nationalpark Neusiedlersee-Seewinkel, extending either side of the national frontier and jointly administered by Austria and Hungary. The aim of the park is to preserve the typical flora and fauna of this transitional zone between the Alps and the Central European plain.

Vienna's "Seaside" – Every village near the lake has a little bathing-beach, normally reached by a roadway between two hedges of reeds. Owing to its proximity to Vienna (50km - 31 miles) it attracts all those who care for aquatic sports and in winter those who are keen on ice sports. Anglers and hunters of wildfowl use flat-bottomed boats to make their way along the canals among the reed-beds.

The Landscape – The eastern shore of the lake has a steppe-like quality, divided up by pools and ponds which have slowly been reclaimed as land for crops and orchards. The western shore is overlooked from a height of about 300m - 1 000ft by the Leithagebirge, at whose foot vegetables, maize, vines and fruit trees (even almonds) flourish in the rich ochre soil and gentle climate.

The vineyards, terraced on the slopes or lying in the plain, enjoy plenty of sunshine and produce famous vintages, the red and white wines of Rust, Mörbisch and Oggau being the most famous for their bouquet. In 1524 the vinegrowers of Rust received royal recognition for the quality of their wine and by virtue of the royal warrant they are entitled to display the arms of the town on the enormous vats in their vaulted cellars.

FROM NEUSIEDL TO EISENSTADT

69km - 43 miles – half a day

Leave Neusiedl northwestwards (if arriving from Vienna by road no 10, make straight for Jois without passing through Neusiedl) and follow the road towards Eisenstadt, bear left 2.4km - 1 ½ miles after Donnerskirchen to Rust.

Rust – Population 1 700. Rust is famous for its storks' nests, to which the birds return faithfully every year. It is a rich wine-growing village. In 1681, it bought its town charter for the price of 30 000l – 6 600gal(UK) of wine and 60 000 gold coins.
This idyllic village has many a picturesque view to offer the visitor: charming Renaissance and Baroque façades with oriels and huge carved doorways, inner courtyards and arcades, and the partially preserved fortified town wall. The considerable architectural heritage preserved in the old town centre has led to its being declared an historic monument.

Fischerkirche – Designed as a fortified church, this irregularly shaped place of worship with its impressive frescoes dating from the 14C and 15C is surrounded by a wall. Note in particular the three statues on the altar to the Three Magi, in the Late Gothic style, in the side aisle.
From the village a causeway through the rushes leads to a landing-stage and to the **Seebad Rust** ⊙, a well equipped bathing resort.
Excursions on the lake are organized in season.

★★ **Mörbisch** – *See MÖRBISCH.*

Return to Rust; bear left for St. Margarethen and Eisenstadt.

Before reaching Eisenstadt, the small capital of the Burgenland, one drives through a hilly district with alternating vineyard and orchards.

Eisenstadt – *See EISENSTADT.*

OBERNBERG AM INN

Oberösterreich – Population 1 680

Michelin map 426 fold 7 – 37km - 23 miles south of Passau – Alt 352m - 1 155ft

The market town of Obernberg, founded in *c*950, was ruled from Passau for many years. In 1779, together with the Inn region, it passed under the aegis of Austria. The town stands on the south bank of the Inn, which marks the frontier between Austria and Germany.

Marktplatz – This large well-preserved market square has at its centre a carved stone fountain. It is framed by elegant houses with brightly coloured façades, some of which are decorated with stucco. Note in particular the stucco façades of the Wörndlhaus, the Apothekerhaus and the Schiffmeisterhaus, which are the work of Bavarian master Johann Baptist Modler (*c*1740). From the middle of the square the fretted gables, and the silhouette of the bulbous belfry of the church, make a pleasant picture.

When driving from Britain to a destination in Austria
*use the **Michelin Road Atlas Europe** ;*
in addition to the maps at a scale of 1 : 1 000 000 or 1 : 3 000 000
there is a selection of 70 town plans
and a wealth of motoring information:
hardback, paperback and small format

OBERTAUERN✳✳

Salzburg – Population 4 000
Michelin map 426 fold 34 – Alt 1 739m - 5 705ft

The holiday resort of Obertauern lies on a broad terrace on the Radstädter Tauernpaß *(see RADSTÄDTER TAUERNPASS)*. In contrast to most of the other Austrian mountain locations, it did not develop from an existing village, but was set up purely as a winter sports location. It is surrounded by one of the most beautiful skiing areas in the northern Alps.

During the summer, Obertauern provides some interesting hiking destinations, in particular the **Seekarspitze peak**★★ (alt 2 350m - 7 710ft; *3 hour 30min return trip*) and the **Gamsleitenspitze-Zehnerkarspitze-Klockerin-Wildsee circuit**★★ *(allow 6 hours 30min for the whole circuit; for experienced hikers only)*.

Day trippers can park at car park P1 at the outskirts of the village.

✳✳ **Skiing area** – The Obertauern (alt 1 650-2 310m - 5 413-7 579ft) area's main attraction is its guaranteed snow, but it can also boast 26 skilifts leading to 120km - 75 miles of piste. Its somewhat modest size is more than made up for by the quality of the facilities. Only a few other Austrian winter sports locations offer such modern, comfortable equipment and pistes and ski-runs of such differing degrees of difficulty.

Experienced skiers can hone their skills on the impressive Buckelpiste, or humpbacked piste, along the Gamsleitenbahn 2, which includes a difference in altitude of 360m - 1 181ft, and on the ski-run on the Hundskogel. For fairly good skiers there are some magnificent pistes in the area of the Seekarspitze summit, whilst for beginners the more or less flat slopes immediately surrounding the village, at Sonnenlift and Kurnenlift, are suitable.

VIEWPOINTS

★ **Zehnerkarseilbahn cable-car** – Alt 2 192m - 7 191ft. *45min return trip.* The cable-car runs to the foot of the Zehnerkarspitze peak (alt 2 381m - 7 811ft). Beautiful **all-round view**★ over the massif around Obertauern from the Seekarspitze to the Gamskarspitze. After dropping 200m - 656ft, the ski-run offers a view of the far-distant limestone massif from the Tennengebirge to the Dachstein.

★★ **Gamsleitenbahn 1 and 2** – *Accessible to skiers.* Turn left at the mountain station of the second chairlift (alt 2 313m - 7 588ft) and approach the furthest end of the piste. Magnificent **view**★★ over Mosermandl and the rocky ridges of the Kesselspitze. The Gamskarspitze and the Plattenspitze peaks tower opposite.

★★ **Seekareck** – *Accessible to skiers using the Grünwaldkopf and Seekareck chairlifts.* Turn left at the mountain station (alt 2 160m - 7 086ft). In a few minutes you will reach a raised bit of ground, from which you can see the Großglockner.

When there is no risk of avalanche and the trail has been cleared, it is well worth climbing up to the peak (alt 2 217m - 7 273ft; *10min on foot*). Wonderful **panorama**★★ over the Radstädter Tauern, the Dachstein and the Hohe Tauern.

★ **Panoramabahn** – Alt 2 208m - 7 244ft. *Accessible to skiers.* The view stretches over the Schladminger Tauern. A wonderful **view**★★ over the Hohe Dachstein and the Radstädter Tauern can be seen from the red piste, which leads along the left side of the Seekarspitzbahn down to the valley.

★ **Hundskogelbahn** – Alt 2 136m - 7 008ft. *Accessible to skiers.* **View**★ over the Bischofsmütze, the Tennengebirge and the Großglockner.

OBERWÖLZ

Steiermark – Population 950
Michelin map 426 fold 36 – 27km - 17 miles northeast of Murau

This small medieval town at the foot of its 12C castle, Schloß Rothenfels, was occupied as early as the Hallstatt period, after which it developed over the course of its eventful history from village to market town, before finally obtaining its civic charter in around 1300. At this time, Oberwölz was a well-off community which owed its wealth to the salt trade and silver-working. Of the fortified town wall built during this period, there remain large sections complete with fortified towers and three gateways. The remains of the wall encircle the pretty historic town centre, which is bright with flowers in season.

★ **Sigismundkirche** – This chapel, which is very close to the Gothic parish church, was founded in the 14C to serve the town's former hospital. The back of the chapel, which housed the patients, consists of an enormous gallery supported by intersecting ribs; this part of the church is roofed by a complex arrangement of rib vaulting rising from three pillars.

ÖTSCHERMASSIV★

Niederösterreich und Steiermark

Michelin map 426 folds 23 and 24

The mountainous area south of St. Pölten, between the Wienerwald and the Eisenerz Alps, is part of the limestone Pre-Alps. The first foothills, which are wooded and 600m to 800m - 2 000ft to 2 600ft high, give way to a succession of minor ranges, reaching an altitude of 1 893m - 6 211ft, at the massive peak of the Ötscher (from an old Slavonic word Otčan = godfather), which can be seen at a great distance, especially when approached from the north.

ROUND TRIP STARTING FROM MARIAZELL

112km - 70 miles – allow half a day

★ **Mariazell** – *See MARIAZELL.*

Leave Mariazell by the road (no 21) east which runs steeply downhill, enters the Salza valley and follows the stream closely. In Terz the picturesque road turns north and plunges into a gorge with rocky sides to which conifers cling.

St. Aegyd lies in the Unrecht Traisen valley, which is lined with factories and sawmills. Beyond Hohenberg the limestone cliffs are broken, here and there, by well-developed natural amphitheatres.

In Freiland turn right into road no 20 to Lilienfeld.

Lilienfeld – Population 3 030. The Gothic church of this Cistercian Abbey is of astonishing size and architectural purity.

From Lilienfeld return south; in Freiland continue southwest (road no 20).

The road, which is pleasant and picturesque, becomes more and more enclosed, first between wooded slopes, then in a rocky gorge where there are outcrops of schist. Reservoirs supply small factories, including papermills at Dickenau. Beyond Türnitz, the well laid road climbs steadily offering wider and wider views of limestone ridges of 1 200m to 1 400m - 4 000ft to 4 600ft. A series of hairpin bends leads to the village of Annaberg, built on a pass at an altitude of 973m - 3 192ft facing the summit of the Ötscher.

Annaberg – Population 1 060. Annaberg has a curious site at the top of a pass, facing a range of mountains from which the Ötscher stands out. The place has long had a pilgrimage church well known to the faithful on their way to Mariazell. The first building, a timber chapel, was erected here in 1217, though the present church is of 14C-15C date. It is dedicated to St Anne, as the Holy Family (15C) at the high altar shows, and still has fine ogive vaulting but was decorated in the Baroque style in the 17C and 18C.

The ceiling of the small south chapel is adorned with frescoes and stucco; cherubs and statues overload the high altar and side altars, and there is a mass of gilding and carving on the pulpit and the organ-loft.

During the hairpin bend descent, the Ötscher, towering 1 000m - 3 280ft above, stands out clearly to the west. Josefsberg is the start of a pleasant run downhill among fir woods, with fine vistas towards the Gemeindealpe (alt 1 626m - 5 335ft) on the right. People throughout this region live on cattle raising and forestry. In the valleys there were once many little forges, working on the Styrian iron ore from the nearby Eisenerz. Today they have disappeared.

To the right of the road lies the artificial Erlaufstausee lake, barring the upper course of the Erlauf. On leaving Mitterbach turn right and drive beside a second lake, the natural Erlaufsee.

Return to Mariazell.

ÖTZTAL★★

Tirol

Michelin maps 426 folds 30 and 31 and 218 folds 9 and 10 (south of Längenfeld)

The Ötztal, which is remembered by mountaineers as a series of shining glaciers – total surface area: 173km² - 67sq miles – is a deep valley running into the Inn and consisting for 50km - 31 miles of ravines separated by isolated basins, where the patriarchal traditions of Old Tyrol have long been observed.

When mountains unite more than they divide – The Ötztal Alps include the highest point in the northern Tyrol, the Wildspitze (alt 3 774m - 12 382ft). Students also learn that the highest parish in Austria, Obergurgl (alt 1 927m - 6 321ft) and the highest permanent human habitation in the country, **Rofen** near Vent (alt 2 014m - 6 608ft), are in the upper basin of the Ötztal.

Until the First World War these places were more closely connected with the Alto Adige to the south, from which their people originally came, than with the Inn valley. For a long time the inhabitants preferred to trudge through snowfields on wide

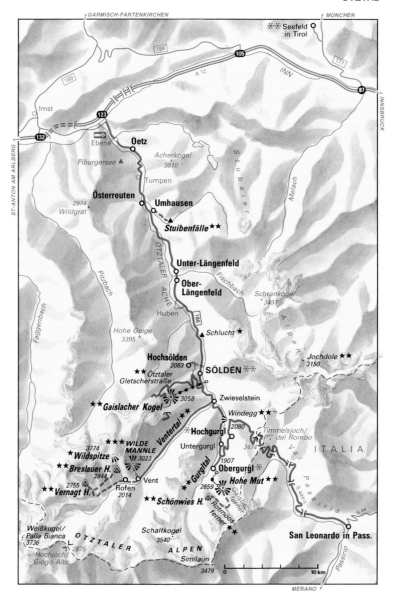

passes like the Hochjoch or Niederjoch, at an altitude of nearly 3 000m - 10 000ft, rather than make their way along the floors of the gorges of the Ötztaler Ache, on unsafe roads exposed to floods, falling stones and avalanches.

When the Timmelsjoch road was completed, in 1969, the isolation of the Ötztal came to an end, at least in summer.

FROM THE INN VALLEY TO SAN LEONARDO IN PASSIRIA
(ST. LEONHARD IN PASSEIER)

88km - 55 miles – allow at least 1 day, to get an overall impression of the area. To include the magnificent Venter valley and the no less beautiful Gurgl valley (with rambles) allow at least 3 days.

On the Italian side the road is generally snow-free from mid-June to mid-October. The route demands care (no crash-barriers) and has an irregular surface, especially in the tunnels. Trailers, caravans, buses and trucks are forbidden. On the Austrian side, however, the road is generally open all year round, at least to Hochgurgl.

The **Ötztalstraße** ⊙ runs through pleasant pine woods among piles of debris brought down from the Ötztaler Ache which has been deeply furrowed by the torrent. This flows beneath the picturesque covered bridge at Ebene to enter the Ötz basin, which is dominated by the rocky tooth of the Acherkogel. Chestnuts, fields of maize and peach and apricot orchards show that the Ötztal corridor, running due south, attracts the warm air of the Föhn *(qv)*.

Oetz – Population 2 000. The town is well sited on the last levels of the sunny slope on which the large church is built. Several buildings have a traditional air, for example, the Gasthof Stern with its flower-decked oriel and painted façade.

The walk to the romantic Piburgersee nearby is popular. The road climbs over a first shelf, crossed by the torrent in a muddy stream. It reaches Tumpen in another basin into which the Tumpenbach, on the right, pours in a series of cascades.

Österreuten – This hamlet is one of the most harmonious architectural groups in the valley. Note the overhanging upper storeys sheltering a veranda, a detail which is found also in the Cortina Dolomites.

Umhausen – Population 2 300. A typical large inn (the Gasthaus Krone) is characteristic of this pleasant village. Customers may ask to see the room with a balcony still furnished in 17C style.

★★ **Stuibenfälle** – *About 1 hour 30min on foot Rtn along a signposted track which begins at the Tourist Office pavilion (Verkehrsverein).* The path leads first to a restaurant-chalet, crosses the torrent and continues up the left bank to the foot of the **waterfall**. A second wooded ravine lies downhill, near the swiftly flowing Ötztaler Ache. The valley widens again to form the Längenfeld basin.

Längenfeld – Population 3 500. This resort is divided into two separate settlements by the Fischbach torrent.

The town nestles in an angle of the valley made by the steep promontory of the Burgstein. There are good walks through nearby larch woods.

The scene has a harsh beauty, for the inner plain of Längenfeld, which still carries a few crops at 1 200m - 4 000ft altitude, is hemmed in between peaks approaching 3 000m - 9 840ft. Many details of the landscape are, however, charming, such as the white 17C Pestkapelle, a votive chapel for delivrance from the plague, in the woods on the opposite slope.

Beyond Huben a long ravine begins, narrowing after the bridge at Aschbach to a **gorge**★ covered with larches.

✿✿ **Sölden** – *See SÖLDEN.*

The valley forks in Zwieselstein: to the right lies the **Ventertal**★★ *(see SÖLDEN)*, the valley which gave access to two of the earliest border passes over the Alpine ridge (Hochjoch 2 875m - 9 432ft, Niederjoch 3 019m - 9 905ft).

This itinerary takes the valley on the left, however, the **Gurgltal**★★ *(qv)* with the famous winter sports resort of **Obergurgl**✿.

After a steep climb the Timmelsjoch road drops briefly to reach the **Windegg viewpoint**★★ (alt 2 080m - 6 824ft) from which there is a view of the Gurgl valley and the Great Gurgl Glacier and, to the north, the cleft of the Ötztal. The road begins to climb once more through an austere landscape up to the Timmelsjoch (2 509m - 8 032ft). On the steeper southern slope of the pass the road, often cut out of the rock, passes through a tunnel 700m – nearly half a mile long, before plunging into the Val Passiria and providing impressive views of the crest marking the frontier, particularly the Monte dei Granati (Granatenkogel) to the south. The road does not descend to the river level but continues along the mountainsides, which are often steep, as far as Moso (there is a view from the terrace of the Gasthaus Saltnuß). The journey then becomes easier as the valley opens out.

At San Leonardo one can join the road from Merano to the Brenner by way of the Monte Giovo (Jaufenpass).

OSSIACHER SEE★

Kärnten

Michelin map 426 fold 35 – Local map under WÖRTHER SEE

A little set back from the Villach basin, the lake of Ossiach, which is as yet largely unknown to tourists, is distinguished from other large lakes in Carinthia by its uniform, rather wild setting between steep, wooded slopes. The south shore is particularly unspoiled and offers some delightful views. The road along the north shore forms a part of the alternative route from Villach to Vienna which bypasses Klagenfurt.

★ TOUR OF THE LAKE

Starting from Villach *66km - 41 miles – half a day*

Villach – *See VILLACH.*

From Villach the road to Vienna (no 94) leads into the alluvial plain partly occupied by the lake. Ahead and to the right the ruins of Landskron stand on a spur. The road skirts the north shore of the lake, at the foot of the steep slopes of the Gerlitzen.

Ossiacher See

★★ Gerlitzen – *From Tschöran, 12km - 7 miles on a toll road – plus 1 hour on foot Rtn. Access and description under GERLITZEN.*

Going round the lake anti-clockwise, the road takes the southern shore, which is slightly steeper and more countrified with its hamlets of old wooden houses (at Altossiach).

Ossiach – Population 570. The Benedictine **Abbey** of Ossiach (now transformed into a hotel) was the centre of the re-evangelisation and Germanisation of Carinthia and Slovenia from the 11C.

In the 16C and 17C it had periods of splendour, as in the summer of 1552, during which the Abbot, when receiving Charles V, sailed a fleet of galleys on the lake for his Imperial visitor.

The monastery **church★** ⊘ suffers a little from having so large a mass for its single clock-tower, built at the crossing of the transept.

Inside, the upper parts were greatly modified by Baroque influences between 1741 and 1749. This is particularly noticeable in the raised **stuccowork★** coloured according to the technique of the Wessobrunn School in Bavaria. The less brilliant decorative painting is the work of the local artist, Joseph-Ferdinand Fromiller, who also worked in the Landhaus at Klagenfurt.

The ancient Gothic chapel, with its baptismal font on the left of the entrance, preserves one of the most precious of the sixty altarpieces dating from the end of the Gothic era, to be found in Carinthia. This masterpiece, which dates from the beginning of the 16C is attributed to one of the St Veit studios. It represents the Virgin between St Margaret and St Catherine, with the apostles, in groups of three, on the panels.

As the tour of Ossiach lake ends, the ruins of Landskron appear once more against the distant crests of the Villacher Alpe.

Burgruine Landskron – *Via St. Andrä by a steep road.* The castle, which in the Middle Ages was one of the strongholds of the Habsburgs in Carinthia, passed in the middle of the 16C to the Khevenhüller family who rebuilt it. The chroniclers of the time described the brilliant life style of Bartholomew Khevenhüller, who also owned the castle of Velden *(qv)*. During the Thirty Years War Landskron castle became the object of endless appropriations and appeals, set in train by the measures taken in Austria against the protestants – the Khevenhüller supported the Reformation – and after the 17C the fortress was no longer maintained. The ruins are now occupied by a café-restaurant and an eagle observation point. From the esplanade there is a wide **view★** of the Villach basin, the Karawanken and Ossiach lake.

The road back to Villach runs parallel to the canal built to drain the lake.

Avoid sight-seeing in a church during a service

PACK- und STUBALPENSTRASSE★

Steiermark und Kärnten

Michelin map 426 folds 36 and 37

Between the valleys of the Mur and Lavant Rivers and the Graz basin rise the gentle, wooded heights of the Pannonian Pre-Alps. These mountains, known as the Koralpe, the Packalpe, the Stubalpe and the Gleinalpe, form a barrier less by their height, which hardly exceeds 2 000m - 6 500ft, than by their solitude. The inter-regional road from Graz to Klagenfurt passes over the Packsattel, whereas the old road from Graz to Judenburg via Köflach crosses the Stubalpe, cutting off the wide bend of the River Mur.

★STUBALPE

From Judenburg to Köflach 44km - 27 miles – about 1 hour

Beware of the steep gradient on the east slope of the Gaberl pass (maximum 1 in 5) between Puffing and Salla valley.

Judenburg – Population 10 580. The town is densely built up on its spur, around the foot of a tall tower which has become the emblem of the town. Judenburg, located at the point where five trade routes converged, is the oldest commercial centre in Styria. From 1103, records show that there was a Jewish community here, which held the reins of the trade and usury activities. In 1496, as elsewhere in Styria, Emperor Maximilian I had the Jews driven out. Numerous old buildings and courtyards from the historic town centre survive, clustered around the **Neue Burg**.

The mountainous stretch of the "Gaberlstraße" begins at the village of Weißkirchen. The tortuous road rises in stages through the fir trees to the crest which it follows nearly to the Gaberl-Sattel. There are many attractive vistas north and south through woodland into the nearby valleys. Behind, the Aichfeld plain (in the Judenberg-Knittelfeld region) lies at the foot of the bare crests of the Niedere Tauern, which stretch northwest. The main crest of the Stubalpe is crossed at the Gaberl-Sattel (alt 1 547m - 5 075ft – *inn*).

On the east slope of the pass, the road drops suddenly into the wild and narrow wooded **Salla valley**, reaching its floor at a tiny village of the same name. Here and there a large chalet or an old mill stand by the torrent. The sawmills and scythe factories *(Sensenwerk)* which introduced industry to the valley, may still be seen, though some are now in ruins. (Styrian scythes have a worldwide reputation).

The valley opens out again.

Köflach – Population 12 000. This is a pretty town, in spite of the opencast lignite extraction nearby (the Köflach deposits are the most productive in Austria).

★PACKSATTEL

From Köflach to Wolfsberg 52km - 32 miles – about 1 hour 30min

Northeast of Köflach (3km - 2 miles) is the Lippizaner Stud Farm at Piber.

Köflach – *See above.*

After leaving Köflach, the route passes the opencast lignite pits and then climbs up the side of an outlying hill a little distance from the main Packalpe ridge. There are good views down into the industrial valley, particularly after Edelschrott; the bright white outline of the pilgrimage church at Maria Lankowitz stands out, as do the chimneys and cooling towers of the thermal power station at Vottsberg. The road runs along the enclosed Teigitschbach valley but the views open out as it begins the final climb up towards the village of Pack.

Pack – Population 530. Favoured by the proximity of the **Packer Stausee** (an artificial lake with boating and bathing facilities), this little place also enjoys a peaceful **panorama**★ of the wooded foothills of the Pannonian Pre-Alps and the Graz plain. The construction of the Graz-Wolfsburg motorway has freed the village from through traffic and allowed it to reclaim its past atmosphere.

In gentle pastoral surroundings the road reaches the Packsattel, which is also known as the Packhöhe or the Vier Töre (Four Gates - alt 1 166m - 3 825ft). The road passes into an even quieter and more thickly wooded zone. A series of hairpin bends below the Preitenegg ridge lends a little variety to this descent of the Carinthian slope, during which one can see, in the distance, the crests of the Saualpe, rising in series to the west. If the weather is clear, the rocky barrier of the Karawanken can be seen, to the south, through the Lavanttal gap. This section of the route ends at the foot of the sombre Schloß Waldenstein. It then winds along the ravine of the Waldensteiner Bach to join the equally deep valley of the Lavant at Twimberg.

* **Lavant Motorway Bridge (Autobahnbrücke)** – 1 079m - 3 500ft long and 165m - 541ft high, this bridge is taller than the Stephansdom in Vienna. It is among the ten longest bridges in Austria and it is Europe's second highest bridge built on piers.

Wolfsberg – Population 28 180. The old, upper town was built at the foot of the château of the Counts Henckel von Donnersmarck, which was reconstructed in the 19C in the Tudor style. The town centre is the Hoher Platz, a square adorned with a column to the Virgin (1718) and surrounded by houses in the Biedermeier style. The lower town is modern, with wide streets and pleasant walks beside the Lavant.

Gestüt PIBER*

Steiermark

Michelin map 426 fold 37 – 3km - 2 miles northeast of Köflach – Alt 503m - 1 650ft

Piber's claim to fame rests on the beautiful Lippizaner stallions, a race prized during the Baroque period, which are bred here. The stallions are sent to the Spanische Reitschule in Vienna, where it is possible to watch them in displays of classical horsemanship.

* **Stud Farm (Gestüt)** ⓥ – A visit to the stables and a walk in the fields nearby will give a close view of the famous Lippizaners. Born bay or black, the horses acquire their white coats between the ages of four and ten. They were brought here in 1920 from the stud at Lipica near Trieste (now in Slovenia), where they had been bred without interruption since the 16C.

  Today's Lippizaners are the descendants of six late 18C strains of Danish, Neapolitan and Arab origin, which all go back ultimately to an ancient Iberian breed already famous at the time of Julius Caesar.

Lippizaner stallions at Piber stud farm

PITZTAL***

Tirol

Michelin map 426 fold 30

The long Pitztal valley, which runs from north to south, is bordered in the west by the Kaunertal valley and in the east by the Ötztal valley. It is famous for the extraordinary Alpine scenery in its upper reaches. It is enclosed by a massive glacier basin, over which towers the 3 774m - 12 382ft high **Wildspitze** peak, the highest point in the Tyrol.

* **Road from Arzl to Mittelberg** – *39km - 24 miles – allow 45min.*

  The road leads through numerous villages and hamlets. After 18km - 11 miles, the glaciers of the Pitztal valley come into view at Hairlach. 4km - 2.5 miles later, the road passes through St. Leonhard, the main holiday resort in the valley. The mountain slopes draw further away from the road. The scenery is characterised by forest, little waterfalls and the broad Pitzbach, which the road follows to Mittelberg, where it ends. From here, lifts take you up to the glaciers.

★★★ **Hinterer Brunnenkogel** ⊙ – Alt 3 440m - 11 286ft. *Around a 2 hour return trip. Anyone wishing to take a trip to the Riffelsee lake (on the same day or on the following day) should buy a combined tourist excursion ticket.*

You should take sunglasses, sturdy shoes which are also suitable for snow, warm clothing (even in summer) and if possible, binoculars.

First take the Pitzexpress funicular railway. After travelling underground for 3.7km - 2.3 miles, you will reach the foot of the Pitztal glacier at an altitude of 2 860m - 9 383ft. Continue on the Pitz-Panoramabahn, the highest cable-car in Austria.

From the mountain station you will reach the peak in a few minutes, and will be able to enjoy the fantastic **Alpine panoramas**★★★. The Hinterer Brunnenkogel is located in a magnificent situation right in the centre of a massive glacier basin. The Wildspitze peak towers majestically over this grandiose landscape. On the right you can see the Taschachferner glacier, which rolls down the slope at the foot of the impressive Hochvernagtspitze peak. In the background you can also see the peaks of the Kaunertal and Ötztal valleys.

In the west a long, rugged rocky face with the Ögrubenspitze and Bliggspitze peaks rises up opposite the Wildspitze. In the north you can see right up to the last hamlets in the Pitztal, flanked by the Watzespitze peak and the Hohe Geige.

✳ **Pitztal glacier skiing area** – A cable-car, four T-bar lifts and a chairlift lead up to the 29km - 18 mile long piste which is well covered in snow. The skiing area, which is normally open from the autumn right up to June, is suitable for skiers of all levels, although easy runs predominate.

★ **Excursion to the Riffelsee** ⊙ – Park the car in Mandarfen, a hamlet 1km – half a mile below Mittelberg. Ride up in the cable-car. This excursion is especially recommended as part of a hike.

During the trip you will enjoy interesting **views** over the valley, and of the Kerlesferner glacier to the south. From the cable-car mountain station (alt 2 300m - 7 546ft), there is a wonderful view over Riffelsee lake, which is surprisingly light in colour and large in size in view of its altitude. The **landscape**★ is dominated by the Seekogel. A walk around the lake is recommended.

Hikers with plenty of stamina can take the Fuldaer Höhenweg ridge trail, which leads southwards directly along the mountainside to the **Taschachhütte** mountain lodge at an altitude of 2 432m - 7 979ft. It is located at the foot of the Hochvernagtspitze peak and the Taschachferner and Sexegertenferner glaciers *(day trips)*.

PÖLLAU★

Steiermark – Population 1 860

Michelin map 426 south of fold 24 – Alt 427m - 1 401ft

Pöllau lies in the heart of a small, undulating region well away from the major tourist routes; it gives the impression of being the capital of this valley, the Pöllauer Tal. Much of the surrounding countryside, which encompasses six townships, has been turned into a game park (124km² - 48 sq miles); it is criss-crossed by 100km - 62 miles of waymarked paths and boasts large wooded areas that are well stocked with animals. The park is dominated to the east by the summit of Rabenwaldkogel (1 280m - 4 198ft) and to the west by the Masenberg (1 261m - 4 135ft), both highly popular areas with walkers.

In an area of limited agricultural activity, vines occupy a significant niche in the local economy. In the season, there are a large number of traditional bars *(Buschenschenken)* to be found in the countryside, serving good quality wines, sometimes to the accompaniment of accordion music.

The charm of Pöllau is due in part to its beautiful old tile roofs.

SIGHTS

Marktplatz – This traditional market place, with its column to the Virgin Mary, is characterised by the southern character of many of its old façades. The narrow streets leading into the square have preserved the provincial flavour of their simple, unsophisticated architecture.

To the north of the square, a door set in a pedimented building adds a note of discreet solemnity to the surrounding rural gaiety. The door opens into the old abbey, a vast, almost circular area, round which the town has grown.

Abtei – This abbey of canons regular under the Rule of St Augustine was founded in 1504 by a nobleman of Pöllau, Hans von Neuberg. The new foundation had a troubled time during the 16C, when Styria was racked by religious disputes and particularly by Turkish raids.

By the end of the 17C the abbey had become prosperous and it was then rebuilt in the Baroque style. Less than a century later, at the time of Austria's secularization in 1785, it was closed down by the Emperor Joseph II and turned into a private residence. The old abbey buildings now belong to the town.

★ **Abbey church** – The plans for this huge building were drawn up by **Joachim Carlone**, a member of the celebrated family of Graz architects. The prior wished the new church to bear as strong a resemblance as possible to St Peter's in Rome. Rebuilding took place between 1701 and 1709 in the form of a Latin cross with a cupola over the transept crossing.

The dimensions are impressive: nave and chancel 62m - 203ft long, transept 37m - 121ft wide, cupola 42m - 138ft high, creating an unusually large space for a community numbering only a few dozen priests.

The remarkable **decor** is a delightful blend of paintings, gold, stuccowork and opulent sculptures. The frescoes in the nave and cupola are by **Matthias von Görz**, a Styrian painter heavily influenced by the Italian artists with whom he worked when he was studying in Italy. The hallmarks of this regional painter are the use of bright colours, a somewhat simple serenity, a passion for light and considerable skill at *trompe-l'œil*. It took him 12 years to finish decorating the church. In the vault of the **cupola**, the nine choirs of angels celebrate the Trinity; from between the eight windows allegorical figures of the virtues look up towards heaven. The vault of the nave is decorated with the fall of the wicked angels, the veneration of the cross, the adoration of the Lamb of God by all the saints, and the Blessed Virgin Mary enthroned and surrounded by her court. The **high altar** is decorated with an enormous painting, representing the martyrdom of St Vitus, executed by the artist Joseph Adam von Mölkh in 1779.

The 24-stop **organ**, built in 1739, stands on an arcaded gallery, beneath a ceiling fresco of David playing the harp.

Pilgrimage church at Pöllauberg

EXCURSIONS

★ **Pöllauberg** – *6km - 4 miles northeast of Pöllau.*
Pöllauberg church, which seems to float in mid-air, in fact crowns the top of a steep hill and is visible for miles around. There can be no place in Styria that is more abundantly decorated with flowers than this tiny village, built in the shadow of the celebrated pilgrimage church which dominates the Pöllau valley. From this natural balcony, it is possible on a clear day to see as far as the Hungarian plain.

★ **Church** – On reaching the top of a flight of seven steps, it is initially surprising to see an elegantly ribbed axial pillar concealing much of the chancel from view. This pilgrimage church was built between 1375 and 1379 according to an unusual design; two naves of equal size and with intersecting ribs in the vaults are separated by three columns, which stand in the central aisle and are so carefully sited in relation to the chancel that there is a clear view of the celebrant from every seat.

The large and sumptuously decorated high altar was built in 1714 around a statue of the Virgin Mary. The pulpit which is lavishly decorated with gold dates from 1730.

★ **Schloß Herberstein** – *23km - 14 miles south of Pöllau. From Kaindorf take the Graz road; in Kaibing turn off towards St. Johann bei Herberstein. See Schloß HERBERSTEIN.*

PÖRTSCHACH★

Kärnten – Population 2 500

Michelin map 426 folds 35 and 36 – Local map WÖRTHER SEE – Alt 458m - 1 503ft

A peninsula jutting into Wörther Lake decided the tourist future of the resort of Pörtschach whose opulent villas and hotels nestle among foliage. The existence of this tongue of land prompted the construction of a long, flower-decked promenade beside the lake.

The little structure known as the "Gloriette", a belvedere overlooking the lake and the Karawanken, is the favourite goal of walks and drives from Pörtschach. It is situated beside Schloß Leonstein, a castle standing on a rock to the southwest of the town.

PULKAU

Niederösterreich – Population 1 740

Michelin map 426 fold 11 – 8km - 5 miles northeast of Eggenburg – Alt 291m - 955ft

Pulkau is a large wine-producing township not far from the Czech frontier, in a hilly area which lends itself to the cultivation of vines. The highest ridges are marked by dark spruce woods and the town itself has the added interest of two unusual churches.

Pfarrkirche – The parish church crowns a hill to the north of the town. It is flanked on the east by a Romanesque tower and is noteworthy for the simplicity of the main building. The north chapel has a few traces of early 14C frescoes; the south chapel has foliated capitals.

In the middle of the churchyard stands a curious **charnel-house** (Karner). This is a 13C twelve-sided building, entered through a Romanesque doorway adorned with statues.

Heilig-Blut-Kirche – This church is an unfinished Gothic building which contains, above the high altar, a fine carved and painted wooden **altarpiece★** made by artists of the Danubian school at the beginning of the 16C. The figures of Christ, St Sebastian and St Bartholomew occupy a central position; the painted panels are decorated with scenes of the Passion.

Bad RADKERSBURG

Steiermark – Population 1 850

Michelin map 426 fold 39 – 32km - 20 miles south of Bad Gleichenberg
Alt 208m - 682ft

Since it was founded in 1265 by Ottokar of Bohemia, Radkersburg has been one of the leading trading centres in Styria. Timber, iron and salt, transported down the Mur on rafts, were traded for farm produce such as wine and honey from the southeast. Most importantly, the town had the right of prior purchase on wine. During the wars against the Turks, Radkersburg was an important bastion, with the result that it was named as an Imperial stronghold at the Augsburg Diet in 1582. The well-preserved **ring of fortifications**, with moats, six bastions and towers all still virtually intact, dates from this period. Numerous mansions and merchant's houses with beautiful stone doorways and courtyards give an indication of the town's former wealth.

Radkersburg was pronounced a spa town on the strength of its springs rich in calcium and bicarbonate.

SIGHTS

Hauptplatz – In the middle of the main square stands the **Pest-und Mariensäule**, a column dedicated to the Virgin Mary which commemorates the town's deliverance from the plague in 1681.

Rathaus – The town hall is flanked by a tall, Late Gothic octagonal tower with a particularly amusing bulbous belfry.

Stadtpfarrkirche – The nucleus of this Late Gothic church consists of a pillared basilica dating from the 14C. At the time of construction, a free-standing fortified tower from the town wall was incorporated into the church building. Inside, the ribbed vaulting above the side aisles contrasts with the barrel-vault above the nave.

Ehemaliges Zeughaus – A covered alleyway leads to a fine arcaded courtyard and the former arsenal. This where the cultural and historical heritage of the town and its surroundings is kept.

★ **Frauenplatz** – This shady square is near the Frauenkirche. A small chapel was put up in front of the newly built Baroque triple-aisled church in 1496. The square church tower, decorated with pilasters and crowned by an onion dome, and the square surrounded by trees and modest little houses make a very pretty picture.

RADSTADT

Salzburg – Population 4 194
Michelin map 426 fold 20 – Local map under SCHLADMINGER TAUERN

Radstadt, built on a regular, square layout by the Salzburg bishops at the end of the 13C, is still enclosed by the original fortified walls with their towers. On the west side, part of the moat has also survived. This pretty town 862m - 2 828ft above sea level lies on the junction of two spectacular scenic roads, the Dachsteinstraße and Radstädter Tauernstraße *(qv)*. To the north towers the Roßbrandgipfel summit, from where there is a breathtaking view of the surrounding mountain ranges, and to the south the Kemathöhe (alt 1 577m - 5 174ft), which is excellent for downhill skiing in the winter. Together with neighbouring resort Altenmarkt, 20km - 12 miles of ski-runs have been laid out.

The charming countryside around Radstadt boasts a number of interesting manor houses, such as those of Tandalier and Mauer, in the traditional Salzburg style (wide, overhanging roofs, corner turrets and watch towers).

★★ **Roßbrand viewpoint** – Alt 1 770m - 5 807ft. *10km - 6 miles steep mountain road (toll payable). From the car park at the end of the road, 15min climb to the Radstädter Hütte mountain lodge and then on to the cross.*
There is a wonderful **panorama**★★ of the Dachstein range, the Schladminger Tauern (Hochgolling, Höchstein), the Ankogel group, the Hohe Tauern (Großglockner, Großvenediger) and the Hochkönig. The most famous of the 150 mountain peaks visible from here can be identified through a panoramic telescope.

RADSTÄDTER TAUERNSTRASSE★

Salzburg
Michelin map 426 folds 20, 34 and 35

This road was much used in the Roman era and is still marked by military milestones which have been recently re-erected. The road, which crosses the summit of the Niedere Tauern at 1 700m - 5 577ft, connects the upper valleys of the Enns and the Mur. In the Middle Ages it was one of the lines of expansion towards the south pursued by the Archbishops of Salzburg.

The **Lungau**, in the upper valley of the Mur, is the only remaining relic of these ambitions. Until the opening of the Tauern motorway, it was one of the most remote and tradition-bound areas of the Alps and is still linked politically with the Salzach region. On arriving at St. Michael, motorists climb the Katschberg, either via the pass or via the tunnel of the same name *(see KATSCHBERGSTRASSE)*, to reach the lakes of Carinthia or the Cortina Dolomites.

FROM RADSTADT TO ST. MICHAEL IM LUNGAU

67km - 42 miles – half a day

10km - 6 miles of narrow, hilly road south from Radstadt.

Radstadt – See RADSTADT.

The run from Radstadt to Untertauern unfolds above magnificent meadows, dotted here and there with big farms. On the horizon, the crests of the Radstädter Tauern stretch in an almost unbroken line. Radstadt remains in sight for a time downstream.

Above Untertauern a series of hills and ravines, cooled by the shade of maples and the Taurach cascades, gives access to the upper part of the valley.

Gnadenfall – This pretty cascade of the Taurach leaps a wooded shelf in two light falls.

Hotels are dotted about among the larches and spruces below the pass (Radstädter Tauernpaß: alt 1 739m - 5 705ft). About 800m – half a mile short of the pass a modern (1951) statue of a Roman legionary stands guard over the bridge.

Obertauern – See OBERTAUERN.

The descent of the south approach to the pass involves a forbidding section but between Tweng and Mauterndorf pleasant clearings appear on the banks of the calmer Taurach. Soon the roofs of the castle of Mauterndorf emerge from the trees.

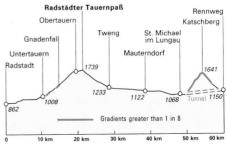

213

★ **Burg Mauterndorf** - *See Burg MAUTERNDORF.*

★ **Tamsweg** - *See TAMSWEG.*

★ **Schloß Moosham** ⊙ – This former fortress of the Archbishops of Salzburg was restored and refurnished last century. In the arolla (pine) panelled rooms on the 2nd floor and in the vaulted chancellery there are considerable collections of furniture and art objects. Ask for the explanation of the comical picture of people classified by their characteristic features in the bedroom on the 2nd floor. The castle's **lower courtyard**★ provides a lasting and picturesque memory: the stillness, the grass and the surrounding wooden galleries. The old well is 64m - 210ft deep.

St. Michael im Lungau – Population 3 250. Benefitting from the exceptional sunshine enjoyed by the upper valley of the Mur, this resort is a busy place with a huge modern youth hostel. Next to the Gothic parish church is the "Wolfgangkapelle", an elegant little building on an octagonal plan.
With its numerous ski-lifts giving access to the fine ski-slopes all around, St. Michael, together with St. Margarethen and Mauterndorf, is a particularly attractive centre for winter sports.

RANKWEIL

Vorarlberg – Population 9 930
Michelin map 426 fold 28 – Alt 463m - 1 519ft

The pilgrims' church at Rankweil rises above the Austrian section of the Rhine valley, overlooking a wide plain covered with orchards (huge pear trees).
This part of the Vorarlberg, known as the "Garden of Vorarlberg", boasts countryside along the road coming from Götzis, via Klaus, which, like the fertile fields on the Swiss bank of the river, resembles parts of England in its greenness.

Liebfrauenkirche or Burgkirche – Elderly or physically handicapped people can reach the church by car up a ramp leading off to the northeast from the ring-road around the castle rock.
This place of worship dedicated to the Virgin Mary was built perched on a steep-sided rock by the Bishop of Chur in the 8C. It was also used as a parish church. After it had been destroyed during uprisings in 1445, it was rebuilt at the end of the 15C and this time fortified by the addition of a ring of defence works, a cylindrical keep and a rampart walk, giving it quite a forbidding character. In 1986 the church was raised to the status of basilica minor.
The **Gnadenkapelle**, or Chapel of Miracles, was built at the same time as the side aisle adjoining it (1658) and houses the church's most precious treasure, a beautiful Late Gothic statue (15C) of the Virgin Mary, attributed to the Swabian school. To the right of the Gnadenkapelle stands the so-called "miracle-working" or Silver Cross, on the front of which hangs the figure of Christ crucified, a Romanesque work dating from the 13C, and which features three reliefs depicting the Entry of Christ into Jerusalem, the Angel Announcing Christ's Resurrection to the Women at the Tomb, and the Ascension of Christ.
A door beneath the gallery leads to the old **rampart walk**★ (Wehrgang), from where there is a marvellous **view**★ of the Rhine plain, ringed by the Vorarlberg and Swiss mountains. To the west and southwest lies the barrier of the Alpstein (Appenzeller Alps) with the Altmann summit (2 436m - 7 992ft), the Wildhaussattel, the jagged Churfirsten and the Alvier group. On the Austrian side, beyond the Ill gap at Feldkirch, The Drei Schwestern (Three Sisters) mark the frontier with Liechtenstein. Through the opening made by a small valley, the Schesaplan summit (Rätikon alt 2 965m - 9 728ft) can be seen.

RATTENBERG★

Tirol – Population 540
Michelin map 426 fold 18 – Alt 514m - 1 686ft

This tiny frontier town was a subject of dispute between the Tyrol and Bavaria until 1505, when Maximilian of Austria annexed the lower Inn valley as far as Kufstein. Rattenberg took advantage of a bottleneck in the alluvial plain of the Inn, which enabled it to control traffic on the road and on the river.

Renaissance townscape – By the 17C the silver mines on which Rattenberg's prosperity had been based were exhausted. In its impoverished state, the town was unable to improve or replace its building stock, which accounts for its appearance today, an almost perfectly preserved example of Renaissance urban design. The old town, squeezed between the Inn and the Schloßberg, forms a triangle whose

Rattenberg

Bohnacker/ÖSTERREICH WERBUNG

longest side, parallel to the river, is barely 300m long. The densely built up urban fabric is articulated by no more than two streets, linked by narrow alleyways. The building of the motorway has happily freed the main street from choking traffic.

Glass-making – Among other Tyrolean specialities, Rattenberg manufactures engraved and finely modelled glassware, both in the town itself and in Kramsach on the north bank of the Inn.

Rattenberg styles itself "the town of glass" (Glasstadt), though the well-known technical college specialising in glass technology is actually in Kramsach.

SIGHTS

★ **Hauptstraße** – The most characteristic houses have plain façades under dull coloured roughcast, adorned with some stucco, with window and door frames in pink marble and crowned with a horizontal pediment. As one can see from the castle *(for access see below)*, the pediment does not conceal a flat roof, which would be unsuitable in an Alpine climate, but a furrowed roof *(Grabendach)* anticipating the trussed roofing of 19C workshops. This division of the roof into several ridges at right angles to the street provided better protection against fire than a single, gabled roof, and did away with the intermediate gutter, which caused trouble between neighbours.

Augustinermuseum ⊘ – *Pfarrgasse 8.*
The Augustinian monastery was founded in 1384. In 1993 a museum was installed on the premises, with the aim of displaying Tyrolean art treasures in an appropriate setting. A large area is given over to Late Gothic sculpture, exhibited in the cloisters. Some excellent examples of local goldsmithing, the master exponent of which was Dominikus Lang, illustrate the very high standard to which this art had been refined.

★★ **Pfarrkirche St. Virgil** – Abutting the castle bluff, this Gothic church of 1473 is remarkable for its fine external stonework of pink marble.
Its twin naves, separated by four graceful columns with capitals of antique design, are bathed in light, making them a harmonious and iridescent confection in pinks and whites. Abundant statuary, delicate stucco work adorning the vaulting, and elegant frescoes make up the scintillating Baroque decorative scheme of about 1730, to which the finest artists of the region made their contribution. The masterly **Last Supper** in the main nave is the work of the Bavarian artist Matthäus Günther; the Transfiguration in the chancel is by Simon Benedikt Faistenberger *(qv)*. The statues around the **altar** in the smaller nave were sculpted by Meinrad Guggenbichler, the famous sculptor from Mondsee.
At the far end of the church, a flight of steps leads to the chapel dedicated to Saint Notburga, born in Rattenberg in 1265.

Schloßberg – *30min on foot Rtn.* Go beneath the railway bridge behind the church and on emerging from the covered way, bear right into the path up to the castle. At the green open space turn right to reach the edge of the terrace at the foot of the tower.

From this vantage point there is a good **general view** of the town, hemmed in between the Inn and the mountain, with the belfry of the Servitenkirche (13C-18C) rising above the roof ridges. Downstream, the Kaisergebirge can be seen.

EXCURSION

Freilichtmuseum Tiroler Bauernhöfe ⊙ – *7km - 4 miles. Leave Rattenberg in the Kramsach direction and cross the Brandenberger Ache (a tributary of the Inn) towards Breitenbach am Inn. The museum car park is on the right shortly after the hamlet of Mosen.*

A good number of farm buildings from most parts of the province have been rebuilt here in a quiet Alpine setting, enabling the visitor to appreciate the phenomenon of the Tyrolean chalet in all its pleasing variety.

REISSECK-MASSIV★★

Kärnten

Michelin map 426 fold 34

The Reißeck massif, which towers 2 400m - 7 874ft over the Möll valley at an altitude of 2 965m - 9 727ft, is one of the most unspoilt places in Carinthia. Since the building of a funicular and the laying of a railway line as part of construction of the power station at Kolbnitz *(see TAUERNTUNNEL)*, the massif has been opened up to the outside world to a far greater degree. Due to its beautiful situation and the good snow conditions, holidaymakers soon began to practise skiing here. During the winter, skiers are able to reach two high altitude ski lifts, which in the summer make the ideal point of departure for hikes to the many lakes and viewpoints of the massif.

★ **Reißeck funicular and railway** – *1 hour return trip with the funicular and 15min on the train.*

The funicular, made up of three sections, is quite spectacular, because of its very steep gradient (up to 82%). A 3.5km - 2.2 mile journey leads up to the Schokerboden station (alt 2 237m - 7 339ft), from where there is a beautiful **view**★ of the valley and the first rocky foothills of the Reißeck massif.

After travelling underground for 3.2km - 2 miles, the train arrives at the Reißeck mountain hotel, which is a pleasant place to stay in both summer and winter.

★ **Walk to the Mühldorfer Seen** – An easy 20min climb leads to the Großer Mühldorfer See, from where there is a **view**★ to the east over the Hohe Leier. After this the trail is quite stony, so sturdy shoes are essential *(follow the red and white markings)*. After 10min the path emerges above the Kleiner See dam. There is a beautiful **open view**★ over both lakes, which lie in an unspoiled rocky landscape. The **Riekentörl pass** (alt 2 525m - 8 284ft), with the Riedbock on its left and the Redlkopf on its right, lies to the north west.

Hikers should unquestionably climb this pass *(it takes an hour over a quite rocky trail, but presents no technical difficulties)*, which offers a magnificent **panorama**★★ over the entire Reißeck massif.

RETZ

Niederösterreich – Population 4 370

Michelin map 426 fold 11 – Alt 252m - 827ft

Retz, near the Thaya valley, is an important wine-growing and farming centre (some wine-cellars are open to the public – **Kellerbesichtigungen** ⊙), in a hilly region which forms part of the Bohemian massif. The **old town** still has its grid plan, ramparts and defensive towers.

Hauptplatz – This is the heart of the old town. It is rectangular, very large, and looks fine with its column to the Holy Trinity. It is surrounded by a few houses which are remarkable for their architecture and decoration: the **Verderberhaus** (north side) is crowned with a gallery and its ground floor pierced by an arched passage; opposite (no 15) is the **Sgraffitohaus**, a handsome building with a carved doorway and a façade covered with inscribed maxims.

The **Rathaus** was created in the 16C by converting a Gothic church; the Lady Chapel has survived on the ground floor.

Schloß RIEGERSBURG ★

Niederösterreich

Michelin map 426 fold 11 – 8km - 5 miles west of Hardegg

The natural and thought-provoking landscape of the north eastern Waldviertel provides a backdrop for the most important Baroque castle in Lower Austria. Visitors are surprised when they come upon this elegant building, a precious jewel which lies hidden in its park in the midst of otherwise rural surroundings. The former moated castle was bought by Sigmund Friedrich Count Khevenhüller, Governor of Lower Austria. He entrusted master builder **Franz Anton Pilgram** with its conversion to a four-winged Baroque palace, grouped around a square inner courtyard. Pilgram was a student of Hildebrandt and was the master builder of the abbey in Göttweig *(qv)*. In the castle at Riegersburg, he demonstrated his expertise. The decoration is rich, but not ostentatious, so that the building heralds the Classical style. The high quality **furnishings★** in the castle, which is still owned by the family, make it a fine example of an 18C country seat.

TOUR ⊙ *time: 45min*

The main façade is divided by a central portico with five columns and round arched windows, flanked by jutting corner pavilions. The typanum shows the coat of arms of the Khevenhüller, above which stands the figure of Atlas carrying the globe. The gable itself bears the statues of Wisdom, Unity, Justice and Honesty. The beautiful sculpted decoration, which dates from 1733, is the work of Josef Kracker.

Detail of portico, Schloß Riegersburg

Staterooms – The **banqueting hall** (Festsaal) is reached via the three flights of the main staircase. It is remarkable that stucco work as a means of decoration has only been used sparingly, and no gilding detracts from the beautiful proportions of the room. A sopraporte shows Count Johann Joseph Khevenhüller-Metsch, Maria Theresa's Chief Lord Chamberlain, whose diaries are said to have inspired the libretto for the opera *The Rosenkavalier*. The paintings of Maria Theresa and her mother Elisabeth Christine are by Martin van Meytens.

The **Baroque room** houses a view of Naples composed of 35 copper engravings dating from 1730-1775, which is a most unusual work since it shows a view from the air. The furniture in the Salon includes Queen Anne and Chippendale pieces, as well as furnishings in the Austrian Baroque style and a handsome tabernacle cupboard.

The **tower room**, hung with toiles de Jouy (plate-printed cotton), houses furniture from the 18C. Note the pretty travelling writing desk from England.

The **dining room** contains French furniture and houses one of the most famous portraits by Austrian painter Auerbach of Prince Eugene of Savoy. Note also the statue of a graceful blackamoor, a Venetian work.

The **stucco ceiling★** of the **Yellow Salon** depicts an allegory of princely virtue. The room is furnished with a Marie Antoinette suite and two beautiful Florentine commodes with delicate inlaid work. The **Chinese Salon** also features a magnificent stucco ceiling. The carpet with its Chinese decorations comes from the manufacturer Zuber in Mulhouse, France. The two commodes with their precious chequered inlaid work were a gift from Maria Theresa.

In the north wing is the elegant **castle chapel**, consecrated in 1755. The altar is integrated into the architectural structure and is surmounted by rich stucco work. The altarpiece depicts Saint Sigismund.

The **castle kitchen** on the ground floor, which was in use up to 1955, and which still has its original appointments, working equipment and the large brick oven, is the only remaining manorial kitchen in Austria.

From the castle café in the right wing, it is possible to gain access to the castle park with its pond.

EXCURSION

Burg Hardegg ⊙ – *8km - 5 miles to the east*. The town of Hardegg, which lies on the Thaya at the frontier with the Czech Republic, is dominated by the fortress of the same name, which is enthroned on a rocky mountain top. Its formidable keep and handsome walls create a great impression of impregnability. The origins of this strategically important fortress – highly prized because of its location in the north of the Ostmark or East March – date back to the year 1000, but records show that extensions were added right up to the 14C.

After a chequered history, the fortress passed into the hands of the Khevenhüller in 1730 and at the end of the 19C it was converted into a mausoleum for the Lower Austrian line of this dynasty. Some of the rooms are dedicated to the memory of the unlucky Emperor Maximilian of Mexico, whose comrade-in-arms and close confidant was Count Johann Franz Carl Khevenhüller.

*The Michelin Red Guide Europe
lists recommended hotels and restaurants
in the cities of Vienna, Innsbruck or Salzburg ;
consult the latest edition*

RIEGERSBURG★

Steiermark – Population 2 550

Michelin map 426 folds 38 and 39 – 10km - 6 miles north of Feldbach – Alt 450m - 1 476ft

Riegersburg, proudly standing on the top of a basalt height nearly 200m - 650ft above the Grazbach valley, is one of the most imposing strongholds to have guarded the eastern frontiers of Austria through the ages. First the Celts, then the Romans, saw the value of this defensive position and dug in there several times. The castle, built in the 13C, successfully withstood the attacks of the Hungarians and the Turks. In 1945 violent fighting took place here between the Russians and the Germans, the latter defending Riegersburg to the last gasp.

★ CASTLE (BURG) ⊙

time: 1 hour

From whatever direction one approaches, Riegersburg's bold **site**★ is a surprise. The village clings halfway up the south slope, 100m - 330ft below the castle.

A steep path climbs to the first line of ramparts; within is a large esplanade, on which stands a memorial to the numerous local victims of the last phase of the War in 1945. The entrance gate bears the coat of arms of the Riegersburg family.

This castle is of interest more for the fine **views**★ it offers of the Styrian countryside than for its architecture and internal arrangements. There is a collection of arms and armour and, in the inner courtyard, a well, surrounded by a graceful wrought-iron grille.

On the north side, the fortress commands the valley from the top of a dizzy precipice.

SAALACHTAL★

Salzburg und Bayern (Germany)

Michelin map 426 fold 19

The valley of the River Saalach, which breaches the Northern Limestone Alps, is served by an excellent road which links Salzburg to Zell am See and the Großglockner. Owing to the clearance made by enormous masses of glacier ice coming down northwards from the Tauern, the most open scenery is to be found near Saalfelden and Zell am See, near the source of the Saalach. Below Saalfelden, on the other hand, the river rushes through a rock cleft which is considered to be one of the most impressive transverse defiles in the Alps. After Lofer the cleft is replaced by a less striking series of basins and small wooded gorges.

FROM SALZBURG TO ZELL AM SEE

95km - 59 miles – about 2 hours, excluding Salzburg

Customs control at the entrance into Germany (Schwarzbacher Landstraße) and at the entrance into Austria (Steinpaß).

★★★ **Salzburg** - *Time: 4 hours. See SALZBURG.*

Leave Salzburg by ③ on the plan and route no 1 going southwest.

★ **Bad Reichenhall (Germany)** - *Description in Michelin Green Guide Germany.*

Branching off at Schneizlreuth from the Deutsche Alpenstraße, the Lofer road runs within view of the distinctive peaks of the Drei Brüder (Three Brothers) in the middle distance to the south. The road then turns away temporarily from the Saalach, as its course is too deeply sunken, and slips into a side valley ending at Melleck. Soon afterwards the Steinbach ravine marks the Austrian frontier. This is the Steinpaß.

Between Unken and Lofer several bottlenecks, especially the Kniepaß, where the Saalach foams close beside the road, give the run a touch of excitement. The northern approach to Lofer provides glimpses, directly after Hallenstein, of the central group of the Loferer Steinberge (Ochsenhorn, Großes Reifhorn, Breithorn); further south rise the Leoganger Steinberge.

★ **Lofer** - *See LOFER.*

Making a contrast with these scenes, the **enclosed section★** from Lofer to Saalfelden, in a former glacial gorge, is strikingly uniform. The Leoganger Steinberger (Lhaner Horn, Großes Rothorn) are particularly visible where the road crosses to the east bank of the Saalach.

Lamprechtshöhle ⊘ - An interesting series of illuminated chambers and galleries leading to an underground cataract.

Seisenbergklamm ⊘ - *500m from the main road, past Weißbach church the road signposted to the Seisenbergklamm ("Naturdenkmal des Landes Salzburg") which leads to a car park.*
Galleries and stairways, hidden by overhanging foliage, give access to the floor of this fissure through which the Weißbach roars.

South of Weißbach the road runs along the floor of a long canyon, whose steeper and steeper sides form part of the Leoganger Steinberge and Steinernes Meer ranges. Note, in passing, the Diesbach cascade. From the Brandlhof bend (chapel built into the rock), which comes a little before the mouth of the ravine, one can see, in the distance, the snows of the Wiesbachhorn and the Kitzsteinhorn (Hohe Tauern) and, in clear weather, as far as the Großglockner.

The Saalfelden basin opens out below the south walls of the Leoganger Steinberge and the Steinernes Meer. This slightly hilly section of the road has wide views. Ahead, the Tauern barrier can be seen clearly through the Zell am See corridor.

Saalfelden - Population 12 000. This market town with twelve centuries of history behind it has plenty to offer visitors: a beautiful site, a historical town centre, four surviving castles and rich and varied leisure facilities. Saalfelden is particularly favoured by cross-country skiers, to whom it offers 80km - 50 miles of ski-tracks.

Towering over the resort are the imposing rock-faces of the Steinernes Meer, shot through with streaks of red from the iron ore they contain, which glow in the rays of the sun. Opposite, the snow-capped peaks of the Hohe Tauern are visible through the dip made by the Zellersee, completing the impressive mountain scene.

Maria Alm - Population 1 740. *Southeast of Saalfelden.* The pilgrims' church, whose sharp spire rises to 84m - 276ft above the ground, looks charming in the foreground against the crests of the Steinernes Meer.

At the end of the run the road skirts the steeper shore of the Zeller See before arriving at Zell am See.

❋ **Zell am See** - *See ZELL AM SEE.*

SAALBACH-HINTERGLEMM ✳✳

Salzburg
Population 2 700
Michelin map 426 fold 19 – Alt 1 003m - 3 291ft

With accommodation for more than 17 000 tourists, Saalbach is without doubt one of the largest winter sports resorts in Austria. It lies at the heart of the **Glemmtal** valley, the upper part of which forms the border between the Austrian provinces of Tyrol and Salzburg. This valley runs along the Pinzgauer Grasbergen on the eastern edge of the Kitzbühler Alps close to the Zeller See lake. Its attraction lies in its wooded rural setting (3 800ha - 9 390 acres of forest) and its harmonious relief with broad, gently falling slopes.

Respite its development as a tourist location, the town has retained its attraction, since buildings are in the traditional style. Saalbach extends from the foot of the Schattberg in the south to that of the Spielberghorn in the north.

The onion tower of the church rises up above the heart of the town, which comprises a steep pedestrianised street with boutiques, restaurants and elegant hotels.

Further up the valley, the town of **Hinterglemm** spreads out at the foot of the Zwölferkogel. It too has developed into an important holiday resort.

Saalbach owes its reputation both to the quality of its accommodation and to its extensive skiing area, in which downhill races are frequently held during the world skiing championships. The winter sports resort obviously also boasts a broad range of leisure facilities (swimming pool, ice rink, indoor tennis courts etc.).

In the summer, Saalbach is a restful summer holiday destination, from where some beautiful excursions can be made, in particular the **Pinzgau hike**★★ *(see ZELL AM SEE)* and the hike to the Tristkogel and to the Torsee lake.

✳✳ **Ski-slopes** – The ski-slopes extend between 900 and 2 100m - 2 953 and 6 890ft in altitude, forming one of the largest skiing areas in Austria. 60 ski-lifts (including 1 cable railway, 9 cable-cars and 18 chairlifts) open up 200km - 124 miles of piste for skiers of all levels.

The snow conditions are generally good from Christmas to April. The lack of altitude is offset by a microclimate, which ensures lower temperatures and considerably more snow than in the surrounding valleys.

This skiing area is of particular interest because it encompasses around twelve peaks between which it is possible to ski, all of which have a difference in altitude of almost 1 000m - 3 281ft. Lovers of wide open spaces will however not find any really high peaks here.

The slopes of the Zwölferkogel and the northern downhill section of the Schattberg-Ost will suit good skiers. Almost the entire skiing area will please skiers who are seeking relaxation, in particular the 8km - 5 mile long run, which links the Schattberg-Ost with Vorderglemm (Mulden and Jausern pistes). They should also try the pistes on the Zwölferkogel (Seekar and family run), the Hasenauer Köpfl (Hochalm piste), the Reiterkogel (pistes 35 and 37), the Kohlmaiskopf (piste 51) and the Bründlkopf. The second run on the Bernkogel is particularly recommended to beginners. Take note, however, that certain unmarked pistes are reserved for snowboarders.

There are far fewer opportunities for cross-country skiing, since only a total of 18km - 11 miles of cross-country track are available between Vorderglemm and Saalbach and above Hinterglemm.

VIEWPOINTS

★★ **Schattberg-Ost** ⊙ – Alt 2 020m - 6 627ft. *45min return trip on the cable railway.* This provides an **overall view** of the Glemmtal valley and its skiing area. In the distance are the limestone massifs of the Loferer and Leoganger Steinberge in the north and of the Hohe Tauern in the south (Wiesbachhorn, Kitzsteinhorn, Großglockner and Johannisberg).

★ **Zwölferkogel** ⊙ – Alt 1 984m - 6 509ft. *30min return trip. Ride up in the cable-car from Hinterglemm or continue uphill from Kolling.* The landscape is dominated by the Hohe Penhab and by the Schattberg-West. The view stretches over the entire area around Hinterglemm.

★ **Wildenkarkogel** – Alt 1 910m - 6 266ft. *45min return trip. Ride up from Vorderglemm on the Schönleiten cable-car.* From the summit, the end of the Karlift ski-lift can be reached in a few moments. There is a good view from here of the Leoganger Steinberge. Walkers may like to follow piste 65 for a while, which forms a pleasant ridge path.

SALZACHTAL★

Michelin map 426 fold 20

The Alpine Valley of Salzach is an artery of the province of Salzburg, whose hooked shape conforms with the bent course of the torrent. Strung out between the Krimml waterfalls and Salzburg is a series of basins, separated by ravines. Until the coming of the railway, each of these isolated sections of the valley tended to lead its own life, quite separate from that of its neighbours.

GEOGRAPHICAL NOTES

The Pinzgau – The roads to the Gerlos *(see GERLOSSTRASSE)* and Thurn *(see KITZBÜHEL)* passes give views of the upper Pinzgau valley (Oberpinzgau), which has been brought out of isolation by the growth of tourism and the construction of hydro-electrical works *(see KAPRUN)*. The region of Zell am See and Saalfelden – the Mittelpinzgau – is more lively. It lies at the foot of the Steinernes Meer chiffs, which here mark the Bavarian frontier.

The Pongau – The bottlenecks of the valley between Taxenbach and Lend, upstream, and between Werfen and Golling, downstream, clearly define the Pongau basin. To the east, the Fritztal and Wagrainer Höhe roads provide easy communications with the upper Enns valley, which explains the attachment of the Radstadt district to the province of Salzburg. Tourist traffic in the Pongau is most intense in the tributary valley of Gastein *(see GASTEINER TAL)*.

The Tennengau – Downstream from the Lueg pass, as far as Hallein, a less mountainous area unfolds. Forest cover and water courses (Golling waterfalls) nonetheless abound. Here the Salzach receives a contribution from the waters of the Lammer, flowing west from the pastoral district of Abtenau and the Salzburg Dolomites. The fine villages of the Tennengau (Abtenau, Golling, Kuchl, etc.), with their pretty painted and flower-bedecked gables beneath wide, overhanging roofs, have many features in common with Bavaria.

The Flachgau – Below Hallein the Salzach enters the flat land of Salzburg and adds a lively note as it flows through the dignified city of the prince-archbishops. After its confluence with the Saalach, the river forms a natural frontier between Styria and Bavaria, passing the Bavarian cities of Tittmoning and Burghausen before joining the Inn.

★☐ FROM LEND TO RADSTADT
via the Hochkönig road and the Wagrainer Höhe
70km - 44 miles - about 3 hours - local map p 223

The mountain section of the route between Dienten and Mühlbach has many bends and is usually blocked by snow in winter.

Hochkönig mountains

W. Geiersper/BILDAGENTUR BUENOS DIAS

221

Lend has an industrial character (aluminium plant) and is also the place where the Gasteiner Ache ends its course in a series of falls. Leave the town on the minor road to Dienten and cross the Salzach.

The hilltop church at **Dienten** soon comes into sight, standing out against the Hochkönig crests whose vertical white cliffs are particularly impressive when lit by the evening sun. Dienten's flower-bedecked farmsteads are spread out along the road, giving way eventually to alpine pastures.

Between Dienten and the Dientener Sattel there is evidence of winter sports activity, with several ski-tows and a modern hotel. The highest point of the route is reached at the Dientener Sattel (1 357m - 4 452ft) at the foot of the rocky barrier formed by the **Hochkönig**.

From this point the road is wider but still has several steep sections. The sharp descent into the resort of **Mühlbach** gives further views of the Hochkönig as well as glimpses of the last ridge of the Mandelwand, to the east. Mühlbach is a good centre for mountain walking, with a number of huts and mountain hotels (for instance, the Arthurhaus) in the area. Copper has been mined in the district since the Bronze Age.

Bischofshofen – *See BISCHOFSHOFEN.*

Take road no 159 then no 311 southwards as far as St. Johann im Pongau.

The countryside to either side of the direct route from St. Johann im Pongau to the Enns valley is most attractive, particularly around the resort of **Wagrain** (population 2 569). After the low pass at **Wagrainer Höhe** there are views of the snow-capped Dachstein (2 995m - 9 856ft) to the northeast; to the south there are glimpses up side valleys of some of the fine peaks of the Radstädter Tauern.

Radstadt – *See RADSTADT.*

② FROM LEND TO SALZBURG

89km - 55 miles – allow half a day excluding Salzburg – local map opposite

The Salzach valley, closely hemmed in as far as Lend *(above)*, opens out north of Schwarzach to form the Pongau basin.

Turn right off the 311 at St. Johann im Pongau, and then take the right fork up towards Großarl and then the footpath to the gorge – allow 1 hour on foot there and back.

Liechtensteinklamm ⊘
– *Allow 45min on foot.*
Walkways with handrails attached directly to the rock enable visitors to walk through the **gorge**★ itself. Sheer, at times over-hanging, rocky walls, an interesting play of light and the unusual formation of the shiny, white-streaked schist rock all contribute to the charm of the gorge, which becomes considerably narrower to-wards the end. Since the last part of the footpath in fact leads through a tun-nel, it is a good idea to take a torch. Re-emerging into the light of day, walkers are rewarded by the sight of a pretty **waterfall**★.

Return to the main road no 311 and go north to-wards Salzburg.

Bischofshofen – *See BIS-CHOFSHOFEN.*

Between Bischofshofen and Werfen, the 16C **for-tress of Hohenwerfen**★ makes a dramatic sight, silhou-etted on its rocky spur and commanding the route through the Salzach valley.

Y. Bontoux

Liechtenstein gorge

★ Eisriesenwelt Caves
– See Höhlen EISRIESEN-WELT.

The road now runs through the Werfen-Golling section of the valley; the sheer walls rear 1 000m - some 3 300ft above the river. This is one of the deepest and most striking of the valleys cutting across the main east-west grain of the Alps and leading to the Lueg pass.

Paß Lueg – The valley makes a sharp bend and narrows even more. The cleverly engineered road leaves the river bank to cross a rise which marks the end of this section of the valley. Level with the pass stands the pilgrimage church of Maria Brunneck, a Rococo building dating from 1766.

In summer it is worthwhile prolonging a stop at the summit in order to go down into the **Salzachöfen** on foot. A steep path *(45min return)*, slippery in rainy weather, leads to a jumble of rocks forming a natural bridge over the Salzach. It is possible, but difficult, to get right underneath the arch of the bridge by following signs marked "Dom".

Lammeröfen ⊙ – *Via the road (no 162) to Abtenau which branches off the main road at the southern end of Golling.* This section of the Lammer gorge is laid out as a pleasant walk.

Golling – Population 3 800. The main street of this busy little holiday resort is lined with pretty, flower-bedecked old houses.

On leaving Golling, turn left, go over the level crossing near the station and cross the bridge over the Salzach. Continue under the motorway bridge and follow signs marked "Wasserfall".

★★ Gollinger Wasserfall – *Leave the car in the Gasthaus Brennerwirt car park.* At the mouth of the valley stands the small Late Gothic church of St. Nikolaus with a marble outside pulpit and beautifully executed Baroque decoration.
The path *(45min return)* leads first to the foot of the lower falls with their pretty, fountain-like effects. It then climbs to the upper cascade.

Between Golling and Hallein the road goes through the most attractive part of the Tennengau with its irregular wooded valley sides. The countryside gradually takes on a less mountainous character.

Hallein and the Dürrnberg Mines – *See HALLEIN.*

There are two charming country houses on the approach to Salzburg, moated **Anif**, with a surprising resemblance to an English manor-house, and **Hellbrunn★** *(qv)*.

★★★ Salzburg – *Time: 4 hours. See SALZBURG.*

The town plans are easily interpreted with the aid of the Key

SALZATAL★★

Steiermark

Michelin map 426 folds 22 and 23

The Salza is a tributary of the upper Enns. Among the last eastern massifs of the limestone High Alps and at the northern foot of the jagged cliffs of the Hochschwab (highest point 2 277m - 7 470ft) it traces a furrow which for 70km - 45 miles is almost uninhabited, except for the tiny villages of Wildalpen and Weichselboden. It offers nature lovers opportunities for delightful expeditions through the woods and along the rapids and pools of the torrent.

FROM HIEFLAU TO MARIAZELL

80km - 50 miles - about 3 hours 30min

The road, although surfaced in some parts, should be taken slowly on account of its uneven nature and its steep gradients (1 in 6). Between Großreifling and Palfau the road is narrow and the surface poor.

Hieflau – *See EISENERZER ALPEN.*

Between Hieflau and Großreifling two dams in part drown the Enns defile. The setting created by these constructions, parallel to the road bridge and the Wandau Dam, is most impressive.

On the section between Großreifling and Palfau the road is steep and follows a winding, uphill course under fir trees or the light shade of beeches. There are several glimpses of the smooth sheet of water below and, later, of the once more swirling torrent.

From Erzhalden to Wildalpen the Salza ravines are clothed in darker forest. Above Wildalpen the river flows near the Hochschwab cliffs. The sides of the Riegerin, eroded into needles, are a strange sight.

★ **Brunn** – From this oratory there is a **view**★ as far as the end of the Brunntal combe, in the heart of the Hochschwab.

After passing the oratory at Brunn, the **view**★★ opens out all along the north slope of the massif, where the rocks are still fantastically shaped by erosion. The cliffs of the Türnach, opposite, are no less curious.

Near the Kläfferbrücke stands a small guardhouse by the conduit which collects the underground waters of the area and supplies Vienna with drinking water.

Prescenyklause – The rock gateway is built in the form of a tunnel. The dam constructed here made it possible to release sufficient water to float logs downstream but it has been out of use since the Salza raftsmen ceased to carry on their dangerous trade.

Weichselboden – The church, set amidst a clump of lime trees, and a hotel, make up almost all the village. To the southeast lies the steep-sided valley known as "In der Höll" (In Hell).

Between Weichselboden and Mariazell the road, passing for a moment out of sight of the Hochschwab, again climbs above the valley, which is now wider but entirely given over to the forest. The landscape becomes gradually less mountainous.

Saw and papermills at Gußwerk mark the return to civilization. The road does not follow the floor of the Mariazell basin but climbs in wide bends to the centre of pilgrimage.

★ **Mariazell** – *See MARIAZELL.*

Salzburg coat of arms

Ⓛ Salzburg – Population 138 210
Michelin map 426 folds 5, 19 and 20
Local maps under SALZACHTAL and SALZKAMMERGUT – Alt 424m - 1 391ft
Hotels and Restaurants: see the current Michelin Red Guides Deutschland or Europe

Salzburg, Mozart's birthplace, is a delight from the first sight of the outline of the Hohensalzburg, the symbol of the power of the prince-archbishops. The fortress rises over the roofs and belfries of the town, through which flow the waters of the Salzach as the river bends in its course.

A soft light bathes the shapes of its towers and churches in a wonderful setting. It enjoys the attraction of the nearby Salzkammergut, and it has the prestige of the festival drawing lovers of classical music in July and August each year.

Its picturesque streets with their wrought-iron signs, its spacious squares with sculptured fountains and the noble architecture of its buildings inspired by bishops with a passion for construction, leave memories which linger for years.

OUT AND ABOUT IN SALZBURG

Tourist Information
🛈 Mozartplatz 5 ☎ 06 62/ 84 75 68
🛈 Hauptbahnhof, Platform 2a ☎ 06 62/ 87 17 12

Motoring information offices near motorway exits

Salzburg-Mitte, Münchner Bundesstraße 1, open all year ☎ 06 62/ 43 22 28

Salzburg-Sud, Park & Ride car park, Alpenstraße, open all year ☎ 06 62/62 09 66

Salzburg-West, Flughafen (Airport), Innsbrucker Bundesstraße 95 (BP filling station), open April to October ☎ 06 62/ 85 24 5

Salzburg-Nord, Rastplatz "Kasern" (lay-by), open Easter to end of October ☎ 06 62/ 66 32 20

Salzburg City Tourist Information
Salzburg information, Auerspergstraße 7, A-5020 Salzburg ☎ 06 62/ 88 98 70, open Mondays to Thursdays 7.30am to 5pm, Fridays 7.30am to 3pm.

Public Transport
Special tickets available include a one-day ticket, the Salzburg-Ticket 1, and a three-day ticket, the Salzburg-Ticket 3, which are valid on the whole of the bus network. The transport authority publishes an information leaflet entitled *Öffentliche Verkehrsmittel*.

Shopping
The old town centre to the left and right of the Salzach, the area around the Getreidegasse, the Mozartplatz, the Alter Markt, the Linzer Gasse, the Makartplatz and the Mirabellplatz.

Post Offices
Residenzplatz, Südtiroler Platz (Hauptbahnhof, open 24 hours), Makartplatz and Schrannengasse.

Information for the Handicapped
A leaflet entitled *Stadtführer von Salzburg für Behinderte* which gives useful information is available from Österreichischer Zivilinvalidenverband, Haunspergstraße 39 ☎ 06 62/ 5 10 44.

HISTORICAL NOTES

The Heritage of the Prince-Archbishops – The See of Salzburg was founded shortly before 700 by St Rupert and was raised in the following century to an archbishopric. In the 13C the bishops were given the title of Princes of the Holy Roman Empire. Their temporal power extended to Italy, while much of their large revenue came from the mining of salt in the Salzkammergut *(details p 34)*. Three of these overlords, while governing their estates with skill, showed a taste for building. In a little more than half a century they converted the little town, with its maze of streets, into something resembling an Italian town, with palaces and open spaces.

Wolf Dietrich von Raitenau was elected Archbishop in 1587. He was a typical figure of the Renaissance: brought up in Rome and closely connected with the Medicis, he longed to make his capital the Rome of the North. When the former cathedral and the quarter round it were conveniently destroyed by fire, he turned to the Italian architect Scamozzi and asked him to build a cathedral larger than St Peter's in Rome. Raitenau's private life was more than averagely active: he had fifteen children by Salome Art, a great beauty for whom he had the château of Mirabell,

on the right bank of the Salzach, built. He was drawn into an un[...]
with the Dukes of Bavaria over the salt trade and lost. He was [...]
Court of Rome and imprisoned in 1612 in Hohensalzburg castle [...]
five years of captivity. His only project to be completed was his l[...]
in the St. Sebastian cemetery.

His successor, **Marcus Sitticus** of Hohenem, undertook to build the cat[...]
modest scale and entrusted the work to another Italian architect, Santi[...]
To the south of Salzburg he had the mansion of Hellbrunn built as a country house,
and the park laid out with fountains.

Paris Lodron took advantage of his long episcopate (1619-1653) to complete the work
begun by his predecessors. He finished the cathedral, and it was solemnly
consecrated in 1628. On this occasion a mass written by the Italian choir-master,
Horatio Benevoli, was sung. It had fifty-three parts; eight two-part choruses, two
string orchestras and two ensembles for brass, woodwind, drums and the cathedral
organ. This remarkable achievement began a musical tradition which was to
blossom in the following
century.

Paris Lodron also completed
the Residence, near the cathedral, a less austere building
than Hohensalzburg castle.
He opened new streets in the
town, creating the face of
Salzburg for generations to
come.

WOLFGANG AMADEUS MOZART (1756-1791)

It was in this bishops' city,
which owed as much to German as to Italian influences,
that Mozart was born on 27
January 1756.

A Child Prodigy – Leopold, a
composer and violinist in the
archbishop's service, soon realized what he could gain
from the exceptional gifts displayed by his son Wolfgang
and his daughter Nannerl,
who was four years older.
Leopold encouraged the development of their natural gifts

Wolfgang Amadeus Mozart

ROGER VIOLLET

– Wolfgang could improvise on the piano at the age of five and played the violin
without ever having been taught. The father began to give his son a serious musical
education and they undertook what was to be a memorable tour of Europe. Between
1762 and 1766, Munich, Vienna, Augsburg, Frankfurt, Paris, London and The
Hague received Leopold and his children with enthusiasm. At Schönbrunn, the
Empress Maria Theresa embraced little Wolfgang. Paris published four sonatas for
piano and violin by the eight-year-old composer, whose talent continued to develop,
being strongly influenced in London by Johann Christian Bach, the youngest son
of Johann Sebastian Bach.

On returning to Salzburg, Mozart stayed for three years, leaving only at the
command of the Emperor Joseph II, to go to Vienna. Mozart defies explanation,
but his success was not due simply to his exceptional gifts. He himself was later
to say "No-one has ever taken greater pains than I to study musical composition
– there are few masters whose work I have not studied intensely".

Kapellmeister at Salzburg – In 1769, at the age of 13, Mozart was made Director
of the Archbishop's orchestra.

Dedication – Mozart's father believed a visit to Italy was necessary to complete a
musician's education. This was where Wolfgang would learn to compose an opera.
Triumph followed him all over the peninsula. In Rome, after hearing it only once
in the Sistine Chapel, the young master wrote out the nine-part chorus of the famous
Miserere by Gregorio Allegri. On his return to Salzburg he composed work after
work.

First Disappointment – Until 1777 Mozart lived most of the time in Salzburg.
Archbishop Hieronymus Colloredo, who succeeded Archbishop Sigismund in 1772,
took a poor view of the constant journeys abroad. Thus, in 1775, Wolfgang had
some trouble in getting permission to go to Munich to present his comic opera,

La Finta Giardiniera (The Feigned Gardener's Girl). In 1777 he had his first quarrel with the archbishop, resigned and left for Paris, accompanied this time by his mother, who unfortunately died on the journey. He came under the influence of Gluck, who had chosen Paris to begin his reform of opera.

During the following years the quiet life he led at Salzburg encouraged the production of many works including religious music, of which the *Coronation Mass* is an example, symphonic and lyrical pieces such as *Idomeneo*, and opera where the influence of the French School appears. In 1781, after a heated altercation between Wolfgang and Count Arco, representing Archbishop Colloredo, the breach was complete. Mozart left Salzburg for Vienna.

Independence in Vienna – On his arrival in Vienna, Mozart, aged 26, had few means of support. It was here, in 1781, that he married Constanze Weber, and here too that he was initiated into the ideals of Freemasonry. Discovery of Handel's oratorios and of further works by Bach, together with the influence of his friend and mentor, Haydn, contributed to the development of his mature style. The public adulation occasioned by "Die Entführung aus dem Serail" of 1781 and the Mass in C Minor of 1783 was not repeated, at least in Vienna, where the public failed to appreciate "Le Nozze di Figaro" (1786) and "Don Giovanni" (1787). A sombre period began, lightened only by his warm reception in Prague.

Destitution (1788-91) – Mozart's career was to end in obscurity. Though nominated "Composer to the Imperial Chamber" by Joseph II, he never received a commission. His final lyric works, "Cosí fan Tutte" (1790) and "La Clemenza di Tito" (1791) met with a cool reception, barely mitigated by the success of "The Magic Flute" (late 1791). The great composer was to die before his time, in solitude and haunted by the fear of death.

On 6 December 1791 the paupers' hearse carried Mozart's corpse to a communal grave in St Mark's Cemetery in Vienna. His remains have never been identified.

Mozart's Music – The fecundity shown by "the divine Mozart" during his short life was equalled only by the ease with which he mastered every form of musical expression: the Köchel catalogue, which contains 626 items, is evidence of this. As for Mozart's style, it has a charm which makes him a favourite with a wide public and is recognized even by the unpractised ear. Pleasant and sparkling motifs ripple beneath a rhythmic counterpoint of charming liveliness.

But spontaneity and *brio* need not mean lack of depth and Mozart is no buffoon or mere comic-opera musician. Though he may attract, at first, simply by easy writing, the listener finds an exquisitely pure melodic line, sometimes tinged with melancholy. Towards the end of his life this vague sadness turned into despair, which gives their full meaning to the Fortieth Symphony in G minor, to *Don Juan*, to the quartets, to the tragic quintet in G (K 516) and to the *Requiem* (K 626) that Chopin wished to be played at his funeral. In it are reflected the emotional frustration of Mozart's life, his struggle against illness and poverty, and from it was to evolve the Romantic Movement.

The Salzburg Festival ⊘ – *See the chapter called Calendar of events at the end of the guide.* Many years were to pass before his native city became aware of Mozart's outstanding place in musical history. The composer's biography was written in 1828 by Georges Nicolas de Nissen, who had married the widowed Constanze in 1809. In 1842 Salzburg put up a statue to Mozart; later the city founded a musical academy named the **Mozarteum**. In 1917 the poet Hugo von Hoffmansthal, the composer Richard Strauss and the producer Max Reinhardt conceived the idea of a Mozart festival.

The festival was inaugurated in 1920. Those contributing have included many of the great names in 20C music, Lotte Lehmann, Bruno Walter, Toscanini, Furtwängler, Böhm... while Salzburg itself has been affected indelibly by the personality of **Herbert von Karajan**, who was associated with the festival for over thirty years and instituted the Easter Festival (in 1967) and the Whitsun Festival (in 1973). The festival is held every year between the end of July and the end of August. The numerous concerts and performances take place at the following locations: the great **Festival Hall** (Großes Festspielhaus – Z), built in 1960 by the architect Clemens Holzmeister and incorporating the old Winter Riding School; the **Mozarteum**, the **Landestheater** (Y), **the Mirabell mansion** (V), and in the old Summer Riding School.

Mozart may be the centre of attraction but other works of the (mostly classical) repertoire are performed by the cream of the world's musical talent; every year there is a performance of Hofmannsthal's *Jedermann (Everyman)* on the cathedral forecourt.

Since the reform begun in 1992, the Festival is placing increasing emphasis on 20C music and theatre.

> **Marionettentheater** (Y) – *Schwarz-straße 24.* The theatre and its extraordinary marionettes performing the grandest of operas have gained a worldwide reputation. On the programme are not only the great Mozartian works like the Magic Flute, Figaro, Don Giovanni, Così fan tutte... but also masterpieces by Rossini, Offenbach, Strauss, Tchaikovsky, recorded by the most illustrious orchestras, and transporting the enraptured audience gathered beneath the Rococo ceilings of the Mirabell mansion into a world of artifice and illusion.

★★ VIEWPOINTS

Marionettentheater, Salzburg

Fine views of the city in its setting can be had both from the Mönschsberg hill whose rocky mass hems in the old town and from the Kapuzinerberg (Hettwer Bastei) on the far bank of the Salzach.

★★ **Mönschsberg** (Z) ⊘ – *Parking: see below.*
From the Gstättengasse (X **12**) a **lift** goes up to a terrace just below the Café Winkler, from which there is a fine general **view** of the city. Modern Salzburg spreads out along the right bank of the Salzach, while the old town, bristling with domes and church towers, lies crowded between the river and the Hohensalzburg fortress. To the south on the horizon are the Tennen- and Hagengebirge, the Untersberg and the Salzburg Alps; eastwards the Kapuzinerberg and, in the background, the Gaisberg, mark the city boundaries.

★★ **Hettwer Bastei** (Y) – *Climb up to the Kapuzinerkirche via the steep ramp reached from the Linzergasse through a covered passageway. From the church, go downhill again for about 50m, turn left and follow the sign "Stadtaussicht-Hettwer Bastei" to the viewpoint.*
The Hettwer Bastei (bastion) on the south side of the Kapuzinerberg gives fine **views** over Salzburg, particularly early in the day, when the morning light enhances the green of the many copper-clad roofs, brings out the textural qualities of the old part of the city, and emphasizes the dramatically sculpted forms of the collegiate church and the cathedral.

Return via the series of steps leading to the Steingasse.

The Steingasse, leading to the 17C Steintor (city gate) is so narrow that the marks made by carts are visible on the walls of the houses.

★★ OLD TOWN *time: 4 hours – plan p 235*

Park outside the old town (pedestrians only) and outside the "blue zones" (east bank); underground car parking (Altstadtgaragen) is available under the Mönchsberg. Walk to the Domplatz.

Domplatz (Z) – Three porticos link the buildings surrounding this square, the cathedral and the former ecclesiastical palaces. In the centre is a column dedicated to the Virgin Mary (1771).

SALZBURG

Bürglsteinstr.	U 5
Eberhard-Fugger-Str.	T 7
Gaisbergstr.	T 10
Georg-Nikolaus- von-Nissen-Str.	U 13
Grazer Bundesstr.	T 14
Hellbrunner Brücke	U 16
Innsbrucker Bundesstr.	U 17
Itzlinger Hauptstr.	T 19
Kleßheimer Allee	T 22
Maxglaner Hauptstr.	U 24
Minnesheimstr.	T 25
Münchner Bundesstr.	T 27
Nonntaler Hauptstr.	U 29
Plainbergweg	T 31
Siezenheimer Str.	T 34
Sterneckstr.	T 38
Vogelweiderstr.	T 42

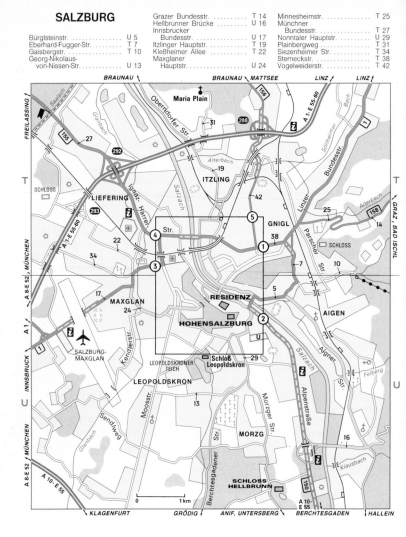

★ **Dom** (Z) – The cathedral, which was built from 1614 to 1655, is a huge construction in which the Baroque style shows through the last features of the Italian Renaissance.

The west front, flanked by two symmetrical towers, is of light coloured Salzburg marble. The pediment between the two towers, dominated by the statue of Christ, is adorned with the coats of arms of Archbishops Marcus Sitticus and Paris Lodron, flanked by statues of Moses and Elijah.

Below them are the figures of the four Evangelists and in front of the main door are statues of St Rupert, St Virgil, St Peter and St Paul. The modern bronze doors (1957-58) in relief have been designed on the theme of Faith *(left)* by Toni Schneider-Manzell, Hope *(right)* by Ewald Mataré and Charity *(centre)* by Giacomo Manzù. The interior is impressive in both size and richness of its marble, stucco and paintings. Mozart was baptized in the Romanesque baptismal font in 1756. The **crypt** was completely remodelled after traces of the Romanesque cathedral had been uncovered (look at the plan of the succession of different buildings on the same spot on the pavement beneath the central rotunda, from the episcopacy of St Virgil in the 8C). The tombs of the prince-archbishops and a Romanesque Crucifix may be seen in the crypt.

Dommuseum ⊙ – Featured here is the cathedral treasure and the Archbishops' gallery of "art and wonders" (Kunst- und Wunderkammer) presented as it was in the 17C. The museum also houses religious art from the Middle Ages to the present from the presbyteries of the Salzburg archbishopric.

In the Kapitelplatz is the Kapitelschwemme, a drinking-trough for the horses of members of the chapter. The trough, built in 1732 by Archbishop Leopold Anton Firmian, is in the form of a monumental fountain.

From the square a street leads uphill to the station of the Hohensalzburg **funicular** ⊙.

★★ **Hohensalzburg** (z) – The former stronghold of the prince-archbishops stands on a block of Dolomite rock, about 120m - 400ft above the Salzach. The castle was begun in 1077 by Archbishop Gebhard, who was an ally of the pope and wished to secure a safe retreat from the threats of the princes of South Germany who were supporting the Emperor in the war between Church and Empire. The castle was frequently enlarged and remodelled, becoming a comfortable residence by the addition of state rooms. The archbishops often resided there until the end of the 15C, reinforcing it considerably by the addition of towers, bastions of cannon and barbicans and the construction of magazines and arms depots.

At the exit from the upper station, turn left to the panoramic terrace from which stairs and a postern lead into the fortress. Go past the ticket office and a little way downhill, bearing right along the lists and round the fortified nucleus of the inner castle until you come out in a square opposite the south wall of the **St. Georgskirche**, which is decorated with two beautiful marble reliefs: a group of statuary in red Salzburg marble of Archbishop Leonhard von Keutschach (1495-1519) between two priests, and above it a Crucifixion.

The door to the right of the church leads to the terrace of the **Kuenburgbastei** from where there is a good **view★★** of the old town, particularly its domes and belfries.

Return to the square (at the end of the tour take the steps "Abgang zur Stadt" at the east end to return into town) and go straight ahead through the castle by the vaulted "Feuergang" passage which is equipped with cannon.

Castle and Museum ⊘ – From the Reck watch-tower there is a **panorama★★**, which is particularly interesting towards the Tennengebirge and the Salzburg Alps (south).

In the castle is a hand-operated barrel-organ dating from 1502. It plays melodies by Mozart and Haydn as well as the original 1502 chorale.

SALZBURG

Auerspergstraße	V 3	
Bürglsteinstraße	X 5	
Erzabt-Klotz-Str.	X 9	
Gstättengasse	X 12	
Kaiserschützenstr.	V 20	
Nonntaler Hauptstr.	X 29	
Späthgasse	X 37	

M³ Salzburger Barockmuseum

The state rooms, formerly the archbishops' apartments, were fitted out by Leonhard von Keutschach and have kept their original decorations of walls adorned with Gothic wood carvings, doors fitted with complicated ironwork and coffered ceilings with gilded studs. In the Gilded Room is a monumental porcelain stove, dating from 1501, the work of a local potter. It is decorated with flowers and fruit, scenes from the Bible and the coats of arms and portraits of sovereigns of the period.

The Hall of Justice has a coffered ceiling on which the beams are adorned with shields bearing the arms of the province and the dioceses or abbeys under the archbishop and those of the dignitaries of his court. The hall also has four red marble columns with twisted barrels bearing the coat of arms (a turnip) of Leonhard von Keutschach.

An interesting **museum**★ (Burgmuseum) may also be visited. Apart from records – plans and prints – showing the development of the town throughout the history of the Salzburg archbishopric, this museum contains a remarkable series of medieval works of art (arms, armorial bearings, etc.).

Go back down the ramps and follow the path on the right to Nonnberg convent.

Stift Nonnberg (Z) – This Benedictine convent was founded around 700 by St Rupert, whose niece, St Erentrud, was its first abbess. It is the oldest convent in the German-speaking world.

The **Stiftskirche**, enclosed by its churchyard, is in late Gothic style and dates from the end of the 15C. The main doorway was built 1497-99; it incorporates the older Romanesque tympanum with its figures of the Virgin Mary flanked by John the Baptist and St Erentrud on one side and by an angel and kneeling nun on the other. The high altar is adorned by a fine carved and gilded altarpiece; in the central section is a Virgin and Child attended by St Rupert and St Virgil, while the wings depict scenes from the Passion. The vast crypt contains the tomb of St Erentrud. The highly compartmentalised vaulting rests on 18 columns. In the **Johanneskapelle** there is a Gothic altarpiece of 1498, attributed to Veit Stoß, with a lively central section showing the Nativity.

Go down to the lower station of the funicular via the Festungsgasse, then into the Petersfriedhof immediately on the left.

★★ **Petersfriedhof** (Z) – This touching cemetery, which evokes the past history of the town, abuts on the vertical rock wall of the Mönchsberg, in which catacombs were hollowed out. Wrought-iron grilles under Baroque arcades enclose the chapels where several generations of the patrician families of Salzburg lie. The 15C Margaretenkapelle is a delicate construction dating from the end of the Gothic period.

★★ **Benediktinerstiftskirche St. Peter und St. Paul** (Z) – The triple-aisled Romanesque basilica was drastically remodelled in the 17C and 18C, with new vaulting and a dome above the transept crossing added, but the serenity and harmony of the Romanesque structure can still be sensed behind the Baroque decor. Entry into the building is via the much restored 13C Romanesque doorway in the west front. Immediately on the right is a chapel dedicated to the Holy Ghost and on the left another dedicated to St Wolfgang.

The best view of the interior is from the gilded **wrought-iron grille**★ separating the porch from the nave. This elaborate work of art dating from 1768 was made by Philip Hinterseer. The building's architectural simplicity, heightened in effect by the white walls, emphasizes the elegance of Benedikt Zöpf's Rococo decoration,

Domes and church towers of Old Salzburg

with its fine paintings and fresh pastel shades, especially pale green, which are used to enhance the delicate stuccowork on the vaulting, the cornices and the capitals.

The ceiling of the nave has frescoes showing scenes from the life of St Peter, the work of the Augsburg artist, Johann Weiß. On each of the walls above the great arches, note, among other compositions, an Ascent to Calvary and a Raising of the Cross by Solari. Beneath the upper windows is a set of paintings by Franz X König representing *(right)* the life of St Benedict and *(left)* the life of St Rupert. The altarpiece on the high altar and those in the nave, with their red marble columns, make an ensemble of great richness. Most of altarpiece paintings are the work of Martin Johann Schmidt *(see KREMS)*. Only the south aisle has chapels. It also contains the tomb of St Rupert, a Roman sarcophagus (3C). In the chapel furthest from the chancel there is a fine marble tomb built by Archbishop Wolf Dietrich for his father, Werner von Raitenau.

Cross the abbey courtyard, turn right into the covered passageway and go along the side of the Franziskanerkirche which is entered through the west doorway.

★ **Franziskanerkirche** (Z A) – The church was consecrated in 1223 but has been remodelled several times since. It offers a comparison between the Romanesque and Gothic styles.

The plain Romanesque nave, divided from the side aisles by massive pillars with capitals adorned with foliage and stylized animals, makes a striking contrast with the well-lit chancel which dates from the final Gothic period, the 15C. The high star vaulting is supported by palm-shaped cylindrical columns.

The impressive high altar is the work of Johann Bernhard Fischer von Erlach in 1708. The finely modelled statue of the Virgin Mary which adorns the Baroque altarpiece of the high altar was formerly part of a Gothic altarpiece made by Michael Pacher at the end of the 15C.

Go out by the side door and follow the Franziskanergasse westwards.

Moderne Galerie – Graphische Sammlung – Österreichische Photogalerie Rupertinum (Z M¹) ◷ – This museum is located in a 17C palace and contains a contemporary art collection. Temporary exhibitions illustrate the avant-garde movements.

North of Max-Reinhardt-Platz stands the massive Baroque Kollegienkirche (University Church), the work of Johann Bernhard Fischer von Erlach. Continue west past the Festspielhaus (Festival Hall).

Ball/BILDAGENTUR BUENOS DIAS

From the Herbert-von-Karajan-Platz (**36**) there is a tunnel (the Siegmundstor), about 135m - 150yds long, which was made in 1767 under the Mönchsberg hill. Look back for a fine view of the Hohensalzburg fortress and the church of St. Peter and St. Paul.

Pferdeschwemme (**Y B**) – This monumental horse trough was built about 1700. It was reserved for the horses in the archbishops' stables and is adorned with a sculptured group, the *Horsebreaker* by Mandl, and frescoes depicting fiery steeds.

★★ **Haus der Natur** (**Y M²**) ⊙ – *Allow at least two hours for the natural history museum's 80 rooms.*
This well-presented exhibition includes a number of lively displays on various aspects of the natural world. Particularly interesting sections are those on dinosaurs, the world of the sea with its large display of sharks, the world of outer space, people, pets, human and animal characters in myth and fable, giant rock crystals, the aquarium and the reptile house.

★ **Getreidegasse** (**Y**) – This is one of the main streets of old Salzburg. Like the rest of the Old Town, which, being crowded between the Mönchsberg and the Salzach, could expand only vertically, it is narrow and lined with five and six storey houses.
A lively shopping street, it is adorned with many wrought-iron signs which provide a picturesque touch, while the houses with their carved window frames lend the street a certain class.

Mozarts Geburtshaus (**Y D**) ⊙ – *Getreidegasse 9.* Leopold Mozart lived on the 3rd floor from 1747 to 1773. It was there that Wolfgang was born on 27 January 1756.

Getreidegasse

In this flat, where Mozart composed many works of his youth, moving mementoes of his life (in particular from 1773-80) can be seen, such as his violins, including the violin he used as a child. His spinet, his piano and musical manuscripts are on display, as well as a selection of portraits and letters. A "bourgeois interior at the time of Mozart" has been installed in the house. The second floor houses a display on the theatre with models of stage sets and literature on Mozart's operas. Particularly passionate Mozart fans may also like to visit the Tanzmeisterhaus *(opposite)*.
Continue along the Getreidegasse past the town hall (Rathaus) on the left and on the right the Alter Markt (Old Market Square), with a fountain to St Florian and a curious **Hofapotheke** (**YZ N**), a chemist's shop with its Rococo interior.

Judengasse (**YZ**). – This street is in the middle of the former Jewish Ghetto. It is narrow and picturesque and, like the Getreidegasse, adorned with wrought-iron signs. At no 4, note a sculptured group in stone representing the Virgin of Maria Plain *(see Excursions below)*.
Through the Waagplatz make for the Mozartplatz; on the north side, instead of roofs and belfries, rises the wooded spur of the Kapuzinerberg.

Residenzplatz (**Z 32**) – Until the 16C there was a cemetery on this site. Prince-archbishop Wolf Dietrich created the present square when he had his cathedral built. It was adorned in the 17C with a fine fountain (group of horses, a Triton and Atlantes). The square is bounded on the south by the cathedral and to the west by the Residenz. On the east is the **Glockenspiel** (**Z**), a carillon of thirty-five bells cast in Antwerp at the end of the 17C and set up in Salzburg in 1705.

★★ **Residenz** (**Z**) – The present buildings, which were modified in 1595, on the initiative of Prince-archbishop Wolf Dietrich, took the place of a building which had been the residence of the prince-archbishops since the middle of the 11C. The northwest wing is late 18C.

In the Conference Hall the young Mozart conducted many concerts before the guests of the prince-archbishop. A door in one of the rooms gives an unexpected view down into the Franziskanerkirche. It was in this palace that Emperor Franz Joseph received Napoleon III in 1867, and the German Emperor, Kaiser Wilhelm I, in 1871.

Residenzgalerie ⊘ – The gallery houses a collection in true princely tradition of important European paintings from the 16C to 19C. A highlight of the collection is the 17C Dutch painting, which includes works by great masters such as Rembrandt, Rubens and Brueghel. The valuable exhibition, which occupies fifteen state rooms, is rounded off with a display of 19C masterpieces.

★ **Mirabellgarten** (V) – Little is left of the Altenau mansion built at the beginning of the 17C by Prince-archbishop Wolf Dietrich for Salome Alt and given the name "Mirabell" by Marcus Sitticus. It was remodelled by the architect Johann Lukas von Hildebrandt in the following century to form part of the great ensemble known as Schloß Mirabell. It was badly damaged by fire in 1818 and subsequently rebuilt in a much more sober style. Today it houses the offices of the city administration.

Of the original building, the monumental **marble staircase**★★ with its sculptures by Raphael Donner still stands, together with the richly decorated Marmorsaal (Hall of Marble), all gilt and coloured stucco, now used for wedding ceremonies and chamber concerts.

The gardens were laid out in 1690 by Fischer von Erlach. With their abundance of flowers, statues and groups of sculpture adorning the pools, they are a favourite place in which to relax. From a terrace there is a fine view over the gardens themselves towards the old fortifications and the Hohensalzburg.

The buildings of the old orangery have been restored and enclose a pretty courtyard with colourful flower-beds. The south wing houses a small museum of Baroque art.

★ **Salzburger Barockmuseum** (M³) ⊘ – This attractive little museum sets out to give a general view of 17C and 18C European art through its highly individual choice of paintings, sketches and sculptures, some of them of remarkable quality.

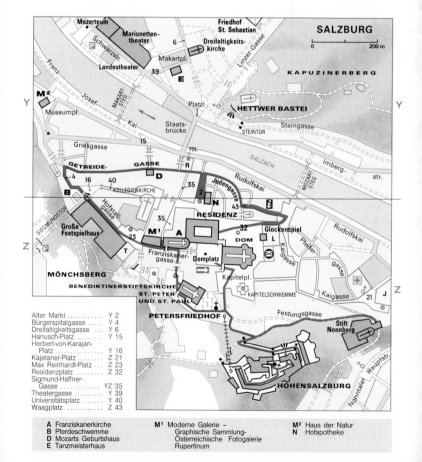

Alter Markt . . . . Y 2
Bürgerspitalgasse . . . . . Y 4
Dreifaltigkeitsgasse . . . Y 6
Hanusch-Platz . . . . Y 15
Herbert-von-Karajan-
  Platz . . . . Y 16
Kajetaner-Platz . . . . Z 21
Max Reinhardt-Platz . . . Z 23
Residenzplatz . . . . Z 32
Sigmund-Haffner-
  Gasse . . . . YZ 35
Theatergasse . . . . Y 39
Universitätsplatz . . . . . . Y 40
Waagplatz . . . . Z 43

A Franziskanerkirche
B Pferdeschwemme
D Mozarts Geburtshaus
E Tanzmeisterhaus

M¹ Moderne Galerie –
   Graphische Sammlung-
   Österreichische Fotogalerie
   Rupertinum

M² Haus der Natur
N Hofapotheke

Tanzmeisterhaus (Mozart-Wohnhaus) (Y **E**) ⊘ – *Makartplatz 8*. The Tanzmeister-haus, which was the Mozart family home from 1773-1787, was destroyed by bombs in 1944, but was rebuilt in 1994 and 1995.

Mozart, who lived in the house until 1781, composed a number of his works here. The museum displays literature on this period as well as a collection of historical keyboard instruments.

The house also contains a "Museum of Mozart Sound and Film", which is open to the general public.

Friedhof St. Sebastian (VX) – Only the doorway in the Rococo style (1752), surmounted by a bust of the patron saint, remains of the original church of St. Sebastian, which was destroyed by fire in 1818 and subsequently rebuilt. Cross the church. Behind a grille is the tomb of **Paracelsus**, a doctor and philosopher of the Renaissance who died in Salzburg in 1541.

Adjacent to the north side of the church are cloisters whose arches shelter funerary monuments and surround a shaded cemetery which in about 1600 was made into the likeness of an Italian *campo santo*. In the centre stands the curious tomb of Wolf Dietrich; the interior is lined with porcelain in many colours. In the central lane of the cemetery are the tombs of Mozart's wife and father.

Dreifaltigkeitskirche (Y) – This church was built from 1694 to 1699 by the great architect Fischer von Erlach.

The oval dome and the interior are in the Baroque style. As in the Karlskirche in Vienna, the originality and daring of this dome make it a perfect francwork for the frescoes by Rottmayr.

EXCURSIONS *local map p 230*

★★ **Road to the Gaisberg** – *16 km - 10 miles. Leave Salzburg on ① and bear right along the road to Graz; in Guggenthal turn right into the Gaisbergstraße, a well-laid road (maximum gradient, 1 in 8), which passes through woods in some places, and is hewn out of the rock in others.*

From the end of the road, go westwards to the edge of the steep slope dropping towards Salzburg (**view**★ of the town, the Salzach gap and the Salzburg Alps); then go northeastwards to the Cross on the highest point, at an altitude of 1 288m - 4 226ft, for a **panorama**★ of the mountains of the Salzkammergut and the Dachstein massif.

★ **Schloß Hellbrunn** (∪) ⊘ – The castle, once the summer residence of Archbishop Marcus Sitticus, was built 1613-16 in the spirit of the great Italian villas of the Veneto.

The banquet hall, with its *trompe-l'œil* painting, and the high, domed Octagon or music-room are most interesting. A tour of the attractive gardens and fountains is full of surprises: fountains and caves are adorned with human figures, a "mechanical theatre" has 113 figures which are set in motion by the action of water to the music of an organ, and fountains suddenly shower the unwary visitor.

Volkskundemuseum ⊘ – The folklore museum is housed on three floors and contains traditional costumes, clothing and a variety of other objects connected with popular religious observances and festivals. The interior of a house from the Salzburg area, together with typical furnishings, is also on view.

A few minutes walk from Hellbrunn stands the so-called **Monatsschlößchen**, built within a month in 1615 under Marcus Sitticus (hence its name – "month castle"), who summoned all the stonemasons in the area to accomplish the task.

Maria Plain (T) – At the exit from a bridge, turn right into Plainbergweg, the road which ends at the church of Maria Plain. This crowns a bluff, to whose slopes oratories cling.

The church, built from 1671 to 1674, has a squat façade framed by two towers. The interior is ornate: the altar in the chancel and the side chapels are adorned with altarpieces, and the pulpit, organ, confessionals and chancel screen were made in the late 17C in an exuberant Rococo style.

Mattsee – *23km - 14 miles. Leave Salzburg on ③ and Itzlinger Hauptstraße. Follow the road through Bergheim, Lengfelden and Elixhausen.*

This pleasant summer holiday resort (population 2 800) with its three lakes (Obertrumer See, Mattsee, Grabensee) offers a variety of leisure activities for water sports enthusiasts.

For those interested in cultural artefacts, there is the **Stift Mattsee**, an abbey founded here in 777: the 14C abbey church features Baroque interior decor and a huge 18C tower; the cloisters house 14C to 19C tombstones; and the priory contains an abbey museum.

★ **Untersberg** ⓥ – *12km - 7 miles plus 1 hour Rtn, including 15min by ᴄ
Leave Salzburg on* ② *towards Berchtesgaden. Just after the major St. Leᴏ.
crossroads, bear right into the road leading to the lower cable-car station.*
At a height of 1 853m - 6 079ft, there is a splendid **panorama** of the Salzburg
basin, the Salzburg Alps (Watzmann, Steinernes Meer, Staufen), the Wilder
Kaiser and the Dachstein.

Schloß Leopoldskron (ᴜ) – Mirrored in its tranquil lake, complete with ducks
and swans, Leopoldskron was built in 1744 as a summer residence for
Prince-archbishop Leopold Anton Firmian by Father Bernhard Stuart, a Benedictine monk from the Scottish St James' Convent at Regensburg, who was also
Professor of Mathematics at Salzburg University. It was acquired in 1918 for
cultural and artistic purposes by Max Reinhardt, one of the founders of the
Salzburg Festival. The castle became famous the world over after it featured
in the film "The Sound of Music". Its charming setting, its car-free lakeside walk,
its modern swimming pool and other recreational facilities make Leopoldskron
a pleasant place to relax in, especially in summer.

The Trapp Family

Rodgers and Hammerstein's Broadway musical *The Sound of Music* (1959,
made into a film in 1965) was based on the true story of a family of Austrian
singers, as told by Maria von Trapp (*The Story of the Trapp Family Singers,*
1949). The romantic tale of how orphan Maria Augusta Kutschera
(1905-1987) was brought up by Benedictine nuns in Salzburg, became
governess to widowed war hero Baron Georg von Trapp's seven children
and finally married the baron himself hardly needs retelling. The family
began singing in earnest – mainly German folk songs and church music – in
the mid 1930s. In 1938, they fled Nazi rule in Austria and emigrated to
the USA, where many of them eventually became US citizens. The Trapp
Family Singers went on a number of international tours between 1940 and
1955 and ran a family lodge and summer music camp in Vermont. The
Trapps set up a relief fund for Austrian families in 1947, the year of Baron
von Trapp's death.

SALZBURGER SPORTWELT AMADÉ✶✶

Salzburg
Michelin map 426 folds 20 and 34

The vast **skiing area** covers a distance of almost 30km - 18.6 miles between the
Tennen range and the Radstädter Tauern. It comprises a group of just under a dozen
small resorts, which however offer a countless range of downhill and cross-country
skiing opportunities to holders of a joint ski pass.
Overall, no fewer than 120 ski-lifts give access to 320km - 199 miles of piste in
the area. In practice however, due to the distances between the individual resorts
and the lack of skiable links between some of the peaks, it is difficult to explore
the entire area on skis. Furthermore, snow cover in the valley is generally only
average, because of the relatively low altitude (around 800m - 2 625ft). Since
there are also no Alpine peaks, none of the ski-slopes has a drop in altitude
of more than 1 000m - 3 281ft. Consequently, despite the area it covers,
Sportwelt Amadé is most suitable for those seeking a comfortable, relaxed skiing
holiday, rather than thrills, on a variety of ski-runs in a pleasant wooded setting.
Two smaller networks of slopes stand out in particular within the overall skiing
area. First of all Zauchensee, Flachauwinkel and Kleinarl (88km - 55 miles of piste
in total) and secondly Flachau, Wagrain and Alpendorf. Each of these areas can be
explored in a single day. The most interesting places are mentioned below.
For cross-country skiers, Radstadt (65km - 40 miles of track), Filzmoos (35km -
22 miles) and Flachau (40km - 25 miles) are particularly recommended.

✳ **Zauchensee** – Alt 1 361m - 4 465ft. Zauchensee is by far the highest-lying
resort in the Salzburg Sportwelt Amadé and consequently offers the best snow
cover in the skiing area as a whole. This small winter sports resort is especially
popular with keen downhill skiers, who are able to indulge their passion here
in a beautiful **low-altitude mountain setting**★ with ski-runs of varying degrees of
difficulty. Those wishing to sample an authentic village atmosphere and a more
extensive range of leisure facilities should visit the charming little village of
Altenmarkt im Pongau (Gothic church), which lies in the valley at an altitude
of 840m - 2 756ft.

.hn cable-car – Alt 2 100m - 6 890ft. *For skiers only.* The cable-car
.·t of the Schwarzkopf, from where there is a magnificent
the Tennengebirge range, the Dachstein and the Radstädter

nountain lodge – Alt 1 890m - 6 201ft. *Travel up on the chairlift.*
.che Dachstein, the Radstädter Tauern and the entire area around
Zauch... ...e.

Flachauwinkl – The pistes are on two slopes, with the A10 motorway running between them. They are connected by a small train, pulled by a tractor.

★★ **Roßkopf** – Alt 1 929m - 6 329ft. *Travel up on the Flachauwinkl cable-car* ⊙. At the top of the cable-car ride there is a remarkable **view★** to the right over Modermandl and Faulkogel to the south.
Then take the chairlift up to the Roßkopf. It is well worth climbing up to the peak itself, which only takes a few minutes, to enjoy the **panorama★★** over the skiing areas of Zauchensee and Flachau and over the Dachstein, the Radstädter Tauern and the Hohe Tauern.
Note that blue piste 21, which runs from the cable-car mountain station down into the valley, can also be tackled on foot, making a long, pleasant **walk★**, for which sticks and waterproof climbing boots are required. The only particularly steep stretch is the final kilometre on the main downhill piste.

Kleinarl – Alt 1 014m - 3 327ft. This attractive village, which enjoys plenty of sun, lies at the foot of a rocky massif with a highly varied relief. The ski pistes on the southern slopes offer comfortable runs for fairly good skiers.

★★ **Mooskopf** ⊙ – *Take the Kleinarl chairlift and then the Bubble-Shuttle chairlift. The peak itself can be reached on foot in just a few minutes.* From the peak a splendid **panorama★★** opens up over the limestone massifs of the Tennengebirge range and the Dachstein to the north, the impressive Ennskraxn massif and the Glingspitze peak to the south, and further to the west over the Hohe Tauern with the Großglockner, Hocharn, Ankogel group and Hochalmspitze peak in the background.

❋ **Wagrain** – Alt 838m - 2 749ft, population 3 000. The holiday resort of Wagrain has the best accommodation and the most generous network of ski-lifts in the entire area. It has acquired a certain fame by being the home of the factory of the largest Austrian ski manufacturer, Atomic.
Wagrain is centrally located within Sportwelt Amadé, but unfortunately suffers, as does its neighbour Flachau, from unreliable snow cover. The busy pistes follow easy routes through dense forest.

★ **Koglalm** – Alt 1 878m - 6 161ft. **Panorama★** over Wagrain, Flachau and Kleinarl with the Tennengebirge range, the Dachstein and the Niedere Tauern in the background. From here, good skiers in the winter and walkers in the summer are able to reach the **Saukarkopf**, where a broader **panorama★★** opens up. A small ski-lift and good snow cover invite skiers to make the most of the pistes here.

SALZKAMMERGUT★★★

Oberösterreich, Salzburg und Steiermark
Michelin map 426 folds 20 and 21

Salt, a traditional emblem of good health and a source of riches, has given the Salzkammergut its name and, until recently, exceptional economic importance *(Salt p 34; Spas p 16)*. In the 20C tourism has helped restore the prosperity of this former salt area of which the long-established resort of Bad Ischl is the centre.
A total of some 76 lakes, together with the massive Dachstein and Totes Gebirge ranges, have contributed to the fame of the area.
Starting from Salzburg it is possible to tour the Salzkammergut in 4 days, by following, in succession, itineraries ①, ②, ③ on day 1, and itinerary ④ on days 2, 3 and 4.

Round the Schafberg – The circular view from the Schafberg embraces a landscape of lakes and peaks which, when split into small pictures like the setting of St. Gilgen, seem to transpose the exquisite urbanity of Salzburg into an Alpine setting. Although the various elements of the landscape are only modest sheets of water and, apart from the north slope of the Schafberg, unpretentious mountains, yet the delicate balance of these scenes, the light in which they are bathed, is worthy of all the publicity put out about the lake of St. Wolfgang and other places.

Along the Traun – From Gmunden to Bad Ischl and Bad Aussee, the scenery is very romantic. The Hallstätter See and Gosausee, the Grundlsee and the Altaussee fill steep-sided hollows. The peaks of the Dachstein and the Totes Gebirge remain mostly out of sight. Great, therefore, is one's surprise to discover, at the end of some cable-car in the region, and especially from the Krippenstein, the rounded shapes of the upper surfaces of these massifs, regular limestone plateaux riddled with basins and caverns, where only a few sharp peaks locate the highest points (2 995m - 9 826ft – at the Hoher Dachstein). The appearance of glaciers in this petrified world – the Dachstein is the most easterly massif in the Alps that boasts eternal snow – is no less strange.

★★ TOUR OF THE LAKES

① From Salzburg to Bad Ischl
84km - 52 miles – about 4 hours – Local map overleaf

Owing to the low pass (alt 608m - 1 995ft) carrying the road over the wooded ridge between Scharfling and St. Gilgen, the route is able to take in both the Mondsee and the lake of St. Wolfgang.

★★★ **Salzburg** – *See SALZBURG.*
Leave Salzburg on ⑤, then take the A1 motorway to the Mondsee exit.

Between Salzburg and Mondsee, the motorway above the little Thalgau valley, is slightly raised and affords open views of the Drachenwand cliffs beyond which, in the middle distance, stands the Schafberg spur. The lake of **Mondsee★** at last appears below the Schafberg.

Mondsee – *See MONDSEE.*

The north shore of the Mondsee, which is calm and welcoming at first, becomes a little more severe beyond the Pichl promontory, where the road climbs over a wooded rise.

Burggrabenklamm – *5km - 3 miles from Au along the road beside the Attersee at the foot of the Schafberg slopes, leave the car in the Gasthaus Zum Jägerwirt car park; 30min on foot Rtn. Unprotected walk on rocks which are slippery after rain.*
Exploration of a ravine as far as a waterfall.

The south shore of the lake of Mondsee between Au and Scharfling is framed by the lower cliffs of the Schafberg; the road passes through sections cut into the overhanging rock and through short tunnels.
The crossing of the pass connecting Scharfling and St. Gilgen is remarkable for the **panoramic section★★** which bends in a curve above St. Gilgen *(car park)*. Beyond the slender bulbous-domed village bell-tower, the **Wolfgangsee★★** lake stretches towards the Rinnkogel massif of which a characteristic peak, the Sparber, seems to form an advanced bastion.

★ **St. Gilgen.** – *See ST. GILGEN.*

Soon the road from Salzburg to Bad Ischl draws away from the lake. The Schafberg, more approachable on this southern slope, is crowned with a hotel served by a rack railway.
To the left a road branches off which leads to the Gschwendt landing stage from which it is possible to reach St. Wolfgang by boat. Leave the main road at Strobl to make the detour to St. Wolfgang.

Strobl – Population 3 300. The main square of the village, the church and the lakeshore with its flower gardens form a quietly graceful scene when traffic allows. In season there is a **regular boat service** ⊘ from Strobl to St. Wolfgang and St. Gilgen.

★★ **St. Wolfgang** – *See ST. WOLFGANG.*
Take the direct road to Bad Ischl, avoiding Strobl.

⌘ **Bad Ischl** – *See Bad ISCHL.*

② From Bad Ischl to Gmunden
34km - 21 miles – about 3 hours – Local map overleaf

⌘ **Bad Ischl** – *See Bad ISCHL.*

This run is marked by a scenic cliff road section along the shore of the **Traunsee★**, the deepest lake in Austria (191m - 527ft). Cliffs rise from the lake waters in tortured shapes.
Below Bad Ischl the Traun corridor, which was one of the great European salt routes, unwinds evenly between the Höllengebirge and Totes Gebirge foothills. Beside the road, at the foot of the west slope, a track follows the course of the saltwater conduit (*Soleleitung – p 35*), which since the 17C has brought the salt waters from Hallstatt to the refinery at Ebensee, whence the salt was at one time sent by boat across the Traunsee. From Gmunden the boats continued on the lower Traun, along a reach which since 1552 has enabled them to avoid the last falls of the river (Traunfall). Glassmaking and chemical factories have set an industrial stamp on modern Ebensee.

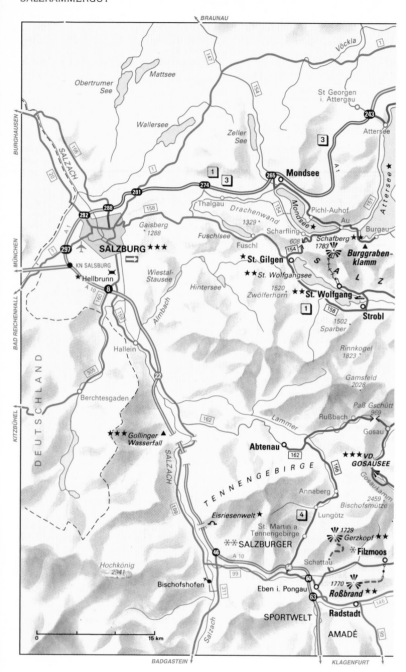

The **cliff road**★ from Ebensee to Traunkirchen is spectacular. From the road, which is hewn in the rock above the Traunsee, one can see the gold peak of the Rötelspitze standing out from the Erlakogel, and then further north, beyond a slope pitted with quarries, the Traunstein.

Traunkirchen – See TRAUNKIRCHEN.

During the last part of the trip through delightful countryside, those who enjoy solving puzzles can pass the time trying to pick out the form of a recumbent woman, the Sleeping Greek *(see GMUNDEN)*.

Altmünster – Population 8 580. Altmünster is home to a Late Gothic hall-church with sumptuous decoration and a stone high altar dating from 1518.

The charming Schloß Ort welcomes travellers to Gmunden.

★ **Gmunden** – See GMUNDEN.

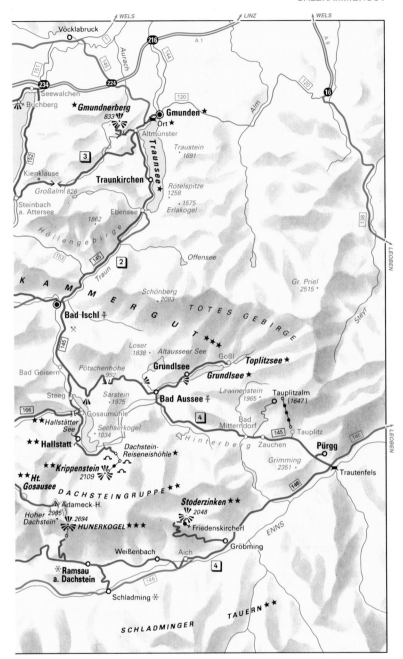

③ **From Gmunden to Salzburg**

117km - 73 miles – allow 1 day – Local map above

The route, which links the three lakes, the Traunsee, the Attersee and the Mondsee, crosses attractive countryside as in the upper Aurach valley or occasionally open countryside as in the Mondsee hollow.

★ **Gmunden** *– See GMUNDEN.*

From Gmunden take the Bad Ischl road to Altmünster.

Altmünster *– See ② above.*

★ **Gmundnerberg** *– See GMUNDEN: Excursions.*

The road leaves the banks of the Traunsee to enter a tranquil hilly region dotted with brilliantly white-washed farmhouses and clumps of huge lime trees. After

241

skirting the hamlet of Großalm to the right the road burrows into the forest which lies within sight of the northern escarpments of the Höllengebirge to reach a pass at an altitude of 826m - 2 710ft.

The descent down the Attersee slope, which is at first very steep, becomes interesting only on reaching the **panoramic section**★ from Kienklause to Steinbach, where the road runs along a bare slope which plunges directly into the lake.

Steinbach am Attersee – Population 950. Holiday resort.

The road runs like a quayside along the **Attersee**★ (or Kammersee), the largest lake in the Austrian Alps *(fishing, boating)* bordered to the south by the last cliff-like slopes of the Schafberg. The west shore of the lake, between the villages of Seewalchen and Attersee, unfolds through a region of charming sundrenched hills where orchards flourish. Only the cliffs of the Höllengebirge, rising up on the east shore lend a note of harshness to the scene. To get a good view of the whole lake, stop at the viewpoint *(bench)* beside the Buchberg chapel.

Attersee – Population 1 350. Holiday resort.

Leave the lake at Attersee and take the motorway towards Salzburg.

The road down towards Mondsee offers a **panorama**★ of the mountains which frame the lake (Drachenwand, Schafberg) and the Salzkammergut Alps.

Mondsee – *See MONDSEE.*

Continue on the motorway to Salzburg.

★★★ **Salzburg** – *See SALZBURG.*

★★ TOUR AROUND THE DACHSTEIN

④ Leaving from Bad Ischl

267km - 166 miles – allow 3 days (day 1: Bad Ischl, Hallstatt, Kripperntein, Gosauseen; day 2: Filzmoos, Roßbrand, Hunerkogel, Ramsau; day 3: Stoderzinken, Bad Aussee, Bad Ischl) - Local map previous pages

⊥ **Bad Ischl** – *See Bad ISCHL.*

Branching off from the Pötschenhöhe route south of Bad Goisern, the road to Bad Ischl at Hallstatt follows the floor of the Traun valley, which is planted with orchards. At Steeg, the road starts along the west shore of the **Hallstätter See**★★, on whose deep blue waters boats with lofty prows can be seen sailing. At the Gosaumühle fork, continue along the lakeside at the foot of a steep slope. Across the water is the Sechserkogel promontory, a spur of the Sarstein. The **view**★ opens out onto the town of Hallstatt grouped below its church; the amphitheatre of Obertraun also appears.

Enter the tunnel to bypass Hallstatt, leave the car at the viewng terrace which at one point makes a break in the tunnels and walk into town.

★★ **Hallstatt** – *See HALLSTADT.*

★★ **Ascent to the Krippenstein** – *Detour south from Hallstatt (6km - 4 miles) and ascent: 2 hours 30min (viewpoint only) to 4 hours (viewpoint and caves) of cable-car and walking - see DACHSTEIN.*

After visiting Hallstatt, continue through the tunnel and on emerging turn round to take the tunnel for south-north traffic only. At Gosaumühle turn left.

After passing under the salt water aqueduct *(Soleleitung – p 35)* the road enters the mountains along the Gosaubach. When the valley widens again, the magnificent crest of the Gosaukamm, bristling with peaks, unfolds on the left above the Gosau basin. Here two almost identical churches are a reminder that Protestant communities have been able to survive in this part of Upper Austria.

Turn towards the lake of Gosau and leave the car at one of the car parks at the end of the road.

★★★ **Gosauseen** – *See GOSAUSEEN.*

Return to Gosau; turn left into the Gschütt pass road.

On the west slope of the pass, the road drops among parklands to the Rußbach hollow, where large peasants' houses with little belfries recall those of the Tyrol; it then crosses the Abtenau depression at the foot of the Tennengebirge.

Abtenau – Population 5 040. This little holiday resort (*Abtenau* – "the abbey meadow") at the foot of the enormous Kogel is popular in the summer and a good departure point for excursions into the surrounding countryside. The Gothic church, with its twin aisles, a former place of pilgrimage, is interesting as much for its graceful outline as for its furnishings (statues of St George and St Florian). The beautifully built priest's house is worthy of the patronage of the abbey of St. Peter at Salzburg.

Return east; turn right to Annaberg, the "Salzburg Dolomites" road.

The furrow of the Upper Lammer, separating the Tennengebirge and Dachstein massifs, begins with a romantic gorge. The most remarkable views of the journey are oriented to the east, especially in the Annaberg-Lungötz section. This is in the direction of the Gosaukamm which is distinguished here by the cleft peak aptly named Bischofsmütze – bishop's mitre. The pass at St. Martin leads into the Fritztal, a tributary valley of the Salzach (views westwards towards Hochkönig).

★★ **From Eben im Pongau to Gröbming** – *1 day. See DACHSTEIN.*

The road follows the valley of the Enns. To the right there appears the massive bulk of Trautenfels castle.

Schloß Trautenfels ⊘ – A fortress called Neuhaus built on a mountain ridge overlooking the Enns valley is first recorded in 1261. The governor of the province of Styria, Siegmund Friedrich von Trauttmannsdorff, converted the fortress to a Baroque country palace in 1664 and renamed it Trautenfels. All that now remains of the interior decor is a number of stucco ceilings with valuable **frescoes** painted by Carpoforo Tencalla and some marquetry doors.

The castle houses a museum of local natural history and folklore, a department of the Steiermärkisches Landesmuseum Joanneum in Graz.

At the Trautenfels crossroads, leave the Enns Valley and take road no 145. The road through the Styrian Salzkammergut massif rises quickly into a ravine carved by the Grimming at the foot of the scaly cliffs of Großer Grimming. To the right the white village of Pürgg dominates the Enns valley.

Pürgg – Population 1 030. *Leave the car at the entrance to the village.* Art lovers should go up to the bluff on which the **Johanneskapelle** stands. The church decoration is typical of a country church of about the year 1200. The **Romanesque frescoes** uncovered and restored (the last time in 1959) depict, in the nave, the Annunciation, the Birth of Christ and its Announcement to the Shepherds, a fabulous fight between cats and mice and the Wise and Foolish Virgins. Figures seen on the triumphal arch are Christ Giving His Blessing, Cain and Abel and the church donors. On the chancel dome the Mystic Lamb is surrounded by the four Apostles, who are symbolically supported by the four sections of the world (on the pendentives). The crucifix on the altar is also Romanesque. The parish church, equally ancient, is curiously built on the mountain slope, so that both the entrances through the façade and at gallery level are on ground level.

The road goes through an enclosed depression known as the Hinterberg Plateau. In the foreground the magnificent chiselled walls of the Grimming face the slab-like shapes of the Lawinenstein. This crest masks the Alpine combe pastures of the **Tauplitzalm** which is popular with skiers in winter owing to the mountain road beginning at Zauchen and a cable-car which travels up from the village of **Tauplitz** (winter sports resort).

Bad Mitterndorf – Population 2 850. Holiday resort.

Through a ravine of the Traun the road approaches Bad Aussee.

⊹ **Bad Aussee** – *See Bad AUSSEE.*

★ **Grundlsee and Toplitzsee★** – *Both lakes are described under Bad AUSSEE: Excursions.*

The Pötschenhöhe (alt 992m - 3 255ft) road provides a short-cut avoiding the great loop of the Traun, partly drowned by the lake of Hallstatt. The east slope of the pass from Bad Aussee forms a small **crest★★** with a panoramic view. The pincer-shaped precipitous promontories of the Loser and the Trisselwand jut out from the petrified surface of the Totes Gebirge. Opposite stands the Sarstein. The west slope of the Pötschenhöhe begins in the pleasant Bad Goisern basin. The last bend, in which there is a space for cars to stop, makes a **viewpoint★** overlooking the waters of the lake of Hallstatt. The lake turns to penetrate the amphitheatre hollowed out by the Traun at the foot of the Dachstein cliffs.

At Bad Goisern turn right into road no 145 to Bad Ischl.

ST. ANTON AM ARLBERG★★

Tirol – Population 2 300

Michelin map 426 fold 29 – Local map under ARLBERG – Alt 1 289m - 4 229ft

St. Anton is something of a shrine for lovers of the sport of skiing. In 1907 Hannes Schneider, pioneer of the Arlberg school of downhill skiing technique *(see Introduction on skiing)*, gave skiing instruction for the first time on the surrounding mountain slopes. From the 1920s onwards, winter sports became extremely popular in St. Anton, made possible thanks to the good transport communications (St. Anton has been accessible by express train from Vienna or Paris, via the Arlberg Tunnel, since 1885) and the extensive skiing area. Today, St. Anton is one of the largest winter sports resorts in the Northern Alps, with accommodation for 8 000 tourists.

ST. ANTON AM ARLBERG

The resort lies in a deeply incised valley and features modern architecture. Those in search of peace and quiet or of unspoilt nature will feel more at home in the nearby village of St. Jakob or at **St. Christoph**, which lies at an altitude of 1 771m - 5 810ft close to the pass.

Nevertheless, St. Anton attracts numerous families, who enjoy its youthful, sporty atmosphere. No other ski-slopes in Austria have as much to offer good skiers, and after a hard day's skiing, the boutiques, bars and restaurants in the pedestrian zone are an ideal place to unwind. St. Anton is also equipped with an ice stadium, several swimming pools, tennis and squash courts.

Summer brings a degree of calm to the resort, although the Arlbergstraße road does attract many passing tourists. Summer visitors are drawn by an 18 000m² - 21 528sq yd leisure park, with its many and varied facilities. There are 90km - 56 miles of trails for hikers, in particular in the Moostal valley. Lake Ferwall is a favourite destination for day-trips.

Arlberg ski slopes seen from the Valluga ridge

Y. Bontoux

✳✳✳ **Arlberg skiing area** – An Arlberg ski pass gives skiers access to the pistes of **Lech**✳✳✳, **Zürs**✳✳ *(see ZÜRS: take the bus there)* and Stuben, besides those at St. Anton. The 500km² - 193sq mile skiing area, which lies at an altitude of 1 300 to 2 650m - 4 265 to 8 694ft, has 260km - 162 miles of marked-out and 180km - 112 miles of unmarked pistes, which are accessed by a total of 88 ski-lifts.

Elsewhere in Europe, only the ski-slopes of the Trois Vallées (Courchevel, Méribel, Les Ménuires, Val Thorens) and Tignes-Val d'Isère in France and St. Moritz, Zermatt and Verbier in Switzerland, are able to offer similar or comparable skiing facilites.

The area around St. Anton is equipped with 44 ski-lifts (five cable railways, one funicular railway and a cable-car). It is especially suitable for experienced skiers, who can ski down the many steep, undulating pistes from the Schindler Spitze, Kapall and Pfannenkopf peaks. Less proficient skiers are also catered for, however, with a number of suitable pistes on the Galzig, Gampen and Gampberg slopes.

Arlberg-Kandahar-Haus – This is a museum on the history of skiing and the development of tourism in the Arlberg area.

VIEWPOINTS

★★★ **Valluga** ⊙ – Alt 2 811m - 9 222ft. *About 2 hours 30min return trip. If possible, take binoculars. In the winter, begin the excursion in the early morning, since there are frequently long waits as there are only a few cable-cars running. Buy a ticket at the machine in the valley station of Valluga I, which will have printed on it the number of the cable-car on which you can travel up. There are mountain inns in the first and second sections.*

First take the Galzig cable-car. From the mountain station, which lies at an altitude of 2 070m -,6 791ft, there is a wonderful **view**★★ over the ski-slopes, from the Schindlerspitze peak to St. Anton, and to the south over the Verwall mountains.

Then take the cable-car Valluga I to the Valluga ridge (alt 2 645m - 8 678ft). The **panorama**★★ from here is very impressive, but you need to travel up to the peak itself with the little Valugaspitze cable-car to enjoy a full 360° **panorama**★★★ *(climb up on foot to the upper viewing terrace).*

To the south the view encompasses the Rätikon (Sulzfluh, Zimba, Madrisahorn), the Montafontal valley (Hochjoch), the Silvretta group and the Bernina (Switzerland) behind the Verwall range and the Samnaun. To the southeast lie the high peaks of the Ötztal (Weißkugel, Wildspitze) and Stubai Alps. The Lechtal Alps (Rote Wand, Omeshorn, Kriegerhorn and Rüfikopf) tower to the north, and in the distance, to the northeast, you can see the Zugspitze.

The various peaks can be made out easily with binoculars.

★★ **Kapall** ⊙ – Alt 2 314m - 7 592ft. *About 1 hour return trip. Ride up on the Kandahar funicular railway or the Gampen chairlift, then take the Kapall chairlift.* You will arrive at the foot of the rocky Weißschrofenspitze peak. There is a very beautiful **panorama**★★ to the south over the whole St. Anton valley as far as the hamlet of Pettneu. The view stretches to the Swiss Alps, the Rätikon (Drei Türme) and the Verwall range. There is a beautiful view straight ahead over the Moostal valley.

★ **Rendl cable-car** ⊙ – Alt 2 030m - 6 660ft. *30min return trip. Sit facing backwards.* During the trip there are several **general views**★ to be enjoyed of St. Anton and its ski-slopes from Valluga to the Kapall. From the cable-car mountain station *(mountain inn)* the view sweeps southwards to the beautiful Moostal valley, which is enclosed by the Kuchenspitze peak, the Küchlspitze peak and their glaciers.

Skiers take a T-bar lift up to the Gampberg (alt 2 407m - 7 897ft), and at the top it is only a short distance to the hill on which the last cable-car support stands. From here there is a broad **panorama**★ of the Verwall range and of the Hochkarspitze peak in particular.

EXCURSIONS

★ **Arlbergpaß** – *See ARLBERGGEBIET.*

Stuben – This little village, which lies below the pass at an altitude of 1 407m - 4 616ft, consists of only a few hotels and is without doubt the most peaceful holiday resort in the Arlberg area. Skiers can travel direct to the St. Anton ski-slopes from here. Zürs can be reached quickly by car. The Albona ridge towers over Stuben, with three chairlifts leading up to it (difference in altitude: 1 000m - 3 281ft). There are also some remarkable opportunities for off-piste skiing, since the mountainside offers vast snowfields with no sudden drops.

★ **Albonagrat** – Accessible for skiers from Stuben. Take the Albona I and II chairlifts, which lead to the Maroj Sattel (alt 2 323m - 7 621ft). Interesting **panorama**★ of the Verwall range to the south and the Arlberg pass to the north, with Zürs and the Widderstein in the background.

Ski down the Albonagrat-Sonnleiten piste and take the chairlift up to the Albonagrat ridge (alt 2 334m - 7 657ft). There is a far-reaching **panorama**★ over the Montafon and Arlberg areas.

Stift ST. FLORIAN★★

Oberösterreich

Michelin map 426 fold 9 – 18km - 11 miles southeast of Linz

The abbey of St. Florian, the largest in Upper Austria and an eminent cultural centre, has been occupied, since the 11C, by Augustinian Canons. The present buildings are in the purest Baroque style, since the monastery was entirely rebuilt (1686-1751) under the direction, first of Carlo Antonio Carlone, then of Jakob Prandtauer. The latter was also the architect of Hohenbrunn, the palatial edifice built nearby for one of the abbey's provosts.

HISTORICAL NOTES

The Legend of St. Florian – Florian was head of the Roman administration in the Noric province *(map p 29)*. He was converted to Christianity, martyred in 304 near the camp of Lauriacum and thrown into the Enns. It was near the site of his grave that the monastery which bears his name was later built. His death by drowning caused him to be invoked against flooding and also against fire, often with the naïve prayer, "Good St Florian, spare my house and rather burn my neighbour's". There is, therefore, hardly a church in Austria without a statue of this saintly protector, in which he figures as a Roman legionary holding a sprinkler or a pail to put out the flames.

Anton Bruckner at St. Florian

Anton Bruckner, recognized as Austria's greatest 19C composer of church music, was born in 1824 at Ansfelden, a little village near St. Florian. His father, a local schoolmaster, died when Bruckner was thirteen. The boy was taken into the choir school at the monastery, where he was introduced to the major works in the repertoire of religious music.

Bruckner trained as a teacher, and after two posts as an assistant teacher, far from the abbey where he felt his real ties were, he managed to win an appointment as teacher at the monastery in 1845, and, to his great joy, he was also appointed its organist. It was at St. Florian that Bruckner made the decision to devote himself to music. He began a course of study on counterpoint under Simon Sechter. In 1956 he was called to Linz as cathedral organist, where he composed a number of masterpieces including his three masses and two of his nine symphonies, and then to Vienna as a professor at the Conservatory. Despite his increasing fame, Bruckner's thoughts kept returning to the abbey at St. Florian, and it was there that he expressed a wish to be buried, beneath the organ which had helped him on the way to success as a composer and performer.

TOUR ⊙ *about 1 hour 30min*

The west façade, which is 214m - 702ft long, is surmounted by three towers. The doorway (Stiftstor) leading into the abbey's inner courtyard (Stiftshof) is particularly elegant, with two superimposed balconies, carved columns and statues.

A remarkable sculptured fountain, the Eagle's Fountain (Adlerbrunnen), and a wrought-iron well-head, dating from 1603, adorn the wide inner courtyard.

Bibliothek (Library) – The fine allegorical paintings on the library ceiling, by Bartolomeo Altomonte, represent the union of religion and science. Marquetry in walnut, encrusted with gold, sets off the valuable early texts, manuscripts and over 140 000 books.

Marmorsaal – The marble hall was dedicated to Prince Eugene of Savoy as a tribute to the leading part he played, as a captain, in the defence of the Austrian Empire against the Turks. It was used as a concert-hall and is adorned with frescoes and pictures. The paintings on the ceiling *(Victory over the Turks)* are by Martino Altomonte.

★★★ **Altdorfer Galerie** – The most valuable pictures in the abbey collection are by Albrecht Altdorfer (1480-1538), master of the Danubian school, who distinguished himself not only as a painter but as a steel and wood engraver and architect.

The fourteen pictures on the altar to St Sebastian, painted in 1518 for the Gothic church of the abbey, form the world's most important collection of Altdorfer's work.

The panels depicting the martyrdom of St Sebastian, and the eight pictures evoking scenes of the Passion, are striking for the feeling in the characters of Christ, the Virgin, Judas and Caiaphas. The background of foliage in shadow lends power to the dramatic scenes.

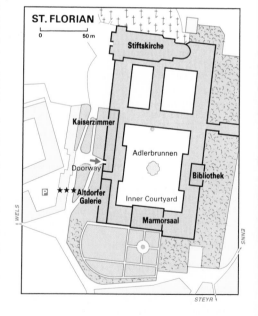

In his devotion to landscape, Altdorfer resembled his contemporary Dürer, and was by several centuries a forerunner of the Romantics. The most attractive aspects of his work are the balanced composition and rich, warm colour.

Kaiserzimmer (Imperial Apartments) – The Imperial apartments are reached by the magnificent grand staircase, which rises through two storeys; the balustrades are adorned with statues and the walls and ceilings embellished with stucco and frescoes. Until 1782 the apartments received such illustrious visitors as Pope Pius VI, emperors and princes.

Amidst a succession of halls and state rooms note the Faistenberger room, the bedrooms of the Emperor and Empress, the reception room and a room known as the "Gobelins" room; they contain rich furniture and interesting stucco work, frescoes and pictures.

Stiftskirche – In designing the interior decoration of the abbey church, Carlone's imaginative exuberance enjoyed free rein. One can only regret the clumsy stucco work and the harsh dominant tones (yellow and violet) of the wall paintings in the nave. The high altar is adorned with a painted altarpiece framed between pink Salzburg marble columns. A fine black marble pulpit, choir stalls ornamented with gilding and carved designs, and altarpieces in each of the side chapels complete this sumptuous display. In the crypt is the coffin of Anton Bruckner.

ST. GILGEN★

Salzburg – Population 3 070

Michelin map 426 fold 20 – Local map under SALZKAMMERGUT – Alt 548m - 1 798ft

St. Gilgen, at the northwest end of the Wolfgangsee, was once an eastern outpost of the prince-archbishops of Salzburg. Together with its setting, it forms one of the Salzkammergut's best-known scenes.

It is worthwhile repeating the family connection of Mozart with this favoured land: his mother, Anna Maria Pertl, was born here in 1720 and his sister, Nannerl, settled here after her marriage to Baron Berchtold zu Sonnenburg, the governor of the district. A plaque on the law courts (Bezirksgericht) recalls this memory, while a fountain (Mozartbrunnen) was erected in 1927 on the central square in front of the Rathaus. St. Gilgen is a delightful sight for anyone coming from Salzburg, or more especially from Scarfling *(route described under SALZKAMMERGUT* **1***)*. The lake attracts numerous watersports enthusiasts, and appeals to sailors in particular not least because of the sudden squalls to which it is subjected, which enable them to test their skill to the full.

A regular **boat service** ⊙ links St. Gilgen's landing-stage (Schiffstation) with St. Wolfgang and a total of nine places around the lake. The veteran paddle-steamer *Kaiser Franz Joseph*, which inaugurated the service in 1873, is still in steam.

ST. JOHANN IN TIROL✳

Tirol – Population 6 500

Michelin map 426 fold 19 – Local map under KAISERGEBIRGE – Alt 660m - 2 165ft

Its location at the intersection of several valleys makes St. Johann a lively place. The wide bowl of the valley – quite a suntrap – is enclosed by the Wilder Kaiser and Kitzbüheler Horn peaks. The market town, which grew up on the site of a scattered village, boasts a number of beautiful Baroque houses with façades decorated with painted, sometimes *trompe-l'œil*, scenes, which are typical of the Tyrolean region and never fail to charm visitors.

St. Johann has evolved into a popular tourist resort, capable of accommodating 6 000 visitors, which offers a wide variety of leisure facilities during the summer catering for tastes ranging from seekers of peace and quiet, to ramblers, to amateur mountaineers. But it is as a winter sports resort that St. Johann has really made a name for itself in recent years. Although there is not as much emphasis on sophisticated après-ski facilities here as in Kitzbühel 10km - 6 miles away, the range on offer is nonetheless the same.

✳ **Ski slopes** – Downhill ski-slopes are concentrated on the north face of the Kitzbüheler Horn. The pistes at Harschbichl, which go up to an altitude of 1 700m - 5 577ft, are well-equipped with 10 ski-tows, 6 chairlifts and 2 cable-cars, which can transport 19 000 people per hour. In spite of the relatively low altitude, there are plenty of challenging ski-runs for competent skiers.

The facilities for **cross-country skiing** are equally impressive. There are 74km - 46 miles of tracks, including two of 16km - 10 miles in length which are classified as difficult, so all are catered for. In association with some of the neighbouring resorts, such as Oberndorf, Going-Ellmau, Kirchdorf-Erpfendorf and Waidring, there are almost 200km - 124 miles of cross-country ski-tracks to be explored!

Pfarrkirche Mariä Himmelfahrt – This Baroque building, designed by the architect Abraham Millauer, dates from 1724-28. Its well-lit interior is remarkable for its paintings; the six decorating the vaults are by one of the masters of the Baroque tradition, **Simon Benedikt Faistenberger**, while the somewhat academic Assumption on the main altar is the work of the Salzburg artist Jakob Zanussi (1679-1742).

Abtei ST. LAMBRECHT

Steiermark

Michelin map 426 fold 36

The Benedictine abbey of St. Lambrecht lies over 1 000m - 3 281ft above sea level in a tributary valley leading off from the Neumarkter Sattel gap. The first record of a church of "St Lambert in the Woods" dates from 1066. Next to this church, the Carinthian ducal family, the Eppensteins, built a family convent in the last decades of the 11C. This foundation was finally granted the status of an abbey by Duke Heinrich III of Carinthia in 1103. The first large Romanesque abbey church, a basilica with twin west towers consecrated in 1160, was replaced in 1327 to 1421 by the present building, a High Gothic triple-aisled hall-church. The abbey buildings were built in 1640 following the designs of abbey master builder Domenico Sciassia. The 17C building had a south wing, with a doorway flanked by statues, added to it in 1730, to close off the outer courtyard on the side of the market square.

The abbey was dissolved in 1786 by Joseph II, but was able to move back into the buildings when the foundation was re-established by Emperor Franz II in 1802.

GEORG MIKES

Benedictine Abbey of St. Lambrecht

TOUR ⏱ time: 30min

Enter the abbey through the great south doorway. To the right stretches the impressive west façade of the abbey building, 135m - 443ft in length, with its harmonious arrangement of plastered walls broken up by marble window jambs. The medieval façade of the west tower was transformed into the Baroque style by Domenico Sciassia. Opposite the west façade, the abbey courtyard is closed off by a bastion adorned with statues by Johann Matthias Leitner in 1746. In the middle of the bastion, an open staircase leads to the Gothic **Peterskirche**. Behind the church stand the remains of the castle. To the north, the abbey courtyard is closed off by the Granarium (1625), the west end of which is adjoined by further ancillary buildings. In the cemetery to the north of the abbey church stands a simple Romanesque **ossuary** (12C).

Stiftskirche – The elaborate marble doorway, built to a design by Sciassia, opens into the narthex, which houses the 14C Lettner crucifix in a Baroque framework. The abbey church itself is an impressive Gothic hall-church with medieval frescoes on the vault above the chancel and on the walls of the nave. The beautiful interior decor is early Baroque. The enormous **high altar★**, 16m - 52ft in height, dates from 1632 and was built after designs by Valentin Khautt. The side altars are the work of Neumarkt sculptor Christoph Paumgartner. The sculpted decoration of the altar to St Emmeramus at the front on the right, the statues of the church Elders on the organ gallery and the Madonna in the narthex are the work of famous sculptor Michael Hönell. The pulpit, richly decorated with figures, and the Mariazell altar in a side chapel are showpieces from the late 18C.

Castle ruins – To the northeast of the abbey stand a square tower and a small chapel, the remains of a castle built in the early 15C, apparently on the site of an older fortress, perhaps that of Count Marward von Eppenstein.

ST. PAUL IM LAVANTTAL

Kärnten – Population 5 770
Michelin map 426 fold 37 – Alt 400m - 1 312ft

The abbey of St. Paul, founded in 1091, half hidden in the trees and slightly above the wide lower Lavant valley, has always been occupied by Benedictines. Its church is one of the finest examples of Romanesque architecture to be seen in Austria.

Stiftskirche (Abbey Church) ⊘ – *To reach the church by car leave St. Paul by the Lavamünd road. At the top of the climb enter the walls through a monumental doorway (the "Hofrichtertor").* The church, construction of which was begun in 1180, ends in a flat chevet from which three rounded apses jut out, their great blind arcades, chequered friezes and cornices above blind arcades, composing a very pure Romanesque decoration. The south doorway features an image of the Adoration of the Magi, and the west door one of Christ in Majesty.

Inside, the Romanesque frescoes behind the altar and the fresco on the north wall of the transept depicting a pair of donors with saints (15C) are particularly interesting.

Abbey buildings ⊘ – These house the famous library and a considerable collection of works of art. There are Romanesque chasubles, a reliquary cross belonging to Queen Adelaide of Hungary (11C), and also paintings (Rubens, Martin Johann Schmidt) and prints (Dürer, Rembrandt).

ST. PÖLTEN★

Ⓛ Niederösterreich – Population 50 000
Michelin map 426 fold 11

St. Pölten, which was founded by the Romans in 1 AD, is the most recently established provincial capital in Austria. The earliest monastery in Lower Austria was established here after 791, so still during the Carolingian era. This monastery was dedicated to St Hippolytus, from which the name St. Pölten is derived.

Baroque city – During the Baroque period, the city flourished. Master builders such as Jakob Prandtauer (who lived in St. Pölten from 1692 to his death in 1726), Joseph and Franz Munggenast, and also famous painters such as Daniel Gran, Paul Troger and Bartolomeo Altomonte, lived and worked here. Evidence of their creativity is found at every turn, so that a stroll around the city centre is something of an intensive course in Baroque art.

Provincial capital – In 1986 Lower Austria, the true heart of Austria, whose first written mention dates back to 996 and which had been without a capital city since 1922 (the area was administered from Vienna), voted by a big majority to make St. Pölten its provincial capital. It was predestined for this role, being the largest city in the province, a major traffic junction and also an industrial location.

SIGHTS

Rathausplatz – In the centre of the square, which is bordered by beautiful patrician houses, stands the **Trinity Column**, created between 1767 and 1782 by Andreas Gruber. The column is made of marble, and the associated fountain arrangement is made of sandstone. It shows St Hippolytus, St Florian, St Sebastian and St Leopold.

Rathaus – The town hall was built in the 16C by connecting two existing Gothic houses. The Renaissance portals also date from the time of its construction. In 1727 Joseph Munggenast, the nephew of Jakob Prandtauer, built the Baroque façade.

Rathausplatz, St. Pölten

Herzberger/ÖSTERREICH WERBUNG

249

Patrician houses – To the left of the Rathaus stands the **Schuberthaus**, in which the composer stayed in 1821, holding "Schubertiade" musical evenings. The building dates from the 16C. The Baroque façade is probably the work of Joseph Munggenast, who is also thought to have planned the **Montecuccoli-Palais** *(Rathausplatz 5)*. His son worked on the houses at nos 6 and 7. The **Stadttheater**, built in 1820 by Josef Schwerdfeger and converted in 1893, has a Classical façade.

Franziskanerkirche – The slightly sweeping façade lends a lively quality to the church built between 1757 and 1768 by Johann Pauli on the narrow north side of the Rathausplatz. The wall, which is concave in the central axis, is divided by flat pilasters. The beautiful statues of St Joseph, St Theresa and the Prophet Elias are the work of an unknown master. The gable area is also decorated with interesting sculpture work. The double vaulted interior with side galleries is beautifully balanced with its Rococo pulpit, the magnificent high altar by Andreas Gruber and the four side paintings by Martin Johann Schmidt, a.k.a. Kremser Schmidt.

Karmelitinnenkirche – Also known as the Prandtauer church after its builder, this church, which was built in 1707, stands to the right of the Rathaus on the south side of the Rathausplatz. It served as a model for the Franziskanerkirche. Inside stands a high altar created in 1712 by Johann Lukas von Hildebrandt for the castle chapel at Aschach in Upper Austria, for which Johann Georg Schmidt, the Viennese Schmidt, painted the altarpiece.

A local museum, the **Stadtmuseum** ☉, is housed in the former Carmelite nunnery, attached to the church. The old post office, **Alte Post**, is only a few steps further on *(Prandtauerstraße 4)*. Take a look inside the pretty inner courtyard in order to appreciate the harmonious balance of this Baroque building and to enjoy the peacefulness of its setting.

★ **Institut der Englischen Fräulein** – *From Prandtauerstraße turn left into Linzer Straße.* You cannot miss the sumptuous **façade**★ which was begun by Jacob Prandtauer, and which is thought to have been extended in 1767-1969 by Mathias Munggenast.

The main colours are white and pink, against which the black of the wrought iron window grilles makes a striking contrast. Four portals, richly decorated with scrolls and busts of angels, divide up the long building. A particularly unusual feature of the façade is its three tabernacle-style niches. At the level of the ground floor, these contain a group of figures between columns, with above them a single figure in a wall niche. The figures depicted are, from right to left, St Katharine of Alexandria with St Ignatius above her; a guardian angel with child, with the Virgin Mary "Immaculata" above, and finally St Anne with the Virgin Mary, with St Joseph above them. This iconography illustrates the vocation of the institute, which was dedicated to the welfare and education of young people. Schools are still housed here.

The **Institutskirche** *(request entry at the gate)* consists of two unequally sized rooms, the smaller of which was designed by Prandtauer. On its 20m - 66ft high cupola is a magnificent fresco entitled *Revelation of the Incarnation of Christ* by Paul Troger. The main room boasts a ceiling fresco by Bartolomeo Altomonte with scenes from the life of the Virgin Mary. The high altarpiece and the paintings in the side altars are by Karl Reslfelder.

CATHEDRAL DISTRICT

★ **Dom Mariä Himmelfahrt** – From the Domplatz, the cathedral building appears almost totally lacking in any decoration. Only the two figures (St Hippolytus on the left, St Augustine on the right) and the Baroque spire alleviate the building's otherwise austere appearance. The core of the cathedral originates from 1150 and the 13C, and the building was modified several times in the 16C and 17C. The splendid Baroque decoration of the interior comes as all the more of a surprise after the sobriety of the exterior.

★ **Interior** – The soft tones of the stucco marble and paintings, the sheen of the liberally applied gilding, the patina of the wood, combine to create an unusually warm red-gold colour effect, which the eye first of all takes in as a whole and only then breaks down into detail. It is difficult to believe that this work of art was contemptuously dismissed in the 19C as a "sign of the reckless energy" of the Baroque period.

The conversion of the cathedral interior to the Baroque style began in 1722 under Jakob Prandtauer and was completed in 1735 under Joseph Munggenast. The high altar painting was executed by Tobias Pock in 1658; it depicts the Assumption of the Virgin Mary. The splendid **choir stalls**★ with their elaborately carved wooden decoration were executed in 1722 by Peter Widerin, who was also responsible for the organ case. Other artists from St. Pölten were involved in the creation of the beautiful pulpit and the confessionals.

The ceiling frescoes and the ten large **wall paintings**★, which depict scenes from the life of Christ, are the work of Thomas Friedrich Gedon and clearly show the influence of Daniel Gran.

During the cathedral's conversion to the Baroque style, the side aisles underwent an interesting transformation, with every second bay being topped by a cupola with a high lantern. The other domes were adorned with frescoes. The first two in the south and north side aisles are the work of Bartolomeo Altomonte, the others, originally by Daniel Gran, were restored in 1949-1950 by H.A. Brunner. Daniel Gran painted the altarpieces in the side altars. The composition of the *Beheading of St Barbara* in the right side aisle is especially beautiful.

The chancel leads into the **Rosenkranzkapelle**. This double vaulted room used to be a separate chapel building, which was incorporated into the monastery church in the 13C. The apse dates from the original period of construction (mid-12C).

Bistumsgebäude - The former Canons' Chapter stands on the north side of the cathedral. It is a large, early Baroque ensemble arranged on five floors. In the east wing of the fountain courtyard there is an ornate **wrought-iron gate★**, which leads to a beautiful staircase designed by Joseph Munggenast.

★ **Diözesanmuseum** ⊙ - *On the upper floor of the cloister courtyard.* This museum houses religious works of art from the Romanesque period to the present. For a proper appreciation of all the treasures, we particularly recommend a guided tour. The crowning glory of the visit, which also includes the Bishops' Oratorium, is unquestionably the sumptuous library, the **Stiftsbibliothek★**, with sculptures attributed to Peter Widerin and frescoes by Daniel Gran and Paul Troger. These depict the four faculties: theology, philosophy, medicine and law.

ADDITIONAL SIGHTS

Riemerplatz - Rathausgasse leads to Riemerplatz with its beautiful houses, some of the basic structures of which date back to the Middle Ages, and which were given Baroque façades in the 18C, for example at no 1 Riemerplatz, believed to have been worked on by Joseph Munggenast. Nos 3 and 4 are attributed to Mathias Munggenast, one of Jakob's sons.

★ **Herrenplatz** - Take Wiener Straße (note some remarkable Baroque façades) to reach this square, which is surrounded by buildings immortalising all the Baroque artists who were active in St. Pölten. An outstanding example is the house at no 2, which features a front gable bearing a sculpture based on the designs of Austria's foremost Baroque sculptor, Georg Raphael Donner. It depicts *Darkness being driven out by Light.*

Before bidding farewell to this lovely capital of Lower Austria, do not fail to take a look at a somewhat original Jugendstil (Art Nouveau) building which caused quite a stir when it was built. One can still sympathize to some extent with the scepticism with which it was received, as the so-called **"Stöhrhaus"** *(Kremser Gasse 41),* which was built in 1899 by Joseph Maria Olbrich, creator of the Vienna Secession building, makes a complete break with traditional architecture.

EXCURSIONS

Schloß Pottenbrunn - *In Pottenbrunn. Take Wiener Straße and Ratzersdorfer Straße heading northeast.* The old moated castle acquired its present Italian style Renaissance appearance when it was converted in the 16C. Especially characteristic are the overhanging arcaded galleries running round the tower and residential building. A bulbous Baroque dome caps the tower.

A museum of tin figures, the **Österreichisches Zinnfigurenmuseum** ⊙, is housed in the castle. Events from Austrian history are shown in tableaux with the help of 35 000 tin figures. The large diorama is especially graphic, showing the siege of Vienna by the Turks (1683). *(For a better understanding of the historical contexts, it is worth buying a catalogue).*

Kirchstetten - *15km - 9 miles east.* This village was for many years the summer retreat of the poet **W. H. Auden** (1907-73), who now lies buried here.

ST. VEIT AN DER GLAN

Kärnten - Population 12 020
Michelin map 426 fold 36 - Alt 476m - 1 562ft

St. Veit was the seat of the Dukes of Carinthia until 1518, when the role of regional capital passed to Klagenfurt. The well-preserved town wall, the picturesque narrow streets, the two town squares with their beautiful houses and arcaded courtyards all contribute to the charming appearance of this town. On the hills round St. Veit stand an unusually large number of castles - no less than fifteen in a radius of about 10km - 6 miles. These provide many excursions and walks for tourists.

From St. Veit road no 94, skirting the lake of Ossiach *(local map under WÖRTHER SEE; text under OSSIACHER SEE),* makes it possible to go quickly to Villach and Italy, avoiding Klagenfurt.

Hauptplatz – *Time: 30min*. This rectangular space, whose longer sides are only infrequently broken by alleys, is the centre of town life. The regular architecture of the houses enhances its design.

Of the three structures which distinguish the square, the most interesting, apart from the traditional memorial column to the plague, erected in 1715, is the fountain called the **Schüsselbrunnen**; its basin is believed to have come from the forum of the Roman city of Virunum *(qv)*. The small bronze statue (1566) surmounting it, the Schüsselbrunnbartele, representing a grotesque figure in 16C miner's costume, is the town mascot. Level with this fountain, at the corner of the street leading to the church, is a 15C statue of St Veit (St Guy), the patron saint of the city. The most distinguished buildings in the square are the **Military Headquarters** (Bezirkshauptmannschaft), in the Classical style (1780), on the short west side of the quadrangle, and, more especially, the town hall.

Rathaus – This graceful municipal building was given its Baroque stucco in 1754. On the pediment is the double-headed eagle of the Holy Roman Empire, embossed, in the centre, with the statue of St Veit. The gateway, which has a Gothic arch and a Gothic vaulted passage, leads to the three-storeyed inner court, decorated will Renaissance arcades and *sgraffiti (1)*. The great hall, or **Rathaussaal** ⊙, is on the 1st floor, under a low Gothic vault to which an 18C decorator has added stucco scroll ornaments.

EXCURSIONS

★ **Schloß Frauenstein** – *5km - 3 miles plus 30min on foot Rtn. Local map right; narrow country roads (passing impossible). Leave St. Veit via Obermühlbach (northwest) and then about 1 500m - 1 mile beyond the village take the second road on the right.*

This well-preserved 16C castle makes a picturesque ensemble with its towers, turrets and roofs of unequal height. Take a look at the pretty, arcaded courtyard.

St. Veit hill country – *Round tour of 25km - 16 miles – about 2 hours – Local map right. Leave St. Veit on the road to Brückl.*

It is not long before the fortress of Hochosterwitz comes into sight, on the right, on the top of a rock, round which winds a fortified access ramp.

About 400m beyond a level-crossing turn right. In the hamlet, at the foot of the rock, turn left up the road to the castle.

★ **Burg Hochosterwitz** – *See Burg HOCHOSTERWITZ.*

Turn back, then follow the direct road to Launsdorf, straight ahead.

Launsdorf – All periods since the Romanesque have left their mark on this appealingly unsymmetrical country church. In the tiny Gothic chancel is a gracious little 15C figure of the Virgin Mary with a Pomegranate.

Return towards St. Veit but bear right to St. Georgen. After 1 300m - about a mile turn right off the by-pass to enter St. Georgen.

St. Georgen am Längsee – Population 3 090. The former abbey for Benedictine noble ladies and oldest surviving convent in Carinthia has kept its original design. A large quadrilateral of buildings encloses a church transformed into the Baroque style about 1720. The inner court is imposing, with large façades pierced by rounded arches. Facing the main door of the church is the Renaissance north gallery (1546) topped with graceful arcatures.

After skirting the little lake of Längsee (right), turn left into the main road to St. Veit.

★ **Magdalensberg** – *15km - 9 miles – about 2 hours – Local map above.*
Leave St. Veit on the road to Klagenfurt. After 7km - 4 miles turn left on to an uphill road on the flank of the Magdalensberg, within view of the Klagenfurt basin and the Karawanken mountain barrier.

---

(1) The "sgraffito" owes its decorative effect to a layer of roughcast limewashed in grey and then scratched off to reveal areas of the original colour beneath.

The road ends at the **Magdalensberg excavations** (Ausgrabungen) ⊘ which have exposed traces of a Noric town inhabited by the first Roman settlers who came as traders in 1C BC.

Walk *(45min Rtn)* up to the top of the mountain (alt 1 058m - 3 470ft), where there is a Gothic pilgrims' chapel dedicated to St Helen and St Mary Magdalene, which houses a beautiful hinged panelled altarpiece (pre-1502) from the woodcarving workshops at St. Veit. There is a majestic **panorama**★ of the wooded Saualpe range, the Klagenfurt basin, the Karawanken and the great semi-mountainous area known as the Nockgebiet, to the northwest. Among the nearest heights is the Ulrichsberg (west) with Celtic temple ruins.

ST. WOLFGANG★★

Oberösterreich – Population 2 480

Michelin map 426 fold 20 - Local map under SALZKAMMERGUT - Alt 549m - 1 801ft

An invasion of visitors is no novelty for St. Wolfgang which stands beside a lake of the same name. It has been a place of pilgrimage since the 12C, and its church is enriched by magnificent works of art. This tradition explains, perhaps, why local life has not been upset by the modern influx of tourists, for whether it would or no the town has now become the country of the "White Horse Inn", of whose beautiful landscape and magnificent **lake**★★ praise was sung in the operetta of that name *(Weißes Rößl)*. The charm of St. Wolfgang is most strongly felt in the less busy periods either side of the main summer season and during the winter.

Access - Parking in St. Wolfgang can be difficult in summer. There are two car parks: at the entrance to the village and at the Schafberg station, 1km - half a mile beyond the church. In the high season a pleasant alternative is to arrive by **boat** ⊘, frequent services operate from Strobl and St. Gilgen and call in at Schafberg and the centre of St. Wolfgang.

CHURCH (PFARRKIRCHE) ⊘ *time: 1 hour*

This church was the successor to the chapel of a hermitage built, according to tradition, by St Wolfgang, Bishop of Regensburg (canonized 1052), who came to seek solitude on the shores of the "Abersee". The present structure dates from the second half of the 15C. Its site on a rocky spur and the need to

Altar by Michel Pacher, St. Wolfgang

accommodate as many pilgrims as possible have given rise to its irregular plan. It abuts on to the elegant structure of the 16C priory, which at one time was served by the Benedictines of Mondsee *(qv)*. The outer cloisters, lined with arcades which yield bird's-eye views of the lake, complete the charming character of the site★★.
Enter the church through the south door.

★★ **Michael-Pacher-Altar** – This masterpiece (1481), showing rare unity in composition and considered to be an outstanding example of Gothic art, was commissioned for the high altar by an abbot of Mondsee and made at Bruneck (Brunico) in South Tyrol, in the master's studio. Subjects for the various scenes were supplied to Pacher by the local bishop, Cardinal Nikolaus Cusanus, famous theologian and humanist of his time. It is certain that the carving of the central panel (Coronation of the Virgin) and the complementary paintings with gilded backgrounds on the shutters showing scenes from the life of the Virgin Mary, are by Michael Pacher himself. An explanation is available on how the various positions of the shutters were arranged to follow the liturgy.
Pacher reveals himself to be a master of perspective and of detail in this work. On the 12m - 39ft high altarpiece both form and expression are reproduced with consummate expertise.

★ **Schwanthaler-Doppelaltar** – This Baroque masterpiece was created by Thomas Schwanthaler in 1675-1676. On the left panel of this double-panelled altarpiece, executed in black and gold and placed in the middle of the nave, the Holy Family is depicted on their pilgrimage to Jerusalem. On the right panel is the figure of St Wolfgang. This exceptionally lively composition depicts more than 100 figures full of life and energy.
It is said that Thomas Schwanthaler dissuaded the abbot of Mondsee from replacing Pacher's altarpiece with his own during the conversion of the church to the Baroque style, but there is no evidence to corroborate this story. Modern visitors have the unusual chance here of visiting a village church and viewing two masterpieces which were created for it at an interval of two hundred years.
A third great artist was active at St. Wolfgang: the Mondsee master **Meinrad Guggenbichler**, to whom the three altars on the north side of the church, including the majestic Rosenkranzaltar, and the pulpit are attributed. His *Man of Sorrows* is particularly heart-rending.
The Schwanthaler family, from Ried in Bavaria, produced no less than 21 artists in a period of 250 years, the majority of whom were sculptors. One such was Ludwig Ritter von Schwanthaler, Court Sculptor to King Ludwig I of Bavaria, to whom we owe the Bavaria on the Theresienwiese in Munich.
After visiting the church, stroll along the lakeshore to the famous **Weißes Rößl** (White Horse Inn).

EXCURSION

★★ **Schafberg** ⊙ – *About 4 hours Rtn, including 2 hours by rack railway and 30min on foot.*
From the terminus, make for the hotel on the summit (alt 1 783m - 5 850ft), a few yards from the impressive precipice on the north face. It is said that from here one can count 13 lakes in the Salzkammergut; the most visible are the lakes of Mondsee, Attersee and St. Wolfgang. In the background, in succession, are the Höllengebirge, the Totes Gebirge, the Dachstein with its glaciers, the Tennengebirge, the Hochkönig, which can be recognized by its large patch of snow, the Steinernes Meer, the Berchtesgaden Alps and the Loferer Steinberge.

SCHLADMINGER TAUERN ★★

Steiermark

Michelin map 426 folds 20, 21, 34 and 35

This mountain chain is surrounded to the west by the Radstädter Tauern and to the east by the Wölzer Tauern. It stretches for 40km - 25 miles and towers over the broad **Ennstal** valley. On the other side of this valley, opposite and parallel to the Schladminger Tauern, is the majestic **Dachstein massif★★** *(see DACHSTEIN)*.
The contrast between these two mountain chains is surprising. Whereas the Dachstein has the appearance of a fortress with its limestone rocks, steep jagged cliffs and the essentially barren landscape which is its distinguishing feature, the Schladminger Tauern are made up mainly of crystalline rocks and are characterised by long, densely wooded and easily accessible valleys, in which there are numerous lakes and rivers.
It is precisely these varied landscapes that lend the Ennstal valley its special attraction, which was further enhanced by the growth in popularity of winter sports in the 1960s. It was then that the outlying slopes of the Schladminger Tauern with their smooth slopes were equipped with the appropriate infrastructure and thus became an important skiing area. Above these foothills of moderate height (peaks of

around 1 850 to 2 000m - 6 069 to 6 562ft), the heart of the chain consists of an Alpine area which towers above the valley, in places, by more than 2 000m - 6 562ft. The most famous peaks, from east to west, are the Hochwildstelle (alt 2 747m - 9 012ft), the Hochstein (2 545m - 8 350ft), the **Hochgolling** (2 863m - 9 393ft) and the Steirische Kalkspitze (2 459m - 8 067ft). Here, the hiker has access to wide-open, unspoilt areas with spectacular views, but only after a long and arduous climb.

The Ennstal valley is the optimum starting point for exploring the Schladminger Tauern and has become, over the years, a large centre for tourism with plenty of hotel and leisure facilities.

HOLIDAY RESORTS

✷ **Schladming** – Alt 745m - 2 444ft. This tradition-conscious town with a population of 4 000, which was established in the 12C, looks back over a turbulent history (to which the museum of local history and culture bears witness). Even in Roman times, silver was mined here. In the Middle Ages, nickel, cobalt and, above all, lead mines came into being; the Augsburg merchants alone are said to have employed 15 000 miners at that time. Yet devastating fires ravaged the town again and again, and the Farmers' Wars of 1525 likewise left their mark on Schladming. Thus, only a few traces of the past have survived. Nowadays, the town, whose main road has been redesigned to form a pedestrian precinct, presents a decidedly bustling and hospitable scene.

The downhill race which has been regularly arranged on the World Cup route since 1973, but above all the World Skiing Championships which were held here in 1982, have given Schladming plenty of publicity. Après-ski entertainment is also provided for, with generous sports facilities (swimming pool, indoor tennis courts, etc.). Schladming is an ideal destination for golfers, too, for whom there is a demanding 18-hole course at Oberhaus. In summer, a number of concerts are given every week in the St.-Anna-Kapelle.

Other holiday resorts in the valley include **Rohrmoos** (with its remarkably restful surroundings), Pichl, **Haus** (with a pretty Baroque church) and Pruggern.

However, many holidaymakers prefer the sunny plateau of **Ramsau** ✷ *(see DACHSTEIN)*, in order to enjoy the unspoilt countryside and enchanting setting of the Dachstein.

DACHSTEIN-TAUERN SKIING AREA

In order to be able to offer holidaymakers the largest possible hinterland, the resorts scattered between the Schladminger Tauern and the Dachstein have joined forces and issue a joint ski pass. The area comprises 78 lifts, 140km - 87 miles of downhill ski-runs and 350km - 217 miles of off-piste slopes. The **downhill ski-runs** ✷ are mainly concentrated on the Schladminger Tauern and consist of five areas: the **Reiteralm** (alt 800 to 1 860m - 2 625 to 6 102ft) above Pichl; the **Hochwurzen** (745 to 1 850m - 2 444 to 6 069ft) above Rohrmoos; the **Planai** (745 to 1 894m - 2 444 to 6 213ft) above Schladming; the **Hauser Kaibling** (752 to 2 015m - 2 467 to 6 611ft) above Haus; and the **Gaisterbergalm** (680 to 1 976m - 2 231 to 6 483ft) above Pruggern.

With the exception of Planai and Hochwurzen, the individual massifs are not connected to each other, which is why buses operate between the locations. The Dachstein-Tauern region is suitable, above all, for moderately good skiers, who will find suitable pistes on each massif, but less so for those who like open spaces and large differences in altitude. Good skiers, however, can try out their skills on the "east slope" of the Hauser Kaibling and on the World Cup piste on the Planai. The pistes along the Weitmoos ski-lift to Schladming and the Rohrmoos II chairlift are suitable for beginners.

The snow cover is good as a rule, but the moderate altitude can pose problems. The snow on the lower pistes, which are equipped with artificial snow cannon, is hard and icy at times and is therefore not suitable for inexperienced skiers. For cross-country skiers, the Schladminger Tauern provide 60km - 37 miles of cross-country ski-tracks all round Rohrmoos in beautiful, sunny surroundings, and a further 28km - 17 miles around Schladming. Cross-country skiers should spend their holidays on the **plateau** of **Ramsau am Dachstein** ✷ *(see DACHSTEIN)*: the internationally renowned **cross-country skiing area** ✷✷✷ there is distinguished by a particularly enchanting setting.

VIEWPOINTS

★★★ **Hunerkogel** – Alt 2 694m - 8 836ft. Wonderful view across the whole Schladminger Tauern chain. *See DACHSTEIN.*

★★ **Roßbrand** – Alt 1 770m - 5 807ft. *1 hour return trip by car (28km - 17 miles west of Schladming) followed by 20min there and back on foot.* Splendid view over the Ennstal valley with the Dachstein on one side and the Schladminger Tauern on the other. *See RADSTADT.*

★★ Planai ⊙ – Alt 1 906m - 6 253ft. *1 hour return trip from Schladming. Take the cable-car up, in 2 stages (sit facing the back). Also accessible via a small mountain (toll) road.*
The view from the mountain station at an altitude of 1 825m - 5 987ft is rather limited. Climb up on foot *(15min)* to the summit marked with a cross, from where there is a wonderful **panorama★★**. In winter, skiers can make the journey via the Burgstallalm piste and also the chairlift of the same name.
To the south, the Schladminger Tauern (Höchstein, Hochgolling, Steirische Kalkspitze) and behind them, further to the west, the Radstädter Tauern (Mosermandl) and the Hohe Tauern (Großglockner) can be seen. To the north tower the Hochkönig, the Steinernes Meer, the Tennengebirge, the Dachstein and the Tote Gebirge peaks.
Hikers can climb up to the **Krahbergzinken** (alt 2 134m - 7 001ft) in 2 hours 30min *(return trip).* An easy nature trail takes you round the summit of the Planai in 45min.

★★ Hochwurzen ⊙ – *Alt 1 849m - 6 066ft. 30min return trip. Accessible from Rohrmoos by cable-car or, in summer only, up a toll road. Climb to the summit up a flight of steps.* Remarkable **panorama★★** of the Dachstein opposite. View of Schladming. Walk as far as the terrace of the mountain inn, from where it is possible to see the heart of the Schladminger Tauern massif with the Hochgolling and Steirische Kalkspitze summits.

★ Hauser Kaibling ⊙ – *Alt 1 870m - 6 135ft. At least 45min return trip. Accessible from Haus by means of the Hauser Kaibling cable-car and also the Quattralpina chairlift. If these are closed, take the Schladminger Tauern cable-car.* **View★** across the Planai area and the Sonntagerhöhe. To the northeast looms the Stoderzinken and, behind it and to the right, the Großer Priel (Totes Gebirge). To the north, the Dachstein stretches as far as the Bischofsmütze.
Skiers should not fail to take the lift to the summit and then climb, in a few minutes, to the actual top of the Hauser Kaibling (Kreuz). Wonderful **panorama★★**, above all of the Hochstein. The view stretches as far as the Großglockner.

HIKES

The villages scattered throughout the Ennstal valley, and especially Schladming, are ideal starting points for **walks and hikes★★** in the relatively low-lying surrounding mountain ranges. A magnificent panorama can be enjoyed from a number of summits (Höchstein, Hochgolling), but because of the long climb involved, it is necessary to plan an overnight stay at the mountain lodge. A

Bodensee

Y. Bontoux

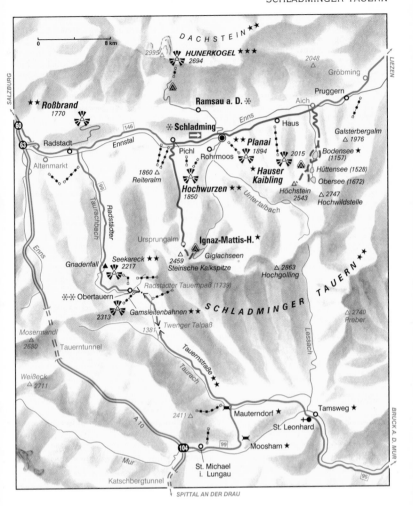

number of easily accessible excursions are described below, which we would recommend, above all, for holidaymakers who are staying in the region for a longish period, rather than for tourists who are only making a brief stay.

★ **Dreiseen-Rundweg circuit** – *45min drive for the return trip (17km - 11 miles east of Schladming). 45min easy walk as far as the sparkling Bodensee lake. For the full circuit round the three lakes, allow for a 4 hour return trip involving some quite taxing walking; the trip leads through a nature reserve. Drive on the E 651 towards Liezen then turn right, level with Aich, and continue on a small toll road towards the Bodensee.* From the car park, a broad trail leads *(15min)* to the **Bodensee**★, which is dominated by a beautiful waterfall. The walk round the lake *(just under 30min)* is a pleasant one. There is an inn on the shore of the lake. People who like hiking and who have sturdy footwear can walk along the western edge *(to the right)* to the far end of the lake and then take an hour or so to climb an arduous trail up to the Hans-Wödl-Hütte mountain lodge (alt 1 528m - 5 013ft) on the shores of the **Hüttensee**, a lake lying in an idyllic **setting**★. A beautiful spruce forest and two waterfalls, which plunge down from the rocky foothills of the Hochwildstelle and the Hochstein, form the backdrop.

In 45min, the trail takes you through luxuriant vegetation as far as the **Obersee** lake (alt 1 672m - 5 485ft), a crystal-clear, shallow expanse of water. Climb down to the Bodensee again and this time walk along its eastern edge.

Those keen on panoramic views may like to climb from the Hans-Wödl-Hütte mountain lodge up to the Hochstein (alt 2 543m - 8 343ft), allowing 6 hours there and back.

★ **Ignaz-Mattis-Hütte mountain lodge** – Alt 1 986m - 6 516ft. *1 hour return trip by car and 3 hours return trip on foot (difference in altitude: about 500m - 1 640ft). Travel by car to Pichl-Preunegg (5km - 3 miles west of Schladming on the E 651). Turn to the left towards Ursprungalm (14km - 9 miles).* **View**★ of

257

the Dachstein. After 6km - 4 miles, there is a toll station. The road is no longer tarmacked but is still drivable. Also accessible by bus *(enquire at the tourist office for departure times).*

From the car park at the end of the road, the picturesque hamlet of Ursprungalm at the foot of the **Steirische Kalkspitze** (alt 2 459m - 8 067ft) can be reached in a few minutes. Walk past the houses on the left-hand trail. After an hour's walk, the Giglachsee-Hütte mountain lodge comes in sight. Turn off to the left and carry on for another 20min to the Ignaz-Mattis-Hütte mountain lodge. From the footpath, there are a number of **views★** of the two **Giglachseen** lakes, set amidst beautiful unspoilt countryside. Climb down from the lodge to the lower lake, walk along on the other side as far as the Giglachsee-Hütte mountain lodge and then return to the car park on the same footpath that you climbed up.

SCHNEEBERG★

Niederösterreich

Michelin map 426 folds 24 and 25

The limestone bastions of the Raxalpe and the Schneeberg *(read pp 20f, An Alpine Country)* are separated by the deep valley of the Schwarza, called the Höllental (Hell Valley). The mountains are much frequented by the Viennese in summer and as soon as the first snows whiten the ski-runs of their summits in winter.

Without climbing these heights, motorists can at least skirt their wooded foothills, cut by wild ravines, by following the route described below.

★TOUR OF THE SCHNEEBERG

From Neunkirchen to Semmering

114km - 71 miles – about 4 hours (excluding the climb to the Schneeberg) – Local map opposite

From Neunkirchen take the road west.

Ternitz – Population 16 154. The chancel of this modern church (1959) is adorned with a large mosaic representing scenes from the Old *(left)* and New *(right)* Testaments. Interestingly, the chancel has been made the focal architectural feature of the building.

From Ternitz a pleasant road, sometimes under trees, runs up the delightful Sierning-bach valley. The Schneeberg can be recognized from afar by its bare slopes. A little before Puchberg rocky shelves become numerous on either side of the road.

Puchberg am Schneeberg – Population 3 190. This pleasant resort at the foot of the Schneeberg has an old castle and a ruined keep.

From Puchberg a mountain railway runs visitors up the Schneeberg.

★ **Schneeberg** ⊙ – *Allow half to a whole day for the ascent (1 hour 15min) from the station at Puchberg, depending on the timetable of the rack railway.* Near the Hochschneeberg terminus (alt 1 795m - 5 889ft), clinging to the mountainside, in a fine position above the Puchberg basin, is a hotel. End the excursion by walking up *(about 2 hours 30min Rtn)* to the **Kaiserstein** (alt 2 061m - 6 762ft – **panorama★** of the Pre-Alps) and to the **Klosterwappen** spur (**view★** of the Raxalpe, beyond the Höllental). This, with an altitude of 2 076m - 6 811ft, is the highest point of the massif.

After Puchberg the road, still picturesque, winds among fir trees, following the courses of torrents with numerous sawmills dotted along their banks.

The route goes round the north of the Schneeberg massif and joins the fine Schwarza valley, which soon narrows, forming the Höllental.

★★ **Höllental** – *See HÖLLENTAL.*

★ **Raxalpe** – This steep sided limestone massif has become a regular climbing centre owing to its proximity to Vienna. Its walls contain several hundred named and numbered tunnels. A much used cable-car, starting above Hirschwang, reaches the edge of the upper plateau at 1 547m - 5 075ft. The upper plateau is a typical limestone shelf, with various **views★**: the Semmering Massif to the south, and the Kaiserstein and the Höllental to the north. Several hotels and refuges are ready to receive tourists.

South of Hirschwang the road leaves the Schwarza valley, and with many bends cuts across a picturesque, rugged region of wooded spurs and ravines. The difficulties of the terrain did not daunt the builders of the Semmering railway, who accomplished monumental engineering feats.

★ **Raxblick** – Between Hirschwang and Orthof, turn off the route for a moment to this spur below an isolated hotel. It forms a viewpoint overlooking the Raxalpe.

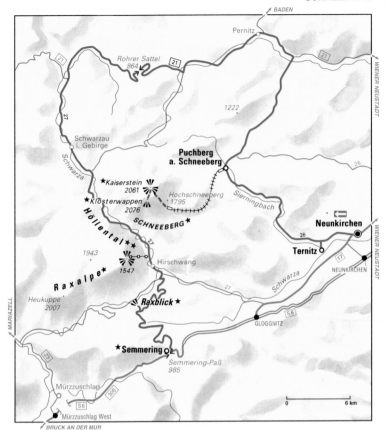

★ **Semmering** – Population 730. This mountain spa and winter sports centre, built on terraces between 985m and 1 291m - 3 231ft and 4 235ft, enjoys a privileged position. It does not suffer from the cold fogs of the valleys and has an exceptionally sunny climate, which helps to make it one of the greatest centres of attraction in Lower Austria. Hotels and villas nestle in greenery on the sheltered slopes of the Semmering pass.

The road leading to the pass was relaid in 1842 on the Gloggnitz slope, with a maximum gradient of 1 in 17. It and the railway constructed in 1854, the first main line in the high mountains in Europe, do honour to the engineers of Imperial Austria.

SCHWAZ★

Tirol – Population 10 930
Michelin map 426 fold 17 – Alt 538m - 1 765ft

From the 15C to 16C when its **silver and copper mines** were in full production, Schwaz was the most densely populated town in the Tyrol, after Innsbruck. The town was well cared for by the Emperor and the financial powers of the period, especially the Fugger family of Augsburg. The degree of prosperity it enjoyed is attested today by the unusual size and the decoration of its most representative buildings, all erected between 1450 and 1520.

This extravagant period also survives in popular tradition, according to which the miners of the past could make the paving of Schwaz ring with the silver nails in their boots.

Modern visitors can get a good idea of working conditions in the mines by visiting a display mine, **Schaubergwerk** ⊘.

★PARISH CHURCH (PFARRKIRCHE) *time: 30min*

The church façade, bristling with pinnacles in the Swabian style, stands at the end of Franz-Josef-Straße. Under a huge roof, covered with 15 000 copper tiles, it shelters four aisles and two parallel chancels, restored in 1912 to their Gothic style of the 15C, with network vaulting. The main south aisle and its side aisle were reserved for the miners' corporation, as certain tombs indicate.

259

The organ-loft shows particularly elaborate Gothic decoration in the vaulting supporting it and in its balustrade. The Baroque organ-case is quite sumptuous. In the main part of the church, there are traces of the Gothic furnishings: the octagonal font of 1470 and, against the pillar separating the two chancels, a Christ with a very intense expression. The finest piece of religious sculpture is the **altar of St Anne** in the south side aisle. Its Baroque altarpiece (1733), honouring the patron saints of Austria, St George and St Florian, frames a fine group of the early 16C: the Holy Family between St Elizabeth on the right and St Ursula on the left.

The gardens climbing up the slope to the south are graced by two fine **cloister walks**★ with pointed vaults.

ADDITIONAL SIGHT

Franziskanerkirche – The Gothic church was finished in 1515. In the layout of its three naves it was in accordance with the strict building rules imposed by the Order. Its conversion to the Baroque style in 1736 destroyed neither its pleasant proportions nor its good lighting. The capitals on the tall marble columns, reduced to simple rings, have a decorative function. The Renaissance **stalls**★ (1618) are the work of a local master-craftsman.

Cloisters (Kreuzgang) – *Entrance through the door of the monastery on the south side of the church.* The cloisters are pure Gothic in style. They contain important remains of wall paintings representing scenes from the Passion (1519-1526), attributed to a brother who came from Swabia. Charming designs of foliage, fruit and birds have adorned the vaulting since the beginning of the 17C. The community of Schwaz is symbolized by various shields: craftsmen and miners' guilds, as well as wealthy shareholders are shown. The Emperor Maximilian is represented by the arms of his hereditary states.

EXCURSION

Schloß Tratzberg ☯ – *5 km - 3 miles. Leave Schwaz on the road to Stans.* Standing half way up the steep slope overlooking the left bank of the Inn, this austere castle is the result of two distinct phases of building. Its severe exterior, still very medieval in appearance, dates from around 1500; other elements, like the painted arcades, were added some 60 years later in conformity with the taste of the Renaissance. For a while the castle was the property of the Fuggers, the powerful merchant dynasty from Augsburg, who had interests in the Schwaz area (*Silberberg* – "silver mountain, mine"). For the last 150 years it has belonged to the ducal family of the Enzenbergs.

The castle's roof is covered in larch shingles. Inside, there is still some original furniture, as well as pictures and weapons. The ceiling of the royal chamber (Königinzimmer) of 1569 is a magnificent timber construction, held together without a single nail. The Habsburg Room is also of interest; it contains a 46m - 151ft long wall painting (dating probably from 1508) which depicts 148 of the Emperor Maximilian's ancestors in the form of a family tree.

Schloß Tratzberg

Abtei SECKAU

The abbey at Seckau, founded in 1140, was run by Augustinian canons, and from 1218 was also diocesan seat, until its dissolution by Joseph II in 1782. The bishop of Styria, who now resides at Graz, nonetheless still has the official title "Graz-Seckau". In 1883, Benedictine monks from Beuron abbey came and took over the abbey at Seckau, thus preventing it from falling into ruin.

The extensive abbey complex, whose corner towers lend it a somewhat military air, stands majestically at the foot of the Seckau Alps (Niedere Tauern).

★ BASILICA *time: 30min*

The body of the church, which dates from about 1150, was built with alternating piers and columns topped with huge square capitals with little decoration, in accordance with the Romanesque German tradition. Since the end of the 15C the internal unity has been broken by the rich network vaulting of the main nave – originally roofed with timber – by the 19C transept and by the changes in the chancel, which the Benedictines, installed in the abbey since the late 19C, ordered in the taste of the period. A simple but moving **Crucifixion** is especially noteworthy; the figure of Christ Crucified dates from 1220, while those of Mary and Joseph probably date from the mid-12C.

Three chapels, of differing periods and arrangements, spring from the north aisle. They are interesting for their works of art. The first one, the **Engelkapelle** (Angel's Chapel), contains a huge composition, inspired by the Apocalypse, by Herbert Boeckl (1960).

Sakramentskapelle – Over the tabernacle in the chapel of the Blessed Sacrament is a 12C alabaster of Venetian origin, representing the Virgin and Child. This is the jewel of the Seckau Treasury and the oldest Marian image venerated in Austria.

Bischofskapelle – The **altarpiece★★** of the high altar (1489) in the Episcopal Chapel, celebrates the Coronation of the Virgin. In a circular framework, which is itself most unusual, the artist has represented the three persons of the Holy Trinity with identical features, in strict conformity with the orthodox definition, three Persons in one God. Stand back a little to see with what talent the sculptor has mastered so difficult a subject, for the slightest error of taste in this group of three heads on one body would have been fatal.

Mausoleum of Karl II – The Mausoleum of Archduke Karl II stands in the chapel which forms a prolongation of the north side aisle. Together they form a decorative scheme which is regarded as a specimen of the transition from late Renaissance to Baroque art. As it was carried out by two Italians between 1587 and 1612, it also marks the beginning of the penetration of transalpine taste into Austria. This influence, which appeared in a dazzling fashion rather later in the mausoleum in Graz of Ferdinand II (the son of Archduke Karl), was naturally felt first in Styria.

SEEFELD IN TIROL★★

Seefeld lies on a broad mountain plateau, well-exposed to the sun, with thick surrounding forest cover and a good view of the rocky ridges of the Hohe Munde, Wettersteingebirge and Karwendel range. It has become one of the most popular cross-country skiing resorts in the Alps.

In the 1930s, Seefeld was already making a name for itself worldwide with the help of local skier Toni Seelos, who had mastered slalom like no other and who made a tremendous contribution to the technique of skiing *(see chapter on skiing)*. The village only really began to develop for tourism in the 1950s and 1960s, however, and its reputation grew even more after it had been the venue for the Nordic skiing events of the 1964 and 1976 Winter Olympic Games as well as for the World Skiing Championships of 1985.

The sophisticated ski resort boasts elegant hotels and restaurants, and a variety of excellent leisure facilities, including a large sports and congress centre, a remarkable swimming pool, two ice-rinks (with a skating school), numerous curling rinks and a casino. In summer these are augmented by an 18-hole golf course, 29 tennis courts and two riding schools.

But the principal charm of this resort lies in the refreshing landscape which surrounds it, which lends itself to walking at any time of year. Seefeld can offer, incredibly enough, 60km - 37 miles of excellently maintained footpaths in winter and 150km - 93 miles in the summer *(maps and guides available from the tourist office)*. The best walk is that up to the **Reither Spitze★** *(see below)*. For those who prefer a less taxing walk, there is the circuit linking the lakes of Wildmoossee, Lottensee and Mösersee *(3 hours walk from the Seekirchl chapel)*.

Ski slopes – Seefeld boasts one of the largest cross-country skiing areas✼✼✼ in the Alps, with 200km - 124 miles of tracks. Good snow cover is usually guaranteed from Christmas to March.

For downhill skiers, the resort has somewhat less potential (only 25km - 16 miles of ski-runs) and is furthermore divided into two areas, each of which requires a separate ski-pass. A chairlift leads from near the Kreuzsee up to the Geschwandtkopf summit (alt 1 500m - 4 921ft). The most interesting slopes are to be found on the Seefelder Joch and more especially the Härmelekopf. The area is ideally suited to beginners or those who prefer gentle skiing.

SIGHTS

Pfarrkirche – This Gothic church was erected, with the generosity of the Princes of the Tyrol, in the 15C, to perpetuate the worship of a miraculous host, which had been an object of pilgrimage since 1384 and was kept until 1949 in the high chapel of the Holy Blood.

The tympanum of the south door represents, on the right, the martyrdom of St Oswald of England, the patron saint of the church, and, on the left, the miracle of the host. Inside there is network vaulting with slender ribs characteristic of the late Gothic style. In the chancel, the mural paintings of the 15C (legend of St Oswald, the Passion, legend of St Mary Magdalene) have been restored. On the right, a picture (1502) of the late Gothic period depicts the miracle of the host.

> The **Golden Chronicle of Hohenschwangau** records the miraculous event. One day, at the conclusion of Mass, the knight Oswald Milser and his armed followers surrounded the priest. His head covered and brandishing his sword, the arrogant nobleman insisted that his rank gave him the right to eat the same special wafer as the priest himself. Forced to comply, the man of God offered it to Milser. Suddenly the ground opened up beneath the feet of the sacrilegious knight. His whole body shaking with fear, he was only just able to cling to the altar, where his fingers left their mark as in wax. The priest retrieved the wafer and the ground became firm again, though the wafer was covered in blood.

Seekirchl – This chapel stands on the shores of the Kreuzsee at the west end of the village. It was built in 1666 and has a ground plan in the form of a rotunda which is most unusual for the Tyrol. The lovely building with its onion domed tower makes a charming sight.

EXCURSIONS

★★ Seefelder Joch ⓥ – Alt 2 074m - 6 804ft. *Take the funicular up to the Roßhütte mountain refuge (alt 1 800m - 5 906).* Then take the Seefelderjochbahn. From the mountain station, it takes a few minutes to reach the cross at the summit, from where there is a beautiful **panorama★★**. To the east are the Karwendel mountains, and to the north lies the Scharnitz pass road. To the northwest towers the long-drawn-out rocky ridge of the Wetterstein range, with the Zugspitze plateau at its edge. To the west, the view covers Seefeld and the broad Inn valley behind it, framed by the Hohe Munde (Mieminger Gebirge) and Rietzer Grießkogel.

Even in winter, it is possible to walk from the Roßhütte down into the valley. Sturdy, waterproof shoes are however essential.

★★ Hike to Reither Spitze – Alt 2 374m -.7 789ft. *For experienced hikers only.* From the Seefelder Joch, follow the ridge path to the Seefelder Spitze (alt 2 221m - 7 287ft), then take the path down to the Reither Scharte. This eventually brings you to the Reither Spitze, from where there is a magnificent **panorama★★** as far as the Ziller valley and the Stubai Alps. Climb down to the Nördlinger Hütte, and then walk on to the Hämelekopf cable-car station. Either walk the final part of the circuit down towards Reither Alm, or take the cable-car.

SEEFELDER SATTELSTRASSEN★★

Tirol und Bayern (Germany)
Michelin map 426 folds 16, 17, 30 and 31

The Seefelder Sattel, or Seefeld Saddle, high above the Inn valley and the Scharnitz ravine, makes a broad breach in the Northern Limestone Alps along the Munich-Innsbruck axis. The road is of great tourist interest but international traffic uses the lengthier but less mountainous motorway route following the Inn valley.

★ ZIRLERBERG

From Innsbruck to Mittenwald

38km - 24 miles - about 5 hours

★★ Innsbruck - *See INNSBRUCK.*

★★ Hafelekar - *See INNSBRUCK: Excursions.*

Between Innsbruck and Zirl the road, following the floor of the Inn valley, runs beneath the steep slopes of the **Martinswand** opposite the tributary valley of Sellrain. This promontory marks the traditional boundary between the upper and lower Inn valley and provided the setting for an episode dear to the hearts of the Tyrolese: Emperor Maximilian is said to have fallen down the cliff in the excitement of the hunt and been saved from a perilous plight by an angel, appearing in the guise of a peasant.

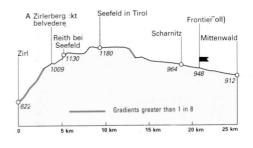

The well known **Zirlerberg**★ slope covers the 500m - 1 640ft difference in altitude between Zirl and Reith bei Seefeld. It was as steep as 1 in 4 in places before improvement – it now being 1 in 7 – and it is said that every weekend spectators posted themselves at vantage points on the lookout for accidents. The only hairpin bend in this section is now an organized **viewpoint**★, with a car park and bar, which has a view of the sawteeth of the Kalkkögel opposite in the middle distance. Higher up in this ascent, in line with the road, to the northwest, is the surprisingly smooth hump of the **Hohe Munde.**

Leave the modern highway for the old road which goes through the centre of Reith.

★ Reith bei Seefeld – Population 790. The church stands in a charming **setting**★ facing the small Roskogel range and the jagged crests of the Kalkkögel, which lie south of the Inn valley.

✵✵ Seefeld in Tirol – *See SEEFELD IN TIROL.*

North of Seefeld the **view**★ becomes extensive and embraces, from left to right, the summit of the Hohe Munde, the **Wetterstein** ridge (except for the Zugspitze), the Arnspitze and the first peaks of the Karwendel. The road drops quickly to the floor of a valley leading to the Isar and reaches the mouth of the Scharnitz ravine, gateway to Bavaria; 6km - 4 miles over the border is Mittenwald.

★ Mittenwald – *Description in the Michelin Green Guide Germany.*

★★ LEUTASCH VALLEY

From Mittenwald to Telfs

32km - 20 miles - about 2 hours 30min - local map overleaf

This route combines a run through the secluded Leutasch valley and a visit to Mösern, one of the most attractive viewpoints in the upper Inn valley.
German-Austrian border between Mittenwald and Leutasch.

★ Mittenwald – *Description in the Michelin Green Guide Germany.*

South of Mittenwald the road comes out of the Isar valley and immediately climbs above the **Leutasch Gorge** (Leutaschklamm) within view of the Karwendel Massif (Viererspitze).

Over a bridge across the Leutascher Ache it runs into the grassy combe of Unterleutasch, majestically bounded on the left by the Arnspitze, and on the right by the rock walls of the Wettersteinwand, from which spring the promontories of the Öfelekopf and the Gehrenspitzen. A few roofed crosses and occasional houses with roofs weighed down with big stones are dotted about this lonely valley, preserving its primitive air. Ahead, the Hohe Munde rises in line with the road.

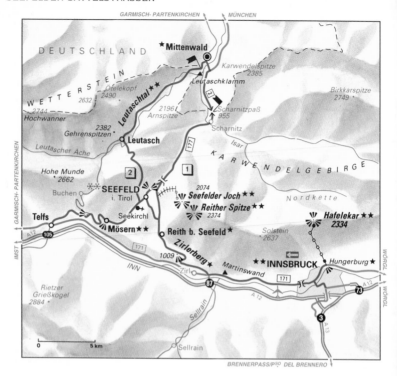

Leutasch – Population 1 670. Holiday resort.

From Leutasch onwards the road runs through a well-wooded area of irregular relief to Seefeld.

※※ **Seefeld in Tirol** – *See SEEFELD IN TIROL.*

A charming rotunda chapel **(Seekircherl)** marks the beginning of a valley which climbs 600m - 2 000ft above the Inn valley.

★★ **Mösern** – Population 130. This is a superbly sited village. It has been identified as forming the background to the Dürer self-portrait of 1498 in the Prado at Madrid. No better place for a picnic!

The **view**★★ is particularly fine. Upstream the Inn can be seen winding along the floor of the Telfs furrow and then slipping into a tangle of crests among which, on the horizon, the Hoher Riffler (alt 3 168m - 10 394ft) stands flecked with snow. Further to the right, the green terrace of the Mieming Plateau (Mieminger Hochland) can be seen at the foot of the Mieming range, which ends at the great dome of the Hohe Munde. South of the valley rise the Sellrain mountains, and, in the middle distance, the jagged crests of the Kalkkögel.

The quick descent, mostly through woods, from Mösern to Telfs is of interest for the panorama in the bend after the Buchen fork (views of the Miemingergebirge).

Telfs – Population 10 180. This market town, first recorded in 1175, has quite an urban character. The local museum contains costumes and masks from the **Telfser Schleicherlaufen** *(see Calendar of events at the end of the guide).*

SILVRETTASTRASSE★★

Vorarlberg und Tirol

Michelin map 426 folds 28 and 29 – Local map under ARLBERGGEBIET

From Partenen to Landeck

73km - 45 miles. A 2 hour drive. Including the hike to the Hoher Rad, allow at least one day. Ischgl is the ideal place to find lodging in the evening.
The actual Silvrettastraße (Partenen to Galtür road) is barred to caravans. There are 30 narrow bends to negotiate on the road on the western slope, which can cause many a surprise for the driver who is not familiar with Alpine roads. The Silvrettastraße is usually blocked by snow from November to the end of May.

The Silvretta-Hochalpenstraße road links the Illtal valley (**Montafon**★ *described under entry of this name*) and the Trisannatal valley (Paznauntal) via the Bielerhöhe pass (alt 2 036m -.6 680ft). The bleak Alpine character of this pass is somewhat softened by a pleasant artificial lake.

In **Partenen** (holiday resort), where a power station uses the water brought up by pressurised pipelines from the Vermunt reservoir, the road begins to climb, covering a difference in altitude of 1 000m - 3 281ft. It leads across a scree-covered valley slope, with nothing very much to soften the inhospitable-looking surroundings. However, the numerous tight hair-pin bends which follow close on one another's heels up the mountainside make the drive quite dramatic.

Vermunt-Stausee – This lake forms an intermediate reservoir between Partenen and the Silvrettatal valley, at an altitude of 1 743m - 5 718ft. The water collected in this artificial lake reaches the power station at Partenen through pressurised pipelines. The **view**★ towards the wild Kromertal valley stretches as far as the mountain ridges of the Großer Litzner and Großer Seehorn (alt 3 124m - 10 249ft).

While the road winds upwards to the mountain pass, which has been polished smooth by glaciers, the Silvretta dam and mountain summit come gradually into view above the upper lake.

Bielerhöhe – The **Silvretta-Stausee**★, at 2 036m - 6 680ft above sea level, blends superbly into the **Alpine landscape**★★. People are glad to take a break here, and mountaineers and those on ski tours use the large hotels as a starting point for their trips around the Silvretta mountains.

The reservoir is the principal component of the power station at Ill. The water collected by the dam reaches the Rodund power station below Schruns in the Montafon region via a number of intermediary reservoirs, and then flows freely on its way again from that point.

A walk along the dam (432m - 1 417ft long and 80m - 262ft high) gives a remarkable **view**★ of the surrounding mountains. The countryside can best be explored on a walk round the lake.

★★ **Walk round the Silvretta-Stausee reservoir** – *An easy hike (about 1 hour 45min).* Walk first along the east shore of the lake at the foot of the dark, pointed pyramid of the Hohes Rad. The route is bordered by several waterfalls and numerous Alpine rose bushes. The return path leads along the west shore, towering above which is the Lobspitze. On this trip there are a number of splendid **views**★★ of

Vermunt reservoir

the Schattenspitze peak to the south, the Klostertal valley with the Tällispitze and Sonntagspitze peaks to the south-west, the Hochmaderer to the west and the Vallüla massif to the north.

★★★ **Ascent to the Hohes Rad** – *Park in the car park at the east end of the lake. The hike (allow 5 hours 30min not including breaks and with a climb to the Hohes Rad of over 800m - 2 625ft) is suitable for experienced walkers. Waterproof climbing boots and warm, knee-high socks are essential. The outstanding beauty and diversity of the landscape are ample reward for the exertion. Those with less stamina should content themselves with the footpath to the Wiesbadener Hütte mountain lodge (allow 2 hours 15min there and 2 hours back).*

It takes about 45min to walk the length of the entire lake. The footpath then leads uphill through the Ochsental valley alongside the gushing waters of the Jil, which is fed by numerous waterfalls and brooks. To the right, the splendid valley is enclosed by an impressive reddish wall of rock. Gradually, all the peaks in the area come into view (the Kleine Schattenspitze, the Kleiner Egghörner, the Schattenspitze, the Schneeglocken with a small glacier and the Silvrettahorn). Most eye-catching of all, however, is the glacial cirque which closes off the valley.

Piz Buin peak and glacial cirque

From the **Wiesbadener Hütte** mountain lodge (alt 2 443m - 8 015ft), there is a wonderful **view★★** of the highest peak in the Silvretta group, the **Piz Buin** (alt 3 312m - 10 866ft), which is flanked by the Vermunt glacier (on the left) and the Oschsental glacier (on the right).

Next comes a 1 hour 30min climb to the Radsattel. Turn left past the mountain lodge and follow the **Edmund-Lorenz-Weg trail** which climbs steeply at first but then leads straight ahead without too noticeable a slope. From this trail, there are a number of particularly beautiful **views★★** of the entire valley. The trail leads down to a small lake (alt 2 532m - 8 307ft), shimmering in amazing shades of colour from orange to green and lying in a splendid setting at the foot of the Rauherkopf glacier. From this point, the trail leads uphill, with one or two steep bends, as far as the **Radsattel** (alt 2 652m - 8 701ft), which forms the boundary between Vorarlberg and the Tyrol. There is a superb **panorama★★**, to the west, of the Großer Litzner and all the glaciers already mentioned. To the east lies the Bieltal valley, which likewise has a glacier towering above it.

The footpath climbs slightly as it leads along the foot of the rocky foothills of the Hohes Rad, before crossing numerous glacial snowfields and then leading over a slight incline until, after 45min, it comes to the **Radschulter★★** (alt 2 697m - 8 843ft). About a hundred metres before the pass, the Radsee lake, with its partially ice-covered waters tinged a dark green, comes into sight beneath the Madlener Spitze peak. From the pass, there is an impressive **view★★** of the Bieltal and Rauerkopf glaciers, which tower upwards out of a rocky, almost lunar landscape.

Experienced hikers, who have a good head for heights and are not too tired by this stage, may like to climb up to the left to the **Hohes Rad★★★** summit (alt 2 934m - 9 626ft). The rocky trail makes this quite a demanding detour, for which you should allow about 1 hour 30min there and back, but at the end of it, a **360°** **panorama** of the Silvretta range and reservoir will make you forget all your exertions.

The walk down from the Radschulter takes 1 hour 30min. The very steep **route**★★ leading between two rock walls is covered by a thick layer of snow well into August *(fold the top end of your socks over your boots so that no snow gets into your boots)*. After the rocks have been left behind, the landscape suddenly becomes green. To the east, the Madlener Spitze peak with its glacier can be seen and (opposite) to the north, the Kleinvermunttal valley, dominated by the mighty Vallüla massif.

For the last part of the walk, the trail is covered with splendid alpine roses and yellow gentians, and provides a number of magnificent **views**★★ of the Silvretta reservoir with the Hochmaderer in the background.

Return to the car.

On the Tyrolean side of the Bielerhöhe, the pastoral valley of Kleinvermunt, in which cattle can be seen grazing, provides a number of views of the Lobspitze and Madlenerspitze peaks.

Turn left. After 5km - 3 miles, the road reaches the **Kops-Stausee**★ (alt 1 809m - 5 935ft), flanked by the Ballunspitze to the south, the Versalspitze to the west and the Fluhspitzen peaks to the north. Return to the main road and drive on to Galtür.

Galtür – Alt 1 584m - 5 197ft. Population 700. This pretty village on the slopes of the Ballunspitze, which can accommodate 3 400 visitors, provides a small but interesting skiing area above the Kops reservoir. 11 ski lifts lead to 40km - 25 miles of piste covering all degrees of difficulty. With 45km - 28 miles of cross-country tracks and good snow cover, it also has plenty to offer cross-country skiers.

Between Galtür and Ischgl, in the upper Paznauntal valley, the forest cover becomes more dense, and stands of larch can be distinguished from the surrounding trees by their lighter colour.

✳✳ **Ischgl** – *See ISCHGL.*

The Trisannatal valley now narrows still further and becomes increasingly picturesque and rugged. Villages lie high up on mountain plateaux or on mountain ledges (such as the holiday resort of **Kappl**). The road leads alongside the mountain torrent, through fairly dense forest. After a long drive, the appearance of the Burg Wiesberg heralds the famous Trisannabrücke bridge.

Towering in the background are the mighty mountain ridges of the Parseier-spitze (alt 3 036m - 9 961ft), the highest peak of the Kalkhoch Alps in the north of Austria.

★ **Trisannabrücke bridge** – *See ARLBERGGEBIET.*

Landeck – *See LANDECK.*

SÖLDEN ✳✳

Tirol – Population 2 761

Michelin map 426 fold 30 – Local map under ÖTZTAL

With an area of 468km² - 181sq miles, only 1km² - 1.2sq miles of which is inhabited, and surrounded by more than 90 summits of over 3 000m - 9 842ft, Sölden is the largest municipality in Austria. This old Tyrolean village, situated 1 368m - 4 488ft above sea level, has developed into an important winter sports and summer holiday resort and constitutes the tourist centre of the **Ötztal**★★ valley *(see ÖTZTAL)*. Sölden lies strung out along a deeply incised, wooded valley, with the Gaislacher Kogel towering over it.

The little village of **Hochsölden** (alt 2 083m - 6 834ft) occupies a beautiful mountain-side site and offers excellent snow cover and extensive views.

Sölden owes its popularity to the quality of its après-ski entertainment. It offers a wide range of sports facilities (an ice stadium and a large sports centre, offering about thirty different types of sport, with a swimming pool and tennis courts), but the winter sports resort is distinguished, above all, by the lively atmosphere of its cafés and discothèques, which are frequented until well into the early hours by crowds of happy holidaymakers.

Ski slopes – Although relatively modest in size (23 ski lifts and 72km - 45 miles of pistes), these are highly regarded because of the considerable difference in altitude they cover (1 377 to 3 058m - 4 518 to 10 033ft). Snow cover is generally good from Christmas to March around Hochsölden. Since none of the pistes presents any special difficulties, they are well suited to a more relaxed style of skiing. Two long descents are particularly worth recommending: that leading down from the Gaislacher Kogel to the valley station of the Stabele chairlift (**view**★ over the Ötztaler glacier road), and that linking the Hainbachjoch with Sölden. Less experienced skiers should use the piste (above Hochsölden) leading along the route taken by the Silberbrünnl chairlift, followed by the broad trail through the woods from Gaislachalm.

SÖLDEN

The **Ötztaler Gletscherstraße★★** ⓥ, one of the highest roads in the Alps (highest point: 2 822m - 9 258ft), is open from spring to autumn. It gives access to a summer skiing area (29km - 18 miles of piste and 10 ski lifts) in a beautiful Alpine landscape on the Rettenbachfern and Tiefenbachfern glaciers.
There is also the possibility of driving to nearby Vent and, in particular, to **Hochgurgl-Obergurgl**⋇, where there are further downhill ski-runs. *However, the Sölden ski pass is not valid here.*
Cross-country skiers have only 8km - 5 miles of cross-country tracks available to them in Sölden, 8km - 5 miles in Zwieselstein and 3km - 1.9 miles in Vent.

VIEWPOINTS

★★ **Gaislacher Kogel** ⓥ – Alt 3 056m - 10 026ft. *1 hour return trip. Sturdy footwear is required for walking on the summit. Ascent via cable-car in two stages.*
During the first section, there is a view of the locality, which is dominated by the Söldenkogel and the Rotkogel. From the mountain station of the second stage the cross at the summit can be reached on foot in a few minutes.
From here there is a splendid **panorama★★** of the peaks and glaciers of the Ötztal alps. In particular, the Wildspitze (alt 3 772m - 12 375ft) can be seen to the south west, following the line of the cable-car. Towering up to the right of it are the Pitztal peaks (the Watzespitze and Hohe Geige). To the left, are the Weißkugel (alt 3 738m - 12 264ft), the Fineilspitze (alt 3 514m - 11 529ft), the Similaun (alt 3 606m - 11 831ft) and the Großer Ramolkogel (alt 3 550m - 11 647ft), all of which have at least one glacier. The skiing area of Hochgurgl lies to the south at the foot of the Kirchenkogel and, in the distance, the Dolomites. To the east, the view stretches as far as the Stubai Alps, the highest mountain of which is the Zuckerhütl (alt 3 507m - 11 506ft).

Giggijochbahn ⓥ – Walk round the terrace of the mountain station, from where there is a beautiful **view** of the Sölden ski slopes, from the Gaislacher Kogel to the Hainbachjoch which, at 2 727m - 8 947ft above sea level, is the highest peak in the Hochsölden skiing area. It is flanked by the Roßkirpl on the left and by the Breitlehner on the right. To the east lie the Söldenkogel, the Rotkogel and the Gurgltal valley.

EXCURSIONS

★★ **Ventertal**

This beautiful long valley is surrounded by glaciers on all sides and provides wonderful opportunities for hiking.

★★ **Road from Zwieselstein to Rofen** – *16km - 10 miles. 20min.* The road leads through a delightful wooded area and, 6km - 4 miles further on, passes through the hamlet of Heiligenkreuz, in which there is a chapel with a pretty, onion-shaped tower.
After a further 7km - 4 miles, the road reaches **Vent** (alt 1 900m - 2 953ft), the only holiday resort in the valley. In winter, Vent is an unpretentious winter sports location which nevertheless has remarkably good snow cover and offers good skiers the challenge of steep slopes. It has 15km - 9 miles of piste at altitudes of between 1 900 and 2 680m - 6 234 and 8 793ft, and 4 ski lifts. In summer, the number of holidaymakers is substantially greater since the opportunities for trips into the high mountains are simply inexhaustible. After Vent, the valley splits into two parts on either side of the imposing Talleitspitze peak (alt 3 406m - 11 174ft). The **Rofental** valley, which is situated on the right, runs alongside the **Wildspitze** (alt 3 768m - 12 362ft) and the **Hochvernagtspitze** (alt 3 535m - 11 598ft) peaks before being blocked by the **Weißkugel** (alt 3 738m - 12 264ft); the **Niedertal** valley on the left of the Talleitspitze peak runs along at the foot of the Ramolkogel (alt 3 549m - 11 644ft) and the Schalfkogel (alt 3 537m - 11 604ft) It ends in the glacial basin of the **Similaun** (alt 3 599m - 11 808ft). All these peaks cause the amateur mountaineer's heart to beat faster since they are, after all, the goal of legendary mountain expeditions.
A road leads as far as Rofen, the highest-lying permanently inhabited hamlet in Austria (alt 2 014m - 6 608ft). The climb to Rofen *(1 hour 30min return trip)* makes a pleasant walk for a family: follow the road and cross the mountain torrent on a small suspension bridge. A good footpath, bordered by ledges, leads back to Vent. It offers picturesque views of the valley floor.

★ **Wildspitze-Sesselbahn** ⓥ – *Leave the car in Vent at the chairlift (there is a charge for the car park). 10min travelling time.* From the mountain station (alt 2 356m - 7 730ft), there is a beautiful **view★** of the skiing area, the Talleitspitze peak and in particular, in the background, the glaciers which surround the Ramolkogel and the Schalfkogel.

A number of hikes starting from the mountain station of the chairlift are suggested below. Fit, experienced hikers may like to climb up to the Wildes Mannle or walk to the Vernagthütte mountain lodge. Less experienced hikers should opt for walking to the Breslau Hütte mountain lodge.

★★★ **Wildes Mannle** - *Climbing boots are essential, and binoculars are recommended. This hike is for hikers with good levels of stamina: 3 hours on foot and a 670m - 2 198ft difference in altitude, going straight there and back. The complete circuit described below, which includes a climb to the Breslau Hütte mountain lodge via the Rofensteig footpath, is recommended only to experienced hikers, since it involves a number of extremely steep, vertiginous passages. Allow about 4 hours - difference in altitude 800m - 2 625ft.*

Walk from the mountain station of the chairlift towards the Breslau Hütte mountain lodge. After half an hour's walk, turn off to the right *(waymarker)* onto a narrower trail. The view becomes more and more breathtaking during the climb. Look out for the markers and "WM" indications. Towards the end, the path gets very steep and rocky, but does not present any real difficulties. From the peak (alt 3 023m - 9 918ft), which is marked with a cross, there is a splendid **panorama**★★★ of about fifteen glaciers belonging to the Ötztal Alps, the most impressive and closest of which is the Rofenkar glacier, covering a difference in altitude of 1 000m - 3 281ft on the slopes of the Wildspitze. Chamois are often to be seen in this region. To the west, notice the Breslau Hütte lodge at the foot of a rocky amphitheatre which is easy to make out because of its reddish colour. A detour to this mountain lodge is a pleasant extension of this hike. Those with a poor head for heights should first follow the same trail as on the way there and then turn off towards the right *(waymarked on the rocks)*. Experienced hikers can take about a 15min walk across the ridge of the Wildes Mannle as far as a metal sign *(towards Breslauer Hütte via Rofenkarsteig)*. But on the way, be sure to pay attention to the markers *(stone cairns)*. At the sign, turn off onto a steep, narrow trail which leads down to the foot of the Rofenkar glacier *(ropes have been fitted in a number of the trickier passages)*.

The path then leads over a narrow ridge to give beautiful **views**★★ of the glacial cirque. Very soon afterwards, turn off to the right *(waymarked "BH" on a rock)* and reach the Rofenbach brook which is crossed in two stages, the last on wooden planks. Then follow the brook for about 10m without attempting to climb the slippery rock walls, before regaining the path, which leads up to the mountain lodge. From here, there is a splendid **panorama**★★ *(see below)*. The climb down *(1 hour)* to the chairlift which will take you back to Vent is easy.

★★ **Breslauer Hütte** - Alt 2 844m - 9 331ft. *A really easy hike, starting from the mountain station of the chairlift. 2 hours 30min on foot for the return trip, and a difference in altitude of 500m - 1 640ft.*

From the hut, there is a very beautiful **panorama**★★ across the Wildspitze and the ridges of the Wildes Mannle to the north, the glaciers above the Niedertal valley to the east and the Kreuzspitze peak and its glaciers to the south.

★★ **Hike to the Vernagthütte** - *This splendid circuit is highly recommended for hikers with stamina. Take the Wildspitze chairlift (outward journey only) early in the morning and walk to the Breslauer Hütte mountain lodge in 1 hour 30min. Then allow 5 hours walk, with almost no uphill sections, but with a drop in altitude of 1 000m - 3 281ft.*

From the Breslauer Hütte mountain lodge, the footpath leads straight across the mountainside. After walking for about 30min, you will reach the Mitterbach brook, which is fed by a glacier on the Wildspitze. This is most easily crossed at a spot where wooden planks have been laid across it further downhill. Return to the footpath.

A little further on, the path leads along a second rocky amphitheatre (Platteikar) and, after a sharp bend to the right, finally reaches a small lake. From here there is a splendid **view**★★, straight ahead and towards the northwest, of the Vernagthütte mountain lodge which lies 250m - 820ft above the valley floor in a gigantic glacial cirque. Stretching out to the right is the Großer Vernagtfern glacier, above which towers the Hochvernagtspitze peak. Rearing up to the left are the Guslarfern glacier and the Fluchtkogel. The **view** to the south is also interesting, taking in the Hochjochfern glacier tongue, which runs down the right flank of the Fineilspitze peak.

The path leads down into the valley below the Vernagthütte mountain lodge. The climb to this lodge *(allow an extra 50min there and back)* is of particular interest to amateur mountaineers, since the lodge is a good starting point for mountaineering expeditions. Those preferring to keep the whole hike a reasonable length should leave out this climb and begin the long trek down to Vent along the banks of the Vernagtbach *(2 hours 45min)*. Along the route are the waterfalls of the Platteibach, Mitterbach and Rofenbach, which was crossed further upstream. In Rofen, rather than following the tarmacked road, cross the brook on a suspension bridge, and take the good footpath leading to Vent.

SPITAL AM PYHRN

Oberösterreich – Population 2 290
Michelin map 426 fold 22 – Alt 647m - 2 123ft

Spital is the halting place, as its name suggests, on the ancient road over the Pyhrn pass (alt 945m - 3 100ft) which connects the Steyr and Enns valleys, and, through them, Linz and Graz. Its old collegiate church is in an unusually unified Baroque style.

* **Stiftskirche** – The collegiate church, built from 1714 to 1730, has a harmonious façade framed by two towers, their height all the more striking by being articulated by three projecting cornices.
The interior of the main building gives an impression of fullness enhanced by the addition to the architecture of decorations which were slightly diminished by a fire in 1841. When Master Schmidt of Krems had finished the paintings on the altarpieces of the side altars, about 1780, no further embellishment in the taste of that time was given to the church. In the chancel, Bartolomeo Altomonte (1693 - 1783) painted a remarkable decoration of colonnades in *trompe-l'œil*, opening at the centre on the scene of the Assumption of the Virgin. This **fresco★** (1740) culminates in the dome with a representation of the celestial Court.

SPITTAL AN DER DRAU

Kärnten – Population 14 770
Michelin map 426 fold 34 – Alt 554m - 1 818ft

The pleasant city of Spittal an der Drau occupies an extensive site at the foot of the Goldeck (alt 2 142m - 7 028ft, cable-car) at the confluence of the Lieser and the Drava (Drau) near the Lake of Millstatt. It is one of Upper Carinthia's main tourist centres.

* **Schloß Porcia** – This cube-shaped structure was begun in 1527; it is framed by corner turrets and is one of the rare specimens of an Italian palace on Austrian soil. It was built for Gabriel Salamanca, a brilliant financier who was General Treasurer to the Archduke Ferdinand until 1526. The palace is now in public ownership and its park, which has become public, is a pleasant place to relax. The **courtyard★**, lined on three sides with Italianate galleries, shows perfect unity of style in its Renaissance decoration, antique medallions, balustrade pillars, door-frames, etc. Theatre performances are held in the courtyard in summer. Splendid 16C wrought-iron gates separate the stairs from the upper galleries.

Bezirksheimatmuseum ⊙ – *On the upper floors of the palace.*
This regional museum houses a detailed and evocative display of the dynastic history and the traditions of the Spittal area. Note the reconstruction of a primary schoolroom of the 1900s. Also presented is an important collection of agricultural equipment and local crafts.

Schloß Porcia

EXCURSION

Teurnia Excavations (Ausgrabungen). – *5km - 3 miles northwest. At St. Peter in Holz, 4.5km - 2.5 miles from Spittal turn off left from the road to Lienz.*
At a bend in the former roadway stand the two isolated buildings which house the **museum** ⊙ of the Teurnia excavations.
Excavations have uncovered the remains of the Roman city of Teurnia, in the shape of two residential terraces, the forum, a bathing house and a temple to the Celtic god Grannus. In the 5C and 6C, Teurnia was a fortified provincial town and episcopal seat. The diocesan church, with its guest house (Hospitium) and two graveyards outside the city walls, dates from this period. Next to the present museum stands the Friedhofskirche, in which a side chapel is decorated with a large **mosaic floor** (5C) featuring animal motifs.

STAINZ

Steiermark – Population 1 996
Michelin map 426 fold 37 – Alt 377m - 1 237ft – 25km - 16miles southwest of Graz
Local map under STEIRISCHE WEINSTRASSE

Lying in the valley and watched over by its ancient abbey, the town of Stainz gives many hints of its past opulence, which was based on the wine trade. It still boasts a number of old houses with smart façades, particularly in the main square, which date from the period of prosperity in the 16C and 17C.
At the northern entrance to the town, the magnificent buildings of the ancient abbey of the Augustinian canons provide a fine setting for the Baroque parish church. In the 18C, at the time of Austria's secularization, the abbey lost its religious function. It was declared a castle and in 1850 was bought by Archduke Johann, who was at the time the town's mayor.

Schloß – Arcaded galleries embellish the two courtyards of the castle; within the walls stand a church and an ethnographic museum.

Church ⊙ – The church, which dates from 1229 and was rebuilt in 1686, has a broad nave which is soberly painted white and lined by side chapels. Only the vault has been decorated – with painted medallions within a stucco composition. The masterly elevation of the high altar (1695) is articulated by columns supporting the pediment and entablature. At the centre is a work by Hans Adam Weißenkircher, who was also responsible for the paintings in the Room of the Planets (Planetensaal) in Schloß Eggenberg. The two towers of the original church survive; their unusual position over the choir is explained by the fact that, when the church was rebuilt in the Baroque style, it was reoriented like the abbey of Rein. The church is dedicated to St Catherine and has been the local parish church since its secularization in 1785.

★ **Museum** ⊙ – *Entrance on the right in the passage to the first courtyard.*
This section of the Joanneum Landesmuseum occupies two floors and contains objects, illustrations, photographs and documents on the subject of Styria's agricultural traditions and local crafts. Items of particular interest include the collection of model equipment from the "Royal and Imperial Agricultural Society" dating from the mid-19C, collected on the orders of Archduke Johann, as well as examples of "popular technology", such as hand-threshing machines and the "Schmeißwachl", a machine for threshing corn. There is a large collection of everyday ceramic ware and traditional country furniture. A press for producing **pumpkin seed oil** recalls this activity widespread in southern Styria; pumpkin seed oil is still considered a great delicacy. The museum also exhibits two original **panelled rooms** from the years 1568 and 1596, and a so-called "Seitenstübel" (side room) from a west Styrian farmhouse complete with a painted ceiling (1796).

Stift STAMS★★

Tirol
Michelin map 426 north of•fold 30

The Cistercian Abbey of Stams was founded in 1273, in the upper Inn valley, by Elizabeth of Bavaria, who, after being widowed, married Count Meinhard II – the pioneer of Tyrolean unity. She built the abbey in memory of her son by her first marriage (to Konrad IV of Hohenstaufen), Konradin last of the Hohenstaufens, who was tortured and beheaded at Naples by order of Charles of Anjou. The majestic architectural ensemble, made ever more striking since the end of the 17C by the two residential towers, is purely Baroque in style. A conventual building houses a ski school where young Tyrolean hopefuls study and ski at the same time.

Stams Abbey

★ TOUR ⊙ 45min

Leave the car on the shady esplanade at the foot of the pretty 14C village church, with Rococo decoration. Ticket office is in the arch of the abbey gateway.

★★ **Stiftskirche** – The present building results from the remodelling in the Baroque style in 1732 of a Romanesque nave without a transept, which was vaulted only in the 17C. The small apses behind the high altar have kept their original appearance but the aisles have been replaced by six side chapels.

Near the entrance, on the right, is the famous **Rose Grille**. This screen, a masterpiece in ironwork dating from 1716, closes the passage leading to the Heiligblutkapelle (Chapel of the Holy Blood) outside.

A balustrade in the nave surrounds the open crypt, where twelve naïve gilded wood statues of the Princes of the Tyrol are reminders that Stams is the burial-place of this dynasty.

The showpiece of the furnishings is the high altar (1613), whose altarpiece represents the Tree of Life in the form of interlacing boughs supporting eighty-four carved figures of saints surrounding the Virgin Mary. On either side of the altar, Adam and Eve represent the beginnings of mankind; at the crown, Christ on the Cross represents the mystery of the supernatural. The work is by B. Steinle. In the monks' chancel a grille marks the tomb of Duke Friedrich the Penniless.

★ **Fürstensaal** – The Princes' Hall is reached from the porter's lodge by an oval shaped **grand staircase** with a fine wrought-iron balustrade. The hall of state, whose ceiling opens onto a balustraded gallery, is decorated with paintings (1722) recalling outstanding episodes in the life of St Bernard.

STEIRISCHE WEINSTRASSE★

Michelin map 426 folds 37 and 38

The **Styrian vineyard trail** is some considerable distance from the major tourist centres and provides the visitor with an opportunity to discover traditional Austria, a tranquil unaltered world in the midst of outstandingly beautiful, picturesque countryside dotted with traditional bars (**Buschenschenken**) where people meet over a glass of wine and listen to music played on the accordion. The people of Graz are very fond of taking Sunday walks to these bars, particularly in autumn when the vines are mature and at their most brilliantly coloured.

The great majority (80%) of Styrian vines produce white wine, Welschriesling, a dry white wine, which alone accounts for 25% of the land planted. 17% of the vines are Müller Thurgau, which produce a sweet, fruity white and are the first to ripen; 10% are Weißburgunder, a Pinot blanc with a subtle bouquet. Zweigelt may be the most important of the reds, but **Schilcher**, a rosé, is better known; the region southwest of Graz where the Schilcher vine is grown is the starting point of the tour.

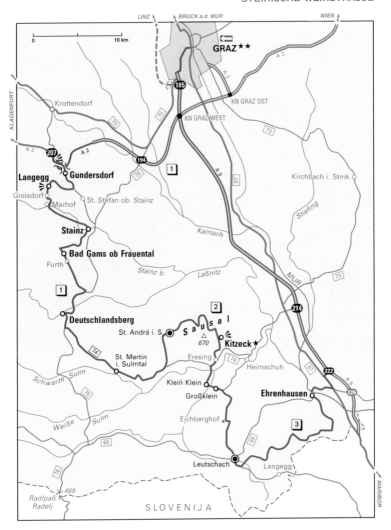

TOUR STARTING FROM GRAZ

180km - 112 miles – 1 day – see map above

Leave Graz on Bundesstraße 70 (AX). Take either the motorway as far as Steinberg or Bundesstraße 70 to Krottendorf, and then follow signs to Stainz.

☐ Schilcher Trail

The Schilcher hills back on to the lower foothills of the Koralpe range, sometimes almost overlapping them. Here the vines are grown on patches of land that are sometimes so steeply inclined that harvesting by machine is impossible. Only south-facing slopes are planted, and one should leave the road to admire the mosaic of the vineyards as they follow the slightest twists and turns of the land.

Schilcher

Schilcher has not always known by this name. It is only since 1976 that this has been the official *appellation* of wine made from the Blue Wildbacher grape variety. Records show that this late-ripening, acidic grape (a distinction is made between the late blue and sloe varieties of Wildbacher), with its characteristic flavour and pretty "onion-skin" colour, has been cultivated in west Styria since as early as 1580. Schilcher vineyards cover about 80ha – 198 acres.

A "Klapotetz"

On leaving the motorway, the road immediately begins to climb, providing charming **views**★★ (left) of the plain of Graz, the undulating hills northwest of the town and, further in the distance, Mount Schöckl (1 445m - 4 741ft) with its flat summit. Chestnut trees soon come into view, just as the vines begin to withdraw from the immediate roadside.

Gundersdorf – Population 400. At the entrance to the village, there is *(right)* a strange wooden stake with a four-bladed helical device on the top *(Klapotetz)*. This is a familiar sight in the vineyards of Styria as its noise scares away the birds during the period from June to harvest time. In the distance, also to the right, can be seen the peaks of Reinischkogel (1 463m - 4 800ft), a local downhill ski resort.

Beyond Gundersdorf, a typical vine-growing village, there is a kind of hinterland which has been shielded from latter-day standardisation and has preserved its old rural dwellings and traditions. The wooden farmhouses, which stand alone or grouped together in small villages, look like so many dolls' houses with their tiny windows adorned with brightly-coloured shutters.

After Gundersdorf turn right, then left towards Langegg and Greisdorf.

Langegg – Population 700. Thirsty travellers can choose from a number of open-air inns *(Buschenschenken)* in this village: the simple wooden platforms attached to wine-growers' houses are a real local institution. Wine may be consumed with **Verackerbrot**, black bread with chopped, spiced bacon, or perhaps with **Brettljause**, a dish of cold meats.
From Langegg there is a delightful **view**★★ of the Mur valley, Mount Schökl (northeast) and the vine-clad hills of Sausal (southeast).

The road between Greisdorf and Marhof runs through maize fields: it is this cereal that is used to make a local speciality, **Sterz**, which is a kind of polenta and constitutes the staple diet of peasants in the area.

Turn left at Marhof and follow the signs to Stainz.

Stainz – *See STAINZ.*

The landscape is undulating and full of charm, with many pleasant walks.

Bad Gams ob Frauental – Population 2 220. The village takes the first word of its name (*Bad* means bath) from its chalybeate springs. The region is, however, also well known in Styria for its traditional pottery; there is a potter's workshop on the outskirts of Furth, a town close to Bad Gams.

The road from Bad Gams to Deutschlandsberg descends into a plain encircled by forests.

Deutschlandsberg – *See DEUTSCHLANDSBERG.*

Rejoin the road from Stainz; continue south in the direction of St. Andrä-Leibnitz via St. Martin; to reach St. Andrä, turn left into the valley road which joins up with the Sausal Vineyard Trail.

② Sausal Vineyards

St. Andrä is the point of entry to the Sausal vineyards which rise to 670m - 2 198ft above sea level and cover a clearly-defined area of fascinating character. The wine most frequently produced in these parts is **Rheinriesling**, a distinguished, semi-sparkling white with an excellent bouquet.

The road winds its way from hill to hill through the overhanging foliage. From time to time there are splendid views down over the plain of Graz (north), the Koralpe range (northwest) and Slovenia (south).

★ **Kitzeck** – Population 1 290. The high-level situation (564m - 1 850ft) of the village, which is set on a ridge in a quasi-mountainous landscape, provides an almost **panoramic view**★★ over a sea of hills (east). It is the highest wine-growing village in Europe, well known for its mild yet sunny climate.

The **Wine Museum** (Weinmuseum) ⊙, which occupies an old wine-grower's house (1726), complete with the main room *(Stube)*, contains articles and tools, handed down from generation to generation of wine-growers, which were associated with the many aspects of vine-cultivation; a reconstruction of a device for smoke-curing, an old press and a wagon for transporting barrels recall age-old systems of working now replaced by modern techniques.

Drive down towards Fresing, on the edge of the Sausal district. Continue to Klein Klein.

A sharp eye will detect, particularly in **Klein Klein**, splendid storks' nests, securely constructed on chimney stacks and occupied between Easter and September. Celtic tombs dating from the 6C-4C BC have been discovered under some tumuli in the forest near **Großklein**, indicating early human occupation of the district. The finds are kept in Schloß Eggenberg.

In Großklein turn left towards Heimschuch; shortly afterwards, turn right to Eichberghof to the south.

The road meanders through wild and hilly country, past the peaks of hills where small south-facing vineyards alternate with fields of maize and wooded areas.

Leaving the Eichberghof Restaurant on the right, follow signs to Leutschach in the south.

③ South Styrian Route

On either side of the road near **Leutschach** the fields are full of hops growing up the characteristic tall hop poles.

In Leutschach turn left in front of the church (green road sign: Südsteirische Weinstraße – South Styrian Wine Route). On leaving Leutschach take the road to Langegg following the Wine Route signs.

This is the most southerly wine-growing area in Austria, where, for several kilometres, the wine route forms the frontier with Slovenia. This region is nowadays known as the **Styrian Tuscany** on account of its sunny climate and its similarity to the Tuscan countryside in Italy.

A forest of conifers gives way to rows of vines which cover the hills with their gentle contours, like waves frozen in the mist. This is the very heart of Welschriesling and Samling country. The road continues among picturesque small hillocks, offering splendid, almost panoramic, **views**★. To the south, at no great distance, are the Slovenian hills. Frequent signs indicate those stretches of road which form the frontier.

Ehrenhausen – *See EHRENHAUSEN.*

Take the motorway back to Graz.

STEYR★

Oberösterreich – Population 43 000
Michelin map 426 fold 22 – Alt 310m - 1 017ft

Steyr had a glorious past, giving its name to the province of Styria and becoming, for a time, a rival to Vienna. It is now Upper Austria's third largest town (after Linz and Wels) and an important economic centre. The old town clusters at the foot of a bluff at the confluence of the Enns and the Steyr. On the edge of town, international firms such as BMW, MAN and SKF have set up in business.

OLD TOWN *time: 1 hour*

★ **Stadtplatz** (Y) – The Stadtplatz, which is a street in the form of a square, is lined with fine late Gothic and Renaissance houses with balconies, supported on corbels, and with projecting first floors. In the middle is a graceful 17C fountain, the **Leopoldbrunnen** (**A**). Two of the buildings in particular, the **Rathaus** (**R**) and the **Bummerlhaus** (no 32), are of outstanding interest. The Rathaus, built in the Rococo style from 1765 to 1771, has a narrow façade surmounted by a belfry; the Bummerlhaus is a fine mansion in the Gothic style, with a gable and the characteristic first floor overhang.

Many of these houses have remarkable courtyards: no 9 has a Renaissance court, with fine pillars supporting two tiers of arcades on which Virginia creeper grows; no 12 has basket-handle arches and large pillars supporting wrought-iron balconies; no 14, of the late Gothic period, has two tiers of balconies and pillars which are sometimes turned or carved, and no 39 has two tiers of Renaissance arcades, adorned with a wooden lean-to roof and *sgraffiti (qv)* decorations.

Marienkirche (Z) – The former Dominican church is flanked on the north side by the **Eisengasse** (Z 4), a picturesque alley going down to the Enns.
The interior Baroque decoration includes a high altar overloaded with gilding, a Virgin and Child of 1704, pictures framed in stucco and a Rococo pulpit.

South of the Stadtplatz is the **Innerbergerstadl** (Z **M**), a 17C granary turned into a local museum. Together with a town gate (the Neutor) and a house flanked with a turret built on brackets, it forms a charming picture.

Go round the Innerbergstadl to the right and make for the parish church along an alley ending in a stairway.

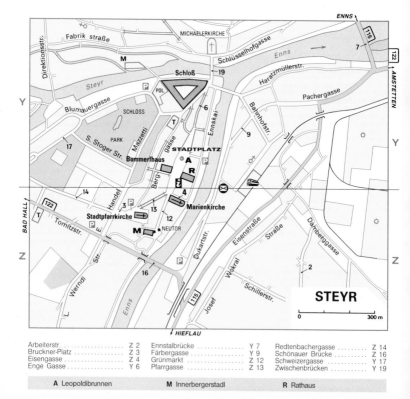

Arbeiterstr.	Z 2	Ennstalbrücke	Y 7	Redtenbachergasse	Z 14
Bruckner-Platz	Z 3	Färbergasse	Y 9	Schönauer Brücke	Z 16
Eisengasse	Z 4	Grünmarkt	Z 12	Schweizergasse	Y 17
Enge Gasse	Y 6	Pfarrgasse	Z 13	Zwischenbrücken	Y 19

A Leopoldbrunnen	**M** Innerbergerstadl	**R** Rathaus

Stadtpfarrkirche (Z) – The church was built in the mid-15C, in the Gothic style, by the architect of the Stephansdom in Vienna, which it resembles both in plan and elevation. This master was also responsible for the **tabernacle★**, with its delicate tracery, and the tripartite chancel baldachin opposite. The font is adorned with 16C low reliefs.

Schloß (Y) – *At the confluence of the Steyr and the Enns.* Records mention a fortress on this spot as early as the end of the first millenium. This castle, which was built in the Baroque style in 1666, was given its present appearance by Linz architect Johann Michael Prunner after a fire in 1727. The oldest part of the building is the keep, or Römerturm.

STUBACHTAL★★★

Salzburg
Michelin map 426 fold 33

The Stubachtal, a valley about 20km - 12 miles long, is one of the most beautiful Alpine regions in Austria. A small winding road leads from Uttendorf (alt 780m - 2 559ft) to Enzingerboden (alt 1 480m - 4 856ft). From this point, a cable-car takes skiers in the winter and walkers in the summer to several mountain lakes and a magnificent glacial massif at the boundary to the Hohe Tauern National Park.

★★ **Uttendorf to Enzingerboden** – *18km - 11 mile return trip.* The road provides a view of the Steinkarlhöhe range and then leads through a beautiful spruce forest. There is a car park behind the reservoir at the foot of the cable railway.

★★★ **Kalser Tauern** – *2 hour 30min return trip, 1 hour of which is on foot.*

Cable-car – *25min ascent.* The first stage of the climb passes over luxuriant vegetation (Alpine roses) with a view of the Grüner See lake at the foot of the Kitzkarkogel. To the left, you can look over the Totenkopf and the lower Riffel glacier. The Rudolfshütte mountain lodge is situated at the mountain station (alt 2 315m - 7 595ft). There is a splendid **view★★** of the Weißer See lake and the nearby **Sonnblick glacier** (alt 3 088m - 10 131ft). A 10min walk brings you to the chairlift lower down.

Medelzkopf chairlift – Alt 2 564m-8 412ft. *15min ascent.* The route leads through a majestic Alpine massif and offers a magnificent **panorama★★★**. At the half-way point, you can look back and see the **Tauernmoos lake and dam**, with the Kleiner Eiser towering above them. On arrival at the top, the **Johannisberg** (alt 3 453m - 11 329ft), enthroned in the centre of the massif, and further to the right the **Eiskögele**, which stands out boldly from the icicles of the Odenwinkl glacier, are the most impressive features of the landscape.

Walk to the Kalser Tauern pass – *45min return. Sturdy footwear needed.* A path, waymarked in red and white, leads through the rocks. Apart from its geological interest, the pass has a beautiful **view★** of the lake and the Dorfertal valley.

STUBAITAL★★

Tirol
Michelin map 426 folds 30 and 31 – Local map under INNSBRUCK

The Stubaital valley is one of the most interesting places in the vicinity of Innsbruck to go for day-trips. In summer, it is an ideal starting point for hiking expeditions, and it also provides one of the largest glacial skiing areas in Europe.

★FROM INNSBRUCK TO MUTTERBERGALM
44km - 27 miles – about 1 hour 30min

Leave Innsbruck via the Brennerstraße *(see town plan under INNSBRUCK)*. After 15km - 9 miles, turn off to the right towards Schönberg.

The broad Stubaital valley with its steadily rising, larch-covered slopes is strikingly peaceful in comparison to the nearby Silltal valley, in which the roar of traffic travelling towards the Brenner pass can be heard.

You will soon see, in the distance, the glacial massif of the **Zuckerhütl** (alt 3 507m - 11 506ft). The road consists of long, straight stretches, leading past various villages including, for example, Mieders on its sunny terrace. The locality of **Fulpmes** specialises in the manufacture of small tools (and also domestic appliances and mountaineering equipment). In earlier times, the most famous metalworkers in the North Tyrol worked here, as the cooperative's houses in the main square testify. **Neustift** is another of the valley's major holiday resorts. Over the last 7km - 4 miles of the journey, the gradient becomes steeper and steeper and the landscape more rugged. The road finally leaves the wood and arrives at Mutterbergalm (alt 1 728m - 5 669ft) at the foot of the rocky cirque which forms the beginning of the valley.

★★ HOCHSTUBAIGEBIET AREA

✷✷ Ski slopes – The ski slopes cover too small an area (18 ski lifts) to attract good skiers for stays of a week or more, but they are ideally suited to weekend skiing breaks. The area's attraction lies in its outstanding snow cover and the diversity of its pistes. Beginners and moderately good skiers will get their full money's worth here. They have numerous practice slopes with gentle gradients at altitudes ranging from 2 300m to 3 210m - 7 546ft to 10 531ft to choose from. Good skiers will appreciate the 10km - 6 mile long **Wilde Gruben** descent, which leads down to Mutterberg through splendid, unspoilt **countryside★★**.

A 4.5km - 3 mile long cross-country course at an altitude of 2 600m - 8 530ft (starting from the Gamsgarten cable-car) is available to cross-country skiers. The Austrian national team often trains here.

The skiing season generally begins in October and ends at the beginning of July on the highest pistes.

The most important viewpoints, which can be reached by lift or on foot, are indicated below *(take warm clothing, sunglasses and thick-soled, waterproof footwear)*.

★★ Eisgrat – Alt 2 900m - 9 514ft. A cable-car in two stages leads to the glacial cirque and the foot of the Stubaier Wildspitze peak (alt 3 340m - 10 958ft) and Schaufelspitze peak (alt 3 333m - 10 935ft). Forbidding **Alpine landscape★★**. Walk round the restaurant to see the lower part of the valley, which is dominated by the Ruderhofspitze peak and the Habicht.

★★ Jochdohle – Trip starting from the Eisgrat. Hikers take the waymarked footpath over the Schaufelfern glacier, which follows the ski piste *(climbing the 250m - 820ft difference in altitude takes about 1 hour; do not leave the footpath; it is possible to hire the appropriate mountaineering equipment at the sports shop in Eisgrat)*.

Skiers travel down to the Gamsgarten restaurant and then take the Eisjoch ski tow (the left-hand lift) which leads to a small pass (alt 3 170m - 10 400ft); **view★** of the Ötztal Alps. Continue by means of the tiny Windachfern ski tow. Finally, you will reach the Jochdohle, where the highest restaurant in Austria is situated (alt 3 150m - 10 335ft).

Rewarding **panorama★★** across the Swiss Alps, the Arlberg and, in particular, the Ötztal Alps, the Ortler in the south Tyrol and, further to the east, the glaciers of the Zillertal valley.

Ski down further on the other slope to the right of the Gaiskarfern ski tow. After completing two thirds of the piste you will see, on the right-hand side and slightly higher up, a place from which is it easily possible to reach the ridges (about 100m from the piste). A signpost indicates the way to the Hildesheimer Hütte mountain lodge. Breathtaking **view★★★** of a landscape of jagged peaks and glaciers, dominated by the impressive Zuckerhütl (alt 3 507m - 11 506ft).

★★ Daunkogelferner glacier – Skiers can reach the glacier (alt 3 160m - 10 367ft) by means of the Daunfern ski tow. Impressive **view★★** over the rocky cliffs which frame the glacier from the Stubaier Wildspitze peak to the Ruderhofspitze peak.

TAMSWEG★

Salzburg – Population 5 260
Michelin map 426 fold 35 – Alt 1 021m - 3 350ft

The approach to Tamsweg on the Mauterndorf road provides a flattering view of the town, which appears to be dominated by the great church of St Leonard, standing alone in the forest on the sloping valley wall.

Tamsweg is the capital of the Lungau and fosters the old traditions: according to a custom reminiscent of that of Flanders, processions take place every year *(see the Calendar of events at the end of the guide)*, headed by a gigantic dummy representing Samson, accompanied by two dwarfs.

SIGHTS

Marktplatz – The regular design of this square, lined with pretty houses, lends distinction to Tamsweg. With the little triangular roof section sheltering the gable, the buildings reflect their origins in the farmsteads of the Lungau countryside. By contrast the **Rathaus** (town hall) in a building dating from the 16C displays corner turrets and closely resembles the style of country mansions commonly found in the Salzburg region. Opposite, stands the old castle of the Kuenburg family, dating from 1742-1749 with stucco work by Johann Androy of Graz. Androy was also responsible for the delicate stucco work in the **Dekanatspfarrkirche**, built from 1738 to 1741 by Fidelis Hainzl.

St. Leonhardkirche – *Drive south from Tamsweg over the bridge over the River Mur (the Murau road). Cross the railway and park at the start of the road (right) which climbs directly up to the church; keep further right into a footpath which is less steep.*

There is a good view of Tamsweg and of the deeply jagged ridges of the Tauern.

The 15C church of St Leonard has kept its early Gothic plan and design – tall light windows, network vaulting, etc. Some of its **stained glass**, which dates from the period when the building was erected, is among the finest in Austria. Note also, immediately to the left on entering (near the gallery), the window of the Tree of Life in which the Virgin of the Annunciation is presented at the foot of the tree, which spreads out on either side, and at its tip forms the arms of the Cross. The "**gold window**" *(Goldfenster)*, on the right of the chancel, is very well known: in a flamboyant architectural setting, it depicts, upwards from the base, the arms of Salzburg borne by two cherubs, St Virgil and St Rupert standing on either side of the donor prelate, the Holy Trinity figuratively represented as the Throne of Grace – the Holy Father presenting Christ – between St Peter and St Paul. South of the high altar, the small altar to St Leonard is surmounted by a statuette of the saint held in the branches of a juniper tree. The discovery of the statuette is the basis of the pilgrimage.

The main through-routes are clearly indicated on all town plans

TAUERNTUNNEL

Michelin map 426 folds 20 and 34 – Between Mallnitz and Böckstein

Until the opening of the Felbertauern tunnel and the Tauern motorway tunnel, the double-track **Tauern railway tunnel** ⊙ (8 550m - 5 miles) was the only way through the Eastern Alps which allowed traffic to flow at all seasons through the particularly impenetrable region of the Tauern mountains east of the Brenner. A rail shuttle service *(Autoschleuse)* has kept the route popular with motorists.

The route described below begins at Spittal an der Drau in the south. It links the warm and well-tilled lower Möll valley, between Spittal and Obervellach, to the Gastein Alpine valley.

FROM SPITTAL AN DER DRAU TO BÖCKSTEIN

39km - 24 miles – about 1 hour not including the railway journey

Spittal an der Drau – *See SPITTAL AN DER DRAU.*

Kolbnitz – Population 1 520. The electrical power station is fed, from both sides of the valley, by pressure conduits collecting water from the Reißeck and Kreuzeck. Seven turbines generate about 307 million kWh/year. This equipment, which was completed in 1959, required the tapping, on the Reißeck slope, of four mountain lakes (Kleiner and Großer Mühldorfer See, Radlsee and Höchalmsee). The maximum drop is 1 772m - 5 812ft.

★★ **Reißeck-Massiv** – *See REISSECK-MASSIV. Allow at least 2 hours 45min for the visit.*

Obervellach – Population 2 715. The **church**★ is a massive building of the late Gothic period (beginning of the 16C). It contains valuable works of art: the 1520 **altarpiece**★ of the Dutch Master Jan van Scorel, on the north side altar, depicting the Holy Family between St Christopher and St Apollonia. Among the surviving wall paintings is the "auxiliary saints" of 1509 in the chancel (from whom the Christian people used to expect cures for the most diverse ills). Also in the chancel is a low relief of the Garden of Olives, and various statues forming an excellent Gothic ensemble of the 16C.

⁕ **Mallnitz** – *See MALLNITZ.*

Take the Tauern railway tunnel to Böckstein.

Böckstein – *See GASTEINER TAL.*

From Böckstein, we would heartily recommend extending your trip to include the famous **Gasteiner Tal**⁕⁕.

TRAUNKIRCHEN

Oberösterreich – Population 1 610
Michelin map 426 fold 21 – Local map under SALZKAMMERGUT
Alt 430m - 1 411ft

On its promontory **site**★, Traunkirchen enjoys a variety of views over the Traunsee, particularly to the south, where the setting is steep and wild. It is a popular stopping-place for visitors exploring the Salzkammergut.

Pfarrkirche – On the northern flank of the rock, the parish church is surrounded by a terraced graveyard overlooking the lake. There are views of the Erlakogel and of the huge dome of the Traunstein. The building formed part of an abbey founded in the 11C and occupied by the Jesuits in the 17C and 18C.

> ### Floating Corpus Christi Festival
>
> Since 1632 a procession whose reputation reaches far beyond the borders of Upper Austria has been held on the lake here every year in celebration of the feast of Corpus Christi. In days gone by, boats called "Trauner" which were used for shipping salt were pressed into service for the procession. Nowadays, these have given way to the rather less romantic motor boat.

In 1632 they rebuilt the church in its present form, and in the same year the first of the annual **Corpus Christi festivals** was held on the waters of the lake. The church has splendid Baroque furnishings, particularly the **Fisherman's Pulpit**★, made in the form of the Disciples' fishing boat, complete with dripping nets, while on the sounding-board is a legendary episode from the life of St Francis Xavier, who introduced Christianity to Japan. In the course of his voyage, the saint was shipwrecked and lost his crucifix, which is shown here being returned to him by a lobster.

Corpus Christi Festival, Traunkirchen

S. Vannini/VIENNASLIDE

TULLN

Niederösterreich – Population 11 290
Michelin map 426 fold 11 – Local map under DONAUTAL – Alt 180m - 591ft

Tulln grew up on the site of the Roman camp of Comagenae *(see map p 29)*, founded here in the 1C AD at this strategic point on the very edge of the Roman Empire. Between 1042 and 1113, the town was the residence of the Babenberg dynasty, predecessors of the Habsburgs, and was thus the capital of Austria until replaced in that role by Klosterneuburg, then by Vienna. This did not affect its prosperity, guaranteed by its favourable location on the banks of the great river.
Tulln even plays a part in popular folklore, as it was here that Kriemhild met Etzel for the first time, in the Song of the Nibelungen.

Roman Tower – The riverbank is laid out as an attractive promenade. By Nibelungengasse stands a square tower (Römerturm), built in the reign of Diocletian (284-305 AD) as part of the fortifications of the Roman camp.

Pfarrkirche – This former Romanesque basilica of the 12C, dedicated to St Stephen, was transformed in the 15C into the Gothic style and then remodelled in the Baroque style in the 18C.

The Romanesque west doorway, framed between two Baroque towers, is adorned with busts of the twelve Apostles and surmounted by a double-headed eagle, the symbol of the Holy Roman Empire, holding two Turks' heads in its talons. The Turks represent the terrible danger of invasion which threatened Austria in the 16C and 17C. The nave and chancel have ogive vaulting and are strikingly spacious. The 1786 altarpiece represents the martyrdom of St Stephen.

★ **Karner** – Level with the chevet of the parish church stands one of the finest funerary chapels in Austria. It is known as that of the Three Kings and was built about 1250. Its outside shape is that of a polygon, to which an oven-vaulted apse is attached. Each face of the polygon is adorned with arches and capitals; under one of the arches is a statue of the donor. The **doorway**★★ is decorated with palm-leaf capitals and geometrical motifs.

Beneath the chapel is a crypt, once used, in accordance with traditional practice, to house the bones exhumed from the graveyard. The chapel itself is roofed with a dome and painted with much restored Romanesque frescoes on the theme of the "Last Things". Following the secularisation decreed by Joseph II in 1785, the building deteriorated, but was eventually restored, first in 1873 and then a century later in 1973.

TURRACHERHÖHE

Kärnten und Steiermark

Michelin map 426 fold 35 – Alt 1 763m - 4 812ft

This small mountain resort has sprung up around lake Turrach close to the Turrach pass, which serves as the border between Styria and Carinthia. It is a well-appointed all-year holiday resort; in summer there is boating and hiking and in winter skiing on slopes that rise from 1 400m - 4 605ft to 2 240m - 7 637ft. The road between Predlitz and the resort at Turracherhöhe passes through a landscape of sturdy forests and Alpine pastures. For a period from the early years of the 17C, the village of Turrach was a mining centre with an ironworks which belonged to the Princes of Schwarzenberg, resident at Murau. The first **Bessemer converter** to be installed in Western Europe began operating here in 1863: it was used to decarbonize cast iron by forcing pressurised air through the metal.

The speed of technical change and the pace of international competition caused the tall furnaces to be abandoned; the last fire died in 1909. Although most of the ironworks has now disappeared, there still stands beside the road near the church the delightful old administration building with its ornamental façade and pilasters, the last remnant of the valley's industrial traditions.

VIENNA★★★

See WIEN

VILLACH

Kärnten – Population 54 640

Michelin map 426 fold 35 – Local map under WÖRTHER SEE – Alt 501m - 1 644ft

Villach, Austria's "gateway to the south", to both Italy and Slovenia, is a major road and railway junction at which the international lines between Vienna and Venice and between Salzburg and Belgrade intersect. The town's favourable site on the banks of the Drava (Drau) must also have appealed to the ancient Celts and Romans, if archaeological evidence of settlement here and in the surrounding area during the Hallstatt and Roman periods is anything to go by. Records mention a bridge (pons) Uillah, from which the town takes it name, in the 9C.

A significant event in the town's history was Heinrich II's gift of it to his newly founded bishopric of Bamberg (Bavaria) in 1007. This was to shape the town's fortunes for the next 752 years, until Maria Theresa bought Villach back in 1759. Frequently referred to as the "secret capital" of Carinthia, Villach is the province's second largest town and the economic and cultural hub of the region. The way the municipality's boundaries have been drawn up means that it stretches as far as the

Faaker and Ossiach lakes, so that it also caters for a variety of sports and leisure activities. Finally, there is the thermal baths with its mineral springs which has also made Villach a certain reputation as a spa resort.

Carinthian Summer – There is a music festival held in Villach and Ossiach every July and August, which offers a wide variety of musical entertainment including chamber music, ballet, puppet shows and opera.

SIGHTS

Old town – The old town of Villach is delimited to the north and east by the Drava. The **Hauptplatz** which straddles it, a square dating from the 12C, is surrounded by a number of houses which essentially date from the 14C to 16C, such as the Paracelsushof *(Hauptplatz 18)*, named after the great physician, who spent his youth in Villach.
The most interesting feature to look out for is the beautiful arcaded courtyards – there are some particularly good examples in the Widmannsgasse.

Hauptstadtpfarrkirche St. Jakob – The simplicity of the exterior of this triple-aisled hall-church makes the complexity of the stellar and ribbed vaulting inside all the more pleasant a surprise. Besides the high altar with its magnificent sculptures, beneath a baldachin, note the stone pulpit dating from 1555. There are also several 15-18C tombstones.

Wallfahrtskirche Heiligenkreuz – This Late Gothic church with its striking outline is in the suburb of Perau, on the south bank of the Drava. The ceiling paintings beneath the organ gallery depict *Christ driving the Moneychangers from the Temple.* Three richly decorated altars and the pulpit dating from the period of the church's construction all add further to the overall harmony of the building.

Relief von Kärnten ⊙ – *In the Schillerpark, Peraustraße.*
This immense relief model of the province of Carinthia is on a scale of approximately 1:10 000 – about six inches to a mile (vertical exaggeration x 2). By studying this tourists can familiarize themselves with the general character of the countryside, often difficult to determine on the spot.

Warmbad – *South of town.* 24 million litres (over 5 million UK gallons) of therapeutic spring water bubbles up daily from the six warm springs (29 °C - 84 °F). When Villach was part of the French Illyrian Provinces between 1809 and 1813, Napoleon nursed plans to develop it into a spa resort of world renown. These came to nothing, but the modern spa at Villach has all the facilities one would expect to find at a well-maintained health resort.

EXCURSION

★ **Villacher Alpenstraße** ⊙ – *16.5km - 10 miles.* This modern mountain road is well laid out along the wooded mountainsides and later along the cliff-like edge of the Dobratsch; many viewpoints have been constructed overlooking the deep Gail valley, facing the jagged crests of the Julian Alps to the south *(make a point of stopping at the car parks numbered 2, 5 and 6).*
On reaching the end of the roadway (alt 1 732m - 5 682ft) take the **chairlift** ⊙ and then climb on foot to the top of the **Dobratsch**★★ (alt 2 167m - 7 107ft). This isolated peak offers a famous **panorama** of the Karawanken, the Carinthian Lakes, the Julian Alps and the Tauern *(about 2 hours 30min Rtn from the end of the road, of which 10min are spent in the chairlift and 2 hours walking).*

★ **Ossiach Lake** – *7km - 4 miles. See OSSIACHER SEE.*

VÖCKLABRUCK

Oberösterreich – Population 12 000
Michelin map 426 folds 20 and 21

Vöcklabruck bestrides the old main road half-way between Salzburg and Linz. The first record of a bridge built here over the river Vöckla dates from 1134 and a century later, in 1246, the town was granted its charter. It was fortified in the early 14C.
The place is still a busy market-town and educational centre for the surrounding countryside with a number of schools and colleges (agriculture, commerce and technology). It benefits too from its proximity to the Salzkammergut to the south, one of Austria's most popular tourist areas. Nearby are the lakes of Attersee and Traunsee with their own range of attractions.

Stadtplatz – As is frequently the case in Austria, the town square is simply a widening of the main road. Much older buildings are concealed by the Baroque façades lining the square. No 14 has an arcaded courtyard very much in the Italian style. The square is closed at either end by rather un-military looking towers. One of them, the **Unterer Stadtturm** (Lower Tower), is decorated with the arms of the various possessions of Burgundy as well as those of the Habsburgs, a reminder that **Emperor Maximilian I**, who owned a house in the town, was married to Mary, daughter of Charles the Bold of Burgundy.

Dörflkirche St. Ägidius ⓥ – *Leave the town via the Unterer Stadtturm and cross the river; the church is just over the bridge on the right.*
This elegant building is the successor to a much earlier church, first consecrated in 1143. It was built in 1688 by the architect **Carlo Antonio Carlone** and decorated by Giovanni Battista Carlone. It was restored to its former Baroque splendour in 1980.

VOLDERS

Tirol – Population 3 550
Michelin map 426 fold 31 – 5km - 3 miles east of Hall in Tirol
Local map under INNSBRUCK – Alt 558m - 1 831ft

This town, first recorded in 1000, was settled even in the pre-Roman period, as a cemetery situated just west of town illustrates.
On the green banks of the River Inn, near the motorway, the Servite church of Volders appears with its red and white decorations as one of the most refreshing examples of Baroque art in the Tyrol.

★ **Kirche zum hl. Karl Borromäus** ⓥ – The church, completed in 1654, is built round a central rotunda in a clover shaped plan. The helmet-like roofs, intricately interwoven and covering the cupolas, and the onion-domed clock tower (1740), its lower part flanked by small towers, give the building a very distinct character. The best general view is from the bridge over the Inn. A passage links the church to the monastery, now used as a grammer school (the Servites are a religious order who, in Austria, devote themselves to the service of the parishioners and to the upkeep of pilgrimage sanctuaries).
What one can see of the church interior, beyond the dividing grille, indicates that the builders engaged the services of excellent artists: outstanding are the paintings of the cupolas and the picture over the high altar of St Charles Borromeo, patron of the church, attributed to Martin Knoller (1725-1804).

Kirche zum hl. Karl Borromäus, Volders

Wiesenhofer/ÖSTERREICH WERBUNG

*If you intend combining a tour of Austria
with a visit to one of the neighbouring countries,
remember to take the appropriate Michelin Green Guide
to Germany, Switzerland or Italy,
or take the Michelin Green Guide Europe*

VORAU

Steiermark – Population 1 503
Michelin map 426 fold 24 – Alt 660m - 2 165ft

On a solitary hillock in Joglland the abbey of Vorau, founded in the 12C, belongs to the monks of St Augustine, who still minister to the needs of several nearby parishes.

Stift (Abbey) – Within the main gateway, the monastery buildings are laid out to a strict plan. The western façade of the church, decorated with fine stucco work and flanked by two towers, is placed between two symmetrical wings.

Stiftskirche – The abbey church was entirely rebuilt in 1660, following the designs of a Swiss architect, Domenico Sciassia, and in 1700 to 1705 the interior was adorned, rather excessively, with gilt, stucco and paintings. The high altar is particularly elaborate.

Freilichtmuseum ⊙ – Close to the abbey is an open-air museum with a collection of traditional rural buildings, a house, a mill, a saw-mill, a press... giving a glimpse of the life of the area as it was lived in the past.

WAIDHOFEN AN DER THAYA

Niederösterreich – Population 5 650
Michelin map 426 fold 10 – Alt 510m - 1 673ft

Waidhofen is situated on the left bank of the River Thaya in attractive rural surroundings of farmland and forest. The town grew up from a fortified settlement, first recorded in 1171, which occupied a triangular site in a field. The parish church stands on the highest point, while the town fortress was built on the lowest ground, to the east.

Pfarrkirche – The church's exterior gives no hint of the interest of the interior decorations, which date from Baroque times. The vault of the nave is decorated with frescoes and surrounded by stuccowork; the pastel tones are dominated by gold and violet. These are the work of Josef Michael Daysinger and depict scenes from the life of Mary. The magnificent **high altar** (1721) fills the chancel with its lofty columns. The beautifully carved **stalls** feature a double-headed eagle on the upper part, which symbolises that the church was an Imperial parish. The pulpit and the organ tribune are worked with great elegance. To the right of the chancel a 17C chapel contains a Virgin and Child (1440), which is charming, despite the stiffness of the pose. The Late Gothic relief on the altar (1510) dedicated to relief from the plague unusually substitutes St Nicolas and the Virgin Mary with Child for two of the Fourteen Auxiliary Saints it depicts.

Old town – The north promenade with powder tower and the south promenade with a partially preserved defence tower are all that remain of the original fortified town wall. There are some interesting old houses along Wienerstraße (no 14, the Heimathaus), Böhmgasse and Pfarrgasse.

Hauptplatz – In the centre of the town square stands the **Rathaus**, a beautiful example of an essentially Gothic town hall, which owes its stepped gables to the Renaissance, however. The ridge turret was added in 1721. The **Dreifaltigkeitssäule** column was put up in 1709, unusually enough not in fulfilment of a vow, but to protect the town from plague, fire and war.

WEISSENKIRCHEN

Niederösterreich – Population 1 060
Michelin map 426 folds 10, 11 – Local map under DONAUTAL – Alt 206m - 676ft

Weißenkirchen in the heart of the Wachau is noted for its vineyards which climb up the sides of the hills and for the charm of its old houses dominated by a fortified church.

SIGHTS

Park by the church.

The church is reached via a 16C covered staircase.

Pfarrkirche ⊙ – Built in the Gothic style in the 15C, the church was fortified in 1531 to resist the Turkish invasions. A Virgin and Child, opposite the pulpit, dates from this period.

Go round the church clockwise and then along the ancient fortifications.

From a little terrace covered with vines, there are views of the east end of the church and the Danube valley.

On returning, take the open air staircase which leads to charming views of the little streets with their overhanging houses.

Wachaumuseum ⊙ – The museum is housed in the Teisenhoferhof, a fortified farm of the 16C, which has a delightful courtyard: arcades support a covered gallery, lined with flowers and sheaves of maize.

The interior galleries contain works by the Wachau painters, a group which was active at the turn of the century.

WELS

Oberösterreich – Population 51 020

Michelin map 426 fold 21 – Alt 317m - 1 040ft

Situated at the junction of ancient trade routes, the small Celtic settlement of Vilabis evolved into the Roman town of Ovilava. Under Hadrian, it was raised to the status of city, while Caracalla made it a Roman colony. By this time, Wels was an important supply centre behind Limes and capital of the Roman province of Noricum. Wherever excavations are carried out inside the boundaries of the town, they uncover yet more evidence of its Roman past. This has resulted in a particularly rich local museum collection. The most important exhibits in the Stadtmuseum are the marvellous **Wels Venus** and the **Wels Genius**.

Wels is now an important towns for trade and trade fairs, which has nonetheless managed to preserve its lovely historical town centre over the centuries.

OLD WELS *time: 1 hour*

Start in Polheimerstraße.

Beyond the **Ledererturm** (Leather Tower) **(A)**, built in 1618, is the elongated **Stadtplatz**★ **(AB)** with its flower-bedecked fountain. There are no Roman remains but the quality and variety of the old buildings of the medieval area around the Stadtplatz make it one of the most evocative of its kind in Upper Austria. No 62-63, once the property of Kremsmünster Abbey, has an imposing Baroque façade.

Go into the arcaded courtyard of no 63.

This courtyard gives a view of the Wasserturm, the reservoir built in 1577 to feed the town's fountains.

Go out of the far end of the courtyard and along the stream to the left.

WELS

Adlerstr.	B
Altstadtgasse	B 2
Bahnhofstr.	A
Dr. Koss-Str.	A
Dr. Salzmann-Straße	A 3
Dragonerstr.	A 5
Eisenhower-Str.	A
Kaiser-Josef-Platz	A
Karl-Loy-Straße	A
Maria-Theresia-Straße	A 6
Maximilianstr.	B
Pfarrgasse	B
Pollheimerstr.	A
Rainerstr.	A
Ringstr.	A
Roseggerstr.	B
Schmidtgasse	B 7
Stadtplatz	B
Stelzhamerstr.	B
Traungasse	B 9
Vogelweiderstr.	A 12
Volksgartenstr.	AB

B Wegkapelle

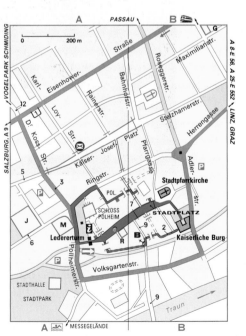

In Traungasse (**B 9**) note the little oratory on the left (**B B**), dedicated to St John Nepomuk; it shelters a fine statue of the saint. Altstadtgasse (**B 2**) runs along remains of the medieval walls. Opposite the west entrance to the Kaiserliche Burg is the Revenue Building, given its present Baroque façade in 1684.

Kaiserliche Burg (**B**) ⊙ – Emperor Maximilian I, the "last knight", died here in 1519. The restored imperial castle now houses three museum collections: the history of the town, with a remarkable display of Biedermeier; agriculture on the theme of the "farmer's year"; and the Austrian museum of bakery, the only one of its kind.

Return to Stadtplatz and the parish church.

Stadtpfarrkirche (**B**) – Behind the high altar in the Gothic chancel are some fine 14C stained-glass windows. Beneath the tower, a beautiful late 12C **Romanesque porch** has been grafted on.

A number of buildings in the Stadtplatz are worthy of attention: the Rathaus (no 1) has a Baroque façade with stucco work and an attic storey topped by four stone urns; there is a Jugendstil façade at no 10; the 1570 paintwork is still intact on the house (no 24) where Salome Alt, Wolf Dietrich's mistress, lived; Biedermeier style (no 49); a lively example of Rococo (no 52); a 16C courtyard (no 34) leads to the Schmidtgasse (**B 7**). To the north of town stands Schloß Polheim (**A**), dating from the 13C and originally the residence of the Counts of Polheim, a local noble family.

On the northwest side of Polheimerstraße is the somewhat pompous façade of the **Stadtmuseum** (**A M**), built 1900-02.

EXCURSION

⋆ **Vogelpark von Schmiding** (Bird Reserve) ⊙ – *7km - 4 miles north of Wels (in Krengelbach).*
This 85 000m² - 915 000ft² reserve with its biotopes and a 3.5km - 2 mile circular path draws 200 000 visitors during the year, who come to watch in peace and quiet the 2 500 birds (350 species) which are resident here. There is a tropical greenhouse and a walk in aviary with birds of prey. Besides birds, the reserve is home to antelopes, gazelles, kangaroos and monkeys.

A resident of Schmiding bird reserve

All aboard the Vienna Prater Giant Wheel

H.A. Jahn/VIENNASLIDE

287

WIEN★★★

Ⓛ VIENNA – Population 1 515 660
Michelin map 426 folds 3, 4 and 12
Local maps under Excursions: Wienerwald below and DONAUTAL
Alt 156m - 512ft
Hotels and restaurants: see Michelin Red Guide Europe

Vienna was the residence of the Imperial court for six centuries and is indelibly stamped with the seal of the Habsburgs. Through the chances of history it is now the seat of a federal government, ruling a much reduced state, but owing to an effective policy of neutrality introduced in 1955, Vienna has retained considerable prestige.

Metternich's famous remark, "The Balkans begin at the Landstraße", is all the more apt when one remembers that "Landstraße", the 3rd district of Vienna, is separated from the centre of the city by the width of a single street. The statesman's dictum has been borne out many times in the course of history. Vienna was an outpost of the Roman Empire, and a stronghold of Christianity against the Turkish assault. Until the collapse of Communism, the city was the Western world's most advanced outpost in Central Europe.

Since 1967 Vienna has been the permanent headquarters of OPEC. In 1979 it became the third UN capital (after New York City and Geneva) with the opening of the International Centre, UN City (BR), in Donaupark. The centre includes the UN Industrial Development Organization and the International Atomic Energy Agency. Nearby is the "Austria Center Vienna", a major international congress centre.

The Austrian capital revolves round its cathedral, the Stephansdom. For many, Vienna suggests the rhythm of the waltz or the shape of the Prater's Giant Wheel. Its prestige, however, is due above all to its buildings, to memories of the Habsburgs, to the treasures in its museums, to the musical tradition preserved by the Opera and its famous choirs and orchestras *(see Vienna Capital of Music below)*, and to the elegance of the shops which line its great avenues.

HISTORICAL NOTES

From Antiquity to the Babenbergs – Since ancient times, the Vienna basin has been a cross-roads of European significance, commanding the neighbouring lands: Bohemia, Moravia, the Hungarian plain and the Alps.

The Romans established their camp at Vindobona facing the territory of the Germanic tribes. It is here that Marcus Aurelius is supposed to have died, and here – according to the Song of the Nibelungen – that Attila and Kriemhilde celebrated their wedding. Later, when the Babenberg family assumed control of the Eastern Marches, its representatives adopted in succession, as residences, Pöchlarn, Melk, Tulln and Leopoldsberg before settling in Vienna. In 1155, Heinrich II Jasomirgott installed his ducal court in the city at a place called Am Hof. The eminence arising from its official function enabled Vienna also to expand as a market town.

Under one of his successors, Leopold the Glorious, Vienna became the capital of the Duchy and was guarded by massive walls with six fortified gateways and nineteen towers. In the centre stood the Romanesque church of St Stephen (it became the bishop's seat only in 1469). By the time Frederick the Warrior, last of the Babenbergs, died in 1246, Vienna had become, after Cologne, the most important German-speaking town. Its growth, from then on, was linked with the fortunes of the Habsburgs, who reigned over Austria from 1273 to 1918.

The Plague and the Turks – In many Austrian towns columns dedicated to the Virgin May or the Holy Trinity were set up at the end of the 17C to recall that the Austrian Empire had escaped two scourges: the plague and the Turks.

The Plague – In 1678, just after the celebrations in Vienna for the birth of a son to the Emperor Leopold I, a terrifying sickness made its appearance. Corpses lay in heaps in the streets or were thrown into the Danube. All who could, fled the capital. Only a few notables, headed by Prince Schwarzenberg, decided to fight the plague. Drastic measures of hygiene enabled them to stop the epidemic, which died out a year after its first appearance.

In 1682 the column to commemorate the deliverance from this plague was erected in the Graben, but another threat, exceptionally grave, loomed on the frontiers of the Empire.

The Turks – An army 300 000 strong, under the command of Grand Vizier Kara-Mustapha, crossed the Danube at Belgrade, heading for Vienna, Prague and the Rhine. Following the green standard of the Prophet was a motley horde of Turks, Slavs, Bosnians, Tartars and even Hungarian rebels.

Although the fate of the Empire and the Christian world was at stake, Leopold had much trouble in organizing resistance. He could not count on the support of Louis XIV, who was pursuing a policy of weakening the Austrian royal house and playing the Turkish card. Of all the monarchs of Western Europe, only Sobieski, the King of Poland, who felt himself to be directly threatened, concluded a pact of mutual assistance with the Emperor.

On 14 July 1683 the Grand Vizier lay siege to Vienna (it had previously been besieged by the Turks in 1529). The town was abandoned by the Emperor and the court and defended only by 24 000 men under **Ernst Rüdiger Count of Starhemberg**. For nearly two months the beleaguered city resisted all attacks. Duke Charles of Lorraine was urged by the Emperor to organize a relief force. King John III Sobieski crossed the river at Tulln and Krems at the head of 80 000 Austrians, Poles, Saxons, Bavarians, Swabians and Franconians on 10 September. The following night he camped on the hill at Kahlenberg and on the 11th deployed his army in the Wienerwald. On 12 September the Turks, caught between two forces, took to flight in a general panic. The famous victory of the Kahlenberg had repercussions throughout Europe. From that time on, the western sovereigns recognized the pre-eminence of the Emperor, who had saved Christendom. The Turkish menace disappeared, broken by Prince Eugene, one of the most famous generals of his time. There followed for the Austrian Empire a long period of prosperity, distinguished by the reign of Maria Theresa.

Maria Theresa "the Great" (1740-1780) – Throughout her long reign the daughter of Karl VI established herself in Europe by strength of character and steadiness in political action which made her famous during the Age of Enlightenment. Her old enemy Friedrich II of Prussia was forced to admit that "When at last the Habsburgs get a great man it's a woman!".

In Vienna the Empress lived very simply in the Hofburg and at Schönbrunn, where she carefully brought up the survivors of the sixteen children she had by François of Lorraine. There she arranged the marriages of her daughters, Marie-Antoinette, the future Queen of France, Maria Carolina, Queen of Naples, and Maria Amalia and Maria Christina, who became respectively Duchess of Parma and Regent of the Netherlands. Meanwhile, the four fair-haired archduchesses led a carefree life, for which Marie-Antoinette was later to pine at Versailles. An anecdote illustrates this happy time; when Mozart, at the age of six, came to Schönbrunn he slipped in a corridor and fell. Marie-Antoinette consoled him and the boy declared: "I'll marry you when I'm grown up!".

Maria Theresa, too, kindly welcomed the child prodigy. As a patron of

Empress Maria Theresa

Trumler/ÖSTERREICH WERBUNG

artists, steeped in French culture, she founded in Vienna the Collegium Theresianum, an astronomical observatory and a library.

The Congress of Vienna – When Napoleon's empire collapsed in March 1814, Vienna supplanted Paris as the centre of Europe. It became the scene of the international congress which was to settle the fate of victors and vanquished. For a year, outside the working sessions of its committees, the Congress of Vienna furnished a pretext for splendid festivities, of which the echoes can still be heard. Here the crowned heads – the Emperor of Austria, Franz I, the young and handsome Czar Alexander I, the King of Prussia, Friedrich-Wilhelm, the King of Württemberg, and many princes and archdukes – made up a brilliant court. Diplomats added their prestige: Lord Castlereagh for Great Britain; Nesselrode for Russia; Wilhelm Humboldt for Prussia; Talleyrand for France; Metternich for Austria.

Receptions and balls were held at the embassies, in the state rooms at the Hofburg, and in the Great Gallery at the Schönbrunn palace. "Le Congrès ne marche pas, il

OUT AND ABOUT IN VIENNA

Area telephone code: 1

Aeroplane:

Tourist information centre at the Wien-Schwechat airport open daily 8.30am to 9pm.

There is a bus link between the airport and the City Air Terminal (at the Hilton Hotel), the Westbahnhof and the Südbahnhof.

There is a rail link between the airport and Vienna-North and Vienna-Centre.

Car:

Tourist information centres for motorists on the outskirts of Vienna:

To the north – Floridsdorfer Brücke, "Donauinsel" exit, open Holy Week to end of September daily from 9am to 6pm.

To the south – on the A2 motorway, "Zentrum" exit, open June to September from 8am to 10pm, Holy Week to end of June and in October from 9am to 7pm.

To the west – on the A1 motorway, Wien/Auhof rest area, open April to October from 8am to 10pm, November from 9am to 7pm, December to March from 10am to 6pm.

Train:

Tourist information centres in rail stations are to be found at the Westbahnhof (open daily 6.15am to 11pm) and the Südbahnhof (open May to October from 6.30am to 10pm, November to April from 6.30am to 9pm).

Tourist Office in Vienna city centre:

Kärntner Straße 38
Wien 1
open daily 9am to 7pm
☎ (1) 21 11 40

Public Transport

Tickets – Tickets are valid on the underground/subway (U-bahn), street trams, express trains (Schnellbahn) and buses. The following tourist tickets are available from most hotel receptions, or from the ticket offices in the underground stations of Karlplatz, Schottentor, Schwedenplatz, Stephansplatz, Landstraße, Westbahnhof, Hietzing and Kagran, as well as from tobacconists:

24-Stunden-Netzkarte (valid for 1 day)
72-Stunden-Netzkarte (valid for 3 days)
8-Tage-Umwelt-Streifennetzkarte (8 day ticket with a band to be validated each day)

There are also individual tickets valid for a single journey within Vienna.

Wien-Karte – This three-day ticket is available from many hotels and from tourist information centres (e.g. Kärntner Straße 38). It offers 3 days unlimited travel on the city's public transport systems, as well as reduced priced entry for some museums and other sights, and some interesting shopping options.

Underground/subway (U-bahn)

- U1 (red) Reumannplatz-Kagran
- U2 (purple) Karlsplatz-Schottenring
- U3 (yellow) Johnstraße-Erdberg
- U4 (green) Heiligenstadt-Hütteldorf
- U6 (brown) Siebenhirten-Floridsdorf

From 1997, line U3 is to be extended from Johnstraße as far as Ottakring. A map of the underground system is given on a city map available from most hotels.

Trams and buses

The city's network of trams and buses covers the whole conurbation, with the exception of the city centre within the Ring. This area has its own minibus service.

A map of Vienna's public transport systems is available from the offices of the transport authorities. ☎ (1) 5 87 31 86.

Children and young adults under the age of 15 travel free of charge on Sundays and public holidays, as well as during the Viennese school holidays.

Entertainments and ticket reservations

The city of Vienna's monthly entertainment programme is available from the **tourist office** (Kärntner Straße 38) from the middle of the month onwards.

Staatsoper, Volksoper, Burgtheater and Akademietheater: Written applications for tickets to performances at any of these four places should be submitted at least three weeks (Staatsoper and Volksoper) or 10 days (Burgtheater and Akademietheater) in advance to the Österreichischer Bundestheaterverband, Hauschgasse 3, A-1010 Wien. ☎ (1) 51 44 26 53 (Mondays to Fridays 9am to 4pm), Fax (1) 51 44 29 69.

If paying by credit card it is possible to reserve tickets by telephone, at least 7 days before the performance, ☎ (1) 5 13 15 13 (Mondays to Fridays 10am to 6pm). Standing places are only available from the evening ticket office, Abendkasse ☎ (1) 5 14 44-29 59 or 29 60.

Spanische Reitschule – Reservations for performances must be submitted in advance to the Spanische Reitschule, Hofburg, A-1010 Wien, or to theatre ticket agencies and travel agents in Vienna. No reservation is necessary for the morning training sessions.

Sung Masses in the Burgkapelle, Hofburg (with the Vienna Boys' Choir) – Places should be reserved at least 8 weeks in advance from the Hofmusikkapelle, Hofburg, A-1010 Wien. They can be collected and paid for at the Burgkapelle on Fridays from 11am to 12noon and on Sundays from 8.30am to 9am. Seats also on sale at the ticket office of the Burgkapelle every Friday from 5pm onwards for the following Sunday.

The following organisation deals with ticket reservations from abroad for various events:

Vienna Ticket Service
Postfach 16
A-1043 Wien
☎ (1) 5 34 17 75 (Mondays to Fridays from 9am to 5pm), Fax (1) 5 34 17 26

Wiener Spaziergänge (Walks in Vienna)

Walks on a given theme, such as Music Capital of the World, Jugendstil, Habsburg Legacy, Viennese Coffee-houses etc., are organised by the tourist office (details and monthly programmes can be obtained from Kärntner Straße 38).

Vienna for the Handicapped Visitor

The Vienna tourist office produces a detailed brochure giving information about facilities available to the handicapped (in stations, hotels, restaurants, theatres, museums etc.) – contact:
Wiener Tourismusverband
Obere Augartenstraße 40
A-1025 Wien

---

danse" (The Congress doesn't advance; it dances), said the old Prince de Ligne maliciously. The remark became famous. More than any other city Vienna could offer choice entertainment to its guests: art collections of rare quality, theatre, opera, concerts of chamber music. Ludwig van Beethoven himself conducted a gala concert and his opera *Fidelio* was received with enthusiasm.

Although Czar Alexander I made himself conspicuous by the brilliance of his receptions and by his libertinism, and though Prince Talleyrand succeeded, by his cleverness and a long experience of European affairs, in acquiring for himself a privileged position among the participating states while defending the rights of minorities, the central figure of the Congress remained Prince Metternich, the Austrian Minister of Foreign Affairs.

Metternich – The career of Klemens Lothar Wenzel, Prince of Metternich-Winneburg, began in 1806, when he was appointed Ambassador in Paris and had every opportunity to observe Napoleon I. In 1809 Metternich was given the heavy burden of directing the foreign policy of his country. It was then that he proposed a *rapprochement* with France and succeeded in making this alliance a reality by negotiating the marriage of Napoleon and the Archduchess Marie-Louise. With remarkable diplomatic insight he made Austria a buffer state between the Russian and French Empires, a third force which might restore the balance of Europe.

Metternich

This policy enabled Metternich to act as mediator at the Congress of Vienna and to have a moderating influence which made Austria, till 1848, defender of order in Europe.

A "Belle Époque" – After the Napoleonic Wars, the Congress of Vienna began a carefree period that the Austrians call **Vormärz**, Pre-March, because it ended with the revolutionary events of March 1848. Wine, women and song – also dancing – seem to have been the chief interests of the Viennese, who lived at that time in a fever of pleasure.

Under the benign dictatorship of Metternich, the idyllic Vienna of the **Biedermeier** consumed mokka, chocolate and pastries at cafés like Hugelmann's, near the Danube, on the road to the Prater. On holidays the Viennese went out among the wine shops *(Heurigen)* of the Danube and Vienna Woods, where they would relax over pitchers of young wine, listening to impromptu poets, violonists and zither players. Anything was an excuse for idling: the parade of beasts being led to the abattoir, the menageries, the boatmen, the changing of the guard to Schubert's dreamy music. People would also meet to hear Schubert's *Lieder,* which were in the repertory of every woman singer in Vienna. The violins sobbed in the Schottenfeld quarter. At the Apollo, a dancehall which could hold 4 000 people and had the biggest floor in Europe, 28 meeting rooms and 13 kitchens formed annexes to the establishment. At the Prater, the waltz was born.

Fashion at the Prater – The Prater was the rendezvous of rank, fashion and smart carriages. Not only the pale, fair-haired Duke of Reichstadt appeared wearing his tight-fitting white uniform, but also the Emperor Ferdinand would stroll, un-escorted, returning the salutes of passers-by.

The comte de St-Aulaire, French Ambassador in Vienna, noted in his memoirs: "At five o'clock in the afternoon, carriages begin to cross the little bridge over the Danube... the procession breaks up only at the entrance to the Prater. Until then they have gone slowly in single file; no one must leave his place. There is no privilege. I have seen the Emperor and Empress obey this rule and, after waiting for a long time, give up hope of reaching the Prater before nightfall, abandon their outing and turn back to the Burg."

Franz Joseph and the Growth of Vienna – After the disappearance of the Turkish menace, a new face had been given to the capital, marked by the influence of Baroque architecture.

Princely palaces, winter residences and churches sprang up; the Schwarzenberg palace (Prince Eugene's mansion) on the Belvedere hill and the Karlskirche. The buildings overflowed the narrow limits of the 17C city walls. New quarters developed and extensive suburbs were established without a definite plan.

Death took Joseph II, "the enlightened despot", by surprise, while he was preparing to transform the whole of Vienna. The difficult period of the Napoleonic Wars did not facilitate the implementation of grandiose projects and the city had to await the reign of Franz Joseph (1848-1916) for the large-scale planning and building that made Vienna what it is today.

The Ring – In 1857 the Emperor signed the decree ordering the removal of the bastions and the formation of a belt of boulevards round the old town. The creation of the "Ring" was to turn the capital into a huge building site. Famous architects and artists, from Austria and abroad, contributed to this great project, which was rivalled only by the transformation of Paris by Baron Haussmann several years later. The great new boulevard is lined by Vienna's most important public buildings as well as by the grand tenement blocks characteristic of the city.

The Gürtel – In 1890, the outer boroughs were incorporated into Vienna and the second ring of fortifications razed, making space for an outer circular road, known as the "Gürtel" (Girdle or Belt).

Augarten Porcelain – The first Viennese porcelain factory was founded in 1717. Following financial difficulties the state took over in 1744, and Maria Theresa made it a national pottery, like Sèvres, installing it in the Imperial gardens at Augarten (**DT**). The porcelain is marked with a Beehive and specializes in flowers and dec-orative gilding.

H. Wiesenhofer/ÖSTERREICH WERBUNG

Augarten porcelain workshop

The porcelain factory made the famous Schönbrunn service for Napoleon. It reached its greatest vogue under the direction of the miniaturist Daffinger, when the Biedermeier style was at its height in the 1820s to 1840s. Following a slow decline the factory closed in 1864 but was reopened in 1923 in the Augarten palace.

VIENNA, CAPITAL OF MUSIC

Refer also to the section on Music in the Introduction.

Venerable traditions – St. Peter's in Salzburg may have been the cradle of sacred music in the German-speaking world but, by the 12C, Vienna under the Babenbergs had become an important centre of secular music. Many troubadours came here, achieving corporate recognition at the end of the 13C. At the end of the Middle Ages, Maximilian I moved his dazzling court choir here from Innsbruck, confirming Vienna's status as a musical capital. The choir became an institution, much admired in the 15C and still arousing the enthusiasm of today's audiences under the name of "**Hofkapelle**".

Music-loving emperors – The Baroque era (17C-18C) saw the arrival of opera, born in Italy around 1600, and ardently welcomed to Vienna by Court and citizenry alike. Generous patrons of music, some emperors were themselves composers of distinction. The most prolific of them, **Leopold I**, left a number of religious works which still form part of today's repertoire. His operettas were sung and performed by the royal family and court. The father of Maria Theresa, Karl VI, was a talented violinist. All received a solid musical education: Maria Theresa played the double bass, Joseph II the harpsichord and cello. Musicians were respected and appreciated, like the young Mozart at Schönbrunn.

The great days of Viennese music – The 18C was dominated by the figure of **Haydn**, the initiator of Classicism in Vienna.
The princely palaces became veritable musical workshops, places for great performers and composers to meet. Haydn's "Seasons" is intimately linked to the Schwarzenberg palace, while **Mozart** discovered the works of Bach and Handel in the house of Maria Theresa's doctor's son and **Beethoven** and **Gluck** were guests at the Lobkowitz palace. With the encouragement of Joseph II, the number of theatres multiplied, helping to bring music within reach of the middle classes.
Around 1825 the musical soirées known as "**Schubertiades**" began, at which Schubert interpreted *Lieder* for a circle of friends and which ended in dancing.
After the revolution of 1848, music societies proliferated, promoting high standards of concert performance and of musical education. The most illustrious of these societies was the "Friends of Music" which numbered the German composer **Brahms** among its conductors. Brahms enjoyed unparalleled prestige, but **Bruckner**, "God's troubadour", who had left his native Linz to become Court organist, found his sacred masterpieces to be beyond the comprehension of the Viennese public. **Mahler** used his 10 years in Vienna as Kapellmeister to undertake the reforms which helped give birth to a new musical era.
By the end of the century music was no longer the prerogative of high society and there was hardly a household in the city which failed to meet at least once a week to make music.

The force of destiny (1770-1827) – One of Beethoven's sources of inspiration was the romantic countryside around Vienna, of which the great composer said, "No-one has loved these places more than I". To the painter Schindler, accompanying him on a walk from Heiligenstadt to Grinzing, he confided, "It is here that I wrote the brookside scene (in the Pastoral Symphony), and the sparrows up there, the quails, the nightingales and the cuckoos wrote it with me".
Irresistibly drawn to the musical metropolis, Beethoven arrived in Vienna at the age of 20. He stunned the city with his ability as a pianist. It was in the city and in the picturesque villages now engulfed in its suburbs that he created the works which revolutionised the language of music: the Eroica Symphony, originally dedicated to Napoleon, the opera Fidelio, applauded at the Congress of Vienna in 1815, the Fifth Symphony, that great drama of a soul in conflict, the Pastoral Symphony of 1808, and finally the "Ode to Joy", the monumental Ninth Symphony, which the master, by now stone-deaf, conducted though in fact the orchestra had to be conducted by an understudy. Deafness had in fact, afflicted him from the age of thirty and led to the deep despair evident in the "Heiligenstadt Testimonies". Later in life Beethoven moved from Vienna to nearby Baden where he would undertake lengthy walks, often by moonlight, through the romantic landscape of the Vienna Woods. After a lifetime of wanderings and disappointments, he died in Vienna on 26 March 1827, saying to his friend Hümmel, "Applaud, my friends, the comedy is over". He is buried close to Schubert in the central cemetery (Wiener Zentralfriedhof).

The triumph of light music

– The sensation of the Congress of Vienna was the **waltz**. This vigorous and light-hearted dance kept the city on its toes throughout the 19C, particularly from 1820 onward when fashioned by the talented and prolific **Strauss** dynasty.

Polished, refined, and made a genre in its own right by **Joseph Lanner** and Johann Strauss the Elder, the waltz was to dominate the dance-floor under Johann Strauss the Younger, whose tributes to the great city like "Vienna Blood", "Tales from the Vienna Woods", were more than amply rewarded by their enthusiastic reception by the Viennese. Strangely enough,

Johann Strauss

Wiesenhofer/ÖSTERREICH WERBUNG

the "Blue Danube" waltz was more successful in Paris than on the banks of the river itself. The ballrooms of Vienna were kept supplied with musicians from among the 300 or so managed by the younger Strauss and his brothers Joseph and Eduard. Today, the statue of Strauss the Younger in Vienna's Stadtpark, which is copied in the souvenir shops, has become one of the city's emblems.

The "New School" of Vienna

– This is the name given to the movement founded by the Viennese **Arnold Schoenberg**, promotor of a veritable musical revolution whose effects would make themselves felt throughout the century.

Originally self-taught, Schoenberg became the pupil of the opera composer Alexander Zemlinsky (1871-1942). His first works, like the *Gurrelieder*, still have affinities with the post-Romantic style. They were soon followed by works like the

---

Viennese Ball Season

During the winter in Vienna, one ball follows close on another. The famous Emperor's Ball is held on New Year's Eve, reawakening the elegance and splendour of the former Imperial court at the Hofburg. During Carnival time (Fasching),

the various associations and professional guilds put on about 300 balls, many in magnificent surroundings (Rathaus, Hofburg, Musikverein), including the Floral Ball, organised by gardeners and florists, the Rudolfina-Redoute Masked Ball, and the balls of the Viennese Coffeehouses, the Vienna Philharmonic Orchestra and the Technicians' Circle. Doctors and lawyers have a ball, and so do hunters and firemen. Guests are welcomed everywhere.

The ball to end all balls in terms of sheer elegance is the **Opera Ball**, held in February at the Staatsoper. This event draws the rich and famous from Austria and abroad, and is the High Society event of the

Ball in the Rathaus, Vienna

P. Koch/RAPHO

year. The ball is opened by ballet dancers from the Vienna State Opera and a committee of young ladies and gentlemen dancing a Polonaise with fans.

First String Quartet (1905), then by the Second Quartet in whose last two movements the boundaries of tonality are left behind. In 1912 his *Pierrot Lunaire*, a melodrama in 21 sections for narrator and five instruments, brought him international recognition. Schoenberg's theories of twelve-tone composition are set out in his *Treatise on harmony* in which he established new relationships between sounds freed from traditional harmonic conventions.

Schoenberg was a born teacher and exercised a profound influence on a number of pupils including Webern and Berg, both Viennese. Of the three composers, it was Webern who went furthest away from classical tonality, while Berg enjoyed the greatest public success with his operas *Wozzeck* and *Lulu*.

After a long period of domination by the theories of the New School, contemporary music is now looking for an approach closer to traditional tonality.

Prestigious institutions – The city's musical life is now dominated by the great institutions like the **Opera** (Staatsoper), whose every performance is oversubscribed.

The yearly waltz soirée known as the Debutantes' Ball is equally popular, tickets for it changing hands at small fortunes.

The fame of the **Hofmusikkapelle** goes back five centuries; its sung Mass on Sunday mornings brings together singers from the Opera and the Vienna Boys' Choir, equally popular are the concerts given at the same time at the **Musikverein** by the Vienna Philharmonic, which has counted Richard Wagner, Johannes Brahms, Gustav Mahler, Richard Strauss, Karl Böhm and Herbert von Karajan amongst its conductors. Contemporary music is given its due by the Vienna Symphony Orchestra at the **Konzerthaus** where, as at the Musikverein, there is at least one concert a day.

Light opera can be heard at the **Volksoper Wien**, while the **An der Wien** theatre, where Beethoven's Fidelio was first performed, is the setting for **musicals**. At the end of the spring, the annual **Wiener Festwochen** charm discerning audiences with a variety of musical events (opera, concerts, ballet), while a few weeks later the Summer Music Concerts can be heard all over town, in various old palaces and town squares.

Musicals

In the beginning was the musical "Cats", which was performed 2 080 times here. Now there are three theatres in Vienna given over to musicals – the modern version of the operetta: the **Raimundtheater**, Wallgasse 18, the **Ronacher**, Seilerstätte 9 and the **Theater and der Wien**, Linke Wienzeile 6.

Ticket reservations (at least three weeks in advance) : Vienna Ticket Service, Postfach 160, A-1043 Wien.

LIFE IN VIENNA

Shopping in Vienna is concentrated around the Hofburg, the cathedral and the opera house, along Kärntner Straße, the Graben and the adjoining streets (all pedestrianised). Here can be found the elegant shops reflecting the city's high standards of taste in clothes, porcelain, glassware, jewellery, books, instruments, antiques and so on.

Other shops, including the big department stores, line Mariahilfer Straße linking the Ring to the Westbahnhof. The amiability and courtesy of the Viennese make it possible for visitors to participate easily in the life of the city.

The coffee-house, a Viennese institution – Among the baggage abandoned by the fleeing Turks in 1683 was a great quantity of coffee beans. The dark-coloured beverage was to become so popular that it even gave its name to the establishments in which it was consumed.

In the 19C the coffee-house became the place for people to meet and to read the newspapers, an indispensable part of middle-class as well as of intellectual life. Many writers like Schnitzler would spend the whole day in their favourite coffee-house, using it as their study.

Famous coffee-houses – The recently restored Café Central was where Trotsky used to come to play chess. Nearby, the Café Herrenhof was a favoured haunt in the 1930s of writers like Musil, while artists like Klimt and Schiele would meet at the Café Museum. Today's artists gather at the Café Hawelka.

The modern coffee-house scene – The city's coffee-houses fill up as the working day ends. Discreetly attired waiters serve the traditional glass of water at the same time as the coffee, which is available in bewildering variety. It can be drunk accompanied by cakes and pastries of equal variety, among them croissants, whose origin is said to go back to the Turkish siege. It seems that it was Vienna's bakers, at their nightly labours, who first heard the Turkish sappers burrowing away beneath the city's

Guide to Coffee, Viennese-style

Listed below are some descriptions of the more commonly served types of Viennese coffee, among the thirty or so preparations which are available :

Großer/kleiner Schwarzer	large/small cup of black coffee
Großer/kleiner Brauner	large/small cup of black coffee with a dash of milk
VerlängerterSchwarzer/Brauner	"Schwarzer"/"Brauner" diluted with water
Einspänner	black coffee served in a glass with whipped cream (Schlagobers)
Fiaker	black coffee in a glass with a tot of rum
Franziskaner	coffee mixed with chocolate chips
Kaffee verkehrt	coffee with more milk than coffee
Kaisermelange	coffee with egg yolk and alcohol
Kapuziner	black coffee with a small blob of whipped cream
Mazagran	iced coffee with rum
Melange	milky coffee (can be served with whipped cream)
Türkischer Kaffee	strong coffee prepared in a small copper coffee pot, served hot in tiny cups

A further tip : never ask for a cup of coffee (eine Tasse Kaffee) in Vienna – it is "eine Schale Kaffee" (literally, a bowl of coffee). Depending on how high a milk content you would like, coffee can be ordered "Braun", or even "Gold".

defences and sounded the alarm. As a reward, Ferdinand I is supposed to have given them the privilege of baking the cresent-shaped rolls which have proved popular ever since.

Once the customer's coffee is finished, the waiter collects the cup and brings another glass of water. He will also keep the customer supplied with newspapers and magazines. The best-known cafés include Dehmel's, Lehmann's, Heiner's and Sacher's. It is not unusual for customers to stay for hours without repeating their order; savouring the passing moment in a leisurely way is an essential part of the Viennese temperament.

Sampling new wine in one of Vienna's Heurigen

Cosmopolitan cuisine – Vienna's restaurants welcome the visitor into their friendly ambience to enjoy dishes from all the countries which once made up Austria's empire, often served to a musical accompaniment. A convivial atmosphere can be enjoyed in a **Keller**, not unlike a German beer-hall, where snacks and cold meals are downed with a glass of beer or wine.

Some establishments (Gasthäuser, Weinhäuser) offering good home cooking are known as **Beisel**. Similar are the taverns *(Weinstuben)* where the Viennese congregate once the working day is over. Then there are the famous wine-pubs; called **Heurigen**, where, by special dispensation, the new wine is served; these cheerful places are to be found in the wine-growing villages on the edge of the city like Grinzing, Nussdorf, Sievering and Gumpoldskirchen. Usually run by the wine-growers themselves, they can be recognised by the pine branch hung up above the entrance. In cosy rooms or leafy courtyards, customers sample the grower's new wine *(Heuriger)*, accompanied perhaps by a snack or simple meal, in an utterly Viennese atmosphere, enlivened by **Schrammelmusik** (played by a pair of violins, an accordion or clarinet plus a guitar).

EXPLORING VIENNA

★ **Tour of the Ring** – *By car or tram (circular routes nos 1 and 2) – Allow an hour. Start at the Stubenring* (HY) *to the east, near the Danube.*
The Ring is particularly attractive at night when the main buildings are floodlit, but it is interesting at any time of day as a preliminary to exploring the historic centre of the city.

Postsparkasse (HY) – On the right stands this important Jugendstil (Art Nouveau) building designed at the very start of the 20C by Otto Wagner. *Description of the interior below, under Jugendstil Buildings.*

★ **Österreichisches Museum für angewandte Kunst** (HY M¹⁰) – To the left is this monumental building designed in Florentine Renaissance style, its stone and brick façade articulated by round-headed bays and twin windows. *Description of the interior below, under Beyond the Ring.*

Stadtpark (HY) – To the south of the museum and flanking the River Wien stretches the attractively landscaped City Park, laid out in 1862; it is famous for its statues of musicians, Bruckner, Lehar, Robert Stolz and, above all, Johann Strauss.

★ **Staatsoper** (GY) – Just after the Schwarzenbergplatz (GZ **120**), which leads to the Belvedere palaces further south, stands Austria's national opera house *(right)* with its elegant arcades. In French Renaissance style, this was the first of the

---

MARKETS

Naschmarkt *Linke Wienzeile*
Several markets are held here :
Naschmarket (fruit and vegetables), Mondays to Fridays from 8am to 6.30pm, Saturdays from 6am to 2pm
Bauernmarkt (local farm produce), Mondays to Thursdays from 6am to 12noon, Fridays from 6am to 1pm, Saturdays from 6am to 5pm
Flohmarkt (flea market), Saturdays from 6.30am to 6pm

Bauern- und Antiquitätenmarkt Freyung *Freyung*
Bauernmarkt (local farm produce), March to October on Tuesdays and Thursdays from 10am to 6.30pm
Antiquitätenmarkt (antiques), October and November on Fridays and Saturdays from 10am to 8pm

K&K-Markt am Donaukanal *near Schwedenplatz*
Trödelmarkt (bric-à-brac), May to September on Saturdays from 2pm to 8pm and on Sundays from 10am to 8pm

Kunstmarkt im Heiligenkreuzer Hof *Grashofgasse and Schönlaterngasse*
Every first weekend of the month on Saturdays from 10am to 7pm and Sundays from 10am to 6pm

Kunstmarkt am Spittelberg *Spittelberggasse*
On Saturdays from 10am to 6pm

Christmas markets

Christkindlmarkt Rathausplatz mid-November until Christmas
Weihnachtsmarkt am Spittelberg end of November until Christmas
Altwiener Christkindlmarkt Freyung end of November until Christmas
Kultur- und Weihnachtsmarkt vor dem Schloß Schönbrunn end of November until Christmas
Kunsthandwerksmarkt vor der Karlskirche end of November until Christmas

great public edifices to be erected along the Ring. The main façade was all that was left standing when the building burnt down in 1945 *(tour of the interior below, under Musical Memories)*.

Burggarten (GY) – Between the Ring and the Hofburg, the palace gardens, first laid out in the 19C, were once the preserve of the Imperial Court. Since 1919 they have been open to the public. At the entrance stands a statue to Goethe, and there are other memorials to Franz Joseph, Franz I (on horseback) and Mozart.

Neue Burg (GY) – The Neue Burg is the most recent wing of the Hofburg. Its semicircular colonnade opening out on to the Heldenplatz (Heroes' Square) is part only of a great building project that was fated never to be completed; another, identical edifice was to have been built to the northwest of the square, turning it, together with the Marienplatz, into a vast "Imperial Forum". The Neue Burg was completed only just before the outbreak of the First World War and the disappearance of the monarchy led to the abandonment of the grandiose scheme. The building now houses a number of museums *(see below, under Hofburg: Interior)*.

Maria-Theresien-Platz (FY) – The square takes its name from the monument erected in 1888 to the glory of the great empress. At her feet are equestrian statues of her generals, Daun, Laudon, Traun, Khevenhüller; other figures represent the statesmen who served her grand designs, like her Chancellor, Kaunitz, Count Mercy-Argenteau and Prince Liechtenstein, as well as the great composers of her reign, Gluck, Haydn and Mozart.

Facing each other across the square are two symmetrical domed buildings, constructed 1872-91 in the official architectural style of the Ring (Ringstraßenstil) to house the imperial collections, to the southeast the **Kunsthistorisches Museum**★★★, to the northwest the **Naturhistorisches Museum**★ *(both described below, under Beyond the Ring)*.

Bounding the square to the southwest is the 18C façade of the Messepalast, designed by Fischer von Erlach as the Imperial stables and now the city's Fairs and Exhibition building.

Rathausplatz, Vienna

Volksgarten (FY) – This quiet park with its pools and statues, a favourite place for a stroll, is one of the most pleasant public open spaces along the Ring. An exotic note is struck by the "Temple of Theseus", a copy of the original in Athens. The rose garden is famous and the park's formally clipped trees frame attractive views outwards.

Parlament (FY) – Opposite the Volksgarten next to the Law Courts stands Austria's seat of government (1873-83) with its elegant Grecian façade.

Neues Rathaus (FY) – The neo-Gothic city hall building is linked to the Ring by attractive gardens. The tower is topped by the famous "Rathausmann" carrying the city flag. Summer concerts are held in the arcaded courtyard. Reception rooms, council chambers and the huge banqueting hall are open to the public. In the basement, as in Germany, is a vast restaurant, the "Rathauskeller". From the tower there is an interesting view over the Heldenplatz and the Maria-Theresien-Platz, while opposite are the three wings of the elegant Burgtheater.

Burgtheater (FY) – The theatre's origins go back to the founding of the "National Court Theatre" on the Michaelerplatz by Joseph II. The present Renaissance style building (1874-88), of modest size but brilliantly decorated, was much criticised for its lack of comfort. It was altered when war damage was repaired.

Universität (FX U) – On the north side of the Rathausplatz stands this neo-Gothic-cum-Renaissance style university building. Behind it, on the left, as the Ring makes its final bend, is the Votive Church.

Votivkirche (FX D) – Two tall spires tower over the entrance to this neo-Gothic place of worship, completed in 1879. Its name commemorates Franz Joseph's escape from an assassination attempt early in his reign.

After passing the **Börse** (Stock Exchange – BX) on the right, the tour ends on the banks of the Donau-Kanal at the Franz-Josefs-Kai.

City viewpoints – There are two splendid viewpoints in the hills overlooking the city from the northwest, the **Kahlenberg★** and the **Leopoldsberg★★** *(see below, under Excursions)* **(AR)**.
The **Donauturm★★ (BR)** ⊘, or Danube Tower, was built on the north bank of the river in 1964. From its two revolving restaurants or its viewing terraces 150m – nearly 500ft above the Donaupark there is a bird's eye **view★** over the city and its surroundings. There is a similar **panoramic view★** from the **Great Wheel** (Riesenrad) in the Prater *(see below, under Beyond the Ring)* **(EU)**.

City coach tours ⊘ – A variety of tours is offered by *Vienna Sightseeing Tours* and *Cityrama*, some of them with particular themes. Tours start from the Staatsoper, the university and the Johannesgasse (Kursalon).

Michaelerplatz entrance of the Hofburg

★★★HOFBURG: a town within a town

The Imperial palace, favourite residence of the Habsburgs, was progressively enlarged during the centuries. The nucleus, built about 1220, was a quadrilateral bristling with towers round a courtyard which later came to be known as the Schweizerhof (Swiss Court).

The presence of successive additions by sovereigns anxious to enlarge and beautify their residence explains the juxtaposition of different styles.

The castle chapel, Burgkapelle, was erected in the mid-15C; the Amalienhof and the Stallburg in the 16C; the Leopoldinischer Trakt (Leopold's apartments) in the 17C; those named Maria Theresa's apartments used by the President, the Reichskanzlei-trakt (Imperial Chancellery), the Spanische Reitschule, where the "Spanish" riding takes place, the Albertina and Österreichische Nationalbibliothek (National Library) in the 18C; in the 19C and 20C, the Neue Burg, whose completion just before 1914 marked the end of the structural history of the palace.

Exterior

The architecture, which is severe and full of majesty, provides remarkable vistas of the intervening courts or the surrounding monuments.

Michaelerplatz façade – The semi-circular façade giving on to the Michaelerplatz is decorated with two monumental fountains, adorned with statues; above this façade rises the dome which roofs the rotunda. The main arches are closed by bronze gilded grilles. It is an inspiration to stand beside the rotunda and see,

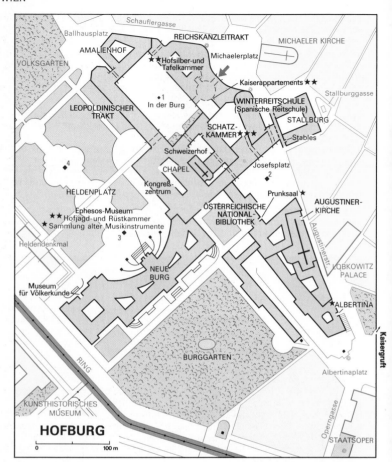

HOFBURG

0   100 m

through a wrought-iron lattice, the steeple of the Michaelerkirche in the distance. The square known as "In der Burg", in the centre of which stands the monument to the Emperor Franz II (1), is reached through this rotunda. From the court a fine Renaissance doorway, bearing coats of arms and inscriptions, leads to the **Schweizerhof**; bordering the courtyard, on the right, are stairs leading up to the Burgkapelle.

Josefsplatz – Arched passageways lead into this elegant square which owes its name to the fine equestrian statue of Joseph II (2), the base of which is adorned with low reliefs in bronze. The pediments of the buildings round it are surmounted by groups of sculpture.

One side of this square is formed by the early 18C **Österreichische Nationalbibliothek** by Fischer von Erlach.

Return to the Heldenplatz.

Neue Burg – The new Imperial palace, which was erected between 1881 and 1908 in the Italian Renaissance style, was intended by the architects to be complemented by a similar wing on the northwest side but this was never constructed. This building presents a concave façade to the view from the Heldenplatz which is bounded on the northwest, beyond the shady Volksgarten, by the steeple of the Neues Rathaus. Here stand the memorials, in the form of equestrian statues, of Prince Eugene of Savoy (3) and Archduke Karl (4), both by the sculptor Fernkorn.

On the southwest side is the monumental gateway, the Äußeres Burgtor, which leads to the Ring (1824). It is now (as of 1934) a war memorial (Heldendenkmal).

Interior: souvenirs of the Habsburgs

★★★ **Schatzkammer** ⊙ – The treasures displayed here recall the long history of the Habsburg dynasty, whose sovereigns amused themselves by collecting these symbols of the power of their family.

The **secular treasure** contains several dazzling pieces, some of them of religious significance. The insignia of the Austrian Empire – crown, sceptre, orb – were produced in the 17C by the Workshop of the Court, in Prague. Rudolf II's crown, surmounted by a splendid sapphire, became, symbolically, the Austrian Imperial Crown from 1804 to 1918 following the dissolution of the Holy Roman Empire.

The **sacred treasure** in rooms I to V includes a number of works of art (12C-19C) taken from the castle chapel and from the Imperial crypt. The insignia of the Holy Roman Empire are also displayed: the famous **10C Imperial crown**★★★, the Imperial sceptre, and even more awe-inspiring the Holy Lance (9C), a kind of military reliquary containing fragments of the Crown of Thorns, supposedly having the power to make its bearer invincible.

Imperial crown

With the marriage of Mary of Burgundy, the daughter of Charles the Bold, to the Archduke Maximilian in 1477, the House of Habsburg inherited the treasures of the Duchy of Burgundy. Since the 18C the treasure of the Order of the Golden Fleece, which includes liturgical relics and insignia used during enthroning ceremonies, has been preserved in Vienna.

★★ **Kaiserappartements** ⊙ – The **Imperial apartments** occupy parts of the first floor of the Chancellery wing (Reichskanzleitrakt) and the Amalientrakt. Of the 2 600 rooms in the palace, about 20 are open to visitors. Luxurious furniture, Aubusson and Flemish tapestries and crystal chandeliers (in the large reception room) are reminders of the people who lived in this part of the Hofburg: L'Aiglon (Napoleon I's son, the Duke of Reichstadt), Karl I, Franz Joseph and especially the Empress Elisabeth (portraits by Winterhalter). The dining hall with its table laid for 20 evokes the sumptuousness of family receptions at the time of the Austro-Hungarian Empire.

★★ **Hofsilber- und Tafelkammer** ⊙ – The magnificent objects on display from the **Imperial porcelain and silver collection** were in regular use at the Imperial table for two centuries until the fall of the Monarchy in 1918.

The modern display includes 18C Chinese and Japanese porcelain, huge gilded centre-pieces, ewers and dishes in chased silver-gilt, and an enormous silver-gilt service for 140 guests, as well as gold knives, forks and spoons, several Sèvres services – a green service of 1776, numerous Empire ones from the Vienna porcelain workshops, and fine sets of glassware.

Hofburgkapelle ⊙ – The Gothic palace chapel was built in the middle of the 15C and later adapted to the Baroque taste. Religious services on Sundays and festivals are a wonderful experience, as they are accompanied by music performed by the Hofmusikkapelle with the famous Vienna Boys' Choir.

Spanische Reitschule ⊙ – The all-white, indoor **Spanish riding school** is the work of Joseph Fischer von Erlach; it is lined by two galleries supported on columns. This interesting creation of Baroque art was built in the early 18C by Karl VI, the father of Maria Theresa. This is where feats of dressage that date back to the second half of the 16C are performed.

The **parades**★★ (Vorführungen) make a fine spectacle. The riders wear brown tail coats, white buckskin breeches, riding boots and cocked hats. The Lippizaner horses *(see PIBER)* are white, with gleaming coats, their tails and manes are plaited with gold ribbons; they dance the quadrille, the gavotte, the polka and the slow waltz.

The **training** session (Morgenarbeit) although less spectacular (without music or chandeliers) shows the horse performing difficult jumps, steps and other movements.

Stallburg – *Entrance: Reitschulgasse 2.* Separated from the indoor riding school by a glazed-in passageway, the Stallburg is composed of three floors of galleries, surrounding a Renaissance courtyard, decorated with a wrought-iron well. The ground floor was transformed by Maximilian II into stables for the horses of his guard. It is still used as a stable by the Spanische Reitschule.

On the second floor is a gallery of 19C European art.

Österreichische Nationalbibliothek ⊙ – The building is the work of the Fischer von Erlach architectural dynasty (early 18C). The core of the collection is formed by the Imperial library, established in the 14C.

The **Great Hall★**, a masterpiece of architecture and Baroque decoration with **ceiling frescoes★★** by **Daniel Gran** in the oval dome and statues by the Strudel brothers, holds Prince Eugene's magnificent library.

Kaisergruft (GY) ⊙ – For more than three centuries the **Capuchin crypt** has been the burial place of the Imperial family. The church was built from 1619 to 1632.

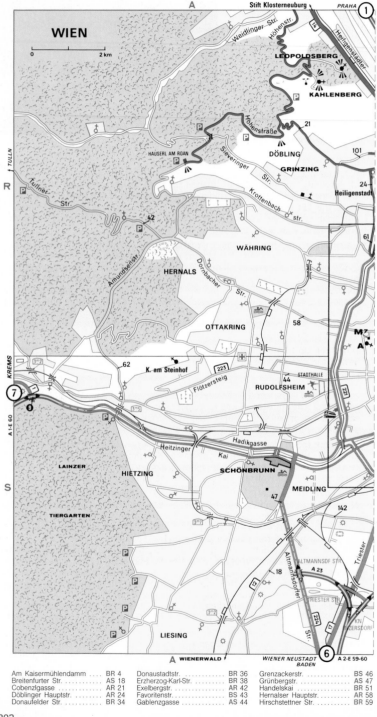

Am Kaisermühlendamm	BR 4	Donaustadtstr.	BR 36	Grenzackerstr. .... BS 46
Breitenfurter Str.	AS 18	Erzherzog-Karl-Str.	BR 38	Grünbergstr. .... AS 47
Cobenzlgasse	AR 21	Exelbergstr.	AR 42	Handelskai .... BR 51
Döblinger Hauptstr.	AR 24	Favoritenstr.	BS 43	Hernalser Hauptstr. .... AR 58
Donaufelder Str.	BR 34	Gablenzgasse	AS 44	Hirschstettner Str. .... BR 59

In a niche on the façade of the church stands a statue of the Capuchin Marco d'Aviano, Papal Legate with the army of Charles of Lorraine, who brought about the unification of the leaders of the Christian armies in the battle to win freedom from the Turks in 1683. The morning after the battle was successfully won, he celebrated Mass on the Kahlenberg hill.

The remains of 12 emperors, 16 empresses and more than 100 archdukes are buried in this crypt; their hearts are in the Augustinian church and their entrails in the catacombs of the Stephansdom. Here lay the bronze coffin of the King

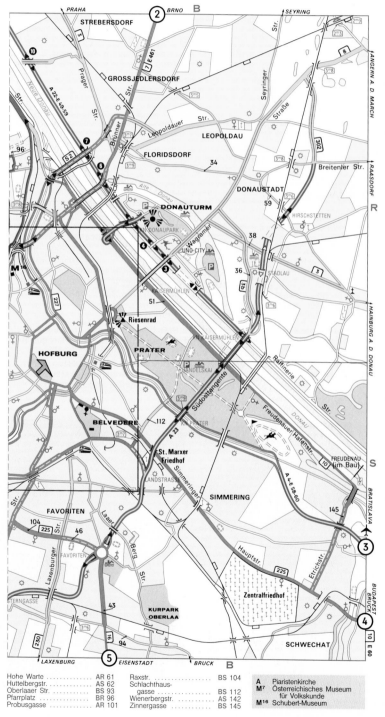

Hohe Warte	AR 61	Raxstr.		BS 104
Huttelbergstr.	AS 62	Schlachthaus-		
Oberlaaer Str.	BS 93	gasse		BS 112
Pfarrplatz	BR 96	Wienerbergstr.		AS 142
Probusgasse	AR 101	Zinnergasse		BS 145

A Piaristenkirche
M⁷ Österreichisches Museum für Volkskunde
M¹⁶ Schubert-Museum

of Rome, Duke of Reichstadt, son of Napoleon I and Marie-Louise, before it was transferred to Paris in December 1940. Of the 139 coffins here (36 of which are walled in), only one does not belong to the Habsburg family: it is that of Countess Fuchs, who brought up Maria Theresa and whom the latter held in such esteem that she granted her this signal honour.

The Empress Maria Theresa and her husband, François of Lorraine, lie in a beautiful Rococo double sarcophagus, the work of Balthasar Moll (as is the sarcophagus of Karl VI, father of Maria Theresa) adorned with busts of the deceased placed symbolically opposite each other and the statue of an angel, ready to sound a trumpet on the day of judgment. The sarcophagus of Emperor **Franz Joseph**, his wife Empress **Elisabeth**, and their son Archduke Rudolf are in a single room, built 1908-1909. The bodies of the heir to the Imperial throne, Archduke Franz Ferdinand, and his wife, both murdered by an assassin in Sarajevo in 1914, are laid to rest at Schloß Artstetten. The so-called Neue Gruft, or new crypt, built in 1961, contains the sarcophagi of **Marie-Louise**, Empress of France, and **Maximilian of Mexico**. The last Habsburg emperor, Karl VI, is still buried on Madeira, but his wife, Empress Zita, was buried in the chapel of the Imperial crypt in 1989.

According to a quaint ritual introduced by Emperor Mathias at the beginning of the 17C, the Imperial remains were brought down to the crypt after the funeral ceremony, accompanied by a final guard of honour. The coffin was carried solemnly down the Staircase of the Dead to the door of the crypt, which was locked. The Master of Ceremonies knocked three times at the door with his staff. The guardian monk demanded to know who was there, whereupon the master of ceremonies gave the name and titles of the deceased. The monk denied all knowledge of the person concerned, so the master of ceremonies knocked three more times, and in reply to the monk's "Who goes there ? " replied, "His Imperial and Royal Highess" – but to no avail, as the monk once again claimed never to have heard of him. A third time, the master of ceremonies knocked three times on the door, and this time, in response to the monk's question, he said, "Your brother X, a sinner", to which the monk replied, "Let him come in." The Church, recognising no authority but that of God, only admitted the deceased in the spirit of humility which befits those who believe in the resurrection of the dead.

Augustinerkirche – Built during the first half of the 14C in the enclosure of the Hofburg, this was the church of the court. In 1784 the Baroque interior decoration was removed and the building thus regained its original Gothic aspect. Many court marriages were celebrated in this church: Maria Theresa and François de Lorraine (1736); the marriages by proxy of the Archduchess Marie-Antoinette (1770), of Marie Louise (1810) and of Franz Joseph and Elisabeth of Bavaria (1854).

Tomb of Archduchess Maria Christina, Augustinerkirche

WIEN

Alserbach-Str.	DT 3	Erdberger Lände	EU 37	Langegasse	CU 77
Billrothstr.	CT 12	Gürtelbrücke	DT 48	Lerchenfelder Str.	CU 81
Brigittenauer Lände	DT 17	Heiligenstädter Lände	DT 56	Rauscherstr.	DT 102
Döblinger Hauptstr.	CT 23	Heiligenstädter Str.	DT 57	Untere Donaustr.	EU 130
		Innstr.	ET 65	Wallensteinstr.	DT 133
		Jörgerstr.	CU 66	Weißgerber Lände	EU 139
		Kinderspitalgasse	CU 74	Wiedner Gürtel	DV 140

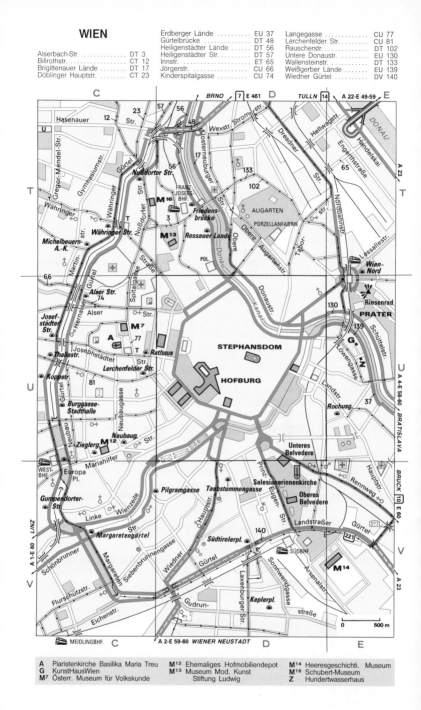

A Piaristenkirche Basilika Maria Treu
G KunstHausWien
M⁷ Österr. Museum für Volkskunde

M¹² Ehemaliges Hofmobiliendepot
M¹³ Museum Mod. Kunst
    Stiftung Ludwig

M¹⁴ Heeresgeschichti. Museum
M¹⁶ Schubert-Museum
Z Hundertwasserhaus

Facing the entrance is the **tomb★** of the Archduchess Maria Christina, favourite daughter of Maria Theresa. This mausoleum of white marble is considered one of the masterpieces of the Italian sculptor Canova, who worked in Vienna from 1805 to 1809. Under a medallion, a portrait of the Archduchess, figures symbolizing Virtue and Christian Love are depicted advancing towards the tomb. The **Loreto-kapelle** ⊙ *(access by the right side aisle)* holds in its **crypt** (Herzgruft) fifty-four urns containing the hearts of the Habsburgs. The Georgskapelle nearby was a meeting place for the knights of the Order of St George, and later for those of the Order of the Golden Fleece. It contains the cenotaph of Emperor Leopold.

★ Albertina ⊙ – The Albertina collection of graphic art owes its name to its founder, Duke Albert of Saxe-Teschen (1738-1822), a son-in-law of the Empress Maria Theresa, through his marriage to Maria Christina *(see above)*. To his personal collection were added, in 1920, the engravings of the former Imperial library assembled by Prince Eugene of Savoy, some of which date from the early 16C. More than 1 000 000 sheets – engravings, old masters' drawings and architectural designs – illustrate the development of the graphic arts since the 14C. The **Dürer collection★**, belonging to Rudolf II, contains such well-known drawings and engravings as the *Praying Hands* and the *Hare*. These are now displayed as facsimiles, the originals only being shown in a special exhibition. In such occasional exhibitions one may also see drawings and watercolours by Rubens, Rembrandt, Poussin, Burgkmair, Fragonard and others.

★★ Hofjagd- und Rustkammer ⊙ – *Neue Burg, main entrance, 2nd floor.*

A display of sabres, swords, helmets, cross-bows, cuirasses, pistols, guns and full-dress harnesses which made up the **armoury** of the Habsburgs during the reigns of Maximilian and Charles V (15C and 16C). They were made by the best arms guilds of Milan, Innsbruck and Augsburg for the royal family and are enamelled, beautifully engraved and delicately carved. Also on display are the hunting arms of the Imperial family and the loot taken from the Turks (end of the 17C) – saddles and scimitars.

★ Sammlung alter Musikinstrumente ⊙ – *Neue Burg, central entrance.*

Displays of old **musical instruments** (16C-19C): wind instruments, percussion or string, played by such famous musicians as Haydn, Beethoven, Schubert, Schumann, Brahms, Liszt, Mahler and various princes of the Habsburg family. The collection is based on instruments collected by Archduke Ferdinand II of the Tyrol and by the Duke of Modena.

Ephesos Museum ⊙ – *Neue Burg, main entrance.*

It was Austrian archaeologists who worked on the important site at Ephesus in Turkey in the 19C, unearthing many significant finds. Valuable archaeological artefacts, now on display in the museum along with a model of the ancient city of Ephesus and relics from Samothrace, were given to the Emperor by the Sultan. In the large entrance hall among the sculpture and reliefs are the eleven marble **Reliefs of Ephesus★★**. These belonged formerly to the mausoleum of Lucius Verus, co-regent with the Emperor Marcus from 161 to 169 AD. The reliefs show the adoption of Marcus Aurelius and Lucius Verus, battle scenes from the wars with the Parthians, and the deification of Lucius Verus.

Museum für Völkerkunde ⊙ – *Neue Burg, side entrance.*

The ethnographic museum contains collections of art from Africa (Benin, among other places) and the Far East (China and Japan) on the ground floor. On the mezzanine level, there are permanent exhibitions on "Polynesians, Pirates of the South Seas", with some unusual items brought back from Captain Cook's voyages in the South Seas, and "Antiquity of the New World – pre-European Cultures of the Americas", with (most notably) the unique Aztec feather head-dresses. The museum also puts on temporary exhibitions.

★OLD TOWN *time: 4 hours, museums not included*

Start from the Stephansplatz (GY 124).

Between the cathedral and the Danube canal lies the heart of Old Vienna – its houses, hotels and long narrow streets, which in spite of reconstruction still evoke a special atmosphere.

★★★ Stephansdom (GY)

– Vienna's cathedral is unique. The great Austrian writer Adalbert Stifter said of it: "As you go around a corner, the cathedral comes suddenly into view. Like a mountain, it is simple and wonderful; its sheer beauty lifts the spirit…" With its vast roof (exactly twice the height of its walls) of variegated and glittering tiles and its mighty south tower (the famous **Steffel** without which the city would lose part of its soul), this is a building without parallel. Often damaged during its eight centuries of existence, but always restored and embellished, the Stephansdom maintains its symbolic meaning for the citizens of Vienna.

Historical notes – On the site of the present building stood a vast three-aisled Romanesque basilica built 1137-47. This was soon replaced by a similar building, in a style anticipating the Gothic style. Of this church, badly affected by the great fire of Vienna in 1258, only the **Giants' Doorway** (Riesentor) and the **Towers of the Pagans** (with their strangely-coiffed figures) remain today.

In 1359 Duke Rudolf IV of Habsburg, wishing to adapt the building to the new Gothic taste, laid the foundation-stone of the present three-aisled nave. A century passed before the vaulting was completed. In response to the request of Emperor Frederick II, the Pope declared Vienna the seat of a bishopric and St. Stephan's became a cathedral.

Damaged during the Turkish siege of 1683, the cathedral fared even worse in 1945, being bombarded by both Russians and Germans. Its former beauty has now been completely restored.

Exterior – The small size of the Stephansplatz, centre of the medieval city, accentuates the great size of the cathedral, whose steeple rises like an arrow to the height of 137m - 450ft (Salisbury Cathedral 123m - 404ft). The north tower remained incomplete for many years, finally being given its Renaissance roof in 1579. Here hangs the great 21 tonne bell known as the **Pummerin**, crudely cast from Turkish cannon captured in 1683.

The Romanesque west door, the **Giants' Doorway**, is crowded with statues: Christ in Majesty on the tympanum, the Apostles at the base of the recessed arches. The decoration is intricately carved.

Go round the cathedral anti-clockwise; at its south-west corner stands the copy of a Gothic lantern of the dead, from the old cemetery of St. Stephan (now the Stephansplatz). In the square, tiles outline the plan of the chapel of St Mary Magdalene which served as a charnel house. Along the south side of the cathedral are tombstones (recalling the former cemetery) and sculptures, unfortunately half-hidden by dirt, and on the south side of the chancel scenes depicting the Visitation and Christ in the Garden of Olives. On the wall of the

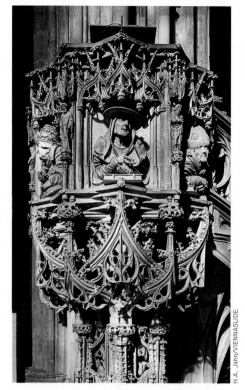

Pulpit, Stephansdom

axial chapel there is an early 15C bust popularly known as the Christ with Toothache and on the north wall a Last Judgement. To the northeast of the chancel stands the "Capistran's Pulpit" on the spot where, on 6 December 1791, Mozart's mortal remains were given absolution.

Enter the cathedral through the Giants' Doorway.

Interior ⊙ – Clearly inspired by the traditional Germanic hall-church, the long nave (107m - 352ft) gives an impression of great majesty. It is ingeniously linked to the three-aisled chancel.

The magnificent carved stone **pulpit**★★★ dates from the early 16C and is the masterpiece of Anton Pilgram, who has portrayed himself, under the ramp, holding his sculptor's tools and looking out of a half-open window. All round are busts of the four Fathers of the Church: St Augustine, St Ambrose, St Gregory and St Jerome. The boldness of its carving and the vigorous attitudes struck by its figures place it among the finest and most sophisticated works of the Flamboyant Gothic style.

The left apsidal chapel, known as the Frauenchor, contains a beautiful altarpiece decorated with carved wood, painted and gilded, known as the **Wiener Neustadt altarpiece**★★. Carried out in the first half of the 15C, it shows a group of figures sculpted in the round on the wooden base; on the central panel are the Virgin and Child flanked by St Barbara and St Catherine and, up above, the Coronation of the Virgin. In the chancel the altarpiece on the high altar represents the stoning of St Stephen.

The right apsidal chapel, the Apostelchor, preserves a remarkable **tomb**★★ of the Emperor Friedrich III, made of red Salzburg marble by Nikolaus Gerhart of Leyden at the end of the 15C. The artist has illustrated the struggle between Good and Evil, symbolizing the evil spirits in the form of noxious animals trying to enter the tomb to trouble the sleep of the Emperor, while the good spirits, represented by local personages, stop them.

Catacombs ⊙ – In the catacombs are urns containing the organs of the emperors of Austria, chapels established since 1945 and traces of the former Romanesque basilica destroyed by fire in 1258.

Cathedral towers ⊙ – The south tower (Hochturm) can be climbed to a height of 73m - 240ft, while the platform of the north tower (which houses the Pummerin bell) is 60m - 197ft above ground. In fine weather there are good **views** over the city, the Kahlenberg heights and the Danube plain to the east.

Cross Stephansplatz to Singerstraße.

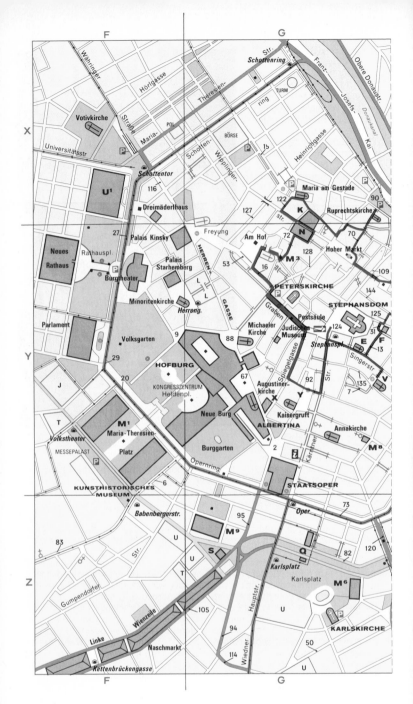

Deutschordenskirche (GY **E**) – *Singerstraße 7*. This church was built by the Order of the Teutonic Knights, a German hospitaller order founded in the Holy Land in 1190 for German pilgrims (it became a military order in 1198 and was consecrated in 1395).

The church, a 14C Gothic building, remodelled in the Baroque style, contains a beautiful 16C Flemish **altarpiece★** at the high altar, which is made of gilded and carved wood, with painted panels.

Treasure of the Teutonic Order ⊘ – History of the Order (seals and coins) and wealth accumulated over the centuries: sacred vases in gold covered in enamel; silver arms decorated in gold and precious stones, crystal, clocks, portraits and uniforms of Heads of the Order.

Franziskanerkirche (GY **V**) – The interior of this church was transformed in the Baroque taste in the 18C. On one of the righthand altars is a painting of St Francis by Johann Georg Schmidt, known as "Wiener Schmidt", and an

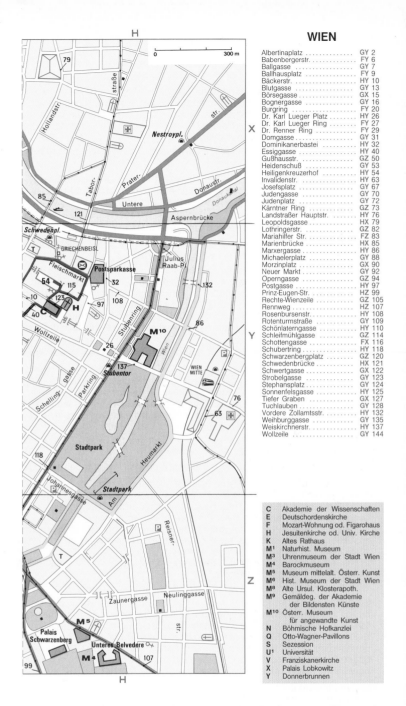

Albertinaplatz	GY 2
Babenbergerstr.	FY 6
Ballgasse	GY 7
Ballhausplatz	FY 9
Bäckerstr.	HY 10
Blutgasse	GY 13
Börsegasse	GX 15
Bognergasse	GY 16
Burgring	FY 20
Dr. Karl Lueger Platz	HY 26
Dr. Karl Lueger Ring	FY 27
Dr. Renner Ring	FY 29
Domgasse	GY 31
Dominikanerbastei	HY 32
Essiggasse	HY 40
Gußhausstr.	GZ 50
Heidenschuß	GY 53
Heiligenkreuzerhof	HY 54
Invalidenstr.	HY 63
Josefsplatz	GY 67
Judengasse	GY 70
Judenplatz	GY 72
Kärntner Ring	GZ 73
Landstraßer Hauptstr.	HY 76
Leopoldsgasse	HX 79
Lothringerstr.	GZ 82
Mariahilfer Str.	FZ 83
Marienbrücke	HX 85
Marxergasse	HY 86
Michaelerplatz	GY 88
Morzinplatz	GX 90
Neuer Markt	GY 92
Operngasse	GZ 94
Postgasse	HY 97
Prinz-Eugen-Str.	HZ 99
Rechte-Wienzeile	GZ 105
Rennweg	HZ 107
Rosenbursenstr.	HY 108
Rotenturmstraße	GY 109
Schönlaterngasse	HY 110
Schleifmühlgasse	GZ 114
Schottengasse	FX 116
Schubertring	HY 118
Schwarzenbergplatz	GZ 120
Schwedenbrücke	HX 121
Schwertgasse	GX 122
Strobelgasse	GY 123
Stephansplatz	GY 124
Sonnenfelsgasse	HY 125
Tiefer Graben	GX 127
Tuchlauben	GY 128
Vordere Zollamtstr.	HY 132
Weihburggasse	GY 135
Weiskirchnerstr.	HY 137
Wollzeile	GY 144

C	Akademie der Wissenschaften
E	Deutschordenskirche
F	Mozart-Wohnung od. Figarohaus
H	Jesuitenkirche od. Univ. Kirche
K	Altes Rathaus
M¹	Naturhist. Museum
M³	Uhrenmuseum der Stadt Wien
M⁴	Barockmuseum
M⁵	Museum mittelalt. Österr. Kunst
M⁶	Hist. Museum der Stadt Wien
M⁸	Alte Ursul. Klosterapoth.
M⁹	Gemäldeg. der Akademie der Bildensten Künste
M¹⁰	Österr. Museum für angewandte Kunst
N	Böhmische Hofkanzlei
Q	Otto-Wagner-Pavillons
S	Sezession
U¹	Universität
V	Franziskanerkirche
X	Palais Lobkowitz
Y	Donnerbrunnen

Immaculate Conception of 1722 by Johann Michael Rottmayr. The nearby **Franziskanerplatz** has a Moses fountain and, like the Ballgasse leading off it to the south, is bordered by picturesque old houses.

From Singerstraße turn right into Blutgasse (13).

Mozart-Wohnung or Figarohaus (**GY F**) ⊘ – *Domgasse 5.*
Mozart lived in this house from 1784 to 1787 and composed *The Marriage of Figaro* there.

Domgasse (31) and Strobelgasse (125) lead to Wollzeile, a busy commercial street in old Vienna. Take Essiggasse (40) almost opposite, turn right into Bäckerstraße (10).

Bäckerstraße contains elegant 16C and 17C houses and the **Akademie der Wissenschaften** (Academy of Sciences – **HY C**) the former university built in the middle of the 18C to plans by Jean-Nicolas Jadot, the French architect attracted to Vienna by François de Lorraine. The Jesuit Church stands in Dr Ignaz Seipel Platz, surrounded by quiet houses and little covered passageways.

Jesuitenkirche or Universitätskirche (HY H) ⊘ – The rich Baroque decoration from the early 18C completely altered the character of this church, which was built in the early Baroque style. Interesting features include the pulpit, inlaid with mother-of-pearl, and the *trompe-l'oeil* fresco on the cupola by Andrea Pozzo, the Jesuit lay-brother who executed the church's transformation (1703-1705).

Take Sonnenfelsgasse (125) and then Schönlaterngasse (110); both streets are flanked by picturesque 16C houses.

Heiligenkreuzerhof (HY 54) – The courtyard, a former dependence of the Heiligenkreuz abbey, is framed by 18C pale coloured façades and the chapel of St. Bernhard, which is a retreat for artists and writers, seeking a peaceful atmosphere.

Take Postgasse (97) to the Fleischmarkt (Meat Market).

At the entrance to the Griechengasse is one of the city's oldest inns, the Griechenbeisel.

Hoher Markt (GY) – Interesting remains have recently been found here of Vindobona, the Roman Legion's Camp which preceded Vienna. In medieval times, this was the heart of the city, the "High Market" and also the place of execution. Today the square is dominated by the **fountain** known as the Virgin Mary's Wedding fountain (Vermählungsbrunnen), the work of Emmanuel Fischer von Erlach in 1732. At no 10 is a Jugendstil **clock** where figures in historic dress come to life every day at noon.

Judengasse (70), where second hand clothes are sold, leads to the Ruprechtskirche.

Ruprechtskirche (GX) ⊘ – Built in the 11C on the ruins of one of the gates of the Roman city, the French church of Vienna is the town's oldest church, but it has been restored several times. The Romanesque clock tower and great roof give it unusual character. The contemporary stained-glass windows are by Lydia Roppolt.

Return to Sterngasse, a narrow street with some steps. Turn left into Fischerstiege, then into right Salvatorgasse.

At no 5 there is the handsome Renaissance doorway of the Salvatorkapelle.

Maria am Gestade (GX) – At the heart of Vienna, on a terrace which used to dominate the main branch of the Danube, a sanctuary called Our Lady of the River Bank or Our Lady of the Steps was started in the 12C on the site of a Gothic edifice of which the general outline is still to be seen.
The western façade, of Flamboyant Gothic style, is ornamented with sculptures and the portal is preceded by a canopy. The seven-sided Gothic tower is surmounted by a beautiful pierced dome.
In the interior, the chancel has interesting stained glass windows, and elegant statues on the pillars of the nave.

Walk down Schwertgasse (122) – Interesting Baroque doorway at no 3.

In Wipplingerstraße, facing each other, are two handsome Baroque buildings: on the left (**Altes Rathaus** GX K), the former town hall of Vienna from the 14C to 19C – in the courtyard is the fountain of Andromeda (1741) by Donner – on the right is the old **Böhmische Hofkanzlei** (Chancellery of Bohemia – GY N) with its outstanding façade by Johann-Bernhard Fischer von Erlach (1714). Skirt the Chancellery to the Judenplatz (72), the heart of the Viennese ghetto in the Middle Ages, then follow the narrow Parisergasse to the Am Hof church.

★ **Uhrenmuseum der Stadt Wien** (GY M³) ⊘ – *Schulhof 2.* A remarkable collection of watches and clocks from primitive clocks to electronic ones; miniature clocks to the wheel works of the Stephansdom; as well as jacquemarts and cuckoo clocks. Note the amazing astronomical clock (18C) by Rutschmann.

Am Hof (GY) – This square is decorated by a bronze column to the Virgin Mary (Mariensäule, 1667). It was here that Franz II, on August 6, 1806, announced the renunciation of the German Imperial Crown, thus ending the Holy Roman Empire.

Take Bognergasse (16) to the Graben.

★ **Peterskirche** (GY) – This beautiful church, which is acclaimed as the most sumptuous of all the Baroque churches of the capital, with its frescoes and gilded stuccos, was built from 1702 to 1708 by Johann-Lukas von Hildebrandt to replace a three-aisled, Romanesque church, which was itself a replacement of the first place of worship in Vienna, a 4C building in the camp of Vindobona. The very short nave is topped by a cupola ornamented with a fresco representing

The Graben, Vienna

the Assumption attributed to Michael Rottmayr. The altarpieces of the side chapels were executed by the most eminent artists of the time, including Martino Altomonte *(Vision of St Anthony – The Holy Family)* and Rottmayr *(St François de Sales).*

Pestsäule (GY) – The plague column, dominating the elegant Graben, was constructed in the Baroque style at the end of the 17C.

Turn right into Spiegelgasse to the Donner fountain.

★ **Donnerbrunnen (GY Y)** – *Neuer Markt.* The fountain was built by Georg Raphaël Donner from 1737 to 1739.

The central statue, representing Providence, is surrounded by cherubs and fish spouting water. The statues (copies in bronze) round the fountain personify the rivers Traun, Ybbs, Enns and Morava (March), symbols of the four provinces nearest to the capital. The original statues in lead are in the museum of Baroque art in the Belvedere.

Return to Stephansplatz via Kärntnerstraße.

The chapter on Art in the Introduction to this guide gives an overall view of the artistic movements in Austria so that buildings and works of art may be placed in context.

Austrian art at first drew on a variety of sources owing to the position of the country in central Europe; it acquired its distinctive characteristics with Baroque art in the 17C and 18C, with the Biedermeier style after the Congress of Vienna (1814-15) and, at the turn of the century, with Art Nouveau and its radical alternatives presaging the modern era.

★★★ KUNSTHISTORISCHES MUSEUM (MUSEUM OF FINE ARTS) (FY) ⊙

The collections of art in this museum, patiently assembled by the art-loving Habsburgs, are among the most important in the world. The whole 1st floor is devoted to paintings – the left wing is reserved for the Flemish, Dutch and German schools; the right wing for the Italian, Spanish, and French schools.

On the 2nd floor, assembled in the annexe (Sekundärgalerie) are many Flemish, German and Italian works of art of the 16C and 17C *(this section is currently closed).*

Work being carried out on the building is likely to last several years and it is possible that galleries will be closed and paintings moved. The accuracy of the information given below cannot therefore be guaranteed.

Italian, Spanish and French Painting
From the entrance hall, take the stairs up to the 1st floor.

The monumental staircase is adorned with a sculpture group of *Theseus and the Centaur* by Antonio Canova.

Gallery I – Works by **Titian** (1490-1576), master of colour and portrait painting: *Ecce Homo, Margravine of Mantua, Young Woman with a Fur, Jacopo di Strada* and the portrait of Prince-Elector Johann Friedrich of Saxony.

KUNSTHISTORISCHES MUSEUM (1 st floor)

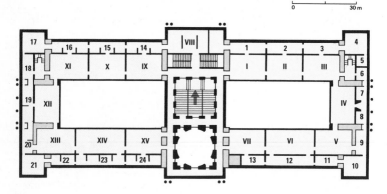

Gallery II – **Veronese** (1528-1588), the virtuoso of tones of colour (his green is famous), excels in compositions where grace of movement is continued in the draping of silk or velvet, as in his *Adoration of the Magi* and *Lucretia*. Portraits of women by Bordone.

Gallery III – **Tintoretto** (1518-1594) shows his profoundly assured technique as a painter in *Susanna Bathing*, and his skill as a portrait painter in *Lorenzo Soranzo*.

Gallery V – **Caravaggio** (1571-1610), revolutionary in his day, is represented by a large altarpiece depicting the *Madonna of the Rosary* and the striking painting of *David with Goliath's Head*, which has some marvellous chiaroscuro effects. Works by painters from the school of Caravaggio.

Gallery VI – Italian Baroque painting (17C masters from Bologna, Florence, Venice, Naples and Milan): **Guido Reni** *(Baptism of Christ)*, Cagnacci *(Suicide of Cleopatra)*, Fetti and Giordano.

Gallery VII – 18C Italian school: **Tiepolo,** Batoni, Canaletto Belotto (views of Vienna). Note the portrait of Gluck by Duplessis, and the portrait of Count Sinzendorf by Hyacinthe Rigaud (1659-1743).

Return to Gallery I, and follow the circuit round the smaller exhibition rooms.

Room 1 – Early Renaissance works from northern and central Italy. Those by great 15C Italian masters include *St Sebastian* by **Mantegna** (1431-1506) and the San Cassiano altarpiece (fragment) by Antonio da Messina.

Room 2 – Works by **Giorgone** (1478-1510), a friend of the young Titian: *Three Philosophers* and the *Portrait of a Young Woman* (Laura). Note also *Portrait of a Lady* and *Portrait of a Young Boy in front of a White Curtain* by Lorenzo Lotto.

Room 3 – Works by **Correggio** (1489/94-1534), whose sfumato technique (blending of tones or colours to soften outlines) was to influence painting into the 18C: *Abduction of Ganymede* and *Jupiter and Io*. Also Parmigianino's (1503-1540) famous *Self-Portrait in a Convex Mirror*.

Room 4 – Paintings by **Perugino** (1448-1523) and **Raphael** (1483-1520), and the Florentine masters Fra Bartolomeo and Andrea del Sarto.

Room 5 – Works by the Milan school (da Preda, Luini), influenced by Leonardo da Vinci, and the Mannerist dell'Abbate.

Room 6 – Works from the High Renaissance in northern Italy (Savoldo, Moroni).

Room 7 – Florentine Mannerist painting with works by Bronzino *(The Holy Family)*.

Room 8 – Works by Mannerists Andrea Schiavone and Jacopo Bassano (1517-1592) and his studio.

Room 9 – Spanish painting. Portraits of members of the Spanish Habsburg family by Coello (16C).

Room 10 – In the works of **Velázquez** (1599-1660) Spanish portrait painting reached its apogee. As Court Painter to King Philip IV of Spain he painted for the most part the Spanish royal family and members of court with great realism and attention to the truth. Note in particular *Philip IV* and the *Infanta Maria Theresa*.

Room 11 – Classical Baroque art. Pietà by Annibale Caracci, *Destruction of the Temple of Jerusalem* by **Poussin**.

Room 12 – Paintings by Domenico Fetti (1589-1623), master of Venetian High Baroque, and by Bernardo Strozzi.

Room 13 – 18C Venetian school with views of Venice by Canaletto and Francesco Guardi. 17C and 18C French school. 18C small-format paintings.

Flemish, Dutch and German Painting

Gallery IX – Dutch and Flemish painting from 1520-1550: *St Jerome in his Cell* by Marinus van Reymerswaele, landscapes by Valkenborch, works by Martin de Vos and Pieter Aertsen.

Gallery X – Works by **Pieter Bruegel the Elder**. This great painter of the Flemish Renaissance excelled in his realistic representation of scenes of popular everyday life and of nature. Admire the early works *The Battle between Carnival and Lent, The Tower of Babel, Hunters in the Snow,* and the famous *The Village Wedding. Massacre of the Innocents* is by Pieter Brueghel the Younger.

Gallery XI – Contemporaries of Rubens: *The Fish Market* by Frans Snyders with figures by Van Dyck; *Twelfth Night, the Bean King's Feast* by Jacob Jordaens.

Gallery XII – Devoted to works by **Van Dyck**: *Portrait of a Young General, Venus in Vulcan's Forge,* large altarpieces.

Galleries XIII-XIV and Room 20 – These contain works by **Pieter Paul Rubens**, master in virtually every aspect of the painter's art. The *St Ildefonse Altarpiece* is a composition whose appeal lies in the artist's masterful rendering of drapery and the richness of his palette. Pictures such as *The Château Garden* (Room 20), a charmingly idyllic scene, and *Festivities of Venus* seem to herald Watteau. Note also *Self-Portrait* and *Hélène Fourment with Fur Cloak,* a picture of Rubens' second wife.

Gallery XV – Works by great names of 17C Dutch painting: **Rembrandt** (large and small self-portraits, *Young Man Reading*), Ruisdael *(The Vast Forest),* Van Goyen *(View of Andrecht).*

After viewing these galleries, return to Gallery IX and on the smaller exhibition rooms.

Room 14 – 15C Dutch and Dutch Primitive painting. Geertgen tot Sint Jans's *Lamentation of Christ.*

Room 15 – Early 16C Dutch landscape painting.

Rooms 16 and 17 – These rooms are one of the highlights of the museum. **Albrecht Dürer**, one of the leading figures of the Renaissance, whose art was still exerting an influence on Late Gothic German art, bears comparison with Leonardo da Vinci as being one of the most complete artists of his time, a "universal genius". He is magnificently represented by the charming *Virgin and Child* of Venetian inspiration, the *Martyrdom of 10 000 Christians* with its background landscape worthy of being a picture in itself, *Adoration of the Trinity* executed in brilliant colour, *Portrait of a Young Venetian Woman* with her enigmatic expression, portraits of Johann Kleberger and, above all, of Emperor Maximilian I.

Besides Dürer and early 16C German art (Holbein the Elder: *Virgin and Child),* **Martin Schongauer** is represented by *The Holy Family.* Works by **Lucas Cranach the Elder** *(Paradise, Deer Hunts of the Prince-Elector of Saxony)* and his studio. **Albrecht Altdorfer** represents the Danube School with *Lot and his Daughters.*

Archduke Leopold Wilhelm in his Picture Gallery by David Teniers the Younger

Kunsthistorisches Museum, Wien/BILDAGENTUR BUENOS DIAS

Room 18 – 16C German portrait painting: works by **Hans Holbein the Younger** *(Portrait of Jane Seymour)*, Bruyn and Seisenegger.

Room 19 – Works by painters invited to Court at Prague by Rudolf II: Bartholomäus Spranger *(Venus and Adonis)* and above all **Giuseppe Arcimboldo,** whose allegories of *Winter* and *Fire* depict fantastic heads made of fruit and vegetables. Series of beautiful flower paintings by Jan Brueghel the Elder.

Room 20 – *Described with Galleries XIII and XIV above.*

Room 21 – **David Teniers the Younger,** Flemish painter of peasant scenes, here shows a different side of his painting in *Archduke Leopold Wilhelm in his Picture Gallery.*

Room 22 – Beginnings of Dutch painting, including four portraits by **Frans Hals** (1580-1666).

Room 23 – Works by Dutch artists in Italy in the 17C and by Rembrandt's successors: Jan Steen, Isaak and Adriaen van Ostade, Aert van der Neer, Jacob van Ruisdael.

Room 23 and 24 – 17C Dutch genre and still-life painting. *The Artist's Studio* is one of **Vermeer**'s most famous works; the harmonious composition, the soft and subtle palette and, above all, the artist's characteristic handling of the light falling on the face of the model and the artist's easel make this work stand out as a masterpiece.

Room 24 – 18C English painting (works by Thomas Gainsborough and Joseph Wright).

Egyptian and Oriental Collection
Mezzanine level, to the right, Galleries I-VIII

This collection was assembled in the early 19C and then substantially expanded by the addition of the Miramar Collection from Maximilian, future Emperor of Mexico. Excavations by Austrian archaeologists and scientists have also enriched it. Monuments from the ancient culture of south Arabia constitute the main feature of the collection. Particularly beautiful exhibits include a mortuary temple from the Giza pyramid complex, the shrine of Horus from the 18C BC, and a majestic pair of figures depicting Horus and King Haremhab from the end of the 14C BC. Impressive Ha-Hat stele from Thebes. Charming blue-glazed Egyptian hippopotamus, dating from about 2000BC. Sarcophagus of Nes-Schu-Tefnuit, numerous uschabti statuettes (servant figures fashioned in the form of mummies).

Antiquities
Mezzanine level, to the right, Galleries IX-XVIII

The foundations of this collection were laid as early as the 16C at the Habsburg Court, but it was mainly in the early 19C that the Imperial family funded its enhancement. It is now one of the most important of its kind in the world. Highlights include the exceptional collection of **cameos and jewellery** (Ptolemaic cameo, Gemma Augustea, eagle and lion cameo, Gemma Claudia) and the exhibits dating from the time of the great invasions and the Middle Ages. The remarkable **Dolichenus treasure,** which includes more than 100 artefacts from a Roman temple of Jupiter, was excavated at Mauer an der Url. The **Theseus Mosaic** comes from a Roman villa near Salzburg and depicts episodes from the legend of Theseus; it is one of the most beautiful mosaics to have been found in Austria. Ornate Germanic fibulae from the 4C and 5C and a magnificent necklace with 52 pendants testify to the immense skill of goldsmiths during this period. The gold treasure, probably of ancient Bulgarian origin, which was discovered in modern Romania and includes 23 gold vessels weighing a total of 10kg-22lb, occupies a place of honour in the exhibition.

Sculpture and Objets d'art (Kunstkammer)
Mezzanine level, to the left, Galleries XX-XXXVI

The Habsburgs' passion for collecting precious objects is legendary, and the quantity and variety of collections that they built up over the centuries as discerning connoisseurs of art defies belief. The art galleries of Archduke Ferdinand II from Schloß Ambras near Innsbruck, of Rudolf II in Prague and of Archduke Leopold Wilhelm in Vienna, as well as the contents of the Imperial Treasury were combined in 1891 and now constitute a collection without equal anywhere in the world in the quality and variety of its exhibits.

Among the huge number of magnificent objects on display, note in particular the 12C griffon aquamanile, *Virgin and Child* by Tilman Riemenschneider (c1495), *Allegory of Vanity* by Gregor Erhart (c1500), Emperor Friedrich III's sundial, numerous masterpieces from the goldsmiths of Augsburg, such as *Triumph of Bacchus*, a drinking game by Hans Schlottheim and the Celestial Globe by Georg Roll (1583-1584). The small domestic altar decorated with Christ and the Samaritan woman, a Florentine work (1600), illustrates a highly developed craftsmanship.

The so-called **saliera** (salt-cellar) depicting an allegory of the planet earth, by **Benvenuto Cellini**, occupies a place of honour. It is the only surviving piece of goldsmithing to have been definitively attributed to this artist. Note also the bust of Emperor Rudolf II by Adriaen de Vries, and a splendid bowl with the Triumphal Procession of Amor by Nuremberg master Christoph Jamnitzer in 1605. Among the ivories, *King Joseph I on horseback*, by Matthias Steinl of the Mattsee, stands out.

The unusual rock crystal pyramid by Dionysio Miseroni, the only work he ever signed and dated, was made between 1651 and 1653. Maria Theresa's famous breakfast service is made of gold, ebony and porcelain. Together with a bathroom set, the 70 piece service represents the pinnacle of achievement of Viennese goldsmithing in the 18C.

Coins and Medals (Münzkabinett)

2nd floor, to the left, Galleries I-III

From the reign of Emperor Maximilian onwards, the Habsburgs showed an interest in coins and medals. Ferdinand I collected coins, as did his son Archduke Ferdinand, and part of their collection is displayed in Vienna (the other part is in the Schloß Ambras near Innsbruck). In the 18C Emperor Karl VI and his son-in-law François of Lorraine, husband of Maria Theresa, turned their attentions to numismatics.

Of a total 500 000 items, about 4 500 are on display:

Gallery I – History of money in all its forms (objects, coins, paper) displayed chronologically.

Gallery II – Medals from the earliest examples to the end of the 19C.

Gallery III – Medals from the 20C.

★★BELVEDERE ⊘

The two palaces of the Belvedere were built by the architect Lukas von Hildebrandt as a summer residence for **Prince Eugene of Savoy** (1663-1736). Of French origin, this greatest of all Austrian military commanders spent much of his life in combat, often against the armies of France, as at the battle of Blenheim (1704) in Bavaria, won jointly with his close friend, the Duke of Marlborough. He was a persistent fighter against the Turks, displaying great gallantry as a young man in helping to raise the 1683 siege of Vienna and later bringing the Sultan's rule to an end in Hungary and beyond (battle of Belgrade 1717).

While the Unteres Belvedere and orangery were being built from 1714-1716 as a summer residence and the Oberes Belvedere from 1721-1723 for the festivities given by the Prince, the Duke of Marlborough was enjoying Blenheim Palace (northwest of Oxford) (1705), a national gift from the English Parliament for his victory at Blenheim.

Beautiful Baroque terraced gardens, from which there is a pleasant **view**★ of Vienna, link the two buildings and the orangery which contain works by Austrian artists or artists who painted in Austria.

Oberes Belvedere (DV)

The Oberes (Upper) Belvedere houses the Gallery of 19C and 20C Art.

★ **Galerie des 19. und 20. Jahrhunderts** – The galleries contain a large number of works which reflect the broad trends in Austrian and international painting in these years.

Ground floor – 20C: Austrian art from the period between the two World Wars and post-1945.

Period between the World Wars: includes works by Oskar Kokoschka, Oskar Laske, painters from the Nötsch school (Anton Kolig, Franz Wiegele), Herbert Boeckl, Josef Dubrowsky, Anton Faistauer, Albert Paris Gütersloh, Rudolf Wacker.

Post-1945 art: Austrian Art Informel, Viennese school of Fantastic Realism, New Painting of the 1980s.

1st floor – In the large red marble room, the State Treaty, ending the occupation of Austria by the Allies, was signed on 15 May 1955. On the ceiling is a fresco by Carlo Carlone – *The Apotheosis of Prince Eugene*.

Historicism, Barbizon School, pre-Impressionists, French Impressionists, Vienna Secession.

Hans Makart *(Bacchus and Ariadne)*, Hans Canon, Franz von Defregger *(The Final Banns)*, Anton Romako *(Admiral Tegetthoff at the Battle of Lissa)*, August von Pettenkofen *(Horse Market in Szolnok)*, Leopold Karl Müller, Camille Corot, Constant Troyon, Emil Jakob Schindler *(Embarcation of Steamers near Kaisermühlen)*, Tina Blau *(Spring on the Prater)*, Olga Wisinger-Florian, Theodor

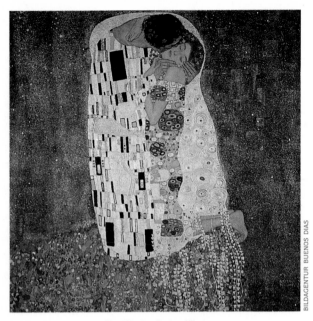

BILDAGENTUR BUENOS DIAS

The Kiss by Gustav Klimt

von Hörmann *(Znaïm in the Snow)*, Karl Schuch, Edouard Manet, Claude Monet *(The Garden at Giverny)*, Carl Moll *(The Naschmarkt in Vienna)*, Vincent van Gogh *(The Auvers Plain)*.

Leading representatives of Jugendstil painting, including **Gustav Klimt** (his dazzling work, *The Kiss*, among others) and Giovanni Segantini *(The Bad Mothers)*.

2nd floor – Classicism, Romanticism, Biedermeier.

Historical, mythological or religious themes: Friedrich Heinrich Füger *(The Death of Germanicus)*, Johann Peter Krafft *(Entry of Emperor Franz I after the Treaty of Paris on 16 June 1814)*, Jacques Louis David *(Napoleon at St Bernhard's Pass 1801)*, Moritz von Schwind *(Erlkönig, c1830)*, Leopold Kupelwieser *(Journey of the Three Kings, 1825)*.

Landscapes: Ferdinand Georg Waldmüller *(Great Prater Landscape)*, Carl Blechen, Rudolf von Alt *(The Stephansdom seen from Stock-im-Eisen-Platz, 1832)*, Caspar David Friedrich *(Rocky Landscape in the Elbsandsteingebirge, c1822-23)*, Friedrich Gauermann *(Landscape near Miesenbach, c1830)*, Joseph Anton Koch, Joseph Rebell, Ludwig Ferdinand Schorr von Carolsfeld *(Great Fir near Mödling, 1838)*, Franz Steinfeld, Adalbert Stifter.

Portraits: Friedrich von Amerling *(Rudolf von Arthaber and his Children, 1857)*, Moritz Michael Daffinger, Franz Eybl, Friedrich Heinrich Füger, François Pascal Simon Gérard, *(The Family of Count Moritz von Fries)*, Angelika Kauffmann, Johann Baptist Lampi the Elder, Ferdinand Georg Waldmüller *(Group Portrait of the Eltz Family)*.

Genre painting: Ferdinand Georg Waldmüller *(Peasant Wedding in Perchtoldsdorf)*, Josef Danhauser *(Wine, Women and Song)*, Peter Fendi, Friedrich Amerling *(The Fisher Boy)*, Michael Neder *(The Coachdrivers' Dispute)*, Carl Spitzweg, Carl Schindler.

Still-life: Ferdinand Georg Waldmüller, Franz Xaver Petter, Josef Lauer, Johann Knapp and others.

Go down to the Unteres Belvedere via the avenue on the right-hand side of the gardens.

Unteres Belvedere (HZ)

The plain façade contrasts with the splendour of the interior, in which works of art from the 17C and 18C in Austria are exhibited to good effect.

★ **Barockmuseum (M⁴)** – Paintings and sculptures are displayed in various rooms, underlining the wealth of variety of the Baroque period by being displayed according to themes such as "Baroque Man", "Man and Destiny", "Everyday life and Festivals", "Power and Powerlessness of Religion". Major painters of this period included **Paul Troger**, in sober or ceremonial mood, and **Franz Anton Maulbertsch**, the "Viennese Tiepolo" who tended more to excess.

The magnificent marble room features a ceiling fresco by Martino Altomonte, depicting the *The Apotheosis of Prince Eugene*. Visitors can also admire the original **fountain**★ by **Georg Raphaël Donner** (1693-1741), a copy of which stands on the Neuer Markt *(Donnerbrunnen)*.

In the Grotesque room, named after the motifs of the stucco work which adorns its walls, there are, besides the wonderfully luminous wall-paintings by Jonas Drentwett, the marvellous **heads**★ by **Franz Xaver Messerschmidt**, who also executed the figures of Maria Theresa and François of Lorraine in the marble gallery. This gallery is home to the famous Herculanean Women.

At the end of the gallery is the dazzling **Gold Room**★ with its mirrors and gilded carved woodwork, in which **Balthasar Permoser's** impressive marble sculpture of *The Apotheosis of Prince Eugene* (1718-1721) is reflected many times over. The sculptor included a figure representing himself at the feet of the prince.

★ **Museum mittelalterlicher österreichischer Kunst (M⁵)** - *In the orangery*. The works are mostly from the Gothic period.

In the first room there is a Tyrolean crucifix, still Romanesque in style, carved in the late 12C and delicate statues by the master of Großlobming (14C and 15C). In the second room is the Vienna altarpiece.

The central room displays, opposite the Vienna altarpiece, 7 panels by **Rueland Frueauf the Elder** representing scenes from the *Life of the Virgin* and *Passion*. On the sides is an excellent selection of **Michael Pacher's** work.

The fourth room contains the *Adoration of the Magi* by the Master of the Scottish Altarpiece in Vienna and a *Flight into Egypt* by the Master of the Mondsee School. The last room marks the end of the Gothic period (early 16C) shown by a concern for detail and a faithful depiction of landscape (instead of the traditional gold background) – the Danube School altarpiece. Admire the two works by **Marx Reichlich** *The Visitation* and the *Virgin Walking up to the Temple* (c1515). The former stable block (Prunkstall) is used to house special exhibitions.

★★★ SCHLOSS SCHÖNBRUNN

U-bahn – U-4 (green line): Schönbrunn or Hietzing stop.

Three centuries ago, the site of Schönbrunn was covered by a vast forest, a favoured hunting ground of the Habsburgs. In 1569 they acquired a wooded estate which had once belonged to a mill. The Emperor Matthias is credited with the discovery, at the beginning of the 17C, of the Schöner Brunnen (Beautiful Fountain) which has given its name to this area of the city (**AY**). The quarter has a fine view over most of Vienna and, beyond it, to the vine-clad hills and the Kahlenberg. In 1683 the imposing hunting lodge was destroyed by the Turks. Once the danger of invasion had passed, in 1695 Emperor Leopold I asked Johann-Bernhard Fischer von Erlach, one of the great architects of the time, to draw up plans for a huge palace for his son Joseph I.

The Emperor wanted Fischer von Erlach to create a summer residence that would surpass in splendour all other royal residences and even eclipse Versailles itself. These grandiose plans were never realized. Every kind of difficulty beset the monarchy, thus more modest building was carried out from 1695 to 1700. After Karl VI, who was not particularly interested in Schönbrunn, his daughter Maria Theresa modified the palace to its present form, after the plans of Nikolas Pacassi from 1743 to 1749, and the park was made by Ferdinand of Hohenberg. Schönbrunn is, nevertheless, an architectural success, particularly when it is viewed in the setting of its famous park.

Historical notes

Many historical memories are linked with the palace and the park. During the reign of Maria Theresa, Schönbrunn was the summer residence of the court. Marie-Antoinette, the future Queen of France, spent her childhood there. It was in the concert room that Mozart, at the age of six, astonished the empress and her courtiers with his amazing talents and, later, in the palace's little theatre, the prodigy directed his opera *Der Schauspieldirektor (The Impresario)* in 1786. Later his work *Don Giovanni* was played there. In 1805 and 1809 Napoleon I set up his headquarters in Schönbrunn. In 1815, during the Congress of Vienna, the Great Gallery was the scene of many magnificent receptions.

After the fall of the French Empire, Schönbrunn served as residence for Napoleon's son, the King of Rome. The boy was placed under the guardianship of his grandfather, the Emperor Franz, who forbade him all contacts with France. In this gilded cage he lived a life of exile, was given the title of Duke of Reichstadt and was immortalized by the French poet and playwright, Edmond Rostand, in his play entitled *L'Aiglon* (The Young Eagle).

It was at Schönbrunn that the Emperor Franz Joseph was born and where he died and it was in this palace that Karl I, last of the Habsburgs, signed the Declaration of Renunciation on 11 November 1918.

Tour

The main part of the building lies behind a façade 180m - 550ft long which has little of the flowing line characteristic of Viennese Baroque at its height in the time of Fischer von Erlach. The harmony of the whole construction is maintained by the ochre colour of the buildings, known as Maria Theresa Yellow, which is heightened by the green of the window frames.

From the façade, giving on to the park, there is a fine **view★★** of the Gloriette, an elegant arcaded gallery, topped by a canopy of stone and surmounted by the Imperial eagle.

★★★ Schauräume (Apartments) ⊙ – A total of 46 rooms out of the 1 440 that make up the palace are open to visitors.

The palace is a triumph of the Rococo style of the 18C – red, white and gold. The detailed elegance of the stucco work, framing ceilings and frescoes with their scrolled whorls, the crystal chandeliers, the richly ornamented faïence stoves, and the priceless tapestries and furniture make these apartments a luxurious and moving link with the past.

The **apartments of Emperor Franz Joseph and Empress Elisabeth** are followed by the **ceremonial rooms** consisting of three rooms decorated by the Austrian painter Josef Rosa, two Chinese chambers, one adorned with lacquer work, the other with porcelain. These chambers lie on either side of the Little Gallery, which communicates through an arcade to the Great Gallery *(see below)* and the Great Ceremonial Hall with its beautiful portrait of Maria Theresa by Meytens.

The **guest apartments** are among the most luxurious of the palace. They include the Blue Salon, hung with Chinese tapestry, in which Karl I signed the Declaration of Renunciation in 1918, the Old Lacquer Room, with black panelling framing remarkable miniatures, the Napoleon Room, decorated with Brussels tapestry, which was the Emperor's bedchamber and where, on 22 July 1832, his son, the Duke of Reichstadt, died at the age of twenty-one, and the Room of a Million with its fine Chinese rosewood panelling framing Persian miniatures painted upon paper.

After crossing a last suite of apartments where one of the rooms has been arranged as a memorial to the Duke of Reichstadt (copy of his death mask) one reaches the Great Gallery, adorned with gilded stucco work and paintings. This is where the delegates to the 1814-15 Congress of Vienna danced their time away. The **baroque theatre** was restored in 1980 and is used for performances in summer.

★★ Park – Designed by the Viennese, Ferdinand of Hohenberg, the park is a remarkable creation of Baroque art, where the Rococo is mixed with a taste for Antiquity. Arbours, veritable cradles of greenery, and vast formal beds of flowers serve as settings for charming groups of allegorical statues and gracious fountains.

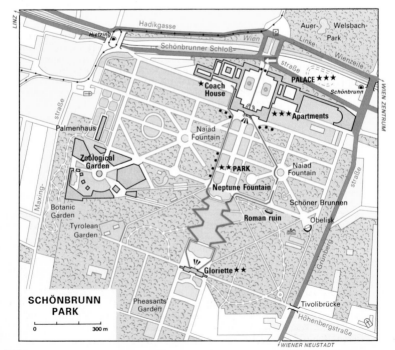

SCHÖNBRUNN PARK

Coach house in Schloß Schönbrunn

Shaded walks lead to the fountain of Neptune (Neptunbrunnen), the Roman ruin (Römische Ruine), and to the **Tierpark** ⊙, a Baroque style zoological gardens laid out in 1752 by François of Lorraine, Maria-Theresa's husband. This is the oldest zoological gardens in the world.

★★ **Gloriette** ⊙ – On its mound rising above the park, this elegant colonnade is crowned by a stone baldaquin surmounted by the Imperial eagle. It was built to commemorate the victory of Maria Theresa's troops over the Prussians at the Battle of Kolin in 1757. Seen against the sky, its famous silhouette evokes some triumphal arch from ancient times abandoned by a long-forgotten deity.
The view from the top of the mound extends over Vienna.

★★ **Wagenburg** ⊙ – The **coach house** contains a very interesting collection of coaches dating from the early 18C to the 20C, which belonged to the court.
Included are those of Maria-Louise, Napoleon, Franz Joseph and Elisabeth, the **phaeton of the King of Rome**, sumptuous harnesses and trappings, and the gilded and ornate **Imperial coach** of Emperor Franz I Stephan, Maria Theresa's husband, which was pulled by 8 white horses.

JUGENDSTIL BUILDINGS

Rejecting the academic architecture of the Ring, the architects of the Vienna Secession designed several buildings to show their theories in practice. Though few in number, they never-theless mark an important stage in the development of modern European archi-tecture.

★ **Wagner-Pavillons** (**GZ Q**) – *Karlsplatz*. Otto Wagner's two highly original Viennese Jugend-stil buildings face each other to the north of the Karlskirche. An extraordi-nary combination of glass, dazzling white marble, gilt, the floral motifs so dear to the Secession, and green-painted metalwork, they were designed to house the entrances to the Vienna Underground. Wagner saw the construc-tion of the metropolitan railway (which he oversaw

Wagner-Pavillon, Karlsplatz

from 1894-1900), predecessor of the U-bahn, as an opportunity to improve the face of the modern city, and applied his genius to the design of the most minor details.

One of the buildings still serves as an entrance to the U-bahn, while the other houses exhibitions and is open as a café in the summer months.

★ **Secession** (GZ **S**) ⊘ – The Secession building in Vienna has been run as an exhibition hall for contemporary art from Austria and abroad by the artists' association of the same name for over 90 years. This Jugendstil masterpiece was built in only six months by Joseph Maria Olbrich, one of Wagner's pupils, based on sketch designs by Gustav Klimt. It was thus ready in time to house the second exhibition of the Vienna Secession in 1898.

The sober forms of this temple of art are crowned by the famous openwork dome of gilt wrought-iron laurel leaves. Beyond the bronze doors are the precisely-calculated spaces of the entrance hall and the **Beethoven Frieze** painted by Klimt on the theme of the Ninth Symphony.

The monumental mural painting, only part of which has survived, was created in 1902 for the 14th exhibition of the Secession.

Linke Wienzeile Apartments (FZ) – It was Wagner's original intention to create a kind of Imperial Way linking Schönbrunn with the Hofburg.

This ambitious project never came to fruition but Wagner nevertheless built these two blocks of flats illustrating the architectural principles of the Secession. No 40 is known as the **Majolica House** (Majolikahaus); the otherwise sober building faced in ceramic tiles appears to have been invaded by floral motifs which flow vigorously across the façade. The gilt decoration of no 38 is equally original. The decoration of the interior is in a similar style.

House designed by Otto Wagner
at no 38 Linke Wienzeile

Postsparkasse (HY **B**) – Otto Wagner built the **Post Office Savings Bank** from 1904 to 1906 and from 1910 to 1912, using the most modern materials (aluminium, glass bricks) and construction methods available at the time. So the marble plaques covering the façade were fixed on with bolts, whose aluminium heads provided a further decorative element. Wagner was also in charge of the interior decoration and fittings. In the cashiers' hall, his use of space was to prove ground-breaking. *The hall is open to the public during the opening hours of the Postsparkasse.*

Kirche am Steinhof (AS) ⊘ – Built 1904-1907 by Wagner to serve as the chapel of the Steinhof mental institution, the church was placed symbolically at the highest point of the leafy hill occupied by the asylum. It was Vienna's first modern church. Its marble sheathing conceals the straightforward brick construction underneath which made it possible to complete the building in the relatively short space of three years (in contrast to the twelve necessary for the buildings along the Ring). The use of tiles, fixed by means of deliberately exposed metal rivets, was a response to the new architectural ideology, with its priorities of speed of assembly and the basing of ornament on constructional features.

Interior – Wagner carried through his scheme for the design of the interior against all opposition, insisting on its functional, rather than its aesthetic qualities. Thus the stoups containing holy water were designed to avoid contamination, the sloping floor is easy to clean, all parts of the building are easily accessible for maintenance purposes and the three entrances facilitated the separation of men and women.

The calm, predominately white spaces of the interior are relieved by mosaics by Jettmar and fine stained glass by Kolo Moser. The altar is surmounted by a gilded canopy.

MUSICAL MEMORIES

A number of great musicians have left their mark on Vienna, musical capital of Europe from the late 18C to the early 20C.

★ **Staatsoper** (GY) ⊙ – Begun in 1861 and formally opened in 1869 by Emperor Franz Joseph II with a performance of Mozart's *Don Giovanni*, the opera house was the first of the great public edifices to be completed along the Ring. Regarded with great affection by the Viennese, it was reopened in 1955 to the accompaniment of much pomp and circumstance.

A symbolic institution – With its unchallengable international reputation, the home of Austria's national opera has counted among its directors such outstanding figures as Gustav Mahler, Richard Strauss, Karl Böhm, Herbert von Karajan, Lorin Maazel, and Claudio Abbado. It has its own orchestra, the **Vienna Philharmonic**, which plays every day in orchestra pits large enough to accommodate its 110 musicians. The orchestra needs four rehearsal rooms to be able to guarantee a performance schedule which changes every day. One room in particular contains an organ with 2 500 pipes. The season lasts from 1 September to 30 June, during which time a cosmopolitan crowd enjoys a total of some 280 performances in this prestigious concert hall.

Technology in the service of music – The lighting, air conditioning and machinery of the opera uses about 9 000kWh/day. Three hundred people is employed, 100 of them involved in the continuous changes of costume and scenery. The larger items of scenery have to be stored at the Arsenal, 4km - 2 ½ miles away. The vans transporting the scenery have their own entrance behind the building and the scenery is moved into place behind the stage by means of special lifts 22m - 72ft high. The huge stage (50m - 164ft deep, 45m - 148ft high) is designed to cope with the needs of today's productions, with an array of the latest machinery including hydraulic jacks, lifts, cranes and a 45 tonne turntable.

Tour – Going backstage complements a visit to the spaces normally accessible to the public. Particularly interesting are the **interval rooms** with their modern Gobelins tapestries, the **tea room**, spared by the fire of 1945 and formerly for the exclusive use of the Imperial family, the original decor in the foyer and the marble room with its marquetry. Completing this sophisticated setting is the horseshoe-shaped main auditorium with its 2 280 seats.

Schubert-Museum (CT M'⁴) ⊙ – The house in which Schubert was born on 31 January 1797 and where he spent the first four years of his life (subsequently he lived at no 4 Säulengasse) has been restored to its original modest state. There is a museum on the first floor.

Mozart-Wohnung or **Figarohaus** (GY F) – *Description above, under Old Town.*

Dreimäderlhaus (FX) – *Schreyvogelgasse 10.*
Legend has it that it was at this house, built in 1803, that Schubert paid court to three young ladies from the same family.
In the nearby Mölkerbastei, there are remnants of the old city walls. No 8 was lived in by Beethoven in 1804, 1810 and 1812.

Palais Lobkowitz (GY X) – Also known as the Palais Dietrichstein, this was built between 1685 and 1687 to the plans of Giovanni Pietro Tencula. In 1709-11 J B Fischer von Erlach endowed it with an attic storey bordered by statues as well as a grand doorway. In 1804 Beethoven conducted the premiere of his *Eroica Symphony* in the palace's great hall (Eroica-Saal).

Zentralfriedhof (BS) – Beethoven, Brahms, Gluck, Schubert and Hugo Wolf all lie in the touching Musicians' Corner (Plot 32A), alongside the Viennese masters of operetta and the waltz: Johann Strauss the Elder and the Younger, Josef Lanner, Karl Millöcker, Franz von Suppé. *A plan of the cemetery is available from the attendant at the second (main) entrance gateway.*

St. Marxer Friedhof (BS) – Buried anonymously in a pauper's grave in 1791, the great composer Mozart has no memorial here other than a solitary stone cherub weeping on an empty sepulchre.

ADDITIONAL SIGHTS

Within the Ring

★ **Herrengasse** (GY) – A pleasant busy street, linking the Freyung with the Michaelerplatz, the Herrengasse (Lords' Street) recalls its aristocratic past. It is an important administrative centre: at no 13, on the site of an earlier 16C building of which the chapel and a Renaissance doorway in the courtyard remain, stands the Landhaus, from where the Revolution of 1848 began. It was built from 1837 to 1848 by Alois Pichl. At no 11 is the seat of the government of Lower Austria; at no 9, the Palais Mollard-Clary, built in 1689 and modified in 1760; at no 7, the old Modena-Palais, with a 19C façade, which now houses the Austrian Ministry of Domestic Affairs.

Michaeler Kirche (GY) – This church is dominated by the semi-circular façade of the Hofburg on the opposite side of the Michaelerplatz. It began as a Romanesque building (nave, transept, right side of the chancel) but the exterior reveals a mixture of styles: neo-Classical façade (1792), tower (1340) with a 16C spire, Gothic apses and side chapels. The high altar owes its profuse decoration to the Fall of the Angels, which was completed in 1781, the last religious work of Baroque style executed in Vienna. In the north transept is the tomb of the Italian Baroque poet, Metastasio, the official author of operas during the reign of Maria Theresa. The Mount of Olives, a magnificent stone sculpture, dating from the end of the 15C, stands against the outside of the south wall of the church. The old tiled roofs of the houses in Stalburggasse frame a picturesque view of St Michael's belfry.

Jüdisches Museum (GY) ⊙ – The Stadtpalais Eskeles in Dorotheergasse dates back to the 15C; it was once the site of a foundation of Augustinian canons. After a turbulent history, the building now houses the collections of the **Jewish museum**: religious and ceremonial objects, documents, paintings and drawings on the history of Vienna's and Austria's large Jewish community. Temporary exhibitions.

Minoritenkirche (FY) – The Minorite church was begun in the first half of the 14C but was altered in the Baroque period. The chevet is flanked by an octagonal tower and the right side by an elegant ribbed gallery. The interior is surprising owing to its almost square design and its three naves of equal height. On the north wall there is a huge mosaic copied from *The Last Supper* by Leonardo da Vinci and executed on the orders of Napoleon I.

Annakirche (GY) – In 1629 this church acquired its present shape and decoration of marbles, stucco, gilding and paintings. There is a fine wooden carving (1505) by Veit Stoss depicting the Holy Family.

Palais Starhemberg (FY) – This majestic 17C palace, now the Ministry of Education, was designed by an unknown architect and belonged to the Count of Starhemberg, the heroic defender of the capital against the Turks in 1683.

Palais Kinsky (FY) – The palace, which was built in 1716 by Johann-Lukas von Hildebrandt for Count Daun, is one of the most remarkable secular buildings of the Baroque period. The façade is richly decorated with armorial bearings, statues, pilasters and sculptured motifs. The doorway and balconies are highly ornate.

Alte Ursulinenklosterapotheke (GY M⁸) ⊙ – Part of the Austrian Folklore Museum, this early 18C **dispensary** houses a collection of religious folk art.

Beyond the Ring

★★ **Karlskirche** (GZ) – The church, which is dedicated to St Charles Borromeo, was built from 1716 to 1737 to plans by Johann-Bernhard Fischer von Erlach, following a vow made by the Emperor Karl VI during the plague of 1713. It is an extraordinary mixture of styles and architectural features.

Exterior – It is said that the inspiration to combine Trajan's Column, a Roman portico and a Baroque cupola came to Fischer von Erlach on the Pincian Hill in Rome. Two columns, modelled on Trajan's Column and ornamented with low reliefs illustrating the life of St Charles Borromeo, flank a portico reminiscent of a temple façade. This central unit is itself flanked by two squat towers with windows in the lower floors.

Karlskirche, Vienna

Interior – In the absence of a nave, the attention is drawn to the huge oval **dome**★★ decorated with frescoes by Johann Michael Rottmayr. All the characteristics of the Baroque are present: an accumulation of ornament, dynamic statuary, indirect lighting of the main altar, effects of perspective. Huge pilasters divide the walls into panels – symmetry and harmony preside over the interior; the chancel relates to the pulpit and portal; two chapels face one another, flanked by two smaller ones. The sole use of pink marble for decoration has a unifying effect. Dominating the pool in front of the church is a monumental bronze by Henry Moore (GZ).

★★ Historisches Museum der Stadt Wien (GZ M⁶) ⊘ - *Karlsplatz.*

Ground Floor - Maps and illustrated summary panels cover the Roman era, as well as pottery, ceramics and low reliefs. From the Romanesque and Gothic periods: parts of capitals, stained-glass windows, frescoes, statues, paintings on wood, arms and banners mostly from the Stephansdom.

1st Floor - Drawings, engravings and plans of Vienna. Souvenirs from the sieges of 1529 and 1683 (booty taken from the Turks); history of Vienna until Maria Theresa's death in 1780.

2nd Floor - The neo-Classical and Biedermeier period is evoked by furniture and by portraits, depicting men of arts and letters (portrait of Grillparzer, the poet, by Waldmüller).
In these early years of the 19C the so-called Vedutenmaler (artists aiming at documentary accuracy) painted fine records of the appearance of their city (*St Stephen's Cathedral* by Rudolf Alt - 1834).
The changes in the layout of the city ushered in by the building of the Ring can be studied in the form of a model. Viennese life in the reign of Franz Joseph is evoked in paintings by Makart and Klimt and the inter-war period by Kokoschka (*Vienna from the Wilhelminenberg* - 1931), while contemporary works testify to the city's continuing liveliness as a centre of culture.

★★ Österreichisches Museum für Volkskunde (CU M⁷) ⊘ - The Austrian folklore museum is housed in the old Schönborn palace built by Johann Lukas von Hildebrandt at the beginning of the 18C. The museum exhibits collections on popular culture of Austria and its neighbouring countries. The new lay-out of the presentation on the ground floor gives an overview of the cultural evolution of popular everyday life and the museum's outstanding collection of popular art. The first floor hosts special exhibitions on folklore.

★ Prater (BR, *plan p 303*/EU, *plan p 305*) - This immense green space, which extends between the two arms of the Danube, was a hunting reserve under Emperor Maximilian II. The benevolent Emperor, Joseph II, opened the Prater to the public in 1766. With its cafés, where they could sing and dance, the Prater was extremely popular during the hey-day of the Viennese waltz. It won world-wide renown when the film "The Third Man" war shot here.
One part of the Prater (the "Wurstelprater") is devoted to travelling fairs. The Giant Wheel *(Riesenrad)* ⊘ (diameter of 61 m - 200ft) has become a familiar landmark of the city.
Adjoining the Wurstelprater is a vast sports ground: Krieau trotting course, indoor cycling stadium, Ernst-Happel stadium, Freudenau galloping course. At the end of the main avenue leading out from the star-shaped cross-roads in the Prater stands the Lusthaus, a summer mansion built in 1781-1783, which is now a café.

★ Gemäldegalerie der Akademie der bildenden Künste (GZ M⁹) ⊘ - The extraordinary **polyptych of the Last Judgement★★** by Hieronymus Bosch (1460-1516) is a terrifying work in which monsters are shown with other horrible phenomena symbolizing the sins and suffering of mankind.
Among the 15C and 16C Italian School are works by Botticelli, and Titian's *Tarquin and Lucretia.*
Lucas Cranach the Elder is represented as much by his early works as by his court paintings *(Holy Family)* and the beautiful enigmatic *Lucretia* (1532). There are also several German primitives such as *The Dormition of the Virgin* by **Ambrosius Holbein.** Flemish Baroque is dominated by **Rubens** *(Oreithyia kidnapped by Boreas)* - note his 14 oil sketches. Other works of the period are represented by Ruben's assistants, Jordaens *(Paul and Barnabus)* and Anthony van Dyck *(Self-Portrait).* Rembrandt's work *(Portrait of a Woman)* is always a pleasure to look at. On display are canvases by Pieter de Hooch, a Dutch genre painter, as well as the Dutch masters, Asselijn and Dujardin, who painted Italianate motifs.
The 18C is represented by 8 *vedute* scenes of Venice by Francesco Guardi (1712-1793).

★ Österreichisches Museum für angewandte Kunst (HY M¹⁰) ⊘ - The Austrian museum of applied arts was completely transformed and reorganised in 1993. With a collection totalling way in excess of 200 000 items, thought had to be devoted to new ways of presenting aspects of the applied arts to visitors in an interesting way. Consequently, the new display presents only the most original, typical or informative exhibits, and the lay-out of certain rooms was entrusted to artists themselves: the displays of Baroque, Rococo and Classical furniture were set

Österreichisches Museum für angewandte Kunst, Vienna

out by **Donald Judd**; the outstanding collection of lace and glassware by Franz Graf; Empire and Biedermeier exhibits by Jenny Holzer; 20C applied arts by Manfred Wakolbinger. A surprise is in store in the display on Historicism and Jugendstil, which Barbara Bloom has reduced to Michael Thonet's famous bentwood chairs (Bugholzmöbel)... and nothing else! A major area is given over to the work of the **Wiener Werkstätten**★★, which makes the heart of any Jugendstil and Art Deco enthusiast beat faster.

The basement is home to **collections of studies** on the subjects of East Asia, furniture, textiles, metal, ceramics and glass.

★ **Naturhistorisches Museum** (FY M¹) ⊘ – On the mezzanine floor the prehistoric section includes numerous objects from Hallstatt and the celebrated statuette of the so-called Venus of Willendorf, about 25 000 years old.

On the first floor there are interesting collections of botany and zoology.

★ **Kurpark Oberlaa** (BS) – *Southeast of the plan p 303.*

South of the city this park has been used in the 20C as a backdrop for numerous Austrian feature films. After being laid out anew, the park hosted the 1974 Vienna International Horticultural Show. Visitors will appreciate the peace and tranquility offered by the variety of paths lined with beautiful flower beds and fountains. Near the restaurant is a beautiful **view** of the surrounding countryside. The Oberlaa thermal baths on the edge of the park are supplied by a hot sulphur spring (54°C – 129°F).

Palais Schwarzenberg (HZ) – The two great Viennese architects of the Baroque period, Johann-Lukas von Hildebrandt and Johann-Bernhard Fischer von Erlach, collaborated in the design of this palace (1697-1723), part of which is now a hotel.

Naschmarkt (FZ) – The fruit and vegetable stalls of the market on the Linke Wienzeile make a colourful picture, full of local atmosphere.

Opposite the market is the Theatre *An der Wien*. The city's Saturday **flea market** *(Flohmarkt)* takes place on the prolongation of the Nasch-markt.

Piaristenkirche Basilika Maria Treu (CU A) ⊘ – The church stands in the centre of the Josephstadt district. Its beautiful transitional Baroque-Classical façade faces the Jodok-Fink-Platz known more familiarly as the Piaristenplatz. The interior of the two great round cupolas is decorated with a fresco by Franz Anton Maulbertsch (1752).

Salesianerinnenkirche (DV) – The Visitandine church was built between 1717 and 1730 under the direction of Donato Felice Allio and is reminiscent of the Karlskirche.

Hundertwasserhaus (EU Z) – *Kegelgasse, 36-38.*

The Viennese artist, **Friedrich (Friedensreich) Hundertwasser**, used this block of flats to express his ideas for reconciling human needs with the environment. Completed in 1984, his colourful, highly unusual building avoids the monotony of conventional mass housing by using a variety of motifs (arcaded loggias, galleries, statues, etc.), an extraordinary range of materials (glass, brick, rendering, etc.), sloping surfaces and lavish landscaping.

KunstHausWien
(**EU G**) ⊘ – *Untere Weiß-gerberstraße 13.*
Hundertwasser's preoccupation with the man-environment relationship *(see above)* is illustrated in the varied and original works exhibited here (paintings, engravings, plans and models). Part of the building is used to house temporary exhibitions.

Museum moderner Kunst Stiftung Ludwig (**DT M¹³**) ⊘ – The museum is housed in the old summer palace of the Prince Johann-Adam of Liechtenstein, ruler of the tiny sovereign state *(see Michelin Green Guide Switzerland)* and a great patron of the arts.

Hundertwasserhaus

The palace, which still belongs to the royal family of Liechtenstein, was completed in 1700, and retains its **Baroque character** in both the layout of the buildings and the interior decor, especially that of the magnificent marble room on the first floor. The perspectives of the original landscaped gardens have not been so fortunate, however.

The **collection of modern art** covers a good cross-section of international 20C art. The various artistic movements are each consigned their own display gallery: works by Jawlensky and Kokoschka represent Expressionism; Fernand Léger, among others, stands for Cubism; Max Ernst and René Magritte for Surrealism; Arman for Nouveau Réalisme; and Robert Rauschenberg and Andy Warhol for Pop Art. Examples of international painting of the 1980s and 1990s include works by Georg Baselitz, Jörg Immendorf and Ernesto Tatafiore.

Heeresgeschichtliches Museum (**EV M¹⁴**) ⊘ – The **army museum** is housed in a beautiful Historicist building designed by Theophil Hansen and Ludwig Förster. Its displays cover the history of the Habsburg monarchy from the late 16C to 1918 in four sections. Part of the museum is given over to the Austrian navy and its expeditions.

Ehemaliges Hofmobiliendepot (**CU M¹²**) ⊘ – Founded in 1750 by Maria Theresa, the **national furniture collection** consists of a series of rooms furnished in 18C and 19C style. The **Biedermeier** pieces are particularly fine; there is also a fascinating Jugendstil drawing room.

Parking in Vienna: special regulations.
Parking at night on tram routes is prohibited in winter.
In short-stay parking zones (Kurzparkzonen) parking is allowed
for a maximum of 1 hour 30min from 8am to 6pm on weekdays
and from 8am to noon on Saturdays using pre-paid parking vouchers
available from tobacconists, service stations and offices
of the Vienna Public Transport Company (Wiener Verkehrsbetriebe).

EXCURSIONS

★★ Tour of the Kahlenberg Heights (AR)
Round tour of 33km - 21 miles – about 2 hours

Leave Vienna on the Heiligenstädter Straße (DT 57), the road to Klosterneuburg, which runs parallel with the railway. By Klosterneuburg-Kierling station turn left into the Stadtplatz and almost immediately left again where the road finally widens; cross the Kierlingbach rivulet and go uphill towards the abbey. Park in the Rathausplatz.

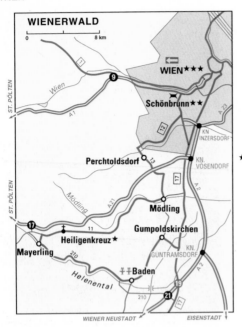

WIENERWALD

0   8 km

WIEN★★★

Schönbrunn★★

ST. PÖLTEN

KN. INZERSDORF

Perchtoldsdorf

KN. VÖSENDORF

Mödling

Gumpoldskirchen

Heiligenkreuz★

Mayerling

KN. GUNTRAMSDORF

Baden

Helenental

WIENER NEUSTADT   EISENSTADT

Klosterneuburg - See KLOSTERNEUBURG.

Leopoldstraße leads south to the Weidlingbach valley; cross Weidlinger Straße into Höhenstraße opposite.

The winding road rises between villas and then enters the woods, emerging with a **view** of Klosterneuburg abbey.

★★ **Leopoldsberg** - This, the most easterly spur of the Wienerwald, overlooks the Danube from 423m - 1 388ft. From the Burgplatz opposite the little church (Leopoldskirche) there is an extensive **view**★★ over the northern and eastern parts of the city and the plain of Wagram, the Leitha-Gebirge and the Wienerwald hills.

Return downhill; turn left into Höhenstraße.

★ **Kahlenberg** - To the right of the Kahlenberg restaurant (483m - 1 585ft), a terrace gives an attractive **view**★ over Vienna. The spires of the Stephansdom and the Ringturm stand out above the city. In the foreground are the vineyards of Grinzing and to the right the heights of the Wienerwald.

Carry on along the Höhenstraße. Stop 500m beyond the left turn into Cobenzigasse.

Level with the Cobenz café-restaurant there is an interesting **view** (left) of Vienna.

Continue on Höhenstraße as far as the guesthouse Häuserl am Roan.

From the car park there is a very fine view of the city of Vienna and the Wienerwald.

Return towards the Kahlenberg; turn right into Cobenzlgasse (AR 21) down into Grinzing.

★ **Grinzing** - Grinzing is probably the best known of Vienna's village suburbs. With its pretty, low-lying houses and friendly atmosphere, it makes an idyllic scene, but its main attraction from the visitor's point of view is the large number of wine-taverns, or *Heurigen*, to be found here.

Heiligenstadt - Admirers of Beethoven will want to visit the central square of this old village (Pfarrplatz) (BR 96) to see the little 17C house (no 2 - now a wine tavern), where the musician lived for some months in 1817.
In Probusgasse (AR 101) stands the **house** (no 6) ⊙ where the composer wrote his famous letter in 1802 called the *Testament of Heiligenstadt* when in despair over his deafness.

Return to Vienna along Hohe Warte (AR 61) and Döblinger Hauptstraße (AR 24).

★ **Vienna Woods** (Wienerwald)

Round tour of 74km - 46 miles - about 3 hours - local map above. Leave Vienna on road no 12 (AS).

The road passes through extensive suburbs before reaching the first vine covered slopes of the Vienna Woods.

Perchtoldsdorf, Mödling - Charming winegrowing villages.

The winding route crosses small rocky and wooded valleys along the banks of the River Mödling and then carries on through the woods as far as Heiligenkreuz.

★ **Heiligenkreuz** ⊙ - The Cistercian abbey of Heiligenkreuz, an important example of middle European architecture, was founded in 1133 by Babenberg Margrave Leopold III. The medieval abbey complex has survived virtually intact. The **abbey church**★ has a Romanesque nave (1187) and a well-lit Gothic hall-chancel dating from 1295, in which the stained-glass windows are the originals. The cloisters was built from 1220 to 1240 in a transitional Romanesque-Gothic style. The

Travelling in style

chapter-house, burial place of the Babenbergs, contains Austria's oldest ducal tomb (1246). The nine-sided Gothic fountain room features beautiful tracery windows with grisaille stained glass and pictures of the Babenbergs.

Mayerling - *See MAYERLING.*

After Mayerling the road follows the little **Helenental** as far as Baden, through rocky, wooded country. The Duke of Reichstadt used to go riding in this little valley.

✚✚ **Baden** - *See BADEN.*

To the north of Baden the road winds between vineyards as far as Gumpoldskirchen.

Gumpoldskirchen - The vineyards of this village produce the famous Gumpolds-kirchner wine, which is much drunk in the local wine taverns *(Heurigen).*
Return to Vienna on road no 17.

WIENER NEUSTADT

Niederösterreich - Population 35 050
Michelin map 426 fold 25 - Alt 265m - 869ft

The town was founded by Duke Leopold V of Babenberg in 1194 as a border fortress against Hungary. Part of the ransom paid for Richard the Lionheart is supposed to have been used to pay for this. Under Friedrich III, between 1440 and 1493, the town was an Imperial residence. In 1459, Maximilian I was born here, and here it is, far from the splendour of his mausoleum in Innsbruck, that he is in fact buried. The town flourished anew during the reign of Maria Theresa, and it continued to prosper into the 19C.
The historic town centre, now an attractive pedestrian zone, still features the regular street layout of the Middle Ages.

SIGHTS

Ehemalige Burg - The core of the castle dates back to the 13C, but it was subject to numerous extensions and modifications. In 1751, Maria Theresa installed a military academy here, which is now recognised as the oldest of its kind in the world.

St. Georgskathedrale ⊘ - The church gable, which can be seen from the first courtyard, is covered with 107 carved coats of arms from the House of Habsburg - known as the "Wappenwand" (15C) - which frame the central window of the church and surround the statue of Friedrich III.
The Gothic hall-church, built during the reign of Friedrich III and completely restored after the Second World War, lies above the arched entrance. The Virgin on the north side altar and some stained-glass fragments (escutcheons), are the most outstanding remains of the original furnishings. Maximilian's mortal remains rest beneath the steps of the high altar.

Neuklosterkirche – *Ungargasse, near the Hauptplatz.*
This Gothic abbey church, in which the chancel (first half of the 14C) is higher than the nave, has Baroque furnishings and decoration. In the apse, behind the high altar, there is the beautiful **tombstone** of the Empress Eleanor of Portugal, the wife of Friedrich III, which was carved by Nikolaus Gerhart of Leyden in 1467.

Hauptplatz – On the south side of the town square stands the **Rathaus**, built in 1488, to which a tower with a rusticated stone façade was added in the 16C, and which was converted to the Late Classical style in 1834. The column to Mary was built in 1678.
The beautiful arcaded houses on the north side of the square date from the Gothic period.

Take the Böheimgasse to the Domplatz (cathedral square).

Dom – The Late Romanesque cathedral building had a Gothic transept and chancel added to it in the 14C. The **Brauttor★**, a doorway on the south side decorated with bands of lozenge and zig-zag motifs, is a lovely example of Late Romanesque architecture. The height of the ceiling inside testifies to the importance of the cathedral during the reign of Friedrich III. The court gallery bears the motto A.E.I.O.U. *(see Introduction p 30)*. Friedrich was probably also the donor behind the twelve larger-than-life-size figures of the Apostles which adorn the pillars, the work of sculptor Lorenz Luchsperger. The **high altar**, with its six Corinthian columns made of red marble, is magnificent without being overdone. The **pulpit** was created in 1609 by Johann Baptist Zelpi and features the statues of Doctors of the Church St Augustine, St Ambrosius, St Gregory and St Jerome.

On the north side of the cathedral square is the **Propstei** (Provost's House), which was the bishop's residence from 1469 to 1785. It has an ornate Baroque doorway with the coat of arms of Bishop Franz Anton, Count of Puchheim.

Abtei WILHERING★

Oberösterreich

Michelin map 426 fold 8 – 8km - 5 miles west of Linz

The church and conventual buildings of the Cistercian Abbey of Wilhering stand on the south bank of the Danube upstream from Linz. The abbey was originally a Romanesque building but over the centuries it was transformed into a masterpiece of Rococo art and today it is one of Austria's most striking examples of that style.

HISTORICAL NOTES

On 30 September 1146 twelve monks from the abbey of Rein came to settle on the edge of Wilhering Forest. Life was so arduous for the newcomers that about thirty years later there were only two monks left. In 1185, at the request of the Chapter General of the Cistercians, Ebrach Abbey near Würzburg in Germany relaunched the foundation and sent twelve monks and an abbot to Wilhering. This time the community was successful and the Abbots at its head acquired great influence. The story goes that one of them, **Abbot Hilger**, one day received a visit from the Duke of Styria. Although the Abbot knew that the Duke suffered from leprosy, he did not hesitate to give him a fraternal embrace. The Duke was so struck by this bravery that he gave the abbey a farm as a gift and took the foundation under his protection.
In subsequent years the Abbey experienced mixed fortunes, particularly during the troubled period of the Reformation in the 16C when one Abbot fled with the abbey's coffers to Nuremburg where he got married.
On 6 March 1733 the abbey and church were badly damaged by fire. It was rumoured locally that the monks had themselves set fire to the buildings so that they could rebuild in the contemporary style. The real culprit was, however, soon found: a twelve-year-old girl by the name of Magdalena Elisabeth Prindlin who had committed the act at the instigation of an unemployed man living in the vicinity. She was condemned to death for her action but was later pardoned. The reconstruction of the abbey was undertaken immediately. It was very expensive, although use was made of the surviving structure. The result was a building of exceptional beauty as anyone visiting the abbey today may testify. The most celebrated architects of the day, including Joseph Mathias Götz, Joseph Mungenast and Johann Michael Prunner, submitted their drawings and plans in the hope of being awarded the commission. Against all expectation, a local craftsman called Johann Haslinger was preferred to his famous competitors. The reconstruction took place between 1734 and 1748. Thorough restoration work carried out between 1971 and 1977 restored the splendour of the 1750s to all the buildings, and in particular to the interior of the church.

TOUR ⏱ 45min

Main Courtyard – The majestic yet sober main courtyard of the abbey is surrounded by monastery buildings arranged in a U shape; the open north side reveals some romantic outbuildings.

On the south side, a pedimented break-front stands out from the central façade. The rough rose-pink rendering of the walls is punctuated by white piers which rest on a stylobate decorated with fine horizontal grooves. The Baroque pomp of the courtyard is stamped with a characteristically Cistercian sense of measure and balance. The church façade, also white and pink, is sub-divided by piers. The portal is the only visible remnant of the original Romanesque church.

★★★ **Abbey Church** – Within the context of European art, this church is probably the most brilliant example of the Rococo style to be found in any of the German-speaking countries. Baroque inventiveness reached its apogee in the Rococo decor of Wilhering. It would be difficult to go further in terms of the profusion of decoration, the richness of colour, the fantasy of the sculpture, the pictorial ingenuity and the delicacy of the stucco work. The whole decor of the church evokes a timeless felicity; the figures – both painted and sculpted – which float and gyrate in space seem to exude heavenly bliss. An imperceptible tremor runs the length of the vault. The church creates a feeling of great serenity, emphasized by the harmony of blues and pinks that is subtly underscored with tiny sea-green touches. Paintings constitute the major part of the decoration at Wilhering Abbey. Stucco work and *putti* supply not competition but a third dimension, that of volume. The gilt on capitals, scrolls and festoons of ovoli catches the light and elegantly enhances the paintings and stucco work, giving them a prominence they would not otherwise achieve.

High Altar — The high altar is designed round a painting of the Assumption of the Virgin Mary by **Martino Altomonte**. It was commissioned by the Abbot of Wilhering in 1637 when the painter, already in his eighties, enjoyed a great reputation. The painting illustrates the theological theme, which was chosen by the Abbot for the decoration of the whole church and inscribed in a scroll on the chancel vault: 'Assumpta est Maria in Caelum, gaudent angeli' (Mary has ascended into heaven, the angels rejoice).

Less than a year later, Altomonte, who lived in Vienna, dispatched the painting by boat up the Danube contained in an enormous wooden case. He asked the outrageous sum of 700 florins, the cost of buying about 50 cows; the Abbot was delighted with the painting and paid up without demur, particularly as modesty had not prevented Altomonte from writing to say that such a work was worth at least 1 200 florins.

During the next six months, Altomonte executed the paintings for the **side chapels★★**. They were his last compositions. When he learned about the huge programme of frescoes planned for the ceilings, he introduced his nephew and succeeded in having him chosen to do the work.

Frescoes – Bartolomeo Altomonte, who was unquestionably less talented than his uncle, was nonetheless a prodigious artist, as he was responsible for more than 450m² – 4 844 sq ft of the ceiling (almost two-thirds of the total area). The nave is decorated with an enormous painting of Mary, Queen of Heaven, surrounded by her court of saints and angels. Altomonte worked closely with stucco artists on this composition which includes paintings of people, a gilt surround and stucco angels all participating in a joint celebration. The chancel ceiling is decorated with a concert of angelic musicians.

Stucco – The stucco artist Franz Joseph Holzinger came from St. Florian with his students to spend three consecutive summers (1739-1741) decorating the church. After an interruption caused by the aftermath of the Thirty Years War, their academic style was considered too rigid and too systematic and all their work was destroyed.

The Abbot at once sent for some young, modern stucco workers who had been trained in southern Germany. These young artists of the Rococo generation had turned their backs on the cumbersome, overbearing compositions of the late Baroque period and had learnt how to apply stucco in moderation and with a delicacy hitherto associated with painting and gilding. It is this subtle harmony of all the decorative arts which makes Wilhering the undisputed Rococo masterpiece that is admired today.

The **cupola** above the transept crossing is the realm of *trompe-l'œil* and illusion. An erudite architectural composition, painted by the Italian Francesco Messenta, opens at the top on a glimpse of sky; the men chained to the Earth by their sins are protected by the Virgin Mary from divine wrath. To the right of the entrance to the monks' choir stands an imposing **pulpit**; it is easy to imagine thunderous sermons being declaimed from this explosion of black and white stucco and gold. The pulpit is a fine match for the **choir organ**, an elegant instrument constructed in 1746 by Nicolas Rumel of Linz, of which the composer Anton Bruckner was especially fond.

Great Organ – The great organ, which is installed at the back of the church, is alive with exquisite detail. The part of the nave, which accommodates the organ, is itself a monumental work of art in which each element contributes to the overall effect: a magnificently worked iron gate, a discreetly elegant gallery which directs the gaze upward and beyond to the three banks of organ pipes. Overhead a clock marks the passing time and a purple curtain in *trompe-l'œil* hangs down from the vault, its heavy folds drawn back to reveal the theatrical scene. It is easy to imagine that, if the curtain were to rise, it would reveal artists putting the finishing touches to the stage set, and that

The organ at Wilhering Abbey

the central bank of organ pipes has just been lowered and the flanking sections moved aside to allow the light pouring through the great window to accompany the thunderous crash of the organ.

Cloisters – The cloisters may be visited through a door (left) from the narthex. A pre-Gothic 13C **doorway** leads into the old **chapter-house**; a series of fine 18C paintings depicts episodes in the life of St Bernard.

WÖRTHER SEE★

Kärnten

Michelin map 426 folds 35 and 36

Wörther lake, stretching between Velden and Klagenfurt and over 17km - 10 miles long, receives little in the way of river floodwaters and is therefore warm (24-28°C – 75-82°F in summer), a fact which has encouraged the development of resorts such as Velden and Pörtschach, very popular with tourists from Germany. A screen of low hills sometimes hides the Karawanken, but a short stroll is generally enough to bring back into view the magnificent splendour of this mountain barrier which extends from Austria into Slovenia and Italy.
Villach is a good centre for visiting both the **Ossiacher See**★ *(qv)* and the **Gerlitzen**★★ *(qv)*.

★SOUTH SHORE OF THE LAKE

From Villach to Klagenfurt

76km - 47 miles – about 5 hours – Local map opposite

At first the route runs through the Drava valley, within sight of the Karawanken (on the way several *Bildstöcke* can be seen). In Velden, instead of following the main road to the resorts of the Austrian Riviera, it takes the road along the south shore of the Wörther See *(narrow roads)*. Note the site of the Maria Wörth promontory and the panorama from the Pyramidenkogel.

Villach – *See VILLACH.*
From Villach take road no 84 as far as the east bank of the Gail.

Maria Gail – Inside this little rural pilgrimage church is an early 16C **altarpiece**★★ from the St. Veit woodcarving workshops; its central panel depicts the Coronation of the Virgin.
On the walls inside are the remains of Late Romanesque frescoes from the second half of the 13C. Besides one or two pieces of Late Gothic woodcarving inside, the church also features some interesting stone sculptures on the outside of its south wall, depicting a sort of Last Judgment scene. These sculptures probably date from before 1300.

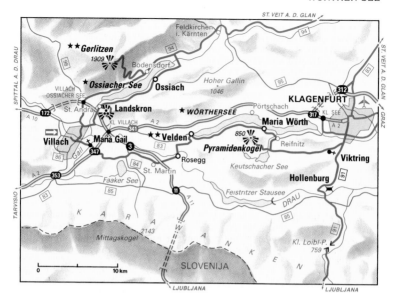

Further east, the road, which continues to rise, gives a wide general view of the Villach basin where the Gail and the Drava converge. Beyond a pinewood, the view embraces the beautiful sheet of water that is the **Faakersee** and the decapitated pyramid of the Mittagskogel, standing quite alone (alt 2 143m - 7 031ft).

The route next descends to the Drava, hidden behind a curtain of trees; 500m before the hamlet of St. Martin *(details on the patron saints p 46)*, a *Bildstöck*, consecrated to this saint, standing at the roadside, depicts in naïve fashion the dividing of the saint's cloak.

Wildpark Rosegg ☉ – *Time: 1 hour.* This naturalistic wildlife park was laid out almost 200 years ago when the old castle at Rosegg was demolished. A great variety of animals can be seen, such as lynx, monkeys, wolves, deer, moufflons, bison, boar, eagles, falcons, etc.

Beyond the Rosegg bridge there are glimpses of the Karawanken range on the border between Austria and Slovenia.

★★ **Velden** – Population 7 980. The elegant, long-established spa resort of Velden lies at the west end of the Wörther See.

Velden on the Wörther See

W. Geiersperger/BILDAGENTUR BUENOS DIAS

It is impossible to miss the yellow castle right on the banks of the river. This was built as a summer residence (Lustschloß) by the local prince, Bartholomäus Khevenhüller, between 1590 and 1603. It was rebuilt after a fire in 1893, but the 17C plan was retained, especially the Baroque fragment formed by the main doorway, surmounted with obelisks and bearing, on the pediment, the family arms. It was at this time that the four hexagonal corner towers with their charming lantern roofs were added.

★★ **Maria Wörth** – Population 1 050. The promontory is dominated by the towers of the two pilgrimage churches of Maria Wörth and the round tower of an ossuary.

In the Romanesque choir of the first little sanctuary, known as the "Winter-kirche", painted murals from the mid-11C depict the Apostles.

The main church, an amalgamation of different styles, is richly decorated inside. There is an early 16C Calvary, a statue of the Virgin Mary above the high altar, and a picture of the Madonna (early 13C), which is a copy of the original in the church of Sta Maria del Popolo in Rome.

Reifnitz – Holiday resort.

Pyramidenkogel – Alt 850m - 2 789ft. A good road leads to the summit, which is crowned with a **viewing tower**, 54m - 177ft high. There is a fine **circular view**★ over the great central valley of Carinthia, the Karawanken mountain barrier and, far to the west, the jagged Julian Alps (Slovenia and Italy). To the northeast lies the Ulrichsberg, looking like a sphinx emerging from the mass of hills. During the Celtic period this was one of the sacred mountains of Carinthia. In the foreground, the peninsula of Maria Wörth juts out into the waters of the lake.

Viktring – *The entrance to the abbey is at the end of the main street of the village which runs north-south.*

Viktring Abbey, founded by Bernard of Sponheim in 1142, is laid out round two vast courtyards with superimposed galleries. It was secularized in 1786.

The church, though shortened in 1847, was closely inspired by the Abbey of Fontenay in Burgundy – the model for Cistercian design. Thus at Viktring, one finds: the blind nave, with its broken cradle-vaulting extending to the crossing, the arched side aisles in transversal cradles buttressing the main nave, and the deep transepts with their square chapels.

The severity of the reformed Cistercian style was tempered during the 14C, when a polygonal chancel replaced the early flat chevet, and also between 1380 and 1390, when the high windows lighting the choir received their beautiful **stained glass**. In the 15C the Chapel of St Bernard, with its network vaulting, was added to the north transept.

Take road no 91 towards the Loibl pass.

Schloß Hollenburg – The massive Hollenburg fortress commands the valley of the Drava, known at this point as the Rosental. The fortress dates from the 14C and 15C. Although the exterior is sober and bare of decoration, the interior courtyard with its Renaissance arcades and outside staircase exudes an almost southern European exuberance. Above the doors and windows are paintings with inscriptions and mottoes. There is a good **view**★ of the Karawanken from the balcony.

So, to visit the castle, when the Loibl pass road begins to go downhill, turn off it to the left into the road that leads to Hollenburg. Park the car a little before the entrance to the fortified covered bridge.

The bridge leads to the inner court which is irregular in shape and picturesque with richly carved arcades. A doorway marked *zum Söller* leads to a small terrace overlooking the Rosental and, opposite, the Karawanken peaks, which look surprisingly close.

Return to road no 91 to enter Klagenfurt from the south.

Klagenfurt – *See KLAGENFURT.*

ZELL AM SEE ✳

Salzburg – Population 7 960

Michelin map 426 – S of fold 19 and N of fold 33

Local map under GROSSGLOCKNER HOCHALPENSTRASSE – Alt 757m - 2484ft

Zell am See enjoys a splendid location in the immediate vicinity of the Großglock-nerstraße mountain road and the beautiful Kapruner and Glemm valleys (Saalbach). The peaks of the Hohe Tauern in the south, which are covered in glacial ice, the rugged rocks of the Steinernes Meer sea in the north and the soft Grasberge mountains define the landscape. Zell am See lies on the west bank of the lake of the same name, at an altitude of 760m - 2 493ft. The lively town has a wide variety of leisure facilities (swimming pool, ice rink, 18-hole golf course and riding centre) and generous provision for accommodation. Anyone who values tranquillity above all else is well catered for in rural Thumersbach on the opposite side of the lake.

Zeller See

The town centre, with its beautifully laid-out pedestrian precinct, has managed to preserve its own character (Romanesque church, 16C town hall, local museum). In summer, Zell am See is the ideal starting point for hiking trips and excursions. In addition to the famous Pinzgauer Weg trail *(see below)*, it is possible to climb up to the **Hundstein★** (alt 2 117m - 6 945ft) in an 8 hour return trip, after having taken the Ronachkopf chairlift up as far as possible from Thumersbach.

In winter, the Schmittenhöhe massif provides a pleasant **skiing area**✳ with fairly gentle slopes at an altitude of between 760 and 2 000m - 2 493 and 6 562ft. It consists of 2 areas (Sonnkogel and Hirschkogel) each of which is laid out in two sections. The upper sections (above 1 400m - 4 593ft) can generally guarantee good snow cover from Christmas to April. The long black pistes, nos 1 and 2, which lead through a beautiful spruce forest, should not be missed. Since long waiting times at the lifts can be expected when there is a large crowd, it is advisable to take the Schmittenhöhe cable-car straight away in order to save time *(car park 2km - 1.2 miles above the town)*.

In order to improve on what it can offer, Zell am See teamed up with **Kaprun**✳ *(see KAPRUN)*. The two towns offer a combined ski pass *(for a stay of at least 2 days)* for the **Europa-Sportregion** ski slopes, which has the advantage of combining two skiing areas with a total of 130km - 81 miles of piste, which complement each other well.

Zeller See – During the Ice Age, the Saalach glacier dug the transverse breach at Zell and the Saalfelden basin at a soft point in the shale massif. When the ice melted, the offshore terminal moraines prevented the water from draining away into what is now the Saalach valley. The water remained, so the Zeller See is not fed either by the Saalach or the Salzach. The lake is 4km - 2.5 miles long and 1.3km - 0.8 miles wide and has a depth of 69m - 226ft in places. Since it likewise receives no melted snow and ice, it very quickly warms up to 25°C-77°F in summer. In winter, it generally remains frozen over until March.

Stadtpfarrkirche – Zell parish church, which dates from the 11C, has a beautiful façade in the Romanesque style. The interior bears the imprint of a number of periods, with a Romanesque nave, narthex and aisles in the Gothic style and Baroque ornamental elements. The interesting frescos from the 16C to the right of the altar and under the diagonal ribs near the choir are worth a closer look.

★★ **Schmittenhöhe** ⊙ – Alt 1 965m - 6 447ft. *2km - 1 miles and then a return trip of 1 hour 30min, of which 15min is a journey by cable-car. Climb to the summit in a few minutes (orientation map).* Splendid all-round view of the bold limestone massifs (Wilder Kaiser, Loferer and Leoganger Steinberge, Dachstein) and the sparkling glacial peaks of the Hohe Tauern (Großvenediger, Sonnblick, Kitzsteinhorn, Großglockner, Wiesbachhorn).

★★ **Pinzgau walk** – *Allow a good day for this walk of about 6 hours, which does not entail any major difficulties or differences in altitude, but which nevertheless demands a certain amount of stamina. A map with a scale of 1: 50 000 is needed. Enquire at the tourist office about the departure times of the lifts and of the buses between Saalbach and Zell am See, so that you will be able to return to the departure point in the afternoon without any problems. Take the Schmitten-höhe cable-car very early in the morning (purchase the ticket that includes the descent to Saalbach by the Schattberg-Ost cable railway).*

The path, which can only be taken in dry weather, is among the most famous hikes in Austria. It lies 1 000m - 3 281ft above the floor of the valley all the way, crosses just under a dozen passes and, on a number of occasions, provides a breathtaking **view**★★ of the surrounding mountains.

Walk down to the Ketting-Hütte mountain lodge and then straight ahead on a footpath which leads through the meadow parallel with the Hahnkopf ski lift. At the summit (alt 1 865m - 6 119ft), go down towards the left and walk on along the slope on a narrow path.

Carry straight on at the Kessel pass (leave the track to the Maurerkogel behind on the right), until you reach the Rohrertörl pass (alt 1 918m - 6 293ft) – after about 45min. From this point, there is a view over the Saalbach area and, in the background, over the rocky barrier of the Loferer Steinberge.

Walk on past the gap in the gorge and then turn right at the foot of the Hochkogel, and climb up to the Klinglertörl in the direction of Schattberg. Climb down *(15min)* to the **Hackelberg Seen** lakes. Then take a bend towards the right and walk along Saalbachkogel and Stemmerkogel. At the Marxtenscharte gap, do not continue onto the path opposite, which leads direct to the Schattberg-West, but follow a track which leads round this summit on the right-hand side *(yellow-blue marking)*. After one last climb, you will finally reach the **Schattberg-Ost**★★ *(see SAALBACH)*.

Travel back by cable-car to Saalbach, and by bus to Zell am See.

ZILLERTAL★★

Tirol

Michelin map 426 folds 31 and 32

The Zillertal is among the most densely populated valleys and most important holiday destinations in the Tyrol. It covers a distance of about 60km - 37 miles from north to south and stetches from the Inn valley to the Italian border.

The upper, wide part of the valley lies in easily accessible low mountain countryside. After Mayrhofen, the most important holiday resort in the region, it branches into four narrow valleys (Tuxertal, Zemmtal, Stilluppgrund and Zillergrund), which are delimited, to the south, by the giant crystalline massif of the Zillertal alps. This mountain chain, with mighty glaciers extending over almost 40km - 25 miles, is dominated, above all, by the **Hochfeller** (alt 3 510m - 11 516ft) and the **Großer Möseler** (alt 3 479m - 11 414ft).

Even in the 19C, the Zillertal, with its unusual and varied landscape, was sought out by large numbers of hikers and mountain-climbers.

In the 1920s, dams and reservoirs for generating hydroelectric power were constructed in the Zemmtal, Stilluppgrund and Zillergrund valleys as well as in the nearby Gerlostal.

But the growth in popularity of winter sports has also made a significant contribution to the valley's economic boom. It has unfortunately not been possible, because of the wayward relief of the region, to set up any integrated skiing area. Instead, just under a dozen, rather scattered massifs of modest size have been equipped with ski lifts. The more interesting sections include the **Tux glacier**✳, **Mayrhofen-Finkenberg**✳, **Gerlos**✳ and **Zell am Ziller**. Ski passes valid for at least 4 days cover all the massifs, between which there are bus connections. In view of the relatively long distances between the individual areas, however, there are only limited opportunities for switching between them in a single day. Also, because of the low altitude in the floor of the valley, good snow cover is not always guaranteed. The Zillertal alps are therefore primarily suitable for a more relaxed style of skiing.

MAJOR RESORTS DOWNRIVER

Zell am Ziller – Alt 575m - 1 886ft. Population 3 500. The capital and main market town of the Zillertal clusters round its **church**★, which was built in 1782, on a daringly innovative octagonal ground plan. The enormous, lantern-crowned dome above the central section was painted by Franz Anton Zeiller (1716-1793) from Reutte, the cousin of the famous Johann Jakob Zeiller *(see FERNPASS-STRASSE: Reutte)*. Characters from the Old and New Testament are depicted, grouped around the Trinity, looking impressively majestic.

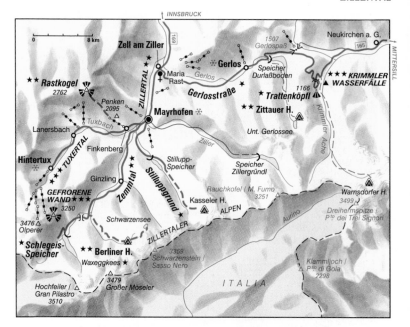

In May, the entire population of the valley gathers in Zell for the traditional "Gauderfest" festival which is celebrated with a procession, wrestling matches on the town green and the consumption of a 20° proof specially brewed beer (Gauderbier).

Besides all this, Zell am Ziller is an ideal winter sports resort for families, with 45km - 28 miles of piste and around 20 ski lifts on the slopes of Karspitze and Kreuzjoch.

The **Gerlosstraße★** *(see GERLOSSTRASSE)* which leads into the Hohe Tauern, also starts here.

☀ **Mayrhofen** – Alt 630m - 2 067ft. Population 3 600. Mayrhofen lies 7km - 4 miles downriver from Zell am Ziller and is indisputably the main tourist centre of the region, with its extensive accommodation facilities (guest capacity of over 8 000 in hotels, boarding-houses or holiday apartments), its many shops lining both sides of the main road and its excellent sports facilities (swimming pool and ice rink).

The village lies in the final flat, broad stretch of the Zillertal, in an ideal location at the foot of the four valleys of the upper reaches of the valley. For over a hundred years it has been highly reputed as a centre for hikers and mountaineers. Peter Habeler who, together with the Italian Reinhold Messner, succeeded in climbing Mount Everest for the first time without oxygen equipment, runs a school for mountaineers here.

Life takes on a particularly lively pace during summer because of the international holiday courses organised by the adult education college, which also ensure that the old customs of the region do not entirely pass into oblivion.

Skiing in winter mainly takes place on the **Penken massif** at an altitude of up to 2 250m - 7 382ft (76km - 47 miles of pistes, in conjunction with the neighbouring locality of Finkenberg) and on the Ahorn massif.

★★★ TUXERTAL

From Mayrhofen to Hintertux

19km - 12 miles - allow half a day, not including the hike up the Rastkogel

☀ **Ski slopes on the Tux glacier** – By virtue of its good snow cover and its large differences in altitude, this area is the most interesting for skiing in the entire Ziller valley. 19 ski lifts lead to 86km - 53 miles of piste at altitudes of between 1 500 and 3 250m - 4 921 and 10 663ft. In winter, really excellent snow cover is found only above the first section (alt 2 100m - 6 890ft), and in summer, only in the fourth section (alt 3 050 to 3 250m - 10 006 to 10 663ft). The pistes at the Kaserer lifts, above all, are suitable for moderately good skiers, while the bumpy slopes on either side of the Lärmstange chairlifts provide good opportunities for experienced skiers.

Tux glacier and the Olperer summits seen from Gefrorene Wand

After Mayrhofen, the valley narrows noticeably and becomes increasingly steeper. Pass through the localities of Finkenberg and Lanersbach at the foot of the Rastkogel massif. The valley broadens out again level with Juns and provides an unobstructed view of the Tux glacier which is situated upriver. The road ends in the small holiday resort of **Hintertux** (alt 1 500m - 4 921ft).

★★★ **Gefrorene Wand** – Alt 3 250m - 10 663ft. *3 hour return trip. Ascent by means of 2 cable-cars and 2 chairlifts. Thick-soled, water- and snowproof footwear, warm clothing and sunglasses are a must.*
From the second section onwards, the eye roves over the icicles of the Tux glacier and the rock face which connects Kleiner Kaserer and Armstange.
From the mountain station of the last chairlift, the view is dominated by the pyramids of the **Olperer** (alt 3 476m - 11 404ft) which towers above the gigantic Tux glacier. The barren alpine setting contrasts with the green floor of the valley, which is dominated by Rastkogel and Kalkwandspitze. When visibility is good, it is possible to make out, to the north, the Kitzbühl Alps, the Karwendel mountains and the Zugspitzplatt. Walk 200m along the ski piste to a rocky peak in the shape of a bird's head.
There is a grand **panorama**★★★ over the Schlegeis-Stausee reservoir, which is dominated by the glacial cirque of the same name and flanked by the Hochfeiler and Großer Möseler. Further to the left, you can see the glaciers of Waxeggkees and Hornkees at the foot of the Tuxerkamm ridge, and also the Schwarzenstein. In the background it is possible to make out the Dolomites (to the south) and also the Stubai and Ötztal Alps (to the west).
From the chairlift, it is possible to climb up to the Gefrorene Wandspitze peak, from where there is a beautiful all-round view. Anyone wishing to go hiking on a glacier can walk down to the third section *(about 20min)*.

★★ **Hike up the Rastkogel** – *5 hour return trip on foot, difference in altitude of about 700m - 2 297ft.*
Travel up from Finkenberg (alt 840m - 2 755ft), initially by cable-car, and then by chairlift to the **Penken** ☉ (alt 2 095m - 6 873ft) *(buy a return ticket)*. From the mountain station, a track leads gradually up to the Wanglalm. The route then continues upwards to the Wanglspitze peak and past the mountain station of the chairlift from Vorderlanersbach to the Rastkogel. There is a beautiful view over the valley at a number of points on the way. From the summit, there is a splendid **panorama**★★ over the Zillertal Alps. Note in particular the Lanersbach ski slopes, framed by the Grünbergspitze and Grüblspitze peaks, the Tuxer Hauptkamm ridge, and the Stillupptal (Tristnergipfel summit) and Floitental valleys.

** ZEMMTAL

* **From Mayrhofen to the Schlegeis-Speicher reservoir** – *23km - 14 miles – toll after 15km - 9 miles – 1 hour 45min return trip. Allow a whole day, if including the hike to the Berliner Hütte mountain lodge. The road is open from May to October. The journey can be made by bus from the station at Mayrhofen.*
Drive upriver from Mayrhofen in the direction of Ginzling. Shortly after that point, a stretch of road only accessible to motor cars cuts its way through narrow, scenic **gorges**★. Anyone travelling in a larger vehicle or wishing to avoid difficult mountain stretches can drive to the left through a long tunnel which, although it makes the journey considerably easier, nevertheless also robs the excursion of a large part of its charm.
After 8km - 5 miles, you will reach **Ginzling**, a peaceful village at the fork of the Floitengrundtal and Gunggltal valleys. The journey continues to the Breitlahn car park, which is the start of the famous hike to the Berliner Hütte mountain lodge. On the far side, our route continues on a single track **toll road**, on which traffic alternates through 2 long tunnels, as far as the Schlegeis-Speicher reservoir. From the final bends in the road, there is an impressive **view**★ of the 131m - 430ft high dam and of the Hochfeiler (alt 3 509m - 11 512ft).

* **Schlegeis-Speicher reservoir** – This artificial lake is the largest in the area, with a capacity of 126.5 million m³ – 165.5 million cubic yds. It lies in a splendid **setting**★ at the foot of the Hochsteller massif and the Schlegeis glacial cirque. The power station, which has 4 turbines, generates 284 million kWh annually and is linked to the other hydroelectric power stations in the Zillertal to create a generating capacity of over 610 million kWh per annum.

** **Hike to the Berliner Hütte** – *Park at the Breitlahn car park (alt 1 257m - 4 124ft, for which there is a charge) by the toll station. Difference in altitude: 800m - 2 625ft. 5 hour 15min return trip on foot, with no technical difficulties, however the hike requires a certain amount of stamina.*
A large part of the route is covered on a beautiful footpath alongside a mountain torrent. It leads through woods and over Alpine pastures. A good hour's walk brings you to the **Grawandhütte mountain lodge** (alt 1 636m - 5 367ft), from where you can enjoy a **view**★ of the impressive rock walls of the Großer Greiner and of the Schönbichl Horn with its small glacier, from which high waterfalls thunder down.
Leaving the lodge behind, the footpath gives numerous beautiful **views**★, along the way, of the valley floor, which is dominated by the Realspitze peak and Federbett glacier. On the climb up to the **Alpenrosenhütte**, the vegetation becomes increasingly sparse and the mountain torrent ever more tempestuous. Immediately after the lodge, the magnificent Waxegg glacial cirque, or **Waxeggkees**★, suddenly comes into view. After a further half hour you will finally arrive, up a steep path, at the Berliner Hütte, an imposing mountain hut dating from 1898. It lies amidst magnificent **Alpine countryside**★★ dominated by the Großer Möseler, the Waxeggkees and the Hornkees.
Hikers with a particularly high level of stamina may like to carry on towards the **Schwarzensee lake**. After only half an hour, there is a beautiful **view**★ of the Schwarzenstein glacier, the Großer Mörchner and the Zsigmondy peak.

* STILLUPPGRUND

From Mayrhofen to the Stillupptal waterfall inn – *9km - 6 miles on a toll road – 45min return trip. Journey by bus possible.*
From the Mayrhofener Hauptstraße, turn off to the left, after a small bridge, into the Ahornbahnstraße. A steeply rising road snakes its way uphill. After passing through a dense wood, this road leads along the slope through small gorges. These are followed by narrow Alpine pastures, crammed in between mighty walls of rock.
The road leads to the far left end of the **Stilluppdamm** (alt 1 130m - 3 707ft), from where there is a beautiful **view**★ across the lake. It continues through a tunnel as far as a pretty inn. After this, the road is blocked to traffic. The lake lies in the middle of a rugged, unspoilt **natural landscape**★ and is framed on both sides by a waterfall.
It is possible to travel by bus to the **Grüne-Wand-Hütte** (alt 1 438m - 4 718ft) and to hike from that point to the **Kasseler Hütte** (alt 2 177m - 7 142ft) in about two hours.

Tourist Information Centres
are located on the town plans by the symbol **🛈**
and the telephone number and address are listed
in the Admission times and charges section of this Guide

ZÜRS✻✻

Vorarlberg – Population 13

Michelin map 426 fold 29 – Local map under ARLBERGGEBIET

Alt 1 716m - 5 630ft

Until the end of the 19C, the barren erosion valley in which Zürs is now situated remained uninhabited throughout the winter. Because of the risk of avalanches, the route over the Flexenpaß was impassable and the snow cover reached a depth of more than 10m - 33ft some years. In summer, the valley merely provided ordinary pasture lands, since the poor soil and the slopes made agricultural exploitation impossible.

These initially unfavourable features of the locality (abundant snowfall, steep terrain without vegetation) finally became a decisive plus factor with the growth in popularity of winter sports. After the building of the road over the Flexenpaß, which was completed in 1900, the valley suddenly benefited from a lively influx of visitors. The first ski competitions were organised as early as 1906 for the local residents. In the 1920s, the pioneers of modern skiing from the Lake Constance area met there. The first ski lifts in Austria were put into operation in the municipality of Zürs in 1937.

After the end of the Second World War, the Arlberg massif was soon regarded as one of the most beautiful skiing areas in Europe. Like its neighbouring municipality of Lech✻✻✻ *(see LECH)*, Zürs consciously decided to limit its growth in an attempt to preserve the surrounding countryside. That is why the resort still consists, even nowadays, of an unpretentious group of about twenty hotels and boarding-houses which blend in with the vast snowfields all around. Its 1 500 beds are generally occupied by a regular clientèle to whom the sporting, lively and fashionable character of the place appeals.

Zürs is endowed with international stature thanks to the Arlberg ski pass, which is also valid for the pistes at Lech, Stuben and St. Anton. After a long day's skiing, holidaymakers can get together in the fitness centre (facilities for tennis and squash), the gourmet restaurants and, until the early hours, the famous Zürs discothèque.

IMPRESSIVE VIEWS

★ **Trittkopf** ⊙ – Alt 2 423m - 7 949ft. *Take the cable-car up to this viewpoint. Allow 20min for the return trip.*
   Beautiful **view** of Zürs and the surrounding area, towering above which are the mighty crags of Hasenfluh, Flexenspitze and Wildgrubenspitze. The Arlberg pass road can be seen to the south with, in the background, the Verwall group, the Rätikon and the Swiss Alps.

★ **Madlochjoch** – Alt 2 438m - 7 999ft. *This viewpoint can be reached by skiers via the Seekopf and Madlochjoch chairlifts.* View of the Schafberg from the mountain station. The Roggspitze peak and Valluga can be seen in the opposite direction.

Zürs am Arlberg

★ **Muggengrat** – Alt 2 450m - 8 038ft. *This viewpoint can be reached by skiers via the Seekopf and Muggengrat chairlifts.* Scenic **Alpine landscape**★, from which the crags of Hasenfluh and Flexenspitze stand out in particular. The view stretches as far as the Verwall range to the south, and Lech and Oberlech at the foot of the Widderstein to the north.

SKI SLOPES

Although the skiing area at Zürs is by no means vast, it is nevertheless of outstanding quality. Skiers glide along on the abundant, light snow as though on velvet and the pistes are remarkably well-managed. The "Rüfikopf", "Family run" and "Muggengrat-Zürsersee" pistes are suitable for beginners, while moderately competent skiers prefer the "Palmen", "Steinmännle" and "Madloch-Zürsersee" pistes. The more proficient skiers can try out their skills on the magnificent **Muggengrat-Täli** piste and the unique run which leads down from the **Madlochjoch** to Lech, giving as an added extra a magnificent **view**★★ over the Lechtal Alps. Besides this, there are wonderful opportunities for off-piste skiing alongside the Madloch and Muggengrat chairlifts.

First and foremost, however, Zürs' location makes it the ideal starting point for excursions into the Arlberg area. The Lech snowfields are a perfect training ground for moderately good skiers, while particularly expert ones prefer to travel in the bus to St. Christoph or St. Anton in order to ski down the steep pistes of the Valluga there. The only drawbacks of the Arlberg district are the lack of skiable links between the individual areas and also the absence of high-altitude peaks.

Stift ZWETTL

Niederösterreich

Michelin map 426 fold 10 – 3km - 2 miles northeast of Zwettl

The great Cistercian Abbey of Zwettl stands in a bend of the romantic valley of the River Kamp just above the Ottenstein Dam.

Stift (Abbey) ⊙ – From the abbey courtyard, which has a fountain at its centre, there is a fine view of the Baroque tower of the abbey church.

An elegant **west front**★ was added to the 14C Gothic church, built of granite from the Waldviertel, in the 18C. It is decorated with larger-than-life-size statues and topped by a slender onion-domed tower.

The Baroque decoration is continued inside where a profusion of marble and statues harmonize with the architecture of the chancel, framed by fourteen side chapels. The altarpieces are by Martino Altomonte, Paul Troger and Johann Georg Schmidt.

The cloisters mark the transition between the Romanesque and Gothic styles. From the monks' hexagonal ritual washing place, projecting outwards, one appears to be surrounded by small columns and capitals.

342   Travelling to Austria

343   Motoring in Austria

344   Accommodation

345   Tourist information
General information

346   Further reading

347   Enjoying the Great Outdoors
Recreation

351   Table of winter sports
resorts

353   Calendar of events

355   Useful vocabulary

357   Admission times and charges

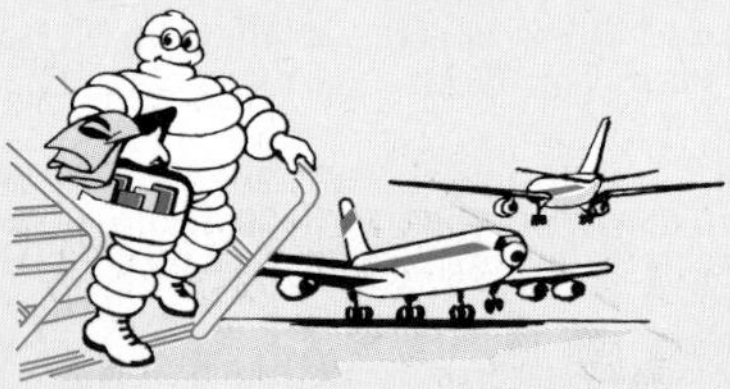

Sundial in the Lech valley

Mallaun/ÖSTERREICH WERBUNG

Practical
information

Travelling to Austria

Formalities – Holders of a valid national passport from a member state of the European Union, from the USA or from some Commonwealth countries (Australia, Canada, New Zealand) require no visa to enter Austria, and may remain there for up to 3 months (British citizens up to 6 months). Visitors of other nationalities should check whether they need a visa with the **Austrian Embassy**.

Austrian Embassy
18 Belgrave Mews West
London SW1X 8HU
UK
☎ (0171) 235 3731

Austrian Embassy
15 Ailesbury Court
93 Ailesbury Road
Dublin 4
EIRE
☎ (01) 269 4577

Austrian Embassy
3524 International Court NW
Washington DC 20008
USA
☎ 202-895-670

Austrian Embassy
12 Talbot Road
Forrest ACT 2603
Canberra NSW
AUSTRALIA
☎ (6) 295 1376

Customs regulations – Since Austria became a full member of the European Union in January 1995, EU nationals travelling in Austria are subject to EU regulations. Tourists are not charged duty on items brought into the country for their personal use. The UK Customs Office produces a leaflet on customs regulations and the full range of "duty free" allowances *(A Guide for Travellers)*, available from HM Customs and Excise, Dorset House, Stamford Street, London SE1 9PS, ☎ (0171) 928 0533. The US Customs Service (PO Box 7407, Washington, DC 20044, ☎ 202-927-5580) offers a free publication *Know Before You Go* for US residents. Further information can be obtained from the Austrian Customs Office in Vienna: ☎ 1/79 59 09.

Travel by air – Scheduled flights are provided by **Austrian Airlines** from London Heathrow to Vienna and on to Linz, Salzburg, Klagenfurt and Graz; by **British Airways** from London Heathrow and London Gatwick to Vienna; by **Lauda Air** from London Gatwick and Manchester to Vienna and Salzburg; by **Aer Lingus** from Dublin to London for connecting flights to Vienna; and by **Lufthansa** from Dublin to Munich (Germany). Contact your travel agent for details.

Travel by rail – From London Victoria via Dover and Ostend to Vienna (direct), Salzburg (change at Munich) or Innsbruck (change at Sargans). The Orient Express travels from Paris (which can be reached via the Channel Tunnel on Eurostar) through Germany to Salzburg and Vienna.
The Arlberg-Express provides a convenient rail link with the Tyrolean winter sports resorts, stopping at Feldkirch, Bludenz, Langen, St. Anton am Arlberg, Landeck, Imst, Ötztal and Innsbruck.
Details of motorail services can be obtained from DER Travel Service in London (18 Conduit Street, London W1R 9TD, ☎ (0171) 290 1116, Fax (0171) 629 7442), and further information on rail timetables and fares from local travel agents or rail companies.

Travel by road – Ostend to Vienna (1 238km - 769 miles) via Cologne, Nuremberg and Linz. Ostend to Salzburg (1 056km - 656 miles) and Ostend to Innsbruck (1 027km - 638 miles) via Stuttgart or Nuremberg and Munich. Calais to Bregenz (873km - 542 miles) via Rheims, Strasbourg and the Black Forest (long non-motorway sections). The shortest land route to Vienna (931km - 578 miles) involves the long sea crossing from Harwich to Hamburg, then travel via Berlin, Dresden and Prague (long non-motorway sections).

Help us in our constant task of keeping up to date.
Send your comments and suggestions to

Michelin Tyre PLC
Tourism Department
The Edward Hyde Building
38 Clarendon Road
WATFORD Herts WD1 1SX
UK
Fax : 01923 415052

Motoring in Austria

Documents – It is necessary to have a valid driving licence (preferably an international driving licence), and third party insurance cover is compulsory. Drivers are advised to obtain the International Green Card from insurance companies.

Highway Code – Traffic in Austria drives on the right. Seat belts must be worn. Children under the age of 12 are not allowed to travel in the front seat. It is compulsory to carry a first aid kit and emergency triangle.

Speed limits – 130kph - 80mph on motorways/highways and 100kph - 62mph on other roads (in the mountainous Vorarlberg region and when weather conditions dictate the fitting of winter tyres, these speed limits are reduced to 100kph - 62mph and 80kph - 50mph respectively); cars towing a load in excess of 750kg - 1 650lb must not exceed 100kph - 62mph on motorways/highways, and 80kph - 50mph on other roads. The speed limit in built-up areas is 50kph - 31mph.

Route planning – The **Michelin map** 426 (scale 1: 400 000) covers the whole country and gives details of likely road closures in winter. The hikers' maps published by Freytag and Berndt are useful for more detailed exploration.

Driving in winter – In snowy conditions winter tyres should be fitted, or chains if conditions are particularly severe. Studded tyres (fitted to all four wheels) may be used between 15 November and 7 April.

Fuel – Petrol (gas) comes in the following varieties:
> *Bleifreies Normalbenzin*, standard lead-free 91 octane;
> *Euro-Super bleifrei*, lead-free 95 octane;
> *Super Plus*, 98 octane.

Caravans – Some mountain roads have gradients steeper than 20% (1 in 5), as well as very narrow stretches. Steep gradients are indicated on Michelin map 426, which also gives dates of likely road closures in winter. Stretches of road which seemingly present no particular difficulties (such as the approach roads to the Tauerntunnel) may be unsuitable for caravans because of the heavy volume of traffic they carry.
The table below indicates the most difficult stretches on the various access routes across the Alps (east to west).

Name of pass	Altitude (metres)	Route	Michelin map 426 fold no	★ road barred ○ not recommended
Hochtannbergpaß	1 679	Reutte – Dornbirn	㉙	○
Bielerhöhe	2 036	Silvrettastraße	㉙	★
Seefelder Sattel *(1)*	1 180	Innsbruck – Mittenwald	⑯	★
Timmelsjoch *(2)*	2 474	Ötztal – Italy	㉚	★
Gerlospaß *(3)*	1 507	Zell am Ziller – Zell am See	㉜	★
Hochtor	2 505	Großglockner – Hochalpenstraße	㉝	★
Radstädter Tauernpaß *(4)*	1 739	Radstadt – St. Michael im Lungau	㉞	○
Katschberg *(4)*	1 641	St. Michael im Lungau – Spittal an der Drau	㉟	○
Turracher Höhe	1 763	Murtal – Carinthian lakes	㉟	○
Kartitsch-Sattel	1 526	Kötschach – Sillian	㉝	○
Loibltunnel	1 067	Klagenfurt – Slovenia	㊱	○
Gaberl-Sattel *(5)*	1 547	Direct link: Oberes Murtal – Graz	㊲	★
Präbichl	1 232	Ennstal – Leoben	㉓	○
Rottenmanner Tauern	1 265	Oberes Murtal – Ennstal	㉒	○
Aflenzer Seeberg	1 253	Mariazell – Aflenz	㉓	○

(1) Easy access to Seefeld when heading from Mittenwald to Innsbruck.
(2) Access for caravans less than 3.4m - 11ft high along the Ötztal as far as Untergurgl.
(3) Easy access to the Gerlos pass and to Gerlos heading east-west.
(4) We recommend taking the A 10 motorway.
(5) Inaccessible in winter; not recommended in summer.

Parking regulations – In the larger cities (Vienna, Salzburg, Innsbruck, Klagenfurt, Graz, Villach etc.) coupons for parking fees can be bought from service stations, tobacconists *(Tabak-Trafik)*, banks and occasionally from ticket machines. Special parking restrictions apply in some towns in the Vorarlberg region (short-stay parking meters). Elsewhere, parking discs are in use; they can be obtained free from tobacconists and should be displayed clearly visible inside the windscreen.

Car hire – Cars are on hire to drivers over the age of 19 who have had a driving licence for more than one year. A minimum age of 25 may be required to hire a larger vehicle. The major car-hire firms (Avis, Denzel Rent-a-Car, Hertz, Interrent etc.) have offices at airports and main stations and in all the larger towns.

Traffic reports – These are given on the hour, after the news bulletin, on radio station Ö3. Information on traffic and road conditions is also available on ☎ (1) 15 00, or from ÖAMTC on (1) 15 90.

Breakdown service – This is provided *(small charge for non-members)* by two Austrian automobile clubs: Ö.A.M.T.C. (Österreichischer Automobil-, Motorrad- und Touring Club, Schubertring 1-3, A-1010 Wien, ☎ 1/7 11 99), ☎ 120, and A.R.B.Ö. (Auto-, Motor- und Radfahrerbund Österreich, Mariahilfer Straße 18/0, A-1150 Wien, ☎ 1/89 12 10), ☎ 123.

Accommodation

Hotels – Austria offers a great variety of hotel accommodation *(see useful vocabulary listed on p 355)*. Lists of hotels can be obtained from the Austrian National Tourist Office or from local tourist information centres *(addresses listed opposite)*.
The **Michelin Red Guide Europe** (for Vienna, Innsbruck and Salzburg) and **Michelin Red Guide Deutschland** (for Salzburg and Bregenz) are revised annually and give a selection of hotels and restaurants based on inspectors' reports.

Farm holidays – These are popular in the Tyrol in particular, and they can often be combined with some sort of course (embroidery, sculpture, riding etc). Details available from the Austrian National Tourist Office.

Bed and Breakfast – Private houses offering this type of accommodation indicate vacancies with the *Zimmer frei* sign.

Camping and caravaning – Lists of sites can be obtained from the Austrian National Tourist Office or from local tourist information centres. Permission must be obtained before pitching camp on private land. With the exception of Vienna and nature reserves, most areas allow visitors to spend the night in a caravan or camping van outside the boundaries of a camp site, as long as no evidence of camping activities is left outside their vehicle.

Tourist information

Austrian National Tourist Offices

Australia: 1st Floor, 36 Carrington Street, Sydney, NSW 2000, ☎ (2) 299 3621, Fax (2) 299 3808

UK *(not open to the public; information by letter or telephone only)*: 30 St George Street, London W1R 0AL, ☎ (0171) 629 0461, Fax (0171) 499 6038.

USA: PO Box 491938, Los Angeles CA 90049, ☎ 310-477-3332, Fax 310-477-5141.

USA: PO Box 1142, New York, NY 10108-1142, ☎ 212-944-6880, Fax 212-730-4568.

Tourist Offices of the Austrian Provinces

Vienna: Wiener Tourismusband, Obere Augartenstraße 40, A-1025 Wien, ☎ 1/21 11 40, Fax 1/216 84 92

Burgenland: Burgenland-Tourismus, Schloß Esterházy, A-7000 Eisenstadt, ☎ 0 26 82/6 33 84, Fax: 0 26 82/6 33 84 2

Carinthia: Kärntner Tourismusgesellschaft mbH., Casinoplatz 1, A-9220 Velden, ☎ 0 42 74/5 21 00, Fax 0 42 74/5 21 00-5

Lower Austria: Niederösterreich-Information, Heidenschuß 2, A-1014 Wien, brochures: ☎ 1/5 31 10-62 00 (24-hour order service), holiday advice: ☎ 1/5 33 31 14-34, Fax 1/5 31 10-60 6

Salzburg (province): Salzburger Land-Tourismus GmbH., Alpenstraße 96, A-5033 Salzburg, Postfach 8, ☎ 06 62/62 05 06-0, Fax 06 62/62 30 7

Styria: Steirische Tourismus GmbH., St.-Peter-Hauptstraße 243, A-8042 Graz-St. Peter, ☎ 03 16/403 03 30, Fax 03 16/40 30 13-

Tyrol: Tirol Werbung, Bozner Platz 6, A-6010 Innsbruck, ☎ 05 12/53 20-170, Fax 05 12/532 01 74

Upper Austria: Landesverband für Tourismus in Oberösterreich, Schillerstraße 50, A-4010 Linz, ☎ 07 32/60 02 21-0, Fax 07 32/60 02 2

Vorarlberg: Vorarlberg-Tourismus, Römerstraße 7/1, A-6901 Bregenz, ☎ 0 55 74/425 25-0, Fax: 0 55 74/42 52 55

Local Tourist Information Centres – These are indicated by the symbol ⎇ on the town plans in this guide. Addresses and telephone numbers are given in the Admission times and charges section.

Foreign Embassies in Austria

Royal British Embassy
Jaurésgasse 12
A-1030 Wien
☎ 1/713 15 75

Embassy of Ireland
Landstraßer Hauptstraße 2
Hilton Center
A-1030 Wien
☎ 1/715 42 46

Australian Embassy
Mattiellistraße 2-4/III
A-1040 Wien
☎ 1/512 85 80

United States Embassy
Boltzmanngasse 16
A-1091 Wien
☎ 1/31 339

General information

Currency – The unit of currency in Austria is the Schilling (S), subdivided into 100 Groschen. In late 1996, the exchange rates were about 16 S to the pound (just over 10 S to the US dollar). Austrian notes are available to the value of 5 000, 1 000, 500, 100, 50 and 20 Schillings, and coins to the value of 20, 10, 5 and 1 Schillings, and 50 and 10 Groschen.

Travellers' cheques and foreign currency can be changed into Austrian Schillings at banks, bureaux de change, railway stations and airports. Credit cards are generally accepted throughout Austria, although it is probably worth checking before making your purchases. On the whole, Eurocard and American Express are more widely accepted than Visa.

Banks are generally open from 8am to noon and 2.30pm to 4.30pm on Mondays, Tuesdays, Wednesdays and Fridays, and from 8am to noon and 2.30pm to 5.30pm on Thursdays. Banks are closed at weekends. Bureaux de change at airports and mainline railway stations are usually open from the first to last plane or train (i.e. 8am to 10pm) 7 days a week.

Post offices – Post offices are open from 8am to noon and 2pm to 6pm on weekdays and (some offices only) from 8am to 10am on Saturdays. Cashdecks close at 5pm. Main post offices in large towns and cities are open all day, and sometimes even on Saturdays. It is possible to change money at post offices.

Letters addressed to a destination in Austria should indicate the international abbreviation A in front of the post code.

Stamps can be bought from *Tabak-Trafik* outlets.

Telephone – Off-peak rates apply daily from 6pm to 8am and at weekends from 6pm on Friday to 8am on Monday. The international dialling code for Austria is 43, after which the zero preceding the local code should be dropped. To telephone abroad from Austria, dial 00, then the international dialling code of the country concerned (Australia: 61, Canada: 1, Eire: 353, New Zealand: 64, UK: 44, USA: 1), then the local code (minus preceding zero) and subscriber's number.

The local area code for Vienna when calling from within Austria is 02 22.

Emergency telephone numbers

Fire: 122 Police: 133 Ambulance: 144

Shops – These are normally open from 8am to 6pm Mondays to Fridays with a break for lunch, and from 8am to 12noon or 1pm on Saturdays (until 5pm on the first Saturday of the month). Check for local variations on this (early closing etc). Shops in popular tourist areas often have special dispensation to remain open longer.

VAT paid on purchases in excess of 1 000 Schillings made at a shop displaying the "Tax Free" sticker can be reclaimed by foreign visitors on completion of a customs declaration.

Public holidays – 1 and 6 January, Easter Monday, 1 May, Ascension Day, Whit Monday, Corpus Christi, 15 August, 26 October (Austrian National Holiday), 1 November, and 8, 25 and 26 December.

Further reading

A Brief Survey of Austrian History by R Rickett
Chronicle and Works (vol 2) *Haydn at Esterházy 1776-1790* H O Robbins Landon
Exploring Rural Austria by G Beer
Fin de Siècle Vienna by C E Schorske
Mountain Walking in Austria by C Davies
Music and Musicians in Vienna by R Rickett
The Fall of the House of Habsburg by E Crankshaw
The Habsburg Monarchy 1809-1918 by A J P Taylor
The Kalkalpen Traverse by A Proctor
Unknown Austria (3 vols) by B Whelpton
Vienna, the Image of a Culture in Decline by E Crankshaw

Literature

Aichinger, Ilse: *Die größere Hoffnung*
Bachmann, Ingeborg: *Malina, Die gestundete Zeit*
Bernhard, Thomas: *Das Kalkwerk (The Limeworks), Die Berühmten (The Famous), Holzfällen (Woodcutters), Heldenplatz (Heroes' Square)*
Freud, Sigmund: *Die Traumdeutung (The Interpretation of Dreams), Das Unbehagen in der Natur (Civilization and its Discontents)*
Grillparzer, Franz: *Das Goldene Vließ (The Golden Fleece), König Ottokars Glück und Ende (King Ottocar, His Rise and Fall), Ein Bruderzwist in Habsburg (Family Strife in Habsburg)*
Handke, Peter: *Die Angst des Tormanns beim Elfmeter (The Goalie's Anxiety at the Penalty Kick), Die linkshändige Frau (The Left-Handed Woman), Publikumsbeschimpfung (Offending the Audience), Wunschloses Unglück (A Sorrow Beyond Dreams)*
Hofmannsthal, Hugo von: *Jedermann (Everyman), Das Salzburger große Welttheater, Der Rosenkavalier (libretto), Chandos Brief (essay), Cristinas Heimreise (Christina's Journey Home), Der Turm (The Tower)*
Musil, Robert von: *Der Mann ohne Eigenschaften (The Man without Qualities), Die Verwirrungen des Zöglings Törleß*
Rilke, Rainer Maria: *Sonette an Orpheus (Sonnets to Orpheus), Duineser Elegien (Duino Elegies)*
Roth, Joseph: *Radetzkymarsch (Radetzky March), Kapuzinergruft (The Capuchin Tomb)*
Schnitzler, Arthur: *Liebelei (Playing with Love), Reigen (Merry-Go-Round), Leutnant Gustl (None But the Brave), Der Weg ins Freie (The Road to the Open)*
Stifter, Adalbert: *Der Nachsommer (Indian Summer), Bunte Steine (Colourful Stones)*
Zweig, Stefan: *Schachnovelle, Sternstunden der Menschheit (The Tide of Fortune), Ungeduld des Herzens (Beware of Pity)*

Enjoying the Great Outdoors

National parks

Nationalpark Hohe Tauern – 800km² - 309sq miles of this Alpine nature reserve lie in the province of Salzburg, 720km² - 278sq miles in the eastern Tyrol and 380km² - 147sq miles in Carinthia.
Information centres:
Nationalpark-Rat, Rauterplatz 1, A-9971 Matrei in Osttirol, ☎ 48 75/51 61 17, Fax 48 75/51 61 2
Regionalverband Nationalpark Hohe Tauern, A-5722 Niedernsill, ☎ 65 48/84 17
Nationalparkverwaltung Hohe Tauern/Kärnten, Döllach 14, A-9843 Großkirchheim, ☎ 48 35/61 61.

Nationalpark Neusiedler See-Seewinkel (Burgenland) – This is the only nature reserve of the steppes in central Europe. It covers 14 000ha - 35 000 acres, 6 000ha - 15 000 acres of which are in Hungary.
Information centres:
Nationalpark Neusiedler See-Seewinkel, Informationszentrum, Obere Hauptstraße 2-4, A-7142 Illmitz, ☎ 21 75/34 42.

Nationalpark Nockberge (Carinthia) – This national park lies between the Lieser valley and the Turracher Höhe range. It was designated a nature reserve to protect its eco-system.
Information centre:
Nationalparkverwaltung Nockberge, A-9020 Klagenfurt, ☎ 4 63/53 63 20 17.
There are plans to set up national parks in the following areas:
Lower Austria: Donau-Auen (Danube plain), Thayatal
Salzburg: Kalkhochalpen
Upper Austria: Kalkalpen

Bird-watching

Burgenland: Neusiedler See; Seewinkel/Lange Lacke; veterinary care centre for storks and other birdlife at Parndorf (A-7111).
Carinthia: Eagle observation point from the castle ruins at Landskron; bird reserve on Großedlinger lake (near Wolfsberg); Völkermarkter reservoir.
Lower Austria: Donau, March and Thaya river plains; Thaya valley near Hardegg.
Salzburg (province): Pinzgau (between the Gastein and Habach valleys); Zeller See (south shore of the lake).
Styria: Mur reservoir (southern Styria).
Upper Austria: Danube plain in the Linz valley; Schmiding bird reserve.

Recreation

See also the map of Places to stay on pp 12-13, which shows spas, winter sports and mountain resorts.

Angling

On the whole, two fishing permits are required: one valid for the whole province and the other a local, private one from the owner of the stretch of water. Further information from Fischwasser Österreichs, Kongreß-Zentrum Seeburg, A-9210 Pörtschach am Wörthersee, ☎ 42 72/36 20 30.
The Carinthian tourist office (Kärntner Tourismusgesellschaft, Casinoplatz 1, A-9220 Velden, ☎ 0 42 74/5 21 00) publishes a brochure, *Fischen*, on the subject of angling in Carinthia, including descriptions of local species of fish, stretches of water, types of bait recommended and times to allow to make a catch.

Cycling

Austria has over 10 000km - 6 200 miles of cycle paths to offer sightseers on two wheels. Some of the most popular include:
Bodensee-Radwanderweg beginning at Bregenz and running round the shores of Lake Constance (120-250km - 75-155 miles)
Inntalradweg from Landeck to Passau (410km - 255 miles)
Tauernradweg from Krimml to Passau (325km - 202 miles)
Salz-und Seen-Tour through the Tennengau (165km - 103 miles)
Donauradweg from Passau to Hainburg (305km - 190 miles)
Kulturradweg via Linz, Steyr and Wels (140km - 87 miles)

Neusiedler-See-Radweg 70km - 44 miles on Austrian and 40km - 25 miles on Hungarian territory

Murradweg from Muhr to Bad Radkersburg (340km - 211 miles)

Thermenradweg from Loipersdorf through southern Burgenland and southeastern Styria (180km - 112 miles)

Karnischer Radweg from Kötschach-Mauthen to Villach (90km - 56 miles)

Drauradweg from Sillian to Völkermarkt (230km - 143 miles)

Guides to these cycle paths can be obtained from "Radtouren in Österreich", c/o Salzburger Land, Postfach 8, A-5033 Salzburg, ☎ 06 62/62 05 06 12.

The following towns are particularly well-adapted to the needs of cyclists: Graz, Klagenfurt, Linz, Salzburg, St. Pölten, Vienna.

Golf

Austria can boast an increasing number of attractively landscaped golf courses and pleasant golfing hotels. In 1994, 73 golf courses were recorded nationwide: one 36-hole; nine 27-hole; 34 18-hole and 29 9-hole.

Further information from Österreichischer Golf-Verband, Prinz-Eugen-Straße 12, Haus des Sports, A-1040 Wien, ☎ 1/5 05 32 45

Hang-gliding and paragliding

The minimum age for learning hang-gliding is 18 years. Reputed schools for hang-gliding and paragliding include those at:

Carinthia – Bad Kleinkirchheim, Katschberg

Salzburg – Dorfgastein, Mattsee, Salzburg

Styria – Gröbming, Ramsau

Tyrol – Galtür, Kössen

Upper Austria – Weyregg

In the Vorarlberg region, paragliding is permitted from certain mountain summits and following prescribed routes only.

Further information from Österreichischer Aero-Club, Prinz-Eugen-Straße 12, A-1040 Wien, ☎ 1/50 51 02 80.

Hiking

With a network of about 50 000km - 31 100 miles of waymarked footpaths, Austria is a hiker's paradise. Ten long-distance footpaths make it possible to explore the entire country on foot, if such is your wish. Three long-distance Euro-footpaths also cut across Austria.

The Austrian tourist authorities publish a leaflet *Wandern* with brief descriptions of hikes in each Austrian province.

Walking in the mountains – Austria boasts about 680 mountain peaks over 3 000m - 10 000ft above sea level and 528 carefully managed mountain huts, offering

Walking in the Dachstein range

R. Lamm/VIENNASLIDE

mountain enthusiasts a wide variety of possibilities for walking and climbing slopes of every imaginable degree of difficulty.

For safety reasons alone, it is advisable to plan the route of any mountain excursions very carefully in advance, and to ensure that you have the correct equipment and that you are in a good general state of fitness. Useful aids to planning your itinerary are the series of hiking maps *(Wanderkarten)* published by Kompass and by Freitag & Berndt.

Lakes – Water sports and boating

Austria might otherwise be known as the "land of 1 000 lakes", as it is home to at least this number, 200 of which are to be found in Carinthia.

There are regular passenger boat or ferry services on some of the larger lakes, such as the Achensee, the Attersee, Lake Constance, the Hallstätter See, the Ossiacher See, the Traunsee, the Wörthersee and the Wolfgangsee. Details available from Erlebnis Bahn und Schiff Österreich, Prof.-Kaserer-Weg 333, A-3491 Straß im Straßertale, ☎ 27 35/5 35 05.

In almost all cases, it is possible to row, sail, water ski or quite simply swim in Austria's lakes. Further information on these possibilities is provided by the tourist offices of the lakeside communities.

Mountain climbing

Mountain guides and climbing schools are to be found in the following areas:

Carinthia – Heiligenblut, Kötschach-Mauthen, Spittal an der Drau, Villach

Lower Austria – Gloggnitz, Puchberg am Schneeberg

Salzburg – Filzmoos, Kaprun, Mauterndorf

Styria – Bad Aussee, Graz, Ramsau

Tyrol – Ehrwald, Ellmau, Fulpmes, Galtür, Innsbruck, Landeck, Lanersbach, Mayrhofen, Obergurgl, St. Anton, St. Johann

Upper Austria – Gosau am Dachstein, Mondsee

Vorarlberg – Bartholomäberg, Brand, Lech, Mittelberg, Vandans

Further information is available from Verband Alpiner Vereine Österreichs, Bäckerstraße 16, A-1010 Wien, ☎ 1/5 12 54 88, or the Österreichischer Alpenverein, Wilhelm-Greil-Straße 15, A-6020 Innsbruck, ☎ 05 12/5 95 47.

Railways – Steam Engines and Tourist Trains

Carinthia
Rosenthaler Dampfbummelzug from Weizelstal to Ferlach along the Rosen valley
Museumstramway from Mariazell to Erlaufsee

Lower Austria
Höllental-Expreß from Reichenau/Rax to Hirschwand
Mariazellerbahn from St. Pölten to Mariazell – oldest electric narrow-gauge railway
Ötscherland-Expreß from Kienberg to Lunz am See
Schneebergbahn from Puchberg to Hochschneeberg mountain refuge – rack-railway
Waldviertler Schmalspurbahn from Gmünd to Litschau, Heidenreichstein or Groß Gerungs
Ybbstalbahn from Waidhofen an der Ybbs to Lunz am See

Salzburg
Pinzgauer Lokalbahn from Zell am See to Krimml via Mittersill
Salzburger Lokalbahn from Salzburg to Oberndorf
Taurachbahn from Mauterndorf to St. Andrä – section of the Mur valley railway (Murtalbahn)

Styria
Erzbergbahn from Vordernberg to Eisenerz – steepest railway in Austria
Murtalbahn from Murau to Tamsweg

Tyrol
Achenseebahn from Jenbach to Seespitz
Giselabahn from Hopfgarten to Zell am See
Stubaitalbahn from Innsbruck to Fulpmes
Zillertalbahn from Jenbach to Mayrhofen

Upper Austria
Attergaubahn along the shores of the Attersee
Schafbergbahn from St. Wolfgang to the Schafberg summit
Steyrtal-Museumsbahn from Steyr to Grünburg – oldest narrow-gauge railway in Austria

Further information from ÖBB, Bahn-Totalservice Wien Westbahnhof, ☎ 1/5 80 03 22 00, or Erlebnis Bahn & Schiff Österreich, Prof.-Kaserer-Weg 333, A-3491 Straß im Straßertale, ☎ 27 35/5 35 05.

Here are some statistics on winter sports facilities in Austria:
22 000km - 13 700 miles of ski slopes
2 700 ski tows
16 000km - 9 900 miles of cross-country ski tracks
900 resorts with cross-country ski runs
400 ski schools with 8 300 ski instructors
500 natural toboggan runs
1 500 curling rinks
14 000km - 8 700 miles of paths cleared of snow

Skiing and winter sports

Austrian districts have set up numerous excellent skiing areas equipped with an infrastructure designed to appeal to visitors. On request, the tourist offices of ski resorts will send out prospectuses with panoramic maps which clearly indicate the main skiing areas.

Year-round skiing is possible at the following resorts:
- in **Carinthia**, Mölltaler Gletscher;
- in **Salzburg**, Kaprun/Kitzsteinhorn;
- in **Styria**, Ramsau/Dachstein;
- in the **Tyrol**, Hintertux/Tuxer Gletscher, Kaunertal, Stubaier Gletscher, Ötztal/Rettenbach-und Tiefenbachferner, Pitztal/Mittelbergferner.

Information can be obtained from Österreichischer Skiverband, Olympiastraße 10, A-6020 Innsbruck, ☎ 05 12/33 50 10.

Information on snow conditions:
- in Lower Austria and Styria, ☎ 01/15 83;
- in Salzburg province, Upper Austria and Carinthia, ☎ 01/15 84;
- in the Tyrol and Vorarlberg, ☎ 01/15 85.

Weather reports for the ski resorts: recorded message on ☎ 05 12/15 67.

All the winter sports resorts shown in the following table have ski schools.

Mallaun/ÖSTERREICH WERBUNG

St. Anton am Arlberg

White water sports

Rafting is only permitted from 1 May to 31 October. Rafting and canyoning are prohibited in the Hohe Tauern national park.

Rivers on which it is possible to go rafting are:
- in **Carinthia**, the Möll, Gail, Gurk and Lieser;
- in **Lower Austria**, the Thaya, Salza, Enns and March;
- in the province of **Salzburg**, the Enns, Lammer, Mur and Saalach;
- in **Styria**, the Enns and Salza;
- in the **Tyrol**, the Inn, Isel, Ziller, Ötztaler and Tiroler Ache;
- in **Upper Austria**, the Enns, Traun and Steyr.

Further information is available from the Österreichischer Kanuverband, Berggasse 16, A-1090 Wien, ☎ 1/3 17 92 03.

WINTER SPORTS RESORTS (1)	No of fold on Michelin map 426	Minimum and maximum altitude of the resort in metres	Cable-cars	Chair-lifts and ski-lifts	Distance (in km) covered by cross-country ski runs	Skating rink	Long-distance skiing	Indoor swimming pool	Distance (in km) covered by footpaths cleared of snow	Sleigh rides	Summer skiing
Aflenz-Kurort St	23	765-1 810		8	18	⛸	×	🏊	20	×	
Altenmarkt/Zauchensee S	20	856-2 240	2	26	150		×	🏊	30	×	
Badgastein/Sportgastein S	34	1 083-2 686	6	25	36	⛸	×	🏊	40	×	
Berwang T	16	1 336-1 640		8	17	⛸	×		5	×	
Brand V	28	1 037-1 920		7	29	⛸	×	🏊	15	×	
Brixen im Thale/Westendorf T	18	800-1 827	1	13	13	⛸			6	×	
Dorfgastein S	34	835-2 027	3	20	20	⛸	×	🏊	20	×	
Ehrwald T	16	1 000-3 000	2	16	50	⛸	×	🏊	31	×	
Ellmau T	18	812-1 550	1	12	10	⛸	×	🏊	55	×	
Filzmoos S	20	1 057-1 645	1	15	40		×	🏊	50		⛷
Flachau/Flachauwinkl S	20	925-1 980	5	46	150	⛸	×		30	×	
Fulpmes/Schlick 2000 T	31	960-2 260	1	8	18	⛸	×	🏊	30	×	
Galtür T	29	1 584-2 297		11	16	⛸	×	🏊	62	×	
Gargellen V	28	1 430-2 130		9	1		×	🏊	8		
Gaschurn/Partenen V	28	1 000-2 300	2	27	45	⛸	×	🏊	10		
Gerlos T	32	1 245-2 300		26	20		×	🏊	20	×	
Gosau O	20	766-1 800	2	35	45	⛸	×	🏊	40	×	
Großarl S	34	920-2 100	3	20	21		×	🏊	40	×	
Heiligenblut K	33	1 301-2 902	3	9	14	⛸	×	🏊	35	×	
Hermagor/Sonnenalpe/Naßfeld K	34	600-2 004		23	200	⛸	×	🏊	55	×	
Hofgastein (Bad) S	34	870-2 300	4	14	37	⛸	×	🏊	30	×	
Innsbruck/Igls T	31	574-2 334	3	7	32	⛸	×	🏊	30		
Ischgl T	29	1 400-2 864	4	36	28	⛸	×	🏊	1	×	
Kaprun S	33	800-3 029	5	19	15	⛸	×	🏊	30		⛷
Kaunertal T	30	1 273-3 160		8	25	⛸	×	🏊	5		⛷
Kitzbühel T	18	800-1 995	3	24	40	⛸	×	🏊	40	×	
Kirchberg in Tirol T	18	860-1 995	1	16	30	⛸	×	🏊	24	×	
Kleinarl S	20	1 014-2 200		8	20		×	🏊	30	×	
Kleinkirchheim (Bad) K	35	1 100-2 440	3	29	20	⛸	×	🏊	40	×	
Kleinwalsertal/Hirschegg Mittelberg Riezlern V	15	1 124-2 030	2	33	44		×	🏊	40	×	
Kössen T	18	600-1 700		5	80	⛸	×		46	×	
Kühtai T	30	2 020-2 520		10	30		×	🏊	2		
Lech/Oberlech V	29	1 450-2 444	5	29	24	⛸	×	🏊	25	×	
Lermoos T	16	1 004-2 250		10	58	⛸	×	🏊	27	×	
Leutasch T	16	1 130-1 600		4	160	⛸	×	🏊	90	×	
Lienz T	33	720-2 278	1	11	60	⛸		🏊	30		
Lofer S	19	639-1 747	1	13	50	⛸			40	×	
Mallnitz K	34	1 200-2 650	1	11	28	⛸	×	🏊	25	×	
Maria Alm S	19	800-2 000	2	33	30		×	🏊	20	×	
Mariazell St	23	870-1 267	1	14	90	⛸	×	🏊	10	×	
Matrei in Osttirol T	33	1 100-2 400		6	29	⛸	×	🏊	5	×	
Mayrhofen T	32	630-2 095	2	31	10	⛸	×	🏊	62		⛷
Mitterndorf (Bad) St	21	812-1 965		20	95	⛸	×	🏊	20	×	
Mühlbach am Hochkönig S	20	853-1 562	1	24	10	⛸	×	🏊	20	×	
Nauders T	29	1 365-2 750	1	15	30	⛸	×	🏊	50	×	
Neukirchen am Großvenediger S	32	856-2 150	2	11	47	⛸	×	🏊	20	×	
Neustift/Hochstubai T	32	1 000-3 250	4	28	20	⛸	×	🏊	40	×	⛷
Obergurgl/Hochgurgl T	38	1 930-3 064	1	21	11	⛸	×	🏊	7		
Obertauern S	32	1 740-2 335	1	24	17		×	🏊	17	×	
Partenen V	29	1 100-2 300	5	27	45	⛸	×	🏊	10	×	
Radstadt S	20	856-1 700		10	150	⛸		🏊	30	×	

WINTER SPORTS RESORTS (1)	No of fold on Michelin map 426	Minimum and maximum altitude of the resort in metres	Cable-cars	Chair-lifts and ski-lifts	Distance (in km) covered by cross-country ski runs	Skating rink	Long-distance skiing	Indoor swimming pool	Distance (in km) covered by footpaths cleared of snow	Sleigh rides	Summer skiing
Ramsau am Dachstein *St*	32	1 100-2 700	1	20	155		×	⛊	70	×	⛷
Rauris *S*	33	950-2 200	1	9	43	⛸	×	⛊	35	×	
Saalbach-Hinterglemm *S*	19	1 003-2 100	9	49	18	⛸	×	⛊	35	×	⛷
Saalfelden *S*	19	744-1 550		5	80	⛸	×	⛊	30	×	
St. Anton am Arlberg/ St. Christoph *T*	29	1 304-2 811	5	37	19	⛸	×	⛊	15	×	
St. Gallenkirch/Gortipohl *V*	28	900-2 370	4	25	30		×	⛊	12		
St. Jakob in Defereggen *T*	32	1 389-2 520	1	8	26	⛸	×		12	×	
St. Johann im Pongau/Alpendorf *S*	20	650-1 850	2	26	25	⛸	×	⛊	25	×	
St. Johann in Tirol *T*	19	660-1 700	2	16	75	⛸	×	⛊	59	×	
St. Michael im Lungau *S*	35	1 075-2 360		11	65	⛸	×	⛊	40	×	
Schladming *St*	21	750-1 894	2	23		⛸	×	⛊	10	×	
Schruns/Tschagguns *V*	28	700-2 380	3	10	13	⛸	×	⛊	35	×	
Seefeld in Tirol *T*	16	1 200-2 100	3	14	123	⛸	×	⛊	60	×	
Semmering *N*	24	1 000-1 340		5	20	⛸	×	⛊		×	
Serfaus *T*	29	1 427-2 684	3	14	42	⛸	×	⛊	36	×	
Sölden/Hochsölden *T*	30	1 377-3 250	3	40	22	⛸	×	⛊	30		
Tauplitz/Tauplitzalm *St*	21	900-2 000		19	95	⛸	×	⛊	20	×	
Turrach/Turracherhöhe *K/St*	35	1 763-2 200		11	30	⛸	×	⛊	15	×	
Tuxertal/Lanersbach *T*	31	1 300-3 250	4	28	18	⛸	×	⛊	55	×	⛷
Wagrain *S*	20	900-2 190	5	44	35	⛸	×	⛊	20	×	
Werfenweng *S*	20	1 000-1 836		12	38		×	⛊	25	×	
Wildschönau *T*	18	828-1 903	1	34	10	⛸	×	⛊	40	×	
Zell am See *S*	19	758-1 949	4	27	38	⛸	×	⛊	30	×	⛷
Zürs *V*	29	1 720-2 450	5	29	4		×	⛊	4		

(1) The letter following the name of the resort denotes the Land in which it is situated:

B Burgenland	**N** Niederösterreich	**S** Salzburg	**T** Tirol
K Kärnten	**O** Oberösterreich	**St** Steiermark	**V** Vorarlberg

Calendar of events

Traditional folk festivals

6 January (every 4 years, next time 1998)

Badgastein . . . . *Perchtenlauf:* carnival procession

February (in turn)

Nassereith map 426 fold 16 . *Schellerlaufen* ⎫
Imst map 426 folds 16 and 30 *Schemenlaufen* ⎬ carnival processions
Telfs . . . . *Schleicherlaufen* ⎭

1st weekend in May

Zell am Ziller . . . . *Gauderfest*

Whit Monday

Freistritz an der Gail
(west of Villach)
map 426 folds 34 and 35 . . . . *Kufenstechen:* a joust using a barrel as target

End of May – every six years (1997, 2003)

Erl (north of Kufstein)
map 426 fold 18 . . . . Passion plays

Corpus Christi (2nd Thursday after Whitsun)

Brixen im Thale
map 426 fold 18 . . . . *Antlaßritt:* procession on horseback
Gmunden . . . . Procession
Hallstatt . . . . Procession on the lake
Traunkirchen . . . . Procession on the lake

Corpus Christi weekend, last weekend in July, 1st Sunday in August

Tamsweg . . . . *Samsonumzug:* procession

Second Friday after Corpus Christi

Tyrol . . . . *Herz-Jesu-Feuer*

24 June

Zederhaus map 426 fold 18 . *Prangenstangentragen:* poles up to 8m – 26ft long, decorated with flowers are carried to the church in a procession and left there until 15 August (the feast of the Assumption)

15 August

Nationwide . . . . Processions in traditional costume

End of September – beginning of October

Burgenland and **Lower Austria** . . . . Wine harvest: processions, wine fountains, fireworks

End of November or beginning of December to Christmas

Innsbruck ⎫
Klagenfurt ⎪
Salzburg ⎬ Christmas markets
Spittal an der Drau ⎪
Villach ⎪
Vienna ⎭

5 December

Bad Mitterndorf
map 426 fold 21 . . . . *Nikolospiel:* street festival in honour of St Nicholas

27 December to 15 January

Thaur (northeast of Innsbruck)
map 426 fold 21 . . . . Christmas nativity scenes are on display in people's houses, some of which are open to the public

"Prangstangen"
from Zederhaus

Moetschtmaier/ÖSTERREICH WERBUNG

31 December to February
Nationwide . . . . *Fasching* (pre-Lent carnival), balls

Music – Opera – Theatre

1 January
Vienna . . . . New Year's Day concert with the Vienna Philharmonic Orchestra

Holy Week
Salzburg . . . . Easter Festival, ☎ 06 62/80 72-0

May to October
Millstatt . . . . International Music Festival

Beginning of May to mid-June
Vienna . . . . Vienna Festival

Second half of June
Feldkirch map 426 fold 14 . . *Schubertiade*, ☎ 05 5 76/20 91

August
Innsbruck and **Schloß Ambras** Festival of Old Music, ☎ 05 12/57 10 32

First weekend in July
Wiesen map 426 fold 25 . . . . Open-air Jazz Festival, ☎ 0 26 26/81 648

June to 15 September
Vienna . . . . Music Festival (200 concerts)

Mid-July to August
Mörbisch . . . . Operetta Festival (by the Neusiedler See) ☎ 0 26 85/6 62 10-0

End of July to end of August
Bregenz . . . . Lakeside Festival, ☎ 0 55 74/22 811
Salzburg . . . . Salzburg Festival, ☎ 06 62/80 72-01

July and August
Ossiach/Villach . . . . Carinthian Summer Festival, ☎ 0 42 43/5 10-502

Second week in September
Eisenstadt . . . . International Haydn Festival in Schloß Esterházy, ☎ 0 62 82/6 18 66

September and October
Linz . . . . International Bruckner Festival, ☎ 07 32/ 2 75 2 75

October
Graz and its surroundings . . Styrian Autumn (Fall) Festival, ☎ 03 16/ 81 05 76

Schleicherlaufen at Telfs

Useful Vocabulary

Hotel terms are underlined

Ansichtskarte . picture postcard
Ausfahrt,
  Ausgang ... exit
Ausflug ...... excursion
Auskunft .... information
Bahnhof ..... railway station
Brücke ...... bridge
Brunnen ..... fountain, well
Burg .... fortified castle
Café .... tea and coffee shop
Denkmal .... monument, memorial
Dom .... cathedral, largest local
        church
Einfahrt,
  Eingang ... entrance
Essen .... to eat (Mittagessen: lunch
      Abendessen: dinner)
Fahrweg ..... suitable for vehicular traffic
Fähre .... ferry
(Wasser) Fall . (water) fall, cascade
Festung ...... fortress, fortified town
Forsthaus .... forestry lodge
Fremdenheim . *pension* – where only
    breakfast is served
Frühstück .... breakfast
Frühstücks-
  pension .... see *Fremdenheim*
Garten .... garden
Gasse .... street, alley
Gasthaus..... café, inn
Gasthof ...... inn
Gaststätte ... restaurant ; buffet
Gebühr ...... tax, tip, toll
Geradeaus .. straight ahead
Geschlossen .. closed
Gesperrt ..... barred, closed
Gipfel .... summit
Gletscher .... glacier
Gobelins ..... tapestry (in general)
Grüß Gott .... "God bless": traditional
    greeting (= "hello")
Guten Morgen/
  Tag .... Good morning/day
Guten Abend . Good evening
Gute Nacht ... Good night
Haus .... house
Hof .... courtyard, hotel, farm
Höhe .... height, altitude
Höhenweg ... high level route
Höhle .... cave
Hütte .... mountain refuge, factory
Jause .... tea, light meal
Kanzel .... pulpit, lookout point

(Musik)
  Kapelle ..... orchestra, fanfare
Kar .... limestone cirque or corrie
Kirche .... church
Klamm ...... gorge, ravine
Kloster .... abbey, monastery
Kofel, Kogel .. dome-shaped mountain
Krankenhaus .. hospital
Kreuzgang .... cloisters
Kur .... cure and place to stay
Landhaus ..... seat of provincial
    government
Landungsstelle . landing stage
Links .... to/on the left
Markt .... market square,
    market town
Maut .... toll (road, bridge)
Mesner ...... sacristan
Münster ..... cathedral
Offen .... open
Postlagernd ... *poste restante*, to be
    called for
Quelle .... spring, fountain
Rathaus ..... town hall
Rechts ...... to, on the right
Schloß .... castle, palace
Schlucht ..... gorge, defile
Schlüssel ..... key
Schwimmbad .. swimming pool
See .... lake
Speisesaal .... restaurant or dining room
    in a hotel
Spielbank .... casino
Stausee ...... artificial lake (reservoir)
    formed by a dam
Stift .... abbey, monastery
Strandbad .... bathing beach
Straße .... road, street
Stube, Stüberl . small dining room in a
    restaurant decorated in
    the local style
Tal .... valley
Talsperre ..... dam
Tor .... gate, town gateway
Treppe ...... steps, stairs
Verboten ..... forbidden
Wald .... forest
Wechsel ..... exchange (money)
Wildfütterung . winter forage point for
    wild animals
Zimmer frei ... rooms to let
    (room available)
Zimmernachweis accommodation bureau

Skiing

Abfahrt ...... departure, piste
Bergski ...... uphill ski
Bindung ..... binding
Eisbahn...... ice-rink
Gondelbahn .. cable-way
Kanten ...... edges
Lawine ...... avalanche
Loipe .... cross-country ski-run
Rutschen .... side-slipping
Schlepplift ... ski-tow
Schneepflug .. snow-plough
Spitzkehre ... kick-turn
Stemmen .... turning position

Schuß .... direct descent
Schutzhaus .... hut, refuge
Seilschwebebahn cable-way
Sesselbahn,
  Sessellift .... chairlift
Skilehrer ...... ski-instructor
Skischule ..... ski-school
Sprungschanze ski-jump
Standseilbahn . funicular railway
Stimmung .... "atmosphere"
Stock .... pole
Talski .... downhill ski

Road Signs

Anfang	start	Rechts, links einbiegen	turn right or left
Aussicht	viewpoint	Rollsplitt	loose chippings
Bauarbeiten	road works	Sackgasse	cul de sac
Baustelle	works	Schlechte Wegstrecke	road in bad condition
Einbahnstraße	one-way street	Schlechte Fahrbahn	
Ende	end of restriction	Steinschlag	falling stones
Freie Fahrt	no restrictions	Umleitung	detour
Frostschäden Frostaufbrüche	icy roads	Verengte Fahrbahn	road narrows
Fußgängerzone	pedestrians only	Vorrang	priority
Gefährlich	dangerous	Vorsicht	caution
Glatteis	black ice		
Kurzparkzone	restricted parking		
LKW	heavy lorries		
PKW	private car		

Culinary terms

Apfelsaft	apple-juice
Backhendl	fried chicken in breadcrumbs (Styria)
Brettljause	cold cooked meat served on a board
Faschiertes	mince, meat-balls
Frittate	pancakes cut into strips and put into soup
Gebäck	rolls, biscuits (in restaurants, bread is charged extra)
Gulasch	stew with highly seasoned sauce
Hirschbraten Rehbraten	roast venison
Kaffee	coffee; see WIEN
Kaiserschmarrn	sweet omelette with raisins
Knödel, Nockerl	dumplings
Kren	horseradish Leberkäse ("liver cheese"); slice of meat or liver paté, served hot
Mehlspeise	collective name for sweet dishes served as a hot dessert
Mus	fruit purée
Palatschinken	thin pancake filled with apricot jam or chocolate sauce
Pfannkuchen	pancakes
Platte	grilled meats, richly garnished
Salzburger Nockerl	sweet omelette
Schlag (obers)	whipped cream
Schnaps	colourless grain spirit
Semmel	bread roll
Strudel	thin pastry rolled and filled
Tafelspitz	boiled beef with a small slice of liver, sauté potatoes, vegetables and tartare sauce
Torte	cake
Wienerschnitzel	Viennese fillet of veal fried in breadcrumbs

Meat can be

gebacken	fried in breadcrumbs
gebraten	roast or braised
geröstet	sautéed
gekocht	boiled
geselcht, geräuchert	salted and smoked
vom Grill, gegrillt	grilled

*The current Michelin Red Guide Europe offers
a selection of pleasant hotels in the cities of Vienna, Innsbruck or Salzburg ;
each entry specifies the facilities available (gardens,
tennis courts, swimming pool, car park)
and the annual opening and closing dates ;
there is also a selection of restaurants recommended for their cuisine :
well-prepared meals at moderate prices ; stars for good cooking*

Admission times and charges

As admission times and charges are liable to alteration, the information below is given for guidance only. The information given applies to individual adults (not including special reductions for groups etc).

Every sight for which admission times and charges are listed is indicated by the symbol ⊙ in the alphabetical section of the guide. The information below is listed in the same order as the entries in the main body of the guide.

Churches do not admit visitors during services (other than to worship) and are usually closed between noon and 2pm. Admission times are given if the interior is of special interest. It is usual for visitors to make a donation, especially if accompanied by a keyholder of the church.

The telephone number, and in the case of larger towns the address, of the Tourist Information Centre is given to the right of the place name, and indicated by the symbol 🛈. These centres provide details of guided tours etc.

NB The feast of Corpus Christi is celebrated on the Thursday after Trinity Sunday (8th Sunday after Easter).

A

ADMONT
🛈 Rathaus, A-8911, ☎ 0 36 13/21 64

Stiftsbibliothek – Unaccompanied visit or guided tour (30min); open May to September from 10am to 1pm and from 2pm to 5pm; April and October from 10am to noon and from 2pm to 4pm; otherwise only open to groups (minimum 20 people, by telephone appointment); closed November to March; 60 S (combined ticket with museum); ☎ 0 36 13/23 12.

ALPBACH
🛈 ☎ 0 53 36/52 11

Stift ALTENBURG

Stiftsgebäude – Guided tour (c 1hr); end of March to mid October, Monday to Saturday, at 10.30am, 2pm and 3pm; on Sundays at 11am and 2pm; otherwise by appointment; 60 S; ☎ 0 29 82/34 51.

Excursion

Rosenburg – Open daily 1 April to 15 November from 9am to 5pm; 65 S; ☎ 0 29 82/23 03.

ARLBERG

Arlberg road tunnel – Toll for private cars: 150 S.

ARTSTETTEN

Erzherzog-Franz-Ferdinand Museum – Unaccompanied visit or guided tour (1hr 15min); open from 1 April to 2 November from 9am to 5.30pm; otherwise by appointment only; 60 S; ☎ 0 74 13/83 02.

Bad AUSSEE
🛈 Chlumeckyplatz 44, A-8990, ☎ 0 36 22/23 23 25 51

Kammerhof (Local Museum) – Open daily mid June to mid September from 10am to noon and 4pm to 6pm; from the beginning of April to mid June and from mid September to the end of October, open Tuesdays from 3.30pm to 6pm, Fridays from 9.30am to noon and Sundays from 10am to noon; closed November to end of March (may be visited by telephone appointment); 40 S; ☎ 0 36 22/ 5 25 11 21.

Motorboat excursions on the Toplitzsee – Tour of 3 lakes (c 2hr 30min); daily from May to September; 70 S; ☎ 0 36 22/86 13.

Salzbergwerk – Guided tour (1hr 15min); May to end of September from 10am to 4pm; daily from October to the end of April at 2pm by appointment; 130 S; ☎ 0 36 22/7 13 32 51.

B

BADEN
🛈 Brusattiplatz 4, A-2500, ☎ 0 22 52/4 45 31

Beethoven-Gedenkstätte – Open Tuesday to Friday from 4pm to 6pm; Saturdays, Sundays and public holidays from 9am to 11am and 4pm to 6pm; closed 1 January and 24 December; 20 S; ☎ 0 22 52/86 80 02 31.

BADGASTEIN
🛈 Kaiser-Franz-Josef-Straße 1, A-5640, ☎ 0 64 34/2 53 10

BISCHOFSHOFEN 🏛 Salzburgerstr. 1, A-5500, ☎ 0 64 62/24 71

BLUDENZ 🏛 Werdenbergstr. 42, A-6700, ☎ 0 55 52/6 21 70

Lünersee cable-car – Operates end of May to mid October from 8am to 4pm; 52 S single trip; ☎ 05 56/7 01 31 67.

BRAUNAU AM INN 🏛 Stadtplatz 9, A-5280, ☎ 0 77 22/26 44

BREGENZ 🏛 Anton-Schneider-Straße 4a, Postfach 187, A-6900, ☎ 0 55 74/4 33 91

Vorarlberger Landesmuseum – Open daily, except Mondays, from 9am to noon and 2pm to 5pm; closed 1 January, 1 November and 25 December; 20 S; ☎ 0 55 74/4 60 50.

Martinsturm – Open May to September, Tuesday to Sunday from 9am to 6pm; 10 S; ☎ 0 55 74/4 66 32.

Cable-car trip to the Pfänder – Operates April to the end of September from 9am to 7pm; otherwise, 9am to 6pm; departure every half hour; closed for 2 weeks in November; 120 S Rtn; ☎ 0 55 74/42 16 00.

BREGENZERWALD

Rappenlochschlucht – Open beginning of May to end of November; unaccompanied visit or guided tour by appointment; ☎ 0 55 72/2 21 88.

BRENNER

Motorway toll – Private cars: 130 S in each direction.

BRUCK AN DER MUR 🏛 Koloman-Wallisch-Platz 25, A-8601, ☎ 0 38 62/5 18 11

D

DACHSTEIN

Ascent of the Krippenstein – The cable-car operates 1 May (1st section), mid May (2nd section) and 20 June (3rd section) to 15 October; departures between 8.40am and 5.50pm (or 5.30pm or 4.50pm according to season), every 20min (more frequently at peak times); 160 to 270 S depending on the journey; ☎ 0 61 31/2 73-0.

Dachstein-Rieseneishöhle – Guided tour (1hr); open daily May, June and September to mid October from 9am to 3.30pm; July and August 9am to 4.30pm; 81 S; ☎ 0 61 31/3 62.

Mammuthöhle – Guided tour (1hr); open daily mid May to the end of June and September to mid October from 9am to 2pm; July and August 9am to 3pm; 81 S; ☎ 0 61 31/3 62.

Koppenbrüllerhöhle – Guided tour; open from end of March to the end of April, Tuesday to Friday from 10am to 4pm; from May to the end of September, daily from 9am to 4pm; 80 S; ☎ 0 61 31/3 62.

Hunerkogel – Cable-car operates mid May to the end of June from 8.30am to 4.50pm; July to the beginning of September from 8am to 5.50pm; beginning of September to the end of November from 8am to 4.50pm; during the winter season, dependent on the snow situation; does not operate from 1 to 20 December and from mid April to mid May; Rtn 250 S; ☎ 0 36 87/8 12 41.

DEUTSCHLANDSBERG 🏛 Mühlweg 2, A-8510 Stainz, ☎ 0 34 63/45 18

DONAUTAL (DANUBE VALLEY)

Burg Clam – Guided tour (45min); April to October from 10am to 5pm; 50 S; ☎ 0 72 69/72 17.

Grein: Rokokotheater – Guided tour (20min); May to October daily at 9am, 10.30am and 2.30pm; 25 S; ☎ 0 72 68/66 80.

Grein: Schiffahrtsmuseum – Open daily May to October, except Mondays, from 9am to noon and 1pm to 5pm; 30 S; ☎ 0 72 68/32 60.

Schönbühel: Church – Admission by telephone appointment; ☎ 0 27 52/84 79; or apply to the presbytery.

Spitz: Pfarrkirche – Open April to October from 7am to 7pm; otherwise from 8am – 5pm; ☎ 0 27 13/22 31.

Archäologischer Park Carnuntinum – Opening times: excavations and information centre April to October, daily from 9am to 5pm; Carnuntinum archaeological museum, daily, except Monday, from 10am to 5pm (7pm on Fridays); closed Good Friday, 1 November; excavations 25 S, museum 50 S; ☎ 0 21 63/3 37 70.

Petronell: Romanesque chapel – To visit the interior, apply to the administrative offices at Kirchengasse 57; ☎ 0 21 63/22 28.

Rohrau: Harrach'sche Gemäldegalerie – Open daily, except Mondays, from Easter to 1 November from 10am to 5pm; 58 S; ☎ 0 21 64/2 25 36.

Rohrau: Geburtshaus Joseph Haydns – Open daily, except Mondays, from 10am to 5pm; closed 1 January, 25 and 26 December; 20 S; ☎ 0 21 64/22 68.

Schloßhof – Open beginning of April to the end of October from 10am to 5pm (closing time of ticket office); 50 S; ☎ 0 22 85/65 80.

DÜRNSTEIN
🏛 A-3601, ☎ 0 27 11/2 19

Pfarrkirche – Open April to October from 9am (10am Sundays) to 6pm; 20 S; ☎ 0 27 11/2 27.

E

Schloß EGGENBERG

Prunkräume – Guided tour (45min); April to October at 10am, 11am, noon, 2pm, 3pm and 4pm (additional visit at 9am Saturdays and Sundays); in March and November, guided tours by appointment; ticket also valid for the Abteilung für Vor-und Frühgeschichte der Steiermark and the Abteilung für Jagdkunde; ☎ 03 16/58 32 64 32.

Abteilung für Vor- und Frühgeschichte der Steiermark – Open February to November from 9am to noon and 1pm to 5pm; entry charge: see above; ☎ 03 16/58 32 64 21.

Abteilung für Jagdkunde – Open March to November from 9am to noon and 1pm to 5pm; entry charge: see above; ☎ 03 16/58 32 64.

EGGENBURG
🏛 Kremser Straße 3, A-3730, ☎ 0 29 84/35 01 40

Pfarrkirche St. Stephan – Keys obtainable from the presbytery or from Kirchengasse 6.

EHRENHAUSEN
🏛 Marktgemeinde, A-8461 – ☎ 0 34 53/43 43

Mausoleum – Guided tour (45min) by appointment with the presbytery ☎ 0 34 53/25 07.

EHRWALD
🏛 Kirchplatz 1, A-6632, ☎ 0 56 73/23 95

Ascent of the Zugspitze – The Zugspitzbahn cable-car departs every 20min from mid May to end of October and from December to 1 week before Easter; closed from November and mid April to mid May; 410 S Rtn; ☎ 0 56 73/23 09 52.

EISENERZ
🏛 A-8790, ☎ 0 38 48/37 00

Erzberg: Open-cast mines – Guided tour (1hr 30min); Open May to October from 10am to 3pm (with additional times if required); 130 S; ☎ 0 38 48/4 53 14 70.

Stadtmuseum – Unaccompanied visit or guided tour (1hr); open May to October, Monday to Friday from 9am to 5pm; Saturdays, Sundays and public holidays from 10am to noon and 2pm to 5pm; otherwise Monday to Friday from 9am to noon; 36 S; ☎ 0 38 48/36 15.

EISENERZER ALPEN

Chairlift up the Polster – Chairlift in operation during summer on Saturdays, Sundays and public holidays from 8am to 5pm; 90 S Rtn.; ☎ 0 38 48/22 24.

EISENSTADT
🏛 Rathaus, A-7000, ☎ 0 26 82/33 84

Schloß Esterházy – Open end of March to mid November from 9am to 4pm; July to September from 9am to 5pm; 50 S; ☎ 0 26 82/6 33 84 16.

Haydn-Saal – The Haydn Quartet plays in period costume in the Haydn Room every Tuesday and Friday at 11am (c 30min); guided tour daily from 9am to 5pm; in the winter Monday to Friday from 9am to 4pm; 50 S; ☎ 0 26 82/6 33 84 15.

EISENSTADT

Haydn-Haus – Open Easter to 31 October from 9am to noon and 1pm to 5pm; closed from November to Easter; 20 S; ☎ 0 26 82/6 26 52 29.

Burgenländisches Landesmuseum – Open Tuesday to Sunday from 9am to noon and 1pm to 5pm; closed 1 May, 1 November, 25 December to 1 January; 30 S; ☎ 0 26 82/6 26 52.

Excursion

Raiding: Liszts Geburtshaus – Open from Easter to 31 October from 9am to noon and 1pm to 5pm; 20 S; ☎ 0 26 19/72 20.

EISRIESENWELT

Access – The caves are open and the cable-car operates from 1 May to the beginning of October; guided tour (about 1hr 15min); July and August from 9.30am to 4.30pm, May, June and September from 9.30am to 3.30pm; 80 S; ☎ 0 64 68/2 48.

Eisriesenwelt-Linie – Bus operates in July and August from 8am to 6.30pm and in May, June, September and October from 8am to 5.30pm; 70 S Rtn.; ☎ 0 64 68/2 93.

Cable-car – Operates in May, June and 1 September to the beginning of October from 9am to 5pm and in July and August from 9am to 6pm; 110 S Rtn.; ☎ 0 64 68/2 48.

ENNS   🛈 Mauthausnerstraße 4, A-4470, ☎ 0 72 23/21 81 24

Basilika St. Laurenz – Some parts of the church may be visited unaccompanied; guided tour (church and excavations: 1hr); for precise details of opening times and other enquiries, apply to the presbytery; ☎ 0 72 23/22 37.

Pfarrkirche St. Marien – Open May to September Monday to Saturday from 9am to 6.30pm, Sunday from noon to 6.30pm; October to April Monday to Saturday from 9am to 4.30pm, Sunday from noon to 6.30pm; guided tour available as part of tour of town or by appointment; ☎ 0 72 23/28 55.

F

FELBERTAUERNSTRASSE

Felbertauerntunnel – Toll: 190 S (summer toll from May to October) and 110 S (winter toll from November to end of April) for private cars.

FELDKIRCH   🛈 Herrengasse 12, A-6800, ☎ 0 55 22/7 34 67

Domkirche St. Nikolaus – Open from 8am to 6pm; ☎ 0 55 22/7 22 32.

Schattenburg: Heimatmuseum – Open Tuesday to Sunday from 9am to noon and 1pm to 5pm; 25 S; ☎ 0 55 22/7 19 82.

Burg FORCHTENSTEIN   🛈 Hauptstraße 54, A-7212, ☎ 0 26 26/6 31 25

Fortress – Guided tour (1hr 15min); April to October from 8am to noon and 1pm to 4pm, otherwise by appointment; 55 S; ☎ 0 26 26/8 12 12.

FREISTADT   🛈 Hauptplatz 12, A-4240, ☎ 0 79 42/29 74

FRIESACH   🛈 Hauptplatz 1, A-9360, ☎ 0 42 68/43 00

Petersberg: Stadtmuseum – Open end of May to the beginning of September from 1pm to 6pm; 40 S; ☎ 0 42 68/26 00.

FROHNLEITEN   🛈 Brückenkopf 1, A-8130, ☎ 0 31 26/23 74

St. Georgskirche – To visit apply to the presbytery; ☎ 0 31 26/24 88.

G

GASTEINER TAL

Cable-car up to Schloßalm – Operates end of May to mid October from 8am to 4pm; December to mid April from 8am to 4pm; 180 S Rtn.; ☎ 0 64 32/64 55.

Chairlift up the Stubnerkogel – Operates end of May to mid October and beginning of December to end of April from 8.30am to 4pm; 180 S Rtn.; ☎ 0 64 32/64 55.

Chairlift up the Graukogel – Operates beginning of July to end of September and mid December to beginning of April from 8.30am to 4pm; 180 S Rtn.

GERAS 🛈 Hauptstraße 16, A-2093, ☎ 0 29 12/2 16

Abbey – Guided tour; Easter to end of October Tuesday to Saturday at 10am, 11am, 2pm, 3pm and 4pm (Sunday at 2pm, 3pm, 4pm); 50 S ☎ 0 29 12/34 52 89.

GERLITZEN

Toll road – Toll payable between 15 May and 15 October; 50 S per private car and driver, 15 S for each additional passenger.

Chairlift – Operates from 9am to 5pm; closed October and November; 160 S Rtn.; ☎ 0 42 48/27 22.

Geras Abbey

GERLOSSTRASSE

Gerlosstraße – Toll payable between the Gerlos pass and Krimml; 90 S per private car.

Bad GLEICHENBERG 🛈 Birkenhof, A-8344, ☎ 0 31 59/22 03

GMÜND 🛈 Rathaus, A-9853, ☎ 0 47 32/22 22

Porsche-Automuseum Helmut Pfeifhofer – Open mid May to mid October from 9am to 6pm; otherwise, 10am to 4pm; 65 S; ☎ 0 47 32/24 71 or 29 71.

GMUNDEN 🛈 Im Graben 2, A-4810, ☎ 0 76 12/43 05

Lake cruises on the Traunsee – Trips on the paddle steamer "Gisela"; July and August on Thursdays, Saturdays, Sundays and public holidays from 2.30pm to 5.15pm; 160 S; Traunseeschiffahrt, Traungasse 12 a, 4810 Gmunden; ☎ 0 76 12/52 15.

Kammerhofmuseum – Open May to the end of October Tuesday to Saturday from 10am to noon and 2pm to 5pm; Sundays and public holidays 10am to noon only; December to mid January also open on Sundays and public holidays from 2pm to 5pm; closed in November, mid January to end of April; 20 S; ☎ 0 76 12/79 42 44.

Scharnstein: Österreichisches Kriminalmuseum – Open daily May to mid October daily, except Mondays, from 9am to noon and 1pm to 5pm; 50 S; ☎ 0 76 15/25 50 or 26 00.

Scharnstein: Reptilenzoo – Open daily May to October, except Mondays, from 9am to 5pm; 50 S; ☎ 0 76 16/81 46.

Cumberland-Wildpark – Open April to October from 9am to 6pm; otherwise, 11am (9am on Sundays and public holidays) to 4pm; 60 S; ☎ 0 76 16/82 05.

GRAZ

Zeughaus – Open (guided tour 1hr) April to October from 9am to 5pm (1pm on Saturdays, Sundays and public holidays); closed 1 May and Corpus Christi; 25 S; ☎ 03 16/80 17 48 10.

Mausoleum – Open May to September from 11am to noon and 2pm to 3pm; October to April, guided tour only (20min) at 11am; closed Sundays and public holidays; 15 S; ☎ 03 16/8 21 68 30.

Stadtmuseum – Likely to be closed for renovation until November 1997; ☎ 03 16/82 25 80.

Funicular up to Schloßberg – Funicular operates May to June from 8am to 11pm, July and August from 8am to midnight, October to March from 10am to 10pm; departs every quarter of an hour; 20 S Rtn.; ☎ 03 16/88 74 50.

Steiermärkisches Landesmuseum Abt. Volkskunde – Closed. Reopening date not known at the time of going to press; ☎ 03 16/83 04 16.

Mariahilf-Kirche: Minoritensaal – Visits by appointment only; enquire at the church office; ☎ 03 16/91 31 70.

Alte Galerie des steiermärkischen Landesmuseums Joanneum – Open Tuesday to Friday from 10am to 5pm; Saturdays, Sundays and public holidays from 10am to 1pm; 25 S; ☎ 03 16/80 17 47 70.

Rein: Stiftskirche – Open daily from 8am to noon and 2pm to 5pm; guided tour (1hr); Sundays and public holidays 3pm or by appointment; 30 S; ☎ 0 31 24/5 16 21 33.

361

GREILLENSTEIN

Schloß Greillenstein – Open July and August from 9.30am to 6pm; April to June, September and October from 9.30am to 5pm; ☎ 0 29 89/8 21 60.

GROSSGLOCKNER-HOCHALPENSTRASSE

Hohe Tauern National Park – For all information, details of nature trails and walks on the glacier or in the nature reserve, as well as activities organised by the park's villages, apply to Nationalparkverwaltung Hohe Tauern Kärnten Geschäftsstelle, Döllach 14, A-9843 Großkirchheim; ☎ 0 48 25/61 61 15.

Toll road – Toll for private cars: 350 S.

Pasterzengletscher – "Gletscherbahn" (funicular) operates June to the end of September from 9am to 4pm; 95 S Rtn.; ☎ 0 48 24/25 02.

GURGLTAL   🛈 6456, A-Obergurgl, ☎ 0 52 56/2 58

Chairlift up the Hohe Mut – The lifts operate from July to the end of September and from December to April (8.45am to 4pm); 80 S Rtn.; ☎ 0 52 56/2 74.

GURK   🛈 9342 – ☎ 0 42 66/81 25

Cathedral interior – Open daily Ash Wednesday to 1 November from 8.30am to 6.30pm (7.30pm on Saturdays); 1 November to Ash Wednesday from 8.30am to 5.45pm (6.30pm on Saturdays); ☎ 0 42 66/8 23 60.

Cathedral crypt – From Palm Sunday to 1 November, may only be visited as part of a guided tour of the interior of the cathedral; 40 S; ☎ 0 42 66/8 23 60.

Episcopal chapel – Guided tour (30min) from Easter to 1 November, daily at 1pm and 3.45pm; otherwise by appointment; 25 S; ☎ 0 42 66/8 5 23 60.

H

Bad HALL   🛈 Kurpromenade 1, A-4540, ☎ 0 72 58/20 31

Pfarrkirchen parish church – The church is currently being restored, but is open to visitors between 9am and 7pm; ☎ 0 72 58/30 20.

HALL IN TIROL   🛈 Wallpachgasse 5, A-6060, ☎ 0 52 23/62 69

Burg Hasegg – Guided tour (1hr); April to October hourly from 10am to 5pm; (from 2pm and 5pm only on Sundays); otherwise by appointment; 35 S; ☎ 0 52 23/5 62 69.

Stadtmuseum – Guided tour (1hr); April to June and October, Monday to Saturday from 10am to 5pm, Sundays and public holidays from 2pm to 5pm, hourly guided tours; unaccompanied visits: July to September daily from 10am to 3pm; closed November to March; guided tours by telephone appointment; 35 S for the guided tour, 20 S for an unaccompanied visit; ☎ 0 52 23/5 62 69.

HALLEIN   🛈 Unterer Markt 1, A-5400, ☎ 0 62 45/53 94

Salzbergwerk Dürrnberg – Guided tour (1hr 15min); April to October from 9am to 5pm; November to March from 11am to 3pm; 170 S; ☎ 0 62 45/8 52 85 22.

HALLSTATT   🛈 Kultur-und Kongreßhaus, Postfach 7, A-4830, ☎ 0 61 34/2 08

Prähistorisches Museum – Open April, daily from 10am to 4pm; May to September, daily from 10am to 6pm; October to March, Wednesdays (daily 26 December to 5 January) from 2pm to 4pm; 40 S; ☎ 0 61 34/82 08.

Salzbergwerk – Guided tour (1hr 15min); April to 15 September from 9am to 4pm; 16 September to 4 November from 9.30am to 3pm; temperature is 8°C – 46°F inside the mine; 135 S; ☎ 0 61 34/82 51 72.

Heimatmuseum – Open May to September from 10am to 6pm; April from 10am to 4pm; 26 December to 5 January from 2pm to 4pm; 40 S; ☎ 0 61 34/82 08.

HEILIGENBLUT   🛈 A-9844, ☎ 0 48 24/20 01 21

Church – Open from 7am to 6pm.

Schareck cable-car – Operates from mid July to mid September and from mid December to mid April; 160 S Rtn.; ☎ 0 48 24/22 88.

HERBERSTEIN

Castle interior – Guided tour (1hr); April to October daily from 10am to 4pm; 98 S; (ticket includes entry to the wildlife park, the castle, Meierhof and Feistritzklamm); ☎ 0 31 76/88 25.

Tierpark – Open April to October daily from 8am to 6pm; 98 S (ticket includes entry to the wildlife park, the castle, Meierhof and Feistritzklamm); ☏ 0 31 76/88 25.

Stift HERZOGENBURG

Monastery – Guided tour (1hr); April to October at 9am, 10am, 11am, 1pm, 2pm, 3pm, 4pm, 5pm; otherwise by appointment only; 50 S; ☏ 0 27 82/31 13 31.

Burg HOCHOSTERWITZ

Castle – Open Easter to the end of October from 8am to 6pm; 70 S; ☏ 0 42 13/20 20.

Bad HOFGASTEIN   🛈 Senator-Wilhelm-Wilfling-Platz 1, A-5630, ☏ 0 64 32/71 10

Schloß-Museum HOHENBRUNN

Jagdmuseum Hohenbrunn – Open daily, except Mondays, April to the end of October, from 10am to noon and 1pm to 5pm; 30 S; ☏ 0 72 24/89 33.

HOHENTAUERNPASSTRASSE

Oberzeiring: Silberbergwerk – Guided tour (50min); open Easter to the end of October from 9.45am to 4pm; 20 December to 6 January from 11am to 4pm; 60 S; ☏ 0 35 71/23 87.

I

INNSBRUCK   🛈 Burggraben 3, A-6021, ☏ 05 12/5 98 50 or
🛈 Hauptbahnhof, ☏ 05 12/58 37 66

Hungerburg funicular – Operates from 7.25am to 7.55pm (every 15min), on weekdays from 6.55am; ☏ 05 12/58 61 58.

Stadtturm – Open from March to October from 10am to 5pm (6pm in July and August); 22 S; ☏ 05 12/57 59 62.

Dom zu St. Jakob – Open from 7.30am to 7.30pm (6.30pm in winter); closed on Friday from noon to 3pm; 35 S; ☏ 05 12/58 39 02.

Hofburg – Open daily May to October, except Mondays, from 9am to 5pm; 55 S; ☏ 05 12/58 71 86.

Hofkirche – Open weekdays from 9am to 5pm (5.30pm in July and August); closed in the afternoon of Shrove Tuesday; 20 S; ☏ 05 12/58 43 02.

Silberne Kapelle – Open weekdays from 9am to 5pm (5.30pm in July and August); closed in the afternoon of Shrove Tuesday; 20 S; ☏ 05 12/58 43 02.

Tiroler Volkskundemuseum – Open Monday to Saturday from 9am to 5pm (5.30pm in July and August); Sundays and public holidays 9am to noon; closed 1 January, in the afternoon of Shrove Tuesday, Easter Sunday, Whit Sunday, Corpus Christi, 1 November and 25 December; 40 S; ☏ 05 12/58 43 02.

Trumler/ÖSTERREICH WERBUNG

Armoury at Schloß Ambras

Tiroler Landesmuseum "Ferdinandeum" – Open May to September from 10am to 5pm (also 7pm to 9pm on Thursdays); otherwise Tuesday to Saturday from 10am to noon and 2pm to 5pm; Sundays and public holidays from 10am to 1pm; closed Mondays out of season; 50 S; ☎ 05 12/5 94 89 84.

Riesenrundgemälde vom Bergisel – Open April to October from 9am to 5pm; 28 S; ☎ 05 12/58 44 34.

Alpenzoo – Open from 9am to 5pm (9am to 6pm in summer); 60 S; access by funicular free of charge if zoo ticket bought at lower station; ☎ 05 12/29 23 23.

Wilten: Stiftskirche – Guided tour by appointment.

Wilten: Basilica – Open daily June to mid October, otherwise visits by appointment; ☎ 05 12/5 83 38 57.

Kaiserjägermuseum – Open March and October from 10am to 3pm; April to September from 9am to 5pm; 25 S; ☎ 05 12/58 23 12.

Schloß Ambras – Open daily April to October, except Tuesdays, from 10am to 5pm; December to March, guided tours only at 2pm (also 3.30pm on Sundays); 60 S; ☎ 05 12/34 84 46.

Cable-car to the Hafelekar – Operating times and prices not available at time of going to press; ☎ 05 12/29 33 44.

ISCHGL

Pardatschgrat cable-car – Operates December to the beginning of May; 385 S (day return).

Bad ISCHGL   🖪 Bahnhofstraße 6, A-4820, ☎ 0 61 32/35 20 77 57

Kaiservilla – Guided tour (40min) May to mid October from 9am to 11.45am and 1pm to 4.45pm; 95 S; ☎ 0 61 32/2 32 41.

Marmorschlößl: Photomuseum – Open April to October from 9.30am to 5pm; 15 S; ☎ 0 61 32/2 44 22.

K

KAPRUN

Kapruner Kraftwerk – Open daily end of May to mid October from 8am to 4pm; 185 S Rtn. (in 3 stations); ☎ 0 65 47/71 51 30 25.

Kitzsteinhorn – The cable-car operates all year round, every 30min from 8.30am to 4.30pm; 250 S Rtn; ☎ 0 65 47/8 70 00.

KARWENDELGEBIRGE

Erfurter Hütte – Rofanbahn (cable-car) operates July and August from 8am to 5.30pm; otherwise from 8.30am to 5pm; closed November to mid December and Easter to the end of April; 160 S Rtn.; ☎ 0 52 43/52 92.

Toll road Hinterriß-Eng – Vorderriß-Hinterriß section: no charge; Hinterriß-Eng section: toll 28 S for private cars.

KATSCHBERG

Katschberg tunnel – Toll for private cars: 100 S.

KAUNERTAL

Wiesenjaggl-Sessellift – Operates from 8.30am to 4pm; ☎ 0 54 75/4 46.

KEFERMARKT   🖪 Oberer Markt 15, A-4292, ☎ 0 79 47/62 55

St. Wolfgangskirche – Open daily from 8am to sunset; ☎ 0 79 47/62 03.

KITZBÜHEL   🖪 Hinterstadt 18, A-6370, ☎ 0 21 55/22 72

Heimatmuseum – Open from 9am to noon; closed Sundays and public holidays; 30 S; ☎ 0 53 56/45 88.

Cable-car up to the Kitzbüheler Horn – Cable-car: (1st section) mountain and valley trip, mid May to the end of October and mid December to mid April from 8.30am to 5pm; (2nd section) mountain and valley trip from 8.45am to 5pm; 160 S; ☎ 0 53 56/5 85 10.

KLAGENFURT
🏛 Neuer Platz/Rathaus, A-9010, ☎ 04 63/53 72 22

Landesmuseum – Open Tuesday to Saturday from 9am to 4pm; Sundays and public holidays from 10am to 1pm; closed Christmas and New Year; 30 S; ☎ 04 63/53 63 05 52.

Diözesanmuseum – Open mid June to mid September, Monday to Friday from 10am to noon and 3pm to 5pm, Saturdays from 10am to noon; beginning of June to mid June and mid September to mid October, weekdays from 10am to noon; 30 S; ☎ 04 63/5 77 70 84.

Landhaus: Großer Wappensaal – Open April to September from 9am to noon and 1pm to 5pm; closed Sundays and public holidays; 10 S; ☎ 04 63/5 36 30 552.

Bergbaumuseum – Open April to October from 9am to 6pm; 40 S; ☎ 04 63/53 74 32.

Excursion

Minimundus – Open April and October from 9am to 5pm; May, June and September from 9am to 6pm; July and August from 8am to 7pm (9pm on Wednesdays and Saturdays); closed mid October to mid April; 85 S; ☎ 04 63/21 19 40.

KLEINWALSERTAL
🏛 Walserstraße 64, A-6992, ☎ 0 55 17/5 11 40 or
🏛 D-Hirschegg, A-87568, ☎ 0 83 29/5 11 40 or
🏛 D-Oberstdorf, Marktplatz 7, A-87561, ☎ 0 83 22/70 00

KLOSTERNEUBURG
🏛 Am Niedermarkt, A-3400, ☎ 0 22 43/20 38

Abbey – Guided tour (1hr); April to November from 9am to noon and 1.30pm to 5pm (Sundays and public holidays from 11am to noon and 1.30pm to 5pm); December to March from 10am to noon and 1.30pm to 5pm (Sundays and public holidays from 11am to noon and 1.30pm to 5pm); closed 25 December; 50 S; ☎ 0 22 43/41 12 12.

KREMS und STEIN
🏛 Undstraße 6, A-3504, ☎ 0 27 32/8 26 76

Historisches Museum der Stadt Krems – Open March to October, Tuesdays from 9am to 6pm, Wednesday to Sunday from 1pm to 6pm; 40 S; ☎ 0 27 32/80 15 67.

Excursion

Stift Göttweig – Open Easter to end of October from 10am to 5pm; 50 S; ☎ 0 27 32/85 12 31.

KREMSMÜNSTER
🏛 A-4450, ☎ 0 75 83/72 12

Abbey – Art collection; guided tour (1hr); April to October daily at 10am, 11am, 2pm, 3pm and 4pm, November to March daily at 2pm; closed 1 January, Good Friday, 1 November, 11, 24, 25, 31 December; 45 S; natural science collection; guided tour (1hr 30min); May to October at 10am and 2pm; 50 S; ☎ 0 75 83/27 52 16.

Excursion

Fahrzeugmuseum im Schloß Kremsegg – Open July and August from 10am to noon and 1pm to 5pm; September to June, Saturdays from 1pm to 5pm, Sundays and public holidays from 10am to noon and 1pm to 5pm; closed 1 November and 24 December to 5 January; 70 S; ☎ 0 75 83/52 47.

KRIMML

Krimmler Wasserfälle – The falls are open to the public all year; 15 S; ☎ 0 65 64/2 23.

KUFSTEIN
🏛 Münchner Straße 2, Postfach 53, A-6330, ☎ 0 53 72/22 07

Fortress: Heimatmuseum und Kaiserturm – Guided tour (1hr 15min); beginning of April to the end of October at 9.30am, 11am, 1.30pm, 3pm and 4.30pm; closed Mondays, except in July and August; 34 S; ☎ 0 53 72/6 70 38.

Heldenorgel – Recitals daily at noon (also at 6pm mid June to the end of August); open July to the end of August from 11.30am to 11.55am and 5.30pm to 5.55pm; ☎ 0 53 72/69 20 44.

L

LAMBACH
🏛 Markplatz 8, A-4650, ☎ 0 72 45/83 55

Stiftkirche – Guided tour (1hr 30min) daily at 2pm; closed 1 November to Easter Sunday; 45 S; ☎ 0 72 45/2 17 10.

LANDECK
🏛 Malserstraße 10, Postfach 58, A-6500, ☎ 0 54 42/23 44

LECH
A-6764, ☎ 0 55 83/2 16 10

Petersboden chairlift – Operates mid July to mid September from 8am to noon and 1.30pm to 4pm; end of November to mid April from 9.30am to 4.30pm; 65 S Rtn.; ☎ 0 55 83/24 48.

Rüfikopf cable-car – Operates July to September from 8.30am to noon and 1pm to 5.30pm; December to April from 9am to 5.30pm; 125 S Rtn.; ☎ 0 55 83/2 33 60.

LEOBEN
Hauptplatz 12, A-8700, ☎ 0 38 42/4 40 18

LERMOOS
A-6631, ☎ 0 56 73/24 01

LIENZ
Albin-Egger-Straße 17, A-9900, ☎ 0 48 52/6 52 65

Schloß Bruck und Osttiroler Heimatmuseum – Open Palm Sunday to 1 November from 10am to 5pm (6pm mid June to mid September); closed Mondays, except mid June to mid September; 50 S; ☎ 0 48 52/6 25 80.

LINZ
Hauptplatz 5, A-4010, ☎ 07 32/23 93 17 65

Pöstlingberg – A tram service links Linz-Urfahr (north bank) with the Pöstlingberg; departure every 20min from "Pöstlingberg-Bahnhof"; Monday to Saturday from 5.40am to 8.20pm, Sundays and public holidays from 7am to 8.20pm; 40 S Rtn.; ☎ 07 32/78 01 74 03.

Alter Dom St. Ignatius – Open from 7am to 12noon and 3pm to 7pm; ☎ 07 32/ 77 08 66.

Minoritenkirchen – Open July to September Monday to Friday from 8am to 4pm, Saturdays from 8am to 11am, Sundays from 8am to noon; October to June daily from 8am to 11am; ☎ 07 32/77 20 13 67.

Oberösterreichisches Landesmuseum – Open daily, except Mondays, from 9am to 5pm (10am to 4pm on Sundays and public holidays); 50 S; ☎ 07 32/77 44 19.

Neue Galerie – Open mid May to mid November, Monday to Friday from 10am to 6pm (10pm on Thursdays), Saturdays from 10am to 1pm; otherwise daily from 10am to 6pm (10pm on Thursdays); closed on public holidays and Sundays from mid May to mid November; 60 S; ☎ 07 32/70 70 36 00.

Stadtmuseum Nordico – Open Monday to Friday from 9am to 6pm, Saturdays and Sundays from 2pm to 5pm; closed on public holidays; 40 S; ☎ 07 32/70 70 19 01.

LOFER
A-5090, ☎ 0 65 88/32 10

Wallfahrtskirche Maria Kirchental – Open from 8am to 8pm (6pm in winter); ☎ 0 65 88/5 28.

M

MALLNITZ
A-9822, ☎ 0 47 84/5 22

Ankogelbahn – Operates July and August from 8.30am to noon and 1pm to 4.30pm; December to April from 8.30am to 4.30pm; ☎ 0 47 84/6 90.

MALTATAL
Malta-Hochalmstraße – Toll for private cars: 160 S.

MARIA SAAL
Am Platzl 7, A-9063, ☎ 0 42 23/22 14

Kärntner Freilichtmuseum – Open daily May to mid October, except Mondays, from 10am to 6pm; 50 S; ☎ 0 42 23/31 66.

MARIASTEIN
Schloßmuseum – Apply to the presbytery for visits; guided tour by appointment; donation; ☎ 0 53 32/64 74.

MARIAZELL
Hauptplatz 13, A-8630, ☎ 0 38 82/23 66

Cable-car to Bürgeralpe – Operates January, February, March from 8am to 5pm; April, May, June, October, November from 9am to 5pm; July and August from 8.30am to 5.30pm; September from 8.30am to 5pm; December from 8am to 4pm; closed April after the Easter holidays and November; 85 S Rtn.; ☎ 0 38 82/25 55.

Schatzkammer der Basilika Mariazell – Open May to the end of October Mondays to Fridays from 10am to 4pm; Easter Day, Easter Monday and 25 December to 1 January Monday to Friday from 10am to 12noon; ☎ 0 38 82/25 95.

Burg MAUTERNDORF
Lungauer Landschaftsmuseum – Open Whitsun to mid September from 11am to 1pm and 3pm to 5pm; 35 S; ☎ 0 64 72/74 25.

MAUTHAUSEN
🛈 Heindlkai 61, A-4310, ☎ 0 72 38/22 43

Konzentrationslager – Open April to September from 8am to 6pm; February to March and October to 15 December from 8am to 4pm; last admission 1hr before closing time; closed 16 December to 31 January; 25 S; ☎ 0 72 38/22 69.

MELK
🛈 Rathausplatz 11, A-3390, ☎ 0 27 52/23 07

Abbey – Open Palm Sunday to the end of April and October from 9am to 5pm; May to September from 9am to 6pm; 1 November to Palm Sunday guided tour only (1hr) at 11am and 2pm; 55 S; ☎ 0 27 52/2 31 20.

Excursion

Schloß Schallaburg – Open end of April to the end of October from 9am to 5pm (6pm on Saturdays, Sundays and public holidays); 80 S; ☎ 0 27 54/6 31 70.

MILLSTATT
🛈 Rathaus, A-9872, ☎ 0 47 66/20 22

Abbey cloisters – Open from 8am to 8pm; 50 S; ☎ 0 47 66/21 47.

MÖRBISCH
🛈 Hauptstraße 28, A-7072, ☎ 0 26 85/84 30 or 82 01

MONDSEE
🛈 Dr.-Franz-Müller-Straße 3, A-5310, ☎ 0 62 32/22 70

Heimat-und Pfahlbaumuseum – Open daily May to September from 9am to 6pm; October only Saturdays, Sundays and public holidays from 7am to 5pm; otherwise by appointment; 25 S; ☎ 0 62 32/22 70.

Freilichtmuseum Mondseer Rauchhaus – Open daily May to September from 9am to 6pm; October only Saturdays, Sundays and public holidays from 9am to 5pm otherwise by appointment; 25 S; ☎ 0 62 32/22 70.

MONTAFON

Kristbergbahn – Operates from 7.50am to 6.45pm; closed Low Sunday (1st after Easter) to mid May and November to mid December; ☎ 0 55 56/7 41 19.

Chairlift up to Sennigrat – Operates mid June to mid October from 9am to 4.30pm every half hour, Christmas to Low Sunday from 9am to 4pm; 57 S Rtn.; ☎ 0 55 56/7 21 26.

Valisera cable-car – Operates mid December to the beginning of April; ☎ 0 55 57/6 30 00.

MURAU
🛈 am Bahnhof, A-8850, ☎ 0 35 32/27 20

Murtalbahn – Operates Tuesdays and Wednesdays from July to mid September, also Saturdays in August (1 trip in each direction every day); 180 S Rtn.; information in Murau; ☎ 0 35 32/2 23 10.

MURTAL

Österreichisches Freilichtmuseum – Open daily April to October, except Mondays, from 9am to 5pm; 60 S; ☎ 0 31 24/5 37 00.

Lurgrotte – Guided tour (1hr or 2hr); March to October from 9am to 4pm; otherwise by appointment; closed on Mondays in March; 55 S (for the 1hr guided tour); ☎ 0 31 27/25 80.

N – O

NEUSIEDLER SEE
🛈 Rathaus, A-7071 Rust, ☎ 0 26 85/2 02 18 or 5 02

Seebad Rust – The access road to the lake is free of charge, but there is a charge for parking; open May and June from 9am to 6pm, July and August from 8am to 7pm; 40 S; boats for hire during the season; ☎ 0 26 85/5 91.

OBERNBERG AM INN
🛈 Markplatz 1, A-4982, ☎ 0 77 58/22 55

OBERWÖLZ
🛈 Hauptplatz 3, A-8832, ☎ 0 35 81/4 20

ÖTZTAL
🛈 Sölden, A-6450, ☎ 0 52 54/2 21 20 or
🛈 Obergurgl, A-6456, ☎ 0 52 56/2 58

Timmelsjoch-Hochalpenstraße – Toll above Hochgurgl on the Austrian side of border; 80 S per private car (including 6 occupants); it is not possible to cross the pass at night, because the border is closed from 8pm to 7am.

OSSIACHER SEE

Ossiach: Church – Visits by prior inquiry at the presbytery; ☎ 0 42 43/22 80.

P

Gestüt PIBER

Stud farm – Guided tour (1hr 10min); Easter week to the end of October from 9am to 11.30am and 2pm to 4.30pm; otherwise group reservations of at least 20 people; 100 S; ☎ 0 31 44/33 23.

PITZTAL

Hinterer Brunnenkogel – The funicular railway and the cable-car operate all year (except June) from 8.30am to 4.30pm; 260 S Rtn.; combined ticket for Brunnenkogel and Riffelsee: 350 S Rtn.; ☎ 0 54 13/82 88.

Riffelsee cable-car – Operates mid June to the beginning of October from 9am to 12.15pm and 1pm to 4.30pm; mid December to mid April from 9am to 4pm; 150 S Rtn.; ☎ 0 54 13/82 97.

PÖLLAU   🛈 Lamberggasse 30, A-8225, ☎ 033 35/41 10

PÖRTSCHACH   🛈 A-9210, ☎ 0 42 72/23 54

PULKAU   🛈 Rathausplatz 1, A-3741, ☎ 0 29 46/2 76

R

Bad RADKERSBURG   🛈 Hauptplatz 1, A-8490, ☎ 0 34 76/25 45

RADSTÄDTER TAUERN

Schloß Moosham – Guided tour (1hr); daily during the season at 10am, 11am, 1pm, 2pm, 3.30pm; in winter at 11am, 1pm, 2.30pm; closed November to Christmas; 100 S; ☎ 0 64 76/3 05.

RANKWEIL   🛈 Ringstraße 27, A-6830, ☎ 0 55 22/41 54 11 23

RATTENBERG   🛈 Postfach 33, Klostergasse 94, A-6240, ☎ 0 53 37/33 21

Augustinermuseum – Open daily 1 May to the 2nd Sunday in October from 10am to 5pm; 40 S; ☎ 0 53 37/26 31.

Excursion

Freilichtmuseum Tiroler Bauernhöfe – Open April to October from 9am to 6pm; 60 S; ☎ 0 53 37/6 26 36.

RETZ   🛈 Lehengasse 10, A-2070, ☎ 0 29 42/23 79 or 27 00

Kellerbesichtigungen – Guided tour of wine cellars (1hr 30min); March to April and October to the end of December at 2pm (also at 10.30am on Sundays and public holidays); May to September daily at 10.30am, 2pm and 4pm; meet in the Hauptplatz in front of the Rathaus; closed January and February; 70 S; ☎ 0 29 42/27 00.

RIEGERSBURG Niederösterreich

Schloß – Guided tour (30min); 1 April to 15 November from 9am to 5pm (July/August to 7pm); 78 S; ☎ 0 29 16/3 32.

Burg Hardegg – Open 1 April to 15 November from 9am to 5pm; 60 S.

RIEGERSBURG Steiermark   🛈 A-8333, ☎ 0 31 53/2 56

Castle – Open April to October from 9am to 5pm; 85 S; ☎ 0 31 53/8 21 31.

S

SAALACHTAL

Lamprechtshöhle – Accessible all year from 9am to 5pm; 35 S; ☎ 0 65 82/83 43.

Seisenbergklamm – Accessible May to October from 8.30am to 6.30pm; 30 S; ☎ 0 65 82/8 35 24 (Weißbach Tourist Information Centre).

Schattberg-Ost cable railway – Operates end of May to the beginning of October and in winter from 9am to 4pm; 160 S Rtn.

Zwölferkogel cable-car – Operates end of May to the beginning of October and in winter from 9am to 11.45am and 1pm to 4.30pm; 160 S Rtn.

SALZACHTAL

Liechtensteinklamm – Accessible beginning of May to mid October from 8am to 5pm; 30 S; ☎ 0 64 12/60 36.

Lammeröfen – Accessible May to the end of October from 8am to 6pm; 20 S; ☎ 0 62 44/84 42.

SALZBURG

Salzburg Festival – Salzburger Festspiele, Hofstallgasse 1, or Postfach 140, A-5020 Salzburg; ☎ 06 62/80 45-0.

Performance of *Jedermann* during the Salzburg Festival

Lift up to Mönchsberg – Trip to the viewing terrace; daily May to September from 9am to 11pm; otherwise 9am to 7pm; 27 S Rtn; ☎ 06 62/6 20 55 10.

Dommuseum – Open daily mid May to mid October from 10am to 5pm; 50 S; ☎ 06 62/8 04 71 27.

Hohensalzburg funicular – Operates all year from 9am to 5pm (9pm May to September) every 10 minutes; closed for around 2 weeks in November and January for maintenance; 32 S Rtn.; ☎ 06 62/84 26 82.

Hohensalzburg castle and museum – Open April to June and October from 9am to 6pm, July to September from 8am to 7pm, November to March from 9am to 5pm; closed 25 December; 35 S; ☎ 06 62/84 24 30.

Moderne Galerie-Graphische Sammlung-Österr. Fotogalerie – Open end of July to the end of September from 9am to 5pm; otherwise from 10am to 5pm (9pm on Wednesdays); closed Mondays (October to July); 40 S; ☎ 06 62/80 42 25 41.

Haus der Natur – Open from 9am to 5pm; 5 S; ☎ 06 62/84 26 53.

Mozarts Geburtshaus – Open daily mid June to mid September from 9am to 7pm; otherwise daily from 9am to 6pm; last admission 30min before closing time; 65 S; ☎ 06 62/84 43 13 75.

Residenzgalerie – Open daily from 10am to 5pm; closed Wednesdays (except April to September); 50 S; ☎ 06 62/84 04 51.

Salzburger Barockmuseum – Open Tuesday to Saturday from 9am to noon and 2pm to 5pm; Sundays and public holidays from 9am to noon; closed 24, 25, 31 December and 1 January; 40 S; ☎ 06 62/87 74 32.

Tanzmeisterhaus (Mozart-Wohnhaus) – Open daily from 10am to 6pm (from 9am to 6pm in July and August); 55 S; ☎ 06 62/84 42 27 40.

SALZBURG

Schloß Hellbrunn – Guided tour (fountains: 35min, castle: 20min); May, June and September from 9am to 5pm (4.30pm in April and October, 10pm in July and August); closed November to March; 90 S fountains and castle, 70 S fountains only; ☎ 06 62/8 20 37 20.

Salzburger Tierwelt Hellbrunn – Zoo open in summer from 8.30am to 5.30pm; in winter from 8.30am to 4pm; 70 S; ☎ 06 62/82 01 76.

Volkskundemuseum – Open from 9am to 5pm; 40 S; ☎ 06 62/84 11 34.

Cable-car to the Untersberg – The cable-car operates July to September from 8.30am to 5.30pm (8pm on Wednesdays); March to June and October from 9am to 5pm; mid December to the end of February from 10am to 4pm; closed for 2 weeks at the end of April and from the end of October to mid December; ☎ 0 62 46/7 24 77.

SALZBURGER SPORTWELT AMADÉ

Flachauwinkl cable-car – Only operates in winter; 80 S Rtn.

Mooskopf – The second section only operates in winter; 120 S Rtn.

SALZKAMMERGUT   🚹 Kreuzplatz 23, A-4820, ☎ 0 61 32/69 09

Boat service from Strobl – Boat trips on the Wolfgangsee: see below under St. Wolfgang.

Schloß Trautenfels – Open May to October from 9am to 5pm; 40 S; ☎ 0 36 82/ 2 22 33.

ST. ANTON AM ARLBERG   🚹 Arlberghaus, A-6580, ☎ 0 54 46/2 26 90

Valluga cable-car – Operates January to the end of April and December from 8.45am to 4.15pm; July to mid October from 8.15am to 4.15pm (departures every half hour); 230 S Rtn.; ☎ 0 54 46/2 35 20.

Kapall chairlift – Operates January to the end of April and December from 8.45am to 4.15pm; beginning of June to the beginning of September from 8.30am to 4.30pm; 200 S Rtn.; ☎ 0 54 46/2 35 20.

Rendl cable-car – Operates December to the end of April from 8.30am to 4.15pm; ☎ 0 54 46/28 89.

ST. FLORIAN

Abbey – Guided tour (1hr 30min); April to October at 10am, 11am, 2pm, 3pm and 4pm; November to March only by appointment; 60 S; ☎ 0 72 24/89 02 10.

St. Florian Abbey Church

ST. GILGEN 　　　　　🅿 Mozartplatz 1, A-5340, ☎ 0 62 27/3 48

Boat service on the Wolfgangsee - See below under St. Wolfgang.

ST. JOHANN IN TIROL 　　　🅿 Speckbacherstraße 11, A-6380, ☎ 0 53 52/22 18

ST. LAMBRECHT

Abbey - Guided tour (1hr 30min); mid May to mid October weekdays at 10.45am and 2.30pm, Sundays at 2.30pm only; 35 S; ☎ 0 35 85/23 45.

ST. PAUL IM LAVANTTAL 　　　　🅿 A-9470, ☎ 0 43 57/20 17

Stiftskirche - Open end of May to the end of October from 9am to 5pm; 75 S; ☎ 0 43 57/20 19 22.

Abbey buildings - As Stiftskirche.

ST. PÖLTEN

Stadtmuseum - Open Tuesday to Saturday from 10am to 5pm, Sundays from 9am to noon; closed 1 May, 1 and 2 November, 15 November, 24 December to 6 January; 20 S; ☎ 0 27 42/3 33 26 40.

Diözesanmuseum - Open April to the end of October, Tuesday to Friday from 10am to noon and 2pm to 5pm, Saturdays from 10am to 1pm, 1st Sunday in the month from 10am to noon; closed all public holidays; 30 S; ☎ 0 27 42/(3)5 21 01.

Excursion

Schloß Pottenbrunn; Österreichisches Zinnfigurenmuseum - Open April to the end of October Tuesday to Sunday from 9am to 5pm; 50 S; ☎ 0 27 42/4 23 37.

ST. VEIT AN DER GLAN 　　　🅿 Hauptplatz 1, A-9300, ☎ 0 42 12/55 55

Rathaussaal - Open Monday to Friday from 8am to noon and 1pm to 4pm; ☎ 0 42 12/55 55 13.

Magdalensberg excavations - Open May to October from 9am to 7pm; 40 S; ☎ 0 42 24/22 55.

ST. WOLFGANG 　　　　🅿 Kurdirektion, A-5360, ☎ 0 61 38/22 39

Boat service on the Wolfgangsee - Beginning of May to mid October; landing stages at: Strobl, St. Wolfgang (village and Schafberg station), Ried-Falkenstein, Ferienhort, Lüg, Fürberg, St. Gilgen; ☎ 0 61 38/22 20.

Church - Open April to October from 9am to 6pm; November to April from 9am to 4pm; ☎ 0 61 38/23 21.

Excursion

Schafberg - Cog railway operates May to mid October; every 60 to 80min from 8.10am; 250 S Rtn; ☎ 0 61 38/2 23 20.

SCHLADMINGER TAUERN

Planai cable-car - Operates from 9am to 5pm in summer; 8.30am to 5pm in winter; closed May to mid June and November; 150 S Rtn; ☎ 0 36 87/22 04 20.

Hochwurzen cable-car - Operates from 9am to noon and 1pm to 5pm in summer; from 9am to 4.15pm in winter; closed May, June, October and November; 110 S Rtn; ☎ 0 36 87/22 04.

Hauser Kaibling cable-car - Operating times as Planai; 140 S Rtn.; ☎ 0 36 86/22 87.

SCHNEEBERG

Ascent with the rack railway - Operates May to the end of October; two departures daily on weekdays, at 8.50am and 11.40am; 250 S Rtn; ☎ 0 26 36/22 56.

SCHWAZ 　　　🅿 Schwaz-Pill, Franz-Josef-Straße 26, A-6130, ☎ 0 52 42/32 40

Silver and copper mines - Guided tour (2hr); May to October from 8.30am to 5pm; 1 to 15 November and end of December to the end of April from 9.30am to 4pm; closed mid November to 26 December; hard hats and outerwear provided for visitors; sturdy shoes are recommended; 130 S; ☎ 0 52 42/72 37 20.

Excursion

Schloß Tratzberg - Guided tour (1hr); April to October from 10am to noon and 2pm to 4pm; closed Mondays; 100 S; ☎ 0 52 42/6 35 66 20.

Abtei SECKAU 　　　　🅿 A-8732, ☎ 0 35 14/2 05

SEEFELD IN TIROL   🛈 Rathaus 43, A-6100, ☎ 0 52 12/23 13 and 23 16

Excursion

Funicular to Seefelder Joch – Operates end of May to mid October Monday to Saturday from 9am to 5pm, Sundays and public holidays from 8.30am to 5pm; closed mid October to the beginning of December and mid April to the end of May; 170 S; ☎ 0 52 12/24 16.

SÖLDEN

Ötztaler Gletscherstraße – Toll for private cars: 210 S.

Gaislacher Kogel cable-car – Cable-car operates end of June to the end of September and end of December to the beginning of April from 9am to 4pm; 210 S Rtn.; ☎ 0 52 54/23 61 21.

Giggijochbahn – Cable-car operates end of December to the beginning of April from 9am to 4pm; 125 S Rtn.; ☎ 0 52 54/2 36 10.

Ventertal: Wildspitze-Sesselbahn – Chairlift operates end of June to the end of September from 8am to noon and 1.30pm to 5.30pm; closed mid April to mid June and beginning of October to mid December; 80 S Rtn.; ☎ 0 52 54/81 54.

SPITAL AM PYHRN   🛈 A-4582, ☎ 0 75 63/2 49

SPITTAL AN DER DRAU   🛈 Burgplatz 1, A-9800, ☎ 0 47 62/34 20

Bezirksheimatmuseum – Open mid May to mid October from 9am to 6pm; mid October to mid May Monday to Thursday from 1pm to 4pm; 45 S; ☎ 0 47 62/28 90.

Excursion

Teurnia-Museum – Open daily May to October, except Mondays, from 9am to 12noon and 1pm to 5pm; 30 S; ☎ 0 47 62/3 38 07.

STAINZ   🛈 A-8510, ☎ 0 34 63/22 03 12 or 22 43

Church – Open from 8am to 7pm; apply to the presbytery at Schloßplatz 2; ☎ 0 34 63/22 37.

Castle Museum – Open April to mid November from 9am to 5pm; closed 1 November; 25 S; ☎ 0 34 63/27 72.

Stift STAMS   🛈 A-6422, ☎ 0 52 63/65 11

Abbey – Guided tour (45min) January to April and October to December on weekdays at 9am, 10am, 11am, 2pm, 3pm, 4pm (also 5pm in May, June and September); July and August weekdays from 9am to 11am and 1pm to 5pm every half hour; closed in the morning on Sundays and public holidays; 40 S; ☎ 0 52 63/55 73 or 5 69 72.

STEIRISCHE WEINSTRASSE

Kitzeck: Weinmuseum – Open April to November Saturdays, Sundays and public holidays from 10am to noon and 2pm to 5pm; otherwise by appointment; 20 S; ☎ 0 34 56/35 00.

STEYR   🛈 Stadtplatz 27 (Rathaus), A-4400, ☎ 0 72 52/2 32 29

T

TAMSWEG   🛈 Marktplatz 134, Postfach 57, A-5580, ☎ 0 64 74/62 84

TAUERNTUNNEL

Railway tunnel – Regular summertime service between Mallnitz and Böckstein; from Mallnitz, 6am to 10pm every hour; from Böckstein, 6.30am to 10.30pm every hour; journey takes 12min; price: 190 S for private cars including passengers (320 S return ticket valid 2 months); details: Böckstein station ☎ 0 64 34/26 63 39 or Mallnitz-Obervellach station ☎ 0 47 84/60 03 90.

TRAUNKIRCHEN   🛈 Postfach 11, A-4801, ☎ 0 76 17/22 34

TULLN   🛈 Nußallee 4, A-3430, ☎ 0 22 72/4 28 50

TURRACHERHÖHE   🛈 A-8864 Turracherhöhe, ☎ 0 42 75/83 92

V

VIENNA

See below under Wien.

VILLACH
 Europaplatz 2, A-9500, ☏ 0 42 42/24 44 40

Relief von Kärnten – Open May to October from 10am to 4.30pm; closed Sundays and public holidays; 20 S; ☏ 0 42 42/20 53 49.

Villacher Alpenstraße – Toll for private cars: 160 S.

Chairlift – Operates mid May to September from 9am to 5pm; in winter, dependent on snow conditions; 75 S Rtn; ☏ 0 42 42/21 95 30.

VÖCKLABRUCK
 Lebzelterhaus, Hinterstadt 13-15, A-4840, ☏ 0 76 72/66 44

Dörflkirche St. Ägidius – If church closed, apply to the presbytery; ☏ 0 76 72/ 7 26 08.

VOLDERS
 Bundesstraße 24 c, A-6111, ☏ 0 52 24/5 27 71

Kirche zum hl. Karl Borromäus – Open daily from 7.30am to 7pm.

VORAU
 Kernstockweg 207, A-8250, ☏ 0 33 37/22 28

Freilichtmuseum – Open 10am to 5pm; closed November to Easter; 25 S; ☏ 0 33 37/34 66 or 23 42.

W

WAIDHOFEN AN DER THAYA
 Rathausplatz 1, A-3830, ☏ 0 28 42/23 31

WEISSENKIRCHEN
 A-3610, ☏ 0 27 15/22 21

Pfarrkirche – Open April to October from 8am to 7pm; November to March Saturdays from 8am to 6pm, Sundays and public holidays from 12noon to 7pm; ☏ 0 27 15/26 00.

Wachaumuseum – Open daily April to October, except Mondays, from 10am to 5pm; 20 S; ☏ 0 27 15/22 68.

WELS
 Stadtplatz 55, A-4600, ☏ 0 72 42/4 34 95

Kaiserliche Burg Museums – Open Tuesday to Friday from 10am to 5pm, Saturdays, Sundays and public holidays from 10am to noon; ☏ 0 72 42/4 34 95.

Vogelpark von Schmiding – Open April to the end of October from 9am to 7pm (last admission 5pm); 90 S; ☏ 0 72 49/4 62 72.

WIEN (VIENNA)
 Kärntner Straße 38, oder Westbahnhof, A-1010, ☏ 01/21 11 40

Donauturm – Open April to September from 9.30am to midnight; October to March from 10am to 10pm; lift: 65 S; ☏ 01/23 53 68.

Sightseeing city coach tours – The companies "Vienna Sightseeing Tours", ☏ 01/71 24 68 30 and "Cityrama", ☏ 01/5 34 13 12, operate the "Große Wiener Stadtrundfahrt" at least once daily (3hr), plus shorter tours (approx 1hr 15min) several times daily; main departure points: Opera and Johannesgasse (Kursalon).

Hofburg: Schatzkammer – Open from 10am to 6pm; closed Tuesdays, 1 May, 1 November, 24 and 25 December; 60 S; ☏ 01/5 33 79 31.

Hofburg: Kaiserappartements – Open daily from 9am to 5pm; 70 S; ☏ 01/5 33 75 70.

Hofburg: Hofsilber- und Tafelkammer – Open from 9am to 5pm; 70 S; ☏ 01/53 33 75 70.

Hofburgkapelle – Open Tuesdays and Thursdays from 1.30pm to 3.30pm, Fridays from 1pm to 3pm, Sundays and public holidays only by appointment; closed January, February, July, August, December and all public holidays; ☏ 01/5 33 99 27.

Spanische Reitschule – Summer break in July and August; for performances (reruns) on Sundays (10.45am) and Wednesdays (7pm), apply in writing as far in advance as possible to: Spanische Reitschule (Hofburg, Michaelerplatz 1, A-1010 Wien – *do not send any money*) or to theatre ticket or travel agencies; advance booking is not necessary for the morning training sessions with musical accompaniment, April to September on Saturdays (10am); tickets are available on the same day at the entrance (Innerer Burghof); performances: 190-240 S, training sessions: 100 S; ☏ 01/5 33 90 31.

WIEN (VIENNA)

Österreichische Nationalbibliothek – Great Hall open June to September Monday to Saturday from 10am to 4pm, Sundays and public holidays from 10am to 1pm; October to May weekdays from 10am to noon; 30 S; ☎ 02 22/53 41 02 77.

Kaisergruft – Open from 9.30am to 4pm; 40 S; ☎ 01/5 12 68 53.

Augustinerkirche: Lorettokapelle – Closed for restoration, probably until May 1997; ☎ 01/53 37 09 90.

Albertina – Open Monday to Thursday from 10am to 4pm, Fridays from 10am to 1pm; 10 S; ☎ 01/5 34 83 45.

Hofjagd- und Rüstkammer – Open daily, except Tuesdays, from 10am to 6pm; closed 1 May, 15 August, 1 November, 24 and 25 December; 30 S; ☎ 01/52 52 44 04.

Sammlung alter Musikinstrumente – Open daily, except Tuesdays, from 10am to 6pm; closed 1 May, 15 August, 1 November, 24 and 25 December; 30 S; ☎ 01/52 52 44 04.

Ephesos Museum – Open daily, except Tuesdays, from 10am to 6pm; closed 1 January, 1 May, 15 August, 1 November, 24 and 25 December; 30 S; ☎ 01/52 52 44 04.

Museum für Völkerkunde – Open daily, except Tuesdays, from 10am to 4pm; closed Easter Day, 1 May, Whit Sunday, 1 November, 25 December; 50 S; ☎ 01/53 43 00.

Stephensdom: Interior – Open Monday to Saturday from 9am to 11.30am and 1pm to 4.30pm, Sundays and public holidays from 1pm to 4.30pm; ☎ 01/51 55 25 26.

Catacombs – Guided tour (30min); Monday to Saturday from 10am to 11.30am and 2pm to 4.30pm, Sundays from 2pm to 4.30pm; 40 S; ☎ 01/51 55 25 26.

Cathedral towers – It is possible to climb the Hochturm on the south side of the cathedral from 9am to 5.30pm; 25 S; ☎ 01/52 55 25 26; Nordturm (high speed lift to "Pummerin" great bell); April to September from 9am to 6pm; October to March from 8am to 5pm; 40 S; ☎ 01/51 55 27 14.

Deutschordenskirche: Treasure of the Teutonic Order – Open May to October Mondays, Thursdays, Fridays and Sundays from 10am to noon, Saturdays from 10am to noon and 3pm to 5pm; November to April Wednesdays, Fridays and Saturdays from 3pm to 5pm; 25 S; ☎ 01/5 12 10 65.

Mozart-Wohnung or Figarohaus – Open daily, except Mondays, from 9am to 12.15pm and 1pm to 4.30pm; closed 1 January, 1 May, 25 December; 25 S; ☎ 01/3 10 45 98.

Jesuitenkirche – Open from 8am to sunset; ☎ 01/5 12 52 32.

Ruprechtskirche – Scheduled to be closed for restoration in 1997; ☎ 01/5 35 60 03.

Uhrenmuseum – Open daily, except Mondays, from 9am to 6pm; closed 1 January, 1 May and 25 December; 50 S; ☎ 01/5 33 22 65.

Kunsthistorisches Museum – Open daily, except Mondays, from 10am to 6pm (9pm on Thursdays); closed 1 January, 1 May; 45 S; ☎ 01/52 52 44 04.

Belvedere – Open daily, except Mondays, from 10am to 5pm; closed 1 January, Easter Tuesday, Whit Tuesday, 1 November, 24, 25 and 31 December; 60 S, ticket valid for the three museums: ☎ 01/79 55 71 20.

Schloß Schönbrunn: Schauräume – Main building, 1st floor, guided tour (45min); April to October from 8.30am to 5pm; otherwise from 8.30am to 4.30pm; ☎ 01/81 11 30.

Tierpark – Open January, November and December from 9am to 4.30pm; February and October from 9am to 5pm; March from 9am to 5.30pm; April from 9am to 6pm; May to September from 9am to 6.30pm; 90 S; ☎ 01/87 79 29 40.

Gloriette – Open April to October from 8.30am to 5pm; November to March from 8.30am to 4.30pm; 80 S; ☎ 02 22/81 11 30.

Wagenburg – Open April to October from 9am to 6pm; otherwise from 10am to 4pm; closed Mondays (November to March), 1 May, 1 November, 24 and 25 December; 30 S; ☎ 01/52 52 44 04.

Secession – Open Tuesday to Friday from 10am to 6pm, Saturdays, Sundays and public holidays from 10am to 4pm; closed Mondays; ☎ 01/5 87 53 07.

Kirche am Steinhof – Guided tour (30min) Saturdays at 3pm; closed 15 November to Easter.

Staatsoper - Guided tour; mid July and August daily at 10am, 11am, 1pm, 2pm, 3pm and 4pm; otherwise all year by appointment; 50 S; ☏ 01/5 14 44 26 13.

Schubert-Museum - Open daily, except Mondays, from 9am to 12.15pm and 1pm to 4.30pm; closed 1 January, 1 May and 25 December; 25 S; ☏ 01/50 58 74 70.

Jüdisches Museum - Open Sunday to Friday from 10am to 6pm (9pm on Thurdays); 70 S; ☏ 01/5 35 04 31.

Alte Ursulinenklosterapotheke - Open Wednesdays from 9am to 4pm, Sundays and public holidays from 9am to 1pm; closed 1 January, 4 April, 1 May, 1 November and 25 December; 25 S; no charge on 18 May and 26 October; ☏ 01/5 12 37 13.

Historisches Museum der Stadt Wien - Open daily, except Mondays, from 9am to 4.30pm; closed 1 January, 1 May and 25 December; 50 S; ☏ 01/50 58 74 70.

Österreichisches Museum für Volkskunde - Open daily, except Mondays, from 9am to 5pm (noon Saturdays, 1pm Sundays and public holidays); closed 1 January, Easter Day, 1 November, 25 December; 45 S; ☏ 01/4 06 89 05 16.

Prater Giant Wheel - Operates May to September from 9am to midnight; October from 10am to 10pm; beginning of November to mid January from 10am to 6pm; 45 S; ☏ 01/5 12 83 14.

Gemäldegalerie der Akademie der bildenden Künste - Open Tuesdays, Thursdays and Fridays from 10am to 2pm, Wednesdays from 10am to 1pm and 3pm to 6pm, Saturdays, Sundays and public holidays from 9am to 1pm; 30 S; ☏ 01/58 81 62 25.

Österreichisches Museum für angewandte Kunst - Open daily, except Mondays, from 10am to 6pm; closed 1 January, 1 May, 1 November, 25 December; 30 S (90 S when there are special exhibitions); ☏ 01/71 13 60.

Naturhistorisches Museum - Open daily, except Tuesdays, from 9am to 6pm; closed 1 January, 1 May, 1 November, 25 December; out of season, first floor only open from 9am to 3pm; 30 S; ☏ 01/52 17 70.

Piaristenkirche – Basilika Maria Treu - Unaccompanied visit or guided tour only by appointment with the presbytery; ☏ 01/4 05 04 25 13.

KunstHausWien - Open from 10am to 7pm (10am to 5pm on 24 and 31 December); 90 S, half price on Mondays; ☏ 01/7 12 04 91.

Museum moderner Kunst Stiftung Ludwig - Open daily, except Mondays, from 10am to 6pm; closed 1 January, 1 May, 1 November, 24 and 25 December; 45 S; ☏ 01/3 17 69 00 31.

Heeresgeschichtliches Museum - Open daily, except Fridays, from 10am to 4pm; closed 1 January, Easter Day, 1 May, Whit Sunday, 1 November, 24, 25 and 31 December; 40 S; no charge first Sunday of the month; ☏ 01/79 56 15 14.

Ehemaliges Hofmobiliendepot - Closed for major refurbishment, probably until 1998; ☏ 01/7 11 00 51 92.

Café Central, Vienna

WIEN (VIENNA)

Excursions

Heiligenstadt: Beethoven-Haus – Open daily, except Mondays, from 9am to noon and 1pm to 4.30pm; 25 S; ☎ 01/37 54 08.

Heiligenkreuz: Abbey – Guided tour (45min); at 10am, 11am, 2pm, 3pm and 4pm; 45 S; closed 24 December; ☎ 0 22 58/22 82.

WIENER NEUSTADT ◼ Herzog-Leopold-Str. 17, A-2700, ☎ 0 26 22/23 53 14 68

St. Georgskathedrale – May be visited at any time; ☎ 0 26 22/3 81 20 30.

Abtei WILHERING

Abbey – Open all year from 8am to 5pm; ☎ 0 72 26/2 31 10.

WÖRTHER SEE

Wildpark Rosegg – Open Easter to the beginning of November from 9am to 8pm (ticket office closes at 5pm); closed November to March; 70 S; ☎ 0 42 74/30 09.

Z

ZELL AM SEE ◼ Brucker Bundesstraße, A-5710, ☎ 0 65 42/26 00

Ascent to the Schmittenhöhe – Cable-car operates mid May to the end of October, departure every 30min from 8.30am to 5pm; December to mid April every 30min from 8.30am to 4.30pm; closed mid April to mid May, end of October to the beginning of December; 220 S Rtn; ☎ 0 65 42/3 69 10.

ZILLERTAL ◼ A-6280 Zell am Ziller, ☎ 0 52 82/22 81

Ascent to the Penken – Chairlift operates end of June to the beginning of October from 9am to noon and 1pm to 5pm; 150 S Rtn.; ☎ 0 52 82/22 81.

ZÜRS ◼ A-6763,, ☎ 0 55 83/22 45

Trittkopf – Cable-car operates December to April from 9am to 4pm; 120 S Rtn.; ☎ 0 55 83/2 38 80.

Stift ZWETTL ◼ Gartenstraße 3a, A-3910, ☎ 0 28 22/24 14 29

Abbey – Guided tour (45min – groups of at least 10 people) May to October Monday to Saturday at 10am, 11am, 2pm and 3pm, Sundays at 11am, 2pm and 3pm (also 4pm in July, August and September); otherwise only by appointment; 50 S; ☎ 0 28 22/5 50 17.

Index

Innsbruck . . . . Towns, sights and tourist regions
8911 . . . . Post code
Steiermark . . . . Federal province *(Land)*
Berg, Alban . . . . People, historical events, artistic styles and subjects covered in the text

Individual sights (mountains, lakes, dams, abbeys, castles etc) are indexed under their own names.

This index, like the other alphabetical lists in this guide, follows the normal German alphabetical order, where the vowels ä, ö and ü are classified under ae, oe and ue respectively, ß is classified under ss, and St. under Sankt (Saint).

A

Abtenau *5441 Salzburg* 242
Achenkirch *6215 Tirol* 12
Achenpaß 152
Achensee 152
Admont *8911 Steiermark* 52
Adriach 98
Aflenz-Kurort *8623 Steiermark* 53
Aflenzer Seebergstraße 52
Aggstein (Castle ruins) *Niederöst* 53
Agriculture 33
Aigen im Mühlkreis *4160 Oberöst* 12
Allio, Domenico dell' 112
Almtal 107
Alpbach *6236 Tirol* 53
Alt, Rudolf von 40
Altaussee *8992 Steiermark* 60
Altausseer See 6
Altdorfer, Albrecht 75, 246
Altenburg (Abbey) *Niederöst* 54
Altenmarkt im Pongau *5541 Salzburg* 13
Altmünster *4813 Oberöst* 240
Altomonte, Bartolomeo 39, 329
Altomonte, Martino 39, 329
Ambras (Schloß) *Tirol* 142
Ammenegg *Vorarlberg* 68
Ankogel 182
Annaberg *3222 Niederöst* 204
Anschluß 28
Arlberggebiet *Vorarlberg, Tirol* 55
Arlberg-Kandahar 15, 55
Arlhöhe 183
Artstetten (Schloß-Museum) 58
Aschach (Power station) *Oberöst* 77

Attersee *4864 Oberöst* 13, 242
Attersee (Lake) 242
Auden, W. H. 251
Augarten porcelain 292
Aussee (Bad) *8990 Steiermark* 59
Außerfern *Tirol* 94
Austrian Democracy 31
Austrian Open-air Museum 200
Axamer Lizum *6094 Tirol* 12

B

Babenberg, House of 29, 288
Bachmann, Ingeborg 35
Bad : *see under proper name*
Baden *2500 Niederöst* 61
Badgastein *5640 Salzburg* 101
Bärenschlucht 122
Bartholomäbergkirche 197
Beethoven, Ludwig van 44, 61, 291 293, 326
Beisel 297
Belvedere Treaty 28, 315
Berg, Alban 45, 295
Berg im Drautal *9771 Kärnten* 13
Bergisel *Tirol* 142
Bernhard, Thomas 35
Berwang *6622 Tirol* 12
Bezau *6870 Vorarlberg* 12, 68
Biedermeier 40
Bielerhöhe *Vorarlberg* 265
Bildstock 46
Bischofshofen *5500 Salzburg* 62
Blauspitze 187
Blondel 81
Bludenz *6700 Vorarlberg* 63
Bodensdorf *9551 Kärnten* 13

Bodensee 257
Böckstein *5645 Salzburg* 101
Bödmen *6993 Vorarlberg* 160
Böhm, Karl 45, 295
Bohemia 29
Bosch, Hieronymus 323
Boulez, Pierre 45
Bourbon-Parma, Zita of 28, 304
Brahms, Johannes 45, 293
Brand *6708 Vorarlberg* 63
Brandhof 53
Brandnertal 63
Braunau am Inn *5280 Oberöst* 63
Bregenz *6900 Vorarlberg* 64
Bregenzerwald 66
Brenner (Pass) *Tirol* 68
Brennerstraße *Tirol* 68
Brettljause 274
Brixen im Thale *6364 Tirol* 13
Bruck an der Mur *8600 Steiermark* 69
Bruckner, Anton 45, 177, 246, 293
Bruegel the Elder, Pieter 313
Brunn *Steiermark* 224
Burgenland 32
Bürgeralpe 185
Burggrabenklamm 239
Buschenschenken 272

C

Coffeehouses in Vienna 295
Caravaggio 312
Carinthia 32
Carinthian Open-air Museum 184
Carlone, Carlo Antonio 87, 245, 283
Carlone, Joachim 211
Carnival 47
Carnuntum 29, 80

377

Cerha, Friedrich 45
Charles V 30
Chemical industry 34
Christkindl *4411*
Oberöst 70
Christopher, St 46
Clam (Burg) 77
Climate 12
Coffee 296
Colin, Alexandre 139
Congress of Vienna 30,
289
Constance, Lake 64
Correggio 312
Crafts 16
Cranach the Elder, Lucas
75, 313
Cumberland Wildpark 108

D

Dachstein 70, 242
Dachstein-Rieseneishö-
hle 71
Danube School of Paint-
ing 75
Danube (Valley) 73
Daunkogelferner (Gla-
cier) 278
Deutschlandsberg *8530*
Steiermark 73
Dienten am Hochkonig
5652 Salzburg 222
Dirndl 47
Dittersdorf, Carl Ditters
von 43
Dobratsch 282
Döllach *9843 Kärnten*
194
Dolomites (Salzburg) 242
Donautal 73
Donner, Georg Raphaël
39, 311, 317
Dorfgastein *5632 Salz-
burg* 100
Dornbirn *6850 Vorarl-
berg* 68
Drossensperre (Dam),
151
Dürer, Albrecht 313
Dürnstein *3601 Nie-
deröst* 81
Dürrnberg (Bad) 128
Dürrnberg (Mines) 128
Durlaßbodensee (Reser-
voir) 104
Dyck, Anthony van 313

E

Eben *Tirol* 152
Ebner-Eschenbach,
Marie von 35
Edelweißspitze 122
Eggenberg (Schloß) 82
Eggenburg *3730 Nie-
deröst* 84
Egger-Lienz, Albin 174

Ehrenbachhütte 157
Ehrenberger Klause 95
Ehrenhausen *8461 Stei-
ermark* 84
Ehrwald *6632 Tirol* 84
Einem, Gottfried von 45
Eisenerz *8790 Steier-
mark* 85
Eisenerzer Alpen 86
Eisenstadt *7000 Burgen-
land* 87
Eisgrat 278
Eisriesenwelt (Caves) 89
Elbigenalp *6652 Tirol*
173
Ellbögener Straße 68,
142
Ellmau *6352 Tirol* 148
Emma, St 125
Eng *Tirol* 153
Enns *4470 Oberöst* 89
Erfurter Hütte 152
Erlaufsee 186
Erpfendorf *6383 Tirol*
148
Erzberg 85
Esterházy family 87
Eugene, Prince of Savoy
315
Europabrücke (Bridge) 69
Europa-Panoramaweg
187
Expressionism, Viennese
41

F

Faakersee *Kärnten* 331
Faistenberger, Simon
Benedikt 156
Fastentuch 125
Fauna 23
Felbertauernstraße 91
Feldkirch *6800 Vorarl-
berg* 92
Fernpaßstraße 94
Fernstein *Tirol* 94
Fernsteinsee 94
Filzmoos *5532 Salzburg*
71
Finstermünzpaß 144
Fischer von Erlach, Jo-
hann Bernhard 38,
317, 322
Fiß *6533 Tirol* 12
Flachau *5542 Salzburg*
237
Flachgau *Salzburg* 221
Flexenpaß 56
Flora 23, 145
Florian, St 46, 245
Föhn 13
Forchtenstein (Burg)
Burgenland 95
Forestry 32
Formarinsee 172
Franz Ferdinand, Arch-
duke 58
Franz Joseph 28, 30,
292
Franz-Joseph-Höhe 123

Frauenberg *Steiermark*
86
Frauenstein (Schloß)
Kärnten 252
Freilichtmuseum Tiroler
Bauernhöfe 216
Freistadt *4240 Oberöst*
96
Freud, Sigmund 35
Friesach *9630 Kärnten*
97
Frisch, Karl von 35
Frohnleiten *8130 Steier-
mark* 97
Fromiller, Joseph Fer-
dinand 207
Frueauf the Elder,
Rueland 317
Fügen *6263 Tirol* 12
Fulpmes *6166 Tirol* 277
Fuschertal 122
Fuscher Törl 122
Fuschl am See *5330
Salzburg* 13

G

Gailbergsattelstraße
Kärnten 98
Gaisberg 236
Gaislacher Kogel 268
Gallspach *4713 Oberöst*
12
Galtür *6563 Tirol* 267
Gams ob Frauental (Bad)
8524 Steiermark 274
Gargellen *6787 Vorarl-
berg* 198
Gaschurn *6793 Vorarl-
berg* 198
Gasteiner Ache (Water-
fall) *Salzburg* 101
Gasteiner Tal *Salzburg*
99
Gefrorene Wand 336
Gemeindealpe 186
George, St 46
Gepatschferner (Glacier)
154
Geras *2093 Niederöst*
103
Gerlitzen *Kärnten* 104
Gerlos *6281 Tirol* 104
Gerlosstraße 104
Gerzkopf 72
Gesäuse (Gorge) *Steier-
mark* 86
Giorgione 312
Glaciers 22
Gleichenberg (Bad) *8344
Steiermark* 105
Gluck, Christoph Willi-
bald von 43, 293
Gmünd *9853 Kärnten*
106
Gmunden *4810 Oberöst*
106
Gmundnerberg 107
Gnadenfall 213
Görz, Matthias von 211
Gößkarspeicher 183

Gössl *Steiermark* 60
Göttweig (Stift) *Niederöst* 164
Goisern (Bad) *4822 Oberöst* 13
Goldenes Dachl (Innsbruck) 137
Goldriedbahn 187
Golling *5440 Salzburg* 223
Gollinger Wasserfall 223
Gosau *4824 Oberöst* 13
Gosauseen 109
Gran, Daniel 39
Graukogel 103
Graz *8010 Steiermark* 111
Greillenstein (Schloß) *Niederöst* 120
Grein *4360 Oberöst* 78
Gries *Tirol* 69
Grillparzer, Franz 35
Grinzing *Wien* 326
Großarl *5611 Salzburg* 12
Großer Ahornboden 153
Großglockner 121
Großglockner-Hochalpenstraße 121
Großklein *8452 Steiermark* 275
Großvenediger 92, 188
Gruber, Franz Xaver 128
Grundlsee *Steiermark* 60
Gstatterboden *8913 Steiermark* 86
Guggenbichler, Meinrad 196
Gumpoldskirchen *2352 Niederöst* 327
Gundersdorf *8511 Steiermark* 274
Gurgltal *Tirol* 124
Gurk *9342 Kärnten* 125

H

Habeler, Peter 14
Habsburg, House of 26, 30
Hafelekar 142
Hahnenkamm 156
Hainburg *2410 Niederöst* 81
Haindlkarbrücke 86
Hall (Bad) *4540 Oberöst* 126
Hall-church 36
Hallein *5400 Salzburg* 128
Haller Silberthaler 127
Hall in Tirol *6060 Tirol* 126
Hallstätter See (Lake) 128
Hallstatt *4830 Oberöst* 128
Hals, Frans 314
Handke, Peter 35
Hardegg (Burg) *Niederöst* 218

Hasegg (Burg) *Tirol* 127
Haselgebirge 35
Haslinger, Johann 328
Hauser Kaibling 256
Haydn, Joseph 43, 81, 87
Hebbel, Friedrich 107
Heiligenblut *9844 Kärnten* 129
Heiligenkreuz *2532 Niederöst* 326
Heiligenstadt *Wien* 326
Heimatwerk 16
Helenental 327
Hellbrunn (Schloß) 236
Herberstein (Schloß) *Steiermark* 130
Hermagor *9620 Kärnten* 13
Herzogenburg (Abbey) *Niederöst* 130
Heurigen 49, 297
Hieflau *8920 Steiermark* 86
Hiking 16
Hildebrandt, Johann Lukas von 39
Hilger, Abbot 328
Hinterer Brunnenkogel 210
Hinterriß *6221 Tirol* 153
Hintersee 92
Hintersteinersee *Tirol* 148
Hinterstoder *4573 Oberöst* 13
Hintertux *6294 Tirol* 336
Hirschegg *6992 Vorarlberg* 160
Hirschwang *Niederöst* 132
Historicism 40
Hitler, Adolf 63
Hochgurgl *6456 Tirol* 124
Hochkönig 222
Hochosterwitz (Burg) *Kärnten* 131
Hochsölden *Tirol* 267
Hochstubaigebiet *Tirol* 278
Hochtannberg 66
Hochtannbergstraße 67
Hochtor 123
Hochwurzen 256
Höllental *Niederöst* 132
Hofen (Burg) 66
Hofer, Andreas 30, 141
Hoffmann, Josef 41
Hoffmann, Leopold 43
Hofgastein (Bad) *5630 Salzburg* 100
Hofmannsthal, Hugo von 35
Hohe Mut 124
Hohenbrunn (Schloß-Museum) *Oberöst* 132
Hohentauernpaßstraße *Steiermark* 133
Hohenwerfen (Fortress) 222
Hohe Salve 149
Hohe Tauern (National Park) 21, 121
Holbein, Ambrosius 323

Holbein the Younger, Hans 314
Hollenburg (Schloß) 332
Holzinger, Franz Joseph 54, 329
Holzleitner Sattel 94
Holzmeister, Clemens 229
Horn *3580 Niederöst* 55
Hrdlicka, Alfred 35
Hundertwasser, Friedrich (Friedensreich) 324
Hunerkogel 72
Hungerburg 136
Hydroelectric power 33, 75, 151

I – J

Igls *6080 Tirol* 142
Imbach *Niederöst* 164
Imst *6460 Tirol* 144
Innsbruck *6020 Tirol* 135
Inntal 143
Iron Mountain 85
Ischgl *6561 Tirol* 145
Ischl (Bad) *4820 Oberöst* 146
Iselsberg (Pass) *Kärnten* 194
Jerzens *6474 Tirol* 12
Jochdohle 278
Jochenstein (Dam) 76
Johann, Archduke 59, 112
John of Nepomuk, St 46
Joseph II 30, 292
Judenburg *8750 Steiermark* 208
Jugendstil 40

K

Kärnten 32
Kärntner Freilichtmuseum 184
Kahlenberg *Wien* 326
Kaisergebirge 147
Kaiserstein 258
Kalsertal 188
Kalser Tauern 277
Kals-Matrei-Törlhaus 187
Kammersee *Steiermark* 60
Kandahar 15, 55, 57
Kanzelkehre *Tirol* 152
Kapall 245
Kappl *6555 Tirol* 267
Kaprun *5710 Salzburg* 150
Karajan, Herbert von 35, 45, 229, 295
Karlesspitze 154
Karwendelgebirge *Tirol* 152

Kasereck 124
Katschbergstraße 153
Kauffmann, Angelika
65, 68
Kaunertal 153
Kefermarkt *4292*
Oberöst 154
Keller 297
Kepler, Johannes 177
Keutschach, Leonhard
von 189, 232
Khevenhüller family
131, 207, 332
Kirchstetten *Niederöst*
251
Kitzbühel *6370 Tirol*
155
Kitzbüheler Horn 156
Kitzeck *8442 Steier-*
mark 275
Kitzsteinhorn 151
Klagenfurt *9020 Kärn-*
ten 157
Klapotetz 274
Kleinarl *5602 Salzburg*
238
Kleinkirchheim (Bad)
9456 Kärnten 13
Kleinwalsertal *Vorarl-*
berg 160
Klein Klein *Steiermark*
275
Klimt, Gustav 41, 316
Klobensteinpaß *Tirol*
160
Klosterneuburg (Abbey)
Niederöst 160
Klostertal 55
Klosterwappen 258
Kneipp, Sebastian 16
Köflach *8580 Steier-*
mark 208
Kölnbreinsperre (Dam)
Kärnten 182
Kössen *6345 Tirol* 160
Kötschach *9640 Kärnten*
98
Koglalm 238
Kokoschka, Oskar 315,
325
Kolbnitz *9815 Kärnten*
279
Koppenbrüllerhöhle
(Cave) 71
Krems *3500 Niederöst*
162
Kremsegg (Schloß) 166
Kremser Schmidt 39,
162
Kremsmünster (Abbey)
Oberöst 165
Kremstal 164
Krenek, Ernst 45
Kreuzjoch 198
Kreuzkogel 102
Krimmler Wasserfälle
Salzburg 166
Krippenstein *Oberöst*
71
Kristbergbahn 197
Krumpendorf *9210*
Kärnten 13
Kühtai *Tirol* 12
Kufstein *6330*
Tirol 166

L

Laas *Kärnten* 98
Längenfeld *6444 Tirol*
206
Lambach *4650 Oberöst*
168
Lammeröfen *Salzburg*
223
Lamprechtshöhle *Salz-*
burg 219
Land (Länder) 32
Landeck *6500 Tirol* 169
Landskron (Castle ruins)
207
Lanersbach *6293 Tirol* 12
Lang, Fritz 35
Langegg bei Graz *Steier-*
mark 274
Lanner, Josef 44, 294
Launsdorf *9314 Kärnten*
252
Lavant Motorway Bridge
209
Lech *6764 Vorarlberg*
170
Lechtal (Upper valley)
173
Lend *5651 Salzburg* 222
Lenzing factory 34
Leoben *8700 Steiermark*
173
Leopold I 83, 293
Leopoldsberg *Wien* 326
Leopoldskron (Schloß)
Tirol 237
Leopoldsteiner See 86
Lermoos *6631 Tirol* 174
Lesachtal 98
Leutasch *6105 Tirol* 264
Leutasch (Valley) 263
Leutschach *8463 Steier-*
mark 275
Liechtensteinklamm 222
Lienz *9900 Tirol* 174
Liezen *8940 Steiermark*
86, 133
Lilienfeld *3180 Nie-*
deröst 204
Limbergsperre (Dam)
151
Linz *4020 Oberöst* 177
Lippizaner horses 209,
301
Liszt, Franz 89
Lochau *6911 Vorarlberg*
66
Lodron, Paris 227
Lofer *5090 Salzburg*
181
Loos, Adolf 42
Lorenz, Konrad 35, 108
Loser Panoramastraße
60
Lower Austria (province)
32
Lueg (Pass) 223
Lünersee 63
Lungau 189, 213
Lunn, Arnold 55, 57
Lunz am See *3293 Nie-*
deröst 12
Lurgrotte 200

M

Magdalensberg 252
Mahler, Gustav 45, 293,
295
Makart, Hans 315
Mallnitz *9822 Kärnten*
181
Maltatal 182
Mammuthöhle (Cave) 71
Mantegna 312
Maria Alm *5761 Salz-*
burg 219
Maria Gail *9500 Kärnten*
330
Maria Kirchental 181
Maria Plain *Salzburg* 236
Maria Rast 104
Maria Saal *9063 Kärnten*
183
Mariastein *6322 Tirol*
185
Maria Taferl *3672 Nie-*
deröst 79
Maria Theresa 27, 30,
289
Mariatrost (Abbey) 119
Maria Wörth *9082 Kärn-*
ten 332
Mariazell *8630 Steier-*
mark 185
Marienwasserfall 186
Matrei in Osttirol *9971*
Tirol 186
Mattsee *5163 Salzburg*
236
Maulbertsch, Franz An-
ton 39, 316
Maurach *6212 Tirol* 12
Mauterndorf *5570 Salz-*
burg 189
Mauterndorf (Burg) *Salz-*
burg 189
Mauthausen *4310*
Oberöst 190
Mauthen *9640 Kärnten*
98
Maximilian I 26, 135
Mayerling *Niederöst* 30,
190
Mayrhofen *6290 Tirol*
335
Meistersinger 43
Meitner, Lise 35
Melk *3390 Niederöst*
191
Mellau *6881 Vorarlberg*
67
Mendel, Gregor Johann
35
Messerschmidt, Franz
Xaver 317
Messner, Reinhold 14
Metternich 30, 291
Millstatt *9872 Kärnten*
193
Minimundus 159
Mining 34, 85, 158
Minnesänger 43
Mittelberg *6993 Vorarl-*
berg 160
Mittelgebirge Region
143

Mitterndorf (Bad) *8983 Steiermark* 243
Mittersill *5730 Salzburg* 92
Möderbrugg *8763 Steiermark* 133
Mödling *2340 Niederöst* 326
Mölck, Joseph Adam von 98
Mölltaler Gletscher *Kärnten* 195
Mörbisch *7072 Burgenland* 195
Mösern *6100 Tirol* 264
Mondsee *5310 Oberöst* 195
Monn, Matthias Georg 43
Montafon *Vorarlberg* 197
Mooserboden Reservoir 151
Moosersperre (Dam) 151
Moosham (Schloß) 214
Moser, Kolo 41
Mountaineering 14
Mozart, Wolfgang Amadeus 44, 227
Mozarteum 228
Mühlbach am Hochkönig *5505 Salzburg* 222
Mühldorfer Seen 216
Mühlviertel 180
Munggenast, Joseph 39, 54
Murau *Steiermark* 199
Murtal 200
Music 43, 227, 293
Musil, Robert von 35
Mutters *6162 Tirol* 12

N

Napoleon Bonaparte 30
National parks 16
Nauders *6543 Tirol* 144
Neßlegg 67
Neukirchen am Großvenediger *5741 Salzburg* 105
Neunkirchen *2620 Niederöst* 258
Neusiedl *7100 Burgenland* 202
Neusiedler See *Burgenland* 201
Neustift *6167 Tirol* 277
Nibelungen, Song of the 74, 288
Nibelungengau 79
Niederösterreich 32

O

Obergurgl *6456 Tirol* 124
Oberinntal 143
Oberlech *Vorarlberg* 171

Obernberg am Inn *4982 Oberöst* 202
Oberösterreich 32
Obertauern *5562 Salzburg* 203
Obervellach *9821 Kärnten* 279
Oberwalder Hütte 123
Oberwölz *8832 Steiermark* 203
Oberzeiring *8762 Steiermark* 133
Österreichisches Freilichtmuseum 200
Österreuten *Tirol* 206
Ötschermassiv 204
Oetz *6433 Tirol* 206
Ötztal *Tirol* 204
Ötztaler Gletscherstraße 268
Operetta 44
Ort (Schloß) 107
Ort, Johann 107
Ossiach *9570 Kärnten* 207
Ossiacher See 206

P

Pabst, Georg Wilhelm 35
Pacher, Michael 254, 317
Pack *Steiermark* 208
Packsattel 208
Palfnersee 103
Pardatschgrat 146
Parmigianino 312
Partenen *6794 Vorarlberg* 265
Pasterzengletscher 123
Penken 335
Perchtoldsdorf *2380 Niederöst* 326
Permoser, Balthasar 317
Pernegg 104
Persenbeug *3680 Niederöst* 79
Pertisau *6213 Tirol* 12
Pestsäule 48, 288
Petersberg 97
Petronell *2404 Niederöst* 80
Pfänder 66
Pfarrkirchen *4540 Oberöst* 126
Pfunds *6542 Tirol* 144
Pians *6551 Tirol* 56
Piber *8580 Steiermark* 209
Pillerpaß-Straße 154
Pinzgau 221, 334
Pitztal *Tirol* 209
Plague column 48, 288
Planai 256
Plansee 95
Plochl, Anna 112
Pöllau *8225 Steiermark* 210
Pöllauberg *Steiermark* 211
Pörtschach *9210 Kärnten* 212

Pöstlingberg 177
Polster 87
Pomis, Pietro de 82, 115, 119
Pongau 221
Pontlatzerbrücke 144
Porsche Museum 106
Pottenbrunn (Schloß) 251
Prescenyklause 224
Prandtauer, Jakob 39, 132
Puchberg am Schneeberg *2734 Niederöst* 258
Pürgg *8981 Steiermark* 243
Pulkau *3741 Niederöst* 212
Pyramidenkogel 332

R

Radkersburg (Bad) *8490 Steiermark* 212
Radschulter 266
Radstadt *5550 Salzburg* 213
Radstädter Tauernstraße *Salzburg* 213
Raiding *Burgenland* 89
Raitenau, Wolf Dietrich von 66, 226
Ramsau am Dachstein *8972 Steiermark* 72
Rankweil *6830 Vorarlberg* 214
Raphaël 312
Rappenlochschlucht 68
Rattenberg *6240 Tirol* 214
Raunacher, Johann Baptist Anton 83
Rauris *5661 Salzburg* 12
Rauz 56
Raxalpe 258
Raxblick 258
Rehberg *Niederöst* 164
Reichenau an der Rax *2651 Niederöst* 12
Reichlich, Marx 317
Reichstadt, Duke of 304, 318
Reifnitz *9081 Kärnten* 332
Rein (Stift) 119
Reißeck-Massiv *Kärnten* 216
Reith bei Seefeld *6103 Tirol* 263
Reither Spitze 262
Rembrandt 313
Reni, Guido 312
Retz *2070 Niederöst* 216
Reutte *6600 Tirol* 95
Richard the Lionheart 81
Riegersburg (Schloß) *Niederöst* 217
Riegersburg *8333 Steiermark* 218

Riezlern *6991 Vorarlberg* 160
Riffelsee 210
Rilke, Rainer Maria 35
Ringstraßenstil (Vienna) 298
Rofen *Tirol* 268
Rohrau *2471 Niederöst* 80
Romako, Anton 40, 315
Romans 29
Rosegg (Wildpark) 331
Rosenburg 55
Roßbrand 72, 213, 255
Rotmoosferner (Glacier) 124
Rottenmann *8766 Steiermark* 133
Rottenmanner Tauern 133
Rottmayr, Johann Michael 39
Rubens, Pieter Paul 313
Rudolf I of Habsburg 26, 29
Rüfikopf 172
Rust *7071 Burgenland* 202

S

Saalachtal 219
Saalbach-Hinterglemm *5753 Salzburg* 220
Saalfelden am Steinernen Meer *5760 Salzburg* 219
Salieri, Antonio 44
Salla (Valley) 208
Salt 34, 60, 238
Salzachöfen 223
Salzachtal 221
Salzatal 224
Salzburg *5020 Salzburg* 226
Salzburg Dolomites 242
Salzburg (province) 32
Salzburger Sportwelt Amadé *Salzburg* 237
Salzkammergut 238
St. Andrä *8444 Steiermark* 275
St. Anton am Arlberg *6580 Tirol* 243
St. Christoph am Arlberg *Tirol* 56, 244
St. Florian (Abbey) *Oberöst* 245
St. Gallenkirch *6791 Vorarlberg* 198
St. Georgen am Längsee *9313 Kärnten* 252
St. Gilgen *5340 Salzburg* 247
St. Jakob in Defereggen *9963 Tirol* 13
St. Johann im Pongau *5600 Salzburg* 12
St. Johann in Tirol *6380 Tirol* 247
St. Kanzian am Klopeiner See *9122 Kärnten* 12

St. Kanzian Lakes 159
St. Lambrecht (Abbey) *Steiermark* 248
St. Leonhard im Pitztal *6481 Tirol* 12
St. Michael *Niederöst* 80
St. Michael im Lungau *5582 Salzburg* 214
St. Paul im Lavanttal *9470 Kärnten* 249
St. Pölten *3100 Niederöst* 248
St. Veit an der Glan *9300 Kärnten* 251
St. Wolfgang *5360 Oberöst* 253
St. Wolfgangsee (Lake) 253
Sarajevo Assassination 59
Sausal Vineyards 275
Saxe-Teschen, Duke Albert of 305
Schafberg *Oberöst* 254
Schallaburg (Schloß) 193
Schareck 130
Scharnstein *4644 Oberöst* 107
Schattberg 220
Schilcher 273
Schindler, Emil Jakob 40, 315
Schladming *8970 Steiermark* 255
Schladminger Tauern *Steiermark* 254
Schloßalm 101
Schloßhof 81
Schmiding (Bird Reserve) *Oberöst* 286
Schmidt, Johann Georg 308
Schmidt, Martin Johann 39, 162
Schmittenhöhe 333
Schneeberg *Niederöst* 258
Schneider, Hannes 55
Schöckl (Mount) 274
Schoenberg, Arnold 45, 294
Schönbergalpe *Oberöst* 71
Schönbrunn (Schloß) *Wien* 317
Schönbühel *3392 Niederöst* 79
Schöneck 123
Schönwieshütte 124
Schößwendklamm 92
Schongauer, Martin 313
Schrammelmusik 297
Schröcken *6888 Vorarlberg* 67
Schruns *6780 Vorarlberg* 198
Schubert, Franz 44, 73, 293
Schubertiades 293
Schwanthaler, Thomas 254
Schwarzau *Niederöst* 132
Schwarzenberg *6867 Vorarlberg* 68

Schwarzsee 157
Schwaz *6130 Tirol* 259
Sciassia, Domenico 185
Seasons 12
Secession 41
Seckau (Abbey) *Steiermark* 261
Seefelder Joch 262
Seefelder Sattelstraßen 263
Seefeld in Tirol *6100 Tirol* 261
Seekircherl *Tirol* 262
Seewiesen *8636 Steiermark* 53
Seisenbergklamm 219
Semmering *2680 Niederöst* 259
Senftenberg *3541 Niederöst* 164
Sennigrat 198
Serfaus *6534 Tirol* 12
Silvretta Nova 198
Silvretta-Stausee (Reservoir) 265
Silvrettastraße 264
Sitticus, Marcus 227
Skiing 15
Sleeping Greek 107
Sölden *6540 Tirol* 267
Söll *6306 Tirol* 149
Soleleitung 35
Sonnenwelleck 122
Spas 16, 99
Spital *Tirol* 148
Spital am Pyhrn *4582 Oberöst* 270
Spittal an der Drau *9800 Kärnten* 270
Spitz *3620 Niederöst* 79
Sportgastein *Salzburg* 101
Spullersee 172
Stadl Paura *4651 Oberöst* 169
Stainz *8510 Steiermark* 271
Stammel, Joseph 52
Stams (Abbey) *Tirol* 271
Stanzertal 56
Starhemberg, Ernst Rüdiger Count of 289
Steiermark 32
Stein *Niederöst* 164
Steinbach am Attersee *4853 Oberöst* 242
Steirische Weinstraße 272
Stemmbogen 15
Sternberg, Josef von 35
Sterz 274
Steyr *4400 Oberöst* 276
Stifter, Adalbert 35, 155, 177
Stilluppgrund 337
Stoderzinken 73
Straßenplatz 48
Strauss, Johann the Elder 44, 294
Strauss, Johann the Younger, 44, 294
Strauss, Richard, 45, 295
Stripsenkopf 150

Strobl *5350 Salzburg* 239
Stroheim, Erich von 35
Strub *Tirol* 148
Strudengau 78
Stubachtal *Tirol* 277
Stubaital *Tirol* 277
Stubalpe 208
Stuben *Tirol* 144
Stuben *6762 Vorarlberg* 56, 245
Stubnerkogel 101
Stuiben (Falls) *Tirol* 206
Styria 32
Suttner, Bertha von 35

T

Tamsweg *5580 Salzburg* 278
Tannheim *6675 Tirol* 12
Tauerntunnel 279
Tauernstraße 133
Tauerntal 92
Tauplitz *8982 Steiermark* 243
Tauplitzalm *Steiermark* 243
Telfes *6165 Tirol* 12
Telfs *6410 Tirol* 94, 264
Teniers, the Younger 314
Tennengau 221
Ternitz *2630 Niederöst* 258
Teurnia Excavations 271
Textile industry 34
Thiersee *6335 Tirol* 168
Thörl *8621 Steiermark* 53
Thurn (Pass) 157
Timber industry 33
Timmelsjoch 205
Tintoretto 312
Tirol 32
Toplitzsee 60
Tourism 33
Trapp family 237
Trattenköpfl 105
Tratzberg (Schloß) 260
Traun (River) 238
Traunkirchen *4801 Oberöst* 280
Traunsee 106, 239
Trautenfels (Schloß) 243
Treffen *9521 Kärnten* 13
Trida Sattel 146
Trisannabrücke 56
Troger, Paul 39, 54
Tschagguns *6774 Vorarlberg* 198
Tulln *3430 Niederöst* 280
Turracherhöhe *Kärnten, Steiermark* 281
Tuscany (Styrian) 275
Tuxertal 335
Tyrol 32
Tyrolean chalets (Museum) 216

U

Umhausen *6441 Tirol* 206
Unterach am Attersee *4866 Oberöst* 13
Unterboden *Vorarlberg* 67
Untergurgl *6456 Tirol* 124
Untersberg 237
Unterzeiring *Steiermark* 133
Upper Austria 32
Ursprungpaßstraße 168

V

Valais 67, 160
Valisera 198
Valluga 244
Van Dyck, Anthony 313
Velázquez, Diego 312
Velden *9220 Kärnten* 331
Vent *6458 Kärnten* 268
Ventertal 268
Verackerbrot 274
Verdun, Nicolas de 161
Vermeer 314
Vermunt-Stausee (Reservoir) 265
Veronese 312
Versettla 198
Vienna *1010 Wien* 288
Vienna, Congress of 30, 289
Vienna (province) 32
Vienna, Treaty of 30
Vienna Woods 326
Vienna Workshops 41
Viktring (Abbey) 332
Villach *9500 Kärnten* 281
Villacher Alpenstraße 282
Virgental 189
Vöcklabruck *4840 Oberöst* 282
Volders *6111 Tirol* 283
Vorarlberg 32
Vorau (Abbey) 284
Vormärz 292

W

Wachau 79
Wagner, Otto 41, 319
Wagrain *5602 Salzburg* 222
Wagrainer Höhe 222
Waidhofen an der Thaya *3830 Niederöst* 284
Waidhofen an der Ybbs *3340 Niederöst* 13
Waidring *6384 Tirol* 148
Walchsee *6344 Tirol* 150

Waldmüller, Ferdinand Georg 316
Walser 67, 160
Waltz 44, 294
Warth *6767 Vorarlberg* 57, 173
Wasserfallboden (Reservoir) 151
Wasserfallwinkel 123
Weather 12
Webern, Anton von 45, 295
Weichselboden *8633 Steiermark* 224
Weißenkirchen *3610 Niederöst* 284
Weißensee *Kärnten* 13
Weißseeferner (Glacier) 153
Weißes Rößl 254
Wels *4600 Oberöst* 285
Werfenweng *5453 Salzburg* 12
Wesenufer *4085 Oberöst* 77
White Horse Inn 254
Wien *1010 Wien* 288
  Albertina 305
  Altes Rathaus 310
  Alte Ursulinenklosterapotheke 322
  Am Hof 310
  Angewandte Kunst (Österr. Museum) 323
  Annakirche 322
  Augustinerkirche 304
  Barockmuseum 316
  Belvedere 315
  Böhmische Hofkanzlei 310
  Burggarten 298
  Burgtheater 298
  Deutschordenskirche 308
  Donauturm 299
  Donnerbrunnen 311
  Dreimäderlhaus 321
  Ehem. Hofmobiliendepot 325
  Ephesos-Museum 306
  Franziskanerkirche 308
  Galerie des 19. und 20. Jahrhunderts 315
  Gemäldegalerie des Akad. der bildenden Künste 323
  Gloriette 319
  Gürtel 292
  Heeresgeschichtliches Museum 325
  Heiligenkreuzerhof 310
  Herrengasse 292
  Historisches Museum der Stadt Wien 323
  Hofburg 299
  Hofburgkapelle 301
  Hofjagd-und Rüstkammer 306
  Hofsilber-und Tafelkammer 301
  Hoher Markt 310
  Hundertwasserhaus 324
  Jesuitenkirche 310
  Josefsplatz 300
  Jüdisches Museum 322
  Kaiserappartements 301
  Kaisergruft 302
  Karlskirche 322
  Kinsky (Palais) 322
  Kirche am Steinhof 320

383

KunstHaus Wien 325
Kunsthistorisches Museum 311
Kurpark Oberlaa 324
Linke Wienzeile 320
Lobkowitz (Palais) 321
Maria am Gestade 310
Maria-Theresien-Platz 298
Markets 297
Michaeler Kirche 322
Michaelerplatz (entrance to Hofburg) 299
Minoritenkirche 322
Mittelalterlicher österreichischer Kunst (Museum) 317
Moderner Kunst Stiftung Ludwig (Museum) 325
Mozart-Wohnung 309
Naschmarkt 324
Naturhistorisches Museum 324
Neue Burg 298, 300
Neues Rathaus 298
Österr. Nationalbibliothek 302
Out and about 290
Parlament 298
Pestsäule 311
Peterskirche 310
Piaristenkirche Basilika Maria Treu 324
Postsparkasse 320
Prater 323
Ring 292, 297
Ruprechtskirche 310
Salesianerinnenkirche 324
Sammlung alter Musikinstrumente 306
St. Marxer Friedhof 321

Schatzkammer 300
Schönbrunn (Schloß) 317
Schubert-Museum 321
Schwarzenberg (Palais) 324
Secession 320
Spanische Reitschule 301
Staatsoper 321
Stadtpark 297
Stallburg 301
Starhemberg (Palais) 322
Stephansdom 306
Uhrenmuseum der Stadt Wien 310
Universität 299
Völkerkunde (Museum) 306
Volksgarten 298
Volkskunde (Österr. Museum) 323
Votivkirche 299
Wagenburg 319
Wagner-Pavillons 319
Zentralfriedhof 321
Wiener Neustadt 2700 Niederöst 327
Wienerwald Wien 326
Wiener Werkstätten 41
Wildenkarkogel 220
Wilder Kaiser 148
Wildes Mannle 269
Wildschönau-Oberau 6311 Tirol 13
Wildungsmauer Niederöst 80
Wilhering (Abbey) Oberöst 328
Wilten 141
Windegg (Viewpoint) 206

Wine 49, 272
Wörther See Kärnten 330
Wolf, Hugo 45
Wolfsberg 9400 Kärnten 209

Z

Zahmer Kaiser 149
Zamangspitze 198
Zauchensee 5541 Salzburg 237
Zdarsky, Matthias 15
Zeiler, Johann Jakob 54, 95
Zell am See 5700 Salzburg 332
Zell am Ziller 6280 Tirol 334
Zemmtal 337
Zillertal Tirol 334
Zirlerberg 263
Zita, Empress 28, 304
Zittauer Hütte 105
Zitterauer Tisch 102
Zürs 6763 Vorarlberg 338
Zuger Hochlicht 171
Zugspitze 84
Zugspitzkamm 84
Zweig, Stefan 35
Zwettl (Stift) 3910 Niederöst 339
Zwölferkogel 220

Vienna Philharmonic Orchestra
New Year's Day Concert

Sacher Torte

Frau Sacher, a leading personality in late 19C Vienna, fed the impoverished Austrian nobility in her famous restaurant long after they had ceased to pay. She was less generous with the recipe for her celebrated torte, but many have tried to equal her pastry prowess.

Preheat the oven to 165°C/325°F (thermostat 3)

Grate 180g/5-6oz semi sweet chocolate.
Cream together until smooth 100g/ ½ cup sugar and 115g/ ½ cup butter,
Beat in 6 yolks, one at a time, until the mixture is light and fluffy.
Add the chocolate and 115g/ ¾ cup dry bread crumbs,
30g/ ¼ cup finely ground blanched almonds, a pinch of salt.
Beat the remaining egg whites until stiff but not dry, fold them in gently.
Pour the mixture into ungreased pan with a removable rim.
Bake 50 min to 1 hour
When the torte is cool, slice it horizontally through the middle
(you may turn the top layer over so that the finished cake is flat on top).
Spread 225g/1 cup apricot jam or preserves between the layers.
Cover with chocolate glaze.
For the genuine Viennese touch, heap on the *schlag* !

Notes

MANUFACTURE FRANÇAISE DES PNEUMATIQUES MICHELIN

Société en commandite par actions au capital de 2 000 000 000 de francs

Place des Carmes-Déchaux – 63 Clermont-Ferrand (France)

R.C.S. Clermont-Fd B 855 200 507

© Michelin et Cie, Propriétaires-Éditeurs 1997

Dépôt légal avril 1997 – ISBN 2-06-150702-6– ISSN 0763-1383

Printed in the EU 03-97/1

Photocomposition : MAURY Imprimeur S.A., Malesherbes

Impression et brochage : AUBIN Imprimeur à Ligugé, Poitiers

Illustration de la couverture par Didier WIBROTTE/Pascal VITRY